OLD FORGE

ROYAL AIR FORCE COLTISHALL

FIGHTER STATION

A Station History

Mick Jennings MBE
Foreword by Sqn Ldr Jason Hughes BSc (Hons) RAF

First Edition 2007

Designed
by
Jupper Peep
studio@jupperpeep.com
www.jupperpeep.com

Published
by
Old Forge Publishing
39 Backgate
Cowbit
Lincolnshire
PE12 6AP
oldforgepub@aol.com
www.oldforgepublishing.org
01406 381313

ISBN 978-1-906183-01-1

Printed for Old Forge Publishing
By

LPPS Ltd
Wellingborough
Northants
NN8 3PJ

01553 764728

Contents

ROYAL AIR FORCE COLTISHALL FIGHTER STATION

A Station History

■ Acknowledgements ■

I am most grateful to those individuals' whose infectious support and enthusiasm made the research and writing of this book such a pleasure.

Sqn Ldr Jack Love RAF (Ret) was the Community Relations Officer (CRO) at Coltishall when I was first posted to the Norfolk Station in 1995. It is down to him that this project took to its wings all those years ago. On many occasions, Jack and I would discuss various aspects of Coltishall's history and inevitably, Jack always came up with an answer, or at least put me in contact with someone who could help. It seemed like he knew everyone that was anyone! He instilled in me the firm belief that it is our history that will fulfill our destiny.

Many other fine people have assisted me with information and encouragement:

Air Historical Branch (RAF), Derek Allnutt, Billy Barstard, Ken Bartram, Jim Bellingall, Allan Bolton, Martin Bowman, Tony Brent, Billy Buck, Wg Cdr Brian Carroll, City of Norwich Aviation Museum, Jim Clarey, Taff Collins, Bob Collis, Jerry Crombie, AM Stephen Dalton,Pete Daviss, Graham Day, Aldon Ferguson, Mark Gauntlett, Alan Hague, Peter Hall, Merv Hambling, John Hambrook, AVM Chris Harper, Paul Hendley, Gp Capt Tim Hewlett, Gp Capt Mike Hobson, Roger Hobson, AVM John Howe, Wg Cdr Barney Hubble, Sqn Ldr Jason Hughes, Dr Rodney Maliphant, Bill Mayes, Dennis Morris, Tom O'Reilly, Joan Osborne-Walker, Ken Ovenden, Photographic Section RAF Coltishall, Derek Pells, Lindsey Pietrzak, WO Steve Roberts, Wg Cdr Paul Robins, Phillip Rounce, the late Bob Sergeant, Philip Smith, Ralph Stone, Sgt Alan Vernon, Sgt Richie Vernon, Max Waldron, David Wade, Reg Wall, Clive Watkins, Frank Webster and WO John Welton. To those I have omitted to mention, I apologize - your contributions, however small, were most gratefully received.

A special thanks to John Evans for proof reading the manuscript and for providing valuable support during the final stages of research. I would also like to thank my wife Ellen and daughter Kimberley for their total support and encouragement and for tolerating my long absences whilst engaged on the research and writing of this book.

And finally to all those who have served at RAF Coltishall over 66-years and for those who are sadly no longer with us - I hope this book does you justice; I salute you all.

The countryside of Britain, in particular the East of England, is littered with disused World War II airfields, which serve as a reminder of the darkest days that our country has ever faced. Originally called 'Scottow' Aerodrome, Royal Air Force Coltishall was envisaged by the Air Ministry as a bomber base in 1936. Set in a beautiful part of Norfolk, adjacent to the Broads, Coltishall was always an undeniably pretty station. When construction started in 1938 the pre-war planners insisted that hundreds of trees were planted, even when the military need was so pressing. This forethought gave Coltishall a far more natural ambience than the industrial feel of more modern stations and allowed Coltishall to blend gracefully into the surrounding countryside.

The increasing threat posed by the Luftwaffe meant that Coltishall's role was to quickly change from a bomber to fighter station and it was declared operational on 23 June 1940. Coltishall was soon pressed into action and some 17 days later claimed the first kill of the battle of Britain. During World War II it became synonymous with Aces such as Bader, Stanford Tuck, 'Cats-Eyes' Cunningham and 'Sailor' Malan, cementing the place in the Nation's history.

Whilst a host of stations across the country were closed in the post war years, Coltishall was spared and, unlike many other surviving stations, retained its World War II heritage. Coltishall was unique in the history of the Royal Air Force, as it remained a fighter station for its entire operational life. Throughout its 66-year operational history the Station hardly changed in its role, layout and more importantly, its character. From the pivotal years of the Battle of Britain, through to the dawn of the jet age, Lightnings and finally 32 years of the Jaguar, Coltishall remained virtually the same. Indeed, it was the World War II design that made living and working at Coltishall such a different experience from other stations. The close proximity of the different squadrons and sections did not allow for isolation and there was always a Common operational purpose, a real sense of Community and genuine fondness for this special place. This was the 'Spirit of Coltishall' - if only you could bottle it.

Those of us who served at Coltishall have many fond memories of the place, but Mick Jennings MBE possesses a burning passion for heritage of this Battle of Britain Station. Mick's encyclopaedic knowledge has produced this excellent book that catalogues every minute detail of Coltishall's history. His work encapsulates the Spirit of the Station, the uniquely strong relationship with the local Community and the vital role it played at the forefront of British Air Power for 66 years.

As a young boy I was inspired by the famous names associated with Coltishall and by the bravery of those who served there. To have joined the list of station commanders of such a famous station was an immense privilege. As I write, the future of the site is still uncertain, but I sincerely hope that after all the years of service that she has given, that a dignified role can be found for her retirement. Like previous station commanders, I have merely been the custodian of this historic site; the custodian of RAF Coltishall's history is now Mick Jennings - it could not be in better hands.

Sqn Ldr Jason Hughes BSc (Hons) RAF

"The Royal Air Force has behind it a tradition no less inspiring than those of the older Services - you will have to shoulder far greater responsibilities than those which your Service had to shoulder in the last war; one of the greatest of them will be the safeguarding of these islands from the menace of the air. I can assure all ranks of the Air Force of my supreme confidence in their skill and courage and their ability to meet whatever calls will be made on them."

H M King George VI
4 September 1939

These stirring words from King George were received by the RAF a day after war had been declared on Germany. The tone and sentiments of the message were, perhaps, the realization that air power in all its destructive forms was going to be one of the decisive elements which would bring this country to victory.

The threat from Germany had been identified many years prior to the declaration of war. The great expansion period for the Royal Air Force in the 1930s saw many new airfields being built in the counties of Norfolk, Lincolnshire and Yorkshire just to name a few. Coltishall's existence stems from this period of growth.

Coltishall was originally designed to fulfill the requirements to support bomber aircraft and the construction work that started in 1939 was to the standard pattern of an expansion period bomber airfield. However, during early 1940, with work well advanced, it was decided that the role of the station would be switched from a bomber base to that of a fighter station.

For many, Coltishall will always be remembered for the wartime exploits of pilots such as Douglas Bader, Bob Stanford Tuck, Max Aitken, John 'Cats Eyes' Cunningham and Johnnie Johnson. Quite rightly, those names should never be forgotten; neither should the memories of all those who have served at Coltishall since the late 1930s, be they aircrew, groundcrew, soldiers, sailors or civilian.

During the war years in excess of 80 Fighter Squadrons called Coltishall, Matlaske and Ludham (the two Sector airfields) home; be it for a few days or many months. Hurricanes, Defiants, Beaufighters, Mosquitoes and the mighty Spitfire; bombers such as the Boston, Stirling, Lancaster, Whitley and Halifax. The United States Army Air Force with P-39 Airacobras, P-51 Mustangs, P-47 Thunderbolts, B-17 Flying Fortress and B-24 Liberator; the list goes on.

On 8 August 1945, Coltishall was re-designated as RAF (Polish) Coltishall. This move saw all the Polish flying squadrons, together with their servicing echelons; re-locate to Coltishall from various other stations throughout the UK and Continent. It was not until January 1947 that Coltishall reverted to full RAF status with the disbandment and departure of the Polish elements.

The jet age came to Coltishall in 1951 with the arrival of the Venom and Meteor. As the experience of jet aircraft evolved, so did the aircraft. The early versions of the Venom and Meteor were replaced by updated versions of the same type. New equipment such as the Javelin and Hunter soon appeared over the Coltishall skyline. The quantum leap however came in 1959 when the Air Fighting Development Squadron received their first English Electric Lightning.

It fell to 74 (Trinidad) Squadron, who had previously operated the Hunter from Coltishall, to introduce the mighty Lightning into full operational service during 1960. The station was to have a long association with this Mach 2 fighter as 226 Operational Conversion Unit (OCU) operated many variants of the Lightning from April 1964 to September 1974. During that period they were responsible for training 810 pilots for front line Lightning squadrons.

Search and Rescue had always played a vital role at Coltishall, from the Walrus amphibian aircraft of 278 (ASR) Squadron during the war years to the Whirlwind, Wessex and Sea King helicopters of 22 and 202 Squadrons; their aims were the same, to save lives.

The wartime exploits of Bader and Stanford Tuck were replayed on a daily basis when the Spitfires and Hurricanes of the Historic Aircraft Flight (HAF) were based at Coltishall in the 1960s and 70s. With the arrival of Lancaster PA474 in 1973 and the re-designation of the HAF to Battle of Britain Memorial Flight (BBMF), it was becoming more and more difficult for the flight to function, especially as the station was building up for the arrival of the Jaguar. To the dismay of many, the BBMF left Coltishall for their new home at Coningsby in 1976.

Since 1974, Coltishall was the home of the Jaguar. From the early days, the station's role was to support the North Atlantic Treaty Organization (NATO) in defending the West from attack by the Warsaw Pact. With the fall of the Berlin Wall and the peace dividends that followed, the Jaguar Force at Coltishall trained for a war that they hoped would never happen. How the world changed. The Gulf War, Operation DENY FLIGHT and Operation WARDEN were just a few of the more public aspects of life at Coltishall. Despite an ever increasing role throughout the world's trouble spots for the British Forces, it was defence cuts and not the enemy that would see the end of Coltishall. In 2004, the Defence Minister, Geoff Hoon, announced that the Jaguar aircraft would be retired early and that Coltishall would be closed by the end of 2006.

As the story of the only station in the RAF to have remained a Fighter Station throughout its existence unfolds, you will see that since 1939 Coltishall has always been a hive of activity. Short-sighted or not, the closure of Coltishall is a sad chapter in the annals of the RAF. History, tradition, ethos and sentiment are all swearwords to those who care little for our heritage. But one thing is for sure; the 'Spirit of Coltishall' cannot and will not be broken.

It is inevitable that in undertaking a task such of this magnitude, many personalities, exploits and tragedies will have been missed and regardless of how much research goes into ensuring that stories and recollections are reported accurately, there will be errors and mistakes. If there are, then I apologies, but sincerely hope that they will not spoil your enjoyment of the book.

For me this is the closure of one of the most memorable time in my life. I am proud to have served at Coltishall both as a member of the RAF and latterly as the CRO. I feel privileged to have been there at the end to represent those that have passed into history. A new life 'Down Under' waits, but the 'Spirit of Coltishall' will go with me as will the memories of the finest Station in the Royal Air Force.

Mick Jennings MBE
Royal Air Force
COLTISHALL

December 2006

Chapter One

THE BEGINNING

The Norfolk Chronicle for Friday 8 July 1938 recorded local attitudes when proposals for the new aerodrome were announced. It was 'understood that the Air Ministry have decided to erect an aerodrome on a site at Scottow.' 'Although the land concerned is urgently needed for the purpose of a Royal Air Force aerodrome, it is hoped that it may not be actually necessary to erect buildings on it, except in case of emergency.'

'A thorough search has been made in the area for a possible alternative site but without success. The site chosen is part of the Scottow Hall Estate and comprises some 530 acres. It is flanked on two sides by the main North Walsham to Norwich road and Scottow to Aylsham road. The Scottow Memorial junction forming one corner. It embraces the whole of Manor Farm (260 acres), the whole of Rookery Farm (72 acres), 55% (100 acres) of Colk's Farm and about 46% (105 acres) of Malthouse Farm.'

'We understand that it will be necessary to remove trees along the Scottow Moors and in Steward's Plantation, but the cutting of trees near Scottow Hall will be avoided unless in the course of time the aerodrome has to be built on.'

The News Chronicle was told by the Scottow Hall estate agent - "The matter is very much in the air. Negotiations are certainly going on, but nothing definite has been decided. The land has been examined by officials, but there has been no enquiry from the Air Ministry regarding the Scottow estate and no official notice has been served on the owner or myself as agent."

"Meanwhile, farmers keep stoically on, hoping that they will be able to reap what they have sown."

Mr Henry Watts of Colk's Farm said, "I have been told that should an aerodrome be built I shall loose 100 acres of my farm, good corn growing land will be taken and will leave me with the 80 least productive acres and my buildings."

At Manor Farm the foreman said: "We don't know what work to do, as we do not know if it will be wasted. At least we hope they will give us time to crop the harvest. When officials were taking samples of water they said this was an ideal spot for an aerodrome."

Mr H G Roberts of Rookery Farm will be hit the hardest. Besides losing the whole of this farm, he is also in partnership with Mr W Blofield of Manor Farm, another holding that will be severely affected. Mr Roberts Commented, "Some of the best agricultural land in Norfolk will be wasted." "There is any amount of scrubland around Cawston and district, yet it must be here, on good productive land that they will build. "This land is heavy and after the rains there is a good deal of surface water which I should think would not be ideal for a heavy bomber to land on. The aerodrome will take my living and clean me out."

At the Malthouse Farm, Mr Roger Gray said: "All the land on this side of the Norwich Road will be taken, but I believe they will leave us a cart track round the farm buildings. This is some of the best land in Norfolk and it seems a great pity to me."

Notwithstanding all these objections from interested parties, the plans for the aerodrome went ahead.

These were the headlines in the Eastern Daily Press (EDP) on 12 November 1938 when local residents found out for sure that an airfield was to be built. The article went on: 'It is understood that the Air Ministry have decided to construct an aerodrome at Scottow, to be known as Coltishall Aerodrome, and work will begin after 21 November.'

The site of from 450-500 acres lies between Coltishall and Buxton roads, which meet at the Scottow War

Memorial cross-roads, and it is two and a half miles from Coltishall, four miles from North Walsham and seven miles from Aylsham, and about nine miles from the coast. The land is flat with a brick earth sub-soil, and there is a good deal of timber in the vicinity.

The first indications of the Ministry's intentions came recently, when farmers received notice that it was not advisable to continue to crop the fields that the Ministry had selected. Mr Alan Blofield of Manor Farm will lose about 230 acres that will leave him with only 30 acres for feeding his cattle. He informed our representatives that he would be more content if allowed to retain 50 acres.

Mr F H Gray of Malthouse Farm is to loose 92 acres out of his farm of 247 acres and there is likelihood that yet more of his land may be required. Mr H G Roberts of Rookery Farm is losing 27 acres.

The agricultural Community regrets that good arable land has to be taken as from their point of view there is suitable waste and park land available that could answer the purpose, but on the whole they were facing the change with a philosophic spirit. Scottow has an area of just over 2000 acres, so the acquisition of the site must make a great difference, and not least of all the pleasant rural picturesque ness of the village.

On Thursday, letters from the Air Ministry caused concern among the tenants of three cottages at Batley Green that is approached by a loke from the Coltishall Road. The news of the impending change has had a serious effect on Mrs T Buck, and old age pensioner aged 83 years who is grieved at the thought of having to leave her home in which she has lived for 64 years, ever since she was married. The widow, who is frail, has children with whom she can live; otherwise she would have to go to the infirmary.

Mr Herbert J Newstead a pensioner aged 66 years, is also perturbed at the prospect of having to give up his smallholding of two and half acres that he has worked for 16 years. This smallholding has enabled him to supplement his income and unless he can find similar alternative accommodation he will suffer seriously. At present, he has the help of his four sons in working the holding.

The third cottager to receive the notice is Mr Harry Forster who has a wife and two children. He is an agricultural labourer and it is expected that Smallburgh Rural District Council will supply him with a cottage.

The letter from the Air Ministry sent to the cottagers merely stated that the owners consent had been given to the Ministry to take over the site of Coltishall Aerodrome as of 21 November in order that preparation of the landing ground may proceed. The letter pointed out that this does not necessarily preclude the harvesting of outstanding roots or other crops, as the preparation, which will in the first place consist in the removal of hedges and trees, will take a considerable time. It was further stated that the Ministry were further in touch with Mr Sinclair, agent to the estate, with a view to the provision of cottage accommodation elsewhere, if this is possible, by arrangements with Smallburgh Rural District Council.

Whilst it is felt, it was added, that the notice of the Air Ministry's intentions is extremely short, it is hoped your occupation of the cottages may be arranged to cease within a reasonable period of that date in order that work of preparing the site is not held up. The letter concluded by stating that fair compensation would be paid for tenant's rights.

It is understood that Bomber Squadrons will be stationed at Scottow. Horsham St Faith's will be a similar station and both will be opened in 1940. The station buildings will in each case be the same as Watton.

Chapter 2

The Early Days

During the 1930s Norfolk, together with Yorkshire and Lincolnshire, was a hive of activity. A large number of airfields were under construction to satisfy the needs of The Royal Air Force during the 'Expansion Period' leading up to the start of the Second World War.

As war deepened in the early 1940s, many more were constructed to support the ever-increasing numbers of Bombers and Fighters being produced to attack the enemy in its heartland. In 1939 when Bomber airfields were considered to be more important than Fighter fields, 'The Men from the Ministry' were busy scouring the Norfolk countryside for suitable sites for their airfields.

As was the intention, Coltishall was constructed to fulfil the needs of an operational Bomber Station for 2 Gp of Bomber command as it was fully accepted that Bomber command would be all-important in the air war that was about to start.

Construction of the airfield started in February 1939 with the design of the field being typical of an 'Expansion Period' layout based around three Type C hangars in a gentle arc on one side of the airfield. The hangars were fronted by a large concrete apron that led onto a well-prepared grass airfield surface. Behind the arc of hangars a further three Type C hangars were planned, but eventually only two were built together with a range of workshops, stores facilities, admin buildings and accommodation blocks. The construction of these buildings was to standardised 'Expansion Period' designs that were said to have been the brainchild of Sir Edward Lutyens.

Many of the buildings, particularly the accommodation blocks, were austere yet graceful in their appearance. Most buildings had an identical interior layout to all other period airfields, thus giving its inhabitants a sense of feeling at home regardless of the Station. The Type C hangars were built with single-storey squadron office accommodation along each side, as was normal for bomber bases.

Later, as the airfield began to expand a further eight Blister type hangars (six type 'O' and two type 'EO') were built to supplement the five 'C' types. The grass runways, as with most bomber bases, were connected by a 50ft wide, concrete perimeter track. The grassed surfaces of the landing strip soon began to deteriorate and a Steel Matting surface, Sommerfield Track, was laid to cover the landing areas during the latter part of 1944. Basically, Sommerfield Mat Type Tracking was made of

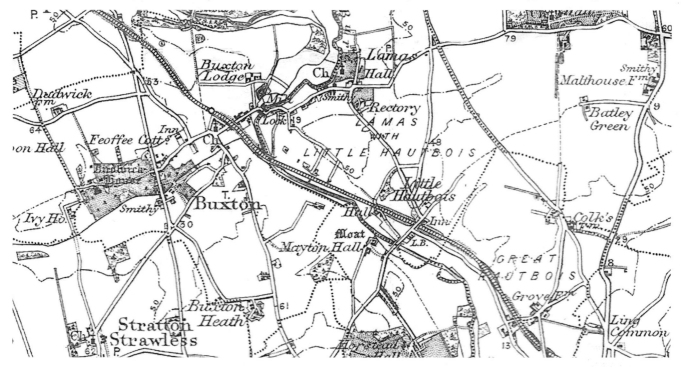

The lie of the land in 1906 many years before the arrival of an airfield

Pilots of 66 Sqn discuss tactics with their CO Sqn Ldr Rupert Leigh, circa 1940.

13 SWG 3" mesh wire netting, reinforced by mild steel rods spaced at 8" intervals. Each roll of netting came in 75" lengths that were fixed by steel spikes driven into the ground at an angle away from the tracking, at 2' intervals along the length of the strip.

Fate destined Coltishall never to fulfil its intended role. The disastrous air campaign over France in the early 1940's caused the Air Ministry to radically review its procedures and tactics. The defence of the United Kingdom was now to be 'priority one' if it intended to stay a free land. East Anglia was by now covered by many bomber airfields, and as such had to be considered as a prime target for the Luftwaffe. At this time, Duxford provided the only top cover for this vast area and it became essential to provide East Anglia with additional fighter stations and squadrons. As Coltishall had not been taken over by Bomber command this new airfield exactly fitted the bill; a Fighter Station.

Coltishall was officially opened in the June of 1940 as a part of 12 Gp Fighter Command that was then commanded by AVM Trafford Leigh-Mallory who, during the Battle of Britain, gained notoriety for his 'Big Wing' concept. However, prior to the official opening of the station, a small number of Blenheims from Watton and Horsham St Faith were dispersed to Coltishall in November and December of 1939. The first recorded aircraft movement was Blenheim IV L7835, flown by Sgt R G Bales and Sgt Barnes.

The first fighters arrived at Coltishall on the 29 May 1940 when Spitfire I's of 66 Squadron, under the command of Sqn Ldr Rupert Leigh, arrived from Horsham St Faith for coastal shipping guard duties. Immediately prior to their arrival, the squadron had been covering the Dunkirk evacuation beaches.

Wg Cdr Harry Broadhurst was to become the first appointed Station Commander for Coltishall. However, on his arrival in early June of 1940, he found no squadrons, not many Officers and very few airmen! In fact, it seemed, from his point of view, that his only command was to be the 'works and bricks' section that were still busy building the place! A day later, he sighted an Air Ministry signal asking for a Wg Cdr for immediate duty in France, for which he volunteered post haste. His AOC, AVM Leigh-Mallory, expressed surprise that Broadhurst should wish a move only two days after his promotion and appointment as Station Commander at Coltishall. He replied that he had no aeroplanes and nothing to command except some building operatives, so could he please go to France! His request was granted and he duly arrived at Lille to find total chaos! Destroyed aircraft, both British and French littered the airfield. For Harry Broadhurst it seemed that he had left one building site for another. However, he did have a squadron to command and his pilots and groundcrew were in good spirit and were determined to fight on whilst they had anything to fly.

Thus, the first officially recorded Station Commander of Coltishall was to be Wg Cdr W K Beisiegal and it fell to him to declare Coltishall fully operational at 0001 hrs on 23 June 1940.

Three days earlier, Coltishall had welcomed its second resident squadron, 242 Squadron. It is ironic that this squadron had suffered horrendous losses during the Battle of France, the reason that the station became a fighter and not a bomber base in the first place. 242 Squadron was manned mainly by Canadian pilots who had joined the RAF prior to the start of the war. Their mount, the Hawker Hurricane, was an aircraft that was to be the backbone of Fighter Command throughout the dark days of the Battle of Britain.

Due to the mauling that 242 Squadron had received in the Battle of France, it was felt that the squadron needed a strong Commander to raise the pilots' morale and to help the squadron regroup and re-establish itself after the horrors of France. The Squadron Leader selected for this difficult and demanding task was a 30 year-old fighter pilot with artificial legs, Douglas Bader.

Sqn Ldr Douglas Bader was a charismatic man whose great weakness, according to his friend, Sqn Ldr Kenneth Cross, was that; 'he knew better than anyone else.' He had never worked in an Operations Room and frequently complained that his squadron was sent up too late. He does, however, have some of the virtues lacked by his AOC, Leigh-Mallory. Extroversion and charisma, but he did lack experience of battle responsibility. If these shortcomings were true to life at the beginning of his time at Coltishall, they certainly changed as he whipped 242 Squadron into shape.

Bader had been told of his new command by AVM Leigh-Mallory, AOC 12 Group, at the Gp Headquarters, Watnall, a camp that straddled the B600 at Watnall, NW of Nottingham. At first, Bader thought he had been summoned to his HQ to explain a landing accident which had taken place the previous day when the Spitfire he was flying overshot in a night landing. The aircraft slid on her belly over the low wall of an aircraft pen, shearing the undercarriage off and jarring to a stop. As the bricks were raining down on the metal of his aircraft Bader just sat there prior to uttering one short, unprintable word!

Without any preamble Leigh-Mallory said: "I've been hearing of your work as a Flight Commander. I'm giving you your own squadron, 242. "Bader replied: "Yes Sir...

Air Vice Marshal Trafford Leigh-Mallory, AOC 12 Gp, Fighter Command.

Sir, there's one thing I should tell you...I broke a Spitfire last night; Overshot my landing." Mildly, Leigh-Mallory replied: "Well, that happens sometimes, you know." After a further briefing on what the AOC expected of the newly promoted Acting Squadron Leader, Bader drove the hundred or so miles back to his base at Kirton-in-Lindsey to pack his bags prior to his journey south to Coltishall, and his new command.

He arrived in the Norwich area at about 2300 hours on a dark, damp night. A local policeman gave him directions on how to get to Coltishall, however just five minutes later Bader was well and truly lost! He asked a local chap, who just happened to be on the road at that time of night, for directions; that request failed, as the man did not know either! He then saw a woman and she fearful of his intentions, fled as soon as he spoke.

With no signposts anywhere, he felt that his chances of finding the base that night were now minimal, but (yet again) he found another man who said suspiciously, "How do I know who you are? You may be a spy; anyway I don't know where the aerodrome is!"

About an hour later Bader's journey around the back roads of Norfolk came to fruition when he came across a barbed wire barrier across the road and behind it, in the light of a red lamp stood an RAF sentry. Bader explained to the sentry that he was the new CO of 242 Squadron. The sentry requested the password of the day. Bader exploded: "How the hell do I know the password, I've never been here before!" "Sorry Sir", replied the sentry, "without the password I can't let you through." Bader simmered at the barrier for another twenty minutes until the guardroom located the Duty Officer, who then ruled that Acting Sqn Ldr Bader could be admitted without the password.

Douglas Bader had worked hard to prepare his new squadron for further action, although not without causing a few headaches to his superiors on the way. At one point he sent a signal to his Group which stated: "242 Squadron now operational as regards to pilots but non-operational repeat non-operational as regards equipment."

Wg Cdr Beisiegal was appalled, and demanded to know why Bader had not shown him the signal prior to its release off the station! Word soon came back that the signal was causing an awful shindig at Group

Sqn Ldr Douglas Bader, OC 242 Squadron.

Headquarters, to which Bader replied: "There'll be an awful shindig at Fighter Command too; I've sent them a copy as well!" A short pause followed this statement until the Engineering Officer, WO Bernard West, broke the silence by saying: "Well Sir, we'll either be getting our tools or a new CO!"

The fall-out from Bader's signal highlighted a serious shortage of support equipment and ruffled the feathers of many within the Group and command. Bader was summoned to Stanmore Park, Fighter commands Headquarters, to explain his outburst to the AOC Fighter Command, ACM Sir Hugh Dowding. Bader explained to the AOC his reasons for bypassing the chain of command in sending the signal. The AOC accepted his explanation and said cheerfully, "All right. Now you come with me and we'll fix this up." At Coltishall the following day, Wg Cdr Beisiegal held an inquiry into the affair of 242 Squadron's equipment. The next morning the Lorries were rolling past the guardroom to the maintenance hangars to offload the piles of spares.

During this time of chaos on the ground, Bader continued to lead his squadron on twice-daily training missions developing the tactics of large formation fighter attacks. Many of the young pilots found training under him to be hard and unrelenting. Bader's nickname, and personal call sign, was taken from his initials 'DB', 'Dogsbody.' It is said that his call sign alone

gave confidence to his young charges. His persistence and bloody mindedness paid off, as on the receipt of the spares he so desperately needed, he reported to Squadron Operations at Coltishall, and sent signals to both HQ 12 Gp and Fighter Command, to say that his squadron was now operational. It has often been said that under Bader's command, 242 Squadron was the best in Fighter Command, "It was the first, the last and at all times the best"

The same night as 242 Squadron became operational; some 70 enemy bombers were plotted. Unfortunately, thick cloud prevented any interceptions. That evening, it became obvious that a switch of targets by the enemy had made East Anglian airfields and the Midlands Industrial areas the main recipients of their deadly cargo.

Derby, Coventry, Debden, Duxford, Coltishall, Bircham Newton, Finningley, Swinderby, Stamford, Lowestoft, Cromer, Wittering and Sutton Bridge had all been bombed that evening. The unwanted visitors to Coltishall on the night of 24 June followed an earlier raid on the night of 21/22 June, when eleven bombs were dropped. All the bombs missed their intended target, exploding at Swanton Abbott where they caused little damage, except to a horse that was killed. Unfortunately, these were only the start!

Early July saw a visit by PM Winston Churchill. Accompanied by the Station Commander and AVM Leigh-Mallory, Mr Churchill visited the dispersals around the Station to speak to the pilots and ground crews. Plt Off Robert 'Bobby' Oxspring of 66 Squadron was amongst those who were presented to the Prime Minister. The PM asked the pilots how things were going and the main complaint to him was the lack of activity which, apart from Dunkirk, they had borne for nearly a year.

Winston Churchill's response was for them all to be patient because very soon they would have as much as they wanted. Just a few days later he made his famous speech to the nation about the defence of our Islands: 'The Battle of France is over, the Battle of Britain is about to begin.' How right he was!

It is generally accepted that the Battle of Britain started in July 1940, but Coltishall's first loss was not due to enemy action. On 8 July Spitfire I, K9914 of 66 Squadron crash landed on the airfield following an engine fire. The aircraft was later recovered and became an instructional airframe.

But the battle was on in earnest the next day though low cloud obscured the English Channel and there were only a few scattered raids. Norwich received its first

Sqn Ldr Douglas Bader with a few of the pilots of 242 Squadron.

attack of the war by two Dornier Do17z bombers at 2100 hours.

Mr Alan Hague, then living at Brundall, recalls that he was about nine years old and cycling home from Thorpe on the Yarmouth road when he saw two aircraft flying towards him. Thinking that they were Blenheims, he jumped off his bicycle and waved to them, but when they were about 400 yards away and at about 500 feet above the ground he saw the German crosses on the sides and immediately leapt into the nearest ditch. The aircraft passed over Thorpe Hospital and disappeared in the direction of Norwich.

Their particular target was the Boulton and Paul factory where the workers were changing shift as the raid started. Twenty bombs were dropped, causing considerable damage to the engineering works and to Barnard's Ironworks on Mousehold Heath, causing 13 deaths with many seriously injured among the workforce. Spitfires of 66 Squadron were scrambled from Coltishall to intercept the raiders, who had managed to attack before any warning could be given. The fighters caught up with one of the Dorniers but despite firing all their ammunition the bomber escaped.

66 Squadron, still under the command of Sqn Ldr

Rupert Leigh, who incidentally was a close friend and old Cranwell chum of Douglas Bader, did not have to wait very long to be called into action.

On 10 July, enemy activity had been recorded since 0200 hours that morning, and the routine defensive patrols being planned for that day gave pilots from the Coltishall based squadrons some indication that action would be almost inevitable at sometime during the day.

After taking off at 0440 hours, Sgt F N Robertson, flying his Spitfire I, N3035 and two further Spitfires flown by Pt Off's C A Cooke and J Mather, climbed to 15,000 feet on their defensive patrol. A half an hour later they were in the clear skies above the murk over Winterton when they spotted a formation of enemy aircraft off the coast.

They attacked immediately, and as the Spitfire formation flew astern of one of the bombers, which at the time was flying above them, the gunner of the enemy raider raked one of the Spitfires with accurate machine gun fire, forcing the Spitfire formation to disengage their attack.

With the damaged Spitfire heading back to Coltishall, the remaining pair pressed home the attack as the bomber turned for home. Sgt Robertson immediately went in for the attack, and after a long single burst from his machine guns, mortally damaged the Do17Z of II/KG3 which crashed into the sea.

Both Spitfire pilots witnessed the Dornier crew swimming clear of the wrecked bomber before they were forced to return to Coltishall running short of fuel. They were both credited with the destruction of the Dornier - the first recorded 'kill' of the Battle of Britain.

Donald Elliott joined the RAF in 1938 and went to 1 SoTT (School of Technical Training), Halton as a boy-entrant from the Sir John Leman School at Beccles. After training as an engine fitter and passing out in the rank of LAC he was posted to 66 Squadron at Coltishall. Throughout his time in the RAF, Donald kept a meticulous diary from which he used to write weekly letters on RAF life to his family. It is from these diaries,

The Dornier Do17z was pleasant to fly but seriously underpowered. It was no match for a determined Hurricane or Spitfire pilot.

now in the possession of his brother Christopher, that we are able to get an insight of life in early 1940 at Coltishall:

"We got to our new stations last night. I am posted to 66(F) Squadron, Coltishall. It's on the main road between Norwich and Mundesley. It's eight miles from Norwich so I shall be about 28 miles from Beccles altogether...It's a five-minute flight from there to Beccles so I may be seeing you sometime."

Action, with Dunkirk just over, came quickly:

"We lost one of our Spitfires over the sea on Wednesday afternoon. His engine seized up and he had to jump....Every little job you do, however small, is done perfectly....The other morning, when that German machine raided Norwich, it could be seen from this aerodrome by our pilots but, as usual, another muddle and they were not allowed to take-off....We have managed to get one or two Jerries in the last day or

two....Yes, of course, I have worked on some of the machines that have shot down the Nazis. I expect I have been on all of them; there's not many of us for the engines of the whole squadron."

"I am still busy as ever. We start at eight in the morning now, and every night it's either been eight or nine before we have packed up. Sunday is exactly the same as any other day up here, so we don't know one day from another now."

Donald Elliott was at the dispersal on the morning of 10 July 1940, the day that 66 Squadron recorded the first kill of the Battle of Britain. His diary went on to tell the story of the damage to Plt Off Cooke's aircraft on his return to Coltishall:

"The Germans burst of gun-fire went straight through the revolving airscrew and into his bullet proof windscreen - it's a piece of glass about three times the size of this paper and is an inch thick. It was like looking at snow though it. It's been fitted since the war started. If it hadn't, the pilot would have got it in the head. As it was, he said that he said his prayers when the windscreen splintered. I have got a piece of it."

From Coltishall on 19 August Donald reported:

"Out of the blue about 3 o'clock this afternoon came one of those....Nazi things. He let go six or eight over the next hangar....I am sorry to say there were about a hundred workmen working on and around it....a few were killed and a good many injured. It shook us up a good bit - some of the boy's couldn't remember where they were and what they were doing before the bombs dropped....The air-raid siren went after all the bombs had been dropped."

His diary for 22 August went on to say:

"Jerry came again yesterday dinner time, only our fighters were ready for him. It was like disturbing a hornet's nest when he came over. Both Squadrons, 66 and 242 - shot up after him and then began a lovely game of hide-and-seek in and out of the clouds over the camp. Presently one of our Hurricanes came back full-out, dived down low over the drome and shot up again, doing a complete role. That's the sign they all give if they have scored a victory."

LAC Donald Elliott left Coltishall with his squadron for Kenley on the 3 September 1940.

The pilots of Green Section of 242 Squadron also found themselves up bright and early on 10 July. At 0820 hours, whilst patrolling at 8000 feet over a convoy ten miles off Lowestoft, the section sighted two Heinkel He111 H-2's of III/KG53.

Plt Off J B Latta spotted the first Heinkel five miles west of the convoy. Immediately increasing his speed he soon closed in on the raider. His first burst of machine gun fire, from the stern quarter, had no effect. The next attack came from astern at a range of 200 yards.

At 50 yards separation the Heinkel sought cover in the cloud layer at 4000 feet, however by this time smoke was pouring from his starboard engine. Plt Off Latta followed through the thick cloud but was unable to spot the bomber again. It was presumed that the Heinkel returned safely on one engine, but like so many other combat reports the actual outcome was inconclusive.

S/Lt R E Gardner, one of three pilots seconded to 242 Squadron from the FAA (Fleet Air Arm), had the most successful outcome of the trio of Green Section pilots. As he headed out to relieve Red Section on convoy patrol, he first became aware of the presence of the Heinkels by seeing Anti-aircraft fire from the Royal Navy ships whilst flying at 15,000 feet above the convoy. No sooner had he set his gyro on intercept course for the Heinkel's, and as he started to climb to 24,000 feet, when he was ordered back to continue his convoy patrol.

Back above the convoy, he noticed another aircraft four miles to the southeast. This time he successfully intercepted the aircraft and shortly after visual identification, he dived into the attack dead astern. For his second pass, he came in fast at an angle of 25 degrees to the port side. Both the port engine and undercarriage-bay of the bomber were hit in this attack. After his third attack, the bomber succumbed to the damage and crashed or pan caked into the sea. It was two or three minutes before the Heinkel sank, by which time one of the crew had taken to a life raft.

The leader of Green Section, Plt Off A F Eckford, saw two bombs drop close to the convoy as it steamed some twelve miles south-east of Yarmouth. He then spotted a Heinkel He111VA as it climbed north from 12,000 feet into the nearest cloud cover. On emerging from his temporary shelter the Heinkel was met with a long-range burst of machine gun fire from Plt Off Eckford's Hurricane, the tracer fire from the Heinkels top gun position was silenced in the attack.

Both aircraft sank back into the cloud and re-emerged, the Heinkel climbing to the south-east trailing white smoke in its wake. Plt Off Eckford then saw the second Heinkel approaching Green Two. He gave chase and went in for the attack, but soon lost it again in heavy cloud cover.

On this day, the Germans mounted many weather reconnaissance flights to assess conditions over the United Kingdom. One such aircraft, a Dornier Do17 of WetterKundungstaffel 261, was off the coast of East Anglia at dawn. Two Spitfires of 66 Squadron, flown by Sqn Ldr Leigh in L3182 and Sgt R J Hyde, were scrambled at 0600 hours to intercept the Dornier

off Great Yarmouth. Having found the bomber, in the ensuing fight the German was damaged, but Sqn Ldr Leigh's aircraft had sustained damage to its oil tank from return fire from the Dornier which then managed to escape into the clouds. Sqn Ldr Leigh managed to coax his aircraft back to Coltishall although the Spitfire sustained further damage on landing.

In early 1940, a public campaign was launched to recruit WAAF personnel from the Norfolk area to work in the Os Room at Coltishall. This campaign was held at the Odeon Cinema in Norwich with Sqn Ldr Bader on the stage to promote recruitment. Those who volunteered were summoned to Coltishall, uniformed and taken straight to the Ops Room with no training for the task or for RAF life in general.

The original Ops Room at Coltishall was soon closed as it was deemed inadequate for the increase in

Heinkel He111 H-2s of KG53 head for an English target.

work generated within the Sector especially with the additional sorties being flown from the satellite airfield at Matlaske. A new home had to be found reasonably quickly to enable the vital work to continue and it was soon realised that the facilities at Old Catton on the outskirts of Norwich were the ideal alternative.

At this time, the facilities were under Care and Maintenance with only the Meteorological Office in residence. Within weeks the new Ops Room was in full swing with the Duty Watch being transported from Coltishall on a daily basis. Soon however, it was decided that the facilities at Old Catton were unsuitable, and more importantly vulnerable, especially after Norwich became a regular recipient of German bombs with the start of the Baedeker Raids on British cities early in the

Stratton Strawless Hall.

war. In fact, the move proved to be prudent, as by the end of the war over 19,000 kilos of high explosives had been dropped on Norwich causing the deaths of 340 citizens and injuring a further 1092.

At nearby Stratton Strawless Hall, on the Norwich to Aylsham road, a new purpose designed Ops Room was built adjacent to the original buildings with Nissen huts being constructed in the grounds to house the RAF and WAAF personnel who, prior to the completion of the domestic accommodation, were transported to and from Coltishall on a daily basis.

Bentley Priory, Fighter commands Headquarters, was the central processor for all information from the air-raid warning system. It sent information along the nerve fibres of the Fighter Command organisation, which was simple and resilient. ACM Sir Hugh Dowding, the C-in-C of Fighter Command, created three groups within the command, each with responsibility for the airspace within their particular areas of responsibility.

Initially there were three groups, 11 Gp responsible for the South East, 12 Gp covering East Anglia and the Midlands and 13 Gp the North and Scotland. On 8 July 1940, 10 Gp was added to Fighter Commands strength to cover the South-West of England with the threat to the southern approaches. These groups were sub-

divided into Sectors that were given letters, Coltishall being 'Sector J' of 12 Gp. However, as was the norm with other Sectors in Fighter Command, Sector J was known by the name of the sector Station, the airfield controlling them; in this instance, the Coltishall Sector. Sectors were able to control up to six squadrons, but most usually controlled two or three.

It was at the filter room at Bentley Priory that all the information on raids was collected, assessed and compared with known friendly flights. A filter officer gave each raid a number; the track of the raid would then be transferred to Ops Rooms and simultaneously to the group controllers, who then in turn passed the information on to the sector Stations.

Fighter Command itself did not make any tactical decisions about the air fighting. Operational command rested with the groups, and it was they who decided when the direction of the raid was clear and when to send up which aircraft. They then passed the orders to the sectors specifying which units to send up and which raids to intercept.

The sectors were then responsible for bringing their units into contact with the enemy, specifying which direction and at which height to fly. Thus, the group made the tactical decision; it determined the targets of its attacks, when to attack and what forces to use. The sector also had the tactical responsibility of bringing those forces to bear by guiding them to a tactical advantage. They were also responsible for getting their pilots back, helping then to navigate and advising them where to land, which at times was not their home airfields.

Plotting was done in a similar way at Fighter Command, by the Groups and Sectors. In the centre of each room was a large table with a grid-lined map drawn on showing the group and sector boundaries and the airfields within the sector. Hostile raids were plotted by WAAFs who worked in three shifts of about ten hours each and were usually known as the 'beauty chorus.' At sector stations such as Stratton Strawless, each of them was assigned to a radar station and Observer Corps centre within the sector. The WAAFs were equipped with telephone headsets and a croupier's rake with which they moved wooden blocks around the table representing each raid. A floor supervisor told the plotters who to plug their telephones.

The blocks representing the raids had numbers slotted into them to show the raid designation; for example, H06 for 'Hostile 6.' Underneath would be the hostile strength, 30+ to show the minimum size positively identified by the Observer Corps posts or by radar return. Arrows were placed behind the blocks to show the direction of the raid. There was a clock on the wall with each five-minute segment colour-coded red, blue or yellow and the arrows were coloured to show during which segment they had been updated. Observers and controllers could therefore see how up-to-date the information on the table was.

Friendly aircraft were plotted in a separate room and other WAAFs put their blocks on the board showing the units concerned, their strength and their height.

Above the tables arranged around a balcony were the men who used the information supplied. At Stratton Strawless there were typically eight, each with a specific role. At the centre sat the Sector Controller who controlled all the aircraft based at the sectors stations under his control; Coltishall, Matlaske and Ludham. At his left sat an Assistant Controller who dealt with other squadrons operating in the sector and to their flanks sat two Deputy Controllers, one listening in to other sectors and the other dealing with air-sea rescue.

On either side of the Deputy Controllers were 'Ops A' who was in permanent contact with group and 'Ops B' who got through to dispersal and actually scrambled the pilots from the airfields. On the wings of the balcony sat

liaison officers who were in direct contact with Observer Corps Headquarters and Anti-Aircraft command respectively.

For those who lived at the hall, or 'Gin-Palace' as it was more popularly known, it was an escape from the inevitable discipline of life at Coltishall. However, on one occasion, the off duty plotters and support staffs were ordered to attend a drill session on the Parade Ground at Coltishall under the direction of the Station Warrant Officer (SWO), WO Mayes. As many of the locally recruited WAAFs had never been subjected to previous drilling activities, let alone understanding the SWO's fearsome commands, the outcome was awful to say the least! The disgusted SWO finally dismissed them all as a disgrace to his sacred Parade Ground!!

One of those who served at Stratton Strawless was a young, locally recruited WAAF, Bunty Walmsley. As a Corporal, she remembers a couple of incidents that typified life at the 'Gin Palace.' Sun bathing on the roof of the hall was a favourite pastime for those off duties or between shifts. This activity was sadly terminated by the actions of over-zealous American pilots who used to make a 'bee-line' for the hall to admire the view! Her

Stratton Strawless Hall Girls.

second memory arcs back to the early days whilst in the Ops Room at Coltishall. Not long after joining up in 1940, Bunty, together with other members of her watch, were suddenly aroused from their beds and told to immediately assemble outside to be addressed by the WAAF CO.

Garbed in various forms of night attire, they all staggered outside looking the worse for wear. The next moment their CO appeared dressed in full uniform, and to their amazement, proceeded to inform them that the Germans had invaded the South Coast, and that further landings were likely. She went on to say that if Coltishall should be involved, she expected each and every one of them to defend the station in the best possible way. Soon after - on reflection, Bunty decided that her only weapon was a poker allocated to her billet! In the morning, they were all due to report for their watch at 0800 hours. On meeting up with some of the RAF section of her watch, the WAAFs discovered that none of them had been disturbed and were equally unaware of any invasion.

Hilda Hatton, then LACW Hilda Addiss from Dulwich in London, worked in the Ops Room at Old Catton as a Fighter Plotter and remembered with fondness her experiences whilst in Norfolk in the Coltishall Sector.

"I was one of a dozen or so WAAFs who were held at Coltishall waiting for the accommodation to be finished at Stratton Strawless Hall. Whilst at Coltishall, I volunteered to work in the Officers' Mess as a waitress rather than being 'volunteered' for something less savoury. I served the Officers' and their ladies at the Christmas party in 1941 where to my embarrassment, on being tasked to collect the glasses from the ante-room; I found that I was too short to collect the glasses placed on the mantelpiece of the fire place - Luckily there was a rather gallant pilot who lifted me up so that I could reach!"

Hilda and her colleagues worked a 'six on - twelve off' shift pattern in three 'Watches'- A, B and C. This shift pattern continued throughout the war years for Hilda, even over the Christmas periods. In 1942 she was on duty over the New Year and remembered that at the midnight hour some of the WAAFs chased the Squadron Leader in charge of the shift down the corridor and cornered him. The entry in the watch log told of him 'being chased by the WAAF and wrongfully seduced!'

The facility at Old Catton was also shared with other air-defence establishments such as 465 Searchlight Battery of the Royal Artillery manned by territorial soldiers of the 72nd Middlesex Searchlight Battery. Amongst their number was Gunner Ted Hatton who was later to become Hilda's husband. He could not remember seeing Hilda whist she worked at the Ops Room itself, even though she used to pass details of 'plots' to the searchlight co-ordinator in the adjoining office on a regular basis. They only became aware of their close working relationship after they met on a bus whilst travelling into Norwich on a night out. The rest as they say is history; they married after the war when Ted returned from overseas.

It wasn't long however before the new Ops Room at Stratton Strawless Hall became ready for use and the facilities and personnel at Old Catton were transferred lock, stock and barrel. The most striking thing for the 'plotters' who had worked at Catton was the sheer size of the new Ops Room. The previous room only had a double deck for the controllers; Stratton Strawless had three, and whilst working on the top deck Hilda often suffered from vertigo as she found the maps to be further away and distant.

She also remembered the numerous visits by Wg Cdr Max Aitken of 68 Squadron. He used to travel to Stratton Strawless from Coltishall to observe his squadron from the decks when they were involved in major operations. With the plots being moved around the tables and the R/T messages coming over the radio, they often felt they were in the aircraft with the crews. This is why Wg Cdr Aitken chose to be at the Ops Room rather than at the airfield when things were 'hot.'

Hilda eventually left Stratton Strawless in 1943 and was posted to Allerton Park Castle in Yorkshire, Headquarters of 6 (Royal Canadian Air Force) Group Bomber command - often referred to as the Canadian Bomber Group. Her new surroundings were much smaller than those at Stratton Strawless; however, being the old ballroom in the castle, much more imposing and grandiose.

11 July 1940 was a memorable day for Sqn Ldr Bader for it was to be the day he claimed his first enemy aircraft. Over the following months he was to claim a score or more, but this one was special - his first. The aircraft, was a Dornier Do17Z of Wekusta Staffel 261, a long-rang weather reconnaissance unit.

Low cloud and rain had prevented any flying on the morning of the 11th, but a call from operations reporting the presence of a likely enemy raider (Raid 22) over the coast spurred Bader into action. Due to the adverse weather conditions, low cloud at about 600 feet and drizzle, Bader prevented the rest of his section from being scrambled and chose to get airborne himself. After breaking the low cloud and murk at around 700 feet he turned north towards Cromer. Very soon he spotted what turned out to be a Dornier Do17Z, 400 yards directly in front of his aircraft. Suspecting that the enemy did not expect to be intercepted at that height and in such weather conditions he closed to within 250 yards.

As Bader re-set his reflector gun sight to 200 yards the rear gunner of the Do17 opened fire. Bader returned fire as the Dornier banked to the left. Descending through 180 degrees, the bomber then started a shallow climb into the cloud with Bader close behind. At this stage a second burst of fire erupted from the Hurricane, again

While different technically in many respects the Bristol Blenheim (above) and the Junkers Ju88 (right) where often mistaken for each other.

without any visible signs of contact with the bomber. As it seemed obvious to Bader that the interception was unsuccessful, he returned to Coltishall where his failure was reported to the Intelligence Officer in the Ops Room. However, on his return to the dispersal, approximately 15 minutes later, he was informed that a Home Guard observation post had reported that the Do17 had crashed into the sea near Cromer at the exact time of the action.

Blue Section of 66 Squadron, between the times of 1509 and 1614 hours on 20 July, intercepted an aircraft identified as a Blenheim. The Spitfires challenged the aircraft as it was a dirty grey colour and bore no markings, but when the gunner replied with tracer fire they soon quickly realised their error. The bomber was left alone to do whatever it was doing, another secret trial?

On 23 July, Flt Lt George S Powell-Sheddon of 242 Squadron destroyed a Junkers Ju88 of 4(F)/122 SE of Great Yarmouth at dawn. Junkers aircraft from this squadron had recently begun daily weather reconnaissance flights along the East Coast. As Flt Lt Powell-Sheddon was dealing with this particular aircraft, a second Ju88 broke through the cloud in an attempt to bomb Harleston. Luckily for the German crew they managed to escape before the Hurricanes of 242 Squadron could catch them.

But the pendulum of attrition swung again on 29 July when Plt Off Leon Collingridge of 66 Squadron was wounded when his Spitfire I N3042 came down at Orfordness at 1405 hours following contact with a Heinkel He111. He was taken to Ipswich Hospital following the crash.

At 1403 hours that day, a Dornier Do17Z of KG2 was so badly shot up by Hurricanes of 85 Squadron who were guarding Convoy 'Agent', 45 miles east of Felixstowe, that it was forced to crash-land at St. Inglevert. With the evidence of the convoy supplied by the Do17 crew, He111's of KG53, 'Legion Condor', set off to attack the ships. The trap was well and truly set with Hurricanes of 17 Squadron attacking the southern flank of the He111 formation, bringing down one of the bombers, while Coltishall-based Spitfires from 'A' Flight of 66 Squadron went in to the attack from the north.

Prior to this sortie many of the pilots of 66 Squadron discussed their frustrations in the extreme to be sitting at Coltishall less than 100 miles away from the hectic air fighting raging in the south with little chance of helping out. But suddenly, during the sortie off Lowestoft, their morale was uplifted.

Plt Off Bobby Oxspring was leading Blue Section

with Plt Off Peter Studd and 'Pickles' Pickering when control vectored them on to a Heinkel He111. The trio spotted it flying at 15,000 feet on a northerly heading a few miles east of the convoy. Plt Off Oxspring put the section into line astern and led the attack in from above. He misjudged the approach and had to close from dead astern to get into range. As they did so, the rear gunner opened fire, his tracers going to Oxspring's right side and below. Closing in to about 400-yards, Plt Off Oxspring let go with a long burst and then broke up and away to starboard. He didn't see any hits on the Heinkel, but its rear fire had ceased.

Plt Off's Studd and Pickering followed in with their attacks and then they scissored the target from the beams. The Heinkel's wheels dropped down as he headed for some stratus cloud around 8,000 feet. They picked him up again underneath the layer of cloud and expended the remainder of their ammunition into him. The aircraft went down with both engines on fire to ditch in the sea. The trio of Spitfire's stayed long enough to see two of the crew clamber out into their dinghy before the aircraft sank from sight. Back home at Coltishall, they submitted their combat reports to the Intelligence Officer claiming their first victim.

The Heinkel, belonging to I/KG53 based at Lille-Nord, Belgium, was shot down at 1445 hours with the loss of the four-man crew; including those who were seen alighting into their dinghy. A second Heinkel from the same Luftwaffe unit was shot down 14 miles off Hammond's Knoll by a Spitfire of 66 Squadron flown by Flg Off E W Campbell-Colquhoun following interception at 1530 hours killing the five-man crew captained by Leutnant Schattka.

In addition to the many engagements with the enemy that both 66 and 242 Squadron dealt with in July, they were often scrambled to intercept aircraft which turned out to be our own Blenheims from East Anglian stations such as Horsham St Faith and Watton. The trouble for those spotters on the ground was that the Blenheim, from certain angles, looked almost identical to the Junkers Ju88. Naturally, the Blenheim crews became a little agitated with the constant interceptions by the eager and vigilant Hurricane and Spitfire squadrons.

A desk-bound boffin then strived to devise a method of identification for the Blenheim crews when they were approached menacingly by friendly fighters. Effectively, the Blenheim rear gunner fired a very pistol which contained the 'colours of the day.' These colours could be a variety of green and red, two greens or two reds. Unfortunately, no one knew what the 'colours of the day' were supposed to be anyway! Even the Luftwaffe adopted these tactics in the hope of luring the unsuspecting fighter's close enough to successfully engage without being fired at themselves. So, as with many ideas of that time, the results were a failure and the boffins returned to square one to try again!

One particular day, the pilots of both 66 and 242 Squadrons at Coltishall, who were at that time at thirty minutes readiness, were playing a game of rounders. The noise of an aeroplane almost overhead caused many of the pilots and groundcrews to look up, and then ignore the interruption, thinking it was only a Blenheim. Only when a stick of bombs fell on the airfield did they realise that the Blenheim was in fact a Junkers Ju88! Furiously the pilots rushed to the dispersal telephone and asked the operations room what was going on!

A few days later another Ju88 appeared. This time, determined not to be caught out twice, both squadrons reacted with full haste sending twelve Hurricanes and twelve Spitfires in pursuit. This time the enemy was in fact, a Blenheim! Acrimonious discussions followed between the Station Commander and his two Squadron commanders, Sqn Ldrs Douglas Bader and Rupert Leigh.

Thankfully, a much better system of early warning was devised, and whilst the interception of friendly aircraft was not eradicated, the frequency was certainly reduced.

It was not only the flying squadrons who were actively settling in to their new surroundings at Coltishall, as many Officers', SNCOs and other ranks of every trade and persuasion found themselves posted to this new Station in deepest Norfolk.

For Len Taylor, a member of the RAF Volunteer Reserve, his time at Coltishall was full of surprises - he recalls: "In July 1940 after 14 days recruit training at Blackpool that included firing 15 rounds on the rifle range, we were sent to Coltishall to form the Station Defence Flight, although that was something we had not volunteered for." At that time, the Station was still in the process of being built and their first two night's accommodation was in one of the newly constructed hangars; their beds, straw filled palliasses. They then moved from the hangar into bell tents located on the grassed area at the top of the Parade Square before eventually moving in to the newly completed No.6 Block.

Members of the Station Defence Flight were issued with Canadian Ross Rifles, Lewis Guns, Boyes anti-tank rifles and later with Vickers water-cooled machine guns that had been mothballed since the First World War. For anti-aircraft defence they had four 20mm Hispano drum fed cannon with solid ammunition. After about four months, they receive four Twin Lewis guns with ring sights. These proved to be more effective and successful as they fired tracer and explosive ammunition.

When the group first arrived at Coltishall they were met by a Leading Aircraftsman wearing First World War medal ribbons. His promotion through the ranks was probably the fastest in the RAF's history, as within a short time he had become Flt Sgt 'Snuffy Joe' Wells. He gave his charges a real hard time as he tried to mould them into an effective fighting unit.

'Snuffy Joe' and another member of the unit who had previously been a gamekeeper used to go off regularly in a van and return with a mixed bag of game birds for the Officers' and Sgts' Messes. Flt Sgt Wells antics soon became known by all, with the Station Concert Party even going as far as to write a song about him:-

> *"Now Flt Sgt Wells he bellows and yells*
> *When Station Defence all fall in*
> *When he goes out poaching*
> *He needs no coaching*
> *He carries his snuff in a tin*
> *You'm on parade, You'm on parade*
> *You'll hear old Snuffy Joes voice*
> *And when he gets posted*
> *His health will be toasted*
> *And the Station Defence will rejoice."*

One morning, just after the Defence Flight had formed up, they saw the SWO, WO 'Tubby' Mayes, coming on to the parade ground accompanied by a cadre of Guards NCOs led by the unmistakeable figure of RSM Britain, whom they all instantly recognised from seeing him on the newsreels of The Coronation and Trooping the Colour. WO Mayes introduced RSM Britain and his NCOs and explained that over the next few days they would instruct those on parade on the intricacies of infantry practice. This would include bayonet-fighting, priming and throwing had grenades and how not to be shot in the backside when crawling!

Len Taylor remembered several 'hit and run' attacks on the airfield by the Luftwaffe. During one attack, bombs struck the new watchtower and a hangar with the Officers' Mess being missed by a matter of yards. Whilst on another occasion the area around the domestic site was showered with incendiaries, many of which fell within the barbed wire defences. This gave the opportunity for many of the individuals who attended

RSM Britain's infantry training to practice their skills at negotiating barbed wire whilst carrying a sandbag!

In August 1940 the Station Defence Flight were put on invasion 'stand-to', given a few extra rounds and told in no uncertain terms what was expected of them and what to expect if they left their posts. The rumour was that the invasion barges had left port and that fuel was being dropped around them and set on fire. After a very long 'stand-to' they were stood down and went back to the routine of training in the morning, 24 hours guard duty followed by an afternoon constructing air raid shelters - 36 hours on duty in each 48 hour period.

The Station Commander, Wg Cdr Beisiegel, insisted on holding church parades. Many of the aircrew officers had absolutely no knowledge of ceremonial parades and so were instructed by the SWO behind closed doors in one of the hangars. One thing was for sure, if ever there had been a hit-and-run raid on a Sunday morning, it would have been a disaster with all the off-duty personnel formed up on the parade ground making an easy target.

The best duty for the lads on the Station Defence Flight was being sent out on detachment to guard the RDF station which at that time was outside the Station boundary and close to the village of Coltishall. Whoever came off the early morning stint at 0600 hours would go down into the village to the back door of the bakery. There they would collect freshly baked rolls and pasties - a luxury in those days of rationing and shortages.

Len Taylor re-mustered to train as a medic in 1941, although his training as a member of the Defence Flight did no go to waste as he ended up in the Far East where all the medics were armed - necessary because the Japanese did not recognise the Geneva Convention.

On Thursday 1 August, while Wg Cdr Beisiegal, the pipe smoking, phlegmatic Coltishall Sector Controller, and known to his friends as 'Bike', was preoccupied with providing escorts for two coastal convoys. During the mid-afternoon, a raid approached the coast without being detected and carried out a swift attack on Norwich. The targets were the Boulton-Paul factory and the Norwich Thorpe railway yards. A timber yard was almost burnt out, Thorpe station was hit and the nearby Prince of Wales Road machine-gunned before the raider made its escape without harm, though leaving 13 dead and 131 injured in the city.

The balance was adjusted slightly later that afternoon when Junkers Ju88s of KG30 from Aalborg in Denmark and Heinkel He111s of KG4 from Schiphol were heading for Convoy 'Pilot.' Which at that time was passing along the Norfolk coast. From 1800 hours, the bombers made 90 minutes of repeated attacks in an attempt to sink the ships. Hurricanes of 242 Squadron 'B' Flight, Green Section were scrambled from Coltishall to the aid of the convoy.

Flg Off G P Christie (Green 1), Plt Off J B Latta (Green 2) and Sgt Richardson (Green 3) headed towards the convoy and at 1810 hours whilst cruising in a climb at 200 mph, Green 1 saw the familiar form of a Junkers Ju88 heading east about 25 miles off Lowestoft. Flying at 800 feet above sea level, the Hurricane approached the Ju88 that was flying about 1000 feet at half a mile distance. At that point, the crew of the Junkers became aware of the Hurricanes and immediately climbed steeply into cloud.

Flg Off Christie was leading his section in open echelon. Leaving the formation, he chased the Junkers and fired a short burst at the enemy aircraft just as he entered the clouds. He then climbed above the clouds hoping to find the Ju88 and, not finding the bomber, he told Green 2 and 3 to take over the convoy patrol whilst he continued the search.

The Junkers broke cloud-level some three minutes later and a couple of miles east of the searching Hurricane. In a repeat of the first encounter, the Hurricane attacked and the Ju88 ran for cover in the clouds. Green 1 continued the search for a little longer but it soon became obvious that the Junkers had successfully escaped and so the Hurricane rejoined the convoy patrol.

15 minutes later, at 1825 hours, Green 1 sighted another Ju88 just at cloud base. The enemy immediately sped into the cloud, this time Flg Off Christie followed on the same course, but this time underneath the cloud base. He soon spotted the Ju88 in light cloud and he pulled vertically into the attack, managing to fire two short bursts into the underside of the Ju88 before his Hurricane stalled in the climb. Once more, he returned to the patrol.

Shortly after, a Heinkel He111-KV appeared out of the cloud directly in front of him. Being caught by surprise, the lower rear gunner on the Heinkel opened up on the Hurricane just as the bomber released its bombs on the convoy - both bombs and bullets missed their target. The He111 was flying west when Flg Off Christie went in for the attack, but yet again the enemy sought the sanctuary of the clouds. This time however, the Hurricane pressed home the attack as the bomber entered the cloud, and Christie witnessed a large piece of the starboard wing detach from the bomber. Encouraged by the positive results of his attack he continued in pursuit of the Heinkel and took a further snap shot at the bomber as it passed through some wispy cloud. Both the starboard wing and engine were damaged, but unfortunately, Flg Off Christie had to end the chase because he was, by now, low on fuel.

Meanwhile Green 3, Sgt Richardson flying P3087, sighted his Junkers Ju88 at 1855 hours with the help of Anti-Aircraft fire from the convoy below. Flying at 700 feet, 15 miles east of Lowestoft, he flew in for a rear quarter attack on the bomber. The Junkers tried in vein to regain cloud cover when the Hurricane broke away to its rear and turned to starboard.

Overtaking the Ju88 on its starboard side, Sgt Richardson made a front quarter attack. He noticed even before pressing the machine gun firing button that the starboard engine on the Junkers had stopped. Pressing home the attack, he saw thick grey smoke billowing from the crippled Ju88. The bomber then began a very shallow dive towards the North Sea where, just above wave height, the nose rose up steeply and the tail struck the sea. The impact caused the bomber to break in two and just thirty seconds later, it had sunk with no trace of any survivors.

Whilst Green 1 and 3 were busy with their respective bombers, Plt Off Latta saw a succession of enemy aircraft which appeared above the convoy at about five minute intervals. They each sneaked out of the cloud cover for no more than a few seconds at a time. On a couple of occasions Green 2 managed to get two or three short bursts into the bombers as they appeared out of the cloud, but as soon as they saw him they would drop their bombs and run for cover. As the Junkers and Heinkels kept breaking the clouds, it was difficult to know exactly how many there were, perhaps it was just a couple of each type.

The three Hurricanes linked up again for their return flight back to Coltishall where they landed at 1920 hours. This eventful patrol was typical of the operations that were to follow over the following months.

Despite early morning cloud and uncertain weather the launching of the first full air assault against the RAF in the Battle of Britain, known to the Germans as 'Adler Tag' (Eagle Day), came on the afternoon of Tuesday 13 August. Some 405 bomber and 1000 fighter sorties were launched by the Luftwaffe against airfields in Southern England to meet the German High command aim of destroying Fighter Command within four days.

Coltishall was too far north to be directly involved though its squadrons ranged far and wide in support of 11 Group in combating raids further south, and in maintaining defensive patrols over coastal convoys.

On the early evening of 16 August, seven Spitfires of 19 Squadron were returning to their home base at Duxford after spending the day on standby at Coltishall. Suddenly, they were ordered to intercept a force of He111s that were approaching Clacton on their way home after bombing targets on the Thames.

The Heinkels were being escorted by 50 fighters, a mixture of Messerschmitt Bf109s of II/JG26 based at Pas De Calais, France and Bf110s of Stab/ZG26 from Crecy in France. The Spitfires immediately directed their attention to the Bf110s. In the fight, Sgt G E Unwin flying Spitfire R6776 and Sgt J A Potter in R6794 both claimed a Bf110 each. A further two were badly damaged although the tally could have been much higher if the cannon on six of the Spitfires had not suffered stoppages.

Interceptions and aerial warfare over the East Anglian coast remained the main occupation for both resident squadrons for the weeks to follow. 66 Squadron were once again in the thick of things and were again involved in actions on Monday 19 August. At 1415 hours a lone Heinkel He111P appeared through the low clouds over Coltishall, in weather that had almost stopped the resident squadrons flying, and dropped five bombs, hitting an unfinished hangar, killing four of the civilian workmen who were completing the structure and wounding many others. The Spitfires of 66 Squadron were immediately scrambled to chase the bomber and Pt Off J A P Studd, a member of the victorious flight on the 10 July, claimed the aircraft of III/KG27 from Rennes shot down into the sea 30 miles east of Cromer. Unfortunately, Plt Off Studd in Spitfire N3182 was also shot down into the sea by another Heinkel He111 at 1720 hours three miles south of Orfordness. He baled out and was rescued by the Aldeburgh lifeboat but tragically, he never regained consciousness.

Following the attack on Coltishall, it was decided to demolish what was left of the damaged hangar as by now the Station was a fully established fighter airfield and the hangar, designed and built for bombers, was not in fact needed. Over the following months, the remains were razed to the ground and buried within the Station grounds.

On 20 August, despite foul weather with heavy rain and cloud almost touching the ground, 66 Squadron were scrambled to intercept a number of Messerschmitt Bf110's attacking Southwold. Plt Off C A W Bodie and Flt Sgt M Cameron each claiming a Bf110 destroyed, with Flt Lt K M Gilles, Plt Off's Cooke, I J A Cruickshanks and H C Kennard each being credited with a half kill on other Bf110s.

In another engagement with a Dornier Do17, 19 year-old Midshipman P J Patterson of 242 Squadron was killed when his Hurricane P2967 dived vertically into the sea and exploded five miles north east of Winterton in full view of a convoy offshore. It was never confirmed if the loss of the Hurricane was due to enemy action and the official cause of the crash was unknown.

Another raid on Coltishall occurred on Wednesday 21 August at 1415 hours when a Dornier Do17Z-3 of 4/KG3 based at Schiphol in Holland attacked the airfield from out of the clouds. An eyewitness recalled that "it was like a hornets nest when he came over." Both 66 and 242 Squadrons were scrambled and began to chase the raider in and out of the low clouds.

Blue Section of 242 Squadron led by Flt Lt G S Powell-Sheddon sighted the Dornier flying at 3500 feet between two layers of cloud. On intercepting the aircraft, Flt Lt Powell-Sheddon fired at the raider before it reached the

He111, one Dornier Do17, one Dornier Do215 and half of a Dornier Do215, all whilst seconded to 242 Squadron from the FAA. That same day other Spitfires of 66 Squadron came upon a Dornier Do17 fifteen miles north of Great Yarmouth. The enemy aircraft escaped into the cloud, though not before a number of hits from the pursuing fighter had been observed striking the fuselage of the Dornier.

Sqn Ldr Bader's luck in finding a target on 11 July was repeated on 21 August. Being warned by Sector Ops of enemy aircraft at 7000 feet over Great Yarmouth, he climbed into the area to find a thick layer of stratocumulus at slightly above the briefed level. On climbing above the cloud layer, he was rewarded with the sight of a Dornier Do17 in front of him crossing from left to right. The Dornier saw him as he attacked and dived for the cloud cover below. With guns firing, Sqn Ldr Bader followed him down but it was nowhere

Dornier Do215.

relative safety of the lower layer of cloud. The Dornier went right through the cloud with the three Hurricanes on its tail.

Plt Off J B Latta (Blue 2) found himself underneath the bomber about 100 yards away. He allowed 25 degrees deflection and gave it a six-second burst. Simultaneously, Blue 3, S/Lt Gardner carried out his own attack. There was no return fire from the cornered enemy. The Dornier's port engine began to burn and there seemed to be a fire in the fuselage as well. The pilot of the aircraft attempted to land but the aircraft crashed in flames.

Soon the Hurricanes returned to report the raider shot down at Sarston near Harleston where it had crashed in a field killing two ponies; S/Lt R E Gardiner was credited with his second victory. By the end of the Battle of Britain, he was to be credited with one Heinkel

to be seen once his Hurricane came out below the cloud layer. Seething with frustration, and being low on fuel, he returned to Coltishall where he was informed the bodies of the Dornier crew had been washed ashore after the bomber had crashed into the sea; Sqn Ldr Bader was credited with its destruction.

Three Spitfires of 66 Squadron, N3043/LZ-K, N3049 and R6715 destroyed Dornier Do215 (0036/G2+JH) of 4 Aufklarling Gruppe off Yarmouth on 30 August 1940 after a long chase across the Norfolk countryside. Of the crew, Ogefr Sonnleiter was confirmed as killed whilst Obfw Weise, Fw Neubauer and Oblt Hefman were reported as missing. One of the Spitfires, R6715 was hit by return fire from a gunner in the Do215; Plt Off J H T Pickering was forced to bale out over the sea 20 miles east of Aldeburgh and was taken aboard a lightship before being collected by a rescue launch.

Other engagements for the Coltishall squadrons that same day resulted in a Heinkel He111 falling to the guns of Sgt R V H Lonsdale (242 Squadron) and Plt Off H R Allen (66 Squadron). Whilst Sgt A D Smith (66 Squadron) shared in the destruction of a Dornier Do17 and Plt Off J H T Pickering (66 Squadron) was credited with a half a share in the destruction of another Heinkel He111.

Sadly, Sgt Smith died seven days later from wounds received on 4 September whilst on patrol near Purleigh in Essex; his Spitfire, N3048, was attacked by a Messerschmitt Bf109 at 1000 hours. Badly wounded, Sgt Smith baled out of his aircraft but lost his fight for life on 6 September.

At 1453 hours on the next day three Spitfires from 66 Squadron (K9823, N3032 and N3035) intercepted a Dornier Do215 reconnaissance aircraft after chasing it from Norwich to 20 miles south east of Felixstowe. Flt Lt K M Gillies, Plt Off C A W Bodie and Sgt D A C Hunt were all jointly credited with its destruction.

Due to its geographical location Coltishall was escaping most of the wrath of the Battle of Britain which had been the daily lot of fighter squadrons in 11 Gp and it was not until the end of August that AVM Leigh-Mallory, hatched the idea of a 'Big Wing.' That was when squadrons based at Coltishall became more involved in this monumental struggle.

Sqn Ldr Douglas Bader, amongst others, was utterly convinced that this was the most effective method of attack. The 'Big Wing' concept was to gather a minimum of three fighter squadrons operating from bases in East Anglia and to the north of London at a designated airfield, in 12 Group's case, Duxford. Each day the selected squadrons would assemble at Duxford in preparation for the day's conflict. From Coltishall, 242 Squadron flew to Duxford ready to carry out their air defence duties.

In fact, the AOC often visited Coltishall to discuss the 'Big Wing' concept with Douglas Bader. As a good leader, Leigh-Mallory knew how to involve himself with his 'team.' This was illustrated on one of his visits to Coltishall when 242 Squadron held a champagne party for the pilots in the Officers' Mess one evening. Leigh-Mallory came over and entered into the spirit of things by doing a Highland fling on a mess table! There was no doubt that he enjoyed being with his pilots and, more significantly, listening to them. He believed that by involving the pilots in lively discussions, be they experienced flight commanders or first tourists; he could develop his own tactics and ideas.

Action came quickly, and on 30 August 1940, the 'wing' was scrambled to engage a large enemy formation between Enfield and Hatfield. Seven Messerschmitt Bf110s and three Heinkel He111s were claimed that day without loss.

Despite its success, 'Big Wing' operations had many opponents. The principal adversary was AVM Keith Park, AOC 11 Gp, Bentley Priory. The personal conflicts that followed caused a great rift between Leigh-Mallory, Park and their respective groups. Despite their differing and often destructive dissent, the concept was continued with success.

Records of airfield defences, anti-aircraft guns and search-light batteries relating to the Coltishall Sector has remained a difficult area to research as no detailed or comparative records of the positioning of these defences remains, even if indeed they were ever compiled. From the little information available, it is known that during

Spitfire I of 616 Squadron on final approach into Coltishall.

the early part of the conflict 340 Troop, a detachment of 121 Light Anti-Aircraft Battery was based at Coltishall with 65 Searchlight Regiment Royal Artillery providing cover from their detachment at Aylsham. By June 1940, 29 Light Anti-Aircraft Regiment, with its Headquarters at Coltishall, took over responsibility for operating within 'J' Sector, responsible for ten detachments ranging from Bircham Newton in Norfolk to Honington in Suffolk. Following the Baedeker series of raids against English cities another major re-shuffle of anti-aircraft defences took place with 41 Brigade taking over responsibility for the Coltishall Sector in mid-May 1942.

By the mid-war period, some searchlight sites, arising from the re-alignment of Fighter Command, were re-deployed especially to the west of the region. In November 1942, Wittering then placed within 5 Anti-Aircraft Group, lost eight sites with many being taken over by Coltishall. At that time, the following sites came under the control of the Coltishall Sector: CS011, South Wootton; CS028, Holme Hill; CS032, Waterden; CS041,

Saxthorpe; CS051 Horning; CS063, Bungay; CS071, Runhall; CS078, Pulham; CS081A, Reymerston; CS1B, Shipdham; CS2A, Hingham; CS2B Deopham; CS3A, Stow Bedon; CS3B, Ovington; CS4A, Horsham; CS4B, Rockland; CS5B, East Harling; CS93A, Rowdhams; CS7A, Stayhill and CS7B, Ixworth.

There are a few records, including the F540 ORB, that actually show how successful the anti-aircraft defences were in and around Coltishall itself. One of note being on 27 October 1940 when a Heinkel He111 was successfully brought down at 1745 hours whilst it was attacking the base from a height of 5000 feet. This was in fact one of many times when the gunners were to engage the enemy, especially as low-level raids against targets in East Anglia became more prevalent as the war progressed.

AC William Baxter was posted to Coltishall on 9 August 1940 direct from the ITW (Initial Training Wing) at Padgate. He was given the trade of Radio Telephone Operator, but there was no time to send him to Signals School and had to be Station trained as it was 'all hands to the pump' at that time; the case for many who joined the RAF during the height of the Battle of Britain. The accommodation blocks had not been completed by the time he arrived and together with others who were posted to the Station in July and August 1940 - sleeping quarters were in the Games Room of the Airmen's Mess. On completion of the limited number

The Spitfire IIA, introduced to Coltishall by 74 Squadron.

of Married Quarters outside the main camp area, a few of the lucky ones, including William, were moved into Quarter No.64. Fate played a part in many wartime romances and for William, 1941 saw 'Cupid's Arrow' strike in a most unusual way. By this time, William was a Radio Transmitter Operator on a Mobile Flashing Beacon that used to ply the roads around Coltishall and North Norfolk providing a valuable navigational aid for aircraft in and around Coltishall. In 1941, the winter was particularly bad, making movement around the narrow country roads almost impossible. However, due to the important nature of their role, the Mobile Flashing Beacon Teams had to persist in getting their convoys to the designated areas around the base. It was during one of these convoys that Williams vehicle lost traction on an ice-covered hill and finished up in the front garden of a house at Skeyton. Luckily, for the crew of the Mobile Beacon and the occupants of the house, little damage was done. On assessing the situation with the tenant and his family, William and the daughter of the home owners eyes met and following a typical wartime romance, they were married on 1 January 1944 at Skeyton Church.

At the end of August 1940, Coltishall was to welcome an individual, who, by the end of hostilities would be the highest scoring Allied fighter pilot of World War II. Plt Off Johnnie Johnson, together with fellow pilots from 19 Squadron at Duxford, was informed that they were to report to 616(South Yorkshire) Squadron at Coltishall immediately. The pilots were told that 616 Squadron had been pulled out of the front line and required time, and pilots, to reform.

On arrival at Coltishall, Johnnie Johnson and his comrades reported to the squadron office where they gave brief details of their flying careers thus far to the Squadron Commander, Sqn Ldr Billy Burton. Burton explained that 616 Squadron had a rough time whilst at Kenley. Having only been at Kenley for a matter of weeks they had lost quite a few aircraft and more importantly, pilots. His job was to get the squadron operational within the next few days.

Apart from the operational flying, training and hard work to bring the squadron back up to strength, the pilots and ground crews were, on occasions, able to enjoy the creature comforts of hostelries, cinemas and dance halls in the local area. One evening Johnnie Johnson and some of his colleagues were enjoying a drink together in the crowded bar of the Bell Inn, Norwich. A short time later their revelry was rudely interrupted by a group of RAF Policemen who ordered all RAF personnel to report back to their respective bases.

As the group made their way back to Coltishall the topic turned to, "what was happening?" On checking in at the gate they soon realised that an Alert No 1 was in force. This effectively signified that an invasion was immanent or probable within the next twelev hours and as such, all of Coltishall's squadrons were placed on the highest state of readiness.

The scene around the base could only be described as one of confusion and totally chaotic, with many versions of what was happening being suggested. The most popular of those rumours being that the invasion was under way and that an actual landing had been reported on the east coast. Later on, however, they were all told that the reports of enemy were false and that a normal state of readiness could be resumed. By that time, the hapless pilots decided it was too late to return to the Bell Inn to finish what had been so rudely interrupted!

In the meantime, 66 Squadron continued with their shipping patrols over the East Coast bagging a Dornier Do17 off Happisburgh. Losses for the Coltishall squadrons at this time were relatively light however, on 7 September 1940, a young pilot, Plt Off Denis Crowley-Milling of 242 Squadron, was shot down near Chelmsford. Prior to becoming a victim himself, Plt Off Crowley-Milling claimed a Messerschmitt Bf110 in the battle over London that day. Luckily, he survived, and went on to serve in the RAF with distinction, retiring as an Air Marshal.

Extracts from Douglas Bader's flying log-book gives some insight as to how 'Big Wings' were operated. The entry for the 9 September 1940 shows that 242 Squadron led a wing comprising of 19 and 310 Squadrons on patrols over London. On this occasion, they intercepted enemy bombers and fighters south of the River Thames. Of the 20 enemy aircraft destroyed on 9 September, eleven were credited to 242 Squadron. Bader himself shot down a Dornier Do215 that crashed in the Thames. During the conflict 242 Squadron losses were Plt Off Selanden who was killed and Sgt Lonsdale who successfully baled out of his stricken Hurricane to safety. 310 Squadron lost two Hurricanes in a mid-air collision with one of the pilots baling out.

Operations on 15 September saw a much larger 'Wing' comprising of 19, 242, 302, 310 and 611 Squadrons. Once again, the patrol area was over London and the tally recorded in Bader's logbook was, 52 Enemy Aircraft destroyed and eight damaged with 242 Squadron laying claim to a total of twelve enemy aircraft for that day.

During the war years, it was very unusual for squadrons to stay at one base for more than a few months and during September of 1940 the first of these transient squadrons flew into Coltishall with their Spitfires. 616 Squadron under the command of Sqn Ldr H F Burton, was one of the many 'Auxiliary' squadrons that had been formed from dedicated 'week-end' fliers. The Auxiliary Air Force started towards the end of 1925 with the

242 Squadron group photograph at Coltishall.

formation of four squadrons, 600 (City of London), 601 (County of London), 602 (City of Glasgow) and 603 (City of Edinburgh). The idea of part-time flyers for the RAF originated in the mind of Lord Trenchard and was placed in front of the politicians because it would not cost too much money. Luckily for our country the politicians raised no objections and the squadrons were already established and ready on the day war was declared. Prior to the outbreak of war, nearly all the auxiliary squadrons were formed as light bomber squadrons, but by wartime, most ended up in Fighter Command flying Gladiators and then Spitfires or Hurricanes. Soon after the war started there was an amusing story circulating in the RAF of a German pilot being shot down by one of the 'Weekend Flyers' in a Gladiator. When picked up and advised of the situation, the unhappy German was reputed to have flung his flying helmet on the ground and uttered the words "fancy being shot down by a lawyer in a bloody biplane!!"

72 Squadron Spitfires at Gravesend.

Towards the end of the war, in July 1944, 616 Squadron was the first squadron in the RAF to receive Jet-Fighters; the Gloster Meteor.

74 Squadron arrived with 16 Spitfire IIAs from Hornchurch on 9 September 1940, under the command of their South African fighter ace, Sqn Ldr Adolph 'Sailor' Malan.

Just one day after 74 Squadron arrived at Coltishall, three Spitfires, led by Flt Lt J C Mungo Park, intercepted and damaged a Messerschmitt Bf110 ten miles north of Happisburgh. Early that afternoon Plt Off B V Draper, also of 74 Squadron, claimed a Junkers Ju88 some 40 miles south-east of Yarmouth just after it had bombed the town with five HE bombs.

242 Squadron continued with their success, and on 14 September action over London resulted in Bader being awarded the DSO. That same day, 74 Squadron was in action off the Happisburgh coast claiming two enemy aircraft, a Messerschmitt Bf110 and Junkers Ju88.

The air battles for the squadrons at Coltishall were not always one-sided. Sgt D H Ayres of 74 Squadron, flying his Spitfire IIA, P7362, was shot down about one mile off Walberswick on 23 September. He baled out of his stricken aircraft successfully, but got into difficulties once he landed in the water. Unfortunately, he drowned and his body was not recovered until 4 October 1940.

September 1940 was a hectic month for Fighter Command, which resulted in the climax of the Battle of Britain. 242 Squadron were despatched to Duxford on 15 September and on that day, as the hectic battles came about, 242 Squadron was successful in shooting down a Dornier Do17z-3 of 5/KG2, Dornier Do17z-2 of 4/KG3, He111 H-1 of KG53, Dornier Do17z-2 from 9/KG76 and a Messerschmitt Me109-1 of 1/JG3. Later that day on another patrol, it claimed two Dornier Do17s, a single Dornier Do215 and 2 Messerschmitt Bf109s. Post-War, the figures claimed for this day were corrected. However, it does indicate the intensity of the action at that time.

At 1010 hours on 4 October 1940, a Junkers Ju88A-1, 3160/3Z+HL of 3/KG77 from Amiens, was despatched by Sqn Ldr Bob Stanford Tuck off the coast of Southwold. Tuck was returning to Coltishall after operational sorties over London when he intercepted the Junkers. The crew of three, Stabsfw. E Hartmann, Ogefr H Hackman and Gefr. A Simbrick were all killed.

On 5 October an intruding Dornier Do17z was destroyed by Spitfires of 74 Squadron patrolling off Harwich, while Flg Off's R J E Boulding and Szczesny shared in the destruction of a Dornier Do215. Misfortune befell the squadron on 8 October when Plt Off D Hastings and Plt Off F W Buckland were killed when their Spitfires, P7329 and P7373, collided in mid-air over Coltishall at 1540 hours whilst practising fighter attacks. Plt Off Buckland had only been on the squadron for eleven days.

A further loss was sustained by 242 Squadron on 17 October when Plt Off Neil Campbell RCAF was killed when his Hurricane V6575 was shot down by a Dornier Do17 at 0925 hours 30 miles off Great Yarmouth. His last message on the radio was that he was attacking - then silence. His body was recovered from the sea and was laid to rest with full military honours in the Scottow cemetery, close to the runway from which he took off on that fateful day. In the same battle, Hurricane P3207, also of 242 Squadron, with Plt Off M K Brown at the controls sustained damage in the cockpit and to his throttle quadrant, but on this occasion the aircraft landed safely back at Coltishall.

October was a busy time for Coltishall with the arrival of two more squadrons. 64 Squadron, with Sqn Ldr A

222 Squadron group photograph at Coltishall.

R D Macdonnel in charge, arrived on the 15th with 72 Squadron, under the command of Sqn Ldr D F B Sheen, taking up residence five days later. On 20 October 1940, Coltishall's first squadron, 242 Squadron and their famous Commander, Douglas Bader, left the base for Duxford.

242 Squadron's replacement, 72 Squadron, wasted no time in getting to grips with the enemy by damaging a Dornier Do17 on 27 October. That same evening, the enemy did not concentrate their actions solely on the London area.

At dusk a Heinkel He111 H-2 of I/KGI from Montdidier swept low over Coltishall and machine-gunned the airfield. Ground defence Lewis Guns around the airfield opened up in reply and the Heinkel later came down in the sea off Lowestoft. This evening raid was repeated when Coltishall was again strafed at 1823 hours on 29 October; this time by a Junkers Ju88 and a Heinkel

257 Squadron on a chilly day at Coltishall.

He111. One of the raiders dropped several bombs on the nearby village of Lamas and the inclusion of the name Miss Clare M Staner on the church war memorial records her death as a result of this action.

Though not attributed to enemy action, the pilot of Spitfire N3293 belonging to 64 Squadron made a safe forced landing near Horsford at 2325 hours on the same day during a routine patrol.

Nuisance raids such as this caused little damage. However, it did highlight the vulnerability of massing fighters in a single area. Satellite airfields were specifically designed so that stations could disperse their assets away from the main base. In Coltishall's case, the first of two satellite airfields was to be Matlaske some twelve miles North-West of Coltishall near the town of Holt.

Effectively the two airfields really operated as one, and by October 1940, Matlaske had two relatively short runways, 1600 and 1300 yards respectively. In retrospect, the haste to get the airfield ready may well have been responsible for the severe drainage problems that Matlaske was to suffer throughout its existence. Living quarters had not been completed by the time the first aircraft arrived during late October.

Nearby Matlaske Hall was requisitioned as living quarters and after the staircase and fire-places were boxed in, became home for both air and ground crews. It was described by its wartime inhabitants as "charming", very different from some of the accommodation at some of the other airfields scattered throughout Norfolk!

Raids persisted, and at 0736 hours on 8 November a single Dornier Do17 on Coltishall dropped ten high explosive bombs on the Watch Tower and surrounding area. The damage caused to this structure and other buildings was sufficient to render many unfit for use and the Watch Tower had to be demolished and re-built.

Rain and low cloud restrained the German activities on 9 November though a few sorties were launched against London and the Home Counties, making use of the cloud cover to evade searching fighters. In the early afternoon however, three Spitfires of 72 Squadron, flown by Plt Off R S Smith, Flt Sgt J Steere and Sgt P Douthwaite intercepted a Heinkel HeIII near Great Yarmouth. In a fierce battle the bomber was shot down into the sea, though return fire seriously damaged Plt Off Smith's aircraft causing him to force land at near Great Yarmouth.

The Spitfires of 222 Squadron, under the command of Sqn Ldr J H Hill, arrived on 11 November to replace 64 Squadron, who had left the day before having been in residence since 15 October. The new squadron had returned to Coltishall after hectic activity in the Battle of Britain with 11 Gp and at one time had been down to three serviceable aircraft. During their rest at Coltishall, they were mainly employed in flying 'Kipper' patrols over the North Sea fishing fleets with their aircraft being detached to operate from Matlaske from time to time.

On 29 November 72 Squadron, who had only been in residence since 20 October, departed north to Leuchars. Since the departure of 242 Squadron, Hurricanes were few and far between at Coltishall however on 15 December 1940 this was to change with the arrival of 257 'Burma' Squadron.

257 Squadron was perhaps the most famous of all squadrons to operate from Coltishall during the war years. It was proud to be known as the 'Burma Squadron' in recognition of the financial support for the aircraft it received from that country. The Squadron Badge was centred by a Chinthe Sejeant, and its Burmese motto 'Thay Myay Gyee Shin Shwe Hti' translated into Death or Glory. A proud motto that the squadron and its pilots lived up to. The squadron was under the command of an equally famous Squadron Leader, Robert (Bob) Stanford Tuck. 257 Squadron was to be resident at Coltishall for almost 12 months, an unusually long occupation, especially as fighter squadrons were moved on a regular basis to satisfy changing operational demands.

On 11 December the radar screen at the coastal radar stations were devoid of enemy aircraft but a number of Junkers Ju88s infiltrated a homecoming bomber stream and dropped bombs on Coltishall before breakfast. More early warning was available on 29 December when the radars picked up a lone aircraft flying at 4000 feet off the coast, south of Great Yarmouth. Despite mist hanging over Coltishall, Sqn Ldr Stanford Tuck and Plt Off Carl Capon were scrambled on an easterly heading to intercept the aircraft. As they crossed the coast, they came into an area of clear sky and saw a Dornier Do17 only a few hundred yards away. Their proximity was due to some precise vectors given to them by the plotters at the sector. Attacking immediately, Plt Off Capon made a beam attack whilst his Squadron Commander fired rounds into the fuselage and the bombers port engine before the Dornier rolled over and crashed into the sea off Great Yarmouth.

At the end of 1940, Coltishall's first operational year, squadrons had claimed 83 Enemy aircraft destroyed, 22 probable and 16 damaged; certainly a premonition of what was to follow.

Chapter 3

1941 - THE FIGHT CONTINUES

The first day of 1941 claimed the life of Plt Off Capon of 257 Squadron. His Hurricane, V7186, crashed on landing after a dusk patrol in atrocious weather conditions; an ominous start.

The following months, in early 1941, saw action centred on enemy aircraft operating off the coast. These duties were known as 'Kipper' patrols, effectively protecting the North Sea fishing fleets that had been receiving excessive attention from the Luftwaffe over the past months. The enemy intruders frequented East Anglian skies on cloudy, rainy days when they knew it would cause the defenders more problems; however, Coltishall's squadrons did their best in difficult circumstances.

As weather conditions improved during the New Year, Coltishall's Hurricanes were used for fighter sweeps over the Dutch coast attacking any enemy target. These raids, known as 'Rhubarbs', were effectively individual low-level attacks over enemy held territory when weather and cloud conditions were favourable.

At 1356 hours on 15 January, 257 Squadron was ordered to patrol over the Honington area in response to an enemy aircraft sighting. The enemy was not seen, but as the patrols were readying themselves to land back at Coltishall, they spotted an aircraft at about 20,000 feet over the Sheringham area. The aircraft, a Heinkel He111, was reconnoitring the coastline. Closing in fast on the enemy, the Hurricanes opened fire and saw smoke coming from the bomber which in turn produced some wild and inaccurate return fire. The He111 was soon lost in thick cloud. This was the nearest that fighters had yet come to 'bagging' an East Anglian raider in 1941.

In the early days before the introduction of ground radars for fighter control the early warning available depended upon the 40 miles range of the coastal sited (AMES) Type 1 or Chain Home radars. Nevertheless, having crossed in over the coast enemy aircraft were usually lost from radar cover and were able to roam almost at will in the cloud layers prevalent over England in winter. Thus it was that three sections of fighters were scrambled from Coltishall on 2 February to intercept a lone Dornier Do17 which had attacked Wymondham at mid-morning. Due to low cloud and the absence of information on their target the Dornier escaped unharmed. Later that day, Flt Lt Van Mentz of 222 Squadron suffered the frustration of missing a raider that actually passed directly over Coltishall.

Sqn Ldr Bob Stanford Tuck, OC 257 (Burma) Squadron.

On 3 February, nine Junkers Ju88s of III/KG30 attacked airfields in Suffolk, and at 1330 hours a single Ju88 was discovered over Harwich by two Hurricanes of 242 Squadron, but this again disappeared into the cloud cover.

In clear conditions on 4 February, Plt Off Barnes in his Hurricane, V7137/DT-G, and Sgt Brejcha in P3705/DT-B, both from 257 Squadron, was ordered to intercept a Dornier Do17-2W which was reported heading for Mildenhall. Once airborne from Coltishall they were soon aware that the Do17 had in fact bombed its secondary target, Lowestoft, with eighteen HE bombs. The Hurricanes intercepted and shot down the bomber half a mile off the coast. Only one seriously injured crew-member survived.

Late in the evening of 10 February, three Messerschmitt Bf110s attacked Coltishall and fired at a Hurricane of 257 Squadron being flown by Sgt Alfred Warminger as he was approaching to land after a night patrol. Sqn Ldr Stanford Tuck was down at his squadron's dispersal when he heard the screaming engines of the raiders just as they dived into the attack. He ran out of his office just in time to see one of the aircraft flash across a patch of moonlight.

Tuck sprinted to one of the defence posts, jumped into a slit trench and began blazing away with a twin Lewis gun. If there was one thing he hated, it was being caught on the ground like this. Flames and dirt rose all around and the air shuddered as the German's cannon shells

Sgt Alfred Warminger.

and bullets raked across the grass and perimeter tracks. There was a stench of cordite as more Lewis guns joined the fight. It was all over in less than two minutes. Holes in the airfield, barrack blocks damaged and one or two airmen injured, but thankfully no one killed.

This event angered Sqn Ldr Stanford Tuck as he had in the previous months tried to organize a raid just like this against enemy airfields on the Continent. He was convinced this was possible, especially as his squadron was now equipped with cannon armed Hurricanes. However, according to the Air Ministry, neither the Hurricane nor the Spitfire could stay in the air long enough, or travel far enough into enemy territory to make such operations worthwhile. Tuck was not convinced and was determined to prove otherwise.

With his engineer Flt Sgt Tyler and Flt Lt Blatchford, his number two, he worked out a system by which they could log the petrol consumption, range and endurance or the Hurricane to the yard and second. From this time onwards, both he and Blatchford snatched every chance to check out their theory. At very low level, they flew in formation up and down a measured stretch of the East Anglian coast, experimenting with different throttle settings, engine performance, fuel mixtures and speed - keeping a meticulous record of each flight.

After about three weeks of experiments between operational sorties, they had amassed enough data to prove, given that all weather conditions were in their favour, that the Hurricane and Spitfire could make the round trip as far as the North of Holland, and even have enough fuel to engage the enemy for ten minutes using full combat power.

Sqn Ldr Tuck prepared his report, attached his data and forwarded his findings to Headquarters 12 Gp at Watnall for approval. Having waited for two weeks for an answer, he decided to plan an attack against ground instillations across the Channel. The answer to his detailed research and his request to carry out this sortie over the Channel soon arrived - his request was refused - as was the data that proved such missions could be launched; disgusted, he gave up the whole idea for the time being.

Even though 242 Squadron had left for Duxford back in October of 1940, and then subsequently moved onto Martlesham Heath later that year, they still worked in the Coltishall Sector. It was on such an occasion that the squadron once again fought over their old stomping ground.

Low cloud persisted for most of February and the same pattern of raids continued, maintaining the frustration for the fighters. Several bombs fell at Oulton Broad at 1547 hours on 14 February but fighters from 242 Squadron were already airborne from Martlesham.

Sqn Ldr Turner and Flt Lt Donaldson spotted a reconnaissance aircraft flying in excess of 29,000 feet. As they climbed to the designated height, it became clear that the enemy was well above the reported altitude. Unable to affect the intercept due to the height, Turner and Donaldson resumed their patrol until Ground Controllers told them that the intruder had descended, this time to 25,000 feet. Again, they climbed expecting to find a Junkers Ju88 or Dornier Do215, types usually involved in long-range reconnaissance flights over the British mainland. This time however, they were very surprised to find a Messerschmitt Bf109 operating at extreme range.

The Bf109 pilot, realising that he had Hurricanes for company, used his superior speed advantage to slip away from the pursuing fighters. This particular flight may well have been the furthest north over Britain that a Bf109 had so far ventured. Whilst the interception proved less than fruitful for the Hurricane pilots, it did give the Intelligence Community a further, valuable, insight into the capabilities of enemy aircraft.

Later that same day Flt Lt Crowley-Milling of 242 Squadron engaged a Junkers Ju88 over the Norfolk countryside, setting fire to its port engine whilst chasing it for more than 40 miles. The chase ended over Aldeburgh when Crowley-Milling was forced to withdraw from the fight with a damaged fuel tank and shattered windscreen on his Hurricane.

The final engagement of the day met with a little more success. Plt Off B P Clee, flying a Spitfire of 222 Squadron, spotted a low flying bomber as it crept over the coast south of Yarmouth. He dived from 7000 feet onto the unsuspecting intruder, and as he closed to within 300 yards, he poured machine gun fire into the fuselage and wings, giving the crew no time to react. The bomber crashed shortly afterwards into the sea.

Better weather on 16 February 1941 assisted the defending fighters. An enemy raid had been operating offshore but was intercepted by Plt Off's Kay and McTyre at low level off Great Yarmouth. Plt Off Bedford of 257 Squadron encountered a Heinkel He111 over Sheringham at midday, but neither of these interceptions proved successful. Later that evening a dozen enemy aircraft attacked airfields in Norfolk, including Coltishall.

Sporadic action continued in daylight of 17 February and at midday aircraft of 222 Squadron damaged a Dornier Do 17 over Marham and another section of the squadron found and destroyed a Junkers Ju88 five miles east of Cromer.

On 20 February another attack was made on Coltishall by a Junkers Ju88 making a low pass over the airfield, damaging Hurricane W9306 in its attack.

At 0945 hours on 24 February, enemy aircraft made landfall over Cromer. In response, two Hurricanes of 257 Squadron were sent to investigate and locate the intruders. At 8000 feet, 15 miles east of Happisburgh, they located a Dornier Do17 of 8/KG3. Plt Off E H Atkins flying P5186, fired at the Dornier before return fire damaged his Hurricane so badly that he was forced to bale out, unfortunately, never to be seen again. The Dornier also badly damaged and on fire, crashed into the sea with no survivors.

Following the frustrations over 12 Group's reluctance in authorising a raid on airfields and targets on the Continent, better news came when on 24 February. Sqn Ldr Stanford Tuck finally received the signal giving him permission for an offensive sortie the next day. He was to lead the first strike against enemy-occupied territories to be made by fighters from East Anglia. On reading the signal, Tuck noted imposed and unexpected restrictions: only two Hurricanes were to take part in the 'experimental offensive', and in no circumstances were they to open fire unless attacked by enemy aircraft.

The objective was a good-sized, triangular area of Holland that included several Luftwaffe airfields, some important railway junctions and bridges plus one or two factories. Their main purpose, as was defined by the orders, was to test the strength and efficiency of the enemy defences. Consequently, Sqn Ldr Tuck and Flt Lt Blatchford spent the evening before the raid mulling over maps of the region and working on their flight plan; double-checking every detail.

The next morning they were greeted by clouds - an almost unbroken layer of stratus that stretched northeast at only a few hundred feet. The Met Office had more bad news for them as they predicted that the cloud extended right over Holland. If there was any good news in the forecast, it would provide them with excellent cover if they needed to make a quick climb-away and, providing they stayed fairly close together, the cloud wasn't thick enough for them to loose each other and risk a collision. The latter proved an important caveat as they had planned the sortie to be in complete R/T silence - at least until they crossed the Dutch coast.

At their aircraft, Tuck and Blatchford were greeted by quite a crowd who had gathered to see them off. It was a long time since any British fighter had flown over the sea into the enemy-held stronghold. This was to be an exciting moment, a minor turning point that gave every

Flt Lt Peter 'Cowboy' Blatchford.

pilot the hope for some action over the Continent in the months to come. Within minutes of take-off, Tuck thought that he might have to cancel the whole operation as, when he throttled back to economical cruising speed, as computed in their flight plan, his Hurricane began to wallow and threatening to stall because of very floppy controls. He quickly checked his instruments - all was well - his engine sounded smooth - what could it be? Lifting his head from the instrument panel, he looked at Blatchford flying along a few feet to his starboard side. Clearly laughing, Blatchford held up one hand, and with two fingers pointing downwards, he waggled them to imitate walking legs. He then nodded down to indicate something on the underside of Tuck's aircraft. The undercarriage - in his excitement and for the first time in his flying career, Tuck had forgotten to retract the wheels! As the undercarriage retracted after Tuck had snatched at the lever in a mild and embarrassed rage, the Hurricane became instantly buoyant again and flying just as expected.

The two Hurricanes were now on their way in the dark and dank cloud. A little way out over the North Sea, they dropped down to wave height and sped their way across to the Dutch coast. The flight itself seemed to take forever, giving both pilots plenty of time to wonder how they might nurse their damaged aircraft back over the sea to safety if they got into trouble. After all the mounted tension, the fifteen minutes over Dutch territory proved to be a big anti-climax! They saw plenty of enemy aircraft, all on the ground. Plenty of Germans too, with the majority taking only a casual glance at the low-flying Hurricanes. Around the airfields and dotted along the coast they spotted plenty of gun positions, but only a few gun crews noticed the British markings and came to life with some wild bursts of fire after the Hurricanes were well out of range. Others actually waved as they flew past, no doubt mistaking them for a couple of Luftwaffe fighters. Not that the Hurricane looked anything like a Messerschmitt 109. Apparently it just did not cross the Germans' minds that British fighters could come that far.

They circled one large aerodrome several times and then flew straight at the control tower a matter of feet above the grass. As they pulled up and banked steeply, both Tuck and Blatchford saw the upturned faces behind the large windows of the towers, oblivious to what was actually happening. Next they saw a party of German troops trudging along a main road. Flying as low as they dared they crossed over the troops causing them to scatter in every direction and duck! Fists were raised but no rifles were fired. For the Dutch people the sight of the Hurricanes, that they immediately recognised, gave cause for hope. Entire families seemed to come out of farmhouses as the roared by, waving towels and aprons with unmistakeable joy. Workers in the fields and people in villages waved them back home to safety - one day, they would be back!

Keeping a weary eye on the time and their critical fuel levels, both Hurricanes worked their way back to their 'exit' point - they crossed the coast of Holland unmolested. As they neared the coast of England, and with plenty of fuel to spare, they spotted a lone Messerschmitt Bf110 away to the north. Turning to chase and using full throttle for four or five minutes they closed in. Then, as the crew of the Me110 spotted

the two Hurricanes, it darted into the cloud and made a hasty retreat. The two Hurricanes turned back, headed for Coltishall, and landed with their gun port shields intact.

Subsequent events showed this to be an historic flight. It set the pattern for the type of operation that the C-in-C, ACM Sholto Douglas, christened 'Rhubarb.' Sqn Ldr Stanford Tuck's report proved that the 'Atlantic Wall' had big gaps. The German radar could be evaded and the Luftwaffe could be caught with their pants down just like anyone else!

As spring approached, better weather deterred the Luftwaffe from heavy daytime activity, with more effort being put into the safer night assaults but the occasional track was detected on the radars and at breakfast time on 26 February Hurricanes of 257 Squadron intercepted a Dornier Do17z six miles south east of Cromer. Flt Lt Peter 'Prosser' Hanks, who was to become the Station Commander at Coltishall in the early 1950s, made several passes without success as the Dornier escaped into the cloud.

Several early morning raids drew the attention of Coltishall fighters on 8 March. At 0840 hours fighters were scrambled to intercept a Dornier circling Norwich, but it had gone by the time they reached the scene.

Later, Junkers Ju88s of II/KG30 drew 222 Squadron into precautionary patrols over Great Yarmouth. On arrival over their designated patrol area, Plt Off B P Clee, flying Spitfire R6596, witnessed a Junkers Ju88 dive through the clouds and drop four bombs in the sea off Britannia Pier. He closed in and poured his ammunition into the bomber as it climbed through 7000 feet.

As his No 2, Sgt R G Morland, in R6684, made three attacks while a gunner in the Ju88 scored hits on R6684's Merlin engine. The action badly damaged the Ju88, coded 4D+DN, and it was finally despatched by Morland who fired his remaining ammunition into the aircraft before it crashed into the sea off Gorleston. Morland's damaged Hurricane made it safely back to Coltishall.

More enemy activity against coastal shipping was countered on 17 March when Flt Lt Van Mentz in P7697 and Plt Off Clee flying P7699 encountered an aircraft at high level over Sheringham. As the Spitfires climbed to intercept, the enemy aircraft dived away from the coast and increased its speed to escape but the Spitfires were able to overtake it and shot the bomber down into the sea 25 miles east of Sheringham.

The next day, Sqn Ldr Stanford Tuck was on patrol at 0825 hours when he caught sight of a Dornier Do17z. In hot pursuit of the enemy, he shot it down into the sea four miles south of the Cromer Knoll light vessel. Flt Lt Peter 'Cowboy' Blatchford, also had similar success that same evening with the destruction of a Junkers Ju88 off Southwold.

In an attempt to counter the night attacks more effectively the first of several detachments of 151 Squadron arrived on 20 March equipped with the Boulton Paul Defiant. commanded by Sqn Ldr Adams DFC, the squadron was based at Wittering, but with trade becoming scarce over the Midlands it was decided to move the aircraft forward to Coltishall to catch the enemy before they crossed the coast.

Four days later 222 Squadron lost Spitfire IIa P7847 which broke up in mid-air over Salhouse, killing its pilot Sgt F J Cockram. This was followed by other losses on 27 March when Spitfire P7857 crashed and P8028 was lost. A week later another Spitfire IIa, P7780 broke up in the air near Southborough, Norfolk; none of these events seemingly caused by enemy action.

Beccles witnessed the end of a Junkers Ju88 of II/KG77 on 1 April after it took off from Rheims for a reconnaissance of North Sea shipping. Two Hurricanes of 257 Squadron were scrambled form Coltishall, flown by Plt Off G North and Sgt Alfred Warminger. Two further Hurricanes from Martlesham Heath based 242 Squadron were also scrambled from their Suffolk base.

When the two Coltishall aircraft reached the target area over the coast they were sceptical of it being a bandit, especially considering the clear skies at the time. Even on sighting the aircraft 2000 feet or so above them, their first reaction was one of caution. Bristol Blenheims looked remarkably like Junkers Ju88s from head-on and at the time were being used for anti-shipping strikes off the Dutch and Continental coasts. Their caution was unfounded - it turned out to be an enemy as on seeing the Hurricanes it immediately dived to increase speed, turning onto a south westerly heading off Caister. Although climbing as hard as the Merlins would allow, the pursuing Hurricanes were still a good 1000 feet below when the aircraft passed overhead. Despite Sgt Warminger standing his Hurricane on its tail, almost on the stall, he could not get sights on the raider. The enemy gunner gave a short burst from his machine guns for good measure. Then the Junkers Ju88 steamed away towards Beccles. Both Hurricanes were then directed by the controller on the R/T to climb up and turn south, thus cutting off the German's seaward escape as the aircraft from 242 Squadron were in a good position to effect their interception. A few seconds later,

the Coltishall pair saw the other Hurricanes which were about to dive on the enemy as he disappeared into a bank of cloud overland. They then heard the satisfactory outcome over the radio. The Ju88 jettisoned four bombs before falling onto the marshes near Basey Fisher Farm, Henstead, only two members of the crew managed to bale out, both landing safely to be taken prisoner.

In April 1941, AC Frank Webster left 151 Squadron at Wittering and was posted to 222 (Natal) Squadron at Coltishall. With two other 'erks', whose final destination was unknown to Frank, a slow train journey across country took them through pleasant, watery landscapes until they eventually alighted at Norwich. It was afternoon and, rightly or wrongly according to RAF dictates, they went to the pictures to cheer themselves up. They saw 'All This and Heaven Too' with Charles Boyer and Bette Davis. They were not cheered up - it was doleful! After this, the three made their farewells and Frank then caught the train to Coltishall. Arriving at his new station, he was to find a more modern complex in comparison to the earlier RAF type buildings he had left behind at Wittering. The barrack blocks were light, airy and more spacious. It seemed, as always, that no sooner had one arrived that the barrack-room intelligence was confiding that they would 'all be moving soon.'

The next day, after traipsing around camp getting his Arrivals Chit signed, Frank, as an Instrument Repairer, was directed to 'A' Flight out at the dispersal following first reporting to the hangar for directions. The eventual acquaintances were made of LAC Ted Matthews and Bob Harris, AC Ron Wharton, Stanley Ball and Cyril Stansmore, all Instrument 'Bashers.' They all worked the Flights and covered different times of the day.

In the Ground Crew Room, all was casual with nods of greeting from other tradesmen. The Flight Office, situated at one end of a Nissen Hut, was led by Flt Sgt (Chiefy) Packham and his NCO's. At the other end of the hut was the Pilot's Crew Room, with a door leading on to the pilot's Kitchen Garden - a pastime they enjoyed whilst awaiting 'scrambles' or other types of aerial activity.

Back in the Flight Office was a telephone manned by an 'erk'; he was also responsible for other admin duties around the office. The ringing of the telephone prompted a quick answer and thoughtful expectation by all who heard it. Often the 'erk' crashed out of the office door to frantically ring the 'panic bell' hanging outside the hut. Immediately the pilots and ground crews who were at readiness went into action. The pilots who had been sitting, reading, chatting or gardening dashed to their aircraft - if they had not been near them already.

The ground crew fitters and riggers were already there. One helped strap his pilot into the cockpit and at 'thumbs-up' the other pressed the 'tit' of the previously connected trolley actuator; the engine roared into life and the aircraft were soon airborne. It all happened in as many minutes. The Form F700 (aircraft log-book) had been signed long before by all the tradesmen stating that the aeroplane was fuelled, armed (fire power being eight machine guns), electrics, sufficient oxygen and wireless working OK. Still very 'green' in service terms, Frank remembered having an 'Alice in Wonderland' approach to such events.

222 Squadron at that time was led by Sqn Ldr Love with Flt Lt Davis as 'A' Flight Commander. The only other pilots names Frank could remember were Plt Off's

the haze to see the dark shape of a Spitfire loom out of the gloom which was then given its Daily Inspection by all trades.

Instrument repairers, along with wireless operators, electricians and armourers were classified 'ancillary trades' to flight mechanics and riggers. Rough interpretation is that fitters and riggers had enough to require their full attention of engine and airframe of one aircraft. Ancillary equipment could be, and was, covered by a lesser number of 'bods' covering the whole flight - about six aircraft. Later on in the war Frank formed the opinion that the United States Army Air Force and the South African Air Force to name but two, used far more men with far less responsibility than RAF ground crews - a fitting tribute to the training instigated by the 'Father of the Royal Air Force' - Lord Trenchard.

151 Sqn Defiant.

Laurie and Clee. Thoughts of Clee were sombre. He was a fresh, fair and stocky character and after one sortie he was describing his experience in typical fighter-pilot language and actions - many 'zoings' (cannon shells hitting his aircraft) and much arm-waving. On his next scramble he flew off into the cloud toward the coast and unfortunately did not return.

When the squadron was flying there was a ground lull, or vacuum, giving time to explore other areas of the dispersal, and that was the operative word. Dispersed in special clearings were more aircraft but which couldn't fly - they were plywood decoys looking like the real thing. Elsewhere were other Spitfires of higher Mark awaiting attention. They were modified with two cannon and four machine guns. For Dawn Readiness, duty ground crew slept, usually fully dressed, in the Dispersal Hut. In the early hours, invariably misty, one had to negotiate

It was on Frank's first Daily Inspection in the mist that he met LAC 'Paddy' McNamara. He was obviously Irish, well built with curly hair and a ready smile. No doubt looking bewildered and lost Frank was helped by his friendly approach and questions asked in a soft brogue; 'Can I help you chiefy?' He could and did help, but that smile and soft voice could be deceptive on certain occasions - he was tough.

He went around with Jock, a small, stocky, dour, also tough Scot and a slim talkative Englishman named Martindale. Martindale's talk usually landed the trio in bother - away from the squadron and against any rivals from any source. They were characters and a variation on a theme - An Englishman, Irishman and Scotsman!

The journey to and from dispersals was made by lorry or wagon. The vehicles passed a gun pit manned by RAF Ground Gunners (forerunners to the RAF Regiment), the Ground Gunners (GG) being interpreted as 'Glamour Girls.' A ritual took place on every journey, shouted insults from the wagon to the GG's were based on 'What time does the gun go of?' to be answered by something like 'Get some service in you Brylcream Boys!'

At the time the RAF Regiment was not sufficiently established to guard Air Ministry property and this was done by the army. Three incidents of that time remained in Frank's memory. One concerned a Welsh regiment. Army privates were paid two shillings a day (AC2 RAF tradesmen got four shillings). With no money for luxuries or the 'high-life' in Norwich, the Welshmen did what they do very well, apart from fighting! They sang, and that was how they spent most evenings in the NAAFI over a pint of beer.

The second memory was of the Rifle Brigade, later residents at Coltishall. They marched at 140 paces to the minute, and for speed no doubt, they marched off from the 'Easy' position. On the command 'quick-march', they came to attention, sloped arms, right or left turned and marched off. For mere mortals in the RAF that would take four commands.

The third recollection concerned an RAF Policeman, not very likeable, even sadistic. At an invitation-boxing tournament, an army private did what many of the RAF lads would like to have done; give the policeman an official good hiding! Frank never saw the fight, but saw the Corporal's face the next day.

Frank's billet was a barrack block opening onto the Parade Square. His room was upstairs with room for perhaps 20 beds. His bed was first right inside the door with the Tannoy loud speaker just above his space. When not on night dispersal duty, lights-out and heads-down was officially 2200 hours. He needed little encouragement in that direction and was soon asleep. On a few occasions, the Tannoy would disturb the slumber with information 'Air Raid Warning, Alert.' That needed no immediate action unless on duty, so the snooze resumed. Then invariably and a trifle more urgent: 'Air Raid Warning, Red.' That was different. Feeling annoyed at the intrusion into ones solitude, individuals had to follow orders that decreed they filed down to the shelter under the barrack block. For Frank that was a change to a similar night incident at Wittering. There had been no warning as they scrambled out into the dark to be instructed to disperse into the countryside unless on duty. A very wise move, considering the casualties and damage done.

Any activity above had to be sat out unless otherwise directed. There was always speculation, some bangs and then the final 'All Clear' with a return, yawning, to ones 'pit.' The next morning, for the non-combatants, was to glean any 'gen' on the upset. One incident concerned the facing barrack block across the square to Frank's. The entrance was damaged and casualties were incurred. Bomb craters on the airfield had by then been filled in by the RAF Works and Bricks Section, the army Pioneer Corps or civilian contractors; take your pick!

Cpl Gale was a fitter who lived in the cubicle leading to Frank's room; he was also the NCO in charge. He was also a jazz enthusiast possessing a gramophone and appropriate records. His music blazed out during off-duty moments and he was lost to the world. Because of his intentionally misleading stories he was nicknamed 'Duff Gen', for example he would introduce Frank to new arrivals with the words: "This is Ben Webster", he plays tenor sax. Frank never did and never felt that he bore the slightest resemblance to the real, talented, Negro American jazz man.

Still on a musical note, a few beds away was Alan Allmark, a wireless operator who in Civvy Street was a professional musician who played the drums. Prior to volunteering, mainly through lack of engagements, he led a sextet under his professional name Alan Holmes, his mother's maiden name. He had an easy smile and was very friendly; Frank remembered seeing his name in the Radio Times. Before joining the RAF he arranged for his vocalist and fiancé Bette Roberts to sing with Joe Loss. They used to hear her on the wireless when the band was broadcasting.

A degree of naiveté on Frank's part inspired an attack of the then preverbal 'ring-twitter!' He used to like to take photographs and took some on the dispersal; there were people in flying kit in or near the Spitfires at the time. For printing and developing he took them to Boots in Norwich where all the others had theirs developed. The following week, Frank caught the bus into Norwich to collect his photographs. Calling at Boots and giving his name, the assistant searched and then said: "Ah yes, they have been sent to the police." Eventually a plain-clothes policeman appeared and was quite affable. Finally, he said: "As a complaint has been made we must follow it up. I will be contacting your unit." Quaking, and with disastrous thoughts, Frank hoped that he wouldn't be dealt with by the Station Headquarters mostly because the SWO was a formidable character.

Back at Coltishall the squadron Orderly Room corporal nabbed Frank and told him to wade through King's Regulations to find a rule that covered such a 'crime.' Still not happy, Frank did however reason to himself

From left to right: AC Cyril Stansmore, LAC Ted Matthews, AC Frank Webster and AC Stanley Ball of 'A' Flt, 222 Squadron.

that the days were passing and that he wasn't 'inside' for treason. Then he was told to get his Best Blue on as the CO wanted to see him; he never saw him that time as he was flying. This happened a few times over a period of days until he was finally marched outside his office in the hangar and waited. Some aircraft landed and the CO eventually dashed past Frank - hatless. An NCO marched Frank in before the Squadron Leader who was sitting at his desk with his hat on. He looked up and dismissed the NCO. That was encouraging because 'prisoners' on a charge had an escort, their hats knocked to the ground; Frank's remained on his head. Sqn Ldr Love gave Frank a gentlemanly dressing down, explaining that he could be sent to prison. He then said: "Although photographs and diagrams of aircraft appear in far more detail in the magazine 'Flight', you should not have a camera on the station." He asked Frank if he still had it in his kit to which he replied 'yes sir', expecting it to be confiscated. The CO told him to get it off the camp and then burn the offending negatives.

Some months later, at North Weald and after 222 Squadron had moved away from Coltishall to Matlaske, Manston and Rochford, Sqn Ldr Love passed Frank at

a dispersal and bid him to follow him back to his office. In those hallowed precincts and wondering what was in store, his CO rummaged under some papers in a wire tray and gave him the prints taken Coltishall that caused him so much trouble!

In the meantime, Coltishall's squadrons were also operating by day and night with considerable success. This was highlighted at midday on 7 April when recently Commissioned Plt Off R G Morland of 222 Squadron was patrolling in the Great Yarmouth area in his Spitfire. He witnessed bomb splashes off the coast amongst ships in a convoy. Calling in his No 2, Plt Off Ramsey, they both sped through the defending Anti-Aircraft fire and shot down the attacker. They witnessed the crew of the bomber take to their parachutes. Sadly, due to the cold of the North Sea they all died before rescuers could get to them.

The 9 April saw further success when a Messerschmitt Me109 was claimed in the day and a Junkers Ju88 that night, the latter shot down into the sea off Lowestoft by 257 Squadron's boss, Sqn Ldr Stanford-Tuck. However, that same sortie also proved it wasn't always going to be in the RAF's favour. As one of Tuck's wingmen, Sgt

Les R Truman in Hurricane V6611 attacked another Junkers Ju88 return fire from the enemy aircraft hit his Hurricane and Unteroffizer Alfons Koster, the pilot of the Ju88, made a claim for 'an unknown single engined machine' on his safe return to base. Truman began his return to Coltishall, but just two and a half miles short of the base, the damage to his aircraft forced him to consider abandoning his aircraft. Unfortunately, before he could do so, the Hurricane spun into the ground in flames and crashed at Duffields Farm, Worstead. Truman was killed.

Enemy raids continued in and around the Coltishall area that month. At 2146 hours on 26 April, 21 people were killed when the Ferry Inn at Horning was bombed by a Junkers Ju88 flying at 500 feet. Amongst those killed was 222 Squadron's Adjutant Flg Off Robinson, one of their pilots, Flt Lt Brian Van Mentz, and the Station Medical Officer Flt Lt Attwell.

Flt Lt Van Mentz DFC was born in Johannesburg in South Africa in 1916. He was Commissioned into the RAF in 1938 after a year with the South African (RAF) Reserve. At the time of his death, Van Mentz, who was 24 years old, had flown 75 operational sorties and had shot down six enemy aircraft. A couple of months earlier on 28 January, Van Mentz along with Sqn Ldr Stanford-Tuck were both decorated by HM King George at an Investiture Ceremony held at the Coastal Command base at Bircham Newton. It was suggested at the time that exposed lights attracted the Germans attention and that the Inn might have been mistaken for Coltishall. However, it was later found that the Luftwaffe were in fact aiming for the Shipyards of H C Banham, a yard that had been used to construct landing craft and other vessels including Rescue Launches for the RAF.

One of those lucky to escape the Ferry Inn bombing was Sqn Ldr Stanford-Tuck. The Squadron Leader, with his fiancée Joyce were enjoying the company of his fellow squadron members when he felt a sudden urge to move on. He suggested to the others that they might all travel into Norwich to see the night out. However, as it was late, the others decided the journey would take too long; therefore, they would stay at the Ferry Inn. Tuck, Joyce and his dog Jack left. It was not until he saw Flt Lt Peter Blatchford very early the next morning that he found out that the Inn had been bombed and that there were casualties.

At dusk on the same day he had been in action off Great Yarmouth. In his Hurricane, Z3152, he intercepted a Junkers Ju88 that was attempting to bomb shipping off the coast. He poured cannon fire into the wing root of the Junkers; however his aim was not up to its usual standard. The flashes caused by Anti-Aircraft fire from batteries along the coast caused problems with his night vision and he found aiming through his gun sight difficult.

The next evening Plt Off's Cowen and Kain, both from 257 Squadron and flying Hurricanes Z3175 and Z3070 respectively, came close to 'bagging' a Heinkel He111 which they had intercepted near Great Yarmouth, firing only as the bomber escaped into the cloud. Their aircraft, cannon armed Hurricane IICs, were received by the squadron a few days earlier and the actions of 26th and 27th were some of the first carried out by the squadron

Les and Nina Truman on their wedding day.

with this mark.

On 3 May, action by enemy aircraft had been reported all along the coast. Fifteen High Explosive (HE) bombs were dropped on Lowestoft in one of these raids. One particular enemy raider was a Junkers Ju88A-5, Wrk No 8180 coded 4D+BH, of KG30. Flying at a height of 23,000 feet it skirted north of the wash. Close to Skegness it was fired upon by a Defiant of 151 Squadron which at the time was detached to Coltishall. Although there was no evidence of battle damage, the Ju88's port engine lost power and its compass began to go haywire. The crew, having not delivered their deadly cargo to its intended target, turned to the south and jettisoned their bombs into the North Sea. Over Norfolk, the starboard engine stopped and the crew, with no real alternative, decided to belly-land the Junkers on Sheringham's shoreline. The crew were soon captured, and their gunner, a 53-year-old Major, later told interrogators that he was on his first operational flight.

At 0145 hours on 4 May, in bright moonlight, a Junkers Ju88C-4 of I/NJG2 from Gilze-Rijen passed low over Coltishall releasing four bombs that fell on the north-west boundary of the airfield. Close on his tail were two

Spitfires of 222 (Natal) Squadron, piloted by Plt Off B P Clee and Sgt J H Burgess. In the pursuit, accurate return fire from the Ju88 hit Clee's Spitfire P7699 'Zanzibar III.' The aircraft crashed in flames just outside the boundary of the airfield taking the life of the pilot. For this, the Junkers pilot, Lt Hans Hahn, claimed a Fairey Fulmar destroyed. This same intruder pilot later shot down Hurricane P3866 of 257 Squadron at 0115 hours as it landed at Duxford, having been diverted from Coltishall during another raid, killing the pilot Sgt R G Parrott. However, by the end of that day 257 Squadron had evened the score by shooting down a Junkers Ju88 of Kustenfliegergruppe 106, a coastal reconnaissance unit, off Lowestoft at 2220 hours.

Living very close to Coltishall at Great Hautbois, twelve year old Alan Spinks was used to the activities on the base and the regular attention shown it by the Luftwaffe. The early morning of 4 May was no different.

Messerschmitt BF109F.

He heard the Junkers Ju88 flying in very low and the subsequent explosions as the bombs went off; it was very difficult to get a good night's sleep in those days! Almost immediately, the distinct sound of a Rolls Royce Merlin filled the sky and he thought to himself that the Spitfires were going to 'bag themselves a Jerry.' On hearing the chatter of machine guns, his hopes were high that they had been successful. However, it was not until the next day that the horrible truth was known. Instead of the German, it was the Spitfire and its pilot that was down.

The night of 4 May also saw Heinkel He111s of KG53 set off from their base in Northern France to bomb Liverpool. One particular aircraft, Wrk No 3235 coded A1+LL, set off at 2100 hours and successfully dropped its bombs on the city. After clearing Liverpool, it made for home over The Wash where it was suddenly attacked by a Defiant of 151 Squadron operating out of Coltishall.

The wireless operator of the He111 was killed instantly as the Defiant's gunner raked the underside of the bomber. Oil loss from the port engine of the Heinkel caused it to overheat very quickly, then the starboard engine lost power giving the crew no alternative but to belly land the aircraft which was successfully carried out at Brunton near Holt, the time, 0104 hours. After the crew dragged their dead colleague from the wreckage, they immediately set fire to the Heinkel. Once they completed burning their documents, they covered nearly eight miles across country from the crash site before being captured. The interrogation of the crew deduced that the improvements to the RAF night fighter techniques were causing the Luftwaffe great concern, making deep penetration raids more dangerous, which in turn forced the bombers to route over water whenever possible.

At 0010 hours the next day, Air Attack alarm was sounded and at 0015 hours seven HE bombs dropped on waste ground between the Officers' Mess and Block No 5, resulting in six casualties, including one dead and two seriously injured. A further Air Attack alarm was sounded at 0130 hours but no bombs were dropped.

With the Defiants carrying out an ever increasing number of night patrols, the home based squadrons, 222 and 257 Squadrons, were now free to handle nearly all daylight operations. There were a few exceptions to this arrangement however, as was demonstrated on 11 May.

Difficult as it was for a single seat fighter without radar to find an enemy aircraft at night, Sqn Ldr Stanford Tuck took off from Coltishall at 2315 hours in Hurricane Z3070 to try his luck. A few minutes later, near Sheringham, he engaged a Junkers Ju88 without success. Twenty minutes later, his luck changed and he successfully shot down another Ju88. Tuck gave the Junkers two short bursts from his machine guns at 200 yards. With its starboard wing well ablaze and nowhere to turn, the raider succumbed to the damage and crashed into the sea.

Flt Lt Blatchford also flew that night. After chasing two enemy aircraft, he came across a lone Heinkel He111 which was approaching the coast from the east. First, he aimed at the engine and then the fuselage, within seconds the Heinkel was a burning mass of wreckage on the water.

Earlier in the evening of 11 May, at around 2145 hours, a single Yellow-nosed Messerschmitt Bf109F of JG51 roared along the front of Aldeburgh at roof top height, firing indiscriminately. Blue Section of 257 Squadron was already airborne, chasing three further Bf109s which had strafed Oulton Broad just prior to the Aldeburgh attack. Confusion reigned amongst the defending forces and fighter response to the numerous attacks was less than successful. This was graphically illustrated by the fact that the Operations Controller at Coltishall stated that the '109's were at 15000 feet instead of the actual height of 150 feet! Earlier seventeen Bf109s dived from such a height onto Rochford and it is possible that this report had been passed causing confusion.

As with most other flying stations in the RAF, Coltishall had a couple of aircraft which were used for communication duties and as proficiency trainers for aircrew being employed on ground tours. During the early stages of Coltishall's existence as an operational station, the Station Flight aircraft were Miles Magisters, a two-seat open cockpit trainer. Towards the end of 1940, the Magisters were replaced by the de Havilland Tiger Moth, a two-seat, open cockpit bi-plane trainer. It was on such a proficiency-training sortie that the Station Flight lost one of their Tiger Moths. N6835 crashed into the sea between Lowestoft and Southwold, just off the Suffolk coast on 19 June 1941. Unfortunately, the pilot, a 26-year-old Czechoslovakian, Sgt Vaclau Brejcha of 257 Squadron, lost his life. His body was recovered from the wreckage and returned to Coltishall where he was finally laid to rest at Scottow Cemetery with full military honours.

At 1330 hours on 21 June, Sqn Ldr Stanford Tuck took off from Coltishall in Hurricane IIb Z3152 on a routine patrol. As he was flying out to sea, at about 1000 feet his Hurricane came under attack and was hit by shells from a Messerschmitt Bf109 that had flown up underneath him without being seen. As he spotted the '109, Tuck dropped the nose of his aircraft and waited until the '109 crossed through the cross hairs of his gun sight, a pure fighter instinct from a fighter genius. He pressed the firing button and was delighted to see the cannon shells striking the fuselage and wings of the hapless Bf109. The German, unable to do anything about the situation, crashed into the sea. Tuck knew that the Bf109 was not a lone raider, and was aware that other fighters would be in the area. As he banked, he saw another Bf109 firing at him and he followed this aircraft down to about 100 feet above the sea. The German pilot put his aircraft into a steep bank and flew round in circles, Tuck following on his tail. As the tail chase continued, the German began to take a little pressure off his banks, probably due to the 'G' forces being exerted. Tuck took full advantage of this error and pressed home his attack, which by now was being played out very close to the water. The attack

was successful and the German crashed into the sea. Just as Tuck pulled up to avoid hitting the sea himself, a third Bf109 attacked the Hurricane head on. Although he managed to hit the '109 on several occasions as they headed for each other, the lucky German managed to pull away and head for home, as did Tuck. By the end of the engagement it became apparent to Tuck that his luck might just be running out. He had been hit quite badly during the attack and apart from losing his canopy; he had sustained cuts to his head from pieces of the reflector gun sight. The aircraft was on fire and bits and pieces were beginning to fall off the crippled Hurricane. Realising that there was no way the aircraft would make it home Tuck baled out and once in the water inflated his dinghy and waited to be rescued. After about half an hour a trawler out of Gravesend, which had witnessed the action, picked him up and delivered him to dry land.

That evening, it was the turn of 151 Squadron to claim an enemy bomber. The Defiant, crewed by Plt Off Edmiston with his gunner Sgt Beale, had taken off from Coltishall on night patrol when they came across a Junkers Ju88 just off the coast. After a short chase, they finally shot down the Junkers five miles east of Cromer.

22 June 1941 turned out to be a marked turning point for Coltishall. For it was on this day that 222 Squadron made their first offensive sweep over France, a welcome change from the usual 'Kipper Fleet' patrols. Success in this raid came with the interception of a Messerschmitt Bf109F, which had to scurry away from the fight having been badly damaged. However, the distance from Coltishall to the French coast made further attempts of this kind difficult without using forward operating bases prior to the actual operation. Instead, a change in direction led to the fighters operating in support of 2 Gp and Coastal Command Blenheim's that were now employed in attacking targets off Holland.

The cinema was one of the most important media for both public entertainment and news during the war years. The Ministry of Information lost no time in exploiting this to both inform the public and to bolster morale. Many feature films were made with the help of the Armed Services at that time, for the RAF, Coltishall and 257 Squadron in particular, the film company 20th Century-Fox from Hollywood used their Hurricanes in the air and on the ground in the making of the film 'A Yank in the RAF.' Fox executive, Darryl Zanuck made this film to urge Americans to help the British in the war and it captured glimpses of the early war from Britain's view. The story line showed how Tim Baker, played by Tyrone

TYRONE **POWER**

A YANK in the R.A.F.

BETTY **GRABLE**

JOHN SUTTON

Reginald **GARDINER**

Produced by **DARRYL F. ZANUCK**

Directed by **HENRY KING**

Associate Producer **LOU EDELMAN**

A 20ᵗʰ CENTURY-FOX PICTURE

Power, violated the American Neutrality Act by flying a plane to Canada and in doing so loses his job, but is then subsequently hired to fly a plane to England for $1,000. From there he joins the RAF, initially to fly bombers but then fighters. The story could be classed as 'typical' Hollywood; Betty Grable providing the glamour and a love angle whilst Reginald Gardiner and John Sutton played alongside Tyrone Power as RAF pilots. However, for many of the American volunteer pilots who went on to join the RAF 'Eagle' Squadrons, the plot of the film was to become almost a reality.

The first camera crew had to leave the film before production started in Norfolk; they went off to film 'One of Our Aircraft is Missing.' The second crew on 'A Yank in the RAF' included a Czechoslovakian cinematographer, Otto W Kanturek and British born John 'Jack' Parry. Kanturek was to have a prominent, but tragic part to play in much of the aerial action that was to take place over Coltishall and the surrounding area. It was on 26 June 1941 that Otto Kanturak climbed into

Anson N9732/MK-V of 500 Squadron from Bircham Newton, flown by 24 year-old Sgt E W J Polden, to film Hurricanes of 257 Squadron in mock attacks against their aircraft. The Hurricanes and pilots chosen for the filming took off from Coltishall at 1155 hours; they were Z3391 flown by Plt Off Hone and Z3164 flown by Plt Off Pearson. Whilst airborne three miles to the south-west of Aylsham at 2000 feet, the Anson was 'attacked' on a number of occasions to allow the cameraman to capture the event as if they were Germans on the receiving end of the Hurricanes attentions. Tragically, on one of the passes the Anson was hit in a mid-air collision by Hurricane Z3391. The Anson fell to the ground with the loss of all on board but Plt Off Hone managed to escape by parachute from his aircraft before it came down at Quebec Farm, Aylsham. Otto Kanturak was interred in the Scottow Military Cemetery just off the end of Coltishall's runway 22 with his grave being cared for by the Commonwealth War Graves Commission to this day. This in itself is unusual, but underlies the importance given by the Government to civilians employed in such important war-work. 'Jack' Parry was buried at Marazion in Cornwall and Sgt Polden, the pilot on that fateful day, was buried at Banksum Park Cemetery, Poole in Dorset. 'A Yank in the RAF' was released in the USA on 3 October 1941.

Many changes were now taking place at Coltishall. Stanford Tuck was promoted to Wing Commander on 4 July 1941 and his place as 257 Squadron's Commander was taken by Flt Lt Peter Blatchford, who by now had also been promoted, this time to Squadron Leader.

Great Yarmouth was on the receiving end of its heaviest bombing raid of the war so far, when on 9 July, fifteen enemy bombers attacked the town. Over 80 HE bombs and well in excess of 1000 incendiaries were dropped during the period of the raid. Despite the ferocity of the attack, only three civilians were killed with a further twenty nine injured. To counter the attack, 257 Squadron and their Hurricanes were scrambled from Coltishall. In the battle that followed, the Hurricanes were successful in shooting down a Junkers Ju88 into the sea off Happisburgh.

The close proximity of Coltishall to the sea made it a prime location, and an ideal base, for Air Sea Rescue (ASR) operations. In July, 5 ASR Flt was formed and shortly after, it received its first aircraft, two Supermarine Walrus amphibious biplanes on 19 July 1941. The flight became a squadron in its own right in October 1941 when it was to form the basis of 278 Squadron at Matlaske, equipped with Westland Lysander ASR IIIs, Defiant ASR Is, Anson

ASR Is and the faithful Walrus. It was to become one of the largest squadrons in the RAF, with detachments at many Coastal Command bases throughout the country, from as far a field as Acklington in Northumberland to Sumburgh in the Shetlands. 278 Squadron used both Coltishall and Matlaske until 21 April 1944 when the squadron moved to Bradwell Bay in Essex.

John Roberts trained as an Instrument maker in the RAF, and following his training course at Melksham he was posted to Coltishall in early 1941 to join 5 ASR Flt, later to become 278 Squadron. He remembers that whilst posted onto the strength of Coltishall he was in fact to spend most of his time at Matlaske. John takes up his own story: 'The squadron consisted of three Lysanders and two Walrus with two Defiants used primarily as escorts. We shared Matlaske with 137 Squadron who were flying the Westland Whirlwind. The site was not large enough for these twin-engine fighters with their rather high landing speeds. As a result, many ended up in the hedges and ditches around the field. In February 1942 we were all astonished when a squadron of Bristol Beaufort torpedo bombers landed for re-fuelling. They were on their way to attack the German Battleships Scharnhorst, Gneisenau and Prince Eugen that were fighting their way up through the Channel. I was one of the airmen sent out to cycle through the village of Matlaske to give warning that the aircraft were landing with 'Torpedoes Up' and that the villagers should get into their shelters or take cover until they had taken-

Sqn Ldr Peter Blatchford.

off. The squadron had to suddenly return to Coltishall in July 1942 and I recall one amusing incident from that time. There was a war-time regulation, because of the danger of invasion, which no one should move into, or visit without good reason, a strip of land twelve miles wide around the East and South-East Coast.

Matlaske fell within this area; but notwithstanding this order, several airman and Officers had their wives and families in pubs and farmhouses near the airfield. When the unexpected order came to move back to Coltishall, no road transport was available to move the families and their odds and ends across the Norfolk countryside where some limited service accommodation was to be had. As a result, when the squadron Walruses flew back to Coltishall and taxied to their dispersal at a remote part of the base and chocked, the rear gun hatches were

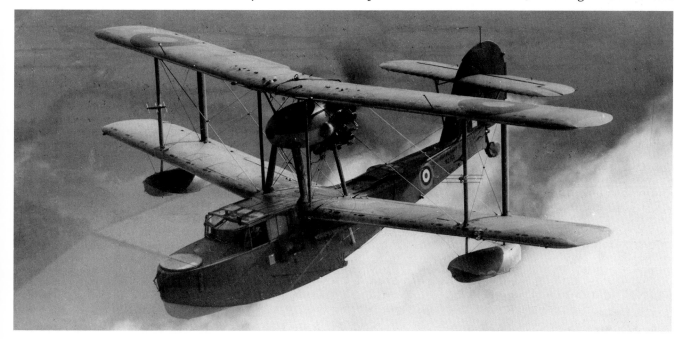

The Supermarine Walrus, affectionately known as the 'Shagbat'.

removed and out came a parade of prams, pushchairs and clothes-horses as well as furniture and fittings!

Coltishall was being used by three other squadrons at that time; 68 and 255 Squadrons flying the Beaufighter, the latter on a detachment basis, and 56 Squadron with Typhoons. One day in January 1942, I was working on a Lysander in what was then 'B' Hangar. Suddenly a great roar shattered the air and a line of 20mm holes appeared across the top of the hangar doors. An armourer, checking one of the Beaufighters, had inadvertently fired the four nose cannon and the tail-down attitude of the aircraft had given just the right elevation to produce the spectacular results!

LAC Wall, who was an armourer with 255 Squadron, also remembered the incident; it was a Beaufighter from 'A' Flight of his squadron. The aircraft was situated on the dispersal area near 'B' Hangar. The armourers were doing their daily inspections before going off night duty when the four 20mm Hispano cannon opened fire on the hangar. At the time LAC Wall was completing a Daily Inspection on a Beaufighter parked next to the said aircraft, when he dived out through the nose hatch believing the airfield was being strafed. With no enemy in sight, he looked around and saw an armourer shaking with fear next to his aircraft. By all accounts he should have checked the firing button on entering the aircraft, as often following the heat of battle the pilots often used to leave the safety button on 'Fire'; he hadn't on this occasion! Whilst it was ultimately the armourers fault, resulting in his transfer to General Duties and posted from the squadron, there are those who think the incident was 'hushed-up' so that the pilot was not reprimanded for not placing the firing button to 'Safe' before exiting his aircraft.

OC 133 (Eagle) Squadron, Sqn Ldr G A Brown.

Pilots of 133 (Eagle) Squadron.

John Roberts also remembered being in the Airmen's' Dining Hall and being asked by HRH The Duke of Kent if there were 'Any Complaints?' Of course there weren't! The Duke was on a visit to the Station that day in 1942 and was tragically killed the next day in Scotland when the Sunderland he was flying in crashed.

During the War, the habit had grown amongst the servicemen that when they wrote home, they would add a word or acronym to the back of the envelope. The most common used was SWALK (Sealed With A Loving Kiss), but some had devised their own, a kind of intimate secret between themselves and their loved ones. The Security Officer at Coltishall told us, in the course of a briefing on security, that when he censored airmen's mail he noticed the word 'NORWICH' printed on the envelope flap and erased it. When it appeared again, always on letters from the same source, he sent for the airman and asked what it meant. Of course, we were not allowed to indicate the whereabouts of our base and with Norwich being so close, it could have been perceived as a breach of security. When asked directly why he had written this word on his letters the man became embarrassed and said it was a private joke between him and his wife. Pressed to explain what it meant, he said it was an acronym in which the letters meant 'Nickers Off When I Come Home.' He added, rather lamely, I know knickers should be spelt with a 'K' and it ought to be KORWICH, but it never seemed to look quite right!

On 29 July 1941, Coltishall welcomed another Hurricane-equipped unit, 133 Squadron, under the command of Sqn Ldr G A Brown. This squadron was formed at Coltishall as the third 'Eagle Squadron', which was comprised entirely of volunteer American pilots flying for the RAF. The squadron was in fact not destined to fly any operational sorties from Coltishall as it was working up to operational readiness prior to its move to Duxford, which took place in mid-August. Also departing in August was 222 Squadron, leaving for Manston on the first of the month, having been resident at Coltishall since November 1940.

During August 1941, Coltishall became home to another squadron which had since May 1941 had been using the base on a detachment basis. 255 Squadron had operated both the Defiant and Hurricane from its base at Hibaldstow in Lincolnshire, and prior to their arrival at Coltishall had re-equipped with the twin engined

255 Squadron aircrew group at Coltishall in the summer of 1941. Wg Cdr J S Bartlett sits behind the squadron mascot, Plt Off Bruce.

Beaufighter. The Beaufighters were based at Coltishall primarily to give night fighter cover to Norwich and the east coast ports. However, in addition to this important task, the squadron was also involved with trials on the newly installed, and still secret, Ground Controlled Interception (GCI) radar at Neatishead. The radar in use at this highly secret and well-guarded unit was the third of its kind to become operational. The first two prototypes were based at Durrington and Sopley on the South Coast.

The Beaufighter had originally been conceived as a long range fighter, but as raids on London in 1940 intensified, the aircraft was unceremoniously rushed into service during September of that year, being the best, and probably the only suitable night fighter available to Fighter Command at that time.

One of the airmen posted to Coltishall with 255 Squadron was LAC Reginald Wall, an armourer with 'A' Flight. He remembers travelling through the night with full kit with a number of his squadron colleagues from Hibaldstow to Coltishall to await the arrival of the Beaufighters the next morning. On arrival at Coltishall railway station they were met by an RAF Policeman who gleefully told them that it was not far to march and to get a move on before their aircraft arrived! The language and gestures in return from the tired and bedraggled airmen was choice, to say the least!

At one stage Wg Cdr Bartlett was in charge of the squadron. He was not known for his prowess in landing the Beaufighter, in fact to his groundcrews and many of his fellow aircrew he was known as 'Kangaroo Bartlett' as he never once landed without a bounce! On one

particular day his landing was so bad that his Radio Operator, Flt Lt 'Kiwi' Heywood suffered whiplash after a landing that would have entered the aircraft into the record books for a hop, skip and jump competition! Flight Lt Heywood ended up being taken to hospital in Norwich and was off flying for a number of days.

Being an armourer, Reg was used to handling all types of weapons and was familiar with every type of gun and rifle on the Station. This familiarity came to the fore on one particular day when the over-zealous Ground Defence Officer decided to hold a 24-hour long airfield defence exercise. Reg was given a Lewis Gun to defend his squadron, a very responsible position to hold. Duly accepting the machine gun he politely asked the Ground Defence Officer for the ammunition to which the reply came: "If the need arose it would be delivered by the army. As this exercise is not for real, and as we don't hold any ammunition for the Lewis Gun on the Station anyway, you'll just have to pretend" - some use if an airborne invasion took place with no notice!

Sadly 255 Squadron had its fair share of fatal accidents and on numerous occasions Reg Wall had the unpleasant task of guarding crashed aircraft around Norfolk. As someone who travelled extensively throughout the County, Reg was asked by the Armaments Officer to go to the Lifeboat Station at Cromer to see Coxswain Blogg and to thank him on behalf of the squadron for their efforts in searching for Sqn Ldr McGevour, who had been lost over the sea a few days earlier on 2 March 1942. On his arrival at the Lifeboat Station, Coxswain Bloggs could not be found but his nephew, Mr 'Shrimpy' Davies, another full-time lifeboatman, was on hand to

The Rolls Royce Merlin-powered Beaufighter IIF.

accept the squadron's thanks. He was also able to show Reg the entry in the logbook that described their search and rescue attempt.

On night shift, especially if it was quiet and night operations were cancelled by HQ Fighter Command, the lads would sneak off camp for a crafty drink at the Crown Inn in Buxton by crossing the airfield and 'escaping' via a strategic and little known route that had been in use for months. Next to the barbed wire where they left the Station, a plank of wood was hidden in the undergrowth that was used to flatten the wire, thus making the crossing easier and less painful. Once out it was a 20 minute hike to the Inn for a well earned pint! On one night, having escaped through the fence, Reg Wall and a half a dozen of his mates were enjoying their illicit pint of beer in the 'snug' next to a roaring fire when suddenly they were stunned to see their temporary CO, Sqn Ldr Bartree and his girlfriend, the actress Deborah Kerr, walk through the door of the Inn. Whilst they hid their faces in the vain hope they had not been 'clocked', there was no way he would have missed them and they knew that. Whilst contemplating the inevitable, a charge on the cards and a few nights in the 'cooler', the lads were shocked when the barman came through and asked if

they would accept a drink from their CO. He was also absent without authority as he was on night duty as well! Obviously, no charges resulted from that evening, but it was a stark reminder to all those involved, including the CO, that they tread a thin line in these unauthorised visits to the Inn!

On a number of occasions there were up to three Lysanders working for the Special Operations Executive (SOE) that used Coltishall as a forward operating base for their clandestine work over enemy-held territory. When the aircraft arrived under the cover of darkness and parked on the far side of the airfield next to the bomb dump, it was the responsibility of groundcrews from the resident night fighter squadrons to see the aircraft in and prepare them for their missions. But as soon as this task had been completed, the engineers were whisked away from the area and only witnessed the arrival and departure of covered vehicles, each containing agents or stores being delivered that night. The area in which these aircraft operated, the far end of runway 33 beyond the bomb dump, was strictly out of bounds with signs being strategically placed at all access points and with armed guards ensuring complete secrecy. People on the Station knew something was happening, but it was never discussed.

For one couple, both based at Coltishall, the area proved to be an ideal location for their courting, as no one dared to venture into this area. Evidently, they must have used the site on many occasions and became complacent in their actions as one evening, when they were sure all was clear, without warning, a full-blown SOE operation took place and they were caught. By the next morning, both had been posted away without ceremony, probably for de-briefing.

Reg Wall also remembers that they had to face up to a problem of rat infestation in the sand-bagged blast pens.

255 Squadron suffered several losses through technical problems with the Beaufighter II.

604 Squadron Beaufighter IF R2102; one of many which passed through Coltishall on detachment during 1940/41.

The pilots complained about the rats running in and around the pens being attracted by the landing lights as they taxied back from sorties. The CO requested that the armourers tackle the problem. As a result of this directive they blocked most of the holes up with soil but left a few open where they inserted 'Smoke Puffs' that were obtained from the Station Armoury, all of which were near their disposal/sell-by date. After the 'Smoke Puffs' were fired, the remaining armourers, donned gum boots and gloves to save being bitten and waited for the rats to come scurrying out of the unblocked holes to meet their fate. This operation lasted several days until the pilots were satisfied the infestation had been disposed of. For a job well done, the CO granted the armourers a seventy-two hour pass, to be taken when duties permitted!

On 13 August, a Wellington IC of 115 Squadron from Marham was returning to the UK after a raid over Essen. Under the command of Plt Off Wood, his aircraft, one of seven in the formation, arrived over Norfolk in the midst of a German Intruder raid that was taking place over virtually the whole of East Anglia. The Germans had already attacked Bassingbourne and Upwood, Cambridgeshire and at Marham as aircraft began to arrive home after raids over the continent. The plotting table in the Ops Room at Coltishall showed no enemy aircraft in the airfields vicinity, the only plot being a Beaufighter returning from patrol. With that information to hand, Plt Off Wood switched on his navigation lights to avoid a collision with the other Wellingtons in his formation making their way to Coltishall. At 3000 feet, a twin engine aircraft approached the Wellington in the dark. With only a Beaufighter reported in the area, the crew did not take any avoiding action. However, when four bursts of machine gun fire raked their aircraft, they soon realised that the Beaufighter was in fact one of the German raiders, a Junkers Ju88C-4 Night Fighter of 1/ NJG2 being flown by Obfw Peter Lufts. The Wellington, T2563/KO-D, which was badly damaged during the attack, overshot the airfield, crashed and burnt out at Smith's Farm, Ashmanhaugh, west of Neatishead at 0220 hours. Sgt Bernard Evans RNZAF, a 25 year old rear gunner was killed and four other crew-members, Sgt R A Hodges, Plt Off A J A Day RAAF, Sgt C D Tavener and Sgt S W Morton RCAF were injured. Plt Off Wood was uninjured. Sgt Evans who hailed from Mount Eden, Auckland, New Zealand, was laid to rest at Scottow Cemetery a couple of days after the incident.

Apart from their Beaufighters, 255 Squadron flew a couple of Blenheim IV's for the aircrew who were

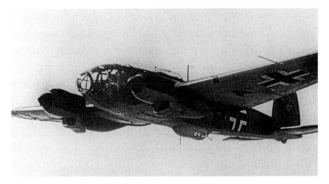

Heinkel He111 H series.

converting onto the twin-engine night fighter. One of the aircraft, L1223 flown by Flg Off James Emmerson, suffered engine failure and crashed on 16 August 1941. The aircraft was in the Coltishall circuit when the engines failed, and whilst trying to make a forced landing the Blenheim hit some trees near the Horseshoes Public House at Scottow before ploughing into the ground. Sadly, Flg Off Emmerson was killed in the crash and was interred in the Scottow Cemetery, a few hundred yards away from where he lost his life.

255 Squadron encountered numerous problems with the Beaufighter, which resulted in many accidents. On 22 August 1941, Beaufighter IIF, R2403, spun into the ground on approach to Coltishall at Sco Rushton. Two local men, Leonard Moore and Cecil Green, ran to the wreck of the aircraft and despite the fire and threatening explosions, managed to drag the badly wounded crew members to safety. For their heroic actions, Mr Moore received the BEM and Mr Green was officially Commended for his bravery. Sadly, both of the crew members, the pilot, and CO of the Squadron, Wg Cdr J S Bartlett DFC, and his Radio Observer, Sgt T R Salked, died later that day from the injuries sustained in the crash.

Sqn Ldr Oats took over command of 255 Squadron until their new CO, Wg Cdr Windsor, arrived from 219 Squadron to take over on 9 September 1941. As with many COs taking over a squadron, Wg Cdr Windsor was greeted with some reservation by the groundcrews. They were all comfortable with their previous boss, Wg Cdr Bartlett, but found their new CO somewhat different. That said, he always stood by those under his command and would act on anything that caused conflict or distress. This was highlighted after numerous complaints about the standard of meals being served up to his men whilst on night shift. It was reported that the meals were always the same and the rumour was that they were recycled from leftovers of the previous days offering. Wg Cdr Windsor took it upon himself to visit the cookhouse unannounced to see for himself. On tasting the 'bubble-and-squeak' he immediately told the duty cook that it was only fit for pigs swill and was not to be served to his men. Immediately he summoned the Catering Officer to report to the cookhouse to explain this most unacceptable situation, and when he arrived, still dressed in his pyjamas, he was taken to task by the Wing Commander. The next night, and for the remainder of their tour at Coltishall, night meals were always prepared and served to the correct ration levels.

Another Beaufighter squadron, 604 (County of Middlesex) Squadron, based at Middle Wallop in Hampshire, had a permanent detachment at Coltishall to cover the eastern sector whilst 255 Squadron worked up to operational readiness. In fact 'B' Flight had been using Coltishall since July 1940, firstly with the Blenheim IF and latterly with the Beaufighter IF. 604 Squadron was the top-scoring night fighter squadron in the RAF, commanded by Wg Cdr John 'Cats Eyes' Cunningham, DSO, DFC.

The detachment was also used to disguise the fact that the squadron was working with the still secret and newly installed GCI Station at Neatishead. This radar was only the third of its type to become operational, after the prototype at Durrington and Sopley on the South Coast. It had a complement of two officers and 40 airmen/airwomen who were billeted in the local village.

On 22 August 1941, Wg Cdr Cunningham and his navigator, Plt Off C F Rawnsley, shot down a Heinkel He111 H-5 of 8/KG40 35 miles North West of Coltishall. Cunningham and Rawnsley were again in the thick of things on the night of 1 September. At 2050hrs their Beaufighter got airborne from Coltishall on a normal patrol off Cromer. Twelve miles NE of Cromer, after being passed to Neatishead's Ground Controllers from their colleagues at Coltishall, they were vectored towards an enemy intruder flying east of them at the same altitude, 10,000ft. As they approached the estimated location of the enemy, their Beaufighter flew through its slipstream, and as soon as Cunningham turned on to the raiders heading, Rawnsley made contact on his AI radar.

By now Cunningham recognised the silhouette of a Junkers Ju88 which was making a rapid descent through 5000ft to escape. At 150 yards astern of the Junkers Ju88, Cunningham opened fire with 46 rounds

Sgt Peter Timothy Vowels.

of 20mm cannon, hitting the doomed bomber between its starboard engine and fuselage. Pulling away from the Junkers Ju88 Cunningham and Rawnsley saw it fall with flashes and flames coming from the damaged areas of the wing. About a minute later they witnessed it fall into the sea and explode some 25 miles east of Winterton.

During 604 Squadron's short stay at Coltishall, Cunningham and Rawnsley had claimed at least two enemy aircraft. On the second occasion, Cunningham invited Coltishall's Station Commander, Gp Capt R Lees, along for a ride to see how the job was done!

In the last two weeks of August 1941, 257 Squadron claimed one of only two raiders destroyed in this period; a Heinkel HeIII shot down sixty miles east of Winterton at 0816 hours on 22 August after a ship had been sunk offshore. On the negative side, 257 Squadron lost another aircraft and pilot when Hurricane Z3448 crashed into the ground on 31 August near Westwick Church whilst carrying out aerobatic practice killing the pilot Sgt P Vowles. Peter Timothy Vowles was born on 4 August 1916 and joined the RAF Volunteer reserve in 1938. He was posted to 257 (Burma) Squadron at Coltishall on 31 December 1940.

It was Sunday, the last day of August 1941. It had been a quiet day and after a pleasant tea in the Sgts Mess, Sgt Peter Vowels walked out to his Hurricane having been briefed to carry out aerobatics. This type of exercise was common, and with currency made a considerable difference to fighter pilot's reactions in a dog-fight. Vowles jumped into his Hurricane Z3448 for that sortie, and his rigger assisted him with strapping in before jumping down off the wing to await the 'thumbs-up' to start the aircraft with the aid of the trolley-acc. After take-off he climbed to over 8000 feet to commence his aerobatic practice. At that height he was able to throw the aircraft around in a series of loops and stall turns. Now west of Coltishall at a lower height, Vowels decided that it was time to make a recovery to base. Whilst in transit he carried out three more loops, all in quick succession. With each loop, his height decreased quite considerably until, after the third loop, and in a desperate attempt to recover his aircraft, he lost it; the aircraft went into a flat spin from which he could not recover.

There were a number of local lads who witnessed the final moments of the Hurricane, one of them being Dan Chapman. He remembered seeing the aircraft coming in

'B', a Beaufighter IIF of 255 Squadron rests on a snow covered dispersal at Coltishall.

from the direction of the coast performing the loops and what he thought was a 'Victory Roll'; this was in fact the flat spin. The aircraft failed to recover and bounced off the top of a tree before hitting the ground at 1845 hours. On impact, the aircraft caught fire and it was not long before the RAF Ambulance and Fire Tenders from Coltishall were on the scene. Unfortunately, there was nothing they could do, as the pilot was pronounced dead. He was an experienced pilot having flown 181 hours on Hurricanes and 125 hours on other types. The subsequent enquiry asked how a pilot with so many hours and familiarity on type should have died in such circumstances. One of the possibilities was that he lost consciousness, possibly due to carbon monoxide poisoning. Sgt Vowles was laid to rest with full military honours at St Michaels Church, Brent Knoll, Somerset; a few miles from Weston-Super-Mare where he was born.

Activity for the fighters at Coltishall in early September was even lower than they had experienced in August. However, there were still isolated attacks on the British mainland by enemy intruders. At the same time, the massive effort by Bomber command against Germany never ceased.

In the early hours of 14 September, an Avro Manchester, L7383/OF-F of 97 Squadron from Coningsby ran out of fuel in bad weather whilst on a training sortie. The aircraft crashed after striking a house in Perch Lane, Westwick at 0232 hrs whilst on approach to Coltishall. Many of the crew were trapped in the wreckage including the captain of the aircraft Plt Off R E Hutchin. Sadly the navigator, Sgt J S Warton was killed in the crash.

Two days later, a single Junkers Ju88 crossed the coast at 2117 hours. Flying low, it headed for Coltishall, where it fired on a Beaufighter which was in the circuit ready to land. This attack was unsuccessful, but un-hindered; the

Ju88 flew back to the coast, and dropped its bomb load on Felixstowe. By this time, luck for this lone raider ran out when it was intercepted and shot down by a Douglas Havoc of 85 Squadron

The 16 September 1941 was a night to remember for the residents of Norwich; they were bombed by the RAF! 93 Squadron, who flew Havocs from their home base of Middle Wallop, had been on detachment at Coltishall since 7 September. The squadron was primarily engaged in Long Aerial Mine laying trials, codename 'Mutton.' The idea was to lay a stream of 92 high explosive charges hung an the end of 2000ft long wires, each suspended from a small parachute in the flight path of approaching enemy bombers. When the enemy bomber struck the wire the drag of the parachute would pull the mine up into contact with the bomber and detonate it. Mine-laying of this type in the East Anglian area was difficult because there were so many RAF aircraft active at night. However, on the 16

257 Squadrons association with Coltishall came to an end in September 1941.

September, 93 Squadron was scrambled from Coltishall to lay their deadly cargo. At 2314 hrs, Havoc DG554, call sign 'Waddle 23' and flown by Plt Off Porter and Sgt Edwards, took off from Coltishall to intercept a raid approaching from the South.

Having been positioned two miles ahead of the raiders by Flt Lt J B Craig, the Neatishead Controller, the Havoc dropped its cargo. Several of the mines detonated prematurely on release and the enemy bombers, on seeing the explosions, turned away and avoided the minefield. Unfortunately due to a change in wind direction the minefield was sown over the south-west corner of the city, and 83 mines drifted slowly by parachute on to the residents of this area. With many reports of parachutes and canisters being reported throughout the area, Air Raid Wardens were kept busy. Unfortunately one of the Wardens, Herbert Batley, later died from the wounds he had received when a canister he tried to move exploded.

Despite this unfortunate incident, the squadron persisted with 'Mutton', but eventually, due to the difficulties in plotting accurately the path of the enemy bombers and of avoiding friendly aircraft, the system was finally abandoned, the squadron returning to Middle Wallop on the 26 October.

604 Squadron finally moved back to Middle Wallop on 21 September 1941 and were succeeded by the now fully operational 255 Squadron, commanded by Wg Cdr Windsor and equipped with the in-line Merlin engined Beaufighter IIF. However, bad weather and aircraft unserviceability kept their activity at a low ebb and it was not until 14 January 1942 that their first victory with a Beaufighter was scored, but that was from a detachment of aircraft flying out of West Malling.

Another visitor on 21 September was a Wellington Ic of 75 Squadron based at Feltwell. R1518 force-landed at nearby Swanton Abbott at 0430 hours after running out of fuel whilst returning from a raid over Berlin. Another loss was Hurricane II Z5045 of 257 Squadron which did

not return from an interception off Happisburgh on 4 October.

Unknown to the squadrons at Coltishall at the time, 12 October 1941 was to be remarkable, as on that day, enemy intruder night fighter operations over the United Kingdom were cancelled. Hitler wanted Allied aircraft to be shot down over Germany where the wrecks could be seen by the German public. There was little propaganda value in wrecks over England. It would be two and a half years before the night intruders would return to the skies over England.

Even without the assistance of night intruders the attrition continued. On 12 October Spitfire IIa P7971 of 19 Squadron from the satellite airfield at Matlaske crashed after hitting some trees on a night approach to Coltishall. The pilot, Sgt Edwards RCAF escaped with his life. The next day a Beaufighter IIF, R2377, of 255 Squadron crashed into the sea off Happisburgh.

On 13 October 1941, a Wellington Ic, T2999/PM-P, of 103 Squadron, being flown by Plt Off Kenneth H Wallis, was returning from a raid on Düsseldorf. His starboard engine had been hit during the raid and fearing the worst, he decided to make for Coltishall. In addition to his engine problems, his intercom, turrets and radio transmitters were all unserviceable. Over the airfield, all Wallis could do was to flash his aircraft identification letters on the downward facing light. By doing so, he was effectively asking permission to land. At first there was no response from the ground, possibly because of the fear that the Wellington might in fact be an enemy raider. However, the second pilot, Plt Off Johnnie Ward, saw a green very light that was followed shortly after by the flare path lights being switched on. Wallis quickly selected his flaps, and at the same time, lowered the undercarriage, concentrating hard on the approach and on getting his crippled aircraft safely down. Well into the approach, Ward became very agitated as whilst looking down through the bomb aimer's window he saw another instrument panel lit up in the darkness. He suddenly realised that they were flying only a few feet above another aircraft! The Wellington slewed off to the right side of the flare path, shuddering violently before dropping so heavily that it burst the tail wheel. Running along the flare path, they saw, close to their aircraft on the port side a Defiant, the aircraft they had almost landed on.

Whilst being de-briefed, the crew of the Wellington learned what had actually happened. The Defiant, which was based at Coltishall, had also suffered communications and radio failure, and the green very light was fired for them. The poor Defiant gunner could see the black outline

The Beaufighters of 29 Squadron were detached to Coltishall several times between April 1941 and May 1943.

Dramatic low-level view of Coltishall via the gun camera of a 255 Squadron Beaufighter IIF. A pair of Beaufighters can be seen, top right, parked in front of a 'C' Type hangar.

of the Wellington about to land on top of their aircraft, but could not tell his pilot of the pending disaster because of their own radio and intercom failure! Needless to say, there was great relief between the two crews and they all enjoyed a rather alcoholic evening together in Norwich to celebrate their lucky escape.

The Wellington was grounded at Coltishall because of the damage, the crew subsequently returned to their own base at Elsham Wolds by train. T2999 returned to 103 Squadron only to crash in a forced-landing two miles from the runway at Elsham Wolds on 26 November whilst being flown by Johnnie Ward.

Mishaps continued on 25 October when a Spitfire Vb, W3215, from Digby-based 411 Squadron was staging through Coltishall to take part in a fighter sweep. Whilst taxiing, the aircraft crashed into a static Hurricane and was damaged.

On 27 October 1941, Handley Page Hampden, AE398, of 44 Squadron joined the circuit at Coltishall after a bombing mission on Hamburg. Being close to the coast, Coltishall was often used as a safe haven for returning bombers damaged by enemy fighters or FLAK. At about 1720 hours the Hampden, with Sgt M Gruber at the helm, crashed close to the Royal Observer Corps (ROC) post on the eastern side of the airfield. Having circled the airfield

for almost 30 minutes in bad weather the engines on the bomber failed which caused the pilot to take drastic action to save his aircraft and crew. In the ensuing crash landing, the Hampden came to rest on the North Walsham road blocking it for many hours. Whilst the aircraft, with only 32 hours on the clock, was totally destroyed, Sgt Gruber and his crew escaped with their lives.

August and September 1941 had been busy months for 257 Squadron, acting as bomber escorts over the Continent, this tailed off in October and a move to Honiley on 7 November further reduced the action.

Their place at Coltishall was taken by 137 Squadron from Charmy Down in Somerset on 8 November, which at the time was equipped with the unique twin-engine Whirlwind I fighter. Under the command of Sqn Ldr H St J Coghlan DFC, the squadron began operations with coastal patrols and convoy escorts almost immediately off Great Yarmouth and the East Coast. Their stay at Coltishall was to be short, as on 1 December, the Whirlwinds moved to nearby Matlaske where they continued operations at a reduced intensity.

During November the attached Defiant night fighters of 151 Squadron had been carrying out a routine programme of dawn and dusk patrols over the North Sea when the inclement weather allowed. On 15 November,

Plt Off I A McRitchie with his gunner Sgt A G Beale took off from Coltishall for a dusk patrol. Their orders were to patrol the outer swept shipping channel and at 1725 hours, while on station at 50 feet, Sgt Beale reported a large twin-engine aircraft on his tail and called to his pilot to make a turn to starboard. The pilot responded immediately with a four 'G' turn just as a burst of enemy cannon fire streamed past the Defiant. Beale identified the aircraft as a Junkers Ju88 and returned fire at 200 yards before the Defiant made another high 'G' turn. Two short bursts sent the Ju88 into the sea, leaving nothing but a patch of oil on the surface. The weather was very bad at the time with mist down to sea level and visibility not more than a mile. The sharp look-out of the gunner without doubt saved the day for the Defiant and its crew.

Analysis showed that the enemy aircraft had been a Junkers Ju88D-1 (M2+DH) of 1/Ku.F1.Gr.106 which probably mistook the Defiant for a Hurricane and reckoned without the fighter's rearward facing guns. That same night another Defiant, AA423 of 151 Squadron, crewed by Sgts Victor Gee and William Bainbridge, was posted missing having presumably crashed into the sea with both crew members lost.

The pressures placed on both Coltishall and Matlaske were now so great that a second satellite airfield was opened on the 19 November 1941. Ludham was to be Norfolk's most easterly airfield, situated about 13 miles to the north-east of Norwich and close to Hickling Broad. Later, Ludham was to see a slightly different use. In 1943, the base was used as a practice bombing range. The local population took their RAF neighbours to their hearts, despite an unfortunate incident when a local farmer narrowly avoided being hit when bombs destined for the Ludham range narrowly missed his car on the Potter Heigham road!

Apart from the satellite airfields of Matlaske and Ludham, Coltishall had two dummy airfields or 'Q' sites as they were known. These sites were night decoy airfields with dummy flare paths; obstruction lights and occasionally dummy buildings. The idea of these 'Q' sites was to draw enemy intruders and bombers away from the main operational airfields. Coltishall's 'Q' sites were at Beeston St Lawrence and Suffield. Ludham was reported to have a 'Q' site of it's own at Somerton.

The end of the year was to see further tragedy for 255 Squadron. On 26 December, the squadron was to loose it's second CO, Wg Cdr Windsor. His Beaufighter, R2398, crashed at Heavingham, killing both himself and his Radio Operator, Sgt Langdon.

Just after 0830 hours on 27 December, Beaufort II, AW248, from 217 Squadron based at Thorney Island, landed at Coltishall. The crew disembarked to brief the pilots of twelve Spitfires which had been detached to Coltishall to escort the Beauforts on a daylight anti-shipping raid off the Dutch coast. Six Spitfires of 152 Squadron, who had taken up residency at Ludham on 1 December under the command of Sqn Ldr J Darwen, the first operational squadron at the base, were to escort the Beauforts out whilst a further six Spitfires of 19 Squadron would see them home.

At 0930 hours, the Beaufort took off with its escorts. Two further Beaufort's of 217 Squadron joined the formation over Coltishall. After a low-level flight over the North Sea, the formation approached the Dutch coast where the Spitfires engaged some Messerschmitt Bf109's as the Beaufort's attacked a cargo ship of about 1200 tons with bombs. From this very successful strike only one aircraft, Beaufort, AW248 sustained damage. The aircraft landed with a feathered starboard engine after being hit by tracer fire from the ship.

Since August 1941 the attached Defiants of 151 Squadron had been co-operating at night with Turbinlite-equipped Havocs. By December, they had developed a flare burning procedure whereby the Havoc would detect a low flying enemy aircraft and drop flares to guide the Defiant into the kill. Unfortunately, the Defiant was no more successful in this than in any other operational role and no kills were achieved with this technique.

Towards the end of 1941 the German low-level mine-laying activity off the English coast and attacks on coastal towns were the greatest cause of anxiety for Fighter Command, with the inability of the coastal radar stations to assist interceptions below 5000 feet or far out to sea. The GCI Stations at Neatishead and Orby were too inland to be able to help, and several of the coastal Chain Home Low reporting stations were equipped for fighter control, notably Happisburgh east of Cromer. Interception experiments were carried out to make fullest use of this increase in the ground control capability, using the Beaufighters of 29 Squadron who at that time were on detachment at Coltishall from their home Station at West Malling.

For the rest of 1941 anti-shipping operations were supported by Coltishall's day fighters while night fighters of 151 and 255 Squadrons maintained night air defence standbys for control by the GCI and Chain Home Low Stations.

Chapter 4

Members of 255 Squadron enjoy a pint or two outside the Adam & Eve pub in late 1941.

1942 - DAYLIGHT OFFENSIVE

The Bristol Beaufort was to be a regular visitor to Coltishall during February of 1942. On 12 February, the base figured in Operation Cerberus. The codename given to operations against the German Battleships, Scharnhorst and Gneisenau, as they made their 'Channel Dash' through the English Channel. Fourteen Beauforts of 42 Squadron had been rushed south from Leuchars, hoping to intercept the ships. Having already been turned away from Bircham Newton because of snow, the aircraft diverted to Coltishall. Three of the aircraft, supposedly loaded with torpedoes, were found on arrival at Coltishall to be unarmed. With the nearest torpedo store over 150 miles away in Grimsby things did not look good. In fact, things got worse! Two more Beauforts developed technical faults, which in turn caused the whole formation to be delayed for their onward flight to Manston.

After about two hours, pressure was applied from upon high to get the Beauforts on their way. The Senior Air Traffic Controller (SATCO) at Coltishall, Sqn Ldr Roger Frankland, instructed the crews of the Beauforts to join up with Hudson's of 407 Squadron over Manston. They were then to follow the Hudsons and attack the ships off the Dutch coast. What followed was a classic example of the chaos that the 'fog of war' can bring about. As soon as the Beauforts formed up behind the Hudsons, the latter broke away and, circling around, formed up behind the Beauforts! This continued for some time as both squadrons had been given the same instructions, to follow each other! Eventually, without the promised fighter escort the bomber formations headed out over the North Sea.

In heavy rain and thick cloud, the unprotected formation went in search of the Battleships. Eventually the German vessels were found off the Hook of Holland

March 1942 saw the departure of 255 Squadron and their Bullmastiff mascot Plt Off Bruce (centre front!).

and six of the Beauforts went into the attack with torpedoes. Without any success, the formation of Hudsons and Beauforts returned to their respective bases without any losses. Whilst this operation was in progress, fighters from Coltishall were scrambled should there be a need to search for survivors from any of the bombers that might have been shot down.

The next day, 86 Squadron arrived at Coltishall with Beauforts to repeat the operation, but they were too late to be of any use as the Battleships had by now sailed to the north east, well out of range. 22 Squadron Beauforts were also unlucky, although they stood by on 15 February for possible action.

On 25 February 1942, Sqn Ldr Clennell, OC 'A' Flight of 255 Squadron, attempted a forced landing in his Beaufighter T3032, due to the failure of the starboard engine. Unfortunately his aircraft struck a tree near White House Farm, Wood Bastwick. Sqn Ldr Clennell and Acting Plt Off H N Vincent were killed in the crash, whilst a third crew member, Plt Off R Wynzar, received concussion and slight facial injuries. His comrades, with full military honours, laid Sqn Ldr Clennell to rest in Scottow Cemetery. Flt Lt F P J McGevor was promoted to Squadron Leader and took over command of 'A' Flight soon after the loss of Sqn Ldr Clennell.

On the evening of 2 March 1942, 255 Squadron were to lose another Beaufighter and its two-man crew. Sqn Ldr McGevor, together with his Radio Operator, Sgt Leonard Barker, were airborne in their Beaufighter, R2333/YD-B, when they reported 'Tally Ho' at 2016 hours. Four

minutes later at 2020 hours they reported that they had successfully shot down an enemy aircraft. At 2028 hours a message was received that his starboard wing was on fire and that his position was ten miles NW of Cromer. Shortly after at 2030 hours, McGevor and Barker baled out of the Beaufighter. Although several aircraft took off in the course of the night and the next morning to search for the crew of the missing aircraft, their efforts were unavailing. As a result of this tragedy, the pressing need of having all Air Sea Rescue Craft (Naval and RAF) fitted with VHF radios, which would enable directions to be passed to the searching aircraft, was emphasised to higher authorities. Sqn Ldr McGevor was never found however the body of Sgt Barker was recovered and was interred at Scottow Cemetery.

In March 1942, 2 Gp resumed its daylight offensive with Douglas Bostons from Swanton Morley, Oulton and Great Massingham. Coltishall's Spitfires participated in all of these actions from the advanced bases. March also saw the departure of 255 Squadron to High Ercall. The road party left Coltishall on the 2 March and the aircrew, with their aircraft, left on the 8 March. On 3 March, a message was received at Coltishall from 255 Squadron at High Ercall to say that the Squadron Mascot, Plt Off Bruce, a Bullmastiff, had gone AWOL after his arrival with the road party. The message requested that if he returned to Coltishall 255 Squadron would be grateful for his return! Luckily, for the hapless 'Mutt', he was found safe and sound at High Ercall and was on hand to greet the aircrew on their arrival.

255 Squadron was replaced almost immediately at Coltishall with another Beaufighter squadron, 68 Squadron. The squadron itself was largely made up of Czech personnel who were commanded by another famous Battle of Britain pilot, Wg Cdr Max Aitken DFC. Aitken was the son of Lord Beaverbrook of Daily Express fame who had also been a member of Churchill's cabinet as the Minister of Aircraft Production in 1940.

One of the Czechoslovakian pilots to serve on 68 Squadron at Coltishall was Jo Capka. His involvement in WWII began on 15 March 1939, when, with other Czech pilots, he stood helplessly by as squadrons of Luftwaffe aircraft landed at his home airfield whilst armed Czech Nazis cordoned off the aircraft he had been trained to fly. Collaboration was not on Jo Capka's agenda so he joined the first Czech underground movement, and when they blew up the Gestapo HQ in his home town of Olomouc near Brno, he fled to Poland by tying himself to the bogeys of a goods train.

The Poles refused to let the Czechs fly with them and he

68 Squadron aircrew at Coltishall on the 28th July 1942.

was told the only chance of leaving Poland and fighting for the Allies lay in joining the Foreign Legion. Jo Capka joined, embarked from Gdynia to Calais and then to Marseilles where he learnt the ways of The Legion. In the blistering heat and under the eye of his sadistic seniors he shifted boulders from one end of the barrack square to the other. He experienced the cruel discipline of a Legionnaire's life in the desert until the Czech pilots were praying for France's entry into the war. When it came, Capka swapped his Legionnaire's uniform for that of the French Air Force, the Armee de l'Air and was sent to an airfield not far from Paris. Here he flew antiquated machines handicapped by frightening bomb aimers in hopeless sorties against the Panzer divisions as they thundered through France. As the Germans advanced his CO counselled surrender, Jo rejected this advice and pleas of a certain Mademoiselle to stay and, with other Czech pilots, travelled through the refugee-stricken roads to Bordeaux where they joined a boatful of Poles and arrived safely in Falmouth.

Now, for the third time, Jo Capka changed uniforms and became a Sergeant pilot in the RAF. He flew Wellingtons in a total of 56 bombing missions that included the famous long haul to Turin, was awarded the DFM and was Commissioned in 1941. He switched to night fighters after hearing that Czech crews were flying with 68 Squadron, and following night fighter conversion training at Charterhall, he got his wish. He continued in this nocturnal role on the Beaufighter through to the Mosquito. Luck always seemed to be on Jo Capka's side; that was until 27 June 1944 when the Mosquito he was flying was machined gunned by a 'Pirate' B-24 Liberator. Blinded with half his face in tatters, he got his observer, Willie Williams, to bale out and then holding the eyelid of one eye open with his fingers managed to see enough to crash-land in an English Wood. Jo survived the crash and after surgery at the hands of Sir Archibald McIndoe, flew again as a 'guinea pig' with a false eye!

After the war Joe Capka returned home covered in glory to run a flying school, but when the Communist coup came in 1948 his friendship with English people and being married to a former Coltishall WAAF, Rhoda Woodhouse, got him arrested as a British spy. Charged with High Treason he was advised to plead guilty and did so. Despite agitation by his wife who had escaped to England, he spent seven and half years in prison of which 14 months was in solitary confinement. Released

Jo Capka in the cockpit of a 68 Squadron Beaufighter.

after the death of Stalin, for many weary months he sought permission to leave Czechoslovakia. His wish was only granted in May 1957 after an interview with President Zapotocky.

Coltishall also became actively involved in the development and trials of radar that would not be affected by 'Window' as it was known that the Germans were developing their own form of radar counter measures. Wg Cdr Aitken, and his squadron, afforded considerable assistance to Wg Cdr D A Jackson of the TeleCommunications Research Establishment (TRE), who at the time, were at an advanced stage in the testing of the operational suitability of the new AI Mk XI radar set. This set had an automatic target following device, and it was hoped that the radar would be able to discriminate between aircraft and the various echoes formed by 'Window'

Operations from within the clutch stations of Coltishall, Matlaske and Ludham were integrated. Squadrons from

Dornier Do217E-4.

Duxford were often moved forward on a daily basis to replace any of Coltishall's resident squadrons that were sent to other sectors. The action at this time can be typified by the following report of 24 April 1942:

"137 Squadron patrolling off Yarmouth and Lowestoft. Sector and convoy patrols continued. A Lysander of 278 Squadron did an ASR search with 154 Squadron's Spitfires. Off Holland 610 Squadron flew a shipping sweep. There was a Wing sweep practice and 37 Squadron made an evening patrol around Hammond's Knoll light. 68 Squadron did a dusk Sector patrol."

On the evening of 27 April 1942, at 2321 hours, air raid sirens in Norwich began to wail. Searchlights lit up and pierced the night sky looking for a sizeable force of Luftwaffe bombers, Dornier's, Heinkel's and Junkers, which were crossing the coast at Wells-next-the-Sea at around 13 to 14,000 feet.

To add to the confusion at that time a force of Junkers Ju88s of KG30 were mining an area between Cromer

and Southwold. By 2335 hours any doubt as to the destination of the main force was dispelled, they were heading straight for Norwich. Their aim was to carry out a raid with incendiaries and high explosives. Once the primary fires had been started, there was a short pause before the main force crossed the City from the west. The gunners operating the Anti-Aircraft Batteries around the City had been ordered to cease-fire at 2350 hours. This was normally the prelude to the involvement of fighters operating in the area. In this case, the fighters consisted of nine Beaufighters of 68 Squadron from Coltishall, ten Spitfires of 610 Squadron out of Ludham and for the first time, a trio of 157 Squadron Mosquito's operating from Castle Camps.

The fighters were ordered to fly a layer patrol with 500 feet vertical separation between operating heights and with fourteen aircraft active at any one time. Unfortunately they were not in position when the first bombs began to explode to the rear of the Drayton Road. At 0045 hours the last bomb fell on Norwich and the raiders headed for home individually. Surprisingly, they had suffered no losses even though Fighter Command had responded with 32 aircraft that had tried to engage the bombers.

During the daylight hours of the 27 April, the defending fighters were more successful. Spitfire Vs of 610 Squadron were scrambled to intercept a bomber formation off the coast that morning. Plt Off Hokan', flying BL267, and Sgt S Creagh in BL484/DW-K', intercepted and successfully shot down a Junkers Ju88D-5 from 3(F)/122 off the coast near Great Yarmouth.

Sadly, success was often tempered by disaster and the 27 April proved no different. At 1600 hours a Beaufighter If of 68 Squadron was lost following an air-to-air firing sortie. T4631, flown by Sgt J Hindle and Plt Off E D Bailey, had been assigned to practice their air firing skills against a target-towing aircraft over the sea. Usually, after the drogue had been fired at, the towing aircraft dropped the drogue and towing cable in a designated area so that the success of the firing could be confirmed. Somehow, on this occasion, during the attack the firing aircraft, T4631, possibly due to excessive zeal or misjudgement, managed to make contact with the wire with one of its wings. Naturally, the drag of the drogue pulled the length of wire, three hundred feet or more, across the wing. The wire cut through the leading edge of the wing and damaged the main spar severely and as Hindle turned into land at Coltishall the additional stress on the wing caused it to fail and break off with catastrophic results.

Two nights later, the Luftwaffe returned to Norwich, inflicting more serious damage. In a repeat of the 27 April, Fighter Command Squadrons were again unsuccessful. Sqn Ldr Henry Donald, the first CO of the Neatishead GCI Station, reported that on the night of 29 April a Heinkel He111 was pursued over Neatishead by a Spitfire being flown by Coltishall's OC Flying, Wg Cdr Peter 'Prosser' Hanks. There was a lot of machine gun fire but no bombs were dropped or casualties sustained.

On 30 April, when the German bombers were homebound from their targets, night fighters from 68 Squadron infiltrated the raid claiming two Dornier Do17's destroyed; one by Wg Cdr Aitken.

Also flying that night was Plt Off Miroslav 'Miro' Mansfield and Sgt Slavomil Janacek of 68 Squadron in Beaufighter If V8246/WH-M. Their AI Mk VIII radar-equipped aircraft tool off from Coltishall at 0110 hours and soon over the North Sea, Janacek acquired a target at a distance of 6000 yards. Under his direction, Mansfield began an approaching climb. At a height of 13,000 feet and a distance of 2600 yards they identified the enemy as a Heinkel He111 and after a slow approach from the rear the pilot opened fire from a range of 300 yards with two short bursts. The starboard engine of the Heinkel exploded followed shortly by the explosion of the whole aircraft. The wreckage fell into the sea 20 miles north-east of Happisburgh. After being notified by GCI that there was another enemy aircraft near their position, Sgt Janacek again perfectly positioned his pilot behind the enemy. The Beaufighter approached the second Heinkel He111 at 500 yards, this time however the crew of the bomber saw the Beaufighter and began their escape by turning to the right in an intense descent. Plt Off Mansfield immediately followed and from 300 yards opened fire with a long burst from his cannon. This one burst of gunfire was enough to hit the enemy in the starboard wing and to cause the engine to explode. The Heinkel then fell into a spiral dive and disappeared 14 miles off Happisburgh.

After a third, this time unsuccessful pursuit of the enemy they landed back at Coltishall just after 0220 hours. But that was not the end of the night for this crew as at 0430 hours they took-off again in the same Beaufighter to an area where another 68 Squadron Beaufighter, X8253/WM-W crewed by Sqn Ldr Vesley and Flg Off Montgomerie, had damaged a single Dornier Do217. In that engagement, Vesley's guns jammed and he had no choice but to hand over to Plt Off Mansfield who it was hoped would finish off the damaged Dornier.

Sgt Janacek began to search on his radar and within no time he identified the track and gave his pilot the co-ordinates to effect another successful intercept. Mansfield took the Beaufighter to within 200 yards and opened fire as he closed to within 20 yards. During this attack, his aircraft was hit by return fire in one wing, but the damage inflicted on the enemy aircraft was more severe with hits being registered on the port wing, fuselage and engine. The results saw the Dornier crash into the sea 15 miles off Happisburgh. The satisfied Czechoslovakian crew landed back at Coltishall following their second successful sortie at 0516 hours.

For their actions that night both Plt Off Mansfield and Sgt Janacek were both promoted and awarded the DFC and DFM respectively. The actions of 30 April/1 May proved to be the most successful night for the Czech night fighters as they had shot down five enemy aircraft and damaged one without loss.

Johnnie Johnson's second encounter with Coltishall came in 1942 when, after promotion to Squadron Leader, he was posted to take command of 610(County of Chester) Squadron. He duly reported to Gp Capt Ronnie Lees, the Station Commander, who gave Johnson a brief sketch of the squadrons under his command. He explained that Max Aitken's 68 Squadron were doing extremely well with their Beaufighters. The Whirlwinds of 137 Squadron at Matlaske, one of his satellite airfields, were being kept busy, as were the squadrons at his second satellite field, Ludham, Johnson's new home.

Gp Capt Lees explained that recent activities of Johnson's new squadron included convoy patrols, enemy shipping reconnaissance off the Dutch coast, a few sweeps with units from 11 Group and plenty of Rhubarbs.

On arrival at Ludham, Johnnie Johnson found that his deputy was none other than the 'Crow', Dennis Crowley-Milling, who had joined the squadron soon after his escape from France the previous autumn. He also found that 610 Squadron was a cosmopolitan bunch of individuals from Canada, Australia, France, New Zealand, Belgium, Rhodesia and Norway. The Norwegian pilot often had to explain his heritage after being mistaken for a member of the Luftwaffe when he used to venture out on his bicycle around the Broads in search of a pint of beer!

This period was particularly busy for Coltishall although a few surprises punctuated the pressure with often amusing consequences. For example on 7 May, six Defiants joined the circuit arriving for 278 Squadron. Unfortunately, the squadron had no fuel bowser, no

After being removed from front-line squadron service early during the Second World War. Many Lysanders found themselves on SAR Squadrons.

100-octane fuel, let alone a 24-volt starter to get them going again!

Respite from the task at hand was short-lived as, on 8 May the Luftwaffe tried again for Norwich. This time the raid was a failure with bombs falling in a wide area around the city. 68 Squadron were scrambled and patrolled the area without success. However, a Dornier Do217E-4 of 1/KG2 was downed near Stoke Holy Cross, either as a result of hitting a balloon cable or by AA fire. The Dornier Do217 had a crew of four, although only three bodies were recovered from the wreckage. By dawn, no less than two Battalions of the Norfolk Division were scouring the countryside and following up countless sightings of the missing airman, all without success. 68 Squadron were again scrambled to intercept a bomber force that was attacking Great Yarmouth. Wg Cdr Aitken claimed a Dornier Do217 destroyed and a Junkers Ju88 damaged. Sqn Ldr Howden and Flt Lt Winward between them accounted for a further Dornier Do217 and Junkers Ju88 in the same raid.

It was not only the Beaufighters of 68 Squadron who were busy. The Spitfires of 610 Squadron were equally involved in the struggle. On 14 May, Sqn Ldr G S K Haywood in his Spitfire V, BL564/DW-E, and Sgt F Mares in W3128/DW-B, caught and badly damaged a Junkers Ju88 which was mine-laying just off shore. The next day, two flights of Spitfires from the squadron were responsible for destroying two Dornier Do217s of 3/KG2.

During the evening of 16 May, Sqn Ldr Haywood in BL564, and Sgt Mares in BL267, were paired again in battle. This time they made a head-on interception of a Junkers Ju88 that appeared out of the cloud off Lowestoft. In the fight that followed, damage was caused to the bomber, but despite the arrival of a third Spitfire,

flown by Coltishall's OC Flying, Wg Cdr 'Prosser' Hanks, the Junkers escaped into the mist, smoke billowing from both of its engines.

A variation for the night fighter squadrons at Coltishall in their nightly search of the skies came with sweeps against German E-boats. Usually, the E-boats travelled fast in 'V' formation and had terrific firepower for their diminutive size. When the squadrons took off on such sweeps, R/T silence was paramount immediately after they had been given the course to fly to intercept the marauding E-boats.

The reflection of the sea itself occupied half the radar operator's screen in the aircraft when they flew, as they did, very low over the waves. The blip of a boat was more like a spot, but they could be picked up. The crews found that the E-boats were inclined to form a circle on hearing the night fighter approach and then with the engines switched off lay in silent wait for the silhouettes of the aircraft to show up, giving their gunners a target to aim at. The aim, therefore, was to catch them underway when the wake could put the crews spot on target with the naked eye.

The FAA operated sea searches from Coltishall at that time and it was from them that the targets were usually identified, leaving the night fighters to hurtle at wave top height after their quarry. The main difficulty, especially if they were stopped, was to pick up the darker patch that was the boat before the aircraft were over the top and away. Unless they fired it was very difficult to spot them, but they usually opened fire first for the simple reason that they saw the approaching fighters first. The night fighters flew at ten-second intervals on these shipping raids giving each a good crack at the target before the next aircraft started its attack run.

It was inevitable that many young airmen and airwomen would find themselves serving at bases in their native County. For one young Norfolk man, Coltishall was to be home from May 1942 to May 1944.

Following the second night of the Luftwaffe bombing Norwich, AC2 Philip 'Ginger' Rounce together with two other East Anglian 'sproggs', AC Class 1 Ronnie Carter from Brandon and Eddie 'Danny' Daniels from Billericay, reported for duty with 5 ASR Flt at Coltishall. On arrival at the Flight's dispersal, on the far side of the airfield, the three young lads were to see for the first time the types of aircraft they were to work on in the Search and Rescue role. The Lysander used for search, marking and dinghy drops and the Walrus, a wood and metal amphibious biplane with a boat-like hull, being used purely for Search and Rescue. There were also a number of Defiants that were supposed to be used for search and escort duties. When 'Ginger' and his mates arrived, they were well and truly grounded, tethered and unused.

Apart from the flying activity, 'Ginge' remembers that Coltishall was also the home of two of his Battle of Britain hero's. OC Flying Wing was Wg Cdr 'Laddie' Lucas. His personal aircraft carried the code 'LL', and by chance, this particular Spitfire was being lovingly looked after by another local lad, LAC Seaton. The second Battle of Britain Ace was Wg Cdr 'Max' Aitken who was in charge of 68 Squadron, a night fighter unit flying the Beaufighter. He also recalls that Sqn Ldr Haley-Bell, one of Max Aitken's Flight commanders, was the brother-in-law of the actor John Mills.

As was inevitable in wartime, certain events remain imprinted in one's memory, and for AC2 Philip Rounce this proved to be true; there were many 'high spots' and an equal number of tragedies. Within a few days of his arrival at Coltishall on 6 June, Philip found himself on the night duty crew as the 'wireless mech.' He vividly remembers cycling back around the peri-track at about 1700 hours to start his duty when he watched in horror as one of 68 Squadron's 'long nosed' Blenheims failed to make it airborne, its undercarriage catching some wires. Needless to say, as was Common with the Blenheim and Beaufighters, it was a right 'burner.' The Pilot and his Armourer passenger were victims; "we could not get near it." The aircraft, a IVf serial number Z5722, the pilot being Sgt Lascelles.

In January 1943, King George VI and Queen Elizabeth visited the Station, accompanied by the Station Commander Gp Capt Donaldson DSO, DFC, the youngest 'Groupie' in the RAF. During the visit they presented the squadron with its new official crest, a seagull within a lifebuoy with a rope in its beak with the motto 'EX MARE AD REFERIENDUM, 'From the Sea to Flight Again.'

"It was about that time that we received our first Avro Anson's to replace the Lysanders for search duties. Whilst the 'Lizzie' did a good job, it was unable to carry the larger dinghies that were needed to drop over downed British and American bombers that carried a crew of eight or nine. On the evening of 4 April 1943, whilst on a search 40 miles South East of Great Yarmouth, the squadron sustained its first operational loss. Anson BG809 was shot down with the loss of the crew. Sadly amongst those who lost their lives was our CO, Flt Lt Phillip Richard Smith, who only weeks before had proudly accepted our new Squadron Badge from HM the King."

"At one stage we shared our dispersal with the Spitfires of 118 Squadron, and it was always a thrill to watch them when they returned from a sweep or from escort duties, coming low over the airfield, wing-tip to wing-tip. One bright summer day in 1943, the 29 July, the Spitfires were returning from Matlaske just down the road. Once again we were all outside watching as they came across the airfield low before peeling off for their landing. On this occasion however, something went horribly wrong; two of the Spits collided and plunged to the ground killing their NCO pilots."

"Life at RAF Coltishall also had its lighter moments, often as good as a comedy programme on the wireless or at the theatre. In fact, Arthur Askey would have been proud of this one!"

"We were all gathered round in the signals workshop when one of the VHF 'Pack Sets' came to life; transmitting details from one of our Walruses that they had just picked up a German pilot and that they were on there way back to Coltishall with their prisoner. The CO of the RAF Regiment formed up to 'arrest the enemy', the party consisted of six of the biggest 'bruisers' in the Regiment armed to the hilt. The 'Shagbat', nickname for the Walrus, taxied into an area in front of Flying Control

Pilots and observers of 68 Squadron relax at Coltishall in May 1942.

where the welcoming party was waiting, prepared to meet their fearsome foe. The rear hatch opened and a pathetic, half-drowned German pilot literally fell out of the aircraft. How we all roared with laughter. Needless to say, the RAF Regiment party and their highly annoyed CO, were not amused, the poor individual needed an ambulance not an armed guard!"

Phillip well remembers a Flying Fortress landing on the short runway across the airfield. It failed to stop in time, crossed our dispersal, and came to a halt when it slid between two oak trees. The impact caused the inner two engines to come loose from their mountings. "I doubt if any aircraft crew ever de-planed quicker!" The date was the 16 December 1943. The aircraft was a B-17F called 'Louisiana Purchase' from the 384th Bomb Squadron based at Grafton Underwood near Kettering in Northamptonshire.

Recalling other significant happenings at Coltishall, Philip recalls the night and next morning of the ill-fated Nuremburg raid when the Met men got it all wrong and Bomber command really 'copped out.' The whole station was brought to readiness in preparation to receive a large number of bombers. The ground handlers managed to park about 40 aircraft around the perimeter of the airfield. "It was my 'black' memory of life on an active airfield", he sadly remembers. "Aircrews were decimated in that most aircraft had terribly injured and dead crews, and I well remember one pal was sick for days after what he had

witnessed. Youngsters of today accuse us of 'celebrating the Anniversary of War' far from it what we do is honour the memory of those dead airmen and thank God for our survival."

"In March 1944 we received our first Vickers Warwick fitted with the airborne lifeboat. It was then decided to move 278 Squadron away from our home of the past two years, with 'B' Flight moving to Martlesham Heath. In the end only six individuals moved to Martlesham with Philip being put in charge of the transfer across the border to the Suffolk base."

"Serving the RAF in East Anglia, particularly at RAF Coltishall, had its moments and I feel privileged to have done my little bit."

For one particular crew from 68 Squadron, the night of 29/30 May 1942 proved to be quite eventful. Amongst others, Plt Off Jock Marshall and his Observer, Plt Off David Haigh, took-off from Coltishall at 2215 hours in their Beaufighter X7692. David Haigh recalls that they disposed of a couple of Heinkels getting a bit 'shot-up' in the process, and through being kept on patrol for too long, had both engines cut when in the circuit to land and crashed in Worstead Park where the Beaufighter was written off. Marshall was off flying duty for six months, with Haigh returning to duty within three weeks of the accident.

Whilst waiting for his 'driver' to recover, David was

asked to take part in an experiment to try controlling direct from a Chain Home Link tube at Happisburgh. The idea at first was that he would mainly be controlling his fellow crews from 68 Squadron, who would have known his voice, and that he might know more of the problems at the other end than the non-flying chaps at that time trying to do the job. In a short time 68 Squadron had three successes whilst David was controlling, and others with different squadrons and aircraft. It was quickly decided by the powers that be, to use other night fighters on 'rest' in this way, and each Chain Home Link got at least one, 'on rest' accordingly.

After a period at other stations, including a year with 125 Squadron, David was sent back to Coltishall with a brief to solve the problems of Divers (V-1 Flying Bombs) launched from Heinkels, in conjunction with 68 Squadron. There were two problems including, accurate height keeping at low level at night solved by radio altimeters, and the sea returns on the radar screen at low levels; the latter being solved by using coloured screens. After much 'trial and error' it was found that orange coloured screens were the best, and these were quickly brought into general use.

David Haigh also recalls another incident that happened on 31 October 1944 whilst on one of their nightly 'anti-diver launcher patrol' detachments from Coltishall to Bradwell Bay. His usual 'driver', Sqn Ldr Eric Barwell DFC had been posted, and the other Flight Commander, Bill Gill, had his navigator go sick with acute appendicitis. He asked David if he could come down to Bradwell for standby; the weather forecast being 'Fog.'

At 1930 hours the crews were asked by Group if they were prepared to fly, as by then the fog was dense. They said that they had suspected 'plots' approaching. Eric and David took-off in Mosquito HK325 on a compass bearing, seeing very little of the runway lights as they became airborne into the fog, with a stark warning that there was little chance of improvement anywhere in the country. They were successful in their aims as they destroyed two Heinkels and ran out of ammunition just as another one they were behind launched its V-1. As luck would have it, there was a brief 'hole' in the fog at Coltishall just as they got into the circuit and landed.

The next day there was an amusing sequel to the previous night's activities. Details of the action were given out in a press release as Bill Gill was awarded an immediate DSO, and his Navigator, quoted as Flg Off Desmond Hutchins, who was in bed in hospital, a DFC. When the error was discovered, Des Hutchins was

allowed to keep his as he was already credited with other 'kills.' David Haigh received his DFC a few weeks later.

Apart from being an ideal airfield for fighters engaged in operations over East Anglia and the East Coast, Coltishall's close location to the sea made it a welcome sight for badly damaged bombers returning from raids deep within the Third Reich. 'Cuckoos', as the damaged bombers were called, were often short of fuel rather than being heavily damaged by FLAK or fighters and an example of this occurred on the night of a 1000 bomber raid on Cologne. A Stirling from Downham Market landed with only enough fuel for a further five minutes flying. That crew was lucky, others were not so fortunate. From the records available, Coltishall received the following RAF heavy bomber 'Cuckoos' during the period of the bomber campaign, all with severe damage, not all landed safely: one Halifax, two Hampdens, four Lancasters, four Stirlings, two Wellingtons and a single Whitley. These only account for RAF bombers as the USAAF became more and more involved in the air war; countless B-17s and B-24s would find themselves in the same situation.

During the war years, many new ideas and inventions were put into practice. One such idea was introduced to assist crews of aircraft returning from night operations. As expected, many aircraft were badly damaged, often with wounded and dead crew members on board and many were hopelessly lost or desperate to find a safe landing site.

Being close to the coast, Coltishall was one of the units equipped as a Homing Airfield. With a Sandra Light beacon close to the airfield, and searchlights spread around in a 20-mile radius of the airfield, all pointing towards the beacon and comparative safety. Many crews returned home, thanks to the inventor of this simple idea.

One night, the Observer Corps HQ at Norwich was informed that a Stirling bomber was reported short of fuel, and would be trying to reach Coltishall. The aircraft crossed the coast at Cromer with its navigation lights on. The flight path of the bomber was plotted, and then the ROC post at Coltishall made a visual contact. Suddenly the lights on the Stirling went out, and its engines stopped. The aircraft, still in the air, glided on and the ROC post saw the silent bomber crossing over the boundary fence, assuming that it had landed safely. To their surprise, they received a telephone call from Flying Control asking whether the Stirling had landed or not as they could not find it!

The mystery was solved at first light. The Stirling was

A still cold night in winter, when I was on night call
"Go at once, about six miles" - a plane was seen to fall.
Off we went in a hurry, the MO and me, in my van
Six miles seemed like sixty, no sign of fire or man.

A shadow there across the field, a shattered bomber, crippled bird
I clutched my torch and blanket, no sound, nothing was heard.
It was so very quiet, uncanny and dead still
"Listen, listen", the MO said, it was so cold and chill.

I shone my torch round this lonely place
My god, a body with no face.
I could not look, I felt so sick
Over here Sir, please come quick.

Another shape just over there
A big ambulance is coming, help is near.
I bend down and fall on my knees
He whispers -"Help me, Help me, please.

He's badly hurt, his hand I hold
I cradle him close to keep out the cold.
Strong men come with tender care
Carry him away on a stretcher they bear.

Our brave young men in Air Force Blue
I'll never forget that night - and you.

At eighty, an old man, cutting the hedge with a sickle
It touched something and he was blasted - was this his war?

They called it a butterfly bomb, but a butterfly is beautiful
This thing hung like a devil, waiting to kill.

We roared down the road to the crossing, a little crowd waited nearby
"Come on man, help us with this stretcher" - they looked the other way.

Struggled with our human burden - the birds were singing once more
We were leaving this scene of carnage - nearly left his leg.

Shut the doors, start her up, into gear, "Get to Norwich as quickly as you can"
Eyes alert, watch the road, forget the sight, five miles to go.

A tap on the Communications window, slide it along, a voice is heard
No rush - take it easy, he's dead. Killed by a butterfly.

found on the opposite side of the boundary fence, having passed right through a group of parked Beaufighters, missing all the aircraft before coming to rest. The crew were all safe, and had to endure a three hour wait until Coltishall personnel found them!

On 18 July, squadrons from within 12 Gp were involved in the raid on Dieppe. Wg Cdr Jameson led aircraft from 411, 485 and 610 Squadrons in support of the operation. The composite wing claimed three Fw190s and two Bf109s for the loss of an equal number of Spitfires.

LACW Winifred Hurren was posted to Coltishall in the summer of 1942 and spent the next eight months carrying out a variety of duties from driving the coal and supply trucks around the Station, driving the CO, Gp Capt Arthur Vere Harvey and the ambulances from the Sick Bay. In those days, the young girls had to face up to many sad occasions and one of the ways that Winifred dealt with such traumas was to write poems about her experiences. (*The poems on the left are just two of many that helped her cope during the dark years of war.*)

The night of 23 July 1942 proved to be outstanding for 68 Squadron and devastating to the Luftwaffe. 68 Squadron that night was claiming five out of the seven kills over East Anglia. Wg Cdr Aitken and his radar operator, Flg Off Higham, destroyed a Junkers Ju88 and a Dornier Do217. WO Bobek with Flt Sgt Kovarik, and Sgt Vesely in a second Beaufighter shot down a further two Dornier Do217's. The fifth aircraft, a Do217, was brought down on its way to bomb an aircraft factory in Bedford by Sgt J C Truscott and his Observer, Sgt Howarth, flying a Beaufighter I fitted with AI Mk IV radar and four cannon.

Guided by the Neatishead Ground Controller, Flt Lt Ballentyne, Truscott was vectored onto a contact at 2300 hours in almost daylight conditions where he quickly established a visual on the enemy raider flying 500 feet below him at 12,000 feet. He dived at full power and closed in astern, throttling back at 150 yards range to confirm it was an enemy Dornier Do217. Truscott then closed the range to 100 feet and, sighting on the port engine, opened fire with two short bursts. The Do217 took no evasive action and the port wing exploded in flames. As the crippled bomber spiralled downwards the Beaufighter had to take violent avoiding action but was able to put in another short burst before entering cloud. After a few minutes there was a glow of an explosion below the cloud layer which continued to burn for some minutes.

Sgt Truscott was immediately given the course to

another intercept but was unable to follow up the chase because his windscreen was covered in oil. He found that by trying to wipe the oil off with his windscreen wipers only made the condition worse and thus was forced to return to Coltishall. The Dornier that Truscott claimed was a Do217E-4/F8+CN of 5KG 40 based at Soesterberg in Holland and it fell to the ground in Fleet Fen, two miles north of Gedney Hill near Spalding, Lincolnshire.

The actions of that night resulted in the award of the DSO for Wg Cdr Aitken, the citation for which, credited him with fourteen enemy aircraft destroyed to date. A further award resulted from the fact that many of his squadron crews were refugee Czechoslovakians and the Free Czech government accordingly presented him with their War Cross. At around 2000 hours on the night of 30 June, operations at Coltishall called 278 Squadron dispersal to say that a Wellington was circling a dinghy 80 miles off the coast; they were therefore to scramble a Walrus and escorts as soon as possible.

At 2050 hours Flt Lt P R Smith and Flt Sgt P N Atkinson took off from Coltishall in Walrus L2238, and vectored to 098 degrees as they passed over the coast. The cloud base at the time was at 400 feet. This cloud base, combined with heavy driving rain, gave very bad visibility for the search and rescue attempt. About ten miles from the coast, the escorting Defiants, also from 278 Squadron, overtook the Walrus. One of the Defiants, AA314, flown by Flg Off E G K Beadman and Flt Sgt S Hurrell, commenced their weaving fight escort flight pattern soon after passing the Walrus. However, after about forty five to fifty minutes into the flight they lost contact over the 'fix' in extremely bad visibility. With an unserviceable fuel gauge to add to their woes, it was decided to return to base.

At about the same time Flt Lt Smith was given another vector, 104 degrees and then 140 degrees for five miles. Within half an hour the orbiting Wellington was sighted, flying around a float flame which was burning on the surface of the sea. Flt Sgt Atkinson signalled to the Wellington by Alddis Lamp to ask if they had seen the dinghy. The reply came "Am orbiting position given to us - no sign of dinghy." The Walrus crew started to make a search pattern; however, the conditions were such that it was almost impossible to see although the water conditions were good and would not prove a problem if they had located the dinghy.

With no success, and with the weather conditions deteriorating by the minute, it seemed that their efforts would be thwarted. In fact, at 2230 hours the crew received a W/T message from Great Yarmouth telling them to recover back to base. Total darkness fell about half an hour before the coast was reached. Flt Lt Smith was flying his Walrus just above the cloud and through constant rainstorms for the whole time. If the weather conditions were not enough to contend with, the crew had to endure friendly fire on three occasions from Royal Navy ships as they approached landfall. Near the coast, the Walrus descended through 1000 feet, and as they broke through the cloud, the 'Canopy Lights' and 'Homing Beams' welcomed the crew back to Coltishall where they finally landed at 2315 hours. Thankfully, the dinghy and survivors were rescued by High Speed Launch the next day, about six miles east of the search area that the Walrus and Defiants had been working the previous evening.

Norwich was yet again the target for Luftwaffe bombers on 26 July when more damage was inflicted on the city. This raid resulted in a rare event for 610 Squadron who were patrolling that evening. The squadron was credited with a Junkers Ju88, which in itself was not so unusual. However, the aircraft was not fitted with Airborne Interception (AI) Radar and so this success was down to the skill of the crew who made an interception virtually blind.

On 29 July, Flg Off Raybould and Flt Sgt Mullaly from 68 Squadron were airborne in Beaufighter X7842/WM-P, a presentation aircraft named 'Birmingham Civil Defence.' They intercepted and shot down a Dornier Do217E-4, 1213/U5+DP, of 6/KG2 that crashed on Salthouse Marshes, Sheringham at 0200 hours; Oblt F Dorflinger, Uffz. Ohnesorge and Obfw J Ziegaus were all killed. Gefr H Skryczak baled out and was later taken prisoner.

There was something unusual about this particular combat as most of the Squadron's victims were either intercepted over the sea and fell into the water or crashed a considerable distance away from Coltishall. This Dornier was intercepted over the sea but crashed on the seashore less than twenty miles from the aerodrome. Thus, on this occasion the successful Beaufighter crew was able to go out in a truck to inspect the wreckage. When Flg Off Raybould and Flt Sgt Mullaly arrived at the crash scene there wasn't much left of the aircraft, but they were able to recover some trophies that found there way back to the Squadron at Coltishall. The tail fin from the Do217 went on to serve as the Squadron scoreboard for the rest of the time they remained at Coltishall. The other item removed; despite strong protests from the guards who said that "intelligence" had not examined the wreckage, was the rear armament, a rather bent and battered Rheinmetall-Borsig heavy machine gun. Even after the

278 Squadron pose in front of a 'Shagbat'.

war, 'The Raybould Gun' was a central part of the annual springtime reunion by the Squadron at Coltishall.

The rear gunner of the aircraft, Gefr Skryczak, baled out at the start of the combat and fell into the sea close enough to the coast to be able to wade ashore. Before being removed to a prison camp he was brought to Coltishall for a meal where Flg Off Raybould was able to meet him. In the conversation that followed, Skryczak said that his crew saw the Beaufighter closing in on the radar but paid very little attention to it as the apparatus was not very reliable. They did however see the attacking aircraft well before the Beaufighter opened fire and thought they had escaped after their violent evasive action. The pilot was even thinking about turning back to the target when the port engine exploded.

What had happened was that the Beaufighter had closed in gently from astern and, as soon as visual contact had been made, dropped below to obtain a clear identifying silhouette against the sky before opening fire. This was standard operating procedure for Flg Off Raybould and other crews, as nine out of ten of all the aircraft they intercepted were friendly and, almost without exception, unaware of the Beaufighters presence. Whilst they were making up their mind that it was in fact a Dornier and about to drop back into a firing position, there was a burst of fire from the rear gunner as the aircraft dropped away

in a steep diving turn. At this stage the Beaufighter crew thought that they had lost their target as he was diving steeply and weaving from one direction to another. They could not see him clearly enough to anticipate which way he was going; then he had the misfortune to cross between the Beaufighter and a bank of cloud which was brightly lit by the half moon. Flg Off Raybould was able to haul the Beaufighter round in a tight turn and fire a wide deflection shot.

When firing at a moving target the crews had to aim where the target would be when the bullets reached it. The bullets were travelling at about three times the speed of the target aircraft and did not arrive instantaneously. The rule of thumb was that they aimed ahead of the target by about one quarter of the range between the attacker and target. Most effective combats took place at about one hundred yards which meant aiming ahead by 25 yards; in this case Flg Off Raybould was at three to four hundred yards which meant aiming about 100 yards in front of the Dornier. His anticipation and aiming was 'dead on' as the port engine of the Dornier caught fire after direct hits from the Beaufighter's cannon. There must have been other damage as well because the Dornier rolled over onto its back and dived into the cloud. Shortly afterward, there was a sudden glow which illuminated the cloud as the plane exploded on contact with the ground.

Flg Off Raybould (left) stands next to Flt Sgt Mullaly with X7842 providing the backdrop.

July also saw the introduction of new types of aircraft to the Coltishall skyline. American-built Mustangs of 268 Squadron based at Snailwell, Cambridgeshire often used Coltishall for refuelling and re-arming prior to, and after, Shipping Reconnaissance missions, or 'Lagoons', as they were more commonly known.

A new type of enemy aircraft appeared in the East Anglian skies on 13 August when a twin engine Messerschmitt Me210 was detected by radar while carrying out a shipping search. Four Typhoons were scrambled to intercept and they soon shot the intruder down into the sea. One survivor was seen climbing into his dinghy, from which he was rescued six days later.

The Dieppe Raid on 19 August required a joint effort from the Coltishall Wing, involving the aircraft of 411, 485 and 610 Squadrons. Under the overall command of Wg Cdr Jameson, the Wing claimed three Focke Wulf Fw190s and two Messerschmitt Bf109s for the loss of five Spitfires.

In an attempt to increase the ability of night fighters to detect enemy raiders on moonless nights, a detachment from 1453 Flt arrived at Coltishall on 24 August from Wittering. Havoc BJ467, crewed by Plt Off's Jack Cheney and James Mycock, plus six groundcrew, were attached to Coltishall for three days to carry out ground control sorties under the direction of their engineer, Flt Lt Derek Jackson. The aircraft was fitted with AI Mk IV radar but in the nose was a 2700 million-candle power Helmore-Turbinlite. The batteries to power this monster searchlight were located in the aircraft bomb bay. This ill-conceived project required a fighter, in this case a Hurricane, to maintain close formation on the Havoc. With the target illuminated, the fighter would then close in for the kill.

To many, the system was deemed a waste of time, especially as the Havoc could position itself with its AI radar to close on the target. Why not dispense with the searchlight and let the Havoc do its own killing with cannon? After their short stay at Coltishall, the detachment returned to Wittering. However, they did return to Coltishall for a few more days to refine their tactics. Eventually the Tubinlite-Havoc Flights were disbanded, after considerable manpower and resources had been wasted on the project.

A new squadron also arrived in this same period when 56 Squadron, equipped with the Typhoon Ia and Ib fighters moved in to the Coltishall satellite airfield at Matlaske on 24 August for what turned out to be an eleven month stay. Equipped with the Typhoon since September 1941, 56 Squadron suffered the problems of an aircraft being rushed into service. The Napier Sabre engine had been installed before its teething troubles were over and a structural defect, later rectified, caused many tail assemblies to part-company with the rest of the airframe. During their time at the Coltishall clutch of airfields 56 Squadron lost 23 aircraft, of which only three were caused by enemy action.

Early in the afternoon of 5 September a pair of 610 Squadron Spitfires at 25,500 feet located two Messerschmitt Me210s, 25 miles south-east of Southwold. One of the Me210s dived away, quickly followed by Plt Off S G Creagh in Spitfire EP253/DW-K and Sgt H R Gregory in AR509/DW-H, each using full-boost to catch the enemy. As the Me210A-1, Wrk No 173 coded 2H+LA, of KG6 raced towards the coast in a vain attempt to escape, machine gun fire from one of the Spitfires ripped into its starboard wing causing the engine to explode. As the battle continued, the Me210 turned onto its back and crashed inverted into the North Sea thirty miles east of Southend. The second Messerschmitt made a rapid exit dropping its bombs on Leigh-on-Sea as it escaped the attention of the Spitfires.

When Sqn Ldr Johnnie Johnson took command of 610 Squadron he made it quite clear to the Station Commander at the time, Gp Capt Lees that his ambition was to take the squadron back to 11 Gp, hopefully to Biggin Hill, Kenley or North Weald. To put the icing on the cake, he also desired the new Mark IX Spitfire to re-equip his squadron when he eventually moved from 12 Group.

Very soon Johnson was to find out his squadron was not going to Biggin, Kenley or North Weald, let alone re-equipping with the Mk IX Spitfire. In fact, they were not even going back to 11 Gp! They were going to change places with a squadron at Castletown, near Thurso, at that time the most northerly base in Scotland! Having promised the squadron a move south, for which all ranks had worked extra hard to achieve, Johnson found this decision a ghastly reward and he was determined to challenge the decision, if necessary at the highest level!

Johnny Johnson flew to Coltishall to see his new Station Commander, Gp Capt C D Harvey to discuss the problem. Whilst sympathetic, the Station Commander pointed out there was little he could do, as it was Fighter Command who decided the fate of squadrons and their postings. Accepting that his Station Commander was

not able to persuade the decision-makers in any way, Johnson then asked if he could put his case to the Group Commander, AVM Saul. Gp Capt Harvey gave the necessary permission, although he did not hold out much hope.

On meeting AVM Saul, Johnson explained his situation and his commitment to those under his command on the squadron. The AOC did in fact think that the decision to send 610 Squadron to Castletown was in fact a stroke of bad luck and had already said as such to Fighter Command. It became all too clear to Johnson that if the AOC had already broached the subject with command it looked ominous that his squadron was on its way to Scotland. However, that said, he did have one more request up his sleeve. He asked AVM Saul for permission to approach the C-in-C. Whilst looking a bit startled at the request, Saul agreed, but was doubtful about the outcome.

A few days later, after taking part in the largest Boeing B-17 Flying Fortress raid on the enemy so far in the war, Johnson rang a Staff Officer at Fighter Command from Biggin Hill to arrange an interview with the C-in-C. It was pointed out that the C-in-C was not in the habit of granting interviews with disgruntled squadron commanders. Johnson then pointed out that he had in fact gone through the correct chain of command and had been given permission by both his Station and Group commanders to make the request. With that reply he was told to report to Bentley Priory at 1400 hours the next day.

North American Mustang I, similiar to those operated by 268 Squadron.

After reporting to Gp Capt McEvoy at Bentley Priory, he explained his reasons for wanting to see the C-in-C. The Group Captain advised Johnson that the C-in-C would see him but it would have to be snappy, as he was an extremely busy man. ACM Sir Sholto Douglas listened to Johnson's well-rehearsed speech on the reasons why the squadron should move south and not north. After a few moments, the C-in-C advised Johnson that he should return to his squadron and tell them that they were going to Castletown. Also, tell them that I have said you will be back in 11 Gp by next spring. If you haven't heard anything by next February, you can come and see me again. By the way, you will find out that Castletown has its compensations!

On 1 October, two Typhoons from 56 Squadron based at Matlaske approached Coltishall and circled the airfield. One of the Typhoons, R7711/US-M, flown by Plt Off Wright, had burst a tyre on take-off from his home base. Sqn Ldr 'Cocky' Dundas, the Squadron Commander, was airborne at the time and decided that the young inexperienced pilot should not attempt an emergency landing on the undulating runways at Matlaske. Therefore, with his squadron Commander at his side, Plt Off Wright flew the few miles to Coltishall to attempt his landing. His approach was fine, but as soon as the wheels touched the grass-covered matting, his Typhoon bounced and turned turtle. His aircraft was a right off but luckily, for the young pilot he escaped without a broken limb. Plt Off Wright was involved in a further two potentially fatal accidents, both times escaping by parachute. In fact, he later boasted that he had broken more Typhoons than anyone else had!

LAC Billy 'Buster' Barstard, born and brought up in Letheringsett near Holt, returned to his native Norfolk when he was posted to Coltishall in October 1942. There he was to join 68 Squadron following his training as a Flight Line Mechanic at Squires gate near Blackpool. Life for 'Buster' on his new squadron proved interesting, as the majority of the crews he was assigned to look after were Czechoslovakian. Early in his time with 'A' Flight, he soon found out that the Czechs had a way with the girls, especially when relaxing in Norwich.

Many of the British ground crews used to illegally wear Czech emblems on their battledress to impress the girls; 'Buster' was no exception. Not saying a word, they walked around the city enjoying the admiring advances of the local girls. This worked well until they met up with some genuine Czech pilots and navigators. On greeting each other, the native Czechs burst into their native language; the young pretenders beat a hasty retreat before they were rumbled!

The Meserschmitt Me210.

The Engineering Officer on 'A' Flight was Flt Lt Lamey, known by all the ground crews as the 'Yellow Peril.' His name came about because of his method of transport, a yellow bicycle that he used to travel between the dispersals keeping an eye on his charges. After the inevitable visit by the 'Yellow Peril' the boys knew they had an hour or so before the next visitation and during that time many 'non-official' methods were employed to keep their Beaufighters in tip-top condition. One particular wheeze was to clean the engines off with surplus aviation fuel that accidentally on purpose spilt whilst refuelling; this saved many hours of hard labour for the overworked mechanics!

With today's jet engines a bird-strike on take-off can result in catastrophe. However, in 'Buster's' days such an event often led to the unexpected. Lapwings were a daily hazard for aircraft operations at Coltishall in 1942/43 and often bird-strikes would result in a messy clean-up for the ground crews. But on certain occasions the bird would remain fairly well intact and would be slowly cooked between the cylinder heads on the engine. The result - added sustenance for the mechanics following their dried eggs and toast offered by the Airmen's Mess!

One morning, following an enemy raid on Coltishall, 'Buster' and other members of his squadron were tasked to assist in the recovery of the Station by filling numerous shallow bomb craters that peppered one corner of the

Douglas Havoc I converted to a Turbinlite.

A pair of official Air Ministry photographs showing the remains of Beaufighter If X7842 of 68 Squadron. On the 5 September 1942 the aircraft caught fire after take-off and crashed near Frettenham. WO Richter and Sgt Kovanda, both Czechslovakians were killed.

airfield. A lone bulldozer joined in this process and was assigned a single crater that straddled one of the runways. At the same time, a lone Spitfire came in to land and out of the 450 acres available he chose to land on the runway being repaired and specifically the ten square yards occupied by the bomb crater and the bulldozer! In the collision that followed the pilot escaped with concussion as his aircraft ground to a sudden halt after hitting the stationary bulldozer. The driver of the machine saw what was about to happen and had made a hasty retreat before the two machines came together!

On a daily basis one of the most important events for the dispersed sites around the airfield was the arrival of the NAAFI wagon delivering the famous 'tea and wads.' As the wagon approached, it was intercepted by enthusiastic individuals on bicycles; just like an enemy aircraft being intercepted by one of their Beaufighters. Before the NAAFI wagon came to a halt bikes were abandoned all over the place in order for the riders to form an orderly queue. The bikes were strewn everywhere, many being abandoned in the path of the NAAFI wagon. 'Buster' and his mates laughed when some poor unfortunate individual's bike was

crushed under the front wheels of the wagon. It was only when he went to retrieve his bike to go back to work that he realised it was his. A long walk ensued back to the dispersal with the remains of his rock cake and his bike!

During the first week of October 1942, a group of American airmen gathered at Coltishall to form the 346th Fighter Squadron (FS) of the 350th Fighter Group (FG), Eighth Air Force. Half of the pilots came from the two Spitfire-equipped USAAF Fighter Groups in England, the 31st and 52nd. The other pilots were former American volunteers who flew with the Eagle Squadrons of the RAF prior to the United States joining the war.

Forty support personnel and engineers assigned to the 346th FS had arrived in England from the US some days earlier on the liner Queen Mary. Like those of their sister squadrons, the 345th FS at Duxford and 347th FS at Snailwell, these Americans were to employ the US built Bell P-39 Airacobra fighters, most of which were still in their crates at various depots throughout the country. The aircraft were delivered to the UK by sea from the US. Unknown to them at the time, they were scheduled to fly to North Africa to support operations one week after a planned invasion by the US and her allies the following month.

While pilots from the 31st and 52nd FGs had flown the P-39 in the US before departing to England five months earlier, the former RAF pilots required initial check out training on the Airacobra. Two P-39s were assigned from RAF stocks and flying began by mid October. However, the air depot did not meet the planned assembly deadline and delivery of any additional Airacobras to the squadrons. In the meantime, pilots continued checkout and re-familiarisation flights in the two assigned P-39s. On 6 November, 2nd Lt Harley J Greenway, who was a former RAF volunteer, was killed when his aircraft crashed on take-off just beyond the airfield boundary.

Two days later the invasion of North Africa took place, however, instead of being prepared to fly to Africa a week later as intended, the only assigned Airacobra was withdrawn a short time later for depot level maintenance and modification.

By mid November, two Spitfires had been acquired from the RAF for pilot flying proficiency. During this period, there were such diversions as a Junkers Ju88 emerging from the mist over the airfield one morning at breakfast time. Strafing the field, the intruder was on the receiving end of the full response of the airfield defences - while on another occasion on 23 November, a 346th FS pilot in his Spitfire Vc, EN867, collided with a visiting Beaufighter VIF, X7924 of 409 Squadron from Colby Grange. It appeared that the Beaufighter had been given permission to take off on a runway heading that crossed a second runway on which the Spitfire had just landed.

By all accounts, both the crew of the Beaufighter and the pilot of the Spitfire were lucky. One of the Fire Pickets on duty that day with 68 Squadron was AC2 Bill Trawford. He remembered seeing the two aircraft collide and the pilots climbing from their burning wreckage; the radar operator of the Beaufighter falling out of the aircraft. Both crews saluted each other and then began to calmly walk away from the carnage! The collision happened only yards away from where he was on duty with 'B' Flight and he was on the scene within minutes. But as was often the case, regulations sometimes defied logic and he was ordered to report to the guardroom for a briefing before returning to finish what he had almost started ten minutes before!

Finally, beginning in the second week of December, 25 new Airacobras were acquired. Despite the mid-winter weather and rudimentary flight and navigational instrumentation, all the pilots began a maximum effort to gain flying time in their assigned aircraft and by the end of the month; most of the pilots had flown in excess 20 hours. The 346th FS eventually moved out to their new, but very temporary, base at Portreath in Cornwall on 2 January 1943; this being their first staging post to their ultimate destination with the Twelfth Air Force in North Africa.

A mysterious event occurred on 13 November when a Lysander of 278 Squadron arrived back at Coltishall with no one in the rear cockpit. The rear gunner, Flt Sgt I L Parsons, had certainly been on board when the aircraft took off, but it was some time before his body was found in the grounds of Blickling Hall, having apparently fallen from the aircraft. Parsons was buried in the Scottow Cemetery.

On 23 December 1942, Wg Cdr Jackson and Dr Arthur Downing, the physicist responsible for much of the AI Mk IX radar design and construction, both acted as Radar Operators on two Beaufighters. Wg Cdr Jackson's sortie started from Coltishall, whilst the Beaufighter with Dr Downing on board took off from Defford, accompanied by a Blenheim V8387 of the same unit. The aim of the exercise was part of the development phase of the trials; to check whether the modifications to their AI Mk IX radar would lock on to the 'Window' instead of the target aircraft.

Disaster struck as the Beaufighters approached the target area. They were attacked by a Spitfire, EP398/VL-E piloted by a Canadian of 167 Squadron based at Ludham on his first operational sortie. One Beaufighter, V8387, with the only example of the AI Mk IX radar set in existence, was shot down and crashed into the sea killing Dr Downing and his pilot Sqn Ldr Henry Mould. The other aircraft,

The Bell P-39 Airacobra.

although badly damaged, managed to recover to Coltishall. Fortunately, the development on the AI radar was at an advanced stage, and when an example of the long awaited American AI arrived in the United Kingdom shortly after the tragic accident of 23 December, it was demonstrated to be the answer to 'Window.'

Russell Reeve, a young lad at the time, witnessed the accident that took the life of Wg Cdr Jackson and Dr Downing and recalls: "I was on the cliff top at Cromer with a colleague when we saw a lone Junkers Ju88 flying towards the coast pursued by two Beaufighters and a number of Spitfires; the time, early afternoon, the weather, good. There were a number of large clouds in the sky moving slowly along the coastline and we were surprised to see the Ju88 climb into one such cloud, in what we thought his flying space would be severely restricted by the size of that cloud. The pursuing aircraft realising where the enemy aircraft had hidden, circled the cloud and waited for him to reappear. Eventually one of the Beaufighter's entered the cloud to flush him out. Suddenly the Beaufighter broke cloud in front of a Spitfire which climbed slightly and fired a very short burst into the Beaufighter's starboard engine. This attack was sufficient to remove parts of the starboard engine and destabilize the aircraft which rolled over onto its back and plunged into the sea. Almost immediately the aviation fuel inflamed a large area of the sea; the chances of survival appeared to be very limited. Nevertheless, I was impressed to see the arrival of the Cromer lifeboat which entered the area of fire in an endeavour to search for possible survivors.

Subsequent to this incident all the aircraft including the Ju88 came down to sea level and flew around the burning wreckage. The Ju88 was in night fighter trim and we could clearly see the identification symbols. I thought at the time the aircraft were flying a 'lufbery' and could not get the Junkers into their sight, but to my amazement the Ju88 eventually broke off the engagement and flew slowly off at sea level with no attempt of a pursuit. We watched until it eventually flew out of sight."

Chapter 5

1943 - THE DRAMA CONTINUES

28 January 1943 was an auspicious day for RAF Coltishall and its resident squadrons. It was on this day that HM King George VI and Queen Elizabeth visited whilst on a tour of Matlaske, Neatishead, Ludham and Coltishall. Lunch was taken in the Officers' Mess soon after the Royal Party arrived at Coltishall. During the afternoon, their Majesties were given an Operation 'Lagoon' briefing at 68 Squadron dispersal followed by visits to the Hunt Range and 278 ASR Squadron.

Whilst with 278 Squadron, the King presented the Squadron Commander, Flt Lt Philip Smith, with the squadron badge, the first occasion when a badge had been personally presented by a Reigning Monarch rather than by the Royal College of Heralds. Those present to witness this unique occasion included Gp Capt A V Harvey, Station Commander, Sqn Ldr C W Cudemore MC, DFC, Camp commandant Matlaske, Sqn Ldr T H V Pickering, OC 56 Squadron, Sqn Ldr H H A Ironside, OC 1489 Flt, Wg Cdr A P Dottridge DFC, OC 68 Squadron and Sqn Ldr E W 'Bertie' Wootten DFC, OC 118 Squadron.

118 Squadron had in fact only been at Coltishall for a matter of days prior to the Royal visit, having re-located from Wittering on 17 January and over the following eight months, whilst operating from the Coltishall Sector, they would see considerable action along the Dutch coast. Most of their operations involved escorting Coastal Command Beaufighters from the North Coates Wing as well as close escort missions for 2 Gp Bomber command Venturas and Bostons. Rhubarb missions

King George IV presents OC 278 Squadron, Flt Lt P Smith with the new unit badge.

The pilots of 118 Squadron.

(Low-level strike operations against enemy targets) were also carried out on a fairly regular basis especially when the weather conditions were suitable.

118 Squadron's first 'kill' in 12 Gp came during an attack on the coke ovens at Ijmuiden on 29 January whilst escorting twelve Venturas of 21 Squadron. Escorting the bombers ten miles overland before turning to commence their bombing run, a group of Fw190s from Luftwaffe Squadron JG1 were seen preparing to attack the bomber formation. Before they could attack, they were engaged by the escorting Spitfires. Sgt Les Lack in Spitfire EN926 fired at one of the Fw190s that was seen to crash into the sea two miles from the target. Sqn Ldr Wootten and Sgt Joe Hollingworth both damaged a couple of the enemy fighters although Hollingsworth's Spitfire, EP646, was hit by return cannon fire. Sadly, Flt Sgt A L Cross in Spitfire EP932 failed to return.

The 29 January also saw the loss of a Miles Martinet target towing aircraft of 118 Squadron. HP138 lost power on take off from Coltishall and crashed after hitting some trees. In addition, Spitfire EN932 from the same squadron failed to return from operations and was presumed shot down by Messerschmitt Bf109s near Ijmuiden.

Another reminder of the early days came when Wg Cdr H P Blatchford DFC was posted back to Coltishall as Wing Commander Flying on 4 February. Another move involved crews from 409 Squadron. With no enemy activity in the local area of Acklington, Northumberland, crews from the squadron commanded by Wg Cdr J W Reid, were sent to Coltishall from February 1943 to May 1944 to fly Ranger sorties, though these proved to be costly in men and machines.

This was a particularly busy period for the station as in addition to the resident RAF squadrons; Coltishall also played host to the Swordfish and Albacore biplanes of 841 Squadron, FAA. These outdated, but very useful aircraft were used by Detachment three of the squadron on night searches and attacks against enemy submarines and 'E' Boats operating in the North Sea off the East Anglian coast.

Another role that the Swordfish of the Royal Navy flew from Coltishall was often cloaked in secrecy. The black painted aircraft operated in the dark of night on low-

The Swordfish, known as the 'Stringbag' was a common sight at Coltishall from 1942 to mid 1943.

level mining missions into enemy held harbours. These Swordfish were specially modified to meet the mission by having one or two of the three man crew positions being taken up by additional fuel tanks enabling them to fly the longer distances over the Continent. Being slow and powered by the relatively quite Pegasus engine it proved to be an ideal platform for this type of operation.

Having arrived at Coltishall in the later part of December 1942, 841 Squadron were to be a familiar sight in and around the base until July 1943 when they departed for Manston.

There was another small RAF detachment based at Coltishall from December 1942 to July 1943. The Mandrel Screen Unit, part of 515 Squadron based at Hunsdon, was a special duties squadron flying Defiant IIs. The Defiants were equipped with a special device known as 'Mandrel', which was designed to jam the enemy early warning radar and prevent the Germans from assessing the route or strength of a bomber force. The Unit's task was to fly ahead of low-level fighter and bomber formations attacking targets in enemy occupied Holland. Weather hampered operations at first; however, by the beginning of March 1943 a total of 58 'Mandrel' missions had been flown. Despite early success, the rapid development of radar counter measures and jamming devices by both sides effectively made the equipment obsolete within a very short time. With these developments and advances, the unit was finally disbanded some seven months later.

From 15 February 1943, 488 Squadron with their Beaufighters started setting up detached flights at airfields in the south of England, the first of three aircraft being detached to Coltishall. These flights would undertake night time Ranger patrols over France, Belgium and Holland attacking any enemy surface transport found. Their first successes came shortly afterwards.

Wg Cdr R M Trousdale DFC led the first detachment to Coltishall. The other two aircraft were captained by Sqn Ldr Rabone and Flg Off J A Gunn who made the first offensive sorties the day after arriving at Coltishall. Rabone encountered bad weather and was forced to

Pilots of 118 Squadron relax between sorties.

return to Coltishall after flying ten miles into enemy territory, but Gunn was more fortunate and recorded the squadron's first success in its new role. Seriously damaging a railway engine and two barges near Nieuport. He was opposed by accurate FLAK and searchlights but had the satisfaction of seeing the barges on fire.

The following night Wg Cdr Trousdale, whilst flying over Belgium, located a train on which he scored cannon strikes; he also shot up two barges. On 19 February, Flg Off Gunn flew the last Ranger patrol of the February moon period when he succeeded in shooting up two railway engines and two barges without encountering any serious opposition. In all, the squadron destroyed 40 locomotives and numerous lorries and barges during the time they were operating away from their home at Church Fenton, with no losses.

In the meantime, 118 Squadron was kept busy with a number of Ramrod (Bomber escort) sorties and the occasional Rhubarb mission. Whilst the latter could on occasion produce useful results, they also added substantially to Fighter Command's losses with many aircraft and more importantly pilots being lost for little or no gain.

On 24 February, Flt Sgt Angus Buglass and Flt Sgt George Croall took off on a Rhubarb from Coltishall in their Spitfire Vb's, EN969 and EP123 respectively, to seek out railway and barge targets in the Bergen area. On reaching the Dutch coast, Flt Sqt Buglass decided that the risks were too great to continue as there was insufficient cloud cover. Just before aborting the mission, his aircraft was hit in the spinner by an accurate FLAK burst. The windscreen on EN969 immediately became covered in oil making it impossible to see through; his airspeed also began to drop so much so that he had great difficulty in maintaining 140 knots. In an attempt to ascertain the damage to his leader's Spitfire, Flt Sqt Croall flew underneath the aircraft, but as he did so his aircraft's starboard wing touched the sea which caused it to turn onto its back and dive straight into the water two miles off Bergen-aan-Zoom. There was little doubt that Croall died instantly.

With the engine on EP969 giving every sign that it would not last for much longer, Flt Sgt Buglass decided to head for the Dutch coast so that he would have a reasonable chance of survival when he baled out. However, try as he may, he could not get his aircraft to climb above 400 feet. After being shot at by a number of German soldiers he decided to turn back over the sea to make one final attempt to make it home. Against the odds, Spitfire EP969 eventually made it to the Newark

68 Squadron Beaufighter, snowbound, cica early 1943.

lightship where Flt Sgt Buglass was able to carry out a successful ditching and having been in the water for about 15 minutes, was rescued by a Walrus of 278 Squadron.

During March 1943, the Beaufighters of 68 Squadron were fitted with new AI equipment, the Mark VIII, with a transmitter power ten times more powerful than the Mark VII equipment. The squadron claimed five enemy aircraft destroyed in their first week of operation with the new radar, one target being detected at seven miles range. However, this was a month of transition as the squadron continued to operate its Beaufighters whilst the Mosquitoes were being modified.

On the night of 18 March another enemy raid was tracked approaching Norfolk. One of the many defenders scrambled to intercept the raiders was a 68 Squadron Beaufighter Mk VI. The aircraft flown by Flg Off Allen and Flg Off Bennett was launched from Coltishall to begin patrolling at 10,000 ft under Neatishead Ground Control. Almost immediately, Allen was given a radar contact some three miles away and well below his patrolling height.

The Beaufighter descended at speed towards the enemy raider, but as they approached, Allen realised he was going to overshoot the target. Despite throttling back and lowering his undercarriage to slow down, he missed the interception and lost contact with the Dornier Do217. Bennett asked Neatishead for further help in relocating the Dornier Do217. After further vectors by the Ground Controllers, contact with the raider was regained at 6000ft some three and a half miles ahead. As the Beaufighter approached within 800ft, the Dornier Do217 made a violent turn to port, unfortunately, in doing so, putting himself in a silhouette between the Beaufighter and the full beam of the moon. Flg Off Allen acted quickly on this error and opened fire with both his

20mm cannon and 0.303 machine guns. Many strikes were seen on the Dornier's port wing and engine which promptly burst into flames. The following explosion severed the wing and the doomed aircraft commenced a deadly spiral into oblivion.

As Allen and Bennett gathered their thoughts, the Neatishead Controllers passed another radar interception. This time another Dornier Do217 was identified some 2000ft away slightly below the Beaufighter's course. The bomber began to weave, and at a range of 700ft, Allen opened fire. Now well ablaze, the hapless Dornier turned steeply and dived, followed by the Beaufighter. Pieces of the aircraft started to break away after further cannon and machine gun shells ripped into the fuselage, some narrowly missing the pursuing Beaufighter. The final death knell came when a large explosion outboard of the port engine caused the bomber to turn on its back and disappear through the 3000ft-cloud base into the sea. The sortie lasted 77 minutes and after landing back

Mosquito II of 25 Squadron.

at Coltishall, Allen and Bennett claimed two Dornier Do217's for the use of 350 rounds of 20mm cannon and 936 rounds of 0.303 ammunition.

Meanwhile, offensive fighter sweeps continued during the daytime. On one such mission, on 18 March, 118 Squadron lost Spitfire V EP228 that was accidentally shot down by anti-aircraft fire from one of the sea forts off Harwich.

Another 68 Squadron Beaufighter mission, flown on the night of 28/29 March by Flg Off Vopalecky and Flt Sgt Huser resulted in half a share of a Dornier Do217 shot down while approaching the Norfolk coast. On the same night, recently commissioned Plt Off Bobek in a Mosquito of the same squadron shared with a Mosquito crew of 157 Squadron in the destruction of a Dornier Do217E-4 of II/KG40 off Southwold.

On 4 April, Anson I, DG809 of 278 Squadron, set out from Coltishall at 2040 hours to assist in the search for a Spitfire pilot who had baled out of his aircraft 70 miles out to sea. The first aircraft to be scrambled, Walrus, L2238, flown by Flg Off W F Sims and Flt Sgt F J Nall, had spotted an oil patch and wreckage on the water close to the reported position. With no sign of the pilot or of a dinghy, it was decided to increase the search area by bringing in the Anson. Sadly, the Anson never reached the search area. The aircraft crashed into the sea after being attacked 40 miles SE of Great Yarmouth with the loss of the crew of five. The body of the pilot, WO Lancelot Telford, was washed ashore on Wells Marsh some two weeks later and was laid to rest in his home city, Newcastle. The four other members of the crew, Flt Lt Phillip Smith, OC of the squadron, WO2 D A Forestell, RCAF, Flt Sgt Johnnie Bartlett, a Newfoundlander and Sgt Gerard Hogan of the Irish Republic all appear on the Runnymede Memorial to the missing.

With all the 'heavy-metal' on the airfield it was something of an anti-climax to report that the squadron hack of 302 squadron from Kirton-in-Lindsey, a Tiger Moth T7458 crashed on 5 April. It was a total loss, but thankfully, Flt Sgt Handzelica and Sgt Makowski survived the take-off accident.

Poor weather in early April gave the resident squadrons a certain amount of freedom when it came to planning offensive sorties and on 10 April four Spitfires of 118 Squadron took off from Coltishall in mid morning to look for potential targets near the Dutch coast. This operation got off to an inauspicious start when Flt Sgt de Courcy's aircraft was damaged by light FLAK just after landfall had been made; but worse was to come.

Whilst attacking several barges and tugs on the canal near Zand, another FLAK post situated on a lock opened up on the low flying Spitfires. Accurate fire hit Spitfire W3429 being flown by Plt Off Alan Beer, RAAF just as he passed over the lock gates. Beer immediately called over his radio that he had been hit and was going to attempt a crash-landing. Sadly, the damage caused him to loose control of his aircraft and it was seen to hit the ground and blow-up, leaving no hope of survival. During the attack, many barges were damaged and one was left on fire. Sgt C Anderton who was flying as Blue 4 on the mission flew so low that his aircraft was splattered by mud and water thrown up by exploding cannon shells!

During such low-level sorties, pilots had to endure the perils of ground fire. Known FLAK concentrations were avoided wherever possible, but 20mm anti-aircraft guns were mobile and could be deployed almost anywhere. The pilots had a healthy respect for the formidable German FLAK capabilities; they were plentiful and deadly effective. What pilots may have thought was a haystack as they sped across the countryside at 100 feet or less could have been a FLAK battery. A dugout in the side of a hill, a church steeple, towers and even flip-sided railway wagons, in fact any innocent looking structure could in fact hide a nasty surprise. Far more pilots and aircraft were lost to FLAK than to enemy aircraft. This was especially true as the war went on and more so after the invasion of the Continent.

Night Ranger (Deep penetration flights to specific areas to engage targets of opportunity) sorties were continually being flown by the Mosquito's of 25 Squadron who used Coltishall as a Forward Operating Location from their home base at Church Fenton. A typical example of this type of operation was recorded on 20 April 1943, a night with a brilliant moon and clear skies. Two Mosquitoes, the first flown by Flg Off Wooton and Plt Off Dymock, took off from Coltishall at 2240 hours for a 'Ranger' sortie in the Osnabruck area. Whilst the second Mosquito, callsign 'Manor 24', flown by Flg Off Jack Cheney and his Radar Operator Sgt James 'Mike' Mycock, flew off to 'hassle' the enemy around Bremen. After a transit flight to the continent across the North Sea at 200 feet, the Bremen bound aircraft pinpointed Vlieland to the starboard and climbed to 4500 feet. The crew altered course for the Zuider Zee dam and crossed the mainland coast at Makkum where a prominent jetty made a good landmark. From there a course was set for Assen and then onto Aschendorf, which was reached just before midnight. The crew followed some railway lines to Papenburg and Leer from the south and then turned in for the attack. Just then, three searchlights illuminated the Mosquito for about 30 seconds. A considerable amount of light flak was directed towards the Mosquito that caused the crew to break off the attack with some violent evasive action.

Having successfully avoided the searchlights and the flak, a new course was set for Zwischenaur Lake, to the West of Bremen, where further along the line a fast moving train was spotted. The stick was gently moved forward and the Mosquito made a head on pass at the train. From about 1300 feet down to about 400 feet the cannon strikes from the Mosquito were observed hitting the train as the aircraft broke away and headed for Cloppenburg. A second train was found soon after passing Furrstenau and this time the attack was made from astern and from the starboard quarter, the crew opening up with a long five-second burst of cannon fire. The slow moving train was hit in the concentrated strike and the ensuing explosions blinded the pilot and his

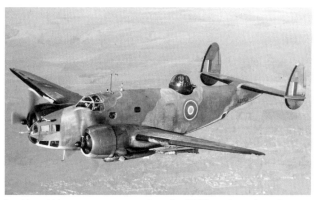

Lockheed Ventura, representative of a 487 Squadron aircraft.

navigator for a split second. The engine became engulfed in clouds of steam and smoke, grinding to a halt and being lit up in a vivid red glow.

It was now time to run for home and as the Mosquito crossed Lingen another barrage of light flak came up from the town and from other isolated gun batteries on the outskirts. Over the Zuider Zee, across the Dutch coast at Ijmuiden and then down on the deck all the way back across the North Sea. The English Coast was reached at Great Yarmouth some thirty minutes later and eventually the Mosquito landed at Coltishall just after 0115 hours after a typical 'Ranger' sortie.

Also on 20 April 1943, Gp Capt G D Harvey handed over as Station Commander to his namesake, Gp Capt A Vere Harvey CBE (Lord Harvey of Prestbury) who was to remain in post for eight months.

On a nostalgic return visit to his old Station in 1986 he was able to point out the exact spot outside No 2 Hangar where his fitter, LAC Sidney Sexton, ensured every morning that his Spitfire, coded 'LL', would be on top line for his immediate use. He also recalled that Wing Operations at 12 Gp orders would be received each evening for the next day's activities. For example, "The Wing will move to Duxford at first light for operations under 11 Gp control" or "The Wing will rendezvous at 1000 feet over Cromer at 0630 hours with Coastal

Douglas Boston IIIA of 88 Squadron, West Raynham.

Lancaster B1 LM310 rests on its belly at Coltishall on the 12 May 1943. Note the black Swordfish in the background.

Command Beaufighters from North Coates for strike against enemy convoy moving southwards from Frisian Islands along the Dutch coast" or "The Kenley Wing will land at Coltishall at "0730 hours for two operations in support of the USAAF."

Two days after the new station Commander's arrival, Beaufighter VIf, V8567 of 68 Squadron spun out of cloud into the ground near Swanton Morley. This was not the end of 68 Squadron's misfortunes as on 24 April 1943, Beaufighter V8736 skidded into an aircraft pen, hitting Spitfre AR423 in the process and was destroyed.

118 Squadron and their Spitfire Vb's were tasked to escort Venturas of 464 Squadron in a raid on the Royal Dutch Steel works at Ijmuiden on 2 May 1943. They flew their customary low-level sea crossing before climbing to bombing height near the Dutch coast. Moderate flak greeted the bombers and their fighter escort and on the return a force of Fw190s intercepted them forty miles off the coast. The Fw190s inflicted damage on two of the Venturas, however in their attempt to down the bombers the enemy lost two of their fighters to the Spitfire escort. The raid caused damage to the coke factory, sulphate plant and numerous storehouses. In the adjacent harbour three ships were hit, two of which sank. Unfortunately, the primary target, the steel works, escaped damage.

Flt Lt R A 'Dickie' Newbury with Spitfire V EN966 'Fiducia'.

The importance of the steel works was such that a further raid was planned for the very next day. This time six Boston IIIAs were tasked to make the low-level attack. The operation was planned to be carried out in conjunction with a diversionary 'Circus' by Venturas of 487 Squadron who were being directed against Amsterdam power stations. Two formations of three Bostons set out from Coltishall and then headed out low-level across the North Sea. The first vic formation, Boston BZ230, BZ241 and BZ220, scored good hits on the switch and transformer stations at the factory but again missed the steel works. Shortly after leaving the Dutch coast, they were set upon by Bf109s and Fw190s, but with skilful flying and successful evasive action the formation escaped.

The second vic scored direct hits on the factory and on turning back out to sea they too were attacked by fighters. Flt Sgt F S Harrop and his crew in Boston BZ227 were lost when their aircraft crashed into the sea in flames. The other two aircraft, BZ223 and BZ351, escaped the battle but on their way home they saw a Ventura plunge into the sea without any sign of survivors. They had in fact witnessed part of an unfolding tragedy.

Prior to leaving their Feltwell base, 14 Ventura crews of 487 Squadron had been briefed to attack the Amsterdam target; to encourage the Dutch Resistance and aid Dutch workers in organising strikes against the Germans. They were to fly below 1000 feet at 190 knots and then climb to their bombing height at a speed of 165 mph. The target was known to be well defended, but the order was to 'press on regardless.' Unbeknown to the 2 Gp planners, a convention of fighter pilots was taking place at Schiphol, into which many of the best Luftwaffe pilots had flown. The assembled fighter pilots were then held on alert for the visit of the German Governor to the town of Haarlem that lay on the Ventura's route to Amsterdam.

Lancaster III ED710 of 100 Squadron after crash landing within spitting distance of Coltishall.

Close up of the damage inflicted on the cockpit of ED710.

At 1643 hours twelve Venturas, under the command of Sqn Ldr Leonard Trent, were airborne and made their way to Coltishall where, at 1700 hours, they were to meet up with their escorts, Spitfire Vbs of 118, 167 and 504 Squadrons. The fighter escort for this mission was under the command of Acting Wg Cdr Blatchford, Coltishall's Wing Commander Flying. As the formation of fighters and bombers headed out to sea a formation of 11 Gp Spitfires, Rodeo 212, were on their way to Flushing as a diversionary tactic to draw the enemy away from the Amsterdam raid.

Somewhere in the planning of this diversionary raid there had been an error, as the Spitfires arrived over Flushing thirty minutes too soon. This error had the effect of putting the enemy radar and fighters on high alert. In response, a total of seventy enemy fighter aircraft in four formations, Fw190s to deal with the Spitfires and Bf109s for the bombers, were scrambled and vectored to Haarlem. The Germans had guessed that the Flushing attack was a bluff and that the main force was out to get the German Governor on his visit. Meanwhile the Venturas pressed on, oblivious of the trap that lay ahead.

As soon as Sqn Ldr Trent saw the enemy fighters he ordered his squadron to close into one formation for maximum protection. Meanwhile over the coast twenty plus enemy fighters swooped down on the Spitfires of 118 and 167 Squadrons which formed the close

protection for the Venturas. A further thirty Fw190s and Bf109s went in after the bombers whilst the Spitfires were engaged in their own scrap. Some three miles behind was 504 Squadron, they entered the fight whilst still climbing from their transit height. Fw190s raced out to meet them and effectively cut them off from the bombers who by now were in a crisis.

Wg Cdr Blatchford desperately tried to recall the Venturas, but by the time they began to respond to his call they were well and truly hemmed in by the Luftwaffe. As the battle erupted, 504 Squadron did a 360 degree turn in the hope of drawing fighters after them, thus away from the bombers, but this ruse did not work. With the fighter escort overwhelmed the Venturas had to go it alone.

487 Squadron proceeded, and one of the first Venturas to be hit (AE916) was flown by Flt Lt Duffill. His aircraft had its hydraulics shot out of action and both engines set on fire. Both his gunners were seriously wounded

and with his aircraft in a desperate state, he was forced to turn for home. As he turned back two of his section followed but they were soon shot down. Seeing the state of Duffill's aircraft, the enemy obviously thought his chances of making it home were nil, and so they broke off the engagement and returned to the main battle. His navigator managed to get the bomb doors open and release the three bombs. As he got further away from the enemy coast, the fires in his engines gradually extinguished and with much skill and luck he eventually made it back to Feltwell, landing at 1855 hours, the only crew from 487 Squadron to return.

Back over Holland, the Spitfires were having mixed fortunes. Sgt R J Flight of 118 Squadron destroyed two Fw190s and 167 Squadron 'bagged' another. However, Wg Cdr Blatchford's Spitfire Vb, EN971/HP-B, was badly mauled and he was forced to make a hasty retreat. He nearly made it back to Coltishall, but the damage was so great that his aircraft came down in the sea some forty miles off Mundesley at approximately 1815 hours. Regrettably, the popular Canadian from Alberta, who had made so many friends during his time at Coltishall, perished in the crash.

The Venturas were being picked off one by one until there were only five left to begin the bomb run. The enemy fighters were relentless and finally only Sqn Ldr Trent's aircraft, AJ209, was left. On his own, he was determined to press home the attack. He did so, only to see his bombs overshoot and explode beyond the target. Now he faced the impossible journey home. Hardly had he bombed when the fighters attacked, ignoring the flak. The controls on his aircraft were shot away and it soon began to dive towards destruction in Kometon Polder. Trent and his navigator were hurled from the wreck at 7000 feet and were eventually captured. The other members of his crew were not so fortunate and were killed on impact. It was not until the end of the war that the full, tragic story of this raid could be pieced together. Sqn Ldr L H Trent was awarded the VC for his actions, a salute to him and all who had taken part in this disastrous operation.

Lancaster BI, LM310/PO-O, flown by Sqn Ldr Keith Thiele and his crew of 467 Squadron, set off from its base at Bottesford for a raid on Duisberg on the evening of 12 May. Whilst on the bomb run the Lancaster was hit by a FLAK burst which blew away the rear half of the starboard outer engine, riddled the starboard inner and shattered most of the Perspex in the cockpit area. Despite being hit on the head by a shell splinter, Sqn Ldr Thiele was able to nurse his damaged Lancaster back to England on just two engines. Unfortunately, on arrival over Coltishall, it was found that the undercarriage could not be lowered as one of the two hydraulic pumps was damaged in the starboard inner engine; the result, a wheels-up landing. Thiele and his crew were collected from Coltishall by their Station Commander, Gp Capt W N McKechnie, in an Anson from Bottesford's Station Flight.

For his act of bravery in bringing his damaged Lancaster back safely, Sqn Ldr Thiele was awarded an immediate DSO, the first such award to an Officer from 467 Squadron. For the Lancaster, despite the fearsome damage, it was repaired at Coltishall and put back into the air with 106 Squadron and finally with 61 Squadron. As QR-E, the Lancaster did not return to Coningsby from an operation over Schweinfurt on 24-25 February 1944. LM310 was shot down over the target area from 20,000 feet with six of the seven-man crew surviving as POW's.

During 1942, RAF aircraft maintenance units called Servicing Commandos, were formed to provide a refuelling and rearming capability at recently captured enemy airfields. Selected aircraft technicians were given commando skills in order to operate under these demanding conditions. All were volunteers and were Group 1 Tradesmen. Upon successful graduation from the course at Inverary, Servicing Commandos were awarded the Special Combined Operations badge. This resulted from a recommendation by Wg Cdr Williams who had been sent by the Senior Engineering Officer (SEO) of Army Co-operation command to observe Servicing commando training at Inverary in March 1943 where he was struck by the tremendous moral effect the 'badge' would have.

Having been trained and prepared for operations many of the Servicing Commandos were then in a state of limbo before being deployed to an operational environment on the Continent or in the Middle East. In fact, in the early stages there was no clear role for personnel trained to commando Status. For many, their first postings following training was to regular RAF Units that operated the types of aircraft that they would be expected to support once in the field. Although strikingly different from regular RAF groundcrews due to their army khaki uniforms, they were appreciated by the squadrons for the extra support they provided whilst attached and awaiting deployment to forward airfields. Servicing Commandos posted to Coltishall joined 3210 Servicing commando Unit that was formed at the base in May 1943. This unit was planned as an integral part of

Combined Operations and its ultimate role was to play an important role in the invasion of Europe. The unit served with distinction during the D-Day landings in Normandy on 6 June 1944 and later in the liberation of Burma, Malaya and Indonesia.

The menace of hit and run raids by Luftwaffe fighter units came to a head on 12 May when a low-level attack was made on Lowestoft that left 23 people dead and 29 seriously injured. 118 Squadron flew anti-Rhubarb patrols up to sixty miles out over the North Sea, but as the enemy raiders always approached their targets fast and low, the chances of being able to successfully carry out an interception was often remote to say the least.

Generally, the best the defending Spitfires could hope for was as a deterrent and this was achieved during a patrol by four aircraft led by Flt Lt R A 'Dickie' Newbury. Flying in Spitfire EP646, he saw three Fw190's approaching the East Anglia coast at about 600 feet above the waves and as soon as they saw the Spitfire's, immediately turned and headed back home at high speed. Flt Lt Newbery led the chase, but even flat out they made no impression on the distance between themselves and their foe, eventually giving up the chase and returning to Coltishall.

Early in the morning of 14 May, Flying Control alerted the fire crews, medics and crash guards that a Lancaster was inbound to Coltishall badly damaged. The aircraft, ED710/HW-D of 100 Squadron, had been on a raid to Bochum when it was hit by flak near Cologne. The crew of the aircraft, under the command of Wg Cdr R V McIntyre, struggled to keep the Lancaster airborne on its long and perilous return home. Wireless operator, Flt Sgt J D W Renno RAAF, was severely wounded in the stomach and thigh but despite losing blood and suffering from relentless pain, he steadfastly refused to leave his post. In doing so, he gave the ASR services a running Commentary on the Lancaster's condition and position, just in case they had to ditch in the North Sea.

As it was, the aircraft successfully made it across the sea and almost made it to Coltishall. Despite all the valiant efforts of the crew, they could not keep their aircraft flying for the last short hop to the safety of the runway at Coltishall. The Lancaster crash-landed at 0430 hours within spitting distance of the field, four hours and 22 minutes after it had taken off from Waltham near Grimsby. For his courage, Flt Sgt Renno was immediately awarded the DFM and for his skill and determination, Wg Cdr McIntyre was awarded the DFC. Both the decorations and citations were published in the London Gazette on 4 June 1943.

Night fighter Fairey Firefly's were first issued to 746

Squadron FAA, the Night Fighter Interception Unit (NFIU), in May 1943. Based at RNAS Ford in Sussex, the NFIU flew alongside the RAF Fighter Interceptor Unit (FIU) in developing night fighter tactics. Flying from Coltishall in late 1944, NFIU Fireflies undertook night patrols to counter V-1 Flying Bombs air launched over the North Sea by Luftwaffe Heinkel He111s. These missions were either flown alongside the Mosquitoes of the based squadrons or as independent sorties; in both cases being known as Anti-Diver missions.

Detachments from 409 Squadron were sent to Coltishall during 1943. Flying their Beaufighter VIf's, they flew Ranger sorties in order to avoid the boredom and loss of efficiency once air activity over the Digby Sector quietened down during the latter months of 1943. Unfortunately, Rangers proved costly for the men and machines of the squadron.

Losses to other than enemy action continued at an alarming rate. On 28 April, two Typhoons of 56 Squadron, whilst on a training flight from nearby Matlaske, were in the Coltishall circuit when one, DN265/US-B exploded in mid-air. The tail and parts of the wings came off and damaged the second aircraft, R8825/US-V as the wreckage plunged earthwards. DN265 crashed on land at Dudwick Farm, halfway between farm buildings and the Aylsham road and was destroyed; the pilot, Sgt D Driscoll was killed. Typhoon R8825/US-Y was able to make a successful wheels-up landing in a field at Bradmoor Farm, North Walsham. Thankfully, Sgt A P McNicol was unhurt. That same day, Mosquito BIV, DZ605 of 139 Squadron at Marham, hit high-tension cables whilst in the circuit and crashed close to Wroxham.

Enemy raids persisted over the area on a daily basis, some successful, others not. On 30 May, the Alarm Controller for the district informed all of the ROC posts in and around Norwich that a Junkers Ju88 had been reported circling Ludham and then as such were to be vigilant as there may well be further enemy activity.

The following evening Observers reported a fire in the Coltishall district to their Alarm Controller. After a few moments, they were advised that the fire was in fact at Overberry Road, Helsdon, where a Hampden had crashed whilst attempting an emergency landing at Horsham St Faith. The Hampden, L4173/GL-T2, from 14 Operational Training Unit (OTU), Cottesmore, had taken off from it base at 2130 hrs the previous night for a raid on Cologne. Unfortunately, the crew, Flt Lt W L Cameron, Flt Sgt M F Porter, Sgts J E Sheridan and E A East all perished in the inferno.

Sgt Driscoll stood no chance when DN265 exploded in mid-air.

Remains of DN265 on land at Dudwick Farm.

The middle months of 1943 found the station extremely busy, in particular 278 Squadron and their ASR aircraft. In mid-June an Anson of 278 Squadron was patrolling an area off the coast. On this patrol they found a Halifax crew that had ditched off Great Yarmouth. The Anson circled the downed airman, awaiting a Walrus amphibian that eventually arrived, and successfully rescued the crew, having been scrambled from its base some 20 minutes earlier. As this ASR incident unfolded, 31 Spitfires of 118, 402 and 416 Squadrons set out to escort home the remnants of a B-17 raid on a synthetic rubber plant at Huls. A busy time for all!

The crash crews at Coltishall were always at standby ready to respond at a moments notice to aircraft accidents on or around the base. With the massive build up of the Eighth Air Force in Norfolk, Suffolk and other counties in East Anglia, inevitably, one day, it would be an American aircraft that they would be called upon to assist.

Early in the morning of 11 June 1943, a force of bombers from the 526th BS of the 379th BG set off from their base at Kimbolton, near Huntingdon, for a daylight raid on Wilhelmshaven. The raid itself was somewhat of a disaster for the group as they lost six B-17 Flying Fortresses over enemy territory. One of the luckier aircraft, although badly damaged, was B-17F, 42-5809/LF-D, 'Mary Jane.' Badly holed by Flak, she managed to escape further attention of the German defences and struggled back across the North Sea to make a safe crash-landing at Coltishall. For six days, the aircraft languished on the airfield before being salvaged by a team of engineers.

On 13 June searching Walrus I, L2268 of 278 Squadron, found a rubber dinghy carrying eight American airmen from a ditched B-17 Flying Fortress. A five-foot sea

made conditions very difficult but eventually the Walrus was able to alight on the water. However, with the extra weight of the rescued airmen the Walrus could not take off in the rough sea prevailing and had to taxi for ten miles to make a rendezvous with a rescue launch. Manoeuvring in the heavy seas, the nose of the rescue launch came into contact with the Walrus and the aircraft sustained some damage, causing a leak in the hull and damage to the leading edge of the port lower wing. Being heavy with water in the rough sea the Walrus took a long time to get airborne before flying back to Coltishall. The pilot was Flt Lt Stanley Trevallion, CO of the squadron, with Flt Sgt Nall as his crewman. For this rescue Flt Lt Trevallion was awarded the United States Air Medal. A week later, an Anson of 278 Squadron found the crew of a ditched Halifax in a dinghy off Great Yarmouth and a walrus was despatched to pick them up.

Late in the afternoon of 14 June, five Beaufighter VIs from Wittering, equipped with serrate and MkIV AI radar, flew into Coltishall to take part in Bomber Support Operations. These aircraft, under the command of 23-year-old Wg Cdr John Braham DSO, DFC, belonged to 141 Squadron, who at the time were the first squadron to be equipped with 'Serrate.'

'Serrate' was a special receiving device which enabled night fighter crews to lock on to the radiation emitted by the enemy aircraft's Lichtenstein radar. These emissions were shown on a small cathode ray tube as a herring backbone. The operator would observe which side of the backbone had the most numerous and largest bones, and then direct the pilot to turn in that direction. When the bones on both sides were equal, it meant the enemy aircraft was dead ahead.

The squadron's first operational sortie commenced at 2335 hours on the day of their arrival. Wg Cdr Braham and his navigator, Flg Off F W Gregory, together with

B-17F 'Mary Jane' displays her war wounds at Coltishall.

The Focke Wulf Fw190.

a second Beaufighter flown by Sqn Ldr C V Winn and Flg Off R A W Scott took off from Coltishall and headed for Holland. In the mean time, a total of 197 Lancasters and six Mosquitoes of the 'Main Force' were en-route to Oberhausen in the Ruhr.

Wg Cdr Braham headed for a German night-fighter base at Deelen near Arnhem. After an uneventful transit across the North Sea they started to patrol over the airfield in wide orbits in the search for enemy fighters. With no 'trade' at Deelen, they flew on to other night fighter bases in Holland and Wesel in Germany before returning to their primary target. However, at 0151 hours Braham decided to head for the coast, as no enemy fighters seemed to be active at Deelen.

At 10,000 feet over Staveren on the northeast coast of the Zuider Zee, Flg Off Gregory caught a glimpse of an enemy aircraft, a Messerschmitt Bf110, to the rear of their Beaufighter on the port side. As Braham hauled his aircraft to port with the aim of getting behind the attacking aircraft, the German pilot also turned to the port. A classic dogfight ensued as both pilots tried desperately to gain the upper hand. It was Braham who finally turned the tide when he managed to get on the Bf110's port beam. Closing to 400 yards he opened up on the enemy with cannon and machine gun fire. The end of the Bf110 came when the Beaufighter closed in astern at 200 yards and pumped a further five-second burst into the full length of the fuselage and port wing, resulting fire erupting in the port engine. Braham throttled back and prepared for another pass; however, by this time the Bf110 had gone into a vertical dive to its destruction some eight miles north of Staveren. Now very low on fuel, Braham and Gregory set course for Wittering where they landed at 0315 hours.

The other Beaufighters who took part in the operation with Wg Cdr Braham that night and early morning had

a very uneventful time. Sqn Ldr Winn and Flg Off Scott, who patrolled the Eindhoven area, did not encounter any enemy aircraft; as was the same for Flg Off R C MacAndrew and Plt Off Wilk who patrolled Gilze Rijen. The fourth Beaufighter to take off, flown by Flg Off B J Brachi and Plt Off A P MacLeod had to return to Wittering due to technical problems. The fifth aircraft flown by Belgian pilot Flg Off Lucien LeBoutte and his navigator Plt Off Parrott also had an uneventful trip over their designated airfields.

This was to be the first of many Bomber Support Operations for the squadron and their serrate equipped Beaufighters. They would in fact fly many of their sorties from Coltishall over the following months. For his part in this first operation, Wg Cdr Braham was awarded a Bar to his DFC.

Russell Reeve, like many young lads in Cromer, were used to seeing RAF fighter aircraft flying around the coast or bombers formating high above prior to making their perilous journeys to the Continent, but on 14 June 1943 at about 1615 hours he was probably the only witness to the tragic loss of Beaufighter R2148 of 68 Squadron flown by Flt Lt Gordon Langley and Flg Off Jack Reade. Russell remembers: "This aircraft crossed the coastline at about 4000 feet with a very low and stormy cloud base. There had been some lightning and heavy rain. As the aircraft approached, a burst of lightning struck the aircraft's port horizontal stabiliser. The aircraft immediately went into a steep dive which appeared to increase in steepness until the aircraft went near vertically into the only piece of vacant land on Cliff Road. It was conceivable that the pilot was instrumental in avoiding the surrounding housing.

I was the first person to reach the scene of this accident. I believe miraculously someone might have survived. There was a significant crater surrounded by multiple pieces of aircraft. While I was in this carnage the whole area became engulfed in a massive flame and I eventually crawled through the wreckage to escape. I recall seeing 20mm cannon shells exploding but without the restriction of a barrel the bullets went no further than twelve inches from the cartridges. I did recall that some Beaufighters were equipped to carry torpedoes but fortunately no further explosions took place.

Distressingly I found pieces of the crew members and a small leather wallet which I was later informed was the property of the pilot. The wallet contained a small amount of money plus a photograph of the pilot's wife whom I understood lived in the North East of England. I later found out that the wallet was returned to her at a later date. The surrounding property sustained considerable damage with broken windows and roof tiles but fortunately with no loss of civilian life.

I was a witness to the crash at the Court of Enquiry held at Coltishall Airfield a few days subsequent to the above. I was 14 years of age at the time and was collected from Paston Grammar School, North Walsham by a Royal Air Force staff car."

An incident on 25 June 1943 forcibly brought home to Coltishall's inhabitants the dangers that all bomber crews faced on a daily basis. A badly damaged B-17 Flying Fortress circled the airfield disgorging its crew with the exception of a dead navigator and its wounded pilot. Once all the crew had baled out, the pilot, realising it was impossible to land his aircraft flew the aircraft out to sea off Waxham, where he finally baled out. This meant a swim for the wounded pilot who on reaching the coast, was taken to hospital.

In the early hours of the following morning it was the turn of another 'Cuckoo' to find Coltishall. This time a damaged Lancaster, whose home base was Langar near Nottingham, landed safely after being attacked and chased home by Fw190s. Among the crew, who all agreed they were lucky to survive, was Langar's Station Commander, Gp Capt McKenna.

It was in July of 1943 that Coltishall became the home of a second pilot who, like Douglas Bader, had lost both his legs as the result of a flying accident; this time whilst serving in the FAA. When Flg Off Colin 'Hoppy' Hodgkinson joined 611 Squadron from 510 Squadron. He was already being talked about as the second Douglas Bader. He joined the squadron to fly Spitfires under the command of Wg Cdr 'Laddie' Lucas and it was not long before his prowess as a fighter pilot became evident.

An example of his flying skill was highlighted when 'Hoppy' joined a flight of Spitfires on an escort mission for 36 American B-26 Marauder bombers who were tasked to attack Bernay airfield near Evneux to the north of Paris in August 1943. The wing had completed their escort mission that had been successfully carried out and were turning for home when more than 50 Focke Wulf Fw190's appeared out of the sun. Wg Cdr Lucas turned all of his Spitfires into the attack; the battle that ensued lasted all the way back to the English coast. 'Hoppy' Hodgkinson had been taught by his father to shoot on their family estate in Somerset and could remember his father's words "swing with it!" Making a well-judged beam-into-quarter attack he hit a Fw190 which was on the tail of Wg Cdr Lucas. The burst of machine gun fire from 'Hoppy's' Spitfire sent the Fw190 reeling uncontrollably to destruction.

A grateful Lucas commented that Hodgkinson's action was an uncommonly quick and accurate piece of shooting, and that he had contributed handsomely to a total of five Fw190s destroyed against the loss of two Spitfires. In twelve eventful minutes Flg Off Hodgkinson had demonstrated that, despite his disability, he could match his skills against the best that JG26 and their CO, Gen Adolph Galland, could offer. This was in fact 'Hoppy's' second kill that day having earlier destroyed an Fw190 just off Brighton Pier.

Whilst on the squadron 'Hoppy' often spoke of his understandable fear of being shot down over the English Channel as, with no legs, he would have been unlikely to have survived. To overcome his apprehension, he stuffed his legs with Ping-Pong balls hoping they would keep him afloat. Once, at 30,000 feet, he took violent evasive action before realising what he had taken to be the clatter of gunfire against the fuselage of his Spitfire was in fact the noise of the Ping-Pong balls exploding at that altitude!

From 14 to 19 June 1943, 118 Squadron and a number of other Spitfire V-equipped squadrons within 12 Group were temporarily withdrawn from the front-line. Their aircraft were sent to 3501 Servicing Unit at Cranfield so that the aircraft could be re-engined with the M-series Rolls-Royce Merlin. When the aircraft returned, most of the pilots were pleasantly surprised by the additional power that the 'cropped-blower' Merlin produced.

Throughout the Second World War, cities, towns, boroughs, companies, organisations and even individuals raised funds to purchase aircraft for the RAF. These were known as presentation aircraft. At least 3000 Spitfires were funded in this way, more than any other aircraft type. For a nominal cost of £5000, each aircraft bought

The fighter pilots of 611 Squadron.

would bear a name suggested by its donor, usually marked in yellow characters on the engine cowling.

There were many such aircraft flying from Coltishall that bore the names of donors. W3320, "The Darlington Spitfire" arrived to join 118 Squadron on 3 July 1943. This aircraft was purchased for £5082 through contributions made by the people of Darlington in County Durham during the town's War Weapons Week of National Savings Campaign in 1940. W3320 found itself the regular 'mount' of Plt Off Flight who had just been commissioned and re-joined the squadron after completing a Fighter Leaders Course at Charmy Down. In his hands, "The Darlington Spitfire" soon found itself in the thick of the action acting as close escort for bombers; the main role of 118 Squadron whilst based at Coltishall.

Operations from Coltishall continued unabated for 841 Squadron FAA who proceeded with their nightly anti-E-Boat sorties. Spitfire squadrons came and went with regularity. They continued to be engaged in anti-shipping strikes, which to the crews were unpopular, however necessary to keep our shipping lanes opens. 118 Squadron, which was still equipped with the older Spitfire Vb, carried on with strikes against enemy shipping, mostly without bomber support. These missions, without the bombers, were called 'Roadsteads.' 118 Squadron, made up mostly of Dutch and Free French pilots, gained a fine reputation for this kind of work whilst operating off the Cornish coast with Coastal Command.

6 July 1943 brought further bad fortune for the Coltishall Sector. Wg Cdr Sandy Rabagliati, Wing Commander Flying, led a flight of seven Typhoons on a shipping strike. The Wing Commander was flying Typhoon EK273/JE-DT, the personal mount of Sqn Ldr Don Taylor, CO of 195 Squadron, based at Ludham. 60 miles from home, Wg Cdr Rabagliati reported mechanical trouble with his aircraft's Napier Sabre engine. He was seen to be climbing, with smoke streaming from the engine, before descending and crashing into the sea. The other members of his flight circled the aircraft before being forced to fly home due to fuel shortage. They were all convinced their 'boss' had scrambled clear, as they saw his dinghy floating near to the impact site.

They duly reported this to the Coltishall sector, and a Walrus, escorted by six Spitfires from 118 Squadron, set out from Coltishall on the rescue mission. Wg Cdr Rabagliati's brother, Flt Lt 'Rags' Rabagliati, was serving on 278 ASR Squadron at Coltishall at that the time and he monitored the rescue effort from the squadron dispersal. By the time the Walrus and its escorting Spitfires reached the search area, the weather conditions were horrendous. With squally rain showers, thunderstorms and high seas, nothing was found of the Typhoon or its pilot. In all 60 aircraft were involved in the unsuccessful search for the dinghy and its occupant.

The day's drama was not yet over. Coltishall had scrambled a further four Typhoons to intercept a flight of Luftwaffe Fw190s near Great Yarmouth. Soon the Fw190s were engaging the defenders and Flt Sgt J K Clusas's Typhoon DN447/US-V was shot down, crashing into the sea. A Walrus searched in awful weather conditions but nothing was seen and the search was abandoned. Things went from bad to worse! Spitfire V EP124 of 118 Squadron, which had scrambled to escort the Walrus, crashed soon after take off. At the same time, an Anson of 278 Squadron was on search and

Wg Cdr 'Laddie' Lucas.

Frank Jones in 'The Darlington Sptifire'.

rescue patrol when the pilot of a Photo Reconnaissance (PR) Spitfire baled out not far from the coast. The Anson crew directed the steamer 'Cagny' to the downed airman to carry out a successful rescue.

Wg Cdr P B 'Laddie' Lucas DFC arrived at Coltishall on 10 July to take over as the third Wing Commander Flying in as many months. The Wing Commander was very well known throughout the RAF and highly respected as a cool, calm and collected leader; those who served with him would have followed him anywhere.

When flying a Spitfire an individual was not only the pilot, but the navigator, the bomb aimer, if carrying a bomb, and the gunner as well. They had to do all these things at the same time in a very tiny cockpit. The Wing Leader had to do exactly the same, but in addition had the responsibility of 24 to 36 aircraft behind him. 'Laddie' Lucas excelled in his role and was an inspiration to his pilots and groundcrews alike.

As with all new leaders, there were areas under his command that needed a fresh approach. In Wg Cdr Lucas's case, it was the flying tactics being used by the Coltishall squadrons that he felt needed immediate attention. Up to his arrival he was somewhat taken

aback to find that his new squadrons were still flying with each section in line astern, a formation first flown by the Biggin Hill Wing over two years before. Wg Cdr Lucas was an ardent believer in the advantages of the open finger four formation and he quickly used his Malta experience to win over his Squadron and Flight commanders in adopting this method of aerial combat; within a matter of days the benefits of the new formation was clear for all to see.

On the afternoon of 18 July, eleven Spitfires of 118 Squadron, including W3320 "The Darlington Spitfire" flown by Plt Off Flight, set off to escort Beaufighters armed with torpedoes. Their target was to have been an enemy convoy. However, as they arrived over the target area the attack was called off when the convoy was seen entering the harbour of Ijkduin. On arriving back at Coltishall the squadron did not have to wait long before being brought back up to readiness for another operation that same evening. Again, they were assigned a similar mission, Group Roadstead No 14, but this time with more success.

A formation, including Spitfires from 56, 402 and 416 Squadrons, rendezvoused with twelve Torpedo-equipped Beaufighters and crossed the North Sea looking for enemy vessels. They made landfall at Bergen on the Norwegian coast and spotted a convoy of 20 ships defended by a fighter escort. The Beaufighters went for the convoy while the Spitfires dropped their long-range tanks in anticipation of the battle with the convoy's fighter escort. In the fight that followed, 118 Squadron were the most successful with three Messerschmitt Bf109s in the 'bag.' Flt Lts R A Newbury and J B Shepherd each claiming an aircraft with the third being claimed jointly by Flt Lt Shepherd and Flt Sgt C Anderton. For good measure, 415 Squadron claimed a fourth victim.

There was no let-up in the pace for 118 Squadron as in

the afternoon of the following day the whole squadron joined in a Roadstead attack on shipping. On reaching Ijkduin the formation split into two flights. Six aircraft under Flt Lt Shepherd flew north and returned to Coltishall without incident. However, for the remaining six Spitfires led by Flt Lt Newbury the results were in complete contrast. The formation went to the south and ran into two vessels of 800 and 1000 tons respectively. The Spitfires dived down into low-level action with cannon fire that left the 800 ton vessel ablaze and the 1000 tonner damaged.

During this fierce encounter, Flg Off F T Brown's Spitfire, EN966/NK-D, another presentation aircraft called 'Feducia' (Royal Army Pay Corps), was hit by FLAK but he continued to press home his attack. However, the damage to his aircraft was so severe that Brown was forced to bale out from 900 feet. Flg Off Brown DFC entered the water and was seen swimming. Plt Off Flight in "The Darlington Spitfire" swept low over Brown and threw out his dinghy that splashed down near the parachute. Sadly there was no further sign of Flg Off Brown and it was assumed he had become entangled in his parachute and drowned.

The Station Commander at this time was Gp Capt Vere Harvey, a successful business man before the war and an Auxiliary Air Force flyer. A tactful man; with a great understanding of just how much he could ask his men to do. He had to use all these qualities on the evening of 25 July, when 611 Squadron wished to go one way and Operations wished it to go another.

That afternoon 611 and 64 Squadron, led by Wg Cdr 'Laddie' Lucas, escorted twelve Mitchells on a mission to bomb Schipol, the Luftwaffe airfield near Amsterdam. The attackers appeared to have the skies to themselves when, just as the last Mitchell finished its bombing run; the wing was attacked by a formation of Bf109Fs. They came down from height but Sqn Lr Jack Charles DFC, the CO of 611 Squadron, broke the formation at exactly the right time and within a few seconds two of the Germans were going down in flames. Another pulled up directly in front of Flg Off 'Hoppy' Hodgkinson's Spitfire and he fired into the Messerschmitts belly, seeing strikes and a great spark from under its yellow spinner.

By now the air was full of aircraft in mortal combat; Flt Lt Colloredo Mansfield, an Austrian Count and CO of 'A' Flight 611 Squadron intercepted one of the Bf109s whilst Sqn Ldr Charles engaged two others; swooping in from the sun, firing continuously at the two aircraft in line astern. The first went up and heeled over in a fiery stall, the second, taking strikes for what seemed to be

a long time, exploding with Sqn Ldr Charles's Spitfire, AR610, right in the line of the Messerschmitts flying debris; it appeared that his aircraft was undamaged. The formation reformed having successfully despatched four Messerschmitts in less than three minutes and headed out over the coast with 150 miles to go for home.

The formation was hardly over the sea when someone called to Sqn Ldr Charles that his aircraft was smoking. He realised that the temperature gauge was going off the clock and he needed to make a quick decision at to his next move. Flt Lt Mansfield suggested that he get further out to sea and ditch; they would then come back to get him. Loosing height fast, his airscrew idling and trailing a thick stream of white smoke, Sqn Lr Charles baled out at 2000 feet. His two escorts, Flt Lt Mansfield and Flg Off Hodgkinson watched as the parachute descended into the water, the yellow dinghy inflated and their CO drag himself into its relative safety. As Mansfield circled, Hodgkinson gained height and sent out a 'May-Day' signal that would set the ASR machinery into motion. Then, setting a very exact course for Norfolk the two Spitfires raced for home. On their way back they assessed the situation; their CO was only ten miles from the Dutch coast, it was a brilliantly clear day and he must have been seen by the Germans. They really didn't give him much of a chance for rescue by a friendly side.

Nor, apparently, did Operations, as they found out when they landed. From so far out, the 'May-Day' had been faint and having no idea of Sqn Ldr Charles's position they refused to scramble the amphibious Walrus which, normally, should already have been sent out to search. All they could do, as they informed Ft Lt Mansfield, was to despatch four Typhoons from 56 Squadron to look for him. Meanwhile, the squadron must re-fuel and hold itself in readiness for another operation in two hours time. They added that any man down in the drink so near to the enemy coast was expendable and that went for Sqn Ldr Jack Charles as well. This statement did not go down too well for 611 Squadron, they had promised their CO that they would be back for him and if it was possible they were going to do just that!

Flt Lt Mansfield soon had to deal with a deputation. To hell with Ops and their show in two hours time, the pilots demanded a squadron search immediately, with or without 12 Group's blessing. Whilst the arguments continued, Flg Off Hodgkinson settled down with slide rule and map to figure out exactly where he had last seen the dinghy. Flt Lt Mansfield rang Group again and again; fruitlessly. Did he not realize what this meant?

- A squadron alone on the other side? - On a clear day? - Within sight of the enemy? - And for just one man? - No, No, And No!

By now the pilots were on edge, standing by the Flight Office in their Mae-Wests waiting for the off. The word had got around outside and the ground crew were drifting over to the dispersal hut in groups. At 1730 hours when they should have been preparing the aircraft for the operation that Group had ordered, two Sgt pilots in Flg Off Hodgkinson's section took him aside. "We won't fly, sir," they said, "not until we've had a crack at getting the Squadron Leader out." It was then that Flt Lt Mansfield rang the Station Commander.

Gp Capt Harvey came over at once and the crowd at the door must have indicated to him what pitch things had come to. Passing through the crew room he then went to talk to Flt Lt Mansfield who briefed him on the situation. When the Station Commander had heard him out he

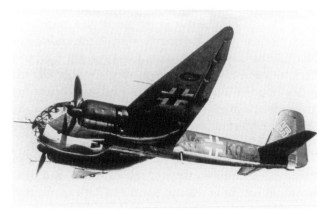

Junkers Ju 188.

picked up the phone himself. The gathered throng knew nothing of the conversation he had with Group, but the Walrus took off almost immediately. Forty minutes later with Flt Lt Mansfield leading, eight Spitfires from 611 Squadron headed out for Holland; it was 1915 hours.

The formation flew at 200 feet away from the sun, dead on the reciprocal course that had brought them home earlier in the day. None of the pilots were happy. It was a flawless evening and it seemed impossible that the Germans were unaware of what was happening. In all probability they had already captured Sqn Ldr Charles and were already waiting for them. Seventy miles out the formation passed the Walrus pressing along at 90 knots. The North Sea seemed vaster than ever, flat calm with a low haze over the surface; each man wondering if they would succeed where the Typhoons had earlier failed. At 2030 hours the Dutch coast was visible and they had still not been attacked. Eyes were straining

and within five minutes four or five of the formation saw the dinghy, just below them and precisely on course. The formation broke and swooped down to greet their leader. He was there, spread eagled in his yellow dinghy, splashing lazily; he looked, to them, more unconcerned than they were! For nearly an hour the Spitfires circled, waiting for the Walrus; they were sitting ducks, too low for the radar to pick them up, but surely someone must have seen them from the coast. They didn't, or if they did, decided to leave the rescuers alone.

The Walrus arrived at last, alighted and taxied up to the dinghy. Sqn Ldr Jack Charles climbed on board and waved his thanks to the orbiting escorts. The Spitfires then turned for home, all out and down at wave height. When they eventually landed they had very little fuel left having been airborne for two hours and fifty minutes, by far the longest flight in a Spitfire for many of the pilots.

It was a great relief to have their Squadron Boss back, but why had they been allowed to mount a considerable operation, on a fine day and within a few miles of enemy occupied territory without being attacked. They might have all been shot down, and in that case, what could Gp Capt Vere Harvey reply to Group? - Nothing, but it was impossible to deny the will of eight men to risk their lives for the magic that lay in one; a minor mystery of the war.

On 26 July 1943 it was 278 Squadron who were again to the fore. The crew of Anson EG496, sighted two dinghies in the sea 20 miles north of Cromer and dropped a smoke float and a Lindholme type dinghy. Two Walrus, call signs Quicksand 6 and 8, were scrambled and vectored to the location whilst the Anson, now joined by Spitfires of 118 Squadron, continued to circle the survivors in their dinghies. At 1850 hours, in thick haze with visibility at about one and a half miles, the first Walrus K8549, crewed by Flg Off William Land and Plt Off Scott, landed in a moderate swell. As the pilot water taxied his Walrus to the dinghies, he found ten men huddled up in sleeping bags, which had been dropped by the Anson in the Lindholme container, uninjured and in good spirits. It was soon ascertained that the ten men were from a B-17G, 'Destiny's Tot', of the 322nd BS from Bassingbourne in Cambridgeshire.

The B-17 had taken part in a raid on a synthetic rubber works at Hanover. Going into the target there was anti-aircraft fire and trouble from enemy fighters. Inevitably, a number of the B-17s had been lost over the target. Lt William H Turcotte and his crew left the target area and made for home. Over the North Sea, the crew started to relax having escaped the period over enemy territory. It came as a bit of a shock to them when the pilot gave the command "prepare for ditching." It had proved impossible to change fuel tanks, and by now the aircraft was running on fresh air.

There was a jolt as the ventral ball turret hit the water first, and the aircraft bounced back into the air before coming down again. The stunned crew gathered their wits and climbed out of the aircraft via the gun mount opening above the radio room, the pilots leaving through the cockpit windows. The dinghies were released, and the crew boarded them, five men in each. Within minutes the B-17 had sunk to the point where the tail plane was beneath the water surface. The weight of the engines and of the water above the tail plane soon caused the aircraft to break its back and then sink rapidly. With the aid of the boathook on the Walrus, Plt Off Scott transferred five men into their aircraft before a take-off was attempted along the swell. Unfortunately, due to the weight of the aircraft and passengers, they could not get airborne. In the mean time second Walrus L2307, crewed by WO George Reeder and Flt Sqt Cyril Rolls, took on the remaining five Americans. The swell was getting quite nasty and a second attempt at taking off by Flg Off Land also failed. WO Reeder did manage to get airborne on his first attempt. However, he soon disappeared in clouds of spray as his aircraft landed back onto the swell; he water-taxied back toward the coast until the rescued crewmen were transferred to a launch. Reeder was then able to get airborne and fly back to Coltishall.

By now the swell had become heavy and as Walrus K8549 prepared for another take-off, a wave came over the rear of the aircraft and tore a piece out of the starboard tail-plane. It was impossible for the crew to assess the damage, so it was decided that the only thing to do was to taxi back towards the coast. The crew attached the two American dinghies to the struts on the wings of the Walrus, and then followed a southeast course on the aircraft compass. As it got dark, the swell subsided considerably and it was about midnight when Plt Off Scott reported that the aircraft was taking on water. Flg Off Land then ordered everyone to sit on the wings, three each side. He opened the cockpit hatch to make a rapid escape should the aircraft capsize.

From time to time, Flg Off Land throttled back to listen for any outside activity. It was a dark moonless night and on the horizon they could see a line of searchlights dipping from the vertical to a horizontal position indicating the direction of Great Yarmouth. They could hear aircraft in the distance; however, being close to the shipping lane known as 'E Boat Alley', they dare not make any visual signals.

At about 0330 hours, just as first light was dawning, a High Speed Launch out of Great Yarmouth intercepted the Walrus. The five rescued crewmen were transferred to the launch and the Walrus placed in tow. The tow itself proved as awkward to control as with the aircraft moving under its own power. It was decided to slip the tow a few miles from the coast and follow the lights of the launch under the power of the Pegasus engine that had behaved faultlessly throughout the whole episode.

The Walrus was taxied into the Royal Naval Base at Gorleston, Great Yarmouth, where the undercarriage was lowered and the aircraft run up onto the beach. The time was 0425 hours. It was estimated that the aircraft had been taxiing for 8 hours at an average speed of about 6 knots, over a distance of about 50 miles. For the latter part of the journey, the Walrus had 18 inches of water in the hull.

After being presented with a very welcome opened bottle of whiskey by the Base Commodore, the crew and their

The 'Destiny's Tot' 50 Franc note.

passengers were taken to the Mess. In addition to their own Fortress crew, there were two further B-17 crews of about 20 men that had been picked up by the launches the previous day. With the Walrus crew being transported back to base, a maintenance crew from Coltishall arrived to drain the aircraft and repair the tailplane. In spite of a few problems with the engine on start-up, the aircraft was floated and flown back to Coltishall without any further mishap. Back at Coltishall, when the engine had been stripped down in the hangar, the cylinders were found to be thickly coated inside with dried sea salt.

The B-17 crew had been flown back to their own base when the crew of Walrus K8549 returned to Coltishall. But as a memento of that long and harrowing rescue, the Americans had left a French 50 Franc note with all their signatures on it; they were: SSgt James A Bowcock, Lt William H Thurcotte, Lt Jack Hargis, SSgt R A Thispen, Lt Carl M Smith, SSgt Albert Dimmond, TSgt Jarvis Allen, Lt Capen R Simmons, TSgt Victor Giganik and SSgt Gerard Tucker.

A Spitfire V of 64 Squadron.

Beaufighter VIf V8619 before it was delivered to 68 Squadron.

Better weather on 25 July enabled Spitfires of 611 Squadron to escort a light bomber force to Holland where they engaged enemy fighters. Thirty miles off the Dutch Coast Sqn Ldr Charles, who had led the 611 Squadron Spitfires into action, went into the sea. Flt Lt Mansfield orbited his position. A further dozen 611 Squadron pilots went to watch over him prior to being relieved by Wg Cdr Chadburn, leading a flight from 416 Squadron, who had escorted the Walrus of 278 Squadron to the spot. The Walrus landed and carried out a successful rescue despite being dangerously close to the enemy coast.

During the evening of 27 July, Sqn Ldr Freeborn, the CO of 118 Squadron, led a total of eleven aircraft from his squadron as part of a close escort for twelve Mitchells on a bombing raid over Schipol aerodrome; the Spitfires being positioned above and to the starboard of the bombers. The ensuing engagement with the defending fighters resulted in a couple of victories for the squadron. This in fact proved to be a cosmopolitan effort with one Messerschmitt Bf109 being destroyed by a Norwegian, 2Lt S K Liby and the second Bf109 shared by Sinhalese Flg Off C Talalla and Plt Off Flight in "The Darlington Spitfire." Plt Off Flight gave a short burst on the starboard beam of the Messerschmitt from 400 yards and then came astern to fire two further bursts into the aircraft. He observed strikes on the fuselage and wing roots, all recorded on his gun camera. Flg Off Talalla made two attacks. When the engagement was broken off at 4000 feet the German was going down in a spin, out of control.

On the night of 27/28 July, Bomber command carried out the second of its four raids on Hamburg. This was the night of the firestorm that caused such enormous destruction. 141 Squadron operated on Serrate Bomber Support on this raid with five Beaufighters flying from

Coltishall as a forward operating location from their home base at Wittering.

Plt Offs Harry White and Michael Allen took off from Coltishall at 2355 hours to patrol an area of the north coast of Holland where several German night-fighter bases were located including that of IV/NJG 1 at Leeuwarden and I/NJG3 at Vechta. They flew over Leeuwarden and then went off to Vechta before returning again to the first airfield. Plt Off Allen was unable to pick up any Serrate signals anywhere.

As dawn was breaking on their way home, skirting the Dutch Islands of Ameland and Terschelling and out over the North Sea, Harry White noticed a tiny light on the sea. They lost height and went down to investigate and found a rubber dinghy with several figures huddled together in it. The Beaufighter circled around and at the same time transmitted a 'Mayday' call on the VHF in the vain hope that the ASR people would come out to rescue them before they were spotted by the Germans and taken prisoner of war. White and Allen had no idea of the outcome of their distress call, as they heard no more after landing back at Wittering after four hours 20 minutes in the air. As Plt Off Allen remembers: "One could only hope they were picked up, if not by us, by the Germans. It was a funny feeling leaving them there as we turned back onto 270 degrees and headed for home."

Improvements to the air defence of the United Kingdom were an ongoing process throughout the war. On the grass airfield at Coltishall runways were being laid with Sommerfield metal tracking and extra Radio Direction Finding (RDF) stations were opened, a total of eleven RDFs being available for use by the Coltishall aircraft. In fact it was whilst the Sommerfield Tracking was being laid that one of the more unusual incidents occurred; or supposedly occurred.

One of the construction workers was George Platton and he remembered an incident where a Dornier had landed at Coltishall by mistake and only when the aircraft was within 20 yards or so of the hangars did the crew realise their mistake. The Germans turned and took-off with all haste. Whilst this incident was never recorded, it is quite possibly true. With Coltishall being close to the coast, and in the heat of battle, it was not unknown for aircrews to fly over a coast and then to turn back, retracing their steps in over the same coastline. Thinking they had crossed over into friendly territory, they would then land in all innocence. A very similar event occurred at Chivenor in Devon on 26 November 1941 when a Junkers Ju88 lost its way whilst on a shipping search operation in the Irish Sea.

On 29 July 1943, 118 Squadron was to take a double blow when squadron aircraft were returning to Coltishall after a couple of Ramrods. Two of their Spitfires collided in a formation break as they readied to land. Both pilots, Plt Off E A Buglass in EP191 which was burnt out and Flt Sgt J Hollingworth in AR447 which simply disintegrated, were killed in the collision.

One individual to witness the catastrophe was 14-year old Alan Spinks who was working in a field very close to the airfield with farmer James Olston carting oat sheaves back to his farm. Mr Olston's first reaction was to tell Alan to be ready to run as a spiralling Spitfire, that seemed to be under some form of control, fell to earth. At the very last minute, just as it seemed that the pilot had gained enough control for a belly landing, the aircraft just fell out of the sky onto its belly. Alan ran across to the wreckage to see if the pilot was OK only to find that he had been thrown from the wreckage and lay motionless about 15 yards from his Spitfire. To his horror Alan realised the body was that of his friend Joe Hollingworth, a man who had always found the time to stop and talk to young Alan when out riding on his motorcycle. Joe Hollingworth lived at Sco Rushton Hall with his heavily pregnant wife and when she heard that a pair of aircraft had collided, she asked Alan for the number of the aircraft; when he told her she immediately knew that it was her husband. Plt Off Buglass's aircraft on the other hand went straight into a dive with no chance of recovery. It impacted the ground near the top end of the thoroughfare close to the end of runway 33. There was nothing anyone could do for the unfortunate pilot.

This was the second crash that Alan Spinks had witnessed as earlier in 1940 both he and his friend George Wines were working in a field close to where a

squadron of Hurricanes were parked. They noticed a single aircraft start-up, taxi and take-off climbing into the low cloud. The next moment the Hurricane reappeared from the cloud and erratically circled around, prompting George to comment that he had never seen an aircraft being flown like that before; it was almost as if the person at the controls had never flown before. With that, just as the Hurricane passed over their heads towards Green's Lane, the aircraft plummeted to the ground with an almighty thump and with no warning. Alan and George ran as fast as they could towards the crumpled mess and saw the pilot motionless in the cockpit with fuel leaking at an alarming rate over the body. In no time an RAF Rescue team arrived on the scene and told the young onlookers to get away from the aircraft as it could explode at any moment. Needing no further encouragement Alan and George withdrew to a safe distance to watch the unfortunate pilot being extracted from the Hurricane. Maybe their initial thoughts on the status of the pilot and his flying abilities were true, as no record was made of the crash apart from the fact that a Hurricane was lost close to the base due to unknown circumstances.

On 30 July Stirling I, EF339/LS-Y of 15 Squadron from Mildenhall belly-landed at Coltishall on its return from a raid over Hamburg and that same day visiting Defiant, T4069/RP-O, of 288 Army Co-Operation Squadron based at Digby suffered a collapsed undercarriage on landing at the airfield; the aircraft being a write-off. On 2 August a Coastal Command Beaufighter from 143 Squadron based at North Coates crash landed at Coltishall; JL881 had been badly damaged by FLAK.

The first few days of August were hectic for Coltishall and the resident squadrons. An Anson of 278 Squadron left the base at 1125 hours on 1 August to search areas H.5829 and H.6829 for a Boston that had been reported as lost over the sea three days earlier. Two sections of Spitfires from 611 Squadron provided the escort and relief escort for the mission. The Anson and its Spitfire escort returned to Coltishall at 1425 hours with no reported sightings of the Boston or its crew. That same day, eleven Typhoons, five of 195 Squadron and six from 609 Squadron were airborne on an offensive shipping patrol off the Dutch coast from 1717 to 1835 hours. The patrol returned safely with no shipping being sighted.

On 2 August, a large section of 51 Spitfire V's of 118, 402, 416 and 611 Squadrons were airborne from 1045 to 1230 as an escort for 33 Beaufighters from North Coates on a Roadstead off Den Helder. A convoy of 18 vessels flying balloons, consisting of merchant and escort vessels, was sighted steaming south in three lines at eight knots. One vessel, a 2000-ton merchantman, was destroyed and several other escort vessels were badly damaged by torpedoes launched from the low-flying Beaufighters. Eight Messerschmitt Bf109s were also escorting the convoy from the air. In the scrap with the Spitfires, Sqn Ldr Northcott, 402 Squadron, destroyed two Bf109's, Flt Lt Rae, 416 Squadron, destroyed another and a fourth was shared by Wg Cdr Chadburn, Plt Off Booth and Plt Off Pow of 16 Squadron. Flt Lt Shepherd probably destroyed a further Bf109 also of 416 Squadron. All the Spitfires returned home without damage although two of the Beaufighters limped home on one engine each and successfully crash-landed at Coltishall. In both cases the crews escaped uninjured.

Shipping Recce's was also being carried out by Typhoons that day. Eight aircraft, four from 195 Squadron and four from 609 Squadron, were airborne from Coltishall at 1255 hours on a reconnaissance patrol from Den Helder to Ijmuiden. Seven coasters up to 1500 tons were seen off Kijkduin Light with a further two coasters and a large tug sighted in Ijmuiden Harbour. Apart from a fishing fleet near Ijmuiden the Typhoons finished their sortie with no other sightings and all returned safely at 1415 hours.

At 2005 hours, 16 Typhoons of 195 and 609 Squadron together with eight Spitfires of 118 Squadron, led by Wg Cdr P B 'Laddie' Lucas, were airborne from Coltishall on a further shipping strike. They over-flew the scene of that mornings shipping attack and saw a balloon flying from a sunken vessel in the area. The other vessels were lying in Den Helder Roads. With no further ships being sighted on this patrol all aircraft landed safely back at Coltishall at 2132 hours.

The Beaufighters of 141 Squadron were once again deployed forward to Coltishall from Wittering on the afternoon of 17 August 1943. This time to escort Bomber commands Lancaster's on a raid against the German V-1 and V-2 experimental rocket base at Peenmünde on the Baltic coast. As night intruders, 141 Squadron's role in Fighter Command was for one flight to escort the bombers out as far as the limited range of the Beaufighters would allow and for another flight to meet the returning bombers as deep into Germany as possible and escort them home. The targets of the escort fighters were the enemy night-fighters that ranged along the bombers route that night.

Flg Off Harry White and Plt Off Mike Allen took off from Coltishall at midnight and 90 minutes later were approaching Hamburg at about 16,000 feet on a clear moonlit night. Allen had picked up a contact on his radar and they set out to investigate. Under normal circumstances the crew would know from the type of their radar contact whether it was hostile - this time they did not. Using the radar, they closed rapidly from two to three miles and had to lose height to put the target slightly above so that they could identify the aircraft visually against the slightly lighter sky. Going 'down hill', they had built up a fair overtaking speed and within moments they saw a dull black shape emerge from the darkness just above the horizon about 1500 feet away. At 500 feet Harry White realised the shape was a Messerschmitt Bf110 night-fighter.

The closing speed was too high for the Beaufighter to open fire and White eased back on his throttles avoiding shutting them up, as if he did, sheets of flame from the exhausts would have given their position away. To help loose speed, White turned hard to port and then back to starboard. It was at that precise moment that the Beaufighter became the target. The Bf110 must have seen the Beaufighter slip out from underneath him and then, slowing down, turn to port and starboard in front of him.

If it had not been for the glimpse of tracer Flg Off White would not have had that split second lead that was needed to get away from the Bf110. If the enemy had not used tracer, only some German night-fighters did, the Messerschmitt would have had chance to correct his aim before the Beaufighter realised it was being attacked. Chastened, breathing deeply, but having evaded the encounter, White and Allen climbed back to their operating height, neither of them in the mood to let matters rest there. Twenty minutes later, using their radar, the Beaufighter crew were closing slowly on what was known to be an enemy aircraft. Even at full throttle it seemed to take an age. The aircraft they were tracking was obviously on his way towards the returning bomber stream. At approximately 900 feet the crew identified another Bf110. At that distance, even at night, it was not an ideal range to intercept. However, White decided to let fire with four cannon and six machine guns. There were strikes, like fireworks and the Messerschmitt dived steeply. The Beaufighter followed but lost sight in the dark. For the crew, they could only claim one enemy aircraft damaged; it might have been destroyed, but could not be confirmed.

Back up to operating height again, the crew re-set their course to meet the returning bombers. Shortly after, another enemy radar contact was made. Again, even at full throttle, it took what seemed to be forever to get within visual range of a Junkers Ju88. Slowly the Beaufighter moved in to 700 feet. A three second, carefully aimed burst of firepower from cannon and machine guns followed, immediately starting a fire in the starboard engine of the Ju88. The fire soon flashed through the fuselage before engulfing the port engine. By now well alight, the enemy aircraft was subject to another three-second burst of cannon and machine gun fire from the Beaufighter. In a blinding flash the Ju88 spiralled down shedding burning pieces and within minutes blew up as it impacted the ground. With fuel now critical, Flg Off White set course for Wittering where they landed two hours later. The score that night was one Beaufighter frightened. One Messerschmitt Bf110 probable and one Junker Ju88 destroyed.

20 August was another busy day for the squadrons at Coltishall. It was on this day that 278 Squadron was involved in its 100th rescue mission. Flg Off Overton of 613 Squadron, just back from a 'Lagoon' sortie, landed to refuel. He brought the news that he had sighted a dinghy 50 miles east of Lowestoft, and had circled it until his fuel had run dangerously low. A Walrus was scrambled, found the dinghy and alighted despite the rough sea. They rescued four Dutchmen of 320 Squadron based at Foulsham. Their Mitchell FR141/NO-B, had ditched due to their port engine being hit whilst returning from Flushing. Luckily for the Captain, J Sillevis, and his crew, the Mitchell remained afloat for eight minutes; long enough to give them time to escape to their dinghy. Yet again the Walrus was unable to take off due to the swell. Flg Off Sims then taxied his aircraft until he found a sufficiently smooth patch to successfully take off and return safely to Coltishall.

At this time enemy activity over mainland Britain increased, including some feeble attempts at intruding by night, often bombing from great height using the new Messerschmitt Me410 and Junkers Ju188. On 22 August, three bombs fell parallel to the flare path just as a Beaufighter of 68 Squadron landed. The bomb that nearly hit the Beaufighter was the last of a string of bombs. At 0210 hours that morning a raider dropped 17 two kilogram anti-personnel 'butterfly' bombs in a field behind the 'Three Horseshoes' Public House at Scottow, adjacent to the end of the runway.

A very different type of sweep, attempted over waters sown with British mines, was intended to destroy enemy minesweepers or aircraft fitted with anti-mine equipment and was known as a 'Distil' operation. One of these was flown on 23 August when 611 Squadron took off from Coltishall and flew at wave-top height across

the North Sea toward the Dutch coast. The Spitfires then turned and flew five miles offshore to Den Helder where two 'M' Class minesweepers and a number of armed trawlers were spotted. Sqn Ldr Davies gave the order to attack, but intense FLAK was very effective, and the Squadron Leader's aircraft, EP393, was hit. He was seen to bale out from about 800 feet and climb into his dinghy. Plt Off J H Gielstrup in Spitfire P8545, named "Indian Telegraph II", was also hit and dived into the sea; there was no further sign of this pilot and he had to be posted missing.

Captain Austeen then attacked and saw hits around the bridge and funnel, thus checking the enemy defensive fire. He was followed by Flg Off Turlington who hit the centre of the vessel closing from 300 to 150 yards and seeing his hits along the superstructure and deck astern; claiming two guns silenced. Many strikes were made on the trawlers and severe damage was considered to have been inflicted on them, but intense FLAK made them pull up to clear the enemy fire.

Sqn Ldr Davies was spotted by several pilots and Flt Sgt Smith confirmed he saw Plt Off Gielstrup's aircraft dip its port wing and then crash into the sea at high speed and break up. He circled for two or three minutes but only saw a large patch of oil and Sqn Ldr Harris confirmed that he saw the Spitfire break up and sink. His body was never found and he is Commemorated on the Runnymede Memorial. Similar operations followed during the next few days, without much result but thankfully without loss to the Squadron.

On 1 September Stirling, EF491/AA-O of 75 Squadron at Mepal, crash-landed at Coltishall after being damaged by a Messerschmitt Bf110 following a raid by 613 heavy bombers on Berlin. Typhoon JP587 from 195 Squadron spun into the ground at Coltishall on 4 September a week later 68 Squadron lost Beaufighter V8562 when it stalled and crashed at Coltishall.

On the 18 September a decision was made to attack six enemy minesweepers seen earlier in the day three miles west of Texel, so at 1715 hours aircraft from 308 and 611 Squadrons took off from Coltishall to escort 24 Beaufighters based at North Coates. Torpedoes launched by the Beaufighters caused severe damage to two of the ships and sank a third. Captain Austeen, the Norwegian OC of 'A' Flight 611 Squadron gave chase to a Messerschmitt Bf109 to which he gave three burst of machine gun fire but was not able to see the results. The next day information was received that a Bf109 had dived into the sea during the Texel operation and this was confirmed by one of the Beaufighter pilots, the circumstances corresponding with Captain Austeen's own combat report that read:

"I was leading Black section at 800 feet as we followed the Beaufighters in on their attack upon the mine-sweepers from coast to sea at 1805 hours. As we passed the target I saw two Bf109Es coming head-on slightly south of my section. I turned right, steeply, to cover the attacking Beaufighters when I saw two more Bf109Es diving from the north on the Beaufighters."

"I dived after them and they broke off the attack. I followed the nearer one which turned left and dived eastwards. I closed to 500 yards and gave a two and three second burst at the enemy aircraft that was at 400 feet but I could not observe the results as I had to break away to avoid other Spitfires and Beaufighters coming out from the attack. The enemy aircraft had clipped wings and I think it was a Bf109E. A Beaufighter pilot, Flg Off Ellsworth of 254 Squadron, reported that he saw a section of Spitfires close on a Bf109 which was attacking a Beaufighter and a moment later the Bf109 flicked over onto its back and dived straight into the sea from 300 feet."

Having previously left Coltishall on 11 November 1940 to move to Hornchurch after the Battle of Britain, 64 Squadron arrived back for the second time on 25 September, this time from West Malling. This time around they stayed until 29 April 1944, with a brief sojourn at Ayr in between. commanded by Sqn Ldr M G L Donnet DFC and Croix de Gurre, and flying Spitfire LFVbs, they carried out bomber escort duties with 'Jim Crow' missions and coastal anti-shipping attacks.

For Sqn Ldr Ioannis Agorastos 'John' Plagis, a Flight Commander with the squadron, his arrival at Coltishall was also a return to operational duties.

'John' Agorastos Plagis was born in Hartley, Southern Rhodesia on 10 March 1919. At the outbreak of the Second World War he tried to join the Rhodesian Air Force but was rejected since, because his parents were Greek; officially he was still a Greek citizen. The RAF at that time, desperately seeking pilots, was not bothered with such minor details and accepted him for training in 1941. By January 1942 he was fully qualified as a pilot and joined 249 Squadron on the aircraft carrier HMS Eagle for their deployment to Malta.

Flying his Spitfire Vb AB346/GN-K off the deck of HMS Eagle on 6 March, four days before his 23rd birthday, he was one of 15 Spitfires flown to the Island from the aircraft carrier. During the next two months he scored the bulk of his victories in the savage dogfights that raged over Malta. He was awarded the DFC following his transfer to another Malta based unit, 185 Squadron. He

'John' Plagis in the cockpit of Spitfire BL734 at Coltishall. Note the 278 Squadron Walrus in the background.

only had enough time to score one more victory before being evacuated to England for rest and recuperation following a total mental and physical breakdown. He resumed operational duties at Coltishall leading a flight with 64 Squadron on bomber escort duties and armed reconnaissance patrols over Europe where he succeeded in shooting down a Messerschmitt Bf109 and Focke-Wulf Fw190 from the cockpit of his personal Spitfire, BL434/SH-B 'Kay.'

John went on to command 126 Squadron, and as a Wing Commander he was awarded the DSO in December 1943. On 17 March 1945, seven days before his 26th birthday, he took part in the famous raid on the Gestapo HQ in Denmark, Commanding the bomber-escort squadrons supporting the Marham based Mosquitoes. Tragically a few years after the war, the Greek/Rhodesian Ace who had flown at least four different types of aircraft in combat, served in two theatres of operations with distinction and earned the respect and admiration of his men, committed suicide, unable to bear the burden of war any longer.

An air raid warning was sounded at Coltishall in the early morning of 28 September, the cause being a lone Halifax JN886/NP-B of 158 Squadron based at Snaith in Yorkshire that was in trouble and being harassed by enemy intruders following an aborted raid on Hanover. Almost at the same time, butterfly bombs and high explosives began to reign down from a force of Junkers Ju88s and Messerschmitt Me410s. The enemy aircraft had penetrated the Norfolk coast under cover of a stream of six to seven hundred Allied bombers recovering to their bases, with the hope of catching them as they alighted. The airfield was closed for almost 24 hours whilst the butterfly bombs were made safe and removed.

The next morning the airfield was declared

JN886 of 158 Squadron after a successful belly landing at Coltishall. The aircraft was repaired and went on to serve with 1666 CU.

unserviceable, partly due to the effects of the bombs, many of which had not exploded, and partly due to the weather. Halifax JN886 that had crashed on its belly at 0023 hours, was also a danger that had to be moved before flying could once again be permitted.

To counter these raids by Messerschmitt Me410s, four Mosquitoes of 151 Squadron were detached to Coltishall, but it was Beaufighter V8619 of 68 Squadron that destroyed a Me410 on the night of 3 October. Flt Lt P F Allen DFC and Bar, with his navigator Flt Lt N H Josling DFC, callsign GRAMPUS 17, was airborne under Neatishead GCI and Searchlight Control, flying between two searchlight beacons at 10,000 feet. The pilot then saw an aircraft coned in the searchlight beams some five miles away, flying large orbits and jinking slightly.

When range was reduced to about three miles at a height of 5000 feet the target flew out to sea for some 15 miles before setting up a patrol parallel to the coast. After a while it turned again and headed inland, being recognised by the Beaufighter crew as a Me410 as it was caught in another searchlight beam. However, the Beaufighter could get a radar contact no closer than two miles. For some three to four minutes the Beaufighter was also held in the searchlight beams, despite the crew's attempts to have the lights doused by firing the colours of the day.

At this point the enemy aircraft began violent evasive action, having seen the Beaufighter in the searchlight glare. After a chase of some 15 minutes Flt Lt Allen was able to close the range to 2000 feet and obtain a visual on the Messerschmitt. As the range decreased to 1500 feet the Beaufighter opened fire with its machine guns and cannon and in a long seven second burst hits were seen on the starboard wing that lead to an explosion. The enemy aircraft then dived, trailing black smoke, crashing into

the sea where it disappeared completely after a violent explosion in contact with the water.

The spell of bad weather persisted for the next few days and caused considerable disruption to the flying operations. The poor weather and bad visibility did not however prevent a football match between the pilots of 64 and 611 Squadrons. The result went in the favour of 64 Squadron 1-0, in spite of the added advantage given by the Station Commander, Gp Capt Harvey, who played on 611's side with great gusto. On occasions however, the play bore a strange similarity to rugby!

Rodney Maliphant was a member of Coltishall's Station Flight from September 1943 to November 1944. Working one day off in 15, he had plenty of time to contemplate what was happening around the base, taking in what was to become an important part of his life.

On arrival at Coltishall his first memories were of the FAA personnel who were there to look after the Swordfish, which in his eyes were strangely antiquated and nothing compared to the Spitfire, Hurricane or Mosquito. However, he soon found out that as a member of the Station Flight he was responsible for looking after an equally ancient aircraft, the Miles Magister in addition to a couple of Airspeed Oxfords used for pilot currency and communication duties.

Daily life for Roy was often boredom interspersed with complete mayhem. One particular occasion found Roy and a colleague on night duty at Station Flight. Nice and cosy in their office, situated within the hangar close to Flying Control, Hangar 1, they were looking forward to a quiet night shift, a repeat of the previous night. However, this was not to be. Just before midnight, they received a call to say that a number of heavy bombers were due into Coltishall having been diverted from their own bases due to fuel shortages after a long and arduous mission over the Continent. As if this were not enough, they were also warned that a squadron of Canadian Mosquitoes would also be joining the circuit at about the same time as the bombers.

Armed only with torches on a very dark night, the pair managed to park what he estimated to be in excess of 30 Halifax and Lancasters. Running up and down the perimeter track in complete darkness to get to and guide what seemed to be an endless stream of large, fast taxiing aircraft with tired crews before they passed the available parking spaces. They managed to park all of the bombers on the grass verges without damage; a result in itself.

Having been engaged in the mayhem of parking the bombers they had completely forgotten about the Mosquitoes that were due down at about the same time. However, as they walked back to the hangar for a well-deserved cup of tea, they concluded that the Mosquitoes must have made it back to their own base as there was no sight of them in the pitch black of night. How wrong they were, as the dawn was to prove.

Neatly parked amongst the Halifax and Lancasters were the Mosquitoes who had parked themselves without complaint or damage! With the uncertainty about numbers and the pressure on space that night they could not afford to park the bombers too loosely. However, in the daylight, they were able to find some wing tips perilously close to each other and how the Mosquitoes managed to weave themselves amongst the four-engine heavies without the help of marshallers remains a mystery to this very day.

Another task the Station Flight had was to provide support to the many transient squadrons who used Coltishall as a stepping-stone to the Continent. The Polish Squadrons in particular always proved interesting. Not necessarily to the flight itself, but certainly to Flying Control when a 'scramble' was called. By all accounts aircraft took off in every direction, not always on the designated runways or under the control of the controllers; fun to watch, but a nightmare for Flying Control!

Photographic reconnaissance aircraft always took priority. Working on the PR aircraft also gave members of the flight the opportunity to look over the latest variants of Spitfires and Mosquitoes that were used for this task. Refuelled at double quick time, Ray often wondered if the oil or fuel caps had been fitted correctly as two or three aircraft took off in formation to carry out their vital high-level work.

One day, and contrary to advice, one visiting American pilot flying the very robust P-47 Thunderbolt, decided that he could take-off immediately behind a flight of three photo-recce Spitfires, only to find the wake turbulence upset his controls to such an extent that he was unable to maintain flight. He made a forced but safe landing on the Station's cabbage patch just beyond the Station Flight Hangar. Apart from explaining to Wing Commander Flying why he had ignored sound advice, he had to explain to the SWO why he chose his cabbage patch to land!

1853161 LAC Maliphant R was posted to the Far East after his tour at Coltishall. He served at Calcutta, Manauri, Burma, Singapore, Sumatra and Penang before going to Celle in Germany where he was demobbed in August 1947.

Whilst on detachment from their home base at Church Fenton, Flg Off V H Linthune and his Navigator/Radar Operator WO J L Paine of 25 Squadron took off from Coltishall at 2020 hours on 3 October 1943 in their Mosquito on Operation MAHMOUD. As they climbed over the North Sea to cross into Holland north of Vlieand at 2102 hours at an altitude of 18,000 feet, fires were observed to the south, probably from Schiphol. From there, they then set course for their patrol area over Kassel where they arrived at 2150 hours.

At 2200 hours contact was obtained at 6000 feet astern, slightly to the south-west of Kassel. Flg Off Linthune did a very steep port turn at full throttle with the contact re-appearing 3500 feet ahead. Simultaneously a second contact appeared 8000 feet astern. The first contact, flying at an estimated speed of 240 knots began jinking, turning slightly to port and lost height to 16,000 feet. The pilot of the Mosquito closed to 600 feet range and got a visual on a twin-engine aircraft 100 feet above and slightly to starboard. Exhausts were not visible, but Flg Off Linthune recognised the aircraft by its silhouette as being a Junkers Ju88 which WO Paine confirmed through his night-vision binoculars.

The Mosquito opened fire from dead astern at a distance of 500 feet closing to 100 feet. The twelve-second burst of 120 rounds from each of the cannon saw strikes on the port engine and side of the fuselage; confirmed by the Cine-Camera-Gun that exposed automatically. The enemy aircraft fell away vertically nose first, as if the pilot were dead or his controls shot away. Then, presumably due to the port engine being disabled, the Junkers went into a violent left hand spin.

Flg Off Linthune was unable to follow the aircraft down visually owing to the second contact having meanwhile closed to 5500 feet astern. WO Paine watched the blip of the first enemy aircraft on his elevation tube and saw it become faint at 9000 feet range below and fade altogether at 13,000 feet range. The speed with which the blip faded and range increased indicated that the Junkers was in an almost vertical fast dive.

In an attempt to intercept the second contact, Flg Off Linthune did a steep turn to starboard. When his orbit was more than half completed, and the blip of the first enemy aircraft had just disappeared, he saw an explosion on or just above the ground about five miles west of the position where the aircraft had begun to dive; the flash was reminiscent of an exploding aircraft. On completing the orbit the second contact had vanished and was not regained in spite of a weaving search.

The Mosquito and its crew set course for home at 2210 hours, landing back at Coltishall at 0130 hours. When interrogated by the Squadron Intelligence Officer (SIO), Plt Off T A Q Lidell, the crew's claim of one Junkers Ju88 destroyed was amended to read 'probably destroyed.' However, Church Fenton's SIO, Flt Lt D L Walters, confirmed that the Ju88 was in fact claimed as destroyed after detailed interrogation and further consideration. The following points being borne in mind:

1. The twelve-second burst of cannon fire (four cannons, no stoppages, 120 rounds each) from dead astern starting at 500 feet and closing to less than 100 feet.

2. The enemy aircraft's 'break away' is not such as would have been attempted, irrespective of height, by any pilot owing to certain injury to crew and aircraft.

3. The speed of descending blip indicates a vertical falling dive.

4. On the blip ceasing it is immediately followed by an explosion as of an aircraft blowing up.

Full confirmation of Flg Off Linthune's claim, that was to be officially recorded, was received by Mr J C Nerve the Librarian at the Air Ministry, in a letter from HQ Fighter Command at Bentley Priory dated 27 October 1943.

On 3 October, Coltishall was again the scene of a crash landing by a crippled bomber. On this occasion Stirling III, EP464/ZO-P from 196 Squadron at Witchford. The bomber was forced to turn back from a raid on the enemy after engine failure following a tangle with a night fighter close to the Dutch coast. The crew attempted to land at Coltishall, but as the port inner failed completely the aircraft crashed at Scottow; the time, 2143 Hours. Sgt T L Dickie was killed in the accident but luckily Flt Sgt G H Kogel, Sgts A W Clarke, R L George, J A Beattie, F Reeves and the pilot, Sgt Williams survived. Williams himself was very seriously injured during the crash, but recovered to return to operational flying. On 8 September 1944, the London Gazette carried the news that Sgt Williams had been awarded the DFM. His citation referred to the accident at Coltishall on 3 October where he was Commended for his skilful flying which had prevented further loss of life to his crew.

October proved to be a busy period for the crash and rescue crews at Coltishall, with many a crippled bombers finding comparative safety after a harrowing and dangerous transit back from their targets over Germany and enemy occupied territory. Just five days after the escapades of Stirling EP464, it was the turn of a 35 Squadron Halifax to call upon the skills of its pilot and the hope of safety at Coltishall.

Stirling III EP464, after crash landing near Scottow.

The crew of Halifax HR777/TL-Y of 35 Squadron based at Graveley in Huntingdonshire took off at 2246 hours on a Pathfinder mission to mark the target of Bremen. What happened over the target was familiar to many a bomber crew, with the official combat report for this mission and particular crew giving a vivid insight to what happened:

Sgt Bent, the rear gunner, saw a Junkers Ju88 at 250 yards on the fine quarter, slightly up and closing fast. Bent told his Captain, Flg Off Melville 'Max' Muller, to 'corkscrew port.' The enemy aircraft opened fire at 200 yards with cannon firing a very dull trace, hitting the Halifax and setting the port outer engine on fire. The rear gunner returned fire with two short bursts, aiming point blank and hitting the fighter, causing it to pull up sharply. The Halifax was now in a spin and the Ju88 appeared to the Rear Gunner to be hanging on its props on the starboard beam. He gave it another very short burst observing strikes and saw it fall away, apparently out of control.

By now the bomber was falling fast in a spin with flames pouring from the outer engine. The pilot eventually regained control after losing over 8000 feet in height. But as the port outer engine was out of action, the port

Another view of EP464 which claimed the life of Sgt Dickie.

inner damaged, with the aileron and elevator controls also severely damaged, the turret being unserviceable and numerous other problems with the aircraft, bombs were jettisoned and course was set for base.

The Bomb-Aimer, 19 year old Sgt Derrick Coleman, recalled that he was terrified during the spin as he was pinned to the floor of his bomb-aimer's position; he thought it was the end. Although the official report states that the bombs were jettisoned, Sgt Coleman was sure that an attempted bomb run was made with a solitary searchlight following their every move.

From the target area, the pilot did a magnificent job in getting his crippled aircraft back to England, gradually losing height all the way and using full right rudder to keep the aircraft flying straight. At one point the Bomb-Aimer tied his intercom lead around the rudder bar to give extra purchase to the constant load that the pilot had to maintain during the transit back.

It was now getting to the stage where some difficult decisions had to be made. With the hydraulic system shot away, fuel being lost from two or three tanks and a bomb door that refused to close causing even more drag to the crippled Halifax, 'Max' Muller asked his crew for their views and opinions on the unpleasant alternatives

Spitfire Vb BM594 of 611 Squadron at Coltishall.

that faced them. Bale out now and risk being POWs, fly on and risk a possible ditching in the North Sea or trying to limp home. After a brief discussion it was decided to fly on.

Throughout the trip Plt Off 'Mac' Maskell, the Wireless Operator maintained radio contact with the formation and his base and as they approached the safety of the English Coast their 'Mayday' was picked up and the crew were directed to Coltishall. The dim lights of the airfield were a welcome sight, but as they prepared for an emergency landing, things went from bad to worse. As if flying on only one engine was not enough, the port wheel undercarriage failed to lock. Additionally, it was

now obvious that the airfield was out of reach, so close yet so far.

By now the Halifax was literally 'hedge-hopping' with the pilot struggling to maintain flight. Eventually gravity beat them and flying through two trees, the wings made contact and the aircraft fell to the ground. Luckily, the impact with the trees slewed the Halifax away from a farmhouse that was in the direct path of the out-of-control bomber. It was a complete write-off, with a least one engine being torn off from its mount and on fire. Luckily, the nose and part of the fuselage remained reasonably intact, enabling the crew to escape injury with the exception of Sgt Tommy Elwood, the Flight Engineer, who sustained a bad cut above his eye during the crash.

For the couple and their son who lived in the House at Bridge Farm, Bradfield, William, Matilda and Jack Gibbons, they initially thought the unwelcome visitors were Germans. But as the fortunate crew scrambled from their burning bomber, they soon realised they were RAF and invited them in for a cup of tea and the warmth of the open fire. Whilst they enjoyed the strong hot tea and sandwiches, they reflected on just how lucky they all were, and there was no doubt in their minds that they owed their lives to the amazing ability and strength of their 'skipper' Max Muller. With no phone in the house, Jack Gibbons had to cycle to the next village of Antingham, and with difficulty managed to arouse the post-mistress in order to phone the police. The Norfolk Civil Defence Diaries record this call as being made at 0438 hours, and show the crash as happening at 0330 hours.

Having been in contact with the bomber ever since picking up the 'mayday' call over the North Sea, the crash crews at Coltishall were on full standby for the arrival of the Halifax. Realising that all was not well with the expected arrival well overdue, crews were despatched along the estimated flight path of the aircraft to hopefully find survivors. Luckily, all ended well for those involved and following a check-up in the Sick Quarters at Coltishall the crew were driven back to Graveley to resume operations with the Pathfinder Force.

Sadly, the trauma of that night for the Gibbons family proved too much. 81 year old William never recovered from the stress caused by the crash and died 55 days later. His 75 year-old wife Matilda also died just seven days after William. They were buried together in nearby Trunch cemetery; their headstone etched with the words 'They travelled together.'

The tide was turned on the enemy on the 12 October

when Flt Lt Allen DFC and Bar of 68 Squadron scrambled and intercepted a Messerschmitt Me410. Chasing it across Norfolk to the coast at Cromer where a trap awaited the unsuspecting intruder.

Flg Off Boyle in a Mosquito of 151 Squadron, another detached squadron at Coltishall, was waiting. Radar operators at Neatishead had advised him of the enemy's position and track. Boyle closed in and went for the kill by giving the Messerschmitt Me410 a short burst from his machine guns. There was an explosion in the fuselage followed by an engine fire. The Messerschmitt went down in a mass of flames into the sea. Fragments from the disintegrating aircraft hit Boyle's Mosquito however he was able to land safely at Church Fenton.

On the 18 October, Bomber command attacked Hanover in Germany with a force of 360 aircraft. 141 Squadron operated that night from Coltishall in their familiar Serrate Bomber Support role with six Beaufighter VIF's that had flown in from their home base at Wittering earlier that day. The six aircraft took off from Coltishall within minutes of each other, but for one aircraft and its crew it was to be their last.

Flg Off C H Johnston with his Navigator/Radar Operator Plt Off A C Watson in Beaufighter V8777 took off from Coltishall at 1832 hours for Bremen where they would patrol ahead of the Hanover bomber force. Shortly after departure they called up Coltishall Operations asking for an emergency landing. This request was passed by the controllers to the Flying Control Officer at 1843 hours. The Beaufighter joined the Coltishall circuit at 1500 feet and to the controllers in Air Traffic Control (ATC), visually all seemed well. Suddenly and without warning approximately when on about a quarter of their circuit the aircraft was seen to fall out of the sky and crash just short of the perimeter track and burst into flames; both the crew were killed instantly.

The other Beaufighters, X8195, V8744, V8499, V8799 and V8402 all landed back safely at Coltishall and Wittering between 2028 and 2225 hours that night with only V8744, flown by Flt Lt H C Kelsey and Plt Off E M Smith, sustaining any damage. Their aircraft had come under accurate and intense FLAK twelve miles northwest of Hanover when they were coned by over 50 searchlights just after 1917 hours. The resulting barrage of FLAK that lasted over ten minutes caused the cockpit to fill with fumes as the aircraft was peppered with shrapnel and buffeted by the exploding shells.

Flg Off Johnston and Plt Off Watson had only joined 141 Squadron on the 14 September 1943 and had carried out two operational sorties; this would have been their

Sqn Ldr Douglas DFC, OC 611 Squadron during the units stay at Coltishall.

third. As they were killed shortly after take off, they were listed as being killed in a flying accident and not being killed on operations.

November was a relatively quiet month for East Anglia, with enemy attacks on only five nights. Against one of these, Wg Cdr Haley-Bell DFC of 68 Squadron with his navigator Flg Off Uezzell in Beaufighter MM844 destroyed a Messerschmitt Me410 six miles north of Happisburgh on 6 November.

On 9 November, four Spitfires of Red Section 611 Squadron, led by Flg Off Colin Hodgkinson took off from Coltishall and headed for Bradwell Bay in Essex. From there they flew a Rhubarb to St Pol and its railway lines. At the Nieuport/Furnes Canal all four aircraft attacked two barges, strikes being seen on both which were left smoking heavily. A small goods train was then attacked and severely beaten-up on the Menin/Armentieres line, with strikes on both the trucks and engine, the latter being engulfed in steam soon after the first Spitfire had carried out its attack. Next in line for the formations attention were two barges on the Merville/Bethune Canal and then to a goods train on the Bethune/Lille

B-17F 42-9733 'Louisiana Puchase' straddling a fighter revetment in November 1943.

railway line. Continuing up the St Pol/Bethune railway line a goods train was seen at five miles east of Bethune. Hodgkinson called up saying that he and his No 2 would take on the engine and told No 3 and 4 to take the FLAK. The train, on being attacked, opened up with Bofors and cannon fire but despite this barrage strikes were seen on the engine and trucks.

Just as the leader told his formation that the train was heavily defended, his No 2, Sgt J V P Daly flying Spitfire AR509, said that he was hit and was climbing to bale out. Sgt Wilson saw Daly's aircraft climb but did not see him bale out and then, at almost the same time saw Flt Sgt Bevan baled out of his Spitfire, EE732. Wilson circled Bevans parachute and saw him land; his aircraft crashing into a wood just west of Bethune. The two remaining aircraft made it back to England independently having both being engaged by intense heavy and light FLAK; Flg Off Hodgkinson landed at Manston with Sgt Wilson landing at Great Dunmow.

This proved to be a very expensive 'Rhubrab' for 611 with two Spitfires lost, Sgt Daly being taken POW and sadly Flt Sgt Bevan killed. Bevan was buried with full Military Honours at Longuenesse (St Omer) Souvenir Cemetery.

By late 1943 there was much concern amongst the higher echelons of the RAF and at the Air Ministry with regards to the long-term welfare of the airmen and airwomen under their command, especially as the war had been ongoing since 1039. A confidential communiqué was issued by the Air Council to all Station commanders highlighting their concerns; Stations were then expected to act accordingly.

The Station Commander at Coltishall, Gp Capt A V Harvey, wrote a letter to all his Section commanders highlighting the concerns of the Air Council and what he expected to happen at his station to address the problem. One such letter was written on 29 November 1943 to Sqn Ldr J W Hendley, OC Engineering:

Dear Hendley,

As you know, the Air Council are much concerned regarding the outlook of airmen and airwomen, and their general attitude towards life at the end of the war when they return to civilian life.

The problem is a difficult one because a number of personnel are becoming war weary and mentally they are tired.

All Stations vary in the amount of thought and trouble given to the subject as a whole, but the Air Council have laid on such things as Discussion Groups which may, to the young officer, appear superfluous, but nevertheless it does give the individual an opportunity to express his thoughts and what is on his mind. For this reason alone I am anxious

Another view of 'Louisiana Purchase'. Note the 64 Squadron Spitfires parked in the background.

that you should play your part in doing what you can with your personnel in fostering the right outlook.

Whilst I am dead against parades and being marched to Church, I nevertheless believe that an occasional visit to a church does not do any harm, and in many cases, will do good. Yesterday I went to our local church and was disappointed to see that only four officers out of some 160 on the Station were present, and there was a poor showing of airmen and airwomen.

Since I have been in command of the Sector, I have hardly ever seen a Squadron or Flight Commander at Church and it must be very galling to an airman or airwoman to be detailed to go to Church and never see their Commanding Officer there.

I should be the last to suggest that operational duties should not in any way come first, but there are occasion - such as yesterday - when the weather is quite unsuitable for flying, that officers could put in an appearance.

From now onwards, I expect Squadron commanders to take a personal interest in this subject and to attend Church occasionally themselves and to see that officers and NCO pilots do likewise.

I do not wish to issue orders on the subject, but I fully expect your co-operation.

Yours sincerely

A V Harvey

At 1100 hours on 29 November 1943, a Lancaster I of 626 Squadron took off from Wickenby on a cross-country exercise. At 1130 hours that exercise came to an abrupt end when the aircraft crashed on landing at Coltishall. Lancaster DV390/UM- with Flt Sgt J T Torrance, RAAF, in command, was extensively damaged when it came to rest. On 2 December a repair party arrived to dismantle the bomber but four days later, during a technical inspection of the wreck, it was decided to reduce the Lancaster to components and scrap.

Air defence activity was even lighter in December, there being only two nights of raids over East Anglia. On the night of 10 December, Beaufighters and Mosquitoes were ordered to the defence. One of 68 Squadron's Beaufighters, MM844, damaged two Dornier Do 217s, but another, V8619 did not return, being shot down in error by a Mosquito over Stowmarket in Suffolk. On that same day Gp Capt A H Donaldson DSO DFC AFC took over command of Coltishall.

Sqn Ldr Douglas DFC, OC 611 Squadron is flanked by (left) Sqn Ldr Nigel Kemp DFC, OC 'B' Flight and (right) Flt Lt G A Jones DFC.

Just a short time after the incident with the Lancaster of 626 Squadron, the crash crews were once again called to the assistance of another bomber, this time a B-17F Flying Fortress of the 544th BS of the 384th BG. On 16 December, the B-17F-70-BO, 42-29733/SU-L, overshot the runway and crashed into the fighter revetments at Coltishall when its pilot, Lt George Cosentine, tried to make an emergency landing. The B-17 had taken off from its home base at Grafton Underwood that morning as part of a massive daylight raid on Bremen.

The aircraft, which was finally recovered from Coltishall by salvage crews on 4 January 1944, had previously served with the 91st BG at Bassingbourn and the 305th BG at Chelveston before being transferred to the 384th BG on 6 November 1943, where she acquired the name 'Louisiana Purchase.'

Little activity took place during the days before Christmas, although 611 Squadron was positioned at Bradwell Bay for an operation that in the end did not take place.

Back at Coltishall on Christmas Day the time-honoured tradition of the Officers' and Senior Non-Commissioned Officers' serving the Junior Ranks was observed. However, the flying and training continued with Sqn Ldr Douglas, 611's CO and one other pilot taking off in the afternoon for a tactical exercise involving two Beaufighters of 68 Squadron also based at Coltishall.

The 27 December saw two Spitfires of 611 Squadron scrambled to find a lame B-17 Flying Fortress that had been involved in a collision and from which the crew had abandoned to 'hit the silk.' Soon locating the bomber over the sea, Flg Off Ronald Graesser had the task of shooting it down by firing a burst into an engine and then another into the tail plane, whereupon it caught fire and plunged into the sea eight miles off Cromer.

Coltishall's MT Section, circa Christmas 1943.

Chapter 6

1944 - V-1 INTERCEPTIONS

It was a filthy night on the evening of Thursday 20 January 1944 when farmer Joe Mutimer and his wife were preparing for bed. At the same time, out over the North Sea, Flg Off Bill Cozens was preparing to land his Halifax V LL191/ZL-N of 427 Squadron, Leeming at Coltishall because of a shortage of fuel.

After crossing the coast and transiting over the Norfolk countryside, the Halifax bomber approached Coltishall far too low and hit some tall trees in a nearby wood; the collision sheared off the left starboard wing together with its two running engines. The remainder of the aircraft carried on through the trees, finally coming to rest in a ball of fire within yards of Orchard House, the home of Joe and Noel Mutimer. The startled occupants immediately got out of bed realising that an aircraft had came close to destroying their home. Joe asked his wife to cycle up the road to alert Mr Eldred, the local ARP man, of the accident. Noel had to cycle to Mr Eldred's because the crash had taken out all the power and telephone lines to the house.

Whilst his wife was struggling on her bicycle in the wind and rain, Joe was performing the bravest feat of his life; he was saving surviving crew members trapped in the burning bomber. For his bravery, he was subsequently summoned to Buckingham Palace to receive the BEM from HM King George VI.

Apart from Joe and Mr Eldred, who responded to Noel Mutimer's plea for help after she had alerted him of the tragedy, Constable Emmerson from North Walsham, who just happened to be passing the scene at the time, also helped in the frantic rescue of the crew, and once extricated, the survivors were taken to Orchard House where Dr Morgan from North Walsham looked after them until the crash crews from Coltishall arrived at the scene to take over.

Thanks to the bravery of those involved in that rescue, four of the seven man crew were saved from the burning Halifax that night; Flt Sgt H P Whittaker, Flt Sgt C L Brenier, Sgt R B Nairn and Sgt W L Stockford. Sadly, the Bomb Aimer, Sgt William Stockford, died from his injuries two-days later. Those killed were the pilot, Flg Off William Authur Couzens, Flg Off Laurence George Biddiscombe the Navigator and Flight Engineer Sgt John McGowan.

Enemy activity over East Anglia on the night of 29 January 1944 commenced at 2027 hours, when a Junkers Ju88A-4, Wrk No 300228 coded B3+AL, of KG54 crossed the coast over Lowestoft on its way to bomb Bury St Edmunds. Flt Sgt Neal and Flt Sgt Eastwood were on night landing practice at Coltishall in their 68 Squadron Beaufighter, callsign GRAMPUS 28 (originally allocated to the experienced Czech crew, Joe Vopalecky and Rudi Husar), when Neatishead Ground Controllers diverted them from their task and vectored them towards an enemy intruder.

The navigator of the Beaufighter, Sgt Eastwood, later recalled that they were a very inexperienced crew, fresh from the OTU and on their first night flight with the squadron. Their aircraft was a Beaufighter VI fitted with AI Mark VIII, very much on its last legs but still fit for breaking in new crews. Their mission detail was practice interceptions against another Beaufighter flown by Flt Sgt Bullus.

The GCI Controller at Neatishead, Flg Off Robertson, had detected an incoming raid which proceeded to sow a 'Window" stream for some 40 miles. The aircraft eventually appeared ahead of its jamming stream and whether by design or by accident, perhaps thinking 'GRAMPUS 28' was an experienced crew, the controller directed the Beaufighter onto the target.

The crew's operational experience was non-existent and they had not seen the effects of 'Window' on their radar before then. The wonderfully clear echo on their AI radar seemed to be more than a mile in length and the crew imagined a trailing wire of this magnitude, complete with radar reflectors, behind the enemy bomber. To evade this mythical wire the navigator directed his pilot to make an approach from behind and above. Slowly overtaking the Ju88 at 210mph, still on a westerly heading, a frantic search then took place as the pilot tried to locate his gun button in the dark; which was the switch for the guns? Navigation lights and every other light in the Beaufighter were switched on and off before the cannon were made live. After, the kill was rapidly completed and the Ju88 was shot down in flames, the interception and despatch being confirmed by Flt Sgt Alf Bullus in the other Beaufighter.

This was the only enemy raider to fall over land that night. Five others were shot down over the sea and less than ten raiders actually penetrated into East Anglia that night. For Flt Sgt Neal the Junkers was to be his first kill on his first operational sortie. Ironically, he had started his service with 68 Squadron as an AC1 electrician. After volunteering for aircrew duties, he had made it his personal ambition to rejoin his old squadron as a pilot.

Red Section of 611 Squadron took off from Coltishall on 31 January at 1100 hours for what they thought was a routine escort of a Walrus of 278 Squadron on an ASR search some 90 miles off the coast. Whilst flying along circling the low-speed Walrus the Spitfires were vectored away onto a B-24 Liberator which had been abandoned by its crew and was circling above Great Yarmouth fully bombed up.

By this time Red Section had been in the air for almost two hours when they were relieved by White Section from the squadron who, within the hour, were ordered to shoot the wayward bomber down as it was now over the sea.

Lt Widerberg, one of 611's Norwegian pilots, came in below the port side of the bomber and fired a short burst into the port outer engine that immediately caught fire. WO Shoebottom then approached from above to fire another burst into the same engine. With this attack the mortally wounded B-24 went into a dive, the wings fell off and it exploded as it hit the sea forty miles east of Coltishall.

The 4 February saw some 60 enemy bombers enter East Anglian air space under the cover of an extensive 'Window' field. The Beaufighters of 68 Squadron were airborne and Flt Lt Karel Seda with Flg Off Hradsky intercepted a Junkers Ju188 that they shot down into the sea off Southwold. This was to be the last operation for the squadron from Coltishall. During their time at the Norfolk base they were credited with a score of 70 enemy aircraft destroyed.

68 Squadron's place was to be taken by 25 Squadron, under the command of Wg Cdr Wight-Boycott, DSO. The squadron arrived at a time when the Luftwaffe was carrying out the 'Baby Blitz' series of raids. Coltishall at that time was thought to be too far north to be involved in these initial raids. However, all changed on 17 March when raiders entered the domain of 12 Gp.

At 2046 hours that night, a twin engine aircraft came in low over Great Yarmouth at 2000 feet and pushed inland as far as Buxton. After circling a couple of times it commenced bombing the quiet village. Shortly after, the raider dropped a container full of 24 bomblets over the south-west corner of Coltishall and into the gardens of nearby houses, damaging two of the cottages. Circling at 5000 feet the aircraft continued its attack against the airfield and then the village of Tunstead. At 2120 hours the crew spotted a brightly lit bus near Heavingham and strafed it twice, luckily without causing any injuries. The

Sqn Ldr E Cassidy DFC was OC 64 Squadron from November 1943 to April 1944.

aircraft then flew further inland towards Swannington where it fired a few shots into huts on the airfield at 2125 hours before finally escaping back to the continent over Great Yarmouth.

Further raids were made on the 19th, and for the Germans, 25 Squadron's intervention proved to be expensive, with the loss of five aircraft. The squadron was again involved in another skirmish on 21 March, when a further two Junkers Ju188s were added to its tally. 25 Squadron had by now reached eleven enemy aircraft destroyed since their arrival at Coltishall.

Plt Off Howe of 64 Squadron had a very lucky escape on 15 February while taking part in a 'Jim Crow', weather and shipping reconnaissance patrol, with seven other Spitfires from his Squadron. Flying at extremely low level, Howe hit the sea with the propeller of his Spitfire. He managed to return and land safely at Coltishall, where to his amazement he discovered that he had in fact lost about nine inches off each propeller blade!

The Mosquito NF.XVII was the mount of 25 Squadron during early 1944.

The night of 20 February saw 95 enemy raiders cross the coast between Hythe and Harwich making their way to London. The Mosquitoes of 25 Squadron were on standby at Coltishall for such an event, and at 2110 hours, a Mosquito NF.XVII, callsign 'GRAMPUS 16', with Plt Offs J R Brockbank and D McCausland at the controls took off into the dark. Flt Lt J Singleton and Flg Off W G Haslam, call sign 'GRAMPUS 20' joined them moments later in another Mosquito. Both Mosquitoes were fitted with the AI.X radar and as yet the Mosquito AI.X radar combination had not been successful in shooting down any enemy aircraft at night.

Soon the Mosquitoes were out of the Coltishall circuit and under control of the Neatishead GCI. 'GRAMPUS 16' was given instructions to climb to 17,000 feet whilst Flt Lt Singleton in 'GRAMPUS 20' was to climb to 18,000 feet on the same heading. At 2143 hours 'GRAMPUS 20' was handed over to the Chain Home Low Radar Station at Happisburgh who gave them vectors to the enemy who were going eastward at 10,000 feet.

Meanwhile, at 2137 hours, the crew of 'GRAMPUS 16' obtained a contact on their radar of an enemy aircraft at seven miles range crossing from left to right directly in front of them. Plt Off Brockbank increased the power of his twin Rolls Royce Merlins and soon gained ground on the enemy. The enemy aircraft was a Junkers Ju188E-1 coded U5+LN and flown by Lt Ewald Bohe of 5/KG2.

In an effort to evade the pursuing Mosquito, Lt Bohe weaved and bucked his aircraft in increasingly violent manoeuvres desperate to shake off the fighter. The Mosquito closed in to 1000 feet on several occasions but was unsuccessful in getting a visual on the Ju188 which caused him to break off the attack. 'GRAMPUS 16' soon lost contact altogether with the enemy aircraft but soon the Neatishead Ground Controller vectored them back onto the hapless enemy.

A single beam from a searchlight illuminated the Ju188 and Lt Bohe corkscrewed his aircraft violently to give himself distance between himself and the Mosquito. The chase went on for 25 minutes and the Mosquito gradually closed in on the enemy aircraft and was soon within 600 feet of the foe. The crew of 'GRAMPUS 16' soon saw the glow from the exhaust stubs of the Junkers.

The Ju188 crossed from port to starboard in front of the Mosquito and as it crossed back Plt Off Brockbank fired two short bursts from his machine guns. At 2203 hours he closed to within 75 feet and poured more rounds into the fuselage and wings of the enemy which caused it to catch fire. The Junkers flew straight and level for a few seconds but soon commenced a steep dive through the clouds to destruction at Park Farm, Whickham St Paul, Essex. 'GRAMPUS 16' headed back to Coltishall and claimed the first night success for the Mosquito NF.XVII.

Whilst 'GRAMPUS 16' was busy with the Ju188 over Essex, 'GRAMPUS 20' was pursuing his quarry at 9000 feet over the sea 50 miles or so off Lowestoft. Flg Off Haslam used night binoculars to positively identify the enemy bomber as Dornier Do217K-1, U5+AR of 7/KG2. At 2236 hours a second success for the Mosquito NF.XVII was recorded when Flt Lt Singleton scored a direct hit on the Do217, sending it to a watery grave. The crew of the Dornier Oblt Wolfgang Brendel, Uffz Heinz Grudbus, Obfw Bruno Schnieder and Fw Bruno Preker were all posted missing presumed killed.

Soon after, 'GRAMPUS 20' was on the chase again; this time a Do217M-1 flown by Uffz Walter Scmidt of KG2 was the target. Flt Lt Singleton eventually caught up with the Do217 within 20 miles of the Dutch coast before he had to break off the chase and return to Coltishall, low on fuel.

Joe Singleton and Geoff Haslam were again in the thick of things on the night of 19 March 1944. Together with other crews of 25 Squadron, they were on readiness at the squadron dispersal at Coltishall, waiting for the scramble bell to ring. A force of 90 plus enemy bombers had been detected crossing the North Sea towards Hull and soon after, the call came through to intercept the force.

At 2055 hours, Flt Lt Singleton and Flg Off Haslam were airborne from Coltishall in their Mosquito NF.XVII, HK255. Neatishead controllers vectored them to 16,000 feet where a contact had been confirmed. At about 8000 feet the radar station at Happisburgh gave them a further vector towards twelve enemy aircraft crossing ahead of them. HK255 was fitted with the American made AI.X radar that had an arc of eight to ten miles under most conditions. At eight miles range Flg Off Haslam established a contact blip on his radar screen. Soon the Mosquito closed in on the aircraft that was visually identified as a Junkers. Flt Lt Singleton closed in dead astern and at 75 yards gave the Junkers a two to three second burst of machine gun fire. The aircraft immediately exploded and the Mosquito was forced to pull up violently to avoid the collision, however it was peppered by flying debris. The enemy aircraft fell into the sea and about 5000 feet above the water completely disintegrated.

The time of this intercept and kill was 2120 hours, some 56 miles NNE of Cromer. Shortly after, the pair was given a further vector by Happisburgh and Flg Off Haslam soon made positive contact at four to five miles range, crossing them slowly from starboard to port. The Mosquito closed in behind and slightly below the enemy aircraft before gaining visual contact at about 1500 feet. The Junkers Ju88 was unaware of the Mosquito and made no evasive manoeuvres. At 2127 hours Flt Lt Singleton took careful aim from 100 yards and fired a two-second burst. The centre part of the Ju88 exploded and the aircraft fell almost vertically into the Wash.

The Mosquito circled the burning wreckage in order for Neatishead to confirm the position, 65 miles NNE of Cromer.

Almost immediately a further contact was made at four miles range. Flg Off Haslam watched the blip crossing right to left on the screen of his AI.X scope. He directed his pilot accordingly and the Mosquito made a hard left turn to the port and followed the blip at 230 knots indicated and at a height of 16,000 feet. Unlike the previous 'sitting duck', this Junkers Ju88 put up a fight. It carried out quite a few violent manoeuvres in a vain attempt to shake off the Mosquito and changed its height several times as the fighter closed to within 1500 feet. At 2133 hours Flt Lt Singleton fired a two-second burst from 125 yards dead astern. The starboard engine of the Ju88 erupted in flames and the pilot fought bravely with his aircraft as it dived to destruction. At 600 yards range Flt Lt Singleton fired another three-second burst which caused the Ju88 to disintegrate in a blazing inferno with debris flying off in every direction. The aircraft eventually hit the sea 63 miles NNE of Cromer.

As the Mosquito levelled out both engines were running very roughly. The indicator on the port radiator dial indicated 140 degrees whilst the starboard indicated 120 degrees. Both throttles were retarded and the radiator flaps opened which succeeded in cooling both engines slightly. Happisburgh were informed of the problems and they responded quickly by giving the crew a vector before being handed over to Neatishead Ground Controllers. The Mosquito crossed the coast at 5000 feet by which time the port engine was very hot and discharging a succession of sparks. At this point Flt Lt Singleton feathered the prop. Doggedly they flew on towards Coltishall with both engines throttled back as far as it was safe to do so without losing too much height. With radiator temperatures already 140 degrees plus, the crew readied to bale out.

Flt Lt Singleton called Coltishall and asked for the lighting to be switched on so that he could see the base from the coast, thus enabling him to make a direct approach. Both engines were still just running, however, the Mosquito was gradually losing height. It was decided to make a landing without flaps and with undercarriage retracted in a vain attempt to keep the aircraft in the air long enough to reach the airfield. But at 1000 feet the starboard engine gave up the ghost and seized, bursting into flames. As the starboard engine fire extinguisher was fired, the pilot increased the power on the port engine, but in doing so this engine also seized. At 140 mph in level flight the Mosquito hit the ground. Flg Off

Haslam opened the top hatch and jumped out with Flt Lt Singleton following close on his heals. They ran 25 yards away from the Mosquito before sitting down and assessing the situation. The aircraft had come to rest at Sco Ruston, just half a mile from Coltishall.

Noticing the engines were still burning at the cylinder heads, Flt Lt Singleton climbed back into the cockpit to switch off the fuel and switches whilst at the same time looking for a fire extinguisher. He could not find the extinguisher so clambered back down and threw clods of earth onto the engines. He had the flames on the starboard engine extinguished by the time the first fire tender and ambulance reached the scene. Both Flt Lt Singleton and Flg Off Haslam were treated for slight head injuries. It was later found that the double engine failure was caused by debris from the Ju88; both glycol tanks had been holed.

That same day saw the early morning arrival of two Lancasters, ME647/AS-J of 166 Squadron, Kirmington and DS629/KO-M of 115 Squadron, Witchford. DS629 had been attacked by three fighters on its return from a raid on Frankfurt and the rear gunner, Sgt Rae, had been wounded in the foot. Its port outer engine had been set on fire and though extinguished was unserviceable, and with no power from its starboard outer engine either, the aircraft landed at Coltishall at 0235 hours.

One of the first flights at 0750 hours the next morning was an Anson of 278 Squadron on an ASR search for victims of the previous night's operations; but nothing was found. Eight Spitfires from 64 Squadron took off for a shipping reconnaissance; seeing nothing except a previously wrecked ship and two fishing boats. In the early evening another shipping reconnaissance this time by Spitfires from 611 Squadron sighted only two very small ships in Den Helder harbour.

During the day the C-in-C Air Defence of Great Britain, AM Sir Roderick Hill, visited Coltishall to congratulate Flt Lt Singleton and Flg Off Haslam on their hat-trick the previous night and a signal was received from AOC 12 Gp sending his 'heartiest congratulations on a magnificent night's work to all ranks concerned at Coltishall.'

Amid these highlights the prosecution of the war continued. On 21 February four Spitfires from 611 Squadron were launched on another shipping reconnaissance, as uneventful as the day before. In the late afternoon five Mosquitoes from 418 Squadron landed to refuel for their night operation. In the event, the main force of bombers was cancelled and only one Mosquito took off, only to return to its base at Ford with an unserviceable gyrocompass.

25 Squadron Mosquitoes were in the thick of it again on 21 March when enemy bombers attempted another raid on London. Upwards of 95 raiders crossed the Suffolk coast and headed for Cambridge where they were to turn onto a southerly heading for the capital. Part of this force acted as a diversion, crossing the coast between Felixstowe and Great Yarmouth.

Two Junkers Ju188's flying at 23,000 feet were intercepted by a Mosquito NF.XVII of 25 Squadron, flown by Flt Lt RL Davies and his navigator Flg Off B Bent. The first Ju188 was successfully despatched 35 miles out to sea south-east of Lowestoft off Dunwich. Two of the crew parachuted from the crippled raider before the aircraft disintegrated and disappeared into the cloud. The second Ju188 fired a Chandelier flare that promptly gave its position away to the circling Mosquito. This aircraft was also shot down into the sea 25 miles south-east of Southwold off Orfordness.

Another large enemy raid of 150 aircraft happened on the night of 22/23 February when eight Mosquitoes of 25 Squadron were airborne on patrol duty. During the patrol, Mosquito NF.XVII, HK283, flown by Flt Lt Ballie and Flg Off Simpson made contact with what they identified at the time as a Dornier Do217.

Although the Mosquito was held in coastal searchlights, the crew was eventually able to make visual contact with the enemy raider at 14,000 feet. After firing a two-second burst, the enemy aircraft exploded and broke up causing severe leading edge damage to the Mosquito as it flew through the debris field. Luckily, the crew were able to coax their damaged Mosquito back to Coltishall where they landed at 0025 hours.

It was not until the official reports of the interception and crash were released that it was found that the aircraft shot down was in fact a Heinkel He177/A3 and not a Dornier Do217 as first suspected.

The Heinkel, Werk No 332227/5J+QL, from the German Squadron 3KG 100, came down at Wolseyhouse Farm, Yoxford in Suffolk. Four members of the crew, Obfw W Ruppe the pilot, Uffz. G Uffz., Uffz. F Beck, Gefr. G Markgraf and Uffz E Werner were all killed, however, the rear gunner, Uffz E Imm survived. The tail section of the aircraft, with the fortunate gunner still strapped in, came down two miles from the main wreckage. It was ten hours later before a local citizen, Mr Kiddle, found the rear section of the aircraft with Uffz Imm still inside.

Whilst awaiting assistance, Mr Kiddle made the gunner as comfortable as possible and provided a mug of tea to ease the pain from two broken legs and numerous lacerations. He was eventually transported to a Military Hospital in Colchester for further treatment.

A propeller blade and boss from the He177 eventually found its way back to 25 Squadron where a brass plaque was attached bearing the names of Flt Lt Ballie and Flg Off Simpson.

Wg Cdr Wright-Boycott, the OC of 25 Squadron subsequently offered the propeller blade to the Norwich Wing of the Air Training Corps (ATC) for use as a sports trophy. The first Wing Sports Day was held at Coltishall during September 1944, with the trophy being presented to the OC 233 Squadron ATC, Flt Lt H J Nursey.

The crew of Mosquito HK283, Flt Lt Ballie and Flg Off Simpson were both killed whilst taking part in an Intruder Operation over Holland on the night of 12/13 June 1944. As a mark of respect for these individuals, the Officers and Cadets of 233 Squadron ATC were photographed with the trophy and framed copies of this event were sent to the relatives of the airmen to commemorate their service and ultimate sacrifice with the RAF.

Unfortunately, the propeller was never again competed for as a Sports Trophy. After the cessation of hostilities, the numbers of cadets joining the ATC declined and this subsequently led to the disbandment of four out of the five Norwich Squadrons. The trophy remained in the custody of 231 Squadron for the next four to six years, being used as a centrepiece for special squadron functions. As the trophy was no longer being used for its intended purpose, the Officers and Cadets of the Squadron decided that it would be a fitting gesture to return the propeller to 25 Squadron to Commemorate its formation as a full flying unit. The trophy was duly returned in January 1990.

The pink button mushrooms that grew all over the airfield were picked on a regular basis by the personnel on the dispersals around the airfield, usually around daybreak before flying started in earnest. AC2 Henry West remembers that when he was with 25 Squadron this practice was a regular occurrence. He recalls that by 'scrounging' some fat, bacon and bread from the mess, acquiring a frying pan and a little stove they we 'in business'! The daily fry-up was done in the bomb shelter close to where their Mosquitoes were parked-up at the dispersal.

Eventually the Station Commander put a stop to the mushroom harvest and illicit fry-ups after an incident early one morning nearly ended in disaster for the mushroom harvesters when a badly damaged bomber made an emergency landing at Coltishall. Henry West

vividly remembers the badly shot up aircraft coming in for its landing at the same time as many 'bods' were out on the airfield picking the button mushrooms. They all had to run for their lives as the stricken aircraft landed on its belly.

On 24/25 March, Coltishall was one of only a few airfields still open in the face of worsening weather. That night the station became host to 33 four-engined bombers, seven intruder Mosquitoes and one Wellington, as well as recovering eight 25 Squadron Mosquitoes. In all, 49 aircraft were landed in 1 hour and 43 minutes, or just over one every two minutes. Parking space was at a premium, but food and accommodation was found for all the crews.

One of the eight 25 Squadron Mosquitoes to be airborne that night was flown by Flt Lt V H Linthune DFC and Flg Off A B Cumbers DFM who had taken off from Coltishall at 2330 hours on patrol over the North Sea. Once clear of Coltishall they were handed over to GCI Neatishead and were vectored by the controllers south west at Angels 10 and when in the south of the Sector vectored east and west. Fires could be seen by the crew to the south but they patrolled for about an hour before any bandits were reported near to their position.

The prototype Heinkel He177.

Flt Lt Linthune was then ordered to proceed east ant an increased speed and was eventually vectored south on to a bandit at their height and travelling east. Contact was obtained at seven miles range 35 degrees to starboard ten degrees above, crossing to port. They increased speed to 250/260 indicated and closed in on a long stern chase. During the chase the gunsight was found to have gone unserviceable and although all the bulbs were changed the pilot was unable to make it operate.

They then saw a yellow light on the starboard side of the enemy aircraft at 2000 feet when the aircraft was 30/40 degrees to port (the light could only be seen from this position). The crew closed in to 800 feet and outlined a visual on the enemy, identifying it through night binoculars as a Junkers Ju188 as it was silhouetted against the dark sky; no exhaust glow was seen.

The Mosquito lined up on its AI Radar, got into an estimated firing position and fired a four second burst with hose-piping action from dead astern. Strikes, followed by a vivid orange-coloured explosion were observed on the starboard engine; the flames however went out. At this stage visual contact with the Junkers was lost as it peeled off to port, jinking violently and losing height. Contact was held on radar and the Mosquito gave chase at 270/300 mph for about 50 miles down to 4000 feet.

The Ju188 then flew in and out of cloud but the light on the starboard side was once again seen giving the Mosquito another chance to obtain a visual from 500 feet astern. Another four second burst was fired with hose-piping action from dead astern and strikes were seen all over the fuselage and wings. The Junkers then did a violent peel off to port; the Mosquito followed it round and it then flicked over onto its back and dived directly below them into the sea where it exploded, lighting up the low haze and cloud for two to three seconds. Flg Off Linthune fixed the position with GCI and returned to Coltishall, landing at 0130 hours. Aircrews of two Mosquitoes belonging to 418 Squadron who landed at Coltishall reported seeing an explosion on the sea in the approximate position and time that the enemy aircraft crashed.

At 0100 hours on 27 March a Lancaster BIII from 49 Squadron crash-landed at Coltishall. ND676/EA-M had taken off at 1955 hours from its base at Fiskerton for operations over Essen. During the flight the Lancaster was intercepted by a German night fighter and was badly damaged. The wireless operator, Flt Sgt M J Herd RAAF, was mortally wounded with Sgt J Hague, the aircraft's navigator being injured. Five of the crew were ordered to bale out over Swanton Morley by the captain, Plt Off A W Swinn, who then made his way to Coltishall for the crash-landing. Damage to the Lancaster was severe enough to warrant its write-off. Flt Sgt Herd was taken to Cambridge City Cemetery for burial.

In the early hours of 31 March, an aircraft swept low over the airfield at Swanton Morley, unseen by personnel on the ground but firing cannon. The air-raid sirens were sounded in Norwich and at about the same time a Lancaster was attacked above the City.

At Coltishall, a Mosquito had just landed and was taxiing towards its dispersal when it was hit by cannon fire from a Messerschmitt Me410 of II/KG51, thought to have been responsible for the attacks on Swanton Morley and the Lancaster above Norwich. The Mosquito NF.XVII of 25 Squadron had just returned from an anti-intruder patrol when it became the victim of its intended target. The port engine and both coolant systems were holed but luckily the two-man crew, Sub Lts Adams and Smith were unhurt.

In the midst of war it is pleasant to record that there was also time for relaxation in a 'Miss Coltishall' beauty contest. The winner was one LACW Peggy Swann, known as 'Swanny' a station MT driver who used to drive the aircrews of 278 ASR Squadron to their dispersals. But war was never very far away.

Coltishall was still on the receiving end of enemy intruders and on the night of 12 April, twelve such raiders had followed our bombers home. Just as a 64 Squadron Spitfire was landing at 0030 hours, with its navigation lights on, it was attacked. The pilot, Flt Sgt Maunders, felt a severe shock through the airframe of his Spitfire Vb, BL581, as it was hit by a burst of machine gun fire from an intruding Messerschmitt Me410 of II/KG51. Instinctively, Flt Sgt Maunders opened up the throttle and began to climb away from the runway to 4000ft. With his engine temperature soaring and flames and sparks pouring from beneath the cowling, the pilot rolled the stricken Spitfire over on to its back ready to bale out. BL581 was by this time in a tight left hand spin and despite the effects of gravity, Flt Sgt Maunders managed to squeeze his way out and parachute to safety as his aircraft plunged to its destruction two miles from Coltishall.

Also in the landing pattern at Coltishall during this attack was a Wellington of 415 Squadron being flown by Sqn Ldr Keillor, which was returning on one engine from a North Sea patrol. Keeping well out of the way of the intruder, the Wellington landed safely.

Many years later a group of aviation archaeologists

decided to investigate the crash site of the Spitfire. Armed with local police reports and with Ministry of Defence permission to recover the aircraft the group arrived at the farm to make some enquiries about the actual site and to seek the landowner's permission to dig. On arriving at the farm they were taken to meet the mother, Mrs Randall and when she was told of the purpose of the visit she immediately said 'you've come to find my engine.' She explained that when the RAF recovery crew had cleared up at the time of the crash they had been unable to recover the engine. They had apparently told her late husband that it was too deep to remove and that it wouldn't be in anyone's way if it were left in the crater.

She recalled that the Spitfire had crashed close to a since felled holly tree; the only problem was finding which of the tree stumps on the ditch edge was the right one. Eventually the impact point was ascertained and at a depth of about eight feet the rear of the Rolls-Royce Merlin 45 was revealed. Another witness related that the RAF team had a small crane on the site with which they had tried to haul out the engine. But by putting the wire cable around the supercharger, all they managed to do was wrench it off the engine.

Once recovered, it was found that the Merlin was in excellent condition apart from the missing supercharger; it even had all the spark plugs and leads in position. After cleaning, the damage caused by the Me410 became evident. A cannon hole was found in the side of the crankcase and a bullet hole in one of the magnetos was also revealed.

With these air attacks the air assault on England was all but over and for the rest of the war the Luftwaffe efforts were directed towards attempting to stem the Allied bomber flow over Germany.

From April to the end of 1944, photo recce Spitfire PR.IIs and PR.XIXs of 541 Squadron from Benson used Coltishall as a stepping stone for sorties over Europe. These operations were often connected with preparing for the invasion of Europe, and latterly, with bombing raids on the V-I and V-2 rocket sites.

Despite a general lessening of activity the Luftwaffe still attempted to maintain pressure on the air defences, with single attacks on bomber bases and 'hit and run' attacks on coastal towns. On 15 April a Focke Wulf Fw190 strafed the beach area near the Winterton Chain Home Link Radar Station, hitting the 'Lacon Arms' at Hemsby. On 8 May a Messerschmitt Bf109 flew along the searchlight beam at Winterton putting the light out of action with its cannon and machine guns. Further strafing attacks on Winterton took place on 6 and 8 June and a Junkers

Ju88 released some bombs near the site on 28 June.

April 1944 also saw another round of squadron comings and goings. 611 Squadron, who had been in residence since 25 September 1943 and 64 Squadron who arrived on 1 July 1943 both left Coltishall. Both Squadrons were moved to the South Coast in preparation for the D-Day landings in France.

611 Squadron became aware that they would have an important part to play in the D-Day landings towards the end of April orders came for them to move from the comforts of Coltishall to the Advanced Landing Ground (ALG) at Deanland in Sussex. There, the Squadron would be an element of 149 Airfield with 64 Squadron who had also moved from Coltishall at the same time. They were joined at Deanland by 234 Squadron from Bolt Head in the South West of England and all three squadrons lived and operated under field conditions. For 64 and 611 Squadrons a culture shock after living on a modern, purpose-built RAF Station at Coltishall.

A Spitfire PR.XIX of 541 Squadron.

The move from Coltishall happened on the 29 April for 611 Squadron when a road party left at 0900 hours, a rail party from Buxton at 1100 hours and the Spitfires departing at 1045 hours. It wasn't until the next day that the tents at Deanland became available; another shock, they had to be erected by their occupants!

Early in the morning of 17 May 1944, Mustangs of 65 Squadron flew from the ALG at Funtington in Sussex to Coltishall to refuel before the Day Ranger (Operations to engage air and ground targets within a wide but specified area) sortie to Denmark. At 0900 hours eight Mustangs left Coltishall and headed for Aalborg. Crossing the Danish coastline at Lild Strand, the formation divided into two groups in preparation for their attack on Aalborg West and Ost airfields.

Flt Sgt Rowland Williams, in Mustang FZ110/YT-S, approached Aalborg from the southwest and spotted a single-engined Junkers W34 south of Limfjord. He

North American Mustang III similiar to those operated by 65 Squadron.

attacked and hit the aircraft several times, witnessed black smoke belching from the stopped engine before he headed off to his next target. He now headed north over the westerly end of Aalborg West and attacked three Heinkel He177s flying in formation. He scored hits on one of them but had to break off as another Mustang piloted by Flt Lt Richard Barrett got in his way. Barratt in Mustang FX993 followed the formation and attacked and damaged one of the Heinkels which was on a test flight following repair. This particular aircraft returned to Aalborg West where it landed with the Mustang in pursuit.

At the same time Uffz. Siegfried Rudchinat of 10/JG11 took off in his Messerschmitt Bf109 and whilst climbing away with his wheels still down caught Flt Lt Barrett in his sights as the Mustang flew across the airfield from the direction of Limfjord. The Mustang was hit and crashed at 1147 hours killing the pilot. Barrett was laid to rest by the Germans with Full Military Honours in Frederikshavn Cemetery on 24 May 1944.

Flt Sgt Williams flew east and fired at two Junkers W34s that were approaching Aalborg West. He then saw

Junkers W34 pre-war airliner.

a Junkers Ju88A-4 flying towards the airfield at low level and opened fire at 370 yards range. The Ju88 returned fire and suddenly pulled up sharply to gain height with the crew bailing out before the aircraft crashed to the ground near the school at Try Rosenby.

The Mustang began to overheat and Flt Sgt Williams was placed in a dilemma; attempt a forced landing or bale out? He chose the former and belly landed his aircraft in a field just east of the farm 'Diget' southeast of Hjallerup at 1130 hours. He alighted from his lightly damaged Mustang and hid in a nearby ditch from where he could watch the Germans search the 'Store Kaersgaard' farm for him. He decided that it would be the best place to hide after the Germans had left. He hid in the barn for a couple of hours before he was found by Sigrid Aaen who was married to the owner of the farm 'Thorvald Aaen.' Williams was moved from the barn to the loft over a cowshed which proved to be a wise decision as the Germans returned to search the barn once again and this time they fired their guns into the hay in frustration.

In the meantime, Oblt Wilhelm Sthal of II/KG30 arrived at the place where the Mustang had landed to inspect the wreck. He found a lower entrance hatch from the Ju88 that the crew had jettisoned before bailing out blocking the radiator of the Mustang - the reason why the aircraft had overheated.

When darkness had fallen on the next evening, Rowland Williams was given a packet of sandwiches by Thorvald and his wife and left the relative safety of the farm moving in an easterly direction. The next morning he entered a barn on the farmstead of 'Little Nedergaard' just east of Stagsted and was soon contacted by the owners Anna and Peter Pedersen who, like his previous contacts, treated him very well. He left the barn early in the evening and walked to Orso where he hid in another barn belonging to the farm 'Store Logtved' owned by Anna Sofie and Knud Nyholm Callisen. It wasn't until the next morning that the family's dog found him asleep in the hay. Following breakfast he was given a map of Denmark and was warned against going further east because there was quite a few Nazi's living around Agerstead.

He decided that the best way to get to Sweden was to travel to Kobenhavn. When he reached the bridge crossing the Limfjord which was heavily guarded by Germans he caught a ride on a truck carrying workers who covered for him. In Aalborg he left the truck and started walking south and after a couple of days he arrived at 'Den Gamle Sognefoged Gard' in Bigum west of Hobro owned by Irma and Anthon Munk. They treated him well and called for Doctor Kund Repholtz to attend to his feet which were not standing up to the constant walking.

Doctor Repholtz's stepson Walter Lonsdale was an active member of the resistance and having made certain that Flt Sgt Williams was in fact a British flyer and not a German agent he was taken to the Doctor's home and taken care of. The next day Williams and Walter Lonsdale left for Hobro by bicycle. In Hobro they got on a train for Randers where the resistance would place the flyer in a safe house. It turned out that the Gestapo had made a raid on the area during the night causing the pair to move on to Aarhus where Williams was handed over to Halding and Ditte Thun who both worked at City Hall.

Later Flt Sgt Williams was moved to the house of Lasse Egebjerg where he stayed for about a week. He was then taken by train to Aalborg and handed over to another member of the resistance called Jens Lyn. A further move was made two days later when he was taken to the vicarage of Aalbaek where the Rural Dean Arne Madsen Hindsholm housed him. On the evening of 5 June Flt Sgt Williams was taken to Saeby and was taken on board the fishing vessel FN336 'Laura of Saeby' and together with other refugees sailed to Sweden with skipper Asa Jens Jensen and his assistant Henry Christensen. They arrived at Gothenberg in Sweden on the morning of 6 June and a month later he was flown to Leuchars in Scotland by a Mosquito to rejoin the RAF and 65 Squadron.

316 (Polish) Squadron, under the command of Sqn Ldr P Niemic, with their Mustang III's, were the first of the Polish Squadrons to take up residence at Coltishall in April. The Poles had exchanged their Spitfire LF.Vbs for the Mustang on the move to Coltishall and their first operation with the new type was carried out on the day of their arrival. At first, East Coast convoy patrols, 'Jim Crows' and escorts to Coastal Command Beaufighter shipping strikes were carried out. But by June, when most of the RAF in the United Kingdom was engaged in the Normandy invasion, the squadron commenced day 'Ranger' sorties over the Low Countries but this activity was soon halted in favour of anti-V1 flying bomb, or 'Diver' patrols.

The first V-1 flying bomb, more commonly known as the 'Doodlebug', to be fired against England from the launching ramps in the Pas de Calais area of France landed on Gravesend at 0418 hours on 12 June 1944. The first in East Anglia impacted at Peasenhall, Suffolk on 16 June at 0028 hours. As with any airborne intruder, defending fighters were called upon to intercept the flying bombs and Coltishall's first alert came on 1 July resulting in the destruction of a V-1 by Mustangs of 316 Squadron five miles off Lowestoft before the missile reached the coast.

On almost every day in July and August about 100 V-1s were launched against England. Of these, fighters bought down about 30 daily. Of the rest only eighteen reached East Anglia in July and thirteen in August. This assault petered out in September as the Continental launch sites were overrun by the advancing Allied troops. The squadron destroyed 50 flying bombs in July and such operations continued until 25 August when the squadron resumed its normal operations in support of the Langham Strike Wing.

Coltishall was also being used by Mosquito squadrons setting out for, or returning from long range 'Ranger' flights. On 16 May 1944 four aircraft from 418 Squadron set off for Lubeck in the afternoon and shot down a Heinkel He111. Near Zingest, a Focke Wulf Fw190 was destroyed and over Kubitzer Bay they shot down a Heinkel He177 and destroyed a Dornier Do18. Then the Mosquitoes moved to Stralsund on the Baltic where they destroyed a Heinkel He111 on the ground and blew up a Bucker Bu131. On leaving they shot down a Junkers Ju86. For all this, Sqn Ldr Cleveland was hit and he had to land in Sweden, becoming an internee.

On 29 May 1944, Wg Cdr C M Wright-Boycott DSO, CO of 25 Squadron, together with Flt Lt D W Reid, was directed by Neatishead Ground Controllers towards an enemy intruder over the North Sea. Their Mosquito soon caught up with the aircraft that was identified as a Messerschmitt Me410, 9K+KP of KG51, flown by Fw Dietrich and Ufz Schaknies.

The aircraft was returning to Germany following an intruder mission in the Cambridge area, where at 0239 hours, Dietrich attacked a Stirling I of 1657 Heavy Conversion Unit (HCU) on approach to Shepherds Grove. The captain of the Stirling, Flg Off W A C Yates and all of his crew perished when the Stirling crashed on to one of the dispersals, hitting and badly damaging a further Stirling to such an extent that it had to be scrapped. The Me410 made a mad dash to safety, but never made it as their aircraft was destroyed by a half second burst of machine gun fire from Wg Cdr Wright-Boycott's Mosquito. The Me410 crashed into the sea 50 miles off Cromer where the wreckage of their aircraft could be seen burning from 20 miles away.

Coltishall had very little to do with the Normandy landings on the 6 June 1944. However, normal air defence tasks were still being carried out over the East Coast. Reports were being received that indicated enemy aircraft were attacking three, night flying, B-24 Liberators. A single Mosquito of 25 Squadron was vectored on to a lone Messerschmitt Me410, which it successfully intercepted, and shot down into the sea 40 miles east of Southwold.

Towards the end of the day on 1 July, two Mosquito NF.XIIs of 25 Squadron were also scrambled from Coltishall to intercept an incoming V-1. However, on this particular occasion, no interception was made as the V-1 was reported to have fallen into the sea before the Mosquitoes came within striking distance.

Eight days later 25 Squadron was again detailed to operate on Anti-Diver (Code name given to operations against V-1 bombs) patrols, this time taking over the duties from 85 Squadron. The Squadron enjoyed some success the following night when six Mosquitoes were operating in pairs at two hourly intervals, patrolling between Deal and Hastings. Sqn Ldr Hoy together with his navigator, Flt Lt Dalton, were airborne at 2221hours when, off Dungeness at 9000ft a V-1 was seen approaching head-on at about 2000ft. Two short bursts from astern brought the bomb down safely into the sea. This success was followed two nights later when Flt Sgt Glossop destroyed another V-1 near Dover. On this occasion the debris from the explosion damaged the starboard engine and holed Glossop's Mosquito in several places. The damage caused a quick diversion and safe landing at Manston.

The dangers to crews attacking V-1s was further highlighted on the 16 July, when a Mosquito of 25 Squadron, crewed by Plt Off's Tait and Letchford, closed in too near to a V-1. The damaged caused by the explosion forced the pilot to crash land the Mosquito near Dover after his navigator baled out just off the coast. The navigator waded ashore and was eventually reunited with his pilot. Upon their return to Coltishall the crew laid claim to two V-1s destroyed during their eventful sortie!

WO Tadeusz 'Tadek' Szymanski was assigned to 316 (City of Warsaw) Squadron at Coltishall. On the afternoon of 12 July, he was flying a Mustang III, modified so that its engine supercharger gave it top speed at 5000 feet, which was the average height and speed that V-1 Flying Bombs could be found. Some 25 miles south of Dungeness, having already engaged a V-1 that afternoon, he engaged a second one, being vectored to the position by Ground Controllers.

His ammunition was soon out, and after being told that there was no one else around to finish the task of destroying the V-1, he moved in close formation on the bomb. He remembered that gyroscopes controlled the V-1s and that if they were turned more than 90 degrees the machine would go haywire and crash. Tadek put enough of the front part of his port wing under the wing of the V-1 and by banking sharply to starboard he hit the bomb. The V-1 lost some height and rolled to the left but gradually climbed and straightened out. By the twelfth attempt the V-1 was approaching barrage balloons near London, but by hitting it hard whilst pulling into a loop it toppled upside down, causing it to dive out of control and crash.

Other initiatives were taken to counter the V-1 menace, including one that involved the Mustangs of 316 (Polish) Squadron during the summer of 1944.

One evening, a large team of engineers arrived at the Station from Rolls Royce with special fuel, oils and various bits and pieces to be fitted to the Merlin engines on the Mustangs. The trials were to prove that the modifications and new fuel would give the engines more boost. The ground crews were warned that if the engines ran at full power for more than ten minutes the engine would be ruined and have to be changed and apart from that, even a small drop of the purple coloured fuel would blister any exposed skin!

The Spitfire IXs of 229 Squadron, commanded by Mjr N F Harrison, arrived at the Coltishall Sector from Gatwick in July 1944 and formed part of the defensive screen covering the Allied landings in Normandy. They carried out a succession of bomber escort sorties, mainly over Holland, a few shipping sweeps along the Dutch coast, and in September some armed reconnaissance sorties giving cover for 100 Gp daylight electronic

The Spitfire IX similar to those operated by 229 Squadron.

countermeasures operations. However, the role of the squadron soon changed when the first V-2 rocket landed at 1630 hours on 26 September 1944.

This event, and the increasing numbers of V-2 attacks on Norwich, heralded an offensive role for all of Coltishall's Spitfire Squadrons. Their task was now to mount armed reconnaissance raids on V-2 launching sites in and around The Hague. Mustangs of 26 Squadron were often detached in to provide scouting cover for the Spitfires, a role that they carried out well into 1945.

Flt Lt Linthune of 25 Squadron was in action once again in his Mosquito NF.XVII on 23 July, this time on an Anti-Diver patrol off the south-east coast under Sandwich GCI control. He recalled on this occasion taking off from Coltishall at 0240 hours with Flt Lt Cumbers as his Navigator to carry out the patrol. This was commenced at 0310 hours at a height of 7000 feet. The patrol was uneventful until 0440 hours when the Sandwich Controller informed him of some trade, giving a vector and telling the crew to put the nose down.

They broke cloud at 2500 to 3000 feet and saw the radar returns indicate the position of the Flying Bomb. It was then visual to the crew at 6000 feet away below the port engine on a course of 310 degrees at an estimated speed of 330 miles per hour. Flt Lt Linthune dived down to 2000 feet and opened fire with three short bursts on the V-1 from 1000 feet closing to 500 feet. Just as they fired the last burst, the fuel tank on the Flying Bomb exploded and almost immediately the ground defences

opened fire. It is believed that the warhead fell into the sea and exploded as a white flash was seen against the cloud as they climbed away from the friendly ground fire. He landed back at Coltishall at 0545 hours. The combat was witnessed by Flt Sgt Glossop, also from 25 squadron, who confirmed that the Flying Bomb blew up before the ground guns opened fire.

On his Personal Combat Report Form 'F', Flt Lt Linthune made special mention of the controlling by the Sandwich GCI who he described as being excellent. Bringing him through cloud and placing the aircraft in a very good position for the interception

Another Polish squadron, again flying the Mustang, used Coltishall as a stepping stone for what was to become a long and eventful mission. It was the early morning of 30 July 1944 that Mustangs of 315 Squadron under the command of Sqn Ldr Horbaczewski took of from Brenzett, an ALG in Kent. All the aircraft

Fighter pilots of 315 Squadron.

121

were fitted with empty droppable combat fuel tanks, an indication of what was to come. An hour after taking off from Brenzett the formation landed at Coltishall and following lunch in the Officers' Mess the crews went back to their aircraft to await the order to take-off. All the Mustangs had been refuelled. The droppable tanks were also full, holding 75 US gallons each and as with the majority of escort missions, there was nothing else to do for the crews but relax in the shade of the aircraft wings before the arduous, five hour long flight.

The Allies had received reports that the Germans were shipping uranium ore from the Bergen region of Norway, along the coast towards the Kattegat and on to Schweinemunde. The British were sending light bomber formations to sink anything that moved along the Norwegian coast.

The Germans posted one Staffel of Messerschmitt Bf109s to Stavanger to protect vital coastal traffic. The British light bombers, mainly Beaufighters of the

315 Squadron Mustang III escorting a Coastal Command Beaufighter.

Canadian squadrons, were taking heavy losses at the hands of the Luftwaffe. To counter these unacceptable losses, the RAF planners decided to surprise the Germans by sending an escort of Mustangs alongside the Canadian Beaufighters.

Finally the control tower ordered take-off and gave directions for a rendezvous with the 48 Beaufighters of five different Canadian squadrons. The main fuel tanks on the Mustang were behind the cockpit, and when escorting other aircraft above 20,000 feet or more, it was the practice to fly for 25-30 minutes on these tanks to make sure the pilots used up a certain amount of fuel. This simple tactic was to eliminate the Mustang's adverse lateral instability. However, on this occasion many of the pilots had to change to the droppable fuel tanks soon after getting airborne as the sped towards the Wash. This, as it later transpired, posed some

difficulties. In addition the formation was to lose one of the Mustangs being flown by Flg Off Czerwinski just after take-off. His aircraft developed a serious engine malfunction and he returned to Coltishall to make a safe landing.

As the formation approached the Wash, the weather began to close in with a rainy, warm frontal system from the west. The Beaufighters were soon spotted at the rendezvous location flying in close formation, low down to avoid radar detection. Sqn Ldr Horbaczewski, with his section of three Mustangs, took up position on the starboard side of the Beaufighters whilst Flt Lt Cwynar went to the port side with Flg Off Maciek Kirste taking up the rear. The weather worsened rapidly as they closed in on the Beaufighters, forming a tight formation around them. Their leader kept a steady course whilst 'hugging the waves.'

Flg Off Kirste soon came through on the radio to inform his leader that he had lost visual contact with the formation. Horbaczewski ordered him to fly back to England. It was dangerous in bad weather or whilst in clouds to accelerate in an attempt to rejoin the formation after losing contact. In fact, instead of returning he continued on to Norway, independent of his comrades. With only six aircraft left, the wingmen were ordered to go echelon port and starboard respectively, and as in cloud formation, held on grimly to the Beaufighter formation. After two hours of total concentration, suddenly it was as if the formation had flown through a curtain or passed over a cliff as they overtook the eastern edge of the frontal system. With the sun behind, the beautiful panoramic view of the Norwegian coast spread out in front of them.

A few miles from landfall, the Canadians turned to the right along the coast in search of shipping. Behind them, slightly above, Horbaczewski tucked in with his section as Flt Lt Cwynar moved to his right with his formation. They changed to main fuselage fuel tanks and waited, keenly observing the Norwegian coast and in order not to betray their position in the sun, they kept the droppable fuel tanks under their wings.

Within a few minutes, one of the leader's wingmen spotted German fighters approaching through a fjord inlet, heading straight for the Beaufighters. There were two groups of four Bf109s each and a formation of Focke-Wulf Fw190s and Messerschmitt Bf110s, leisurely carrying out a left hand turn to take up positions to attack the Canadians. Jettisoning their fuel tanks, the Mustangs attacked, with Sqn Ldr Horbaczewski going in first attacking the inner group as Ft Lt Cwynar's flight engaged the outer formation.

The Germans were taken completely by surprise at first, but having learned a few tricks in battles over France, they immediately turned towards the Polish escorts. They had been told that the Spitfire shuddered when diving, but with the aircraft approaching out of the sun, the Germans had not recognised they were Mustangs.

In the fight that followed over the Lista Peninsula, the Polish shot down seven aircraft without loss. Sqn Ldr Horbaczewski, one and half Bf109s: Flg Off Nowosielski, half a Bf109: Flt Lt Cwynar, one and a half Bf109s: Pt Off Swistun, half a Bf109: WO Jankowski, one Bf109 and one Fw190 and finally WO Idrian, one Bf110.

On 6 August, over the sea 15 miles off Hastings, Master Pilot Tadeusz Szymanski once again got into a tangle with a V-1. Having successfully intercepted and destroyed a V-1, he then came to the assistance of his wingman. His wingman, having used all of his ammunition in the engagement without causing any substantial damage to the V1, watched helplessly as the rocket continued on its programmed journey. Szymanski passed his wingman and pulled alongside the V-1, giving it a heavy swipe with his wing tip as he pulled up. Over the bomb went, and into the sea it crashed. This method of dealing with the V-1 was not 'officially' encouraged, but for some of the pilots the technique proved very successful.

Don Crosby was posted to Coltishall from the ITW at Arbroath in August 1944. Whilst on the station strength at Coltishall, he spent most of his time at Camp 'O', the Sector Headquarters at Stratton Strawless Hall. He remembered that unlike any normal outstation, the facility had no resident Officers and was effectively run by a Flt Sgt. Accommodation also proved unique with the males being billeted in the old stables whilst the WAAFs resided in the main hall itself. Apart from the 'plotters', the only other residents were the cooks.

The social life was lively, with the Heavingham Fox being the local watering hole. From the Fox, the local bobby often chased the airmen and airwomen on his bicycle as they raced back to the hall on their own bikes; without lights. The challenge was to get back, throw the bikes down and then leap into bed fully clothed ready for the Bobby and the Duty NCO to come in looking for the culprits!

Don remembered that work in the Ops Room was critical to the successful mission of the Sector, but at the same time could be really boring. For example, working in the DF Room where an eight-hour spell may or may not have an enemy 'fix.' But on the other hand, the operatives may well have found themselves directing rescue craft to a downed aircraft in the North Sea. To the other extreme, the plotting station could be frantic with plots coming in from every direction; you just didn't know from one minute to the next.

Directing Anti-Diver missions proved to be very satisfying for the plotters as they could almost see the end product of their work. Don remembers one particular event in late 1944 when they plotted some Heinkels which appeared on their screens off the Norfolk coast, releasing the deadly V-1 Doodlebugs over East Anglia towards London. As soon as their deadly cargo had been released, the bombers turned for home. But for the plotters, their next move came into play, as on identifying the tell-tail 'blip', Mosquito night-fighters would have been scrambled from Coltishall for the intercept. One night Don and his shift witnessed the demise of a Heinkel mother ship and the V-1 at the hands of a single Mosquito that they had launched once the enemy had been sighted. By the time Don left Stratton Strawless in 1945 his parent unit was Horsham St Faith as by that time Coltishall had become a Polish Unit.

A Heinkel He111 just after it releases a V-1 Flying bomb.

The 14 August 1944 was to witness the first operation by Czech fighter pilots flying from Britain over German territory. At 1450 hours, 312 Squadron took off from Coltishall to carry out a fighter sweep over the Ruhr in conjunction with the Spitfires of 229 Squadron. In the Hamburg area seven enemy aircraft were spotted but evaded the attention of the eager Czech pilots. At 1620 hours, a further two Spitfires of 312 Squadron took off from Coltishall. However, on this occasion, their task was to escort one of their fellow pilots, Flg Off Liskutin, over the last few miles back to base after he encountered engine trouble on return from the Ruhr mission.

On 25 August, the Spitfires of 312 Squadron set out once again from Coltishall on an airfield attack to Steenvyk in Holland. At 1755 hours, Flt Lt O Smik in ML296/DU-N, Flt Sgt J Konvicka in ML261/DU-P, WO V Ruprecht in ML245/DU-R and Sgt V Angetler in MK670/DU-Y set off on their operation. As no enemy aircraft were spotted on the airfield they set their sights on three trains standing in the station at Raatle. After the first attack the centre train caught fire and the flames soon spread to the other locomotives. Shortly afterwards an explosion, with smoke and debris being thrown up to 5000 feet, erupted from the railway track as the trains succumbed to the attack. The smoke pall was visible to the returning pilots a full 70 miles away. This successful mission was marred however when WO Ruprecht's Spitfire was seen to spin into the North Sea about 55 miles East of Great Yarmouth. Unfortunately no parachute was seen and the pilot's body was never recovered.

Another aircraft making use of the forward position of Coltishall in an emergency was the Mosquito NF.XII of Wg Cdr Karel Ranoszek, the OC of 307(Polish) Squadron based at Church Fenton. Wg Cdr Ranoszek was 'intruding' on 1 September when his aircraft had been repeatedly hit by a German FLAK ship north of Kiel. On his approach to Coltishall, selection of flap for the landing caused the aircraft to nearly turn over onto its back and a fast flapless landing was carried out. Later inspection of the airframe showed a large hole in the port wing where a German shell had missed the main fuel tank by inches. The groundcrew counted up to 300 bullet holes in the aircraft but neither the pilot or his navigator were harmed; the aircraft however was a write-off.

On 14 September, Spitfires of 126 Squadron from Bradwell Bay landed at Coltishall on a navigation exercise. One of the aircraft, Spitfire Mk XI NH406/5J-V, struck an air raid shelter on take off and was totally wrecked. On 20 September Mustang III, HB877 of 316 Squadron, suffered an engine cut on approach to the airfield and the aircraft was seriously damaged when the undercarriage collapsed following a heavy landing.

The night fighters of 25 Squadron were often involved in the night pursuit of flying bombs, though occasionally the target turned out to be a manned aircraft and not always one of an enemy. In the last two months of their stay at Coltishall 25 Squadron began to receive the Mosquito NF.XXX with AI Mk X radar and it was with these aircraft they saw out the war, though they departed Coltishall on 1 October 1944, though, not before losing three of their Mosquito NF.XVIIs. HK300 missing on patrol on 24 September, HK305 on 26 September when it dived into the sea during an air-to-air gunnery practice three miles off Wareham, Norfolk and HK265 the same day when an undercarriage leg jammed and the aircraft was abandoned near Coltishall.

On the 25 September, it was the turn of 25 and 409 Squadron's Mosquitoes to claim their first Heinkel He111-22, V-1 mother ships, over the North Sea. Four days later, 25 Squadron was to record further success.

On this occasion, a Mosquito NF.XVII, fitted with AI.X radar and flown by Wg Cdr L J C Mitchell and Flt Lt D

Mosquito NF.XXX of 25 Squadron.

L Cox, took off from Coltishall at 0055 hours to patrol, and hopefully intercept, anticipated raiders over the North Sea.

At 3500 feet, 40 miles east of Great Yarmouth the crew witnessed a V-1 being launched from the He111 mother ship. As Wg Cdr Mitchell dived on the enemy, 'Greyfriars' Control informed them that the He111 was also making a port turn. The Mosquito levelled off at 600 feet in a turn and Flt Lt Cox made contact with the enemy on his AI.X. The 'blip' on the radar identified the raider as being at two and a half miles range. The Mosquito descended further to 200 feet above the waves, and at 1300 feet away from the Heinkel they gained visual contact. With his night vision glasses, Flt Lt Cox confirmed the contact as a He111-22. From 400 feet dead astern, Wg Cdr Mitchell let fly with a short burst from the Mosquito's guns, scoring a direct hit. The Heinkel exploded disgorging debris and wreckage into the path of the Mosquito. Mitchell turned hard right to avoid the mortally wounded He111. Turning full circle the Mosquito crew saw the doomed bomber crash in flames into the North Sea where it burned for a few minutes before sinking.

The Mosquito and its crew returned to their dedicated patrol area and shortly afterwards saw another V-1 being launched. As he descended towards the V-1 mother ship, they informed Greyfriars Control of their position and bearing. The Ground Controllers vectored the Mosquito towards the area of the V-1 launch and eventually Flt Lt Cox obtained a 'blip' on his AI. Wg Cdr Mitchell converged on the He111 until his range closed to about one mile. He then carried out a hard port turn and closed in behind the enemy.

The Heinkel was steady on course at about 180-190 mph, totally unaware of the approaching Mosquito. The Mosquito in the mean time was now flying at 220 mph, 150 feet above the waves in pursuit. At 1500 feet range they gained visual confirmation that it was a He111 and at that second let loose with a short burst of fire from 600 feet astern. Pieces began to detach from the Heinkel as the cannon shells found their mark. At 400 feet Wg Cdr Mitchell fired another short burst into the port engine which immediately burst into flame. The Heinkel by now was in its death throes and shortly after crashed into the sea engulfed in flames. The Mosquito circled the wreckage for a while to confirm that there were no survivors. At 0615 hours they left the area having satisfied themselves that no one had survived.

A V-2 missile came close to falling on Coltishall during the evening of 29 September 1944. All V-2 missile

602 Squadron Spitfire at Coltishall with Johnnie McMahon at the controls.

attacks on the UK were recorded as Big Ben incidents; the Coltishall attack was to be Big Ben 34. At 1945 hrs the missile exploded near to the Manor House, Coltishall. Luckily the explosion caused only superficial damage to the house and minor injuries to two individuals. Scientific Observers estimated that the firing point of the missile as in a 5km area to the west of Apeldoorn/Arnhem. This estimation was probably correct, as at 1940 hrs the crew of a 125 Squadron Mosquito, on a defensive patrol over Holland, witnessed what was thought to be the launch of Big Ben 34. 20 miles West of Arnhem the crew saw a V-2 launch at a bearing of 330 degrees magnetic from their position and followed the red glow of the speeding rocket until it disappeared from sight into cloud. On return to base, at the de-briefing, their estimation of the actual launch site agreed with that of the Scientists.

The arrival of the rockets, which had been expected by the Intelligence people, provided a new task for the Spitfires of 229, 453 and 602 Squadrons. Armed reconnaissance sorties from these squadrons concentrated in searching for any evidence of V-2 launching sites in Holland, followed up with bombing attacks when they were found. This task continued well into 1945 with attached Mustang Is of 26 Squadron scouting for the Spitfires. This continued until the advancing Allied ground forces overran the launch sites. During the V-2 campaign from 25 September 1944 until 21 March 1945 thirteen rockets fell within ten miles of Coltishall, though after 12 October only one of these impacted in the area.

303 (Polish) Squadron arrived at Coltishall from Westhampnett, Sussex on 25 September 1944 equipped with Spitfire IXs. Four days after their arrival, 453 Squadron, a Canadian unit, moved in from ALG B70 at Deurne, the

Excellent informal group shot of 303 Squadron at Coltishall with the Station Commander, Gp Capt Donaldson in the centre. The Squadron OC, Sqn Ldr Drobinski is on his left.

airfield for Antwerp; they remained at Coltishall until 6 April 1945.

Coltishall was to host a number of aircraft from other units on 30 September as they prepared for Day Ranger sorties to the Continent. Amongst their number was a pair of Mosquito VIs of 418 Squadron who flew in to Coltishall early that morning from Hunsdon, Hertfordshire.

Together with a Mosquito piloted by Flt Lt Miller, Mosquito NS906/TH-W crewed by Flt Lt Robin Thomas and his navigator Flg Off Gilbert Allin, took off from Coltishall at 1423 hours for their Day Ranger to Denmark. The two Mosquitoes crossed the Danish west coast near Thorsminde and passed the airfield at Grove on the way to Aalborg where Flt Lt Miller claimed a Messerschmitt Bf109. At 1658 hours they attacked a train south east of Roskilde on the island of Sjaelland. The aircraft passed Vaerlose airfield and at 1830 hours a FLAK battery east of Kobenhaven open fire.

Shortly after, at 1835 hours, NS906 hit the tree tops of Grib Skov forest, lost a wing and crashed to the ground. The crew were thrown clear of the wreck and were found seven yards away from the remains of their aircraft. Burning fuel from the Mosquito had however spread from the ruptured fuel tanks and had consumed the bodies. It was impossible for those local people who responded to the crash to do anything other than watch in horror.

Soon German troops from the local garrison, under the command of Lt Schmidt, arrived and the area was sealed off until a detachment from the Luftwaffe airfield at Vaerlose arrived to take over. The charred remains of Flt Lt Thomas and Flg Off Allin remained where they lay until the next day while the Germans started to search the Mosquito wreck for anything of interest to the intelligence corps. Forest supervisor Arendrup and the Reverend Magelund requested that they should have the bodies handed over for proper burial. The Germans who stated that they would give the flyers a proper Christian burial with Full Military Honours denied their request; this did not happen.

In 1947 the British troops found a German report stating that Flt Lt Thomas and Flg Off Allin had been buried not far from the crash site. Subsequently, on 15 September 1947, a full search was mounted by the British close to the memorial that the local people had

A sad end for Coltishall Stafion Flight Tempest V JN794 after being struck by Mosquito XII of 307 Squadron on the 5th October 1944.

erected on 22 July 1945, but with no avail. To this day the bodies have never been found.

On 4 October a Spitfire IX, NH254 of 453 Squadron, suffered an engine failure on approach to Coltishall leading to a belly-landing a half-mile east of the airfield during which the aircraft was damaged beyond repair. Another needless accident occurred on 10 October when Mosquito NF.XVII HK514 from 29 Squadron at Hunsdon stalled while chasing a Mustang and spun into the ground one mile north west of the airfield at Skeyton. Yet another engine failure caused the loss of a Spitfire IX of 602 Squadron when it came down whilst in the circuit. MK729 was at 800 feet when the engine failed; the Spitfire crash-landing near North Walsham

In 1944 Sqn Ldr H F O'Neill was given a temporary position at Coltishall between postings as deputy to Wing Commander Flying. The Station Flight had a variety of aircraft that pilots could use for Communications flights or just to keep their flying skills in check whilst off front line duties or holding at the unit awaiting posting, as in Sqn Ldr O'Neill's case. His personal favourite was a silver coloured Tempest Mk V, JN794. A sleek aircraft all the more so because

of it's unique colour scheme. On 5 October 1944, as was the norm at that time, the Tempest was parked outside ATC ready for the next day's tasking.

Arriving at work the next morning, Sqn Ldr O'Neil was confronted by a scene of carnage with his Tempest lying in two bits close to where he had parked it the night before. Apart from this aircraft, another Tempest, EJ689, belonging to 274 Squadron was also damaged and by following the line of the wreckage the culprit was found. Attached to the side of the hangar No 1 was Mosquito XII, HK179, of 307 (Polish) Squadron from Church Fenton. Apparently the aircraft swerved on take-off and collided with the two Hawker Tempests and a lorry before coming to rest near the fire exit of the hangar. One can only imagine the conversation between Wing Commander Flying at Coltishall and his counterpart at Church Fenton!

On 7 October 1944 nine Spitfire IXFs led by Flt Lt Kedzierski of 303 squadron set off at 0620 hours on Ranger Mission No.52. Flt Lt Zmigrodzki with Flt Lt Zenon Krzeptowski, Sgt J Wierchowicz and Sgt L Bisannz made up the sorties members as Blue Section.

The formation sighted two goods trains south of Leeuwarden, one on the mainline and the other in the marshalling yards. There was also a passenger train sighted Southeast of the town. Two aircraft attacked the passenger train twice, with the train stopping on the tracks after the first attack. White smoke was seen to come from the engine at the same time as light FLAK was fired from the train's tender. The attacks on the train were made from 6000 feet with the aircraft pulling out at around 500 feet, a typical profile for a Ranger Sortie.

On landing, the Blue Section's aircraft were refuelled, rearmed and prepared for another mission; this time a Ramrod to escort Lancaster and Halifax bombers against targets in Holland. Ten Spitfires led by Flt Lt Szaposznikow DFM took off from Coltishall at 1250 hours.

The intelligence reports show it was difficult to assess the effectiveness of the mission; however, thick smoke rising above 4000 feet was sighted. The section remained over the target for another 18 minutes flying at 14,000 feet and sighted no enemy aircraft in the vicinity of the target area. There was heavy and intense FLAK over the target up to 18,000 feet with one Halifax taking a direct hit. This aircraft disintegrated, but thankfully parachutes were seen as the crew escaped. Blue Section landed back at Coltishall at 1510 hours.

Coltishall welcomed another squadron who were destined to stay at the base until April 1945. 125 (Newfoundland) Squadron arrived from Middle Wallop in Hampshire on 18 October 1944 equipped with the Mosquito NF.XVII. Whilst at Middle Wallop, the squadron were heavily involved in operations within 10 Gp Fighter Command and their move to 12 Gp saw no break in their operational activities. The day after their arrival, Flt Lt R W Leggat and Flg Off E J Midlove successfully intercepted and despatched a V-1 into the sea. Six days later, Flg Offs W A Beadle and R A Pargeter destroyed a Heinkel He111 whilst on a nocturnal 'Anti-Diver' patrol over the North Sea just after the bomber had released its deadly V-1 cargo.

Though the German flying bomb campaign launched from the Pas De Calais area had ground to a halt as the Allied troops overran the launch sites, another solution had been found by the Germans to continue waging the assault. Air launching the missiles from beneath the wings of mother aircraft, the Heinkel He 111. The flying bomb was mounted under one of the wings of the He111 and carried across the North Sea at night at low level to escape the British radars. From 100 feet the Heinkel had to climb to 1500 feet and accelerate to 150

mph to ignite the bombs pulsejet engine before it could be released about 50 miles from the East coast.

It was only in these seven minutes of climb and acceleration that the Heinkel appeared on the radar screens and only then could the patrolling night fighters be vectored onto their target. But this could only be successful in the time available if the nightfighter happened to be within 25 miles of the detected plot as it commenced its climb, and numerous standing patrols by the Coltishall night-fighters were required. The Mosquitoes soon found that they had difficulty in keeping down to the 110 mph climbing speed of the Heinkel combination and often found that they overshot whenever they were in AI contact. However, the FIU at Ford in Sussex still had a Beaufighter on strength which could maintain this slow speed and this unit was despatched to Coltishall.

Sqn Ldr Jeremy Howard-Williams of the FIU and his radar operator, Flg Off F J MacRae, flew just such a mission. On 4 November they caught a He111 in the acceleration phase passing 1500 feet at 140 mph when they shot it down. This performance was repeated on another occasion but in due course the Beaufighter was returned to Ford.

Not so fortunate was the Mosquito NF.XVII HK348 of 68 Squadron which went missing on 4 December whilst on an V-1 patrol. It was presumed that the Mosquito had fallen into the sea with the loss of WO J K Brill and Flt Sgt J H Walker.

On 5 November a successful interception was carried out by an AI equipped Mosquito NF.XIX (WM-Y) of 68 Squadron. The crew, Flt Sgt Neal and Sgt Eastwood, were given their first contact at one and half-mile range at 1000 feet above the sea. The Mosquito was at 100 feet, but they overshot the target at 160 mph and lost contact. The second contact was at two miles range, both aircraft at the same height of 500 feet, but the target commenced a climb. Flt St Neal followed the contact at a range of 1500 feet and extended the Mosquito's wheels and flaps to prevent overshooting but stayed above the stall.

In a short while the Heinkel released its V-1 flying bomb which caused Flt Sgt Neal to loose his night vision temporarily in the glare of the jet exhaust. Fortunately the mother plane flew straight and level for a while so that visual contact could be made, just as the Heinkel turned starboard for home and started a rapid descent to get below the radar cover. The Heinkel was unlucky as the Mosquito was already on the scene, with the bomber silhouetted against the cloud, lit up by the V-1s pulse jet exhaust. A two-second burst at high deflection, with both aircraft down at 900 feet above the sea, was sufficient for the destruction of the Heinkel, which was confirmed by a fishing boat in the area.

Five days later on 9 November, an AI.X equipped Mosquito NF.XVII, this time of 125 Squadron flown by Flt Lt Simcock and Flg Off N E Hoijne, callsign 'GOODWILL 27', caught another Heinkel in the launch phase. Whilst on patrol under the control of Hopton CHEL, the pilot saw what looked like a V-1 being launched, about 100 miles east of Hopton, but below their radar cover. On investigation, Flt Lt Simcock detected a Heinkel He111 at 1500 feet making a wide turn to port and descending, all illuminated by the glare of the launched flying bomb.

In a heavy rain shower below 10/10ths cloud with a base of 800 feet the Mosquito stalked the bomber as it made for home. But with more heavy weather ahead, Ft Lt Simcock decided to end the chase and open fire at 600 feet range, closing to 400 feet, by which time the Heinkel was down to 100 feet above the sea. Many strikes were seen on the bomber but apart from a large yellow flash there were no flames. Still at 100 feet the bomber then went into a steep port bank and the Mosquito was forced to break starboard to avoid a collision. By the time that Simcock had regained course there was no trace of the Heinkel in the air, or in the sea which was very rough with white caps to the waves.

On the evening of 14 November, two members of the United States Navy (USN) attached to 68 Squadron at Coltishall to gain experience in the night-fighting field were scheduled to fly together on an operational sortie. Lt Joseph Francis Black and his navigator Lt Thomas Newkirk Aitken were assigned to Mosquito NF.XVII, HK289/WM-K, call sign 'FERRO 17.' A very short time after take-off, Ground Controllers at Neatishead warned them of an approaching enemy aircraft. Lt Black turned the Mosquito onto the interception course as relayed by the ground controller, shortly afterwards Lt Aitken registered the target on his AI radar set.

Ignoring the fleeing bomber, the crew concentrated on intercepting the 'diver', despite instructions that their primary target was the launching Heinkel. In their determination to destroy the V-1, they pursued the missile back across the coast. Very soon, they were caught in the beam of a searchlight and then others converged to trap their 'victim' in a pool of light. Now the Mosquito was fast approaching an anti-aircraft gun zone, and the gunners, assuming the aircraft held within the searchlight cone to be hostile, opened up with deadly accuracy.

Residents of the Somerleyton district, NW of Lowestoft, heard the howl of the Mosquito as it plunged earthwards. Witnesses on the ground saw the aircraft, which they thought to be German, recover momentarily from its death dive then drop into a field at Home Farm, Somerleyton, setting fire to a haystack. Local village folk were soon at the scene but realised that no one could have survived the impact.

Others who risked the same AA barrage that night soon realised how lucky they were. Mosquito NF.30 MV526, crewed by Wg Cdr Mitchell and Flt Lt D L Cox of 25 Squadron, was hit forcing the crew to bale out to safety. The loss of the two Mosquitoes that night was subject to Courts of Enquiry; the outcome of the tragedy, and the lessons learned, were quickly incorporated into operational procedures.

Lts Black and Aitken were both posthumously awarded the Purple Star and Air Medal in recognition of their valour. At a service held at Somerleyton Church on 31 December 1944, a memorial was unveiled close to the scene of the tragedy.

A second USN crew, Lt Sam Peebles and Ensign Dick Grinnals were also killed in action on 22 November 1944. This left only one USN crew with 68 Squadron of those sent to Coltishall to gain night-fighting experience, Lt John W Kelly and Lt Tom Martin; both were recalled to the United States two days after the loss of Peebles and Grinnals.

125 Squadron at Coltishall were only a few miles away from the Newfoundland Army Depot that had only recently moved from Sheringham on the North Norfolk coast to Sprowston just outside Norwich. This move presented a good opportunity for the airmen of 125 Squadron to meet their fellow countrymen who were based at the Depot, either as permanent staff or as new recruits from their home province in Canada. In fact seven officers and 66 airmen from 125 Squadron and 6125 Servicing Echelon paraded on 14 December 1944 at the Sprowston Depot with their army colleagues to mark the occasion of the visit by Newfoundland's Trade Commissioner to London, Mr Davies, who took the salute at the parade.

About a week before Christmas 1944, it fell to a Newfoundland pilot to engage the enemy in one of the very few encounters by 125 Squadron during that month. In the early morning of 17 December a Mosquito piloted by Plt Off K D 'Denny' Goodyear and his navigator, Plt Off J Burrows, were patrolling under control from Hopton, a Chain Home Low Station on the Suffolk coast near Great Yarmouth, when they were vectored towards three enemy aircraft at a range of two and half to three miles. Goodyear intercepted the trio of Heinkel He111s and engaged. After about eight minutes from the time of the vector from Hopton, one of the Germans broke away from the formation to starboard; Goodyear followed. In an attempt to evade the persuing Mosquito, the Heinkel pilot began to climb and then dive, all to no avail. Shortly after 0600 hours the Mosquito crew were close enough and with daylight now on their side, to intercept and confirm the identity of the Heinkel from 1000 feet. Closing fast, Goodyear opened fire from below and astern, both he and his navigator witnessing the resulting flash from the Heinkel's starboard engine. The Heinkel dived from an altitude of 700 feet down to 300 feet in a matter of seconds and then climbed up steeply to between 5000 and 6000 feet with the Mosquito close on its tail.

At a range of 600 feet, Pt Off Goodyear could see the white glow of an intense fire burning in the engine he had hit. He opened fired again, but within seconds of this event, his Mosquito went into a violent uncontrollable spiral as the aircraft flew through the slipstream of the Heinkel and he only managed to regain control just 200 feet above the icy waters of the North Sea. So violent was the encounter that the 'G' force had broken loose a large part of the radar equipment in the nose of his Mosquito. This in turn had rendered the electrical system to his guns useless, putting them all out of commission. It would have been futile for Goodyear and his navigator to continue the pursuit; therefore they returned to Coltishall and claimed one damaged Heinkel when debriefed by the Squadron Intelligence Officer.

Between September 1944 and January 1945 a total of 881 V-1s were plotted of which 387 were destroyed, 70 of these by fighters. 26 He111 'mother ships' were also destroyed.

Fighter and fighter-bomber attacks continued on the V-2 sites in Holland throughout the latter part of 1944 with the Spitfires of 12 Gp which operated from bases in East Anglia bearing the brunt of the offensive.

The Coltishall Wing led by Wg Cdr T B Fitzgerald DFC, a New Zealander who transferred from his native air force to the RAF in June 1938, did particularly good work. In the last six weeks of the year, its pilots flew 470 sorties and dropped over 54 tons of bombs on the rocket targets.

Two other New Zealanders flew from Coltishall at that time with Wg Cdr Fitzgerald; Flt Lt B J Oliver DFC, a native of Christchurch was a Flight Commander with 602 (City of Glasgow) Squadron, and Flt Lt H J Burrett

Spitfire bombed up.

who led a flight of 229 Squadron. Their Spitfire XVIs could carry two 250-pound bombs and extra fuel tanks to operate direct from England; by refuelling at advance bases in Belgium, they could dispense with the extra tank and take twice the weight in bombs.

Targets were attacked with notable skill and precision. On 24 December bombs were hurled into a block of flats in the centre of The Hague that was being used by the Germans to accommodate V-2 launch troops. A few weeks later two factories in Holland suspected of manufacturing fuel for the rockets were successfully attacked; storage depots, railway sidings and road bridges were also frequent targets.

Missions continued for the squadron's right up to Christmas. In fact, on Christmas Eve the pilots of 229 Squadron were readying themselves for an operation over Holland. Flt Lt Bob Sergeant of 229 Squadron remembered what happened on that day.

"The day of the eve of Xmas gave us a clear sky and a hard frost on the deck. It was a perfect day to execute the Ramrod that had been hanging fire for some time. With the sun just over the horizon several V-2 trails were seen from the dispersal. This was a fitting prelude to the day's operation."

"The eleven aircraft on this mission were all carrying one 500-pound and two 250 pound bombs each and were airborne from Coltishall at 1010 hours. Wg Cdr Fitzgerald, Wing Commander Flying Coltishall Sector, and myself as his No 2, preceded them with our aircraft fitted with a long-range drop tank and two 250 pounders. The operation concerned the 'pranging' of a block of flats around a courtyard 100 yards by 80 yards lying between The Hague and Wassenar. 229 Squadron was the first on target followed by 455 and 602 Squadron at five-minute intervals. At this rate the highlight of the V-2 concerned would be on the receiving end of 16 tons of well aimed High Explosives, for the target was the HQ and billets of the 'gas main' gunmen."

"In the circuit after take-off the engine of Plt Off Bill Doidge's kite cut out completely, luckily he managed to land his dead aircraft on the extension strip outside the dispersal. The gravity of the situation was apparent when one mentions the fact that the strip in question ran at right angles to the runway in use at that time! Practically everyone on the dispersal was outside watching the squadron form up when Bill Doidge came in steep and fast. On making contact with the ground the undercarriage collapsed and the aircraft slid on its belly for approximately 100 yards. The 500-pound bomb came adrift and bounced along behind the kite with obvious malignant intent. One of the 250-pound bombs fell away too. This was the signal for general panic amongst the onlookers, the word 'bombs' together with suitable service adjectives being freely used! Most of the crowd ran away from the crash but the usual half-dozen 'mad types' ran to the rescue."

"Fortunately there was no rescuing to be done for the bombs remained silent and Bill Doidge emerged from his cockpit under his own volition, white and shaken but nevertheless the same old Bill. He immediately gave a quiet discourse concerning angle of dive etc! Meanwhile the armourers were unobtrusively removing the bits and pieces that made the bombs 'tick.'"

"Flt Sgt Wheatley also returned with engine trouble. He had three times switched to his overload tank and each time the engine cut out. This was not surprising for it had already been mentioned that 500-pound bombs were being carried instead of the overload fuel tanks!"

"The remainder of us crossed in south of Zandvoort 40 minutes after take-off at 10,000 feet. When over the Haarlem/The Hague main road we turned south and flew straight into the target. Visibility was unlimited and it was easy to identify the buildings. Wg Cdr Fitzgerald and I bombed first in a dive from 8000 to 3000 feet. We soon reformed north of the target and orbited to witness the activity of the main party. The squadron bombed at approximately 1104 hours. Strikes were seen, the southwest corner of the target receiving direct hits. Smoke and dust prevented detailed observation but small fires were seen to break out. Most of the bombs appeared to fall in a confined area from the southwest corner to the centre of the courtyard. 229 Squadron pulled out to the east of The Hague where they reformed to fly south to Landing Ground B67 at Ursel where they landed at 1140 hours."

"Meanwhile the Wing Commander and I remained over the target to watch the bombing of 453 Squadron. After a further ten minutes we flew northwest to cross out just north of The Hague at 1115 hours at an altitude of 6000 feet, landing back at Coltishall just after 1155 hours."

"Over the target a moderate amount of fairly accurate light and medium (self exploding) FLAK had been experienced. Unfortunately, 453 (RAAF) Squadron lost Spitfire SM187/FU-N when it was hit by FLAK over the target. The pilot, Flt Lt W R Bennett, baled out of his aircraft near Haguerharlot and was taken prisoner."

"It had been the intention to bomb up again when at Ursel and to attack three separate targets before returning to Coltishall. Unfortunately there were no bombs so those who took-off from Ursel had to be content with strafing these targets as they made their way home."

From January 1945 the main effort was concentrated against the wooded parkland near The Hague known as the Haagache Bosch which was the principle firing area for the V-2 rockets. Severe winter weather restricted operations for the Coltishall Wing against the V-2 targets but towards the end of February the Germans were forced to abandon The Hague woods and improvise firing facilities in the racecourse at Duindigt to the north. The fighter-bombers followed them there and practically drove them out by the middle of March. By that time the target area was heavily pitted with craters and, according to one observer, 'looked as if Bomber Command and not Fighter Command had been attacking it.' Thereafter, the German V-weapon campaign became one of retreat and abandonment, with the last few spiteful missiles being fired from open roadways.

WO Tom 'Paddy' O'Reilly arrived at Coltishall with 229 Squadron on 2 December 1944. On his arrival from Detling, the squadron was equipped with Spitfire IXs. Whilst flying from the grass airfield in Kent, Paddy and his squadron had been flying Ramrods and patrols over the 'Sword' and 'Juno' beaches in support of the D-Day invasion of Normandy.

He remembers that the squadrons role was to fly dive-bombing missions with their newly acquired Spitfire XVIs against the V-2 sites along The Hague in Holland. The Spitfire XVI could carry one 250lb bomb under each wing with either a 500lb bomb or a 90-gallon overload tank situated under the main fuselage. Their daily routine was that the Immediate Readiness Section would be scrambled to fly what was called a 'Jim Crow' (weather reconnaissance) over the potential target area. If it was clear of cloud the code "OK for Betty" would be transmitted. Alternatively, if the target area was partially covered in cloud the codeword "OK for Roderick" (overload tank) was passed. This state of

WO Tom 'Paddy' O'Reilly.

readiness was always changing and was referred to as the 'Yo-Yo' state.

'Paddy' remembers that they had a magazine called 'Tee-Emm' with the main character being the fictitious Plt Off Prune who was guilty of every possible clanger. Each month a pilot on the squadron who dropped a worthy 'clanger' was nominated to receive the Honourable Order of the Irremovable Finger. One of his colleagues, who shall remain nameless, received the award for returning to base being unable to turn over to his overload tank (which happened to be a 500lb bomb) due to the 'Yo-Yo' state being changed whilst he was airborne!

He also remembers occasionally being called upon to fly a bomber escort mission and on one occasion he remembers witnessing a visiting squadron's aircraft crashing that killed the pilot. On that same evening whilst awaiting the signal to start engines for a bomber escort mission, his thoughts dwelt for a short while on what might have happened, and for a short moment, he wished he was somewhere else.

The majority of the time the squadron flew from Coltishall but occasionally from the two satellite airfields of Matlaske and Ludham with most of the sorties being dive-bombing over Holland. However, as the front line moved rapidly through Europe, 'Paddy' often landed between missions at either Ursel or Maldagen in Belgium to refuel and re-arm before continuing with further attacks. This might happen five or six times on a single day before returning to Coltishall.

Whilst at Coltishall he acquired an Armstrong Siddeley 21-hp car from a local undertaker which had been up on blocks due to petrol rationing. Tom had no such problem as he could supplement his meagre ration with the occasional top-up of 100-Octane aviation fuel! His, and as it was to pass, the squadron's adopted Armstrong was to become known as 'Paddy's Hearse!

Often the operational squadrons at Coltishall were called upon to assist 278 ASR Squadron in SAR missions and on 5 December 303 (Polish) Squadron were called upon to assist in the search for a downed Mosquito. Flt Lt Krzeptowski and Flt Sgt Z Bartkowiak took off from Coltishall at 1055 hours for a search area on a bearing of 100 degrees then 140 degrees to rendezvous over the area where the Mosquito was known to have lost contact. Despite continuing their search 15 miles west of Westhoofd off the Dutch Coast nothing was found

Spitfire IX MA158 of 303 Squadron about to depart a snow covered Coltishall on a SAR sortie.

and due to fuel priority, they were recalled by the controller and landed back at 1330 hours with nothing found.

The weather throughout December was rather poor with rain, thick fog and winds plaguing much of the United Kingdom. Thick fog was covering most of the country on the 21 December except for Coltishall and its sister airfields in Norfolk, which were still relatively clear, at least until the early morning hours of the 22 December. Due to the fog, many heavy bombers were being diverted to Norfolk airfields from their home bases in Lincolnshire and Yorkshire, Coltishall being no exception.

Several Lancasters, with Canadian crews, diverted to Coltishall from their base in Lincolnshire. Out of the goodness of their hearts, the Officers Mess brought out their stocks of Gin and Scotch for the benefit of their gallant Bomber Command comrades. These valuable stocks of spirits had been saved for months, ready for the Xmas celebrations. Yet in three short days, the bomber crews had drunk the lot! After the bombers took off for their own bases, and Christmas celebrations, the Coltishall lads were left spiritless.

Sgt Polilejko in MH910 of 303 Squadron.

Chapter 7

THE WAR ENDS - CHANGING TIMES

The closing months of the war saw no let-up for East Anglia's most active airfield. Apart from the resident Spitfires, the Mosquito Mk 30s of 307 (Polish) Squadron together with the Mustangs of 303 and 316 (Polish) Squadrons were also present. 303 Squadron was under the command of Sqn Ldr B H Drobinski DFC. His squadron, the most famous of the Polish squadrons, was formed in August 1940 and quickly brought into action during the Battle of Britain. 'Gandi' Drobinski was no stranger to Coltishall having flown from the base in 1943.

It was from Coltishall in November 1943 that his luck nearly ran out. His Spitfire was hit by 'Flak' whilst patrolling near The Hague. He commented; "I felt as though I had been hit by a hammer on my head. I blacked out, plummeted from 23,000ft to about 5000ft, and I was spinning. I felt whistling wind going through my hood, I saw the propeller turning as my Spitfire was diving toward the sea, but I couldn't hear any engine noise. I was down to 1000ft before I managed to regain control and restart the engine. I told myself that if I could climb to 30,000ft and be halfway between Holland and England over 110 miles of North Sea, I could glide to the English Coast if the engine should fail. I had no R/T and no wingman. With freezing hands and shaking knees I gained height, and after what seemed to be an eternity I landed back at Coltishall."

After landing he found a piece of shrapnel had carved a furrow through the top of his leather helmet, there was a gaping hole in the fuselage and the controls had been very nearly shot away!

The V-2 menace continued to cause major problems for the Eastern Counties and South Coast. A special radar watch, with a series of stations stretching from Lowestoft to Dover, aimed at pinpointing rockets launched from the European mainland was introduced. At one point it was planned to increase the Anti-Aircraft barrage along the coastal

The long serving OC of 303 Squadron, Sqn Ldr B H Drobinski DFC.

strip in a desperate attempt to blast the rockets out of the sky as they passed overhead. This futile gesture was fortunately shelved owing to the possibility of general alarm and damage to property that would have been caused by the falling shrapnel. Apart from that, the speed and trajectory of the missile in flight would have made it impossible to intercept.

During the short lifespan of Walter Dornberger and Dr Wernher von Braun's brainchild, a total of 1115 V-2 rockets landed on Great Britain.

Over this period a series of intensive search and destroy operations were evolved by the RAF against the V-2 sites. One of these was carried out on 14 February 1945 by 'A' Flight of 602 (City of Glasgow) Squadron. Flt Lt Raymond Baxter led a flight of Spitfire XVIs against a target situated in wooded dunes a few miles north of The Hague. After attacking the site several times, the airmen were somewhat taken aback to see, rising out of the woods, a V-2 rocket. Flt Sgt 'Cupid' Love saw the rocket in his line of sight and blasted off a short burst of cannon fire to no effect. As Flt Lt Baxter later recounted - "Thank goodness he didn't hit anything vital, or we wouldn't be here today to tell the tale."

The V-2 menace wasn't the only thing that occupied the minds of the attacking and defending forces, as the V-1 Doodlebugs were still a cause for concern.

To improve the UK coastal radar cover and increase the time that the Heinkel He111/V1 combine was visible, a trial was conducted using a Wellington equipped with centimetric Air Surface Vessel (ASV) radar, the Wellington flying at about 100 feet and the accompanying night-fighter half a mile astern at 50 feet. Thus any target detected by the bomber would be silhouetted against the sky rather than be lost in the sea returns on the Mosquito's radar. The Wellington then flew a racetrack 30 miles off the Dutch coast across the routes flown by the Heinkels.

On 2 January 1945 Sqn Ldr Howard-Williams of the FIU, in a Mosquito

NF.XXX with AI Mk X radar, patrolled behind the Wellington but no targets materialised. Three nights later in a Beaufighter equipped with the older AI Mk VIII, Howard-Williams was scrambled from Coltishall, but this time the Wellington's ASV radar was unserviceable. A week later, they were more successful, but this time the trial was operating out of Manston in Kent.

On 5 January, a Mosquito NF.XVII, HK296 of 68 Squadron, flown by WO A R Brooking and Plt Off R B Finn, reported a similar success. Unfortunately, after a brief message reporting their success, nothing more was heard from this crew.

On 10 January 603 (City of Edinburgh) Squadron under the command of Sqn Ldr Tommy Rigler DFC DFM and equipped with Spitfire XVIs arrived at Coltishall. They operated from both Coltishall and Ludham escorting Beaufighters on shipping strikes and also to indulge in dive-bombing attacks on the Continent, principally on V-2 sites. Holland provided most of the squadron's targets and as the spring weather opened up so the squadron became busier; in fact, on 10 March it dropped 20,000lbs of bombs, a record that many light-bomber squadrons could be proud of. Ten days later came their busiest day with 56,000lbs of bombs being dropped on enemy targets. This was in effect the squadron's last offensive activities for it soon transferred to withdrawal escort duties as targets were now beyond the range of UK based Spitfire units. 603 Squadron's short association with the Coltishall Sector ended when they transferred to Turnhouse on 28 April 1945.

On the same day as the arrival of 603 Squadron, 125 Squadron lost a Mosquito NF.XVII, HK238, when it had engine trouble, followed by a diversion to the nearby USAAF base at Rackheath where the aircraft belly-landed without injury to the crew. Another 'arrival' at Coltishall was P-51D Mustang 44-14628 of the 504th FS of the 339th FG which had been escorting American bombers on their return from Germany. The aircraft force-landed at Coltishall on 16 February but the pilot, Lt Gilbert G Cohen, was unhurt.

Occasional intruder nuisance raids were still making their presence felt. On the evening of 22 February 1945, an enemy intruder shot down a four-engined aircraft near Bury St Edmunds. Two Mosquitoes of 125 Squadron flying practice interceptions were vectored immediately to the area, but were unsuccessful in making contact. That same day Mosquito NF.XVII HK262 from the squadron went missing whilst on an evening interception sortie. WO M Woodthorpe and Flt Sgt D J Long were both lost.

Raymond Baxter (Second Left) and pilots of 602 Squadron.

The 26 February 1945 saw 30 year old Sgt Clemens Prusank in Spitfire IX MA814/RF-Q of 303 Squadron take off from Coltishall for the USAAF base at Harrington near Kettering to carry out some fighter affiliation with the B-24 Liberators of the 801st BG based there. However, a burst tyre on landing prevented Prusank from returning to Coltishall that day and an overnight stop was authorised

Douglas D Walker, a young American GI based at Harrington recounted that it was a sunny morning on 27 February when he and a couple of friends were strolling to the mess to have some lunch. They noticed the Spitfire close to where they were; this in itself was not a surprise as many English pilots landed at the base to purchase American cigarettes and candy bars.

He remembered the pilot hopping out of his aircraft and making his way towards the group where he stopped for a chat - Walker and his pals invited him to join them for lunch. During lunch, they learned how, as a child he fled from the Germans when they had invaded his country

Sqn Ldr Tom Rigler DFC, DFM, OC 603 Squadron.

and how he had waited impatiently to be old enough to join the Free Polish Air Force so that he could gain revenge for what they had done to his beloved Poland.

As they parted company he told the group to watch him as he was going to perform a 'fly over' and show them some 'fancy flying.'

True to his word, shortly after take-off they watched as he skilfully threw his Spitfire into a series of aerobatic manoeuvres until, in horror, they witnessed him dip too low to the ground. A wing ripped through a tree, and then parts of the aircraft smashed into the Finance Hut before burying themselves in a large crater left by the impact.

Douglas Walker and his mates ran with disbelief toward the mangled burning wreckage, but soon realised the hopelessness of the situation. They all watched helplessly as the poor pilot was pronounced dead by the medics at the site. Fortunately, the loss of life was limited as the two men normally in the Finance Hut were in the Mess Hall when the accident happened. Sgt Clemens Prusank, born 22 November 1914, was laid to rest in the Newark-on-Trent Cemetery with full military honours.

On the 3 March 1945 a Court of Inquiry was convened at Coltishall by order of the AOC 12 Gp. Flt Lt C J Maltby of 124 Squadron was appointed President of the Inquiry. There were a total of seven witnesses called to attend the court to investigate the circumstances behind the accident. They included Sqn Ldr Drobrinski, 303 Squadron's CO and Flt Lt Socha, the Commander of 'B' Flight who authorised Sgt Prusak to fly the sortie on that fateful day. From the American base at Harrington witnesses included Lt R F Hook, the Flying Control Officer, Capt P M Silkbaken the Group's Communications Officer and 1st Lt J M Dushman the Group's Assistant Photo Officer. Lt Hook was on duty at the time and recalled that the Spitfire took off at 1421 hours on runway 30. Following this, the tower lost sight of him and did not witness the crash. Capt Silkbaken stated that it was approximately 1440 hours on 27 February 1945 that he came out of the Ops Block and noticed a Spitfire aircraft doing aerobatic rolls at about 300 feet altitude.

These aerobatics were being conducted to the south of his position and after completing the last roll it disappeared from sight behind the Headquarters building that was directly in front of him. His first thoughts we that he intended to 'buzz' the Headquarters area. However, a split second later he heard a blinding roar and crash as the Spitfire went streaking across the ground in a northerly direction approximately thirty or forty yards to his right. The wreckage burst into flames immediately and came to rest approximately 100 yards north of the HQ building.

Other witnesses painted a similar picture detailing the last moments of the Spitfire. For the President of the Inquiry the cause of the accident was because of the pilot flying illegally at low altitude; striking a tree that he intended to clear resulting in the loss of control. Gp Capt A H Donaldson, the Station Commander at Coltishall, concurred with Flt Lt Maltby's findings, adding: "it was obvious that this NCO was lacking in flying discipline having been court-martialled on 28 August 1943 for low-flying."

On 2 March 1945, WO A Rutecki of 303 Squadron led a flight of four Spitfire IXF's on an Armed Reconnaissance and Bombing Mission. The flight took off at 1240 hours and crossing the coast between The Hague and Katwijk at 10,000 feet and flew straight to the target area. They attacked their target, a railway marshalling yard, in steep dives NE/SW from 5000 feet down to 1000 feet using cannon and machine guns.

After the attack the Spitfires turned inland and climbed to 6000 feet as they flew along the main road between The Hague and Gouda. At the next target area, they found a stationary electric train with three carriages containing troops. Two Spitfires attacked the train and about a dozen troops were seen to scatter and take cover as the middle carriage became engulfed in flames. Three aircraft attacked the power generation plant for the railway line at the same time as the strikes on the train - another successful attack with strikes being confirmed against the plant.

The section had been over the target area from 1316 to 1350 hours, and on leaving, they crossed the coast at Kateijk where they were subjected to moderate FLAK from the town. On their way home, they saw six or seven barges facing out to sea, but following the intense battle over the previous few minutes they did not have the ammunition to carry out any attacks on the barges. They landed back at Coltishall at 1430 hours.

The night of 3/4 March 1945 was a night of considerable enemy intruder activity and this was possibly the reason for Mosquito NF.XXX, NT365 of 68 Squadron being shot down by friendly anti-aircraft fire at 2019 hours. The crew baled out to safety and their aircraft, which was hit twice by AA fire, crashed to the rear of Grange Farm, Martham, approximately 14 miles from Coltishall.

At 0359 hours on 4 March, another Mosquito NF.XXX, NT357, of 68 Squadron, flown by Flg Off Aust and Halestrap, was returning to Coltishall after an uneventful anti-intruder patrol. Over the airfield an engine failed and the undercarriage refused to lower. Flg Off Aust attempted to fly another circuit of the airfield but sadly failed with the aircraft crashing in flames at Horstead Hall, tragically, both occupants were killed.

Between midnight and 0400 hours that morning, the RAF lost a total of four aircraft over Norfolk in addition to the two 68 Squadron Mosquitoes.

At 0010 hours Mosquito XIX, MM640/VI-H of 169 Squadron from Great Massingham crashed at The Avenue, Lodge Farm, Buxton. The Mosquito was on return from a bomber support and intruder patrol sortie over Kamen and was itself the victim of a German Junkers Ju88 night-fighter on a late-war intruder operation code-named 'Gisela.'

It is believed that the Mosquito broke up in mid-air before crashing. Both the crewmembers, Canadian pilot Sqn Ldr V J Fenwick and his Navigator/Radar Operator, Flg Off J W Pierce were killed. At the time of the loss, the Mosquito was being diverted from Great Massingham to Coltishall owing to the presence of enemy night-fighters over the area.

At 0025 hours Halifax III, NA107/T of 171 Squadron based at North Creake, was shot down by a night intruder and crashed, on return from a 'Mandrel' sortie, at Walnut Tree Farm, South Lopham. Of the eight crew, five baled out and the remaining three, including the pilot, Sqn Ldr P C Proctor, were injured.

A further Halifax, LV255/G of 192 Squadron from Foulsham, also fell to a night fighter, the aircraft crashing at Ainlies Farm, Fulmodeston, at 0059 hours. Flg Off R G Todd baled out prior to the crash that cost the lives of five crew members. The pilot, Flg Off F D Roberts and his Mid-Upper Gunner, Sgt K A Sutcliffe, were both seriously injured.

The last, (not counting the Mosquito crash at 0359 hours) and most costly of that morning's incidents over Norfolk happened at 0118 hours when Lancaster I, NG325/CA-H of 189 Squadron dived into the ground near East Rudham Railway Station. Flg Off S J Reid, pilot, Sgt F N Benson, Sgt R W McCormack, Flg Off J T Nelson, Sgt M R Bullock, Flg Off H G Harrison and Flt Sgt G F Coley were all killed.

The next day, 125 Squadron lost another Mosquito NF.XVII when the undercarriage of HK287/VA-S jammed and the aircraft belly-landed on the airfield.

Another feeble attack was made at Coltishall on 17 March when an enemy intruder passed low over the airfield firing at a lorry and dropping anti-personnel bombs on the south-west corner of the airfield damaging two cottages. It then dropped bombs on Coltishall village before escaping unscathed out over the coast of Great Yarmouth before midnight.

With the dearth of enemy aircraft over East Anglia the day fighters were becoming more involved in sweeps over the Continent. On one of these armed reconnaissance missions Spitfire XVI SM405 of 603 Squadron was hit by FLAK over Wassanaar on 9 March. The pilot WO Godfrey, managed to fly his badly damaged aircraft back to Ludham where the Spitfire was declared damaged beyond repair (DBR).

A week later, on 17 March SM473/XT-H from the same squadron at Ludham was lost with its pilot, WO J D Green RAAF. Green was on an armed reconnaissance sweep when the aircraft was hit by FLAK during an attack on vehicles near Barandrecht. The same day Spitfire SM388 from 602 (City of Glasgow) Squadron had its engine cut out on take-off from Ludham and the undercarriage was raised to stop, the aircraft becoming damaged beyond repair in the resulting crash.

The next day another Spitfire XVI SM233/FU-P, being flown by Flg Off E W Tonkin from 453 Squadron was hit by FLAK whilst attacking a train junction and had to force-land near Gouda in Holland. The uninjured pilot managed to evade capture and was soon reunited with his squadron. On 20 March, 453 Squadron lost another Spitfire XVI when SM188 suffered engine failure causing its pilot Flg Off N Marsh to abandon the aircraft six miles off Scheveningham, Holland; the aircraft had been hit by FLAK near Noordwijk. Flg Off Marsh was taken prisoner when he was rescued from his dinghy by a German Red Cross boat.

On 22 March B-24 Liberator 42-51150 of the 579th BS, 392nd BG, from Wendling caught fire in the air and crash-landed at Horstead whilst returning from a raid on Germany. Eight crewmen were killed though four baled out before the crash. Two days later, two Spitfire XVIs, both from 603 Squadron, collided in mid-air whilst in formation near Sea Palling. SM396 came down on the foreshore and TB396 crashed two miles north-west of Sea Palling. The next day, on 25 March, Coltishall had a narrow escape when two B-24 Liberators, 42-50804 "Pleasant Surprise II" and 42-5134 from the Horsham St Faith based 752nd BS of the 458th BG collided in cloud whilst assembling for a raid. Four crew-members managed to bale out of the doomed bombers before impact with the ground. One of the aircraft came down at Skeyton just a mile or so away from Coltishall. This collision cost the lives of sixteen men.

The final march-past of Polish Air Force personnel at Coltishall. AM Sir James Robb takes the salute.

The last enemy aircraft to be destroyed near Britain in World War II, believed to have been a Junkers Ju88 from an unidentified Luftwaffe unit, was shot down in flames into the sea ten miles NE of Cromer. A Mosquito XXX from 125 'Newfoundland' Squadron intercepted and shot down the Ju88 on 20 March 1945. Gun camera film from Mosquito, NT450/VA-T, flown by Flt Lt 'Ken' Kennedy and Flg Off Tony Morgan confirmed the claim.

The last wartime change of Station Commander took place on 25 May 1945 when Gp Capt Donaldson left Coltishall to be replaced by Gp Capt P H Dunn DFC who was to see the airfield pass from war to peace.

So ended, the Second World War in Europe. The wartime claims total for Coltishall was 207 enemy aircraft destroyed, 48 probably destroyed and over 100 damaged. However, there was a debit-score as well. The most visible being the tiny cemetery at the threshold of Runway 22. Here, 56 white gravestones record just part of the human sacrifice that accompanied the unfolding story of a station at war

A fitting tribute to the wartime exploits of the station was a visit on 27 July 1945 by Gp Capt Douglas Bader when he returned to Coltishall to put a Spitfire through its paces; the first time he had flown since his capture and release from Colditz Castle. Bader had a great affinity with Coltishall and felt it most appropriate to make this historic flight from the Station where he commanded 242 (Canadian) Squadron back in 1940.

The usual jockeying of Mosquito, Spitfire and Mustang squadrons continued until the base settled down to its peacetime role as a night fighter base. Even in the safety of peacetime operations, flying accidents were still in evidence. 316 Squadron lost a Mustang, HB944, on 4 July 1945 when the aircraft crashed just beyond the East Side of the airfield. WO Tomaszuski failed to bale out of his doomed aircraft and perished in the crash.

On 8 August 1945 changes were made in the organisation, which in turn designated the Station RAF Coltishall (Polish), under the command of Gp Capt T H Polski. This change was to see the transfer of personnel from 133 Polish Wing HQ, 306, 309 and 315 Squadrons in addition to 6306, 6309 and 6315 (Polish) Servicing Echelons. The new units quickly settled in to their new surrounds and by the end of the year had attended Armament Practice Camps (APC) at Bradwell Bay and Fairwood Common.

One of the Polish pilots who remembered those times was Tony Brent, a Warrant Officer with 306 Squadron. He recalls moving from Andrews Field in Essex to Coltishall in May 1945 and as soon as they arrived, hardly having time to unpack, they flew to South Wales for Gunnery School. They took off from Coltishall as a Wing, three squadrons, and made their way down to Fairwood Common. This particular destination had always proved interesting, as the airfield possessed quite a few peculiarities that kept the pilots on their toes; the runway undulating laterally as well as up and down being just one!

Gunnery School for the 'old sweats' proved a bit of a chore, especially the ground lectures, but as soon as this phase had been completed, the air-to-air firing against a target being towed 500 yards behind a target tug proved more interesting. The Poles were always renowned for their calm and relaxed attitude in this discipline and in turn, this always resulted in good results for the students.

The Gunnery School was also used to teach the relatively new art of rocket firing and quite naturally the Poles were interested in this method of warfare. To help the instructors passed on the knowledge required, a dissected example of such a weapon was on display in the main lecture room.

Opinions were divided amongst the Polish pilots as to the effectiveness of the rocket, and more importantly for those present, whether the dissected rocket on display was real or just a wooden mock-up. To prove their scepticism on the latter count, one of the pilots placed the burning end of his cigarette on the 'wooden' propellant of the sectioned rocket. It wasn't long before smoke and the flames took hold. Tony escaped without witnessing the result; as did the other 25 students, but the answer as to whether it was a real example or just a wooden mock-up was there for all to see! As Tony put it, a little amusing incident!

Back at Coltishall, the days were taken up with normal peacetime training and formation flying. But at the same

309 (Polish) Squadron was one of three units which made up 133 Polish Wing at Coltishall in August 1945.

time, AOC 12 Gp, known to the Polish and many others as 'Mr Officious', dictated that weekends should start at 1200 hours on a Saturday in his Group. To ensure this was enforced, he used to insist that all squadrons within the Group flew on a Saturday morning over his Headquarters at Watnall near Nottingham; a spectacle that he viewed from his balcony. He dictated how the formations were to be flown, where squadrons would be located in the mass formation, at what time and at what height. Sometimes he would insist on twelve aircraft flying line-abreast, a very difficult formation to fly, especially for the pilots flying the inner slot where in a turn their aircraft could stall.

All the pilots knew that once they returned to their respective bases, a detailed critique of the formation would be waiting. If the AOC was not pleased, the Squadron commanders certainly knew about it! If this were the case, the following week would see formation practices to ensure that the AOC was not disappointed again!

The Polish took to their new surroundings and neighbours with the same tenacity and enthusiasm that they had shown throughout their involvement in the war. They were self-sufficient in virtually all respects,

including the establishment of their own butchers shop in a Nissen hut close to Black Cottage. The Poles turned the hut into a well-established and efficient operation, and for many families scattered around the base, the extra meat provided by the Poles in exchange for other goods provided a popular addition to their meagre rations. After a while the local farmers wondered why some of their prime bullocks, pigs and sheep suddenly went missing, prompting quite a few visits by the local constabulary to the station! Of course, nothing was found, as the efficiency of the butchers shop during their nocturnal operations proved watertight!

As 1945 gave way to 1946, there was a distinct drop in the number of flying hours allocated to the Polish Wing at Coltishall. That said non-official flying hours could be accumulated by squadron pilots by visiting friends or relations on training sorties where there was no need to refuel due to the distances involved.

Tony Brent managed to maintain his flying hours by visiting friends in Lancaster, using the airfield at Manchester as his drop-off point. After one such sortie he reported to ATC to advise them of his departure time when he was asked if he could 'do something special' for those at the airfield. On this occasion he elected to fly a slow roll after raising his undercarriage, positioning himself for the manoeuvre over the airfield, he began to roll. However, as he passed through the inverted, the roll stopped and Tony was unable to right himself. Only a few seconds had elapsed when he realised that the greatcoat he was wearing to keep warm had tangled in the controls. Quickly he released the offending clothing and made his way back to Coltishall - a timely wake-up call!

The practice of using the Mustangs as taxis soon came to a halt following a visit by one of the pilots to a friend in Dorset. Soon after his weekend jaunt, a bill found its way back to the squadron at Coltishall for fuel and landing fees. This from an airfield, now in civilian hands, that had been used by the squadron only weeks before as an RAF airfield!

Things were getting quite desperate for the pilots at Coltishall as flying decreased to almost nothing; in fact sometimes with no flying for weeks on end. The pilots were losing their touch; their reactions were beginning to wane. Tony himself found to his cost on two occasions the need for constant practice. Luckily, both incidents ended without loss or damage, but the same could not be said for other unfortunates who perished in aircraft accidents; some mechanical, but others due to lack of flying practice.

Tony's first incident happened during take-off in a tight formation. The plan was to get airborne and turn back over the airfield before flying off on the sortie over the North Sea. As the formation turn was completed just after take-off, his Mustang's Packard-Merlin engine stopped. Tony advised his formation leader that he was going to attempt a forced landing back at Coltishall. At the time, the Glycol coolant began to boil over resulting in his windscreen being totally covered apart from a small section in the lower left-hand corner. It was through this miniscule gap that he saw the boundary fence of the airfield pass under his wing. Loosing height, he dropped the undercarriage and lowered the flaps just before touching down.

Tony thought at that moment that it was a good thing that he was in a Mustang and not in a Spitfire as the undercarriage came down immediately. From a previous experience, he remembered that a Spitfire's main undercarriage legs would often come down independently before locking into place. If he had been flying a Spitfire on this occasion, the result may have ended in tragedy.

The second incident also happened in the climb, this time however at 12,000 feet. On this occasion, smoke in the cockpit was the cause for concern. Even on pure oxygen, Tony could smell the acrid smoke even though there were no signs of fire. Realising he had to do something quickly he broke formation and headed back to Coltishall. On the way back he reported his emergency before switching off all his non-essential electrics; almost immediately the smell disappeared.

He landed safely back at Coltishall and only then thought of what might have happened if he had been forced to parachute out to safety having never 'taken to the silk' in his flying career. He was proud of that fact, having only come close whilst based at Abingdon. It was there that he worked very hard to avoid a 300-foot jump from a tethered balloon at the end of a five-day course. He, like many others, avoided the wish of the Chief Flying Instructor (CFI) that all students should experience a parachute jump, even though it was from a balloon. Reports from those who had experienced both the balloon jump and then abandoned their aircraft for real, said that it was much worse from the balloon; for Tony, that was justification enough not to have felt guilty about 'working his ticket' to avoid the balloon at Abingdon!

Tony Brent remained in the RAF post-war and retired as a Flight Lieutenant from the Metropolitan Communications Flight at Northolt in September 1967. During the post-war years, he served with Flying Training Command, Transport Command, Far East Command and on the staff of the RAF College at Cranwell.

During 1946 the Mustang equipped squadrons maintained their flying and exercise commitments, and were joined at Coltishall in April 1946 by 318 Squadron. They arrived from Treviso, Italy with their Spitfire IXs. In December, the Squadrons started to deliver their Spitfires and Mustangs to 33 Maintenance Unit (MU) at Lyneham, and on the 16 December the personnel of the now disbanded 318 Squadron moved to Framlingham, a Polish Resettlement Corps camp.

The last two Mustangs were delivered to Lyneham from Coltishall on the 22 December. Gp Capt A K Gabszewic DSO DFC, the last Polish Station Commander, handed Coltishall back to the RAF on 13 February 1947 when a formal parade was held to mark the end of Polish occupancy. AM Sir James Robb, AOC-C Fighter Command took the salute on behalf of a grateful nation. By March, all of the Polish Squadrons and their personnel had all departed the Station.

Polskie Sily Powietrzne was the name of the Polish Air Forces (PAF) formed in France and the United Kingdom during World War II. The core of the Polish air units

From left to right: Sqn Ldr Berezecki, OC 318 Sqn, Sqn Ldr T Andersz, OC 306 Squadron, Station Commander, Gp Capt A K Gabszewic DSO DFC, Sqn Ldr H Pietrzak DFC, OC 309 Squadron and unknown Polish officer. Possibly Sqn Ldr J Siekierski, OC 315 Squadron.

fighting alongside the allies were experienced veterans of the Invasion of Poland in 1939 and made a large contribution to the victory in the Battle of Britain; they also took part in most of the wartime air operations.

After the joint Nazi-Soviet victory in the Invasion of Poland, a large part of both the flying and technical personnel of the PAF were evacuated to Romania and Hungary, from where hundreds of them found their way to France. There, in accordance with the Franco-Polish Military Alliance of 1921 and the amendments of 1939, Polish Air units were to be re-created. However, the France headquarters was hesitant in creating large Polish air units and instead most of the Polish pilots were attached to small units called 'keys.' Only one large unit was formed, the Groupe de Chasse Polonaise 1/145 stationed at Mions airfield. It was not until 18 May 1940 that the squadron received their first aircraft and even then, they were the obsolete Caudron C714 fighters. After only 23 sorties the bad opinion of the aircraft was confirmed by the front-line pilots; it was seriously underpowered and was no match for the enemy fighters of the time. Because of that, only a week after it was introduced into service with the Polish elements, the French Minister of war, Guy la Chambre, ordered all of the C714s to be withdrawn. That said, since the French authorities had no other aircraft to offer, the Polish pilots ignored the order

and continued to use the type. Although hopelessly outdated compared to the Messerschmitt Bf109s they faced, the Polish pilots nevertheless scored twelve confirmed and three unconfirmed victories in three battles between 8 and 11 June, losing nine in the air and nine more on the ground.

After the collapse of France in 1940, large parts of the PAFs were withdrawn to the United Kingdom, but the British command did not want to accept the independence and sovereignty of the Polish forces and initially Poles were only admitted to RAF units. Because of that, the majority of the much more experienced Polish pilots had to wait in training centres; learning English procedures and language at the same time as the RAF were suffering heavy losses due to the lack of experience of their pilots. However, on 11 June 1940, the Polish and British authorities that finally allowed for the creation of two bomber squadrons and a training centre to be part of the Royal Air Force signed a preliminary agreement.

Initially the Polish airmen were compelled to wear British uniforms, fly British flags and pass two oaths, one to the Polish government and the other to King George VI. However, after the evacuation of the British Expeditionary Force (BEF) from Dunkirk and the arrival of hundreds of Polish airmen from France, the situation changed. On 5 August, the British government

Polish pilots prepare to deliver their Mustangs to Lyneham on the 22 December 1946.

finally accepted the PAF as a sovereign, allied military formation. From then on, the airmen were part of the Polish Army, flying to their own standards and wearing British uniforms but with Polish insignia. Although still subordinate to British command, the Polish units were directly subordinate to a Polish Inspector of the Air Forces, who in turn was responsible to the Polish government. On 6 April 1944, a further agreement was reached and the PAFs in Great Britain came under Polish command, this time without the attachment of RAF officers.

Without doubt, the PAF had a significant impact on Coltishall throughout the war years and during the time the station was in Polish hands. The respect and gratitude of the British towards the Poles during those dark days cannot be underestimated.

Following the departure of the Polish elements, several Mosquito NF.36s of 141 Squadron arrived at the station on 17 June 1946, with 23 Squadron, another Mosquito NF.36 equipped unit, arriving on 23 January 1947. With these two squadrons in residence, Coltishall now became a Night Fighter Station within 12 Gp of Fighter Command.

Apart from their night fighting Commitments, the squadrons also took on daily Meteorological Flights. These flights were made up to 30,000 feet and were carried out by both squadrons on monthly rotation continuing well into 1950.

The night of 23/24 September saw the Station rescue

The last Polish parade and handover back to RAF control on the 13th February 1947.

and medical crews in full action when they were called upon to assist at the scene of a crash at Mautby. Avro Lincoln RE373, of 97 Squadron from Hemswell, crashed with a crew of seven plus two passengers. Unfortunately, the rescue effort was in vain as all the occupants of the bomber had perished in the accident.

Ken Ovenden, then a young SAC MT Fitter, remembered his first encounter with life at Coltishall following his posting from Hethel in late 1946 when that base closed.

Our new MT Section at Coltishall was run by Plt Off Smith and Flt Sgt Richardson, both ex Hethel. We had a lot of work to do at that time as the PAF had just departed Coltishall and most of the vehicles were left unserviceable. Following an intensive build up for our section and the rest of the base, it was time for flying to start. Unfortunately, it was found that there were no serviceable Fire Tenders to allow the planned flying to begin. Flt Sgt Richardson remembered that there were two unserviceable tenders at Hethel and I was despatched back to try and make one out of the two; the deadline was Monday, this was the Friday.

My team managed the near impossible by swapping an engine from one tender to the other. Our journey back to Coltishall along the back roads of Norfolk also proved eventful, as a terrific storm had descended on us during the journey. It was so bad that we had to stop at Horsham St Faith as trees were coming down all over the place. Eventually we arrived back at Coltishall at 1300 hours with flying Commencing at 1400 hours, a close shave!

Life then went on normally until the bad winter of 1947/48. All of the personnel that could be, were sent home. However, we poor MT lads were left to drive the snowploughs. At that time, there were still German POWs awaiting repatriation and eight were assigned to me to help clear the roads around the Coltishall area to allow GPs and the emergency services to travel around as best they could. It was a long six weeks for all. We often travelled to Norwich through snow banks eight to ten feet high. It became so bad around the country that those who were stuck at home were ordered to report to their local Labour Exchange for snow clearing duties.

Wg Cdr Stanford-Tuck was the CO at Coltishall and every Monday morning he took-off in his Spitfire for an hour or so to keep his hand in. He was liked by all

and unlike many post-war stations moral was always good. It may have been the CO, but then again it could just have been Coltishall.'

LAC Peter Hall, a Flight Line Mechanic (Airframes) was posted to Coltishall in December 1947 and served for about 18 months on 23, 141 and 264 Squadrons maintaining their Mosquito NF.36s.

Prior to being called-up, Peter worked for Marshall's Flying School at Cambridge where he was employed in the engineering section, modifying Mosquitoes for night flying duties by replacing the clear windscreens with amber or green screens to assist the crews with their new nocturnal duties. On arrival at his new squadron at Coltishall, he was able to witness at first hand the work he had carried out on the actual aircraft he helped modify at Cambridge a couple of months before.

At that time, there were many ex-wartime pilots based at Coltishall who were waiting for de-mob. To keep their flying skills honed, just in case they chose to stay in the RAF, these particular pilots were given the role of test flying the Mosquitoes just out of servicing or following repair. Peter flew on many occasions recording technical data and performance parameters with these pilots and on more than one occasion, when the situation permitted, experienced the thrill of simulated air combat against the Meteors based at Horsham St Faith. Even then, against the superior performance of the jet-powered Meteor, the Mosquito held its own and often out-flew the jets especially when in the hands of an experienced pilot.

On 16 November 1948, Peter was part of the see-off crew for one of the Station Flight 'Hacks', Mosquito T.3 VT614. At the controls was the Station Commander, Wg Cdr Dennis Spotswood, with the Station Adjutant in the navigator's seat.

Following all the pre-flight checks, the aircraft left the parking slot and made its way to the in-use runway, 10-28; a grass strip that dissected the airfield from the main camp to the south of No 1 Hangar across to the north of the bomb dump. This particular runway had a hump almost in the middle of its 1400-yard length and had the reputation of catching unwary pilots out, especially if the aircraft's speed at that point was insufficient. Effectively, the aircraft would be launched at that point regardless of speed. The result at best would be a bounce back to earth before becoming airborne, at worst a crash.

A pair of Mosquito NF.36s prepare for take-off from Coltishall.

VT614, the all yellow Mosquito, known by all as the 'yellow peril', started it take off run, gradually gaining speed along the grass runway. Through the corner of his eye Peter saw the yellow machine pass behind a building before, to his horror, it reappeared cart-wheeling across the airfield. The Station Commander and his Adjutant fell foul of the dreaded hump and bounced with insufficient speed to remain airborne; they were now just along for the ride. Luckily, both he and his passenger escaped the disaster with only minor injuries, extracting themselves from the mangled wreckage just before the rescue crews arrived at the scene.

Tall tales were often the norm for the ground crews whilst waiting for aircraft to return from their training sorties. For Peter Hall and those on shift during a quiet, peaceful and warm summer night awaiting the return of three Mosquitoes the tales of a certain Cpl Jacobs had them all listening with a little scepticism.

Cpl Jacobs regaled them with tales that he had heard whilst serving in Ireland about the 'Leprechauns and de little people' with much emphasis on the spooky bits, when first one and then the second of their Mosquitoes came home and their ground crews went off to bed leaving Cpl Jacobs and Peter to await the third aircraft. Eventually it landed, taxied up to the hangar and whilst the Corporal did his thing in the hangar, Peter went out to marshall and 'chock' the aircraft before fitting the crew ladder to allow the pilot and navigator to climb out.

In the distance a church bell rang three times, the Merlin engines were ticking and clicking as they began to cool, the noises of the night were deafening.

The instruments, dials, levers and switches etc were luminous and when Peter got into the cockpit everything was winking and blinking at him. Undeterred by stories of 'de little people' Peter got on with the job of fitting the bobbin that secured the rudder pedals. As he leant over the pilot's seat, 'someone' blew into his left ear! He shot up, looked around and saw nothing. "Don't be daft", he said to himself, there are no such things as Leprechauns or ghosts so he proceeded with the operation again and the same thing happened.

At this point, he switched on every light so that he could find and solve the problem. The pilot's Sutton Harness left leg strap carried the radio jack plug and oxygen supply tube and in his haste to get to bed the pilot had not turned off the oxygen completely so it was coming out in puffs every ten seconds or so. Having solved the problem without sight of a Leprechaun Peter closed the aircraft and went off to bed!

On 13 January 1948, the Coltishall Mosquito Wing was brought up to full strength with the arrival from Wittering of 264 Squadron, also equipped with the Mosquito NF.36. The wing continued with its normal training schedules that included the annual detachment to Acklington for the APC. As with 23 and 141 Squadrons, 264 Squadron also began to take their share of the daily Met Flights.

Flying accidents, as in the war years were not uncommon. Both 23 and 141 Squadrons suffered accidents in May 1948. The accident involving one of 141 Squadron's Mosquitoes, RK995, happened on 25 May 1948. The Mosquito collided in mid-air with Percival Proctor C.4 NP349/TS-M, of 4 Radio School (RS) from Swanton Morley. The collision resulted in the

Wg Cdr Stanford-Tuck served as Coltishalls Station Commander during 1947 and 1948.

tragic loss of the Mosquito and its crew, however, the Proctor managed to struggle back to Swanton Morley.

23 Squadron suffered an accident with one of their Mosquitoes, RK974, at Coltishall on the same day when the aircraft overshot the airfield on a night landing.

An unusual method of bird control was started at Coltishall when the Experimental Falcon Scheme was established on the Station in 1948 under the command of Flt Sgt Viles. A veteran of 26-years service, the Flight Sgt flew on Coastal Command aircraft as an Air Gunner during WWII and was an accomplished boxer at squadron and RAF level. Prior to taking up this very unusual post, Flt Sgt Viles attended the RAF Falconry School to learn about his new charges.

His falcons were trained to climb to anything up to 1000 feet and wait until they located a bird flock close to the aircraft operating areas. The raptor would then swoop down into the flock and a feathered battle would Commence. In addition to Coltishall, Horsham St Faith, Cottesmore, Syerston and Waterbeach all had Falcon Units, and whilst the Falcon Schemes at these units were considered a 100% success, they discontinued in 1949, as they were deemed too expensive to sustain. Today, Falcon Units can be found at many military and civil airfields throughout the world as they are assessed as being the most successful and cost effective method of bird control.

For many of the young airmen at Coltishall on National Service, sports and other pastimes were a welcome relief from their primary duties. For Ralph Stone, an Aircraft Electrician at Coltishall during 1948/9, sport was his

escape. Being a bit of a sportsman and organiser, Ralph soon became a member of the Coltishall Sports and Entertainments Committee.

Table Tennis was one of the popular pastimes of the day, and with the Coltishall team boasting an exceptional player from nearby Neatishead, Ralph took it upon himself to organise a 'do' that brought the World Doubles Table Tennis Champions to the base.

Just four days before the 1949 World Championships at Wembley, the World Champions, Victor Barna and Vera Dace, gave some entertaining and skilful demonstration matches to the members of the station during their visit. Coltishall's team member Fred Viner and another RAF player, Johnny Leach, who was at the time an England International, provided the opposition.

Johnny Leach eventually went on to become World Table Tennis Champion, the only RAF person to have held this honour. For Coltishall's star player Fred Viner, following his National Service, he eventually became the Head of the BBC TV's Sportsview programme prior to emigrating to Canada where sadly he died in 1995.

For Ralph Stone his National Service soon came to an end, but his 'coup' in attracting World Champions to Coltishall is his most treasured memory. Post war he settled in Norwich where he continued to use his sporting and organisational prowess as the Founder Member and Chairman of the 'Harford Tornadoes - Anglia Floodlight Youth Football League.'

During August, the Wing carried out practice interceptions on USAF B-29 Superfortress bombers at altitudes up to 30,000ft. These practice engagements led to further liaisons with USAF B-29 Squadrons. In January 1949, the Station carried out affiliation exercises with four B-29s from Marham and visits were exchanged between the aircrew of the two Stations. On each occasion, aircrew from Coltishall flew as observers in the B-29s.

February 1949 saw three accidents in quick succession, one with fatal results. On 1 February, Mosquito NF.36 RL244, of 23 Squadron, crashed one mile West of Coltishall during a night flying test. The second, and fatal incident, involved Plt Off Cox of 264 Squadron. Whilst flying his Mosquito NF.36 RL143, over the Paston Ranges on an air-sea firing practice on 4 February; he lost control and crashed into the sea. The last of the months accidents happened on 14 February when Mosquito NF.36 RL249/YP-E, of 23 Squadron crashed into woods adjacent to the airfield just after take-off. For the pilot of RL249, Flt Lt Dickie Colbourne, the night take off was supposed to be a normal practice gunnery sortie over the Wash on the Holbeach ranges. However, a couple of minutes after take-off, both Merlin engines on his Mosquito failed causing him to make a crash-landing in a plantation of trees four miles WSW of the airfield. The aircraft suffered severe damage, immediately catching fire. Having survived the crash, Dickie Colbourne, dazed and disorientated, called out to his navigator, Navigator 2 William Kirby; a reply appeared to come from outside.

Colbourne's legs were trapped, but as the fire intensified, he finally got clear of the aircraft and smothered the flames on his clothing. On failing to find the navigator, Flt Lt Colbourne realised that he must still be trapped in the wreckage. Despite his injuries, and knowing the aircraft was loaded with high explosive ammunition, he climbed back into the burning wreckage and found the navigator trapped in the aircraft's shattered nose. At this point the aircraft exploded. Although severely burned, Colbourne freed his comrade, dragging him clear and stripping him of his burning clothing. Despite his own

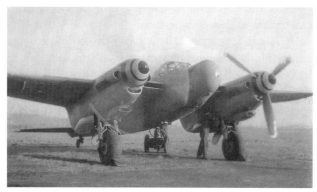

Mosquito NF.36 of 264 Squadron.

severe injuries, he refused to be assisted into a vehicle for transfer to hospital until he was satisfied that his navigator was receiving medical attention. Throughout the difficult journey to hospital, Colbourne remained conscious and offered encouragement to his navigator. Both men were placed on the 'dangerously injured' list; sadly, William Kirby died 20 hours later. Flt Lt Dickie Colbourne remained in hospital for many months.

For his bravery, Colbourne was awarded the George Medal. The citation for which concluded: "Colbourne showed great fortitude, personal courage and devotion to duty under conditions of extreme danger when he was in considerable pain from his own injuries."

During the war years, Dickie Colbourne had flown Walrus amphibians from Coltishall whilst with 278 Squadron, helping to rescue downed airmen from the sea around East Anglia and along the English Channel.

November 1949 saw the Mosquito wing move north

to Church Fenton, whilst the main runways and station infrastructure were upgraded prior to their return in September 1950. An asphalt runway had been constructed and a Control Tower, a Villa Type, was built to the pattern 2328/39. By November, the squadrons had settled back into their 'upgraded' surrounds. They participated in exercises with the FAA that entailed the despatch of four 'Hookah' equipped aircraft to RNAS Culdrose.

Prior to graduating from his basic National Service Officer Training at Kirton-in-Lindsay in Lincolnshire, Off Cdt Philip Smith asked his Course Commander if, assuming he graduated, he could be posted to RAF Germany. "What on earth do you want to go to Germany for?" He replied that he had always liked the German language and would like to be able to learn it. At the completion of his training, having come ninth out of 72 graduates, the Course Commander said: "Ah, Smith - you wanted to go to Germany" - "Yes Sir." - "Well you're going to Norfolk" - "Very Good Sir!" Thus, Philip Smith came to Coltishall; far from being disappointed given that it was a famous Fighter Station.

On arrival at Coltishall on 25 January 1950 as a newly Commissioned Pilot Officer in the Education Branch, he learned that the resident squadrons had been detached to Church Fenton in Yorkshire because the Coltishall runways had still consisted of grass overlaid with steel mesh. This had been fine for the relatively lightweight Spitfires and Hurricanes but would have been quite incapable of receiving the Venoms and Meteors with which the Station was to be re-equipped. Thus the Station had a relatively skeletal complement. Wasting little time in settling into his new home, he soon acquired several inventories and became the Rugby Officer (an interesting secondary duty having never played the game in his life and being of small stature), Sailing Officer and a couple of other portfolios to ensure he was not under-employed!

He remembered detecting a transitional mood in both the Commissioned and non-Commissioned ranks on the Station. The majority of the Officers had seen wartime service as also many of the NCOs. One noticed a certain disillusionment amongst many; "Should I have taken De-Mob?" Visions of a settled married life in 'Civvy Street', coupled with the absence of operational priorities and, worst of all in the eyes of a good few, the re-introduction of promotion exams, morale not being improved when some failed to clear this 'academic hurdle' as they saw it. A few became disillusioned with the Service they had known.

But on the other side of the coin it seemed that quite

a few who had taken the De-Mob suit felt the loss of the sense of camaraderie in the Services, and the Air Ministry ran a very successful campaign aimed at the more skilled Other Ranks, in which an Aircraft Fitter was pictured working on a mainframe with the caption, "Gingers Back" on the poster. Quite a few did come back.

Another factor was that wartime had seen accelerated promotion for the more successful officers, some reaching Wing Commander and even Group Captain by the age of 26; these were known as 'War Substantive' ranks and come the advent of peace time, officers had to return to lower rank. One detected on the Working Tunic sleeves and Battle Dress epaulettes the marks left by a removed ring. Philip readily understood that it must have been hard to have one's 'Scrambled Egg' removed from one's peak if one had been a Groupie. It was usually one rank down, but there were instances where Group Captains reverted to Squadron Leader, but not at Coltishall.

Operationally, the Flying Wing at Coltishall felt that their colleagues at Horsham St Faith were far better provided in that all of St Faith's squadrons were equipped with the shiny new Gloster Meteors. Whereas Coltishall's pilots felt they was very much limping along with there ageing Mosquito Night-Fighters. The serviceability of the Mosquito was a constant headache for the Engineering Wing and a permanent source of frustrations for the pilots and navigators. So much so that there was always tremendous competition amongst the squadrons to be given the daily 'Met Flight' where one Mosquito would carry out a slow circling climb to 32,000 feet.

Philip Smith remembered many of the Coltishall personalities of that time with affection. On his arrival the Station Commander was Gp Capt Denis Spotswood. He recalled him as very tall, somewhat austere, and broody, sporting a large 'Yard Broom' moustache that a more junior officer would probably have been told to smarten up! On the occasion of the monthly Mess

23 Squadron Mosquitoes parade for the AOCs Inspection in 1947.

However, set against this undercurrent of morale decline, in some cases the operational tension was rekindled by the onset of the so-called Cold War, because incredible as it may seem after Nazi Germany's ambitions of territorial acquisition, if not Western World domination, it was genuinely thought by the Governments of America and Britain in particular, that Russia was not without its own agenda of world influence and its own military might was in no way doubted.

This situation resulted in a major challenge for East Anglia's two main Fighter Stations; Horsham St Faith and Coltishall. These two crucial arms in the British Defence capability were charged with conducting a 24 hour Defence Alertness Programme, dubbed Exercise EMPEROR, where Coltishall was concerned with maintaining a Dusk to Dawn defence with Horsham St Faith maintaining the Dawn to Dusk defence; there was no mistaking that the threat from Russia was considered to be very real.

Night, a different Denis Spotswood emerged. After the formal dinner and the games of 'High Cockalorum', various other games and 'recitations', the CO was known to ask the Adjutant, "Adj, who's retired to bed?" The unfortunate Adjutant had perforce to divide his loyalties and name one or two whose faces were no longer to be seen. Denis Spotswood would proceed to grab one of the fire extinguishers in the corridor, enter the unfortunate officer's bedroom and give him a dowsing. The next morning, the CO resumed his austere demeanour!

Philip also remembers that there was a very portly Squadron Leader by the name of Groom, whose branch he could not recall. They learned one day that he had been posted off to the Middle East. The next morning he appeared at breakfast, somewhat to their surprise; they enquired cheerily 'Not Off Yet Sir?', 'No', he rather grumpily replied. It transpired that he was being taken to Norwich Thorpe Station in one of the Camp's 'Tilly'

Mosquito NF.36 RL243 parked on a Coltishall dispersal minus any squadron markings. The aircraft actually served with 23, 141 and 264 Squadrons.

(Utility) Hillmans. His WAAF driver took one of the sharper bends in the road and concentrating on the road as she was, did not notice that whilst going around the bend, Sqn Ldr Groom's centrifugal force carried him straight on, the car's door having swung open and there were no seatbelts in those days! A little further on she realised she was driving on her own and returned to find her passenger climbing out of a ditch! This caused rather a hoot in the MT Section!

At some stage they saw the arrival of a non-denominational Padre, a Squadron Leader who Philip remembered as MacDonald, though he was not certain. He had rarely met a more 'Commercial' operator, still less for a man of the cloth! He was always talking in the Mess, he appeared to know everything about everything and like Oscar Wilde's description of a person; "Knew the price of everything but the value of nothing." This Padre would buy and sell most things, cameras, cars you name it!

On one rewarding occasion, there was a Station Hockey match and Philip found himself drafted into a team on the premise of 'you can play hockey can't you Smithy?' with no time to reply. He was playing right half, the Padre was at centre forward (of course!). Philips team was moving forward and he produced a really good hard pass forward, and it so happened with no intent that his pass planted itself firmly between the buttocks of the Padre! There was a resounding cry from the touchline spectators of "Up the Padres Chuff!" Philip hastened to add that he was convulsed with Mirth!

The use of radar was spreading and Coltishall's night-flyers were being introduced to Ground Control Approach (GCA) guidance where they would be beamed in to the runway by a chequered Black and White Caravan on the end of the runway. The crews were meant to fly 'blind' and touch down on the caravan's instructions. One evening at dinner in the mess, Philip and his colleagues heard a Mosquitoes engines particularly loud and low. The next morning one of the pilots said to Flg Off Parkinson, "Was that you coming in low over the mess last evening Podge?" he replied "Yes", "the caravan guys told me I was slap over the runway and I could touch down; bloody good thing I looked over the side of the cockpit, or I should have landed in the middle of you lot eating your Shepherd's Pie!" Gradually the GCA technique improved at Coltishall!

Cars and transport were a challenge for those at Coltishall during this period. The mention of 'Johnnie' Gibson's new car was a good point for Philip to mention the virtual absence of cars on the camp. Very, very few members of the Officers' Mess had a car because (a) pay was such that they were still considered a luxury and (b) new cars were just not generally available unless one had 'contacts.' A Car Auction Mart had begun to develop at Mile Cross in the City but then spares were seldom available. He remembered Gibson's Minx as being the only car regularly parked outside the mess.

Flg Off Goose, an Engineering Officer had them all cooing with envy as he had got to know that a very elderly living locally had lost he husband and she could not drive. She sold her two-seat Rolls Royce Saloon of 1926 vintage to Goose. It was a beauty, complete with running board and a set of chromium-plated spanners housed in a velvet lined box. Apparently he paid very little for his Rolls!

There was no bus service to Norwich and on Saturdays a farmer from nearby Buxton/Lammas would clear the floor of his lorry, set up a number of wooden 'changing-room' type benches and put on a 'Liberty Boat' run to the City. He would charge sixpence a time, dropping his passengers off at Bishop's Palace Road, next to the Maid's Head Hotel, at around 1400 hours. His charabanc would be there to set off back to Buxton at 1830 hours; the return fare was included in the sixpence!

Having mentioned that cars could mostly not be afforded, the pay of a Squadron Leader in 1950 was 33/6d a day (£1.65 roughly in today's currency) and Philips pay as a Pilot Officer was 10/6d a day (51 pence) from which he had to pay six shillings (30 pence) a day mess charges. On becoming a Flying Officer his pay rose to 13/6d a day (about 67 pence).

The following article appeared in the second edition of the new Station Magazine 'Gen Only', the magazine for Coltishall, Neatishead and the outstations at Stoke Holy Cross, West Beckham, Hopton and High Street. The magazine was the brainchild of Philip Smith who became editor of the publication for only two editions prior to his posting to Stoke Holy Cross. The name given to the magazine was taken from the only 'Girlie' magazine published at the time, a very innocuous magazine called 'Men Only.'

Mosquito NF.36 RL193 pictured at Church Fenton on the 15 September 1950, prior to returning to Coltishall.

CHRONICLES OF THE YEAR 2100A.D.

The Polar Cap of the 1950-51 Ice Age is receding in Norfolk, and archaeologists are very interested in a strange community-dwelling which has been revealed about twelve miles north of Norwich, and about centrally placed between those three permanent landmarks: The Anchor, the Goat and the Horseshoes. It is believed that it may be the second Pompeii, for it has buildings mostly of rectangular shape, and there are four very large buildings with roofs like a vast furrowed potato field. There are strange machines inside these large buildings, but it is understood on good authority that, although it may be possible for them to fly after the fashion of our commonplace Saucers, they are seldom known to leave the ground.

It is also rumoured that this community is inhabited by creatures resembling human beings, and they are clad in blue. Professor Axel Baring, the renowned demographist, says they are obviously of Pagan descent, because at intervals they perform a ceremonial rite on a large square space outside the nodal point of

Coltishall's Villa Type Control Tower in the 1950's.

the camp (a building with symbols N.A.A.F.I above the entrance). On the square during such rites, there are various Totem Poles with flags on them, and the largest one is in the centre of the poles has a large flag with a striking design on it. These Blue Men, reminiscent of Boadicea's tribes, tramp around the square, or at other times, stand very still. A body of Minstrels, also dressed in blue, stand on one side of the square and make loud cacophonous noises with various instruments which, with a stretch of the imagination, may be called musical. Professor Bearing has not yet concluded whether the tramping of the Blue Men is a sign of anger at the noises made by the Minstrels, or whether in fact the noises are supposed to accompany the tramping.

The nodal point mentioned earlier in this chronicle - the place called N.A.A.F.I - is the scene of two major activities. Once a week, the Blue Men are assembled and are given small metal discs and pieces of paper for which they seem grateful. This occasion is another ritual. Each Blue Man goes up to the table behind which sit four very wise men, and he raises his hand as if to strike the wise men; but he then drops his hand down to his side. He is then given discs and pieces of paper - known as Akkers - and he bites the discs and holds the paper up to the light and then turns away, retaining his exuberant happiness until he has left the N.A.A.F.I. The rest of the week the Blue Men spend these Akkers in the N.A.A.F.I, where a form of edible rock is sold. This fact is one of great interest to archaeologists too.

The symbol N.A.A.F.I, after much graphological research, has been deciphered as meaning "Never Ask Again For Inything." Their position above the entrance is without doubt the origin of the verse "Five for the symbols at your door" in one of our oldest folk songs.

RAF Coltishall Officers Mess, circa 1950.

Until further research is made, no other details of the camp can be given except, perhaps, that a guess can be made of its name. From the scant records to which access has been possible, it would seem that this community goes under the name of Coltishall.

9 March 1951 saw a visit from the C-in-C Fighter Command, AM Sir Basil Embry KBE CB DSO DFC AFC. During his visit, Sir Basil briefed aircrew on the future of the night fighter/all weather force, a prelude to the arrival of the Jets. Sir Basil Embry became the C-in-C of Fighter Command in April 1949 at a time when Russia was warming up the Cold War. By sealing off Berlin, it was clear that the actual threat to the United Kingdom could come in a matter of hours. The question was asked at that time - "Could Fighter Command cope?" Possibly, but with Korea and the surprise arrival there of the Mig-15 in large numbers it was realised that whilst Russia's Mig-15 and America's F-86 Sabre were in large-scale production, they were both vastly superior to the best fighter the UK had, the Meteor F.8. At that time there was not even a successor to the Meteor flying in prototype form.

This was not the only cause for disquiet. The whole control and reporting system was still very much as it was at the close of the war yet aircraft speeds had risen by 50 per cent and the need for early interception was transparently a greater necessity. Therefore a complete overhaul and modernisation of the radar and control systems was set in motion, with the target of bringing the lapsed time before first warning of approaching enemy aircraft and interception to the minimum. But such a task also took time, and the early fifties were an anxious time for the occupants in authority at Bentley Priory, Fighter Command's Headquarters.

As proven in WWII, the restless and brilliant leader, impatient of opposition, was just the man to set the command bustling into its new task and to persuade his governing masters of the necessity to order some F-86 Sabres from America. This would bridge the gap in supersonic defence until British industry was allowed and able to get its new aircraft into service.

Sir Basil ensured that his visit to the Station laid out his vision for Fighter Command's future and the role that Coltishall would have in this transition and implementation. Those who were present and listened to Sir Basil's briefing were under no illusion that Fighter Command would be on a different level in the near future.

23 Squadron 'Mossies' at Coltishall in 1951.

Chapter 8

THE JET AGE

Coltishall said farewell to a trusted stalwart during 1951. The Mosquito first saw action at Coltishall during WWII and ever since that time had served with various squadrons in many forms. The Mosquito NF.36s of 141 Squadron left in September of that year and were dispersed to other Mosquito-equipped squadrons and to various MUs for scrapping. In fact, the aircrew of 141 Squadron remained away from the base whilst they re-equipped and trained on their new aircraft, the Armstrong Whitworth Meteor NF.11.

23 Squadron, under the command of Sqn Ldr V S H Duclos, saw a similar change in 1951 when their Mosquito NF.36's gradually gave way to the de Havilland Vampire NF.10. It was not until May 1952, and under the command of a new squadron boss, Sqn Ldr A J Jacomb-Hood, that 23 Squadron ended a ten-year affinity with the 'Wooden Wonder.'

Many National Servicemen who hailed from Norfolk found themselves posted to Stations in their native County including Coltishall. One such individual was posted to the Station following his induction at Padgate and his basic training at Melksham. AC2 Derek 'Del-Boy' Pells was employed as an Admin Orderly working initially in the cookhouse washing plates and cutlery. Over the years, and on promotion to AC1 Class, Derek was employed as a cook for the remainder of his National Service.

Many memories came flooding back in September 2005 when he paid a nostalgic visit to his old Station. One of his most vivid was the time when he and two colleagues received 14 days 'jankers' for sleeping-in after a heavy session at the Three Horse Shoes Inn at Scottow. The three concerned were rostered to be on duty in the cookhouse at 0400 hours on Christmas Day, the morning after their extended drinking session at the pub! By the time Cpl Pickles, the shift NCO, woke the sleeping beauties from their bunks armed with a bundle of F.252's (Charge Sheets), it was 0700 hours and the WAAF's on their shift had already prepared and were serving breakfast to the Christmas Day workers.

As with many RAF Stations at that time, Coltishall had its own pig farm on the far side of the airfield. The pigs, fed on swill from the messes on the Station, provided some of the best pork in the county with the whole process from breeding to slaughter and then butchery

One of the last photos of 23 Squadron 'Mossies' at Coltishall.

being done on the base. Much of this process was carried out by those who worked in the cookhouse, including Derek.

Derek was also a drummer in the Station Band and at one time he was the only male musician. This arrangement proved to be headline news for many of the local and even a couple of national newspapers. Time off for band practice often caused conflict with his primary duties especially with staff shortages in the cookhouse. However, the prestige to the Station of the band ensured his absence; as he put it: "being the only male, I had an important role to play!"

He finished his National Service in 1953 and returned to his native Norwich where he worked as a painter and decorator, continuing with his apprenticeship that had been interrupted by his call-up and as with many who initially dreaded the thought of National Service, he often wished that he had remained in the RAF.

The year ended tragically when Sgt Jennison and Flt Sgt Shipman of 141 Squadron were killed when, during formation practice, their Meteor NF.11, WG936 crashed inverted after they broke away from the formation at Horsham St Faith.

A detachment from 228 Operational Conversion Unit (OCU) from Leeming, arrived on 26 February 1952. The pilots and navigators, who flew their ten Mosquito NF.36s to Coltishall, under the command of Sqn Ldr P G Hill, should have been completing conversion training to the Meteor NF.11. Due to various delays into service of the Meteor, and the build-up of crews training on the Bristol Brigand at Leeming, it was decided to delay the retirement of the Mosquitoes until the Meteors could

Mossies replaced by jet power; 141 Squadron line circa 1952.

Meteor NF.11 WD608 (right) of 141 Squadron on the line at Coltishall. (R C Sturtivant)

be fully integrated into the jet conversion course with the OCU.

To make room for the detachment, 23 Squadron moved to Horsham St Faith on 15 January. Whilst at Coltishall, 228 OCU also began to convert to the Meteor NF.11, and by the end of June 1952, the squadron had received their full strength of 24 aircraft. The Mosquitoes of 228 OCU, together with their support crews, finally left Coltishall on 26 April 1952, thus enabling 23 Squadron to re-locate back to the base during July.

On 24 July, pilots from the wing suspended normal training to assist in the search for a 141 Squadron Meteor crew, whose aircraft had crashed into the sea whilst on a live air-to-air firing exercise. Meteor NF.11 WD608 had been lost while attacking a towed target 15 miles E of Happisburgh.

During the subsequent enquiry into the accident of the Meteor, it was discovered that the dinghy in the pilot's seat had inflated. The inflation pushed the pilot into his seat harness, restricting his movements, as well as forcing the control column forward. This control restriction caused the aircraft to dive, giving the crew no chance of recovery or escape. As a result, locally produced stiletto knives were made by the armoury and fitted to the aircraft just below the canopy. The aim was to puncture the dinghy if a similar incident should occur.

The passenger in the Meteor on this fateful day was SAC Nobby Clarke, a Fighter Marshaller at Neatishead. He had been given the opportunity to fly and experience what actually happened in the air while individuals in his position directed the fighters from the ground.

On that same day, search crews were called upon to assist in the search for a pilot of an F-86 Sabre after he had baled out of his aircraft over the Wash. Regretfully, his body was never found.

In August, the FAA once again flew from the airfield. This time, De Havilland Sea Hornet NF.21s of 809 Squadron came to work up to operational readiness by co-operating with 23 Squadron in practising night flying techniques. Having successfully gained the necessary experience the squadron flew out to Malta in January 1953.

The end of 1952 saw the arrival of visiting squadrons from home and overseas. Between the 27 September and 15 October, Coltishall hosted eight Meteor NF.11s of 87 Squadron, who were detached from their home base in Germany to take part in Exercise 'Ardent.' During November, the unit hosted a second Meteor unit, 85 Squadron who were detached in for two weeks whilst runway repairs were carried out at their home base of West Malling.

On being posted to Coltishall in December 1952, Ken Bartram from Norwich remembers that his railway warrant was from St Athan to Buxton Lammas but on arrival at Norwich Station he was advised that Buxton Lammas had in fact closed 10 years previously! An interesting start to his time at Coltishall; one wonders how many more were sent to the non-existent railway station on posting to the Station? As part of his arrivals procedure, Ken visited the SWO who, noticing his Norwich home address, informed him of the acute accommodation shortage on the Station and asked if he would like to live out at the same time as granting a ration and cycle allowance if he agreed. Having only just been married and with no chance of being allocated a married quarter during his two years National Service, how could he refuse!

The SWO, noticing his service number 3137449, enquired of Ken's career with the ATC. He replied that he had been a member of 231 Squadron in Norwich and attained the rank of Sgt Trumpeter in the band. A

809 Squadron Sea Hornet NF.21.

second break in addition to living out was also about to be proposed, as there was an urgent need for more members in the Station Band. He was advised that if he joined it would mean out of hours practice but would be compensated by no guard or fire picket duties; again how could he refuse!

In Norwich, during the Quarterly Assizes, the Senior Judge attended Sunday morning services at the Cathedral with all the local dignitaries arriving in horse drawn carriages. It was then the tradition for the Judge and his entourage to be welcomed by a fanfare and it was often the case that trumpeters from the Station Band were present for this event. For Ken Bartram and his colleagues, their first indication that they were to provide the fanfare for the Quarterly Assizes was when they were summoned to the Station Commander's Office and advised of this most prestigious honour. Gp Capt P P 'Prosser' Hanks made it clear to both the trumpeters and their respective sections that this was a most important task and an honour to the Station and leading up to the event regularly visited Norwich to watch the musicians during the practice sessions; he personally inspected the group before they left the Station for the actual event.

On the Monday morning following the Cathedral service, the four trumpeters played another fanfare outside the courthouse for the Judge's arrival to begin the proceedings. The pomp and ceremony impressed the Judge so much that they were asked to stay at the courthouse that day to play another fanfare on his departure. Before agreeing, the Corporal in charge requested that the Clerk of Court contact Coltishall for permission for the trumpeters

AC2 Ken Bartram.

to be absent from their place of duty to carry out this request. On contacting Gp Capt Hanks, the clerk was advised that permission was granted for the trumpeters to remain at the court for as long as necessary and for this particular session this meant absence from duty for three or four days. From that point on Ken Bartram and his fellow trumpeters appeared at three more Assizes.

During the first two weeks of February 1953, the station provided emergency support to the local community, when personnel were sent to assist in rescue work connected with a flood disaster. At 0210hrs on 1 February, a telephone call requesting the urgent assistance from Coltishall, was received from the Police at North Walsham. They reported to the Orderly Officer that a breach in the sea wall had occurred at Sea Palling. Rough seas backed by a high spring tide and strong winds had caused the breach. A party of three officers and seventy airmen responded to the plea for help and were on the scene for two weeks until 15 February.

Ex-Cpl Roger Hobson served at Coltishall during his National Service from April 1953 to December 1954 as an Ops Clerk. During this time, 23 Squadron with their Vampires and Venoms and 141 Squadron with the Meteor were the main source of his employment.

At the time he remembers serving with another young airman, also on National Service, called Brian Clough. 'Cloughy' went on to become one of the most charismatic characters in English Football in later years. During his time at Coltishall, even with the rigours of National Service, football still beckoned even to the point that on most weekends, when most were confined to camp, Brian would be away playing football for Doncaster Rovers.

Just after arriving at Coltishall Roger found out that 23 Squadron were in the process of converting from the Mosquito to the Vampire and as each new aircraft arrived a Mosquito was flown out to Defford for scrapping. Defford being close to his hometown of Kidderminster gave him the idea of 'cadging' a lift on one of the 'one-way' flights, however it wasn't to be; something he regrets to this day.

Other significant memories for Roger during his short time at Coltishall included the Queen's Coronation Flypast over Odiham in 1953 where both 23 and 141 Squadrons took part. Unusually, 141 Squadron was led on this occasion by Mjr Merle Allen, an American Exchange Officer. Out of all the

RAF Coltishall Band circa 1953.

tragedies that befell the Station on a seemingly regular basis at that time, especially during the early jet period, Roger remembers the accident involving 23 Squadron's CO, Sqn Ldr Jarcomb-Hood DFC who was killed near Kings Lynn when his Venom crashed on 21 January 1954. He vividly recalls that the mood of the Station was profoundly affected, as the news of the tragedy became widely known.

The training routine for the flying squadrons continued throughout the year. Late February witnessed the resident squadrons engaged in fighter affiliation against the Canberra bomber, which had been recently introduced to front-line RAF service. The Coltishall Wing practised quarter attacks on the Canberra at high altitude, by day and night. On 21 July, both squadrons participated in a similar exercise against American and French B-26 Invaders, which at the time were being used for mine-laying. This particular exercise proved less than successful for the Meteors in the anti-mine-laying role.

July also witnessed the arrival of the Bristol Sycamore HR.13 SAR helicopters which were on detachment from

The breach at Sea Palling in 1953.

275 Squadron at Horsham St Faith. The prime reason for using Coltishall was to support and provide, SAR cover for Exercise 'Coronet.' At the same time the Coltishall Wing took full advantage of the SAR helicopter presence, and practised live dinghy drills, as well as testing the recently introduced exposure suits.

John Hambrook was posted to Coltishall to work in the Equipment Section following his recruit training and remembered two specific incidents that had an impact on his three years at the base and throughout his twelve years of service in the RAF. On the 10 August 1953 he got off the train at North Walsham Railway Station where he met another airman destined for Coltishall who alighted from another compartment; AC Alan Knox.

After being collected from North Walsham by Station MT, the pair was unceremoniously dumped at the Main Guardroom. From there, they both made their way to the Orderly Room to collect their 'arrival chits.' They were then directed to the Transit Accommodation, down past the Airmen's Mess and NAAFI to the hut situated to the right of Aitken Block. Following their long railway journey and the trials and tribulations upon their arrival, both Alan and John enjoyed a quick breather before they thought of sorting out their kit bags and going for a bite to eat.

The catnap did not last long, as a Tannoy message called out their names, ordering them back to the Orderly Room. Wondering what on earth was happening, and whom they had crossed or upset, the pair rushed to find out how much trouble they were in! In fact they were not in trouble. It transpired that an aircraft had crashed and only a matter of an hour or so after arriving, the pair was detailed to join the crash guard. They were ordered to go for an early tea, collect some Wellington Boots from Clothing Stores and report back to the Guard Room for further orders.

The aircraft they were to guard over the next few days was a Meteor T.7 of 141 Squadron from Horsham St Faith, being flown by 20 year old Plt Off George Beaton and Flg Off Derek Gowan. The Meteor had been on a normal GCA back into Horsham St Faith when at about half a mile from touchdown the pilot was advised that he was approximately 40 feet below the glide path. The pilot was given instructions to look ahead and to execute an overshoot. Almost immediately radar contact was lost and the aircraft was found to have struck the ground and disintegrated 200 yards short of the runway threshold. Plt Off Beaton and Flg Off Gowan were both killed. From the evidence presented to the Court of Enquiry, it appears that the safety pilot may have advanced the throttles too quickly, causing the port engine to flame-out and for control to be lost at the most critical stage of the overshoot.

For John Hambrook and Alan Knox, this was a traumatic introduction to life as servicemen in the early 50's. Sadly, many aircraft from Coltishall were lost through accidents on an all too regular basis during their time at the base.

In 1955, towards the end of his posting at Coltishall, the pair were to witness an altercation between two airmen that later was to become a case of attempted murder. It was teatime in the Airmen's Mess on that day, with it being so busy that the queues stretched outside the main doors with airmen four deep waiting to be served. There was plenty of bumping and banging with patience being tested for all. For one young lad the jostling and waiting proved too much and he 'pricked' another lad in the leg with his fork.

Having finished his dinner, the injured party went to Gibson Block to find his assailant armed with a 0.303 rifle. Having found his attacker, he fired a round into his shoulder, threw down his rifle and ran out. The manhunt was on, but it was not long before Sgt Gray of the Guardroom Staff caught the gunman and placed him under arrest. The young lad ended up in prison for a number of years on an attempted murder charge. But for John and the others who witnessed the attack in the Mess, they all wondered how he managed to acquire the live rounds in the first place.

Sadly, in the years that followed, there were two further incidents that ended with the murder of two young and innocent lives; not servicemen, but the children of Coltishall personnel. The tragic and senseless loss of 18-year-old Rachel Lean on 5 September 1995 and 5-year-old Lauren Creed on 21 October 1997 has had a profound impact on everyone at Coltishall. The memory of these young innocent people lives with us all.

Sycamore HR.13 XD196 of 275 Squadron.

During the period 9 to 18 November, 264 Squadron were attached to the Coltishall Wing to participate in Exercise 'Egg Basket', a local trials and development exercise involving a high intensity of aircraft operating from the Station. During 'Egg Basket', a Gee Coding Trial, Intermezzo II, was also trialled successfully. Just before this exercise, 141 Squadron lost Meteor NF.11 WM164, when Flg Off R G Dawes ran out of fuel whilst carrying out practice approaches. He was forced to land his aircraft one-mile short of the airfield perimeter.

November saw 23 Squadron replace their original Vampires with the new and up-rated Venom NF.2. However, tragedy soon struck, when on a delivery flight from 48 MU, Hawarden, one of the Venoms, flown by Flg Off Towle, crashed on 29 November, killing the pilot. Even with the start of a New Year, 23 Squadron's fortunes were not to change. The Venom was proving to be a difficult and temperamental aircraft to maintain, with its radar being particularly troublesome. The numerous problems were summed up during Exercise 'Kingpin' when the squadron managed just two sorties with the only Venom with serviceable radar. However, this aircraft went unserviceable shortly after take off on its third sortie!

As if the problems encountered with their aircraft were not enough, the squadron was to lose their Squadron Commander on 21 January. Sqn Ldr A J Jarcombe-Hood and his navigator, Flg Off A E Osborne, were both tragically killed when their Venom WL828, crashed near Kings Lynn whilst on a weather test.

Witness to the crash, Mr F T Jude of Kings Lynn, who was working on the roof of a new house close to the crash

Line of Venom NF.2s of 23 Squadron at Coltishall.

site, reported that he saw the aircraft diving out of the cloud, although its dive was not too steep. It looked to him as if the plane was doing the same as many others, a mock attack, but sadly on this occasion it failed to pull out of the dive and went straight into the ground. Several other witnesses said that the Venom was on fire before it hit the ground. Mr Clarke of South Wootton reported that the aircraft came out of cloud with orange flames coming from it; "it was alight in the air", he said.

By October, 23 Squadron possessed ten Venoms that had been modified with new canopies and revised tail planes. These modifications contributed greatly to better reliability, and more importantly, serviceability. In the meantime, 141 Squadron had increased its number of Meteor NF.11s to sixteen aircraft.

During Exercise BEWARE in October 1954, two Gloster Javelin Interceptors, XA554 and XA559 arrived at Coltishall. Fitted with 250 gallon ventral tanks, the pair were part of the Ministry of Supply fleet, and were

One of many exercises involving Coltishall during the 1950s was Operation Dividen. 410 RCAF Squadron with the F-86 Sabre is pictured in July 1954.

attached to the Coltishall Wing as part of the acceptance trials for the aircraft. The Javelin, a large twin engined delta winged fighter, with a crew of two and armed with four Firestreak air-to-air missiles was, in later years, to become a part of everyday life with the squadrons at Coltishall.

Both 23 and 141 Squadrons were now introducing more air-to-air firing to their training schedule. 23 Squadron gained the most benefit from these sorties, especially as their Venoms were becoming more reliable, and the crews more efficient flying the aircraft.

One of the armourers who served with 141 Squadron for 18 months of his National Service was Allan Bolton. He remembers that many of the groundcrews assigned to Coltishall were somewhat heavier than other Stations due to the rich supplies of mushrooms on the airfield. Just like the wartime days when it was not unusual to see thirty or forty people out on the airfield in the early morning mist or late in the evening, the 1950's proved no different.

Once a good amount of mushrooms had been collected, the lads would return to their remote dispersal to start their feast. Firstly they would invert an iron that had been misplaced from their Barrack Block and then jam it between two small lockers; with a knob of butter from the mess, they would then fill a billycan with mushrooms. As Allan recalls; "took a feast of mushrooms for breakfast like nothing I've tasted since." "How Charlie's late night pie van at the main gate made a profit I don't know!" Another memory of his time at Coltishall was during the annual air-firing exercises held whilst on detachment with the squadron at Acklington in Northumberland.

In the 1950s there was still to be had a prize for the most successful air-firing crew and a good rollicking for

A Venom NF.3 from an angle which belies the aircraft Vampire roots.

The remains of WX879 at Meeting Hill.

failure. How easy it would have been for an armourer to redress the balance when a pilot or navigator gave them a hard time at a bullnight or during an inspection. An individual armourer could have quite easily put the coloured ammo of his favourite officer in the offender's complement, especially if the latter proved to be a better shot! But as Allan said, "No armourer worth his salt would stoop to such a thing, would he?"

141 Squadron had an almost perfect flying safety record. However, in November, the squadron was to suffer two accidents whilst on detachment to Ahlhorn in Germany. The first accident occurred during a formation break of three aircraft, when the second aircraft in the formation flew through his leader's slipstream on the approach. This caused the aircraft to stall and crash, 500 yards short of the runway. Luckily, the crew escaped uninjured. In the second incident, the pilot, Flg Off Hall, made an inadvertent wheels-up landing whilst under GCA control, once again the crew escaped without injury.

March 1955 proved to be an interesting month for the Coltishall Wing. On 14 March, Exercise COVERPOINT was held to investigate the method of scrambling aircraft using only the Type 80-radar equipment. Three days into this exercise, a crew from 23 Squadron successfully intercepted a Valiant flying at 47,000ft by this method.

At the end of March, 23 Squadron was again taking part in a further two exercises; 'WILD DUCK' and 'SKY HIGH.' Exercise WILD DUCK proved to be particularly useful in gaining experience and information on intercepting high-flying jet bombers, which were taking evasive action whilst using Radar Warning Equipment. Exercise SKY HIGH, an interception exercise against Canberras, which at the time were flying higher and faster than any

previous aircraft, proved very useful in the development of tactics, which would be used, in a further interception exercise, Exercise BEWARE.

141 Squadron began to convert to the Venom NF.3 after the first of the type arrived at Coltishall on 21 June. Some of their pilots had already received single engine training on the Vampire T.11, and by the end of the month they had eight pilots in the final stages of their single engine conversion. That month saw Squadron navigators begin training on new equipment when the Bristol Brigand 'circus' arrived from Colerne on a two-week detachment. The 'circus' returned again in August, when it was the turn of 23 Squadron's navigators to fly their five sorties prior to conversion on to the Venom NF.3.

On 13 September, the Prime Minister, Mr Anthony Eden, visited Coltishall. AOC-in-C Fighter Command, AOC 12 Gp and the Station Commander, Gp Capt P P 'Prosser' Hanks met him. After a short tour of the station, the PM departed for Neatishead and Trimingham by helicopter, where he observed Fighter Controllers at work under exercise conditions. On his return to Coltishall, he spoke to the personnel who had taken part in Exercise ADEX, congratulating them on the way the exercise had been conducted.

The weather during January 1956 was poor, which in turn severely curtailed the flying programme and the build up of the operational status of the Venom NF.3. Both Squadrons lost aircraft during the first couple of months of 1956.

The first Venom WX879, of 23 Squadron, dived into the ground shortly after take off from Coltishall on 2 January 1956. The aircraft came down and exploded as it crashed into a clump of trees on land belonging to Mr

C E Bacon of Lilac Farm, Worstead. Mr Bacon actually witnessed the crash that cost the lives of the crew, Flg Off L G M Jarvis from Grays in Essex and Plt Off H V Parsons from Eltham, London. He reported that the plane was flying very low and then went up a little as if trying to gain height. As it did so, it began to wobble first one way and then the other; the pilot seemed unable to get it under control before it crashed into the trees.

Mr G W Kirk of North Walsham saw the plane "toppling over and over in the air" and realising it was going to crash, jumped into his van with the idea of giving assistance. He temporarily lost sight of the Venom and when he saw it again it seemed to have changed direction. This made him wonder if the pilot did his best to keep the plane out of the way of the houses and village of Meeting Hill. Fourteen days later, on 16 January, Venom NF.3 WX795 of 141 Squadron, crashed following engine failure in the Coltishall circuit.

23 Squadron finally became operational on the Venom during April. On the 20 April the squadron was detached to Wattisham for a week to participate in Exercise FABULOUS. On this occasion, the squadron was not called upon to scramble any aircraft in support of this exercise. However, it did take the opportunity of carrying out practice interceptions on Vickers Valiants of Bomber command, which at the time were carrying out sorties not connected to the ongoing exercise.

When Venom WX881 crashed on 5 June 1956, about a mile from Buxton, off the Buxton to Coltishall road, four local men working in the vicinity ran to the assistance of the two American occupants who were injured and still strapped in the smoking aircraft.

Just after getting airborne from Coltishall, the 23 Squadron Venom being crewed by Capt White and Capt Castleberry, crashed into a field, bounced into an earth mound, skimmed over the road and came to rest 50 yards from the road facing at right angles to its direction of travel. The wreckage was strewn over a 50-yard radius with the cockpit section containing the two crew badly smashed.

A rescue helicopter from Horsham St Faith was scrambled and landed near the crash site and flew White and Castleberry to the Norfolk and Norwich Hospital where both underwent operations for serious injuries.

Gp Capt J C Sissons, Coltishall's Station Commander, praised Derek Wymer, Geoffrey Bunting, John Hazell and Sidney Edwards for their brave and prompt action in extricating the two seriously injured airmen from the burning wreckage. Their actions undoubtedly prevented further injury.

141 Squadron were to encounter considerable trouble with the Mk.5 gunsight fitted to their Venoms during an APC at Acklington. The closing speed for the Venom during this particular practice camp was 300 knots. The Mk.5 gunsight, developed by Ferranti, was designed for a closing speed of 500 knots, a fact that was discovered only after the problems encountered by the squadron at Acklington. With the discrepancy highlighted,

Runway extensions under construction in early 1957.

modifications were introduced to both the gunsight and the standard operating procedures for the aircraft.

In September 1956, a contract was awarded to John Laing and Co.Ltd. for the strengthening of the runways and taxiways. On 13 October, five days prior to the planned start of the construction work, the squadrons, Technical Wing and Station Flight, moved the short distance to Horsham St Faith. To relieve the overcrowding that was expected at Horsham, 'D' Flight, 275 Squadron, with their Sycamore HR.13 helicopters, moved in the opposite direction to Coltishall on the 12 October. The Sycamores were in fact to return to Horsham St Faith the following month, as it was felt that the helicopters were interfering with the ongoing construction work.

During their short stay at Coltishall, Sycamores carried out two operational SAR sorties. The first was to the RAF Hospital at Ely with a Corporal technician who had suffered severe acid burns. The second involved the Captain of the merchant ship 'Wimbledon.' The Captain had been washed overboard when his vessel got into difficulty six miles off Cromer. Prior to the arrival of the helicopter, the crew of the vessel 'Elenor Brook' had picked him up. At the scene of the rescue, a medical officer was lowered on to this vessel from the helicopter, unfortunately only to find that the Captain was already dead.

Whilst detached to Horsham St Faith the two squadrons had no difficulty in converting to the Javelin FAW.4 and in doing so, became the first Javelin Wing

QRA aprons taking shape at the end of the main runway.

in Fighter Command. The flight commanders had been posted to 46 Squadron at Odiham to fly the aircraft so that they could pass on the experience they had gained on the type. This re-equipment enabled the RAF to take over the night standbys (known as 'Fabulous') from the Americans, with two aircraft positioned at the end off the runway with the crews in their seats and the tele-scramble line plugged in. Two more aircraft stood by with the crews at readiness; whilst 'Fabulous' was active, crews in the cockpit would change every hour.

Hunter F.6s of 74 Squadron during their twilight days at Horsham St Faith.

The Gloster Javelin FAW.7 and another new era for Coltishall.

With the gradual arrival of the Javelin it wasn't long before the last of the Venoms were flown to the MU at Shawbury directly from Horsham; the last departing on the 23 May 1957.

On 29 May 1959, the majority of the wing returned to Coltishall. 23 Squadron actually returned home on 4 June, followed four days later by 74 Squadron, with their Hawker Hunter F.6s, also from Horsham St Faith. This move effectively ended a long association for the RAF with Horsham St Faith. The base, being close to Norwich, was often criticised by local residents for the noise associated with a jet fighter station and so the departure of all the fighter units came as a welcome relief for all those living near by.

74 Squadron soon settled in to life at Coltishall, and were especially delighted to welcome one of their former Commanding Officers and old friend of Coltishall, 'Sailor' Malan, who paid a visit on 17 August. The highlight for the honoured guest on this visit was a solo display by a Hunter F.6 of 74 Squadron followed shortly after by a display of a Spitfire from Martlesham Heath. In 1959, the squadron provided four of their Hunters for aerobatic displays throughout the country, with a solo display normally being flown by Flt Lt Ted Nance. In between this hectic schedule, the team, together with other squadron pilots, flew their Hunters at the APC at Acklington, as well as day-to-day training and operational sorties from Coltishall.

On 25 August 1959, 74 Squadron was to suffer a major tragedy when two of their Hunters, XF502/K and XF425/H, collided shortly after take off from Coltishall. One of the pilots, Peter Rayner ejected safely, however the second pilot, Peter Budd, having no time to react to the collision, failed to initiate the ejection sequence and died in the crash. Just a few days later, on 1 September, 23 Squadron, now equipped with an updated version of the Javelin, the FAW.7 were to suffer a very similar accident when XH775/E and XH781/J collided in mid air over Brundall, south of Norwich.

Despite the accidents, both squadrons continued with the rigour of combat training and operational sorties. However, commitments in flypasts, Battle of Britain Displays and the making of a documentary at Church Fenton, in addition to numerous unserviceability problems with the Javelin, began to seriously impinge on the operational status and daily training requirements of the squadrons. Due to these problems, the commitments for the following year were considerably reduced.

Chapter 9

THUNDER AND LIGHTNING

The year 1958 saw extensive alterations to the station in preparation for the arrival of the Air Fighter Development Squadron (AFDS) of the Central Fighter Establishment (CFE) and the very first English Electric Lightnings into RAF service. The first of the pre-production Lightnings to be delivered was XG334/A, which arrived at Coltishall on 23 December 1959 followed by XG335/B and XG336/C a few days after Christmas.

Prior to their arrival there were many concerns about the new fighter and the ability of the station to support such a potent machine of war. One of the greatest concerns was about the stopping ability of the Mach two fighter, even though the runway had been extended to 7000 feet plus.

Pete Daviss, a civilian MT driver became heavily involved in trials to estimate how the aircraft would stop in wet conditions. He would, together with other water tanker drivers, follow 'Crash One' along the runway dumping thousands of gallons of water to simulate the worst-case scenario under these conditions. After they had cleared the area a Supermarine Swift from the RAE (Royal Aircraft Establishment) would land on the flooded runway to test the braking performance. No problems were ever encountered, and as the Lightning was equipped with a brake parachute under normal circumstances the Station was given the go-ahead for Lightning operations.

It was towards the end of 1959 when Coltishall's resident Hunter unit, 74 Squadron, were informed that they were to be the first front-line operational squadron in the RAF to be re-equipped with the Mach two Lightning. Ironically, ever since the Lightning had appeared with the AFDS/CFE for evaluation and acceptance trials many of those Hunter pilots wished they too could get their hands on the aircraft. Soon they would have their chance!

During April 1960, 23 Squadron started to replace their Javelin FAW.7's with the FAW.9. Apart from being the most advanced version of this delta-winged fighter, the aircraft was fitted with a refuelling probe.

Training in the refuelling technique progressed through June and July 1960, in conjunction with Valiant tankers of 214 Squadron from Marham. Most of the Javelin crews had progressed from 'dry' to 'wet' hook-ups, and had completed a range of checks before the end of July. In August, two crews participated in Exercise FUNFAIR that involved a deployment to Cyprus to prove the refuelling concept. Tanker unserviceability resulted in a broken probe and a diversion to the French Air Force base at Orange on the return leg.

The culmination of all this activity came in October when six Javelins deployed to Singapore to participate in Exercise DYKE. Valiants of 214 Squadron provided the refuelling with Hastings and Britannias carrying the groundcrews and spares for the deployment.

The Coltishall Wing on the 19th May 1960. AFDS Lightning F1 XG336 leading with 74 Squadron Hunter and 23 Squadron Javelin.

23 Squadron Javelin FAW.9 rests under a Middle Eastern sun.

The first pair of Javelins staged via Orange, Luqa, El Adem, Nicosia, Diyarbakir, Mehrabad and Sharjah to Mauripur, arriving on 2 October; their objective was to provide a spare aircraft for the final flight to Singapore. In fact they returned un-needed following the same route with an additional stop at San Gusto. They finally landed back at Coltishall on 17 October. The crews for these legs were Flt Lts G Jonas, D J Castle, H Fitzer and D B Collins with Sqn Ldr D J Keats replacing Flt Lt Fitzer for the return flight.

The second pair of aircraft, flown by Sqn Ldr M H Miller and Flt Lts G Kaye, L T Authur and J B Matthews followed the same route out to Karachi, but the third pair, Wg Cdr G I Chapman, the Squadron CO, with his navigator Sqn Ldr J E Jeffries together with Flt Lts P L Tindall and P F Harris, flight refuelled to Mauripur, landing only at Akrotiri.

These four aircraft then flight refuelled to Changi, Singapore, landing only at Gan in the Indian Ocean en-route. On 17 October all four Javelins left Changi for Butterworth in Malaysia where they met up with the Valiants for the return refuelling flights via Gan and Mauripur to Tehran. They then staged back to Coltishall arriving home on the 26 October.

Being able to maintain the original itinerary except for the loss of one day due to Valiant crew fatigue, not only reflected on those who supported them throughout the deployment, but also to the entire squadron who worked tirelessly to ensure the aircraft were able to undertake this historic deployment. The whole exercise was obviously a success and the congratulatory signal from the AOC-in-C concluded with. 'As usual my confidence in 23 Squadron has been fully justified, well done!'

25 May 1960 saw the arrival at Coltishall of the first full production Lightning to the AFDS. The aircraft, XM135/D, apart from being the last F.1 in RAF service when retired on 20 November 1974, is probably more famous for it's unplanned flight at 33 MU, Lyneham, at the hands of Wg Cdr Taffy Holden, an engineer at the MU! Today this aircraft can still be seen at the Imperial War Museum (IWM) Collection, Duxford. In addition to XM135, Four further F.1s remained in use with the AFDS until early 1963 when the surviving airframes were all transferred to 74 Squadron.

The next mark of Lightning to join the fleet of the AFDS was delivered in August 1962. The two T.4s, XM973/K and XM974/J were used for service trials, dual checks and continuation training. XM973 stayed for just under a year whilst XM974 continued with the work on AFDS until it departed for pastures new in early 1966.

Prior to this time, during the Experimental and Development stages of the Lightning programme, many of the pre-production examples of the new fighter were based at Coltishall with the CFE. A graphic example of the dangers in the testing and development of new aircraft happened on 5 March 1960. Sqn Ldr Harding, of the CFE, was airborne in XG334, the 18th pre-production Lightning, when, on selecting the undercarriage down for landing his port leg would not lower beyond 30 degrees. The emergency system was initiated without success and after a series of slow fly-bys over the airfield to allow engineering staff to assess the situation as best they could; the aircraft was flown out to sea and abandoned.

Sqn Ldr Harding ejected safely with slight bruising and mild shock and into the bargain, gained the dubious distinction of being the first RAF pilot to be involved in the loss of a Lightning! Ironically, two more pre-production Lightnings, XG311 and XG335, were abandoned under similar circumstances during the latter stages of development, in both cases without loss or major injury to the test pilots.

As expected, 74 Squadron was to be the first operational squadron within the RAF to receive the Lightning. With such a quantum leap in performance over their old steed, the Hunter, the pilots chosen to fly the new beast had to undertake a five-day aviation medicine course at Upwood. On their return to Coltishall, a further seven days of lectures on such subjects as aircraft systems and emergency drills, followed by the simulator phase, during which time ten hours were flown in the Lightning Mk.1 simulator. All pilots were reminded that, as yet, there were no two-seat conversion trainers, thus their time on the simulator was of the utmost importance!

The first squadron aircraft to enter RAF service, XM165, was delivered to Leconfield, which at the time was being used by Coltishall squadrons whilst their home base was being upgraded. The aircraft, flown by Wg Cdr R P Beamont, arrived late in the afternoon of 29 June 1960. Coltishall's Station Commander, Gp Capt H Bird-Wilson, Wg Cdr David Evans, Wing Commander Flying and the first squadron Commander, Sqn Ldr John Howe of 74 Squadron, were on hand to accept XM165.

Sqn Ldr Howe flew the first squadron sortie in a Lightning on 14 July 1960. By 22 July, all of the squadron pilots had completed conversion training. In addition, Wg Cdr Evans, OC Flying, had flown at least one sortie. The second Lightning for the squadron, XM164, arrived on the 15 July, but squadron training was severely hampered by lack of spares and unserviceability.

By the end of August, 74 Squadron had increased its Lightning complement to seven, but at times only one was available for flying. With such a poor serviceability record, the squadron was more than a little concerned when they were asked to provide four aircraft for the September show at Farnborough. Hard work on behalf of the groundcrews enabled the squadron to accept the commitment, and to their credit, provided a four-ship display on every day of the show except one, when the weather was too bad.

The AFDS continued to make use of the Lightning, though not without problems. During August all four of the AFDS fleet of Lightnings received modifications to their nose wheel undercarriage assemblies to preclude the possibility of the nose wheel centring mechanism disconnecting during take-off. This type of problem, and modification, was typical of the work carried out AFDS on many types of aircraft during the initial development and acceptance prior to entering squadron service.

The AFDS lost Lightning XM138, on 16 December 1960 when it caught fire on landing. The pilot, Flt Lt Hopkins, was unhurt although his aircraft suffered Cat 4 damage and was written off, having only amassed 75 hours flying time.

On 24 December, Sqn Ldr Howe and three of his pilots from 74 Squadron flew a 'Box' formation around the bases of East Anglia, proudly showing off their new machines.

23 Squadron with their Javelins were often overshadowed by the new Lightnings of 74 Squadron. However, they did steal the limelight in the opening weeks of 1961 when the Javelins were put to good use as snow clearing machines on the main runway! The natural nose-up attitude of the Javelin ensured the jet efflux was directed onto the runway, thereby assisting in dispersing the snow! So, on this occasion, it was the Javelins that helped the Lightnings get into the air!

XM135 also served with 74 Squadron at Coltishall.

By the end of April 1961, all of 74 Squadron pilots were operational on the Lightning, and cleared to fly both by night and day. During the summer of 1961, operational training had to take a back seat to displays and publicity events as the RAF were very keen to introduce their new aircraft to the British public.

Sqn Ldr John Howe had enormous enthusiasm for the Lightning and for its potential for display flying. He was instrumental in forming the 'Tigers' as a full-blown aerobatic display team. At the Farnborough Airshow in 1961, he astonished onlookers with a stream take-off in which each Lightning rotated quickly into a 30-degree climb, increasing to near vertical, that they sustained as they reached 250 knots. The leader, by the time his No 9 left the runway, had already passed 5000ft! The roar of eighteen afterburning engines left the crowd in no doubt that the Lightning had arrived.

Apart from the resident squadrons, Coltishall was often the host of other Lightning units who operated from the airfield whilst their home bases were being upgraded or modified.

XM165 leads a 74 Squadron trio over Coltishall.

OC 74 Squadron, Sqn Ldr John Howe.

Firestreak equipped Spitfire!

In 1961, 56 (Fighter) Squadron from Wattisham spent a two-month detachment at Coltishall; amongst their numbers was SAC Nigel Lodge. He remembers:

"It was during the 1961 detachment that some of my colleagues, realizing the paucity of "Firestreak" equipped aircraft, set about updating the Station Gate Guard Spitfire so as to be 'ready for front-line service' in the then Cold War."

"The then Station Commander, Gp Capt H 'Birdy' Bird-Wilson, we were told, almost had apoplexy upon opening his copy of the EDP and seeing a photograph of 'his' aircraft so modified!"

"Of course, we had to make amends on the afternoon following our antics and 56(F) Squadron servicing personnel as a collective, there being no admission to the deed or otherwise claim to fame/notoriety, marched in funeral procession, at the slow-march, with the missile held shoulder high."

"I have to deny any participation in the modification but do, after so many years, admit to having been the photographer. The film was handed to the EDP for processing thus avoiding direct contact and the risk of Gp Capt Bird-Wilson's wrath!"

Flying in close formation with the Lightning was not always without incident. Flt Lt Jim Burns was part of a close formation of four aircraft practising a high speed low level pass along Coltishall's runway on 16 May 1961 when his aircraft, XM141/D started to yaw badly. Observers on the ground initially thought that he had suffered a bird strike, but as pieces of the aircraft started floating down to the ground in front of them they soon realised that the airframe was starting to break up.

It was another of the formation pilots, Flt Lt Alan Wright, who first realised that most of the fin and rudder on his colleague's Lightning was missing. Unfortunately, in addition to the fin and rudder, part of the spine suffered damage which included the radio aerial, this effectively preventing communication between XM141 and the other aircraft as well as ATC.

Flt Lt Burns pulled away from the formation, not realising the extent of the damage. He eventually landed his aircraft safely after a long straight-in approach using aileron control alone. The ensuing investigation into the incident identified that the effects of the aerodynamic pressures which had built up during the high speed low level manoeuvre by four aircraft in close formation had exposed a structural weakness in the fin and caused it to shear off. Subsequent to this all Lightnings were modified and Jim Burns gained the nickname 'Finless Jim' on the Squadron.

As was to be expected with a new aircraft of such performance, this was not to be the last incident. On another occasion, Flt Lt Tim Nelson's drag chute failed to deploy on landing. Mindful on the restrictions on braking, he put the aircraft into full afterburner to go around again. Just as he rotated, the chute deployed and was immediately engulfed by the reheat! As every Lightning pilot knew, landing without a brake chute was a hazardous undertaking that often resulted in brakes being burnt out. Thankfully this time, with the aid of the complete length of Coltishall's runway and the close support of the Fire Section, he landed safely without further incident.

Sqn Ldr Peter Botteril took command of 74 Squadron on 12 December 1961. In fact his first flight in a squadron aircraft was not until 26 March 1962 when he flew XM146. This was in effect an air test, as the Lightnings in RAF service with 56 and 111 Squadrons, as well as those with 74, had been grounded for some time whilst they were being modified following the discovery of some potentially dangerous flaws in the build programme.

During this time all of the squadron pilots had been making heavy use of the flight simulator and before each pilot was allowed to fly a Lightning again he had to complete a conversion programme of at least three sorties in the simulator. These sorties consisted of a comprehensive review and practice of all the known emergency situations, an air test and a high-level sortie profile. Additionally, over a two-day period, 19-20 March, most of the pilots flew the Lightning Mk.2 simulator at Leconfield. Unlike the example at Coltishall, the simulator at Leconfield incorporated a thirty-degree bank movement either way thus giving a more realistic return.

By early May, sufficient aircraft had been recovered from the modification programme to train a team of pilots to undertake an important role as the squadron was tasked to provide a fly-past at the British Trades Fair in Sweden.

On 23 May an advanced party left Coltishall for Vasteras and on the following day eight Lightning's flew to Sweden, staging through Karup in Denmark. After performing over Stockholm as part of their ambassadorial duties, the aircraft left Vasteras on 1 June and flew to Gardermoen in Norway where six aircraft performed at an air display two days later. The squadron returned to Coltishall on 6 June having successfully demonstrated their new aircraft to an appreciative audience at the Trade Fair and at the other locations during their mini-tour.

After returning from their Scandinavian tour the Squadron began work on its full display routine as they had now been officially appointed by C-in-C Fighter Command as the official Fighter Command Aerobatic Team. In fact, after a one-day stand-down following their return from Sweden, work-up commenced for a full aerobatic display with five Lightnings at Upavon scheduled for 16 June.

Another result of their successful Scandinavian tour was the opportunity for their Swedish Air Force counterparts to visit Coltishall in 1961. Eight SaaB Drakens from two wings of the Swedish Air Force based at Norrkoping and Uppsala flew to Coltishall on a five-day exchange.

The Drakens were escorted into Coltishall by a Lightning and two Javelins of 23 Squadron having been met 30 miles off the coast as they entered UK airspace. Their arrival was witnessed by the Swedish Detachment Commander, Air Cdre N M von Arbin, who had arrived

Fin and rudder of XM141.

earlier in a Dakota, together with Air Cdre Scott Malden, Chief of Staff at 12 Gp, the Station Commander Gp Capt Malins and the Swedish Air Attaché, Lt Col Niels Dahl. They were all on hand to formally welcome the detachment to the United Kingdom.

The visit was very much a social occasion but also coincided with the 50th Anniversary of military aviation. For the pilots, a programme had been arranged that included a trip to London, a visit to the V-bomber base at Wittering and an evening at many of the local public houses of which there were none in Sweden.

On the final day the two Air Forces held a mini-Farnborough over Coltishall when Sqn Ldr C Jernow and Flt Lt Eriksson from the Uppsala squadron looped-the-loop and executed high speed turns with only five feet separation between their two aircraft; the general opinion of those watching was "first class." Flg Off Max Carlberg also demonstrated the double-delta fighter to its full capability in a solo demonstration. The British flag was flown by Flt Lt Geoff Brindle who ably matched the Drakens capabilities in a Lightning.

On 7 August 1962, Coltishall was to welcome another famous display team in the form of nineteen Hunters of 92 Squadron, The Blue Diamonds. They arrived at Coltishall to begin practising with 74 Squadron on an ambitious display routine, co-ordinated by Sqn Ldr P G Botherhill. This time with sixteen Hunters and seven Lightnings!

About this time, the 'Tigers' borrowed a Lightning T.4 from the AFDS which was put to good use checking squadron pilots as, prior to this, check-rides were either made in the simulator or by the check pilot following the procedures in a Hunter! After the display season was over, the squadron once again tried to catch up with their day-to-day operational and training commitments, which by this time included operational Quick Reaction Alert (QRA) training.

During Exercise MATADOR, 74 Squadron, with their powerful new Lightnings, had to take a back seat and watch in envy as the Javelins of 23 Squadron were scrambled many times a day on practice interceptions. As it was, the Javelin was still the primary air defence aircraft in the RAF's inventory and whilst the Lightning had been involved in air defence exercises prior to MATADOR it was still taking second place to the Javelin in the overall scheme of things. But not for long.

Changes were beginning to take place at Coltishall once again. During October 1962, the CFEs small fleet of Javelin FAW.8s, various marks of Hunters together with a few Meteor 'hacks' and the Lightning F.1s and T.4s of the AFDS made the move to Binbrook. Once there, trials on further marks of Lightning F.2s, F.3s and F.6s, were carried out until 1 February 1966 when the AFDS was re-named the Fighter Command Trials Unit (FCTU).

The work of the FCTU continued in its own right until the unit was disbanded on 30 June 1967. Its fleet of Lightning F.6s being dispersed to 23 Squadron at Leuchars and the two remaining F.1s of Coltishall vintage being used to form the Binbrook Target Facilities Flight (TTF).

On 18 March 1963, 23 Squadron left Coltishall and brought to a close a 16-year association with the airfield and Norfolk when the Javelins departed for Leuchars in Scotland. The squadron's departure from Coltishall was the result of a reorganisation of Fighter Command. The last five remaining Javelin FAW.9s were led away from the Station by the Squadron Commander, Wg Cdr A J Owen in Javelin XH889 with the pilots and navigators being the last of about 40 aircrew to leave.

Air Cdre L D Scott-Maiden, the AOC, was on hand to see the squadron takeoff for their new Scottish home whilst at the same time a less formal farewell came from their sister squadron at Coltishall, 74 (Tiger) Squadron who sent up one of their Meteor Target Tugs trailing a target banner that was inscribed "Bye 23."

This left 74 Squadron as the only operational squadron at Coltishall, however, they were kept busy, participating in many Fighter Command and NATO exercises. These included Exercises BARRAGE, TOPHAT, QUICKTRAIN and KINGPIN.

The squadron lost their first Lightning, XM142/B on 26 April 1963 when the pilot Flt Lt Jim Burns, ejected safely. The aircraft was on an air test following a 400-hour servicing. After rolling out of a ten-second inverted run, the hydraulic warning captions indicated a failure of both systems. The aircraft was still over land, but pointing out to sea when the pilot made his escape. He was picked up from dry land by a helicopter from 228 Squadron and was back on duty within 24 hours of the incident.

In May 1963 a new night flying programme was introduced and it became necessary to introduce a shift system on the squadron to enable the target of twelve sorties per night to be met. The accent on night flying, coupled with new standard operating procedures for visual identification, witnessed the beginning of a training period that was designed to bring the Squadron up to full operational night-capability with regard to its primary role of intruder identification.

The Squadron participated in two major exercises during July. The first, called on 10 July, was Exercise TOPHAT; a NATO alert exercise. For the first time since the inception of the TOPHAT exercises, a survival scramble followed by a blind scramble was given. In a real life scenario the survival scramble would have been carried out when indications had been received that a full-scale attack on the UK had been launched, thereby, hopefully, enabling the aircraft to take-off and return within a short specified timescale.

Following the scramble, the lead aircraft would fly a set pattern, climbing to a predetermined height. Thereafter, each of the following aircraft climbed 1000 feet higher than its predecessor and added thirty seconds to the outbound leg, which in theory spaced the aircraft at one-minute intervals for recovery to base with the leader returning 25 minutes after take-off. A blind scramble might then follow if there was no control available and when sufficient time had elapsed to allow any manned-bombers to come into range.

The second exercise that month was Exercise MYSTIC, Bomber command's summer exercise for 1963 that

The Hunters of 92 Squadron taxy past the 74 Squadron line.

took place on 27 July. Participants from West Germany, flying the F-86 Sabre, were at Coltishall for the ten days of the exercise, following in the footsteps of Dutch and Belgian Air Forces who flew the Hunter.

The third annual 'Tiger Meet' took place on 30 August 1963 at the Belgian Air Force Base Kleine Brogel. 74 Squadron, being the UK's 'Tiger' Squadron, participated with four aircraft led by their Commanding Officer, Sqn Ldr Botterill. By all accounts 74 Squadron once again managed to 'steal the show.' At the evening reception, Flt Lt Martin Bee was presented with the Tiger Meet Medal for the best flying display which, he performed in XM137/D.

After nearly four years of Lightning operations from Coltishall, 74 Squadron made their way north to Leuchars on 28 February 1964. An eight aircraft formation, six Lightnings and two Hunters, over flew Coltishall before setting off on their journey to Scotland. Arriving over their new station, the formation performed the obligatory flypast before landing to be greeted by the AOC, the Station Commander and the Station Pipe Band. This formation had been preceded earlier in the day by four Lightnings which had been at Valley on an APC since 10 February; these aircraft flying direct from the Welsh airfield to Leuchars. To the great credit of all those concerned, the Squadron was declared operational within five hours of their arrival.

13 April 1964 saw the arrival of 226 OCU from RAF Middleton St George. The OCU was equipped with an assortment of Lightning marks and an equally assorted bunch of pilots eager to fly the Mach Two fighter. Lightning pilots were trained by the OCU at Coltishall right up to September 1974 when the unit left with the Lightning for the final time.

Whilst at Coltishall, the OCU had the task of taking pilots from advanced pilot training and converting them onto the particular mark of Lightning that they would fly on their operational squadron. The new pilot, after extensive preparation in the Ground School, was first taught to fly the Lightning as a new type of aircraft. The second phase of his training was aimed at making him thoroughly familiar with the complex weapons system and all aspects of the air-to-air Guided Weapons, the 'Firestreak' and 'Red Top.' The third and final stage of his training consisted of ground briefings and flying exercises which were designed to give the pilot a sound knowledge of interception techniques dealing with both supersonic and subsonic targets.

In addition to this long conversion course, the OCU trained experienced Lightning pilots to become Instrument Rating Examiners and Interceptor Weapons Instructors, to achieve standardisation in flying training on the Lightning force. The skill and experience of the instructors at Coltishall, coupled with the fact that

Lightning trainers were fully operational, was put to full use during National Emergency and NATO exercises. The OCU formed 145 (Reserve) Squadron during such times, and with quick reaction training carried out at regular intervals, ensured that the squadron could be brought into first line service with minimum delay.

Coltishall had for many years been the Parent Unit to the nearby radar base at Neatishead; providing administrative support, accommodation and transport services. Daily journeys to and from Neatishead were carried out by the Coltishall MT drivers, delivering everything from official correspondence to hot-lock meals and personnel. Pete Daviss remembers the early afternoon of Wednesday 16 February 1966 when an urgent call was made to the MT Section to get as many coaches to Neatishead as were available at that very moment.

With the urgency of the call, all of the drivers, including Pete Daviss realised that something was amiss. It was certainly nothing to do with the regular exercises that were held at that time. Asking no questions, but wondering what was happening, the drivers and their coaches departed for Neatishead at full speed.

As the coaches approached Wroxham, it became very apparent to the drivers that with the number of Fire Engines racing along the country roads, something serious was happening. In fact, their role that day was to evacuate hundreds of personnel from the site back to Coltishall as fireman bravely fought what turned out to be a deadly fire in the main control room at Neatishead.

Neatishead was at the front-line of Britain's Air Defences, being part of a network of radar bases that stretched the length of Great Britain, tracking the movement of Soviet aircraft during the height of the Cold War. At the heart of the facility was 'The Bunker', where 250 plus individuals worked, monitoring the numerous screens and analysing the information being returned from the radar.

The bunker itself was built to withstand a nuclear attack. With walls and roof being ten feet thick and capped with a further 20 feet of earth on top of the bunker's reinforced concrete roof, it would have survived all but a direct hit. From the outside, the facility was well hidden from prying eyes with its entrance being through what looked like an inconspicuous bungalow. For those who worked in the bunker, the entrance staircase through

74 Squadron prepare for take off. XM142/B , in which Flt Lt Jim Burns ejected from on the 26 April 1963 is second from the front.

the bungalow led down through a long tunnel. Every 20 or 30 feet, the tunnel changed direction at right angles to reduce potential blast damage from within or outside of the facility.

On the day in question, a fire broke out in the officer's rest room and adjoining storeroom at around lunchtime; two storeys down and 300 feet from the entrance. The smell of burning was first noticed in the bunker at 1247 hours. Three minutes later the fire alarms sounded and a control panel indicated the source as being the rest and storerooms. As a general evacuation was called, a number of airmen tried to tackle the fire that was by now burning fiercely. They were soon joined by Neatishead's own firemen, who fought the fire bravely until relieved by their civilian counterparts.

The severity of the blaze and the nature of the building itself, highly polished floors of teak and linoleum, insulated with cork and sealed by pitch with dividing walls made of timber and fibreboard, made the bunker a firetrap. The result for the firemen involved was smoke so thick that they could not see in front of their hands.

The intensity of the fire, smoke and heat caused Divisional Officer Gordon Dix from Holt to collapse at the bottom of a staircase. A rescue party was sent in to rescue Mr Dix but they had to abandon their attempt part way up the stairs. Exhausted, the rescuers had to retire, with one collapsing and having to be rescued himself.

A second team of four men were dispatched and managed to get Mr Dix out. They tried desperately to resuscitate their colleague but sadly on arrival at hospital he was pronounced dead. Just after Mr Dix was loaded into the Ambulance, it was realised that two members of the second rescue team were also missing. They were Leading Fireman Herbert Durrant and Fireman John Holman, both from Acle. A further search was made for them but had to be abandoned shortly after because of the horrific conditions that could so easily have claimed more lives if the attempt had continued. With only 30 minutes of breathing air available it was known that there was no chance of survival.

A difficult decision had to be made to prevent further loss of life and the order was given for the bunker to be flooded. Over the next 24 hours over one and half million gallons of water was pumped in to extinguish the fire. It took a number of days for the water to be pumped

23 Squadron Javelin in the foreground, 74 Squadron line and even a Whirlwind taxying in the background!

'The Tiger's. 74 Squadron display team in casual formation.

Virtually the whole of 226 OCU taxy out for the days training sorties.

back out and for the bodies of the missing firemen to be recovered; Mr Holman on the 19 February and Mr Durrant the following day.

This event also turned out to be a landmark in fire service history and amongst the recommendations that followed the inquiry, was for automatic water sprinklers to be installed in all underground sites. It also changed fire service procedures, leading to the wider use of breathing apparatus and the need for fire retardant furniture and materials to be used in such facilities.

With tight security and vigilance within the facility, the most likely reason for the tragic events sadly pointed towards arson. Within days of the fire, the RAF Police began their investigations, looking specifically at who had access to the rooms where the fire started. By looking at the key register they identified the last person to have come out of the room; LAC John Cheesman. The 22 year-old was arrested and taken to Coltishall where he was later handed over to the civilian police. Under interrogation he admitted to maliciously setting the fire in the bunker. On 20 April 1966 at Norwich Assizes, he was sentenced to seven years in prison by Mr Justice Phillimore.

In 1966, Brian Marston held the Chairmanship of the Norwich Branch of the Royal Air Forces Association. In a discussion at City Hall with the Lord Mayor of Norwich,

Mr Harry Perry, during the Battle of Britain Week that year the two pondered how the City could mark the celebrations for the following year. Brian suggested the 'Freedom of Norwich' for Coltishall, especially as the Station had been directly involved with the battle in 1940. Delighted with the suggestion, Mr Perry immediately started to make the arrangements:

Thus, in an impressive ceremony saddened only by frequent showers, Coltishall was given the Freedom of the City of Norwich on 6 April 1967. Standing on the dais in front of the City Hall, the Lord mayor, Mr Harry Perry, said "Today marks another page in the history and traditions of this great city of ours."

The ceremony, watched by large crowds of people in spite of the heavy rain, started with the No 1 Regional Band of the RAF and Coltishall personnel moving into position in front of City Hall. Led by the Chief Constable of Norwich Mr Frank Brown, the Lord Mayor and other dignitaries came out of City Hall. Mr Perry, accompanied by the Station Commander, Gp Capt Mike Hobson AFC, inspected the parade. Four Lightnings and three Spitfires then flew over the City just before the Town Clerk, Mr Gordon Tilsley, read the illuminated Deed of Grant.

This was the fourth time that the City had granted The Freedom of the City to the military and was the first time the honour had been granted to the RAF. The first grant was on 3 October 1945 when the City honoured the Royal Norfolk Regiment. On 17 October 1963 the honour was transferred to the 1st East Anglian Regiment Royal Norfolk and Suffolk before being transferred once again to the 1st (Norfolk and Suffolk) Battalion of the Royal Norfolk Regiment on 2 July 1964.

In reply to the Lord Mayor's speech, Gp Capt Hobson said that it was a very great honour. "It was most certainly a distinction since no other RAF unit had the marching freedom of the City of Norwich. For many of my men and women this has been a very intimate and personal action which they very much appreciate."

The Freedom Scroll, borne by Flg Off G H Lock, proclaimed:

TO THE OFFICER COMMANDING, GROUP CAPTAIN M E HOBSON AFC AND ALL RANKS of Royal Air Force Station Coltishall.

We the LORD MAYOR, ALDERMEN AND CITIZENS of the City of Norwich being desirous of marking both the affection in which we hold the Royal Air Force and our admiration for their glorious achievements in Peace and War

And being also desirous of recognizing the close ties of friendship which bind together the Royal Air Force Station and the City

Do Hereby Confer upon the Officer Commanding and All Ranks of the Royal Air Force for the time being stationed at Coltishall the privilege, honour and distinction of marching through our said City on all ceremonial occasions with bayonets fixed, colours flying and bands playing

In Witness Whereof we have caused our Corporate Seal to be hereunto affixed this sixth day of April in the year one thousand nine hundred and sixty-seven.

Signed Harry Perry, Lord Mayor - Gordon Tilsley, Town Clerk

In 1968, the OCU was to provide aircraft and pilots for various displays and flypasts throughout the country. April of this year celebrated the 50th anniversary of the formation of the RAF, and more than twenty Lightnings were deployed to Wyton for two weeks of intensive training prior to the Royal Review. The OCU was required to provide four boxes of four Lightnings over Abingdon on 14 June for the flypast.

Formation flypasts were also flown to mark the demise of Fighter Command and as part of the official Queens Birthday celebrations. OCU staff went one better for the annual Battle of Britain display at Coltishall, when for the first time ever, they flew a sixteen ship Lightning diamond formation!

Plt Off Whyer about to embark on her record breaking flight.

A special flypast was made at Coltishall on 26 February to mark the end of Fighter Command. With the amalgamation of Fighter and Bomber commands, Strike command was to come into force on 25 April 1968. Five Lightnings, four Hunters, two Meteors, one Canberra and two of the Historic Flight's Spitfires and a single Hurricane were involved, representing Fighter Command past and present.

Lightning T.55 four ship on their way to Coltishall.

Coltishall was to witness a second special event on 29 February when 19 year old Plt Off Vivienne Whyer, an ATC Officer based at Coltishall, became the 1000th, and youngest member of the RAF's 'Ten Ton Club.' Membership of this elite club is limited to those individuals who have handled the controls of an aircraft at 1000 mph. Plt Off Whyer was flown at this speed in an OCU Lightning T4, XM970, by the Station Commander, Gp Capt Mike Hobson. The 1000-mph barrier was exceeded at 1142 hours over the North Sea when Gp Capt Hobson passed the controls to his passenger for this historic milestone. Prior to this flight eight females, including a former ATS pilot Mrs Diana Barnato Walker, the first female to join the 'Ten Ton Club', had achieved this landmark.

February 1968 also saw the arrival of four Lightning T.55s of the Royal Saudi Air Force (RSAF). 55-711/A, 55-712/B, 55-713/C and 55-714/D were all allocated to 3 Squadron of the OCU. With six Saudi pilots on the staff, 3 Squadron was given the commitment to train Saudi pilots on the new marks of Lightning, the F.53 and T.55, which the Saudis had bought to replace their early mark F.52s and T.54s.

With the addition of the four Saudi Lightnings, Coltishall's strength was 44 aircraft, including aircraft that were undergoing major servicing at 60 MU at Leconfield. This number was to drop by one on the 21 June 1968 when XM188 was written off. After landing Sqn Ldr Arthur Tilsley taxied back to the dispersal on his No 2 engine, his No 1 engine having been shut down; normal practice whilst returning to the dispersal after landing. Unfortunately for the Squadron Leader, he did not realise that his No 2 services hydraulic pump was u/s. This meant that the wheel brake accumulator was the only thing left for his differential braking.

The accumulator failed just as the aircraft was about to negotiate the last bend in the taxiway prior to the squadron dispersal.

Having failed to negotiate the bend, the aircraft went straight across the grass and buried itself into the aircrew office at the end of No 1 Hangar. Sqn Ldr Tilsley vacated his aircraft by climbing onto the roof of the offices and quickly vacated the area. The throttle on No 2 engine jammed open in the collision and continued to run at 60% power. XM188 promptly began to devour the hangar, office contents, window frames, glass and furniture, throwing chewed bricks and mortar back towards ATC and causing a column of dust some 200 ft high! Finally a brave technician calmly disconnected a vital component that manually shut the Avon 210 down.

Lightning pilots trained at Coltishall were posted to their various operational air defence squadrons throughout the country, or to one of the overseas bases that operated the Lightning. There, the pilots would take their turn on QRA. Normally this duty lasted for a 24-hour period with the pilot being on constant readiness with his groundcrew and fully armed Lightning. Often this duty was carried out in a purpose designed QRA complex situated close to an operational runway, ready for the 'scramble' orders to come from one of the chain of radar stations which guarded our skies from unwanted intruders.

Coltishall, unlike the other Lightning bases in the UK, did not possess a QRA complex. As a training unit, Coltishall did not expect to be involved in operational sorties from the base. However, in 1971, the OCU was declared to Supreme Allied Commander Europe (SACEUR) as an operational squadron in its own right, and as such, could be called upon to carry out intercepts of unidentified aircraft.

Immediate aftermath of XM188 excursion into 3 Hangar.

Another view of XM188's accident.

Prior to this declaration, the OCU wore the shadow markings of 145 Squadron. However, as soon as they were declared to SACEUR, the aircraft began to sport the insignia of 65 Squadron; their new war role number plates. The first time that a scramble was initiated from Coltishall was before the OCU had been declared as an operational squadron. This happened during the evening of 8 September 1970.

Saxa Vord was one of a chain of UK radar stations whose task was to keep an eye on the skies around the northern approaches, identifying aircraft that approached or entered the North Sea or the sensitive 'Icelandic Gap.' 1970 was at the height of the Cold War with Russian aircraft making regular flights into the North Atlantic to test NATO's reaction.

At 2017 hours on the 8 September, a radar operator at Saxa Vord picked up a contact of an unidentified aircraft over the North Sea between the Shetland Islands and Norway. The contact was monitored at a steady speed of 630 mph at 37,000 feet travelling on a south-westerly heading. The contact was then seen to turn 30 degrees to head due south with its speed increasing to 900 mph and its altitude climbing to 44,000 feet.

The normal procedure for Saxa Vord was to now order a flash message to the nearest QRA flight. This urgent message was duly sent to the QRA flight Leuchars on the East Coast of Scotland. Within minutes two Lightning's were airborne and heading out across the North Sea. For all concerned the radar operators, pilots and groundcrew, this was just another routine scramble, but then the radar plotters noticed something on their screens that left them a little concerned. Up to this point the unidentified aircraft had been travelling at speeds and altitudes consistent with known Russian warplanes, however in a split second the blip on the radar had turned through 180 degrees and disappeared from the screens.

During the next hour the contact reappeared several times, and each time the Lightnings were vectored to investigate but then as quickly as it appeared it disappeared again. By this time two McDonnell Douglas F-4 Phantoms of the USAF from Keflavik in Iceland had been scrambled to assist the Lightnings in trying to intercept the intruder. The F-4s with their sophisticated radar were able to track the intruder themselves without the assistance of the ground radar controllers, however as they attempted to close on the contact they found that they had no more success than the Lightnings. The incident was now beginning to cause alarm to those in high places with the contact being monitored by various organisations within the NATO chain of command.

As more and more organisations became involved the Lightnings and Phantoms continued with their cat and mouse game. They made repeated attempts to close on the contact, but as they approached it disappeared. Eventually, the Lightnings recovered back to Leuchars leaving the Keflavik Phantoms to continue with the patrol.

At 2139 hours, the controllers picked up the contact again. This time the intruder was decelerating to 1300 mph which was almost the limit of the Lightnings and Phantoms. It was now tracked off the northern tip of Denmark at an altitude of 18,000 feet. By this time it was decided to 'scramble' two Lightnings from Coltishall to form a Combat Air Patrol (CAP) some 170 miles east of Great Yarmouth. To enable the thirsty Lightnings to maintain their CAP a Handley Page Victor tanker was scrambled to support them. With a further two Lightnings from Leuchars maintaining a CAP on a 50 mile east-west front, 200 miles north east of Aberdeen the contact was now between the two lines of fighters. At 2145 hours it was decided to 'scramble' a further Lightning from Binbrook to join in the search for the intruder. This aircraft, Lightning F.6 XS894, was flown by an American pilot on exchange with 5 Squadron, Capt William Schaffner. By the time he arrived on patrol, in addition to his machine, four further Lightnings, two Phantoms and three tankers were airborne on the alert and a Avro Shackleton from Kinloss joined them shortly after.

The outcome of this interception, which involved the Lightnings from Coltishall, is subject to much conjecture and differences of opinion. However, one thing is fact; the 5 Squadron Lightning F6, XS894 crashed on the night of 8 September 1970 with the loss of Capt Schaffner. Despite an intensive search by helicopters and Lifeboats from Bridlington, Filey and Flamborough, his body was never found.

Flt Lt Brian Carroll was an Instructor and Central Flying School (CFS) Agent on the OCU from 1970-73. His recollections of his time at Coltishall graphically illustrate the impact that operating a Lightning, in realistic operational conditions, had on one particular trainee pilot who was about to start his conversion flying with the OCU.

At this time, late 1971, 65 Fighter Squadron operated the Lightning T.4 trainer along with an assortment of F.1 and F.1As. As the squadron had been declared to SACEUR, they were also tasked as a front-line squadron, and as such were subject to alerts and Tactical Evaluation Exercises (TACEVAL) in just the same way as the full-time front line squadrons.

XMM3 belonging to 226 OCU.

Brian recalls that the OCU had recently received a new intake of pilots just out of Hunter flying at Chivenor. "They had completed their initial ground school programme of lectures and were reasonably conversant with the Lightnings systems and operating procedures; they had also started Flight Simulator sorties. All had also been airborne in the Lightning on Exercise 1, this was by way of an "Instructors Benefit" sortie during which the full potential of the aircraft was demonstrated, and all manoeuvres, needless to say, were within the approved flight envelope. We were just into the third week of October, the time, 0300 hours when a TACEVAL was called. The weather was cold and wet with steady rain that had been falling all of the previous day and was to continue for the next 48 hours. The cloud was extensive, the lowest as I recall being around 800 to 1000 feet and going all the way to 30,000 feet without a break, just the weather that fighter pilots dream about, well maybe on a bad day!

Within a very short time, the squadron was a hive of activity, the ground crews were working at a feverish pitch, pre-flight inspections were being completed as rapidly as possible, aircraft were then positioned in their pre-determined slots, ready for the pilots to mount up. Weather and exercise briefings for the aircrews were well under way, emergency and other procedures were all covered and we then awaited the first call from the operating authority to start the ball rolling. Meanwhile the new courses of students were being kept busy with routine jobs in operations and in the coffee bar. Operating as we did a number of two seaters, it was decided that we would fly as many of the new course students as possible in the right hand seats to let them see what operating a Lightning as a weapons systems was all about. They had of course no knowledge at this time of the radar, so it was left to each instructor to attempt to brief on that aspect during the sortie.

Word finally came through to bring a number of crews to cockpit readiness, I had been allocated a T.4 and so had a student with me. I had already carried out my own pre-flight inspection so we were able to climb straight into the cockpit. Strapping in only took a few moments, helmets were plugged into the telebrief, ground power was on line, radio frequency selected and flight instruments erected, weapons checked, all ready to start engines as soon as the scramble instructions were received. We had only been strapped in a few minutes when instructions came to scramble. Eagle 04 (my call sign) vector 120, make flight level 220, contact when airborne on Stud 7, SCRAMBLE.

Post declaration to SACEUR, the OCU aircraft wore the markings of 65 Squadron.

Three minutes later we entered the active runway, applying full power and accelerating as only the Lightning could. The rain was still falling; runway lights were blurred as we raced into the darkness. Now airborne, gear retracted, radar scanning, a hard turn onto our designated heading of 120 degrees and into a standard climb out as we changed frequency to Stud 7. Now snug and warm in what I called my 'airborne office', (it was nice to be out of the rain!), I explained briefly what the radar picture was showing, though I doubt that my passenger was able to make much of the orange scene displayed. Less than two minutes had passed since we entered the runway when we levelled off at 22,000 feet. Our target was said to be at 25,000 feet some 40 miles away crossing our track from right to left. To this day I do not think that my student actually saw the contact on the radar, even though I talked the attack through to the kill. We were of course in thick cloud so never made visual contact with the hostile intruder. As I broke away from this interception new instructions were passed from the Ground Controllers to take another target. This one was at high level and closing fast, re-heats were engaged and a rapid climb made to 36,000 feet, speed was increased to Mach 1.3. The weapons were rearmed and as we closed from astern I pulled the aircraft into a steep climb in an attempt to scan the target on radar. A good contact was made and the target was 'splashed' (destroyed) at 47,000 feet.

Back to cruise power and a gentle descent to 35,000 feet, briefly enjoying a clear sky above, well splattered with stars but no moon, the night was really very dark. I was beginning to think that we would be allowed to recover to base when another target was allocated, (they did actually ask if we had sufficient fuel for one more interception, we did). This next interception was at low level, apparently bent on attacking our base, so a rapid descent was required. Back on the power to idle/fast idle, air brakes extended and with gravity on our side we were soon plunging into the cloud layer at 30,000 feet - levelling off shortly after at 2,000 feet. To start the search for our third target we were vectored towards the intruder, finally catching up with him at 500 feet some 15 miles from the coast. This had to be a 'guns' kill as I had used all the available missiles on the first two interceptions. Closing with a degree of care, I finally made contact at around 200 yards, success number three. We were now cleared to recover to base. Briefly back to 3,000 feet to intercept the Instrument Landing System (ILS), we were cleared into the approach pattern. By now we were very low on fuel and as such had to make the first approach count. The rain was still falling as we

XM172 whilst serving with 65 Squadron. This Lightning was destined to spend many more years at Coltishall.

broke out of the overcast at 800 feet, the runway lights, as always a welcome sight, came into view and then 50 minutes after take off we touched down. Taxiing back to the dispersal I asked the student what he had thought of the sortie, he was remarkably quiet for some time. Eventually as we were walking back to the operations building he looked at me, shook his head and said that there was no way that he could ever do a sortie like that. From take off to recovery he reckoned not to have caught up with what was going on, even though I had told him as much as I could, bearing in mind the fact that my workload was high and left little time for chat. I did emphasise at that point that he would not undertake a mission of that nature for quite some time to come, but it did give him some food for thought as he progressed through the course. Some months later, he successfully completed the conversion and weapons course and finally proceeded to his first operational Lightning Squadron.'

226 OCU line.

Many of the ground crews who serviced the Lightning remember vividly their 'love-hate' relationship with the aircraft. Deep down however, they still look back with grudging respect and fondness for the experience of working on such a demanding machine.

John Welton recalls his time with the Lightning at the beginning of his career in the RAF. He could not believe his luck; after passing out from apprentice training at 1 SoTT, Halton, he found himself posted to Coltishall. A home posting and more to the point, going to work on the most dramatic and awe-inspiring aircraft; the Lightning. John takes up the story.

"As a boy living in Lowestoft I was used to the occasional sight of the silver interceptors flying up and down the coast and my annual treat was a visit to Coltishall for the Battle of Britain at Home Days. By the age of eleven, I could recite the details of most of the RAF's aircraft (any one else's hardware was of no interest!) and had made the appropriate Airfix models. As the years went by, I grew more and more convinced that I wanted to be an aircraft engineer, I never wanted to be a pilot but wanted to follow my father's example and tinker with machinery and find out how it worked.

A period of leave followed after passing out and then several other very new Junior Technicians and I reported to Coltishall to begin our careers in earnest. I presented myself to Flt Sgt 'Doc' Findley, (no, I didn't call him that to his face!) in the Engineering Wing Disip Office. When the proverbial riot act had been read as was his wont, I was told to report to 1 Aircraft Servicing Squadron to work on the F.1A and T.4 Lightnings of 145 Squadron, part of 226 OCU. Now, as any serviceman or woman will tell you, military life is full of 'formative' experiences and my first day in the hangar was no exception. Having donned my overalls and been issued with my tool tags on a pin attached to my lapel, I climbed on to the wing of a T.4 and stood next to the team Sergeant. I paused for a moment to drink in the experience; I remember it vividly even after all these years. The general hubbub of aircraft engineering activity throughout the hangar; voices around me discussing technicalities and the aircraft lurking in the shadows of the vast building. I can remember thinking at that moment that I had well and truly arrived and felt smugly self-satisfied that I was now working at the place where I had spent wide-eyed hours as a lad wondering at the marvels of the RAF.

Then I came back to reality with a bump. As I leant forward to inspect the mighty Rolls Royce Avon engine in its bay, my tool tags fell off their pin and clattered onto the wing. All the experienced heads turned towards me in consternation. One of the tags landed on the side frame of the open engine bay and rolled along its full length. Needless to say my heart went into my mouth as impending disaster loomed. Luckily the rolling tag fell outboard onto the wing and the threat of an engine removal (and my untimely death!) receded, much to my relief. Lesson number one - dropping anything into a Lightning always caused grief and hours of searching.

After my somewhat shaky start, I settled into the routine of scheduled servicing (it wasn't called serving in those days) on Blue Team lead by an amiable Chief Technician called Hughie Brown. To say that the Lightning was a technically challenging aircraft is an understatement! One looks at the hands and forearms of any RAF aircraft tradesman and you could spot the scars inflicted by the beast. Everything you needed to get at, appeared to have been hung on a piece of string at Warton and the rest of the airframe built around it! Indeed, certain tradesmen developed the knack of doing some component changes to such an extent that often a specialist would be called in to do the job. For example, SAC 'Nobby' Clarke was the Cold Air Unit expert and he could change one faster than anyone else, so much so that he would be called in off another shift to do the work rather than someone else struggle if we were in a hurry.

In between the routine of second line servicing, and when the 'aeros' pilot was practising or the airfield was busy, I would often stand outside on the airfield side of the hangar and watch the aerial goings on. Several of my friends had been for flights, not so difficult as the OCU had lots of T.4s, and I resolved to have a go at getting myself a trip. My best chance, I thought was if I was suitably trained and had all the ticks in the right boxes, namely, a decompression ride at the Aviation Medical Training Centre at North Luffenham and dinghy drills in the station swimming pool. If you had shown willing in this way, the QFI's on the squadron were far more amenable. I completed both exercises and duly had my name appended on what some in the hangar regarded as the 'Suicide List' in squadron operations. Incidentally, my decompression training had other consequences that I will relate to briefly.

A F.1A (I believe it was XM172 that now adorns the main gate) returned from a series of sorties with the pilots reporting stiff controls. Each time a thorough check of the control runs, associated bell cranks and bearings revealed nothing. Finally, we had an idea. Just behind the rear cockpit bulkhead were glands where the control rods passed through. The gland was packed with grease to form a seal to prevent loss of cabin pressure. It was possible that the grease was contaminated with water then it may freeze and stiffen the controls. A major clue was that the pilots were reporting that the problem only occurred at high altitude. Our plan was to simulate the freezing temperatures of the stratosphere by letting off a CO2 fire extinguisher close to the gland whilst someone operated the controls to see if the stiffness could be reproduced on the ground.

All we needed was a willing volunteer to sit in the cockpit, on oxygen in the freezing cold to move the controls. Guess what, I was the only one qualified to be the hangar pilot! After a medical check, which I unfortunately passed, I sat, somewhat apprehensively in the cockpit with the lid closed, power, hydraulics and the intercom on and breathing rather heavily on 100% oxygen. Surrounded by grinning faces peering through the Perspex I felt very alone and still being the new boy, expendable! With a crack and a hiss, the extinguisher went off behind me followed by a total white out as the cramped cockpit filled with CO2 gas; faces outside grinned in devilish glee as I disappeared in the mist of the freezing gas. I moved the controls forward and back then side-to-side as smoothly as I could and occasionally used a spring balance to check the effort required. Sure enough after a few minutes the controls stiffened and we had solved the problem. If I remember rightly, our investigation led to an instruction to check all Lightnings and replace the glands if the grease pathways were blocked preventing regular replacement of the grease.

Not long afterwards I got my first flight in a T.4. Preparation included the obligatory medical, kitting out and the ejection seat briefing, which included the usual humorous aircrew jokes such as 'If I say eject don't say pardon 'cause you'll be talking to yourself' and 'The last to leave is always the captain so if you hear a bang and a whoosh, you're captain.' I strode across the taxiway, as best I could in all the flying clothing, with my pilot Sqn Ldr May. As we strapped into T.4 XM995, the ejection seat jokes rolled about my head as I tried to concentrate on absorbing every moment of the experience. Finally the engines were wound up and we began taxiing out to the southern end of the runway. We held at the threshold and completed some more pre-flight checks and watched to our right as a student in an F.1A came down the glide path jinking to keep on the right approach line. I can remember Sqn Ldr May giving a running critique of the student's approach which became even more agitated as the single-seater progressed on its shaky way until it's main wheels smashed down into the earth just short in

the undershoot. Luckily for the pilot, the beast leapt back into the air slightly and settled onto the runway and continued rolling apparently non-the worse for the agricultural excursion. At this point my pilot suggested the student had a somewhat low IQ and was of unmarried parentage; at least that was the gist of it! He also suggested that I might like to breathe out, as my oxygen doll's eye had been permanently white for some time!

We were soon roaring down the runway and with the massive push of the reheated Avons we leapt into the air. The exhilaration was tremendous. Feeling the 'G' come on as we turned onto the departure heading and out over the North Sea, climbing all the way. Finally at about 20,000 feet the T.4 flipped upside down to round off the climb and I looked up (or was it down?) at the oil and gas exploration rigs on the surface below. This was a general handling sortie as we carried out some

Lightning T.4 XM995 went on to serve with 92 Squadron at Gütersloh and Wildenrath in West Germany.

aerobatic manoeuvres and charged up and down the East Anglian coast. Ground Control Approaches and circuits followed this. On the approach, I was amazed how much the pilot stirred the control column around to complete, much to my relief, a much smoother landing than the one I had witnessed earlier. Even so, I could understand why a Lightning landing was referred to as a 'controlled crash.'

The sortie was over far too quickly and as I stood on the pan with legs like jelly, listening to the clinking of the engines as they cooled, I knew that no matter how many aircraft I flew in during my career, none would compare with the Lightning. I also vowed that I would try for another and after de-kitting in the flying clothing section I went straight across to Squadron Operations and put my name on the 'Suicide' list again!

As the Flight Sergeant in charge of the Jaguar Aircraft Maintenance Flight (AMF) at Coltishall, I have the very strong feeling that I've come home. Each morning as I come through the main gate, I pass XM172 on its plinth (pointing earthwards, I always thought this was totally in appropriate!) and think of my time on the OCU. In the hangar is the nose section of XS899, which AMF is helping the author of this book restore to static display standard, which reminds me of my two tours at Binbrook. It is heartening to know that like me, and quite a few old Lightning hands now back at Coltishall who won't admit it, others share the enthusiasm for this aircraft and will ensure that the powerful presence of the Lightning will not be forgotten.'

The 1970 Battle of Britain Air Show held at Coltishall on the 19 September resulted in the loss of a Lightning T.4 XM990 and damage to a Lightning F.1A XM180. It had been decided to perform a diamond 16 flypast for the Battle of Britain Open Day. The week prior to the display, XM990 was undergoing checks to solve control problems, which added to the already high workload the engineers were under to prepare sixteen, plus Lightnings for the flying display. After an air test and practice for the formation, XM990 was declared ready. Large crowds enjoyed the open day and the flying, highlighted by the 16 aircraft flypast. Late in the afternoon, one of the Lightning F.1As, XM180, flown by Flt Lt Eric Hopkins, encountered starboard brake failure on landing which in turn caused the tyre to burst and the aircraft to leave the runway and end up stranded on the grass. The incident was serious enough to close the airfield and caused the remainder of the formation, including XM990, to divert to Wattisham.

It was early evening before Coltishall became operational again and clear for the diverted aircraft to return from Wattisham. As XM990 approached the airfield the aircraft began to corkscrew without warning, losing height with every revolution. Swiftly assessing the situation, the pilot applied power and pulled the aircraft up at the top of each corkscrew, gaining precious height. To the crowds on the ground it appeared that the pilot was staging an impromptu display of his own, but inside the aircraft the crew of Flt Lts Brian Fuller and John Sims knew otherwise, they were in fact out of control!

Eyewitnesses watched as something appeared to fall from the Lightning; it was, in fact, the canopy, followed shortly after by the first of the crew members. The pilot in control had to time his escape on the next upward corkscrew of the aircraft, which by now was getting perilously close to the ground. As he left the aircraft the Lightning only had height left to complete one and a half turns before crashing inverted into a small wood bordering the A1140 Norwich to South Walsham road very close to the village of Little Plumstead. Part of the tail was hurled across the road, only inches in front of a car which stopped with debris and soil covering the bonnet.

Local residents hurried to assist the crew. One had parachuted into a wood and was located in a small clearing, having removed his helmet and life jacket. He was complaining of pains to the back of his neck but was more concerned about the other crewman and the location of the crash. As he was speaking, the other crewman came into the clearing looking for him. It was a great relief to both of them that they had survived and that no one was hurt or killed on the ground or that any major damage was caused. The SAR Whirlwind soon arrived from Coltishall and whisked them off to hospital, one on a stretcher. The crash site was cordoned off for nearly a week while the RAF examined the wreckage before it was removed, along with tons of topsoil. The board of inquiry, following the crew's evidence, concentrated on the controls and control surfaces. Helped by the lack of a major fire, it was found that one of the aileron linkages had not been securely fitted and had vibrated out with the aileron movement causing the loss of control.

Gp Capt John Jennings, Station Commander, performed a unique presentation on behalf of President Richard Nixon, President of the United States of America, on 19 March 1971. Capt Edward Jordan was awarded the Air Medal and the United States DFC by command of the President for "Extraordinary Achievement whilst serving in South-East Asia." At the time of the promulgation of these awards, Capt Jordan was undergoing conversion training on the Lightning OCU prior to beginning an exchange tour with 29 Squadron at Wattisham.

The citation for the Air Medal said that Capt Jordan had been awarded the medal for "Meritorious achievement whilst participating in aerial flying. Outstanding airmanship and courage were exhibited in the successful accomplishment of important missions under extremely hazardous conditions. The highest professional efforts of Capt Jordan contributed materially to the mission of the USAF in South-East Asia."

His DFC citation read: "Captain Jordan distinguished himself by extraordinary achievement while participating in aerial flight as an F-4D aircraft Commander near Ph Ba Bai, Cambodia on 15 May 1970. On that date Capt Jordan led a strike mission of two F-4Ds against an active anti-aircraft gun position which he quickly destroyed, under covering at the same time a jungle infiltration track and large supply column. Despite a malfunctioning aircraft fuel system, Jordan pressed the attack as long as possible, causing heavy casualties amongst the hostile forces and destroying several vehicles and many hundreds of pounds of critical equipment. The professional competence, aerial skill and devotion of duty displayed by Capt Jordan reflect great credit on himself and the USAF."

At the beginning of 1972, the runways at Coltishall were in need of repair and resurfacing, so 65 Squadron and 2(T) Squadron, the F.3 and T.5 element of the old 145 Squadron, dispersed to Honington and Binbrook respectively. The OCU returned to Coltishall on 1 September, when they caused quite a stir as many of the local populace thought the airfield had been closed!

The RAF's Lightning display pilot for the 1973/74 season was Flt Lt Peter Chapman who was an instructor with the OCU. Peter was renowned for his scintillating performances in displaying the Lightning, whenever possible, flying his favourite mount an F.3, XP696. For his final display season XP696 sported a white fin and dorsal spine. The conclusion of the 1974 display season also saw the disbandment of 226 OCU in September of that year. Many of the OCU's Lightning F.1As and T.4s were withdrawn from service and scrapped. The same fate befell XP696, possibly due to Flt Lt Pete Chapman's performances!

During his tour at Coltishall as OC Operations Wing and Chief Flying Instructor for the Lightning OCU, Wg Cdr Dave Seward also found time to run the Battle of Britain Memorial Flight (BBMF). He took up his

XM180 leaves the runway after failure of the starboard brake.

appointment in April 1972 and during his two-and-a-half years at Coltishall flew 307 hours on Lightnings and 212 hours with the BBMF. His historical flying had been on all the Flight's aircraft with the exception of the Lancaster.

Wg Cdr Seward, "The Lone Kestrel", had flown immaculate displays in the Spitfire and Hurricane at more than 80 airshows during his tenure at Coltishall with the highlight of his display flying having been the 1973 Paris Air Show and two shows at Farnborough in 1972 and 1974. He also staged the only two large formation sorties flown by the flight when five of the aircraft flew over East Anglian airfields on 2 September 1972 and again when all six fighters were launched for a photographic session on 25 October 1973.

Wg Cdr Seward's enthusiasm for flying these wonderful aircraft was not dampened by the grey, dismal weather when he took to the air in Spitfire Vb AB910 on his last

XM990 on the line at Middleton St George.

XP696 on final approach in Coltishall.

day as OC BBMF on 18 October 1974. Everyone watching on the ground appreciated how he must have felt as he performed his last victory role over No 4 hangar. The bottle of champagne that he was presented with by Chief Technician Dick Melton after the flight was a token of appreciation form the groundcrew. This helped offset the sadness of the occasion for Dave Seward himself.

The Lightning training commitment was transferred from Coltishall to 'C' Flight 11 Squadron at Binbrook, which later took on the name Lightning Training Flight (LTF). From 13 April 1964 to 30 September 1974, 226 OCU flew a total of 64,457 hours on the Lightning and trained 810 pilots to fly Great Britain's last single seat fighter.

Devoid of its Lightnings, Coltishall's runway is resurfaced in 1972.

Chapter 10

MEMORIAL FLIGHT

Another resident with great significance to the heritage of the RAF was based at Coltishall from April 1963. The Historic Aircraft Flight, later renamed the Battle of Britain Memorial Flight, which could trace its origins back to June 1957, arrived from Horsham St Faith with Hurricane IIC LF363, and Spitfire PR.XIX PM631.

In 1965 the British Aircraft Corporation (BAC) presented its Spitfire VB, AB910, to the RAF. Vickers Armstrong Ltd and BAC having maintained the aircraft in airworthy condition since the late 1940s. AB910 was delivered to Coltishall by the famous Spitfire test pilot, Jeffery Quill, on 16 September 1965. 1968 saw a period of high activity for the Flight. During that year, they not only performed their usual roster of air display appearances, but all three Spitfires and the Hurricane were used in the filming of the epic aviation movie Battle of Britain. The aircraft operated out of the old Battle of Britain airfields at Duxford, Hawkinge, North Weald and Northolt, even venturing to the south of France during August 1968 to complete the aerial dogfight scenes of the film.

At the end of the filming schedule the Flight was to gain another Spitfire, this time a rare IIA which had actually seen operational service during the real Battle of Britain in 1940 with 266 (Rhodesia) Squadron which at the time was based at Wittering. P7350 had been part of the Colerne Museum for many years until it was surveyed by Simpson Aero Services for possible use in the film. It was found to be in remarkable condition for its age, and was restored to flyable condition at Henlow prior to extensive use in the filming. Out of the 11,939 Spitfires built by Vickers Armstrong at Castle Bromwich, P7350 was the 14th to roll off the production line in 1940.

During March 1972 IIC PZ865/G-AMAU joined Hurricane LF363. This aircraft, the famous 'Last of the Many', had been part of the Hawker Aircraft Company's Flying Museum which consisted of Cygnet G-EBMB, Hart J9941/G-ABMR and the Hurricane. As such these aircraft made several demonstration flights at rallies, garden parties and airshows over the years. These continued until the gradual wind-down of the Hawker Company in the early 1970s. Hawker gave the Hurricane a major overhaul and then presented it to the Flight on 30 March 1972, thus doubling the Flight's compliment of Hurricanes.

In 1973 the Flight took on it largest aircraft to date, Avro Lancaster I, PA474. The Lancaster was built as a

PM631 and LF363 north of Coltishall photographed from the Station Flight Avro Anson. (via Gerry O'Neill)

Four airworthy Spitfires of the BBMF at Coltishall in 1973. PM631 is in the foreground alongside AB910.

basic B.1 reconnaissance/bomber for use with the Far East Tiger Force, a role that it never achieved. Instead it was re-modified as a photographic reconnaissance aircraft and was issued to 82 Squadron in 1948. The aircraft spent the next four years undertaking a photo-survey of Africa, after which it was allocated to Flight Refuelling Limited, moving on eventually to the College of Aeronautics at Cranfield. It was probably this move that secured the aircraft's long-term future as it spent the next ten years as a flying test-bed for laminar wing research which was being undertaken at that time. In 1964, PA474 was replaced in this task by Avro Lincoln, RF342, and then the Lancaster was taken on

by the Royal Air Force Air Historical Branch. After being flown to 15 MU at Wroughton for re-painting in wartime camouflage the aircraft was flown to Henlow to be placed in open storage for the proposed RAF Museum at Hendon.

The following year 44 Squadron at Waddington, which was the first squadron to operate Lancasters during World War Two, offered to look after PA474 and possibly restore the aircraft to full airworthiness. The Lancaster was ferried to Waddington on 18 August 1965 and a team of volunteers worked on the bomber straight away. Two years of hard work culminated in its first post-restoration flight on 7 November 1967, having undergone what was virtually a total re-build. The aircraft, after satisfying the test flight schedule, was painted in the markings of Sqn Ldr John Nettleton's aircraft on the famous Augsburg raid, coded KM-B. After gaining the necessary Air Ministry approval the Lancaster was flown by 44 Squadron on the display circuit, crewed by 230 OCU Hastings personnel from Scampton, captained in the main by Sqn Ldr Ken Sneller, but operated out of Waddington.

In 1973 the Ministry of Defence (MOD), as the Air Ministry was now known, chose to pool all of its historic piston engined aircraft at Coltishall and therefore the Lancaster joined the Historic Aircraft Flight on 20 November 1973. With the addition of the Lancaster the name of the unit was changed to 'Battle of Britain Memorial Flight.'

Gp Capt Arthur Griffiths, the Station Commander of Waddington, flew the Lancaster the 45 minutes from Waddington to Coltishall. His wartime colleague from Bomber command, Gp Capt John Stacey, Coltishall's Station Commander, took to the air in one of the flight's Spitfires to escort the Lancaster in.

Apart from being an historic moment for both the

PZ865 whilst still owned by Hawker Siddeley in the early 1970s.

Gp Capt Griffiths after delivery of PA474 to Coltishall in 1973.

Memorial Flight and Coltishall, two former Lancaster pilots were VIP visitors to the base that day to witness the arrival of PA474. For Mr Eric Parker of Hellesdon, who during the war was based in Lincolnshire with 626 squadron and completed 33 operational sorties, it was the first time he had seen a Lancaster since leaving his old squadron.

The second former Lancaster pilot, Mr Denis Claxton of Ormesby St Margaret who flew 30 operations with his crew, recalled the long perilous nights over Germany. On one occasion he remembered when his port fin was shot completely away by an attacking German fighter.

Whilst at Coltishall, work on the Lancaster concentrated on bringing the aircraft back to its wartime B.1 configuration, a task which continues to this day. In 1975, a mid-upper gun turret was discovered in Argentina, a country that flew the Lancaster well into the early 1960s. The turret was brought back to the UK aboard HMS Hampshire, and was fitted to PA474 during the winter months at Coltishall, thus completing the external restoration of the aircraft.

That same year, the City of Lincoln adopted the Lancaster, and a strong bond was formed between the city and the BBMF, the aircraft then being named 'City of Lincoln.' Lincolnshire had been a stronghold of Bomber command during the Second World War and so this was seen as a fitting tribute.

During the Memorial Flight's stay at Coltishall, they averaged 72 displays throughout the year. The popularity of the Spitfires, Hurricanes and the Lancaster ensured that Coltishall was now famous for both its Lightning's and historic aircraft.

However, this was soon to change as the last of the Lightnings left the base in 1974 to be replaced by the Anglo-French Jaguar. Inevitably, with the need for more space at Coltishall after the introduction of the Jaguar,

it was decided that the BBMF would move to Coningsby, Lincolnshire. Despite a public outcry and a determined effort by the local press to overturn this decision the flight moved in March 1976. Prior to leaving, 7000 local people gathered at Coltishall to pay their respects to the flight and their historic aircraft. Apart from this moving gesture, the flight was also to say farewell to Flt Lt Peter Gostwick, who flew his final Hurricane display on this day after completing 39 years service in the RAF.

PA474 basks in the sun at Coltishall in 1975.

Chapter 11

SEARCH AND RESCUE

Search and Rescue has always featured in the history of Coltishall. During the Second World War, 5 ASR Flt, and then 278 Squadron, carried out this vital task.

From mid 1956, Whirlwind HAR.2s of 22 Squadron were detached to on SAR standby until being replaced in October of that year by a detachment of Sycamore HR.13 and HR.14s of 275 Squadron from Horsham St Faith. In the 60s and early 70s, the Westland Whirlwind HAR.10s of 202 Squadron were continually at 15 minutes readiness for any emergency, just as the Walrus and Anson's had been with 278 Squadron during the war years.

The Whirlwinds of 'D' Flight, 202 Squadron, arrived at Coltishall on transfer from Horsham St Faith, now Norwich Airport, on 30 August 1964, after being re-numbered from 228 Squadron. Whirlwinds of 'B' Flight, 22 Squadron, replaced those of 202 Squadron on 21 April 1974, and remained on continuous standby at Coltishall until 5 April 1979.

SAR operations have always caught the public interest. During the early days of SAR at Coltishall, much of the work carried out by the helicopters and their crews

A familiar site for many years around the country's coastline. The Westland Whirlwind operated from Coltishall for over two decades.

drew praise and admiration from those involved in specific incidents and from those who learnt of the rescues through the media. Most, if not all, of the crewmembers from the Coltishall SAR squadrons over the years became personally known to those involved with the many lifeboat and coastguard stations that were scattered around the East Anglian coastline. They all had a Common aim, to save lives, and as such became very close both professionally and socially.

The nature of their task, be it helicopter rescue, lifeboats at sea or coast guards operating from the land, always carried the element of danger. When any of these professional lifesavers lost their lives in the line of duty, all felt the shock. An incident on 22 June 1967 cost the lives of three such individuals. This time, those concerned were on a training sortie rather than on operations.

Whirlwind HAR.10, XJ414, had taken off from Coltishall on a routine patrol around the coast. At the controls was Flt Lt Archie Gavan, and joining him on this fateful flight was Flt Lt Gil Pink and Master Navigator Harry Crossman. The Whirlwind flew parallel to the beach off Yarmouth with the crew waving to holidaymakers who in turn acknowledged their friendly greeting. Suddenly, one of the main rotor blades detached from the rotor hub and severed the tail as it flew from the helicopter. With such a catastrophic failure, the pilot was unable to do anything, and about 150 yards off the beach the Whirlwind plunged into the sea.

Despite a further helicopter being scrambled from Coltishall and lifeboats being launched from various stations close to the crash scene it was obvious that there were no survivors. A Royal Navy diving team travelled throughout the night from Portsmouth and they finally recovered the crew from the tangled wreckage the following day.

The news of the tragedy not only shocked all those at Coltishall, but it had an equally devastating effect on the fishing industry of Lowestoft. Mr F E Catchpole spoke on behalf of the community by saying that they knew these men and admired them for their skill and courage. 'Many Lowestoft fishermen owed their lives to these men, and their families will, I know, wish to join us in expressing our heart felt sympathy to the relatives of these three men who have died and to whom we owe so much.'

Whirlwind HAR.10 XJ414 landing at Coltishall.

Military SAR units, which covered the length and breadth of the United Kingdom, were primarily established to give SAR cover to downed military aircraft over land and sea. However, it was the rescue of civilians and their involvement in shipping incidents that principally drew the news for the Squadrons.

Typical of this type of rescue happened on 2 April 1973. Three Whirlwind HAR.10s, two from Coltishall and one from Leconfield, were scrambled to render assistance to the 2000 ton collier 'Amberley', which had got into difficulties near the Dudgeon Shoal off Wells-next-the-Sea. The ship encountered a severe storm with 60-knot winds and 30-foot waves off the North Norfolk coast which had caused her cargo to shift, pushing the collier over onto her beam ends. With her funnel nearly awash and all her lifeboat stations smashed, the ship was in a very dangerous situation. In answer to her MAYDAY call, the two Whirlwinds from Coltishall, crewed by Flt Lts Jim Ross and Tony Cass and Master Signaller Ken Meagher in the first aircraft; Flt Lts Ian Christie-Miller and Don Arnold and Sgt Dick Armor in the second, set off in the direction of Wells. A Shackleton was vectored to the rescue location to give navigational assistance to the Whirlwinds. In addition a USAF HH-53 'Jolly Green Giant' from Woodbridge, Suffolk was also scrambled to assist in the rescue if needed.

In addition to the 60-knot winds, violent hail showers added to the pilot's increasing problems as they approached the ship. The winching process also presented all the problems imaginable with the 'Amberley' lying on her side and heaving vertically through the 30-foot swell. One by one the crew of the stricken ship were brought up, some of them in double-lifts. Six survivors were loaded into the Leconfield Whirlwind with the remaining eight being lifted by the two Coltishall machines. The rescue had been executed just in the nick of time because the 'Amberley' was

A Coltishall based Whirlwind carries out an RNLI exercise off Cromer.

now well awash with the seas pouring into her holds. Just as her master, Capt J Black, was lifted to safety the ship rolled over and sank in the area known as the Blakeney Over-Falls. A total of five commendations were awarded to the crews of the Whirlwinds that night, including the AFM to Sgt Dick Armor and the Queen's Commendation for Bravery to Flt Lt Tony Cass.

During May 1979, Westland Sea King HAR.3s of 'C' Flight, 202 Squadron, replaced the Whirlwinds of 22 Squadron. The Sea King was a quantum leap forward over the Whirlwind in its search and rescue capability. In addition to greater range, passenger carrying capacity and an advanced avionics suite, enabling the aircraft to fly in conditions which would normally keep the Whirlwinds grounded. It was powered by a pair of Rolls Royce Gnome engines which gave it a greater safety margin over the single engined Whirlwind. It was not long before the Sea Kings from Coltishall became involved in SAR missions around the Norfolk coast; however its first real test was to come early the following year.

SAR operations of any kind could be hazardous. However, when confronted with the conditions in which the Sea Kings and their crews found themselves on the 27 March 1980, during the rescue of survivors of the 'Alexander Kielland' Hotel Platform disaster, a whole new meaning to the word 'hazardous' becomes evident.

Flt Lt Jim Bellingall, the captain of the Sea King, described the conditions of the rescue as the worst he had ever been in. Having scrambled from Coltishall at 1930 hours, Flt Lt Bellingall with his crew, Flt Lt Adrian Nockles, Co-Pilot, Master Aircrew John Reeson, Radar Operator and their Winchman, Master Aircrew Ted Berry fought their way in atrocious weather conditions to the search area which was almost two hours away.

The Sea King then conducted the search under an 80-foot cloud base and over mountainous 30-foot waves. The helicopter was in a search pattern three to five miles away from the incident; however the crew could only rely on the radar to see what was happening at the disaster site. The search area, approximately seven miles by three miles, was covered in debris from the platform. They spotted four ten-man dinghies in the

water but they were all empty. In addition there were lifejackets, empty life rafts and general wreckage but to the surprise and disappointment of the crew, no people.

The Sea King continued the search for around two and a half to three hours before going to Boulmer for a refuel and for the crew to grab three hours precious sleep before resuming the search the next day.

Just before dawn on 28 March, a second Sea King was scrambled from Coltishall to join in the desperate search. Flt Lt Dave Carey with his Co-Pilot Flt Lt Paul Martin, Radar Operator Sgt John Brookes and Winchman Flt Sgt Mel Ward, were joined by Sqn Ldr Peter Coles, Station Medical Officer (SMO) and Sgt Rick Skelton as an extra look out. After more than seven hours in the air the Sea King landed back at Coltishall to refuel. Flt Lt Carey described the weather conditions in the area as 'not bad at all', unfortunately no survivors were spotted.

In the meantime Flt Lt Bellingall and his crew had resumed their search after a well-earned rest at Boulmer. During the flight, their Sea King developed a fault and they made a cautionary diversion to the

The highly versatile Westland Sea King replaced the Whirlwinds in May 1979.

oilrig 'Albuskjell F' to refuel and have the aircraft checked. It was on this rig that Flt Lt Bellingall talked to a North Walsham man who said that he was due to go to the 'Alexander Kielland' on 27 March, but the storm had stopped all helicopter flights between the rigs. This was also the reason why so many men were aboard the hotel platform, where two oilrig crews were waiting for the weather to ease. A total of 89 lucky individuals owed their lives to the crews of RAF and Royal Norwegian Air Force Sea Kings, who, in gathering darkness and gale force winds on that fateful day managed to reach the scene of the disaster from their bases nearly 200 miles away on either side of the North Sea.

Tragedy struck Coltishall, and the SAR fraternity, on 18 November 1980 when Master Air Loadmaster (MALM) David Bullock, a winchman on 202 Squadron, lost his life while trying to save the life of an American airman, Lt Col William Olson.

Lt Col Olson's Fairchild A-10A Thunderbolt II collided with a similar aircraft in mid-air over Itteringham. The pilot of the other A-10A ejected over the collision scene and parachuted to safety. In the mean time, Olson attempted to fly his aircraft back to Woodbridge. Near Winterton, he lowered the undercarriage on his A-10, but the damage sustained in the collision allowed all the hydraulic oil to drain away, making his aircraft totally uncontrollable. He was then left with no alternative but to eject over the coast and was quickly blown out to sea in the 40-knot winds.

With the Sea King scrambled from Coltishall they were soon on station over the downed airman. MALM Bullock was lowered into the sea near the unconscious pilot. As gales whipped up 15-foot seas MALM Bullock hooked himself onto the pilot and proceeded to cut away the entangled parachute which by this time was inflating in the gusting winds. Despite the numbing cold, MALM Bullock almost succeeded in detaching the parachute when another gust of wind caught the inflated canopy with such force that it caused the rescue cable from the Sea King to snap. MALM Bullock tried desperately to keep the pilot's head above water, but eventually succumbed himself and lost consciousness as the parachute continued to drag them both under the water.

With the Sea King out of action due to the winch cable snapping, the two airmen were finally recovered by a CH-53 'Jolly Green Giant' from the rescue squadron at Lt Col Olson's home base at Woodbridge.

For his supreme sacrifice in this tragic rescue, MALM

202 Squadron Sea King at Coltishall in June 1979.

Bullock was posthumously awarded the George Medal, one of the countries highest awards for bravery. The citation said that he could have saved his own life, but consciously and with conspicuous courage chose to remain with the pilot in the hope of saving his life.

On 29 October 1981, Mrs Patricia Bullock and her two children, Richard and Melanie, went to Buckingham Palace to be presented with her late husband's George Medal by Her Majesty the Queen. In addition, the USAF bestowed one of their highest honours, the Airman's Medal. The Medal was presented to Mrs Bullock by Gen Baxter, 3rd Air Force Headquarters Commander, at Mildenhall on behalf of a grateful USAF. The Prince Philip Helicopter Rescue Award and the Sir James Martin Memorial Medal was also presented to Mrs Bullock on behalf of her late husband.

On 13 August 1981, Sea Kings from Coltishall responded to one of the worst helicopter disasters in British history when a Wessex 60 of Bristow Helicopters crashed seven miles off Bacton with the loss of 13 lives. One Sea King scrambled soon after a distress call was received by ATC at Coltishall from the stricken Wessex. The Sea King, captained by Flt Lt Stuart Mould, took off from Coltishall at 1647 hours with its normal crew of four plus a doctor. They reached the scene of the crash, seventeen miles away, in just eight minutes. On arrival Flt Lt Mould described the area as 'looking pretty disastrous', the Wessex having completely broken up on contact with the water. The winchman, MALM Keith Mursell, eventually winched eight bodies into the helicopter before transferring them to waiting ambulances on Lakenham playing fields just after 1800 hours. A second Sea King from Coltishall was also re-routed to the scene whilst flying an injured man with a severed finger from a gas rig to hospital.

Immediately after the Falklands Campaign in 1982, 'C' Flight was deployed from Coltishall with their Sea Kings to provide SAR cover in the Falkland Islands. With this re-location came independent unit status, when the detachment was renumbered 1564 Flight. On 1 August 1983, 'E' Flight of 22 Squadron was again to reform at Coltishall with the Wessex HAR.2.

SAR operations around the coastline of East Anglia, as well as many inland taskings, kept 22 Squadron busy on their arrival back at Coltishall. Once again the 'shouts' involving civilian rescues tended to highlight the role of SAR squadrons to the general public. However, in July and August 1984, Coltishall's Wessex were called to provide the service for which they were established, the SAR support to downed military airman. Ironically both incidents involved Jaguar aircraft from Coltishall.

The first incident occurred on 12 July 1984, when

22 Squadron Wessex replacing the Sea Kings of 202 Squadron.

Jaguar GR.1, XZ393, of 54 Squadron, was involved in a mid-air collision with Tornado GR.1, ZA408, of the Tornado Weapons Conversion Unit (TWCU) based at Honington. At approximately 1600 hours, the two aircraft collided twelve miles north of Coltishall, over the costal town of Sheringham. The pilot of the Jaguar ejected just prior to his aircraft plunging in flames into the sea. A Wessex that had been scrambled to the scene moments earlier rescued him from his dinghy. The pilot was transferred to the RAF Hospital at Ely for observation having only suffered slight injuries caused during the ejection sequence.

The two-man crew of the Tornado abandoned their aircraft prior to it crashing into a field at Becketts Farm, Hempstead. A second Wessex from Coltishall collected the crew, who were also only suffering slight injuries, from the crash scene and transported them to hospital for observation.

Ironically the collision occurred close to the spot where on 19 August 1968, Victor K.1A, XH646, of the Tanker Training Flight (TTF) and Canberra B(I)6 WT325 of 213 Squadron collided at 12,000 feet with the loss of all seven crewmembers.

Just one month later, on 22 August, Jaguar GR.1 XZ395 again from 54 Squadron, crashed 20 miles off Cromer during a routine exercise. The pilot ejected safely from the Jaguar following the loss of control of his aircraft just after 1300 hours. Once again the Wessex was scrambled from Coltishall as soon as his Mayday was received. After a short time in his dinghy, the pilot was winched to safety and returned to Coltishall, none the worse for his experience.

'E' Flight was to provide 24-hour cover at Coltishall for almost two years until its eventual move to Manston on 1 September 1985. That same day, 'C' Flight of 202 Squadron returned to Coltishall with their Sea King HAR.3s. The Sea Kings were to be a familiar sight once again at the base and around the East Anglian coastline and, as with previous incumbent squadrons based at Coltishall in the Search and Rescue role, were kept busy with 'shouts' to both military and civilian incidents.

The AFC was awarded to one of 202 Squadron's winchmen, MALM Mel Ward, for his part in the rescue of 32 crewmembers of a burning oil tanker in January 1986. The Greek registered, 73,000 ton oil tanker, 'Orleans' had been holed and caught fire in a collision with a trawler in the North Sea, 65 miles off Great Yarmouth.

The Sea King was scrambled from Coltishall to assist in the rescue with a crew consisting of Flt Lts Martin Powell and Charles Gillow, pilots, Master Aircrews John Reeson, Radar Operator and Mel Ward, winchman. Despite burning oil and snowstorms, which made visibility difficult, MALM Ward risked his life three times. First he volunteered to be lowered onto the deck of the blazing ship. Contending with the language barrier and severe breathing difficulties due to the acrid smoke, he calmed four of the crew and winched them to safety. During the rescue attempt the Sea King was forced to move away, but MALM Ward decided to stay on board to launch a life raft from the stern of the ship after hearing explosions below deck. He then briefed the remaining crewmembers to follow him in pairs. He then jumped 80 feet into the water from the stern of the tanker. However, none of the terrified crew followed.

MALM Ward swam clear of the stern of the ship and its turning screws before being winched back into the safety of the Sea King. Once again he volunteered to be winched on to the deck of the ship despite having swallowed large quantities of seawater and oil. Once on the deck the hysterical crew mobbed him as he prepared the first two members for winching. During the first lift the cable became tangled in the superstructure of the ship and broke leaving the two men suspended over the sea. MALM Ward recovered them by climbing over the rail and dragging them on board. The Sea King was damaged by the whiplash from the broken cable that made the helicopter uncontrollable for a few seconds. Luckily the cable disintegrated, although the rotor head was badly damaged. The pilot of the damaged Sea King managed to reach a nearby oilrig and land his disabled aircraft on the helicopter platform of the rig.

Meanwhile back on the 'Orleans' MALM Ward organised the panic-ridden crew into launching another lifeboat from which a rig support vessel, subsequently rescued all the remaining crewmembers, and MALM Ward.

MALM Ward was unaware that his colleagues in the Sea King had made it to safety, as he was sure that the damage caused by the whiplash of the broken cable was sufficient to cause the helicopter to ditch. Until the support vessel crew told him that they were in fact safe, he was convinced the Sea King had ditched. The citation for MALM Ward's AFC paid tribute to his determination, resourcefulness and courage in the operation to evacuate the crew.

'C' Flight, 202 Squadron, continued in their vital role until the Flight moved to Manston on the 28 August 1988 as part of the relocation of SAR assets following the Herald of Free Enterprise ferry disaster. 'E' Flight, 22 Squadron once again took up residence at Coltishall with the Wessex HAR.2.

Mercy missions flown by SAR helicopters and their crews were often difficult and always varied. On 9 February 1991, Flt Lt Gerry Crombie and his crew flying in a Wessex from Coltishall airlifted a seriously ill 14-month old girl on a desperate 150-mile flight from The James Paget Hospital at Gorelston to the Great Ormond Street Hospital, London.

Doctors decided that the airlift was a safer and

MALM Mel Ward AFC.

quicker option due to the torturous road journey that an ambulance would have to face due to the region's snow-clogged roads. Flt Lt Crombie described the conditions as like 'driving on a motorway in snow; you just cannot see.' The Wessex was forced to fly at around 500 feet, at a speed of 40 knots due to the treacherous conditions before landing at Regents Park. Under normal conditions the flight would have been made at 500 to 1000 feet at 100 to 110 knots. Even then they were only able to find the park using an Ordnance Survey map because normal navigational methods were hampered by the weather. Unfortunately the mercy dash was in vane as the young girl lost her fight for life early the next morning.

'E' Flight remained on standby at the base until 18 July 1994, when they too left Coltishall for the last time. Today, the nearest SAR cover is provided by a Detachment from 22 Squadron, flying their Sea King HAR.3s out of the Army Air Corps base at Wattisham.

Chapter 12

GATE GUARDS

The first recorded gate guard to be allocated to Coltishall for display purposes was Gloster Meteor F.3 EE424, which arrived in October 1955. This aircraft, prior to being moved to an unknown location, was joined by a similar Meteor, EE419 which was resplendent in her colours of the RAF High Speed Research Flight. EE419 stood guard from July 1960 to late 1969 when it was moved to Abingdon as a travelling display airframe.

During 1960-62 Spitfire LF.XVIe TE476, was also on gate guard duty with EE419 until it was moved to Neatishead, however the exact dates are unknown. In the latter part of 1960 Spitfire XVI, SL542, arrived from Horsham St Faith and guarded the entrance until 1988. The aircraft carried the code 4M-N of 695 Squadron until it was finally moved to St Athan for storage. Prior to being allocated to Coltishall, SL542 had served with 595 and 695 Squadrons, 1 and 2 Civilian Anti-Aircraft Co-operation Unit (CAACU), Duxford Station Flight and Horsham St Faith.

Prior to moving to Horsham, SL542 was used as a display airframe at Duxford during the last years of RAF occupation of the famous wartime airfield. The Spitfire was eventually moved to St Athan for storage when it was decided to replace 'real' aircraft on display at various RAF Stations with glass fibre replicas.

Eventually, the Spitfire was used as a swap by the RAF Museum for a Handley Page Hampden that had been recovered from Russia. SL542 was sold to a collector in the USA who planned to return the Spitfire to airworthy condition as N2289J. However, SL542 was once again to change hands when it was sold to a Canadian enthusiast, Anthony Jurak. Presently, January 1998, the aircraft is with Henry Stenger at his Spitfire Restoration Centre,

Lady Bader and Johnnie Johnson unveil Hurricane I replica V7467 in July 1989.

Bartow, Florida, where the aircraft is once again airworthy.

The Hurricane Mk I replica V7467, LE-D, which guards the entrance today carries the markings of Douglas Bader's aircraft when he flew from the station with 242 Squadron. His widow, Lady Joan Bader, unveiled the aircraft in July 1989 in the presence of Sir Denis Crowley-Milling and many of Sir Douglas's old wartime comrades.

Gloster Meteor F.3 EE419.

Spitfire XVI SL542.

Lightning F.1A XM172.

The other aircraft which guards the station to this day is Lightning F.1A, XM172. The English Electric Company at Salmesbury in Lancashire built this aircraft. It made its first flight on 10 October 1960, when it was delivered from Salmesbury to English Electric's test facility at Warton. 56 Squadron was the first unit to receive the F.1A, and in fact XM172 was the first aircraft to arrive at Wattisham on 14 December 1960. Whilst with 56 Squadron, the aircraft regularly flew with the 'Firebirds', the squadron's aerobatic team.

In February 1965, XM172 was transferred to Coltishall to join 226 OCU. With the OCU, the aircraft was to fly with both of the shadow squadrons, 65 and 145 Squadrons. On 11 August 1965, XM172 was flown to 60 MU at Leconfield for major servicing. XM172 did not return to Coltishall until September 1966, when it rejoined 145 Squadron.

October 1973 was to see the aircraft return to Leconfield, this time for disposal. Saved from the scrapman's torch in early 1974, XM172 again returned to Coltishall, this time as a display aircraft. After a considerable amount of equipment had been removed from the airframe, XM172 was placed on display on 24 September 1974 in the markings of 145 Squadron. As a display aircraft, XM172 was issued with the maintenance serial, 8427M. The aircraft was formally unveiled on the 30 September 1974, ironically the last day of Lightning operations from Coltishall, by AVM R W G Freer, AOC 11 Gp. In April and May 1989 the aircraft underwent a total repaint and the markings of 145 Squadron were replaced by those of the OCU.

As a result of the disastrous 'one gate guard' policy, introduced in 1989, XM172 was put up for disposal. Thankfully a collector rather than the scrapman, a fate that befell many other historic aircraft preserved as gate guards at that time, purchased the Lightning and the aircraft remained on display just outside the main gate for another 11 years. XM172 was eventually moved to Booker Airfield in Berkshire by Parkhouse Aviation in 2000 with the hope that one day it would be displayed on a roundabout at Farnborough. That wish never came to fruition and the airframe is now privately owned by a collector in Cumbria.

XW563 was on display from September 2001 until the stations closure in 2006.

The last aircraft to carry out Gate Guard duties was a type linked to Coltishall for over 32-years; the Jaguar. GR.1 XW563 was one of eight prototype aircraft developed jointly by the BAC and Breguet of France and made its maiden flight from Warton on 12 June 1970.

After 678 hours of flight-testing, including operational trails using a newly built motorway, the aircraft was retired in 1977 and used as a weapons load trainer. Following this training role, XW563 new role was as the Gate Guardian for Brüggen in Germany where it remained on display from October 1985 until August 2001. Following the closure of Brüggen, the aircraft was moved to Coltishall where it replaced the Lightning. Prior to being placed on display, the airframe was cleaned, repainted in a gloss-grey finish and remounted complete with drop tanks and under wing electronic defensive pods and was unveiled by the Station Commander, Gp Capt Chris Harper, on 14 September 2001.

In addition to its role as a Gate Guard, the aircraft was dedicated as a permanent memorial to those members of the Jaguar Force who have lost their lives during the course of their duties.

XW563 on the gate. Today, she resides outside the County Hall in Norwich.

Chapter 13

THE JAGUAR ERA

It was in 1962 that the UK and France found themselves separately looking for a high-performance jet trainer. The RAF wanted to replace the Folland Gnat and the Hawker Hunter in about 1975; the Armèe de'l Air desired an aircraft to bridge the gap between the Fouga Magister and the Dassault Mirage III with an enter-service date of 1970.

Denis Healey publicly revealed that an agreement in principle had been forged between the UK and French governments on 28 February 1965. A Memorandum of Understanding (MoU) was then signed on 17 May 1965 for the development of what was to become the Jaguar, a name given to the aircraft just in time to be advertised at the Paris Air Show in 1965.

Each nation undertook to buy 150 Jaguars. The UK required their aircraft for the RAF and the Royal Navy, whilst the French opted for 75 single and 75 two seat Jaguars. On 9 January 1968, a new MoU was signed covering production increase commitments for both countries to 200 Jaguars each, with the UK opting for 90 of the new strike version. In October 1970, the UK position changed once again. There would now be 165 strike Jaguars and 35 two-seat trainers, all to be issued to front line squadrons and a single OCU. However, none were destined for advanced flying training as was first envisaged.

The original collaboration success of BAC and Breguet in the design and development of the Jaguar was taken as a model for future ventures. In May 1966 BAC and Breguet formed a joint company which was registered in France as SEPECAT (Sociètè Europèenne de Production de l' Avion d' Ecole de Combat et d' Appui Tactique).

Eight Jaguar prototypes were built of which three were produced in the UK. The first prototype, two-seater E01/F-ZWRB accomplished its maiden flight on 8 September 1968 from Istres, near Marseilles, with French test pilot Bernard Witt at the controls. Jimmy Dell, the first Briton to fly the aircraft, made his first flight from Istres in a single seater prototype, A04/F-ZWRE on 27 May 1969.

The British test programme began with Jaguar S06/XW560 flying from Warton near Blackpool on 12 October 1969, with Jimmy Dell in command. On 12 June 1970, S07/XW563 flew with Europe's first digital inertial navigation system. The first British built two-seater, B08/XW566, took to the air at Warton on 30

The first of many; the prototype Jaguar E01 at Istres.

August 1970, this time with Paul Millett at the controls. Testing of the British prototypes and development aircraft continued from the company airfield at Warton, and from the aircraft establishments at Boscombe Down, Bedford and Farnborough until the first squadron aircraft were accepted into the RAF with 54 Squadron in March 1974.

A total of eight front-line RAF squadrons and an OCU were to be equipped with the Jaguar. In addition to 54 Squadron, there were two further UK based operational squadrons, 6 and 41, all based at Coltishall. 226 OCU, responsible for training all the pilots onto the Jaguar, was based at Lossiemouth in Scotland. The five remaining operational squadrons were assigned to RAF Germany. The strike squadrons, 14, 17, 20 and 31, were all based at RAF Brüggen, whilst 2 Squadron, the Tactical Reconnaissance Unit, was based at Laarbrüch.

Since 1974, Coltishall has been the UK home of the Jaguar. The first Jaguar squadron, 54 (Fighter) Squadron, arrived at Coltishall on 8 August 1974. The squadron, under the command of Wg Cdr Terry Carlton, was established at Lossiemouth on 29 March 1974, almost a month before disbanding as a Phantom FGR.2 operator at Coningsby on 23 April.

Wg Cdr John Quaterman led 6 Squadron south from Lossiemouth in November 1974, from where it had re-equipped with the Jaguar from the Phantom FGR.2 in June 1974. The final Jaguar squadron to arrive at Coltishall, on the 1 April 1977, was 41 (Fighter) Squadron. 41(F) Squadron was also a convert from the Phantom FGR.2, and like 54(F) Squadron, it had previously been based at Coningsby.

On 20 October 1975, Sqn Ldr Peter Orme of 6 Squadron received a top award from the French in Paris for his part

Jimmy Dell demonstrates XW560 in Lancashire skies; circa 1969.

in flying a badly-damaged French Air Force Jaguar safely back to its base following an incident that took place the previous April. Sqn Ldr Orme, a Flight Commander with 6 Squadron, had been on a routine exchange with a French Air Force Jaguar unit stationed at St Dizier when the Jaguar he was flying in with commandant Claude Gautier was hit by a ricocheting cannon shell.

During the training flight they used the Suippes weapons ranges to fire the aircraft's 30mm cannon. Whilst in a gentle climb at 300 feet and flying at nearly 500 mph the aircraft was hit by a spent cannon shell which shattered the Perspex canopy and hit commandant Gautier's helmet. The clear Perspex screen between the front and rear cockpits was also shattered causing needle sharp fragments of Perspex to hit Sqn Ldr Orme in the face and on his body.

Commandant Gautier slumped in his seat and the aircraft rocked violently, momentarily out of control. As the aircraft lost power, Sqn Ldr Orme took control and during the 15 minute flight back to St Dizier he was able to re-start one of the engines although he was unable to control the other engine which continued to loose power and overheat until the Jaguar was flying at under 200 mph. The French pilot was able to retake control and land at the base despite blood pouring from a serious head injury.

XW563, the platform for Europe's first digital inertial navigation system.

The United States Ambassador to Britain, Mr Elliot Richardson, visited Coltishall on 31 October 1975 he was met by the Station Commander, Gp Capt Leslie Swart and the AOC 38 Gp, AVM P G K Williamson. Mr Richardson was accompanied by AVM D B Craig, Assistant Chief of Air Staff (Operations) and Col Tom McInernrey, the US Air Attaché in London, on his visit to Coltishall to see the RAF at work. During his visit the Ambassador saw the Jaguar in action with a simulated attack on a tank column on the airfield. He also had the chance to make a closer inspection of the RAF's modern and historic aircraft in a static display.

A Buccaneer, Harrier and Jaguar, plus equipment and missiles, were all shown and explained to Mr Richardson who took the chance of a first-hand look at the controls of a Jaguar from the cockpit. But the aircraft of most historic interest to the distinguished visitor was undoubtedly the Spitfire IIa of the BBMF. The highlight of the Ambassador's visit came during the afternoon when he took a three-quarter hour flight in a Harrier T.2 of 233 OCU based at Wittering piloted by Sqn Ldr Chris Marshall.

Europe's Supreme Allied Commander, Gen Alexander Haig, visited Coltishall on 11 February 1976. The four-star NATO General was on his first visit since the station re-equipped with the Jaguar. During his visit, hosted by the AOC 38 Gp and the Station Commander. The General was shown many aspects of the working life of Coltishall.

A further distinguished visitors to Coltishall in 1976 saw Princess Margaret fly in for a five-hour inspection of the station on 30 June. Although the Princess was surrounded by an impressive display of military hardware, she also found herself listening to a child's nursery rhyme. The toddlers of the station's nursery school had been rehearsing the rhyme for weeks. Right up to the last minute no one was sure whether Princess Margaret would be able to stop and listen to the rendition. As she reached the nursery school section of the hangar display she paused and readily agreed to stop for a moment to listen to the rhyme about a caterpillar. The Princess gave the Royal seal of approval with a smile and a laugh.

Princess Margaret arrived at Coltishall just before midday in an Andover aircraft of the Queen's Flight and was met by AM W J Stacey, Deputy C-in-C Strike command. The Princess's host and guide for the day was the Station Commander, who accompanied her in an open-top Landrover along the lines of Jaguar aircraft that flanked either side of the procession's route.

Following the inspection she was briefed on Coltishall's part in Britain's and NATO's defence network, visited the Junior Rank's No1 Club and after lunch in the Officers' Mess toured displays in one of the hangars. These included engineering, Search & Rescue as well as station clubs and societies.

After a quick look at a Jaguar and support systems in a camouflaged hide, Princess Margaret settled down to watch a military exercise mounted by several RAF squadrons and soldiers of the Royal regiment of Wales. The display featured Coltishall Jaguars, Harriers, Hercules transport aircraft, Phantom photo-reconnaissance aircraft as well as Gazelle and Puma helicopters. The exercise, complete with pyrotechnics, was designed to show the Princess how the RAF would combine with the Army units in halting an enemy advance.

Many people were presented to Her Royal Highness during the visit including Capt Michel Ballu of the French Air Force who was based at Coltishall flying Jaguars on an exchange tour and whilst Gp Capt Swart was on hand to greet Princess Margaret it was his ten-year-old daughter Elizabeth who presented the Princess with a bouquet of flowers just before she left the station.

Just a year after 6 and 54(F) Squadrons were declared operational the Station suffered two losses during the NATO Exercise, TEAMWORK 76. On 15 September 1976, 6 Squadron lost Jaguar XX735, in a fatal crash at Eggebeck in Germany. Two days later, 54 Squadron lost XX120, and its pilot, when it ditched off Samose Island, Denmark. These two tragic accidents highlighted, that even during peacetime, the risks of operating in the ground attack role have always been great, and the dangers still exist even with complicated and sophisticated systems which are employed to assist the pilots.

About 120 veterans of the Royal Flying Corps (RFC) and the Royal Naval Air Service (RNAS) met at Coltishall on 1 April 1977 to mark the 59th anniversary of the amalgamation of the two services to form the RAF. The veterans, most in their 80's, travelled from as far afield as Surrey, Sussex, Essex, Cambridgeshire and Lincolnshire for their reunion which was organised by the Lions Clubs in Norfolk, Suffolk and Cambridgeshire.

Jaguar GR.1 XX121 of 54 Squadron at Coltishall in 1976.

The large centre line recce pod gives this Jaguar away as belonging to 41(F) Squadron on finals into Coltishall.

The youngest was aged 76; he joined the RFC as a boy entrant in 1918. The oldest was 94-year-old Wallace Tipple from Redisham near Beccles. Tipple was a balloon observer with the RFC in Palestine in 1917. The reunion brought together flyers and ground staff of all ranks from a Private Second Class to a Group Captain.

During their day long-visit to the base the veterans were invited to inspect the Jaguars from the three resident squadrons. For one of them, 80-year old Capt E N Griffith who travelled from his home at Bishops Stortford, there was an opportunity to climb into the cockpit. In 1918, Capt Griffith was the Commander of 'C' Flight, 48 Squadron RFC based at Bertangles, North Amiens, on the Somme and flew Bristol Fighters.

Another highlight of the day was the presentation of some of the flying records of a World War I pilot who won the DFC for a night reconnaissance mission in 1918. The presentation was made by Mrs Joan Copeland-Sexton who's farther, Lt Clifford White was one of six flyers who took part in the mission over St Quentin, France on 14 June 1918. Lt White, who became Sheriff of Norwich in 1941-42, and his five colleagues were each awarded the DFC. Mrs Sexton presented her fathers flying records, together with a special tie which was produced when the six reunited later, to 83-year old Wg Cdr T E Guttery. The wing Commander represented the Shuttleworth Collection at Old Warden, Bedfordshire where the artefacts were placed on display following the reunion.

Following the severe gales and floods that hit Norfolk on the night of Wednesday 11 January 1978. Coltishall was requested by the local authorities to dry out flooded houses at Kings Lynn, Wells-next-the-Sea, Overy Staithe, Bacton and Walcott. Parties of up to six men of the Mechanical Engineering (Ground) Section

equipped with aircraft heaters were deployed to help the local authorities for twelve days after the floods. Each day the teams set out from Coltishall at 0700 hours and were then directed by the police, special service representatives and local government officials to houses that were to be dried out.

The aircraft heaters proved to be ideal equipment for the job, but there were a few problems. Before the heaters could be switched on, the residents of the house had to go outside, as the temperatures inside soon became unbearable. The heaters could raise the temperature throughout the inside of the house to 120 degrees (F) within ten minutes. In one house the heat caused a thermometer to rise above its maximum and 'blow its top'; many candles and chocolate biscuits were also melted by the heat.

The men heard of some amazing exploits like the lady of 85 who waded waist-deep in water to rescue her dog from her garaged car. Although the flood victims faced up to their situation with the usual British resolve, they were still left with much to do after the aircraft heaters had finished. Two heaters were used to dry out the carpets at a Kings Lynn factory, but many owners were still left with furniture and carpets that had been ruined by the mud and salt water. Some houses with newly decorated rooms were left with a tidemark nine feet up the wall.

However, on the lighter side, there was a pub that was dried out in more ways than one, and a wooden leg was found floating in one room. One garage in Wells had its forecourt of cars replaced by a forecourt of boats!

Whilst the men were in Kings Lynn, they were visited by Her Majesty the Queen Mother who had travelled from Sandringham to inspect the flood damage for herself. Although the local authorities paid for the assistance, it proved to be a superb boost for the reputation of Coltishall and the RAF as a whole. Whilst many Norfolk inhabitants resent the low-flying Jaguars, others remembered how useful the aircraft heaters were and how cheerful and helpful those individuals from the Station were in their hour of need.

Two Jaguars of 54 Squadron crossed the Atlantic on Friday 14 July 1978, to re-create to the day a similar event that happened 30 years previously. On that occasion, Vampire fighters from the same squadron made the very first transatlantic crossing by jet-powered aircraft.

Two Victor tankers of 57 Squadron from Marham also flew the 2260 miles to Goose Bay, refuelling the Jaguars, piloted by the squadron boss, Wg Cdr R J 'Kip' Kemball and Flt Lt John Butler, six times each during the five hour 43 minute flight.

The six Vampires, which made the original flight, did not re-fuel in the air and had to take a roundabout route via Iceland and Greenland before touching down at Goose Bay some eight hours and 16 minutes after leaving the UK.

During the NATO Exercise ARCTIC EXPRESS in 1978, it was the turn of 41(F) Squadron, the newly formed Jaguar Squadron at Coltishall, operating in the tactical reconnaissance role, to highlight the effectiveness of the Jaguar Wing from Coltishall. Detachments of fighter aircraft from a variety of NATO countries were deployed during the exercise. Six Jaguar GR.1s and a T.2 of 41(F) Squadron were based at Andoya on one of Norway's offshore islands. They were employed in a variety of tactical reconnaissance, armed reconnaissance and simulated attack sorties. The squadron mounted up to fifteen sorties per day and achieved rapid response times from origination of task to time over target.

12 June 1978 saw the arrival at Coltishall of 18 RF-4C Phantoms from the 62nd Tactical Reconnaissance Squadron (TRS) of the 363rd Tactical Reconnaissance Wing (TRW) at Shaw Air Force Base (AFB), South Carolina under the deployment name 'Coronet Heron.' The aircraft flew across the Atlantic for a two-week stay at Coltishall as part of a NATO-inspired tactical deployment exercise aimed at making American-based aircrew familiar with operations outside the United States. Leading the squadron in at the end of their eight-hour flight was the Squadron Commander, Lt Col Mike Pavich. The Station Commander, Gp Capt G C 'Bob' Honey, greeted him as he climbed down from his aircraft.

363rd TRW line at Coltishall in 1978.

One of the 18 Phantoms, 67-0466JO, on its way into Coltishall for the exercise, landed at Norwich Airport after the pilot had experienced trouble with the jet's generators. For the pilot of the aircraft, 1st Lt Rick Conniff and his crewman instructor, Capt Lynn Oveson, an informal presentation was made at Coltishall after his aircraft finally joined the rest of the squadron. Rick Conniff was presented with a broken warning light from Norwich Airport, which either his drag chute or jet-blast damaged during landing. The light, together with an accompanying inscription, which read, "Welcome to the 04 Club, Member Number 2", was made by a RAF pilot who explained that 04 was the runway you landed on at Norwich. Your membership is No 2 because the first member was in fact the pilot who was making the presentation. As a Lightning pilot, he did exactly the same in 1968!

Following this presentation, the Lord Lt of Norfolk, the chairman of Norfolk County Council, Lord Mayor of Norwich and other local dignitary's visited the American squadron. Lt Col James Rhodes, the 363rd TRW Operations Officer, presented the Lord Lt, Sir Timothy Coleman, with a squadron plaque. Lt Col Pavich then handed a key to the city of Sumpter, near Shaw AFB, to the Lord Mayor of Norwich, Dr Peter English, and then received a plaque bearing the city's crest in return.

The detachment started at the end of May with the arrival of five Lockheed C-141 Starlifter transport aircraft; four full of equipment and one full of men. A total of 52 twelve-man tents were erected on the main sports fields by 41 members of the Prime Beef (Base Engineering Emergency Force) Contingency Team from Ramstein in Germany. Apart from the tents, the team were responsible for the deployment electrics,

One of five C-141A Starlifters which supported 'Coronet Heron'.

carpentry, plumbing, heating, refrigeration, pavement and grounds; the majority of the 'tent city', including showers, latrines and laundry facilities were all in place within two days of their arrival. They left Coltishall for their return journey to Shaw AFB on 26 June using the callsigns 'Huss 11-16, 21-26 and 31-36'; however, three of the aircraft diverted to Alconbury, completing their homeward flights by the 1 July.

The following years saw the Coltishall Jaguar Wing carrying on its training task at home and overseas. The Wing participated in the annual ELDER FOREST and MALLET BLOW exercises at home, and exercises overseas, principally in Norway. However the highlight has always been the challenges of MAPLE FLAG in Canada, and the ultra low-level missions flown over the Nevada Desert during the RED FLAG exercise, operating out of Nellis AFB, close to the city of Las Vegas.

The following summary, made by an experienced USAF Aggressor pilot during a de-brief after a sortie flown during Exercise Red Flag February 1981, is just about the best accolade any pilot or combat aircraft can receive. His comments typify the role of Coltishall, the Jaguar, the pilots, ground crew and support staff who to this day continue the traditions formed during the earliest days of the station:

"Those Jaguars pose us problems! The RAF boys truly part the sand and shave the rocks, they have a nice aeroplane; they fly it aggressively and their low-level tactics are good...very good! They have got the hang of terrain-masking their Jaguars. Yes, they gave us problems...We find them hard to acquire visually and when we do pick'em up, they're surely no 'easy' kill. We've flown against the best...for my money your Jaguar boys are as good as any of 'em and better than most!"

During May 1980, 54(F) Squadron hosted the first ever exchange visit to the UK by a Hellenic Air Force fighter unit when 345 Mira deployed four Vought A-7 Corsairs to Coltishall under the command of Maj Demetrius Gioltapoulos. Whilst flying from Coltishall during their week-long exchange they flew various sorties with their hosts in what was described as a valuable exercise and following the visit a contingent of Jaguars from 54(F) Squadron spent a few days with the Greek Air Force squadron at their home base at Souda Bay on the Island of Crete.

In January 1982, a report and study identified Coltishall as a possible site for Bloodhound anti-aircraft missiles. A Whitehall spokesman confirmed that up to 20 missiles could be re-located to Coltishall from their current bases in West Germany to bolster Britain's air defences.

A flight of missiles usually comprised of two or three sections with eight missiles in each of the sections. The Bloodhounds would form part of Britain's third line of defence in wartime. Providing firstly a 'no-go' zone for enemy combat aircraft and secondly a sanctuary for friendly aircraft. As it was, Coltishall was not chosen to join West Raynham or Watton in having Bloodhound missiles as part of the UK lines of defence.

5 May 1983 was to witness the first official visit to Coltishall by Her Majesty the Queen, although she had flown from the base on previous occasions. The Queen and the Duke of Edinburgh watched a 17-minute flying display which consisted of 20 Jaguar's taking off at ten second intervals followed by a SAR demonstration by a 22 Squadron Wessex. The finale to the flying display was a diamond nine flypast by Jaguars over the Royal Dais. The Royal couple arrived just before 1100 hours in an Andover of the Queen's Flight. The Lord Lt of Norfolk, Mr Timothy Coleman and his wife, the Station

Commander, Gp Capt Richard Profit and the AOC in Chief Strike command, ACM Sir David Craig, met them. The Royal party inspected 18 Jaguars and a Wessex together with their air and ground crews from the four resident squadrons prior to inspecting various ground displays that were set up in the hangars. After the tour and talking to crowds of well-wishers the Royal party retired to the Officers' Mess for lunch before departing the station.

The legendary film actor James Stewart was an unexpected visitor to Coltishall for the annual Familie's Day held in May of 1983. He joined many members of the 2nd Air Division Association who made a trip to the station as part of their 36th annual convention. Jimmy Stewart was the CO of the 703rd BS based at Tibenham during World War Two. The former US airmen and their families were among the 5000 visitors to Coltishall for the display.

After two very successful and enjoyable events for those based at Coltishall in May of 1983, a tragic event in the Black Forest of Germany on 21 May plunged the station into shock and disbelief. It was on this fateful day that the station lost five of their colleagues from the 41 Squadron Reconnaissance Intelligence Centre (RIC) when the bus they were travelling in crashed and overturned near the small town of Sasbach-Walden twelve miles south of Baden-Baden. The coach was carrying 40 personnel who were on exercise with the Canadian Air Force at Baden Sollingen. In addition to the five Coltishall personnel who were killed, SAC Peter Fox, Sgt Brian Rose, JT Michael Messenger, SAC Stuart Winship and SAC Paul Armstrong, a sixth, SAC Derrick Swash from North Humberside, was also killed with many being injured, some seriously.

A memorial stone was erected in the front of the Airmen's Mess as a permanent reminder and for the everlasting memory of those killed in this tragedy.

The sight of a Hurricane flying over Coltishall was nothing new, but on 20 September 1983, a flypast over two new barrack blocks was poignant, as, standing below, watching the aircraft from the BBMF, was the widow of Sir Douglas Bader and a colleague from his days at Coltishall in early 1940. Lady Joan Bader and AM Sir Denis Crowley-Milling opened the two £280,000 blocks at the base named 'Bader' and 'Crowley-Milling' in their honour.

Greeted by the Station Commander they paused outside the new building to wait for the flypast of the Hurricane that was greeted with applause as it flew low over the distinguished guests. It was the same type of aircraft that Sir Denis flew in the Battle of Britain from Coltishall when he was a member of Sir Douglas Bader's 242 (Canadian) Squadron.

Sir Denis said that it was an enormous privilege to have a block named after him and that it was marvellous to be back at Coltishall on this particular occasion. He added that his nickname had always been 'Crow', so he hoped that it would always be known as 'Crows Block.' Lady Bader told everyone: "I know Douglas would have been very proud" and that she hoped all those who were accommodated in the new blocks would be happy.

Looking back to his wartime days with 242 Squadron, Sir Denis said that at one time he was one of the 'lowest forms of animal life, a Pilot Officer' - while Sir Douglas had been a great squadron Commander.

He remembered coming to Coltishall in May 1940. Douglas Bader had taken over the squadron about a week later - "and of course we had never heard of him, we wondered how well he could fly. He arrived here, climbed into a Hurricane, took off and by God he showed us how well he could fly. And we never looked back; he was a most wonderful leader." One thing he always remembered about Sir Douglas was whenever he landed after a flying operation; he would always have a good look at his tin legs: "He secretly wondered if he would ever get a bullet through one of them so he could cock a snook at the Germans."

On 10 November 1983 Coltishall became the latest target for peace demonstrators in a week that saw over 100 military establishments targeted throughout Britain where 24-hour peace camps were set up in support of the women at Greenham Common. At Coltishall the main entrance was blocked by demonstrators staging a sit-in protest and traffic had to be diverted to the Filbey Road entrance. One group of demonstrators marched into the base, but were later shepherded back to the main gate. It was a peaceful demonstration with both the civil and RAF Police maintaining a low-key watch on the proceedings. A petition, addressed to the Station Commander and deploring the deployment of Cruise missiles was circulated amongst the people gathered outside the gates.

A wartime pilot fulfilled a long-held ambition with a flight in an ASR Wessex from Coltishall on 17 September 1984. But it was no ordinary pilot who took to the skies over Norfolk. During the Second World War, 80-year old Mrs Elizabeth Shaw of Grange Farm Scottow was for a short time a member of a small band of women who worked as ferry pilots.

41(F) Squadron Jaguar in company with a TTTE Tornado GR.1.

She learned to fly in 1932 in a Tiger Moth and flew all round Europe. Then, during the war, her own plane was blown up by German bombs whilst she was living in Northamptonshire and on becoming a ferry pilot she managed just two or three trips before the Ministry decided that it was too dangerous for a mother of five to put herself at such risk.

Living so close to Coltishall she often yearned to experience a flight in a helicopter, something she had never flown in. When the RAF learnt of her wartime exploits and ambition they made the arrangement for the flight that took her over her own farm, on to Cromer over her daughter's farm and then out to sea. The crew of the Wessex from 22 Squadron was Flt Lt Martin Temple, Flt Lt Jim Bellingall and Sgt Dave Walmesley.

Realistic training for the Jaguar and its crews is not without risk. On 7 October 1985, three Jaguar GR.1s of 6 Squadron were flying a low-level sortie that consisted of attacks on Holbeach and Cowden Ranges followed by low-level tactical flying training. The formation was west of the Pennine Ridge heading in a northwestly direction. The No 2 aircraft, XX731, was flying on the starboard side, slightly behind his leader who was flying XX728. As the leader crossed in front of the No 2 at a pre-planned point, the aircraft collided. The pilot of XX728 was incapacitated during the collision and was killed when his aircraft impacted the ground near Aston in Cumbria. Luckily, the pilot of XX731 was able to initiate a successful ejection sequence, although by this time he was at a dangerously low level.

The years 1987, '88 and '89 all witnessed tragic accidents involving Jaguars from Coltishall. The first on 17 April 1987 cost the life of Flt Lt Andy Mannheim of 41 Squadron. He was killed on a low level training exercise in the Lake District when his Jaguar GR.1, XZ116/D, collided with a Laarbrüch based Tornado GR.1 ZA493. The two-man crew of the Tornado ejected and escaped with minor cuts and burns to their faces. An extensive search of the crash scene was made in the vain hope of finding the Jaguar pilot; this involved two Sea Kings and a Wessex as well as mountain rescue teams and many local volunteers. Unfortunately, Flt Lt Mannheim had no time to initiate his ejection sequence and died in the impact.

The second incident involved two-seat Jaguar T.2, XX834, which was lost close to the town of Claw near Stuttgart, West Germany. The aircraft was being flown by Coltishall based pilot, 27 year old Flt Lt Paul Nelson with his passenger, a pilot in the USAF, when it was seen to hit a high voltage power line prior to crashing. The passenger managed to eject just after the collision and landed safely with minor injuries. Unfortunately, Flt Lt Nelson was not so lucky and died in the impact.

The third accident in this tragic series happened on 13 April 1989, to the north of Berwick-on-Tweed. Sqn Ldr Paul 'PV' Lloyd of 54 Squadron in Jaguar GR.1A XZ359 lost contact with his No 2 in dense fog whilst flying over the coast. Shortly afterwards his No 2 backtracked and spotted the wreckage on the

Jaguar GR.1A XZ359 on one of many detachments in Norway during the 1980s. Sadly, the aircraft was lost on the 13 April 1989.

cliff tops four miles north-west of St Abbes Head, near Wheatstock. A Wessex from Leuchars and a Sea King from Boulmer were scrambled to the crash site. Together with a mountain rescue team they scoured the area in the vain hope that Sqn Ldr Lloyd had ejected and survived, alas he had not, his body was found and recovered a short time later.

Wg Cdr 'Laddie' Lucas CBE DSO DFC RAF (Rtd) returned to Coltishall on 10 July 1986 at the invitation of the Station Commander, Gp Capt Mike French. A former Walker Cup golfer, Fleet Street journalist and Conservative MP for Brentwood & Chiswick (1950-1959). 'Laddie' Lucas celebrated the bicentenary of the Royal Cromer Golf Club that morning and came to Coltishall in the afternoon to see how the Station had changed.

A well known and distinguished World War II leader in the RAF, contemporary, friend and biographer of the legendary Douglas Bader, 'Laddie' Lucas commanded 249 Squadron in 1942 during the Battle of Malta and the Coltishall Wing in 1943. He was remembered as "a marvellous Wing Commander Flying, having a busy time Commanding three Spitfire Squadrons, two nightfighter Beaufighter Squadrons and an ASR unit, 278 Squadron."

During his visit to Coltishall, the former Wing Commander Flying was entertained to lunch in the Officers' Mess by Gp Capt French and his executives including Wg Cdr John Collier, the current holder of the wing appointment. 'Laddie' Lucas was shown the Jaguars and Sea King helicopters being employed on the Station that had changed little since 1943. The highlight of his visit was a fly past in his honour by Jaguars from the resident Jaguar squadrons.

'Laddie' Lucas on top of Coltishalls tower in July 1986.

For two weeks in September 1986 whilst the resident Jaguar Squadrons were away on exercise in Norway, Coltishall played host to a detachment of the Alabama Air National Guard (ANG). In the space of three days, Coltishall dispatched the last of the Jaguar Squadrons and became for the ensuing two weeks a 'Phantom Unit' as eleven RF-4C Phantoms belonging to the 117th TRW of the 9th Air Force, based at Birmingham, Alabama 'took over' the airfield for Exercise CORONET MOBILE.

Whilst the resident squadrons climbed aboard the Lockheed C-130 Hercules for their journey north to Norway. The American Guardsmen arrived in C-141 Starlifters and a chartered Douglas DC-8. The Phantoms flew directly from Birmingham, refuelling at Gander and in-flight over the Atlantic. Unfortunately one of the Phantoms was unable to make it over 'the pond' and had to return to Gander. However the crew managed to hitch a lift aboard an RAF Hercules and after landing at Lyneham completed their long journey to Coltishall by road.

RF-4C of the 117th TRW on Coronet Mobile.

The ANG is the Air element of the reserve forces of the USA with many of the Squadron and Wing members being part-timers. As the term suggests, but all members are experienced and in some cases battle-hardened servicemen. They are supported by a full compliment of Officers and SNCO's, who, although they wear the uniform of the USAF, are in fact in English terms civil servants in uniform and unlike their regular counterparts are not classed as on 'Active Duty.'

The excellent September weather, unusual even by our standards, ensured that the Phantom crews were able to capitalise on their seemingly high aircraft serviceability states, although one aircraft failed to return after a weekend route trainer to Moron in Spain. Moreover, the dry weather to some extent compensated for the dramatic climate change experienced by the visitors; it was 90 degrees (F) in Alabama when they left and at first 58 degrees (F) when they arrived.

Of particular note during the Americans' stay was the high degree of camaraderie that made a lasting impression of goodwill on both sides. Moreover many of the Guardsmen commented about the overwhelming hospitality extended by all Coltishall personnel. Although it was a busy detachment for the Americans they managed to find time to support local charities, attend the Battle of Britain celebrations, a visit to London and other notable local attractions. Tech Sgt Bobby Wise even visited the Children's Ward in the Norwich and Norfolk Hospital dressed as a clown. A memorable day for the children and the kind-hearted Guardsman from Alabama.

On Thursday 9 July 1987 Coltishall played host to HRH The Princess Royal. Following her arrival in a Wessex helicopter of the Queen's Flight, the Station Commander, Gp Capt Frank Hoare, escorted the Royal visitor to the Saluting Dais where at the General Salute a flypast was provided by four Jaguar aircraft from 41(F) Squadron.

The purpose of the visit was the opening of the new £75,000 Amenities Centre marked by the unveiling of a commemorative plaque inscribed: 'Royal Air Force Coltishall Amenities Centre. This centre was opened by HRH The Princess Anne on July 9 1987.'

The idea to convert the three-story building was the brainchild of Coltishall's former Station Commander, Gp Capt French, who had left the Station a month before the opening. Mrs Jean Hoare, the Station Commander's wife and President of the Wives Club, invited The Princess Royal to tour the Amenities Centre, a centre that was the home to two clubs, three youth groups, the station Thrift Shop, Nursery School, Crèche and the families' and Padre's Offices.

The Scouts, Cubs and Brownies of Coltishall were introduced to the Princess by Sqn Ldr Trood, leader of the organisations at Coltishall. Although the Youth Club was dormant at the time of the visit, Mrs Jean Hoare invited Sqn Ldr (Reverend) Andrew Lane, the Church of England Chaplain, to speak about the future of the club in its new home. At the Nursery School, Mrs Felicity Petengell, the Headmistress, introduced the 64 children of the school and nine members of staff to Her Royal Highness and then watched the children sing a song of welcome to their distinguished guest.

Mrs Zara Anderson, Chairman of the Thrift Shop spoke to the Princess about the sum of money raised by the shop over the previous year and the charities that had benefited. Indeed, Mrs Niki Peganll, Chairman of the Wives Club, had much pleasure in presenting Her Royal Highness with a cheque for over £3000 the result of the Station's fund raising, in aid of Save the Children Fund, of which the Princess Royal is President.

Having visited both the Sgt's and Officers' Mess where Her Royal Highness enjoyed lunch. The Princess Royal then toured No 4 Hangar to view displays arranged by various sections. Finally, a flying display led by Wg Cdr Brian Pengall, OC 54(F) Squadron, and a SAR demonstration by a Sea King of 'C' Flight 202 Squadron, flown by Flt Lt Martin Temple, was watched with avid interest by Princess Anne.

The sight of civilian airliners making approaches to Coltishall runway on training flights has been a fairly common occurrence, especially with Norwich Airport being so close. However, on 11 July 1987, a rather special civilian airliner caused the roads around Coltishall to be clogged with an estimated 1000 cars. Their occupants waiting for the arrival, for the first time at the base, of the 'Queen of the Skies', Concorde. This elegant airliner landed at Coltishall at the end of a special journey for the 100 or so passengers who disembarked that day. They had been on a ninety-minute flight from London Heathrow, over the North Sea at supersonic speed before recovering to Coltishall after turning finals over the City of Norwich. The visit also gave the opportunity for visitors to photograph the airliner with the Jaguars, as well as causing the Engineering and Movements staffs a minor headache in the handling of such an aircraft!

For one of those on board for this majestic aircraft, the flight into Coltishall proved to be even more heartfelt. Joan Osborne-Walker had served at Coltishall during WWII as a steward in the Officers' Mess. To return after all those years in such a manner was something she was never to forget:

"After our bus journey from Wymondham in deepest Norfolk, we all duly checked in at Heathrow's 'Island E' and then waited patiently for the Boarding Gate number to come up on the VDU opposite the name Coltishall. We all felt very chuffed at seeing that name up there and decided that all the rest of the travelling public were wondering in what exotic part of the world that was. At last the magical '7' appeared and we were able to prance down to the appropriate departure lounge where we found some VIP treatment laid on in the form of refreshments tea, coffee, soft drinks and huge piles of Danish Pastries. Then, the moment we had all waited for with the announcement for us to precede out of the lounge and down the steps to the buses waiting outside, collecting on our way our model of Concorde we clutched the precious blue boxes as if they were gold!

Then at long last, after a brief journey around the tarmac aprons, we were confronted with this most prestigious of aircraft, the CONCORDE, in all its elegance it was the moment heartbeats quickened and, to use that most hackneyed of phrases, as the adrenalin began to flow it was all I could do to stop myself jumping up and down! Instead I managed to take a couple of snaps with shaking hands, I fear. And then it was up the steps and into the interior hardly wider than the coach we had travelled on being greeted by the stewards and being directed to our seats.

We swiftly stowed our gear and fastened our seat belts. While doing so, the voice of Capt David Leney came over the intercom welcoming us aboard Concorde G-BOAB and from then we were given an intensely interesting blow-by-blow account of everything that was happening from start to finish. At 1035 we were given permission to taxi out and subsequently, to take-off. The sudden, powerful acceleration and steep rate of climb to 3000 feet in a matter of seconds was incredibility exciting and exhilarating, and the ground was rapidly dropping away beneath us with every succeeding second.

Instantly, the cabin staff moved smoothly into gear and began serving our meal. No plastic rubbish on this aircraft, crisp, white linen napery, fine cutlery and glass and a first class meal plus a pink carnation. Whilst scoffing our delectable cold roast beef and turkey, salad, delicious roll and butter, fresh fruit salad, cheese and biscuits, chocolates, and quaffing seemingly unlimited champagne, we cross the coast at Clacton and were heading out over the North Sea, still climbing and increasing our speed to Mach one, with scarcely the smallest tremor to indicate our passing through the sound barrier. Meanwhile the commentary continued and, at last, we reached 55,000 feet and were cruising at twice the speed of sound, Mach two, or, as it was put into perspective for us 23 miles a minute at twice the height of Everest! Yet the champagne in our glasses never wavered. It was just too unbelievable for words, as was the very deep blue of the sky it was the most ultimate and ecstatic experience of my life!

With the last remnants of the meal cleared away, we were given the treat of a rapid visit to the Flight Deck, a pair at a time; it was quite awe-inspiring. The Captain was by now, gradually losing height and decreasing speed, and drew our attention to a Lightning aircraft weaving from one side of us to the other, possibly taking photographs or just giving us the once over?

The sea was now shimmering below us as we crossed over one of Norfolk's lovely sandy beaches, we were talked down every step of the way, our height, our speed, our distance from the runway at Coltishall, and as we passed over the perimeter of the airfield we could see masses of cars and upturned faces watching this most fascinating of birds gliding gently and smoothly into land at precisely 1205 hours. Our dream flight had come to an end.

Landing at Coltishall was especially poignant for me if I could have foreseen the future when I was stationed there over forty-odd years ago, I would have dismissed it as sheer fantasy!

There were eager, shining faces and cameras on all sides following our taxiing progress around the perimeter until we came to a rest near the hangars tremendous excitement was engendered both inside and outside the aircraft as it came to a standstill. Before disembarking I made a further excursion to the Flight Deck for the Captain and First Officer to sign my Certificate and they both agreed it was tremendously rewarding to them to give such pleasure to so many people.

There were masses of people milling about and I was torn between collecting my case and coerced into a group photograph for the EDP photographer, and between the two, had a brief encounter with Sqn Ldr Jack Love, the Community Relations Officer the CRO. Then it was on to the coaches, speedy farewells, and back to the humdrum world!"

In June 1984, the Airmens' Club, known as the No 1 Club, at Coltishall, suffered a major fire that was to leave the junior ranks serving on the Station without any proper club facilities for more than three years. Months before the fire, major preparations had been made to provide the junior ranks with a night of entertainment to celebrate the much-awaited Summer Ball for that year. Everything was ready well ahead of time and the tickets went on sale early. There was less than a week to go before the event of the year, when, one quiet Saturday afternoon, just after the bar had closed and the staff had all gone home, a fire broke out in the main function room.

The fire quickly spread, destroying the whole of the interior and leaving nothing but a burnt out shell. That was not the end however, for, during the early evening, fire broke out again in the Tavern Bar and completely destroyed the remainder junior ranks' facilities. Naturally, the Summer Ball for that year was sadly cancelled. The upstairs dining room of the Junior Ranks' Mess, although by no means ideal, was quickly utilised and made into a provisional bar and club facility until sufficient funds could be released to rebuild and refurbish the burnt-out shell.

Owing to several delays in the planning and redevelopment stages of the re-build programme, work on the new club did not commence until March 1987. Once the contractors had started however, there was a

Concorde G-BOAB on the pan in July 1987.

growing air of excitement at the prospect of having new premises in which to hold a belated but much-desired Summer Ball.

At last, on 20 August 1987, the club was ready for use and the official opening ceremony was carried out by Gp Capt Frank Hoare and Gp Capt P J P Hutchings, the COs of Coltishall and Neatishead respectively. Gp Capt Hoare had the pleasure of pulling the first pint from the pumps at 2000 hours that evening.

The new club boasted a very modern bar, a raised floor-seating area, a large stage and dance floor, elaborate disco lighting and equipment and a video machine with computer printer. Both the Services Institute Fund and NAAFI helped considerably in providing the funds needed to purchase the new equipment that amounted to an expenditure of well over £200,000.

At the invitation of the Chief of Air Staff, Mr Roger Freeman, Under Secretary of State (Armed Forces), visited Coltishall on 10 September to fly on a Jaguar sortie at low-level and see for himself the preparation required to execute a typical mission.

The Minister was met by the Station Commander, Gp Capt Hoare who himself was planning a sortie to Tirstrup in Denmark. After a briefing by Wg Cdr Dave Milne-Smith on the role of 41(F) Squadron, it was down to work with the detailed planning and briefings required to support the mission, flying clothing fitment, medical check and finally the sortie itself. Sqn Ldr Jon Butler, 41 Squadron's Executive Officer, had selected two targets to demonstrate the dual recce and attack role of the squadron.

Post flight, the Minister said: "It was a most impressive and incredible experience. I have seen the difficulties and problems you experience at first hand in training at low level. I am a robust supporter of the need for low-flying training and very much take note of the trouble you take to avoid people and property on the ground."

Mr Freeman took the opportunity to talk at length with the squadron pilots particularly on the difficulties they experienced, the work load and flight safety aspects associated with their low-level role. Before the Minister left, he was presented with a jaguar certificate to record his flight. Good humouredly, Mr Freeman quipped: "I wish I could have returned the compliment and given you a signed picture of the House of Commons!"

The AOC-in-C Strike command, ACM Sir Peter Harding honoured 54(F) Squadron at Coltishall by presenting them with a new Squadron Standard. On Thursday 21 January 1988, a brilliant sunny day, Sir Peter took the salute before 75 members of the Squadron. The squadron

Summer camp of 2 AEF in the Summer of 1986.

Commander, Wg Cdr Brian Pegnall led the parade with Flt Lts Rob Last and Geraint Herbert bearing the old and new Standards respectively. The Service of Consecration was conducted by the Venerable G Renowden, Chaplain-in-Chief of the RAF.

In his address, Sir Peter Harding outlined the glorious history of the Squadron, including the various 'firsts' and the fact that it was the top-scoring fighter squadron during the Battle of Britain. The event was made even more special by the presence of no less than twelve previous squadron commanders including ACM Sir David Harcourt-Smith, AVM M D Lyne and AVM F D S Scott-Maiden. Also present were AVM C J Thompson, AOC 1 Gp and Sqn Ldr Clive Francis RAF (Retd), who had been the Squadron Commander in 1963 when the old Standard was presented at Waterbeach.

Retired RAF pilots often joined the RAF Volunteer Reserve to help give air experience flights to Air Cadets and members of the Combined Cadet Force. The cadets are flown in the piston-engined Chipmunk, a tail wheeled aircraft that reminded many of a bygone era. Flt Lt Stan Hayward had been flying the cadets since the Air Experience Flights (AEF) began in 1958, having previously served in the Second World War as a Spitfire pilot. 64 year-old Stan, who had flown over 3100 hours with the AEF was due to retire in September 1988. As a fitting reward and to say 'thanks', the Cadet Forces laid on a trip in one of only two remaining two-seat Spitfires. During July 1988, one of these Spitfires belonging to Mr Charles Church and flown by Gp Capt Reg Hallam, the Officer Commanding Experimental Flying Department at Farnborough, visited Coltishall and for 30 minutes transported Stan back through 40 years.

Understandably moved by the gesture, Stan confessed that he had never expected to have another chance to fly in a Spitfire after last doing so in Berlin shortly after the war. He said: "If you've flown a Spitfire, it's a drug, you never forget it. It smells different and it's an absolutely vice-less aeroplane."

It wasn't quite the same for WO James 'Tubby' Mayes MBE who revisited his former wartime station some 44 years later. Gone were the extra pounds compared to the photograph that he brought along with him. Instead it was a fit, lean but still upright man who swept into the Station Commander's office on 27 July 1988 after having held all the attention of his hosts at a special lunch in the Sgts' Mess. A backward glance at the main supporting beam in the Mess as he left had prompted him to ask, "What happened to the words I painted during the last war? 'Abandon hope all ye that enter here.'"

Making a mental note instead of relying on his Sgt Discip to make the report, he felt it was his duty to set the record straight as he leaned forward to speak to Gp Capt Frank Hoare, "Your record of Station commanders in the foyer isn't correct" said Tubby. The CRO, Sqn Ldr Jack Love and the incumbent SWO both reached for their notebooks, relegated to the role of Tubby's adjutants. "The honour board is missing."

Tubby Mayes didn't miss a thing as he went on to describe how the Station had blossomed from agricultural land into an operational Station. With unerring accuracy the former SWO rattled off the Station and Squadron commanders who became household names both at home and overseas. Lucas, his-brother-in-law Bader, Aitken, Hanks, Donaldson, Harvey. Fondly, and with great pride Tubby showed the Station Commander his autograph book bearing those famous names.

Then it was off on a tour of the Station accompanied by WO John Caisley, the current SWO to see the old and the new. The barrack blocks now holding a fraction of their former numbers (in wartime up to 40 persons per room!). The Jaguar aircraft looking sleek in comparison to the broad nosed 100mph Blackburn aircraft that he had flown in as an Air Gunner after joining the RAF in 1921. The Flight Systems bay was a quantum leap from the basic navigational instruments bench that serviced those lumbering but fondly remembered aircraft that Tubby Mayes once flew.

Suddenly the day had gone. 'Tubby' Mayes was absolutely delighted when the Station Commander presented him with an engraved Station plaque. The young 84 year-old ex-Coltishall SWO was still enthusing as his friends Colin and June Crowhurst drove him away from the Station. Colin, who was instrumental in ensuring Tubby received his Czech medal in 1985 (awarded in 1945!) after enlisting the help of the Rt Hon Edward Heath, presented WO Caisley with a 1940 calendar and to the CRO a model of a Vickers Wellington made by a Polish airman.

Another member of the Mayes family who remembered Coltishall with fondness was his son Bill. Having first set foot on the Station back in 1940 when his father became the SWO, Bill Junior has visited the Station on many occasions with his wife Davinia during the annual visit to Norfolk and to Neatishead where his wife served before they were married.

Bill recalled: "Early in 1940 my father was appointed to open up Coltishall as the first SWO, a position he held until 1944 when he went as SWO to HQ Fighter Command at Bentley Priory."

To open up the station Bill remembered that his father had a small group of experienced NCOs plus an intake of recruits. The new arrivals mostly came into the local LNER railway station, close to where he and his Mother lived in a rented cottage. They often witnessed the new recruits detrain and wondered what their first impressions were of North Norfolk, having travelled for many hours from all parts of the country.

"In his role as SWO my father was increasingly required on duty and he managed to take over the only Warrant Officer's married quarter on the perimeter of the base and my mother and I moved in. I can still identify this house as it still has the traces of camouflage paint. As we lived on the very edge of the camp, I was able to walk along inside the boundary and visit the ASR Flight with their Lysanders and Walruses."

"Many years later, when my father took part in a 'This is your Life' programme on Douglas Bader, he, DB, said to me "I remember you on the airfield, you little bugger, when you were so high." I was eight or nine years old then."

"Dad was keen to make the most of the various open spaces on the station and many of these sites were cultivated to grow vegetables for the messes. In addition hens were reared and fed on canteen waste. Dad appointed a Corporal I/C Gardens, a Cpl Buck, to whom was sent defaulters to work on the gardens."

Bill Junior served in the RAF himself during the early 1950's and it came about that his Flight WO, 'Bill' Bailey, was a Sgt Armourer at Coltishall when his dad was the SWO. This connection brought back many memories for Bill Senior and Junior as well as WO Bailey.

Two former fighter pilots relived wartime memories on 9 June 1989 as they returned to Coltishall, an airfield that was to be home for both of them during the 1940's. Alfred Warminger and Charles Berry Savory joined a host of former fliers at Coltishall as the widow of Sir

Douglas Bader unveiled a replica of the Hurricane her late husband flew; V7467/LE-D. As Lady Bader unveiled the aircraft, a flying example from the BBMF, passed overhead in salute.

The former Sheriff of Norwich, Mr Warminger, who flew Hurricanes with 257 Squadron, Commented that it was still nice to see the Hurricane flying, "it brings back some nice memories." Mr Warminger was joined by Mr Berry Savory who briefly flew Hurricanes with Sir Douglas's 242 Squadron. The pair trained together at the old Mousehold airfield and were called up together at the outbreak of war.

The occasion also supported a two and half million appeal by the Douglas Bader Foundation to build a special care centre for the rehabilitation of amputees at Stoke Mandaville Hospital in Buckinghamshire. Lady Bader said that Sir Douglas, who fought to help fellow amputees, had many happy memories of Coltishall. "I know this was one of his favourite places."

In the 1940s, and subsequently with the HAF and the BBMF, the Spitfire was a familiar sight over Coltishall. However on 3 may 1990, the Station was to become the home to a further example of Reginald Mitchell's

RN201 is delivered by a Belgium Air Force C-130.

masterpiece when Spitfire XVI variant of the fighter flew into Coltishall in the hold of a Belgian Air Force C-130 Hercules.

Belgium's Ministry of Defence exchanged Spitfire RN201/SG31 from Beauvechan Air Base for Fairey Battle R3950, of the Historic Aircraft Collection of Jersey (THAC). The Battle was to form the centrepiece of

Freshly painted 'Desert Pink' Jaguars on the line early August 1990.

an exhibit to mark the 50th Anniversary of the invasion of Belgium. That day, a flight of Belgian Battles was put up to repulse the enemy. After the delivery flight, Spitfire RN201 initially went into store in Norfolk with two other examples of the breed owned by THAC, namely Spitfire SM969 and TE566, all of which have since returned to the air.

The Jaguar in RAF service had never been used in anger; however the Iraqi invasion of Kuwait on the 2 August 1990 was soon to change this situation. Once the backbone of the RAF Ground Attack Force, the Jaguar had largely been replaced by the Tornado GR.1. Despite its age, the Jaguar could offer vital low-level ground attack capability as 'Tank Busters' or 'Can Openers', to take the WWII nickname of 6 Squadron, should the Iraqi Army advance into Saudi Arabia.

As more comprehensive plans emerged from the 'Bunker' at Headquarters Strike command in High Wycombe. Coltishall very quickly began to assemble a composite squadron of aircraft selected from all three squadrons, together with 300 personnel to support them.

The desert pink paint arrived shortly before midnight the day before the Jaguars departure. It was all hands to the pump to start the painting process, including the employment of ATC cadets on Summer Camp and the arrival of a Hercules with additional painters and finishers from Brize Norton. Remarkably twelve aircraft were sprayed in less than eight hours. At first, the horde of media, representing local, national and overseas interests refused to believe that those sandy coloured weapons of war which taxied out on the morning of 11 August had not been hidden away until they were shown the spray equipment in No 3 Hangar.

The Jaguar Wing, under the command of Wg Cdr Jerry Connelly, together with the supporting transport aircraft left Coltishall on 11 August 1990. After a stopover in Cyprus they proceeded to the Gulf region and then flew south to Oman and their new home for the next few weeks, Thumrait, 40 miles inland in the coastal region of Salalah.

The use of Thumrait as a base was a sensible move as the Omani Air Force operated the Jaguar as well from this desert airfield. The training between the two air forces was of mutual benefit as many of the RAF pilots had not experienced flying in desert conditions. The Omanis initially provided the lead in the desert flying environment and then acted as simulated air threats against the RAF Jaguars during the work-up period. It was at Thumrait, within a few days of their arrival, that the detachment had given itself the title of the Desert Cats.

The Jaguar Wing ready to depart Coltishall, supported by RAF Hercules and ex-RAF Belfast.

The heat of the desert caused many problems to man and machine alike, the main concern being heatstroke among the pilots and groundcrews. With temperatures exceeding 100 degrees in the baking sun, the canopies on the Jaguars were expanding and locking adding to the discomfort of the pilots who stood-by in the cockpits of their aircraft waiting for 'the off.'

To overcome this problem, the lads back at Coltishall were asked to come up with a solution. Tubing and canvas was purchased and a design for a desert canopy was soon on the drawing boards. They even went as far as making a video to show how their elaborate 20-foot high canopy was to be constructed. Unfortunately, whilst it worked well in the UK, they couldn't take into account the strong winds that often prevailed over the deserts in Oman and with the strong winds they were soon disappearing over the runway.

Whilst intensive training in theatre continued, the pace at Coltishall also ran into overdrive. Modifications to the next wave of aircraft to be flown out to replace the first batch continued. The rapid modification was to become one of 'Operation Granby's' most remarkable features as far as the RAF was concerned. The official name of the modification programme was 'Fast Track', although those on the ground soon realised the change of name to 'Operation Goalpost' was more appropriate, because the size kept changing!

With the arrival of the USAF at Thumrait, and the relocation of assets to meet the operational needs, the Jaguars moved north to Muharraq in Bahrain. It was from this base that the Jaguars took part in Operation GRANBY/DESERT STORM with great distinction; not only in the ground attack and reconnaissance roles but also in the unfamiliar anti-shipping role.

Operations for the Jaguars began on 17 January 1991, with four aircraft being part of the first wave to go into action. The first air strikes were carried out at night because of the superior night vision capabilities of the Allied aircraft and because they were going in low. The plans for the attack against their first target saw top cover being provided by four to six F-15 Eagles and around half a dozen Wild Weasel F-4G Phantoms and F-16s to suppress surface-to-air missile systems. All this, in addition to tanker support, AWACS and the other allied aircraft being part of that night's incredible show of air power. The scale of the offensive was unprecedented and during the first 18 hours alone some 18,000 tons of bombs were delivered. Thereafter, Allied air operations continued at an average of 2000-3000 sorties a day.

6 Squadron Jaguar rests between training sorties at Thumrait.

In her element!

By 19 January the counter-air and strategic bombing campaign had achieved a sufficient measure of success to allow the Allies to begin shifting the main weight of their air attacks against Iraqi supply lines. On into Kuwait and against the Iraqi army in the field and it was that day - Day 3- that was to see the Jaguars' first full day of operations when they launched five missions of up to eight aircraft each against positions near the Kuwait border.

The RAF's main strength were the ground attack aircraft, the principle being the Tornado GR.1 and GR.1As of which there were over 40 in theatre. The Coltishall Jaguars at Muharraq complemented these aircraft. This powerful force was further augmented in the following weeks by a third squadron of Tornado GR.1s and a detachment of Buccaneers; the latter operating in the laser designator role.

Whilst the Tornados flew by night, the Jaguars flew by day, tasked with attacking a variety of targets including interdiction targets, supply dumps, surface-to-air missile sites, artillery, surface-to-air missile sites, Silkworm missiles. The Jaguars distinguished themselves admirably, particularly in the maritime arena using the newly acquired Canadian manufactured CRV-7 weapon, a high-velocity rocket with a very flat and thus accurate trajectory. The aircraft/CRV-7 combination proved extremely effective against Iraqi naval targets. An example of their maritime prowess coming on Day 14, 30 January, when two Jaguars sank a Poinochney C-class landing craft with CRV-7 rockets and 30mm gunfire.

Even in times of war other milestones were celebrated and one such event was held at Muharraq to congratulate Sqn Ldr Dave Bagshaw who clocked up 4000 hours on the Jaguar shortly before the hostilities started. At that time he was the only pilot to have achieved that number of hours on the Jaguar.

On Day 13, 29 January, the Jaguars continued with attacks on Silkworm sites as a matter of priority and in conjunction with Allied naval forces, attacks against Iraqi naval targets. It was also on this day that the Jaguars first used the American CBU-87 cluster bombs instead of the usual Hunting BL755 units. Jaguars raided ammunition dumps south of Kuwait City on 3 February and dropped 1000lb air-burst bombs successfully on six artillery emplacements on the Island of Faylakah.

The Gulf conflict ended on 27 February 1991. The Jaguar force flew a total of 615 sorties and 915 hours of flying, which included 31 reconnaissance flights. Ordnance expended was 750 x 1000lb bombs, 385 x CBU-877's, 8 x BL755 cluster bombs, 608 x CRV 7 Rockets, 3 x AIM9L Sidewinders and 9600 rounds of 30mm ammunition.

The only tragedy of Operation GANBY for the Jaguar Force was the loss of 26-year old Flt Lt Keith Collister, a pilot with 54 (F) Squadron. He was killed instantly when his Jaguar XX754/EQ, hit the crest of a sand dune in Qatar during low level training with six other aircraft prior to the start of the conflict. Operation GRANBY's first casualty.

In one magnificent week, the pilots, ground crews and support personnel of the Jaguar unit from Coltishall, the 'Desert Cats', came home to champagne receptions. Eighty men arrived on Monday 11 March in a VC10 and as the aircraft came to a stop on the Northern ASP the anxious eyes of waiting families were directed to its passenger doors. Suddenly a whoop went up from the crowd as they gained their first glimpses of their loved ones; mothers, children, girlfriends and station personnel surged forward in a mixture of pride, love and most of all great relief.

These scenes were repeated the next day as four Jaguars arrived and on the Wednesday when eight more Jaguars and another VC10 touched down. As well as the families and well-wishers the Chief of the Air Staff, ACM Sir Peter Harding, was on hand to greet the airmen, saying: "I salute every one of you."

The VC10 captain, Wg Cdr John Brown spoke of his amazement at the large crowds surrounding the airfield. An estimated 1000 cars had brought the narrow roads to a standstill. With the television, local and national press and an abundance of photographers on hand much interest was focused on the nose art applied to the Jaguars, but as one's eye swept along the fuselage the tally of bombs dropped and rockets fired was a sobering reminder of the missions flown and armaments expended.

The Jaguar Detachment Commander, Wg Cdr Bill Pixton spoke of the team spirit and morale that helped bring his pilots through the conflict. During the fighting phase 22 pilots flew more than 600 combat sorties in twelve Jaguars, all of which came home unscathed. Sipping a can of beer after his flight home, he said: "We learnt a lot about tactics, about newer weapons and about human nature."

The detachment brought together pilots from four different squadrons, which could have been a recipe for problems. "There could have been some petty jealousies, but they all gelled. In that situation you do all pull together, your dislikes and differences disappear", said the Wing Commander. He added; "We all came home. You can put that in capital letters. That was my main aim."

Nine awards were made to Coltishall personnel at the end of hostilities. The DFC was awarded to Wg Cdr Bill Pixton, Sqn Ldr Michael Gordon, both from 41(F) Squadron and Flg Off Mal Rainier, 54(F) Squadron, who at the time was the youngest single-seat fighter pilot serving with the British Forces in the Gulf and the youngest recipient of the DFC since World War Two. The AFC was awarded to Wg Cdr Jerry Connolly OC 6 Squadron and MBEs to Sqn Ldr Les Hendry and Flt Lt Chris Boyce. Three pilots were Mentioned in Despatches, Flt Lts Toby Craig, Peter Tholen and Craig Hill.

Flg Off Rainier was not only the youngest single-seat fighter pilot to serve in the conflict, but also flew the most missions. He was singled out for praise for knocking out an Iraqi anti-aircraft position which was throwing out heavy fire against his formation. Part of his citation read: "Showing great presence of mind and undeterred by the obvious danger, Flg Off Rainier promptly engaged the threat and scored a direct hit, eliminating the danger to the rest of the formation. Flg Off Rainier has proved to be a most capable pilot whose bravery, leadership and airmanship are in the highest traditions of the RAF."

Wg Cdr Pixton was praised for showing outstanding leadership and fortitude in leading and pressing home attacks against heavily defended targets whilst Sqn Ldr Michael Gordon was commended for repeatedly pressing home attacks on Iraqi targets with "devastating

The first wave of the Jaguar Wing is welcomed home.

All but one pilot, sadly lost during training over Qatar, returned home safely to their families and Coltishall.

accuracy" and whilst leading the first Jaguar mission of the conflict saving another pilot's life by drawing away anti-aircraft fire.

Whilst many were away in the Gulf region, Coltishall played host to a number of visitors who specifically wanted to reach out to those left behind. On one such occasion, Wednesday 6 February 1991, The Duchess of York flew into the Station and listened intently whilst 60 excited toddlers told her about their brave mums and dads in the Gulf.

During her three-hour visit the Duchess expressed her admiration for all those who were deployed to the region on operations. She met 120 of their wives and girlfriends at St Michael's Church, including Mary Pixton, the wife of Wg Cdr Bill Pixton who was in charge of the Coltishall detachment at Muharraq.

At the Coltishall Airfield First School, the children gave the Duchess a rousing welcome and presented her with a bouquet and tea towel designed by the pupils. Head Teacher Mim Ransby told the Duchess that her visit had been an occasion which the children will be able to remember with happiness during a time, which for some of them, was difficult and confusing.

Since the end of the hostilities in the Gulf, all three of Coltishall's squadrons have participated in United Nation operations. The first, Operation WARDEN, was a United Nations response to the attacks against ethnic minorities by Saddam Hussein after his humiliating defeat in the Gulf War. The Kurdish population fled to the mountainous regions in the north of Iraq bordering Iran, Turkey and Syria, which resulted in massive refugee problems for those three countries. The UN was quick to respond by establishing a safe haven and Security Zone for the Kurdish people. An area of Iraq above 36 degrees North was also designated an air exclusion zone to Saddam's Air Force. To ensure compliance with the UN resolutions, a Coalition Task Force was formed to patrol the area primarily to discourage Iraq from infringement, but also to respond in the event of any flagrant disregard of the UN edict.

With a vested interest in the stability of the region Turkey agreed to join the coalition force, comprised of the USA, UK and France, in operations to be conducted from the Turkish Air Force Base at Incerlik. The USAF provided the air defence and fighter-bomber role, shared with the Turkish Air Force, whilst the UK and France provided tactical photographic and reconnaissance cover as the USAF did not have this component in Europe. The UK committed eight Jaguar GR.1A aircraft and the French a similar number of Mirage F.1CR's both dedicated to observe and record Iraqi military activity within the exclusion zones.

The UK commitment was formed during August 1991 under the command of Gp Capt John Morley. The Jaguar GR1.A was selected as the most suitable aircraft as its photographic systems recorded their imagery on film unlike the Tornado GR.1A that used video cameras. The eight Jaguars were drawn from all three squadrons based at Coltishall, and were painted in the now familiar 'Desert Pink' scheme.

The first four aircraft departed Coltishall on 4 September followed by the remaining aircraft some five days later. 41 RIC, plus support personnel and equipment were flown out to Turkey by Hercules. In addition, the VC10 tankers of 101 Squadron which supported the initial deployment of the Jaguars in their non-stop flight were to stay in theatre to provide air-to-air refuelling cover for the duration of Operation WARDEN.

Although 41 Squadron was the only Jaguar unit dedicated to photographic reconnaissance, both 6 and 54 Squadron pilots had been trained to undertake this role with each squadron providing aircrew and groundcrew on a two monthly rotation.

41 Squadron Jaguar in company with a 101 Squadron VC10 over Northern Iraq during Operation WARDEN.

The Jaguars were required to regularly over-fly all known military sites and photograph the activities to provide constantly updated intelligence. Targets included Iraqi troop concentrations, air defence sites, military airfields (at least five were located within the no-fly zone), railway termini, barracks and vehicle parking areas. All of the targets were located within Iraqi territory and were potentially hostile. Because of this, the Jaguars were fitted with defence packages consisting of over-wing mounted AIM-9L Sidewinder missiles, 30mm Aden cannons (an integral part of the aircraft), electronic countermeasures suite which included the PHIMAT Chaff/flare dispenser and a jamming pod, both of which were fitted to under-wing hard points. Periodically, 1000lb bombs replaced the Reconnaissance Pods, demonstrating to the Iraqis that the coalition was ready and willing to respond with force if needed.

The French Mirage F.1RC's invariably performed their reconnaissance task in the mornings whilst the Jaguars flew slots later in the day. The location of each target to be photographed was carefully plotted on large maps to determine their exact positions. The number of aircraft required to perform the mission was also determined by the quantity of subjects that needed to be photographed, although the normal sortie rate saw the Jaguars working in pairs with up to six aircraft flying per day.

The personnel of 41 Squadron were the first to deploy on 'Operation Warden' during the late summer of 1991 and were the last of Coltishall's squadrons to participate prior to being replaced by the Harrier Force in April 1993.

Tragedy struck Coltishall a hard blow on 29 August 1991. The bravery and pain endured by a heart and lung transplant patient who fought his way back to flying fitness was cruelly ended when the Jaguar aircraft he was flying in crashed.

Wg Cdr John Mardon MBE underwent the double transplant operation at Papworth Hospital, Cambridgeshire, after five long years of illness. He

54 Squadron Jaguar taxys from a Incerlik HAS.

carried on working for as long as possible at a desk job at Coltishall whilst waiting for the operation. During the operation itself, his heart, which was perfectly healthy, was used in a separate transplant operation to give a desperately ill man a new lease of life.

His Jaguar T.2, XX843/GT, collided with a civilian Cessna 152 near Carno in Powys, Wales. Wg Cdr Mardon had been passed fit to fly with another pilot just one year after his operation. His pilot, Gulf Veteran, Wg Cdr Bill Pixton DFC, ejected to safety seconds after the collision suffering only a broken arm. Wg Cdr Mardon and the civilian Cessna pilot were both killed instantly. It was ironic that earlier in the month of this untimely and tragic accident, John Mardon had cycled the 90 miles from Coltishall to Papworth Hospital to raise well over £26,500 for the hospital and the donor family's chosen charity.

The future of Coltishall looked bleak in December of 1991 due to deep and far-reaching defence cuts. Speculation was rife that the station would close and the three squadrons would be moving to Bentwaters in Suffolk once the USAF vacated the base in September of 1993. The uncertainty was fuelled by an announcement that two other airfields, Honington and Wattisham, were to face virtual closure under the sweeping cuts. At that time the future of the SAR unit, which was also based at Coltishall, was to be looked at separately from the fast-jet squadrons.

The news dismayed local residents who had relied on the base from its earliest days as it contributed millions of pounds directly and indirectly into the local economy in addition to giving employment to over 130 local civilians. However all turned out well, when on 21 August 1992 it was announced that Coltishall had been saved from closure. The announcement was based on the fact that to move the Jaguars from Coltishall to Bentwaters would have been too costly.

Raising money for charity has always been high on the agenda of those serving at Coltishall. Many thousands of pounds have been raised for RAF and local charities over the years. Events such as football matches, sponsorships in marathons, darts and bowling tournaments have all featured high in the moneymaking stakes. Many individuals have raised vast amounts of money for their chosen charities in solo efforts.

A typical example of the unselfish dedication to tasks that individuals show for the good of others was the epic journey undertaken by Sgt Colin Robilliard, a Movements Controller of the Supply and Movements Squadron. Colin had been detached to Incerlik in Turkey to support the Jaguar Force who was then on operations over Northern Iraq in support of the United Nations. As he neared the end of his three-month long stay, he decided to take the scenic 2350-mile route home by bicycle rather than joining his colleagues on the five-hour Hercules journey back to Coltishall.

His aim was to raise money by sponsorship for the National Asthma Campaign. His daughter Clare was a sufferer of this incapacitating disease and he wished to help other sufferers. He set out from Incerlik on 4 February 1992 and aimed to complete his journey by the 29 February. His wife Suzy was unaware of his intentions at first, but thought that something was afoot when he asked her to provide details of Youth Hostels on the route. It came as no surprise to her as Colin was a keen cyclist. He had already broken the surface speed record for the 450-mile journey across the Pyrenees in 1989.

Colin eventually rode through the gates of Coltishall to a hero's welcome, just two days later than he had estimated. For his efforts a cheque for £1317.81 was presented to the National Asthma Campaign.

It had been over a half a century since the P-39 Airacobras of the 346th FS, USAAF, left Coltishall for North Africa, the date, 2 January 1943. Some of the original members of the 346th, together with comrades from the other squadrons within the 350th FG, returned to Coltishall in October 1992 to recall all those memorable times of challenge and sacrifice. Amongst the distinguished visitors was the first Commander of the 350th FG, Lt Gen Richard P Klocko. The General, whilst leading his group, was shot down over Tunisia in 1943 and made prisoner of war from February 1943 until May 1945.

Other members of the squadron who served at Coltishall at the reunion were; Col Hugh D Dow, Lt Col George W Miles, Lt Col Leo C Wells, Mr Clarence B Dickinson, Mr Authur N MCKelvey, Mr Charles L Banks, Senior Master Sgt Benjamin A Davies and Mr William H Pettitt. Prior to leaving Coltishall, to visit Duxford and Snailswell, the other two airfields in the Fighter Group during the war, Gen Klocho presented a Commemorative plaque to the Station Commander, Gp Capt Dacre. This plaque is still proudly displayed in the Station Headquarters building at Coltishall.

Tributes were paid to a Norfolk display pilot who was killed when his Hawker Hunter T.7 crashed in thunderstorms over South Yorkshire on 11 June 1993. Wallace Cubitt, from Foulsham, was on his way to the Blackpool Air Show in his recently restored aircraft when it crashed on remote moorland on the edge of the Peak District having taken off from Coltishall that

41 Squadron Jaguar at Gioia del Colle.

Friday afternoon. Mr Cubitt bought the Hunter (XL595/ G-BTYL), which had been in storage since being retired from the RAF, in October 1991 and restored it to perfect flying condition at Coltishall. It was Gp Capt Phil Dacre, Coltishall's Station Commander, who took the controls of the aircraft on its first flight in December 1992.

The 9 July 1993 saw a two-day visit to Coltishall by military representatives from 31 nations to witness the three Jaguar squadrons demonstrate their operational role. The station was chosen as the first one in Britain to open up its gates under the Confidence and Security Building Measure (CSBM). The overall aim of CSBMs is to develop greater openness and promote transparency in the military field in Europe. It comes under the Vienna Document 1992 with over 50 states having signed up to the agreement; these include NATO members, the remaining European countries as well as those from the former Warsaw Pact.

Gp Capt Phil Dacre and his staff at Coltishall designed a programme that showed how the base trains for and operates from a deployed area. After touring hangar displays the group, that included additional observers from Egypt, Jordan, Oman, Tunisia and Israel, witnessed Jaguar and Tornado aircraft 'attack' the airfield. Other demonstrations illustrated operations in Arctic and desert conditions. The perfect summer weather enabled the Red Arrows to provide a grand finale to the action-packed programme and also enabled the Mobile Catering Support Unit to put on a splendid barbeque on the eve of the busy day.

Yet another major deployment fell to the Coltishall Wing, which would see the Jaguar in combat again, this time over the former Yugoslavia. In July of 1993, nine Jaguars left Coltishall for the Italian Air Base at Gioia

del Colle in southern Italy. The Jaguars were supported by 36 Hercules loads of personnel and equipment that was deployed to support the force in 'Operation Grapple/ Deny Flight.'

The Jaguars at Gioia were representative of the Coltishall Wing, although, with the application of a new colour scheme, Alkaline Removable Temporary Finish (ARTF) light grey, the only method of determining squadron ownership of the aircraft was by the two-letter code on the tail and nose-wheel door. The aircraft were fitted and prepared to 'Operation Granby' standard, which included the full air defence package as well as the defence and countermeasure suite. Two of the aircraft were permanently configured for 'wet film' photographic sorties. One with a LOROP (Long-Range Oblique Photography) pod and the other with a BAe podded F.126 general survey camera.

A RIC was set up at Gioia to handle 'wet film' processing and subsequent interpretation. This information was then passed to the 5th Allied Tactical Air Force (ATAF) for future mission planning, particularly in the event of a Close Air Support requirement.

Unlike the Tornados, the Jaguars were tasked during the daytime only and they could fly anything between four and eight sorties a day including reconnaissance missions. The medium-level recce sorties were flown with three aircraft, one acting as 'shot-gun', with up to ten targets per sortie. The Jaguars at Gioia were involved in two air strikes whilst detached away from Coltishall.

The first, on 22 September 1994, was in support of French UN personnel who called for air support following a Bosnian Serb rocket attack. Subsequently, a Serb T55 tank was destroyed near the village of Osijek in the Sarajevo exclusion zone by a pair of Jaguars, each dropping 1000lb bombs.

Potuguese Air Force Corsair II det at Coltishall in 1995.

The second mission was as the result of Serbian actions on 19 November. Two Bosnian Serb Orao aircraft, based at Udbina air base in the disputed Krajina region, attacked the Bosnian safe haven of Bihac in northwest Bosnia. In response to a UN request, a NATO raid on Udbina was planned by the Dutch contingent using photographs taken by the Jaguars on previous reconnaissance sorties. The raid itself was planned for 20 November, but subsequently cancelled because of high cloud over the target area.

The following day, a package of over 50 aircraft attacked Ubdina airfield from the direction of the Dalmatian Coast. The strike package consisted of US, Dutch, French and RAF strike aircraft. Support elements being provided by the airborne controllers in their E-3 Sentry's and EF-111A Ravens of the USAF and EA-6B Prowlers of the USN in the Electronic Countermeasures (ECM) role were tasked to strike the runways and taxiways on the airfield. Included in the package were four Jaguars, two dropping 1000lb bombs on the airfield with the other pair tasked to carry out post-strike reconnaissance.

Flt Lt Chris Carder was detailed to lead the pair of Jaguars for the reconnaissance flight over Udbina. The pair were tasked to get post-strike Bomb Damage Assessment photographs using the LOROP at a height of 15,000 feet, four to five miles off the target. To support the Jaguars a Tristar tanker was on hand to refuel them on the way in to the target.

Additional tankers were stacked up to refuel supporting USAF F-16s, USN and Marine F/A-18s and French Mirages. The controlling AWACS cleared the package through to the target with a warning that enemy triple-A and man-portable shoulder launched missiles were known to be operating in the area. It was also agreed that if the defences proved to be heavy the post-strike reconnaissance mission could be postponed. As it was the mission went ahead. Light triple-A greeted the mission as they flew in, the target identified by palls of smoke. With successful results the pair of Jaguars returned to Gioia De Colle, this time without the tanker support.

In late July of 1995 Harrier GR.7s from Wittering replaced the Jaguars. The Jaguar Force had flown some 3000 operational sorties over Bosnia, comprising more than 5000 flying hours. Not a single Jaguar was lost due to enemy action during this time. However, one aircraft, XZ373/GF was lost on 21 June 1995 during a training sortie whilst being flown by a USAF exchange pilot with 6 Squadron. After a successful ejection over the Adriatic Sea, a Royal Navy Sea King that had been scrambled from the NATO base at Split eventually rescued the pilot.

Coltishall hosted some seldom-seen overseas guests during early July 1995 in the shape of four A-7P Corsair II aircraft of the Portuguese Air Force. A deployment of six aircraft had originally been anticipated, possibly comprising of the four Corsairs, also two of the newly acquired F-16A Fighting Falcons. But in the end, the quartet of aircraft operated by 304 Esquadra based at Monte Real arrived for the exchange visit with 54 (F) Squadron. The Jaguars of 54 Squadron were regularly seen flying with the A-7s until the Forca Aerea Potrugesa detachment departed on 12 July.

It had been almost 22 years since an RAF aircraft had crashed at Coltishall. Then, Lightning F.3 XR719 of 2T Squadron from the Lightning OCU, made a very heavy landing which damaged the aircraft to such an extent that it was deemed beyond economical repair and scrapped; the date 5 June 1973.

On the 23 January 1996, three Jaguars GR.1's were tasked to fly to Lossiemouth on a regular training mission. The first two aircraft were airborne and on there way when the third, XX733/ER, started his take-off run just before 1100 hours. The pilot, 28-year-old Flt Lt Greg Noble of 41 Squadron, experienced problems which caused the aircraft to crash just beyond the end of the runway close to the small cemetery at Scottow. Tragically Flt Lt Noble died in the accident.

The funeral of Flt Lt Greg Noble.

Very soon the news of the accident was known throughout the station. Being a small and close community, the service and civilian personnel on the base shared in everyone's triumphs and tragedies, and because the accident had happened so close, the feelings of helplessness and sorrow were even more acute. The station had all but come to a standstill in shock. Following a private funeral service at the Roman Catholic Cathedral in Norwich, Flt Lt Noble was laid to rest with full Military Honours in the small cemetery at Scottow, within yards of where he lost his life.

Coltishall came to the aid of the civilian community on the 19 February 1996 when stretches of the North Norfolk coastline were at the mercy of the sea after storms smashed the ailing sea defences. In a repetition of the high tides of February 1953, when personnel assisted the local community of Sea Palling, volunteers

were this time busy filling in excess of 3000 sandbags to bolster the sea defences at Salthouse.

On 19 April 1996, the skies above Norfolk saw a family first for father and son Jet pilots, Dick and Chris Hadlow. The two generations of RAF fighter pilots were matched by two generations of jet aircraft that they flew on that day. The Vampire and Jaguar. Dick Hadlow, a retired Squadron Leader, flew into Coltishall in Vampire FB.6, G-BVPO, of the Royal Jordanian Historic Flight.

The afternoon sortie saw the Vampire in close formation with 6 Squadron Jaguar GR.1, XX729/ER, being flown by his son Flt Lt Chris Hadlow. Talking about the flight, Dick Hadlow commented that the idea of the formation seemed to evolve especially with the close links that 6 Squadron has with Jordan. To have a father and son formation was indeed a unique event. Prior to joining the Royal Jordanian Historic Flight, the Vampire served

XZ367/GP in 'Jagged Sphinx' paint scheme for the Egyptian det.

with the Swiss Air Force as J1106. Modifications to the Vampire included a new nose and RAF-style drop tanks, more in keeping with the type operated by the Royal Jordanian Air Force.

The beginning of December 1996 saw the Jaguars, aircrew and groundcrews of 41(F) Squadron, together with support elements, deploy to Cairo West AB, Egypt, for Exercise 'Jagged Sphinx.' This occasion was the first time that RAF fighters had been in Egypt since the Suez Crisis of 1956. The deployment was the result of a Memorandum of Understanding signed between the two nations in November of 1996.

The squadron left Coltishall on 29 November for the six-hour flight to Cairo for a stay that lasted two weeks. Two of their aircraft, XZ113/FD and XZ367/GP, were painted in temporary sand camouflage, similar to that adopted by the Jaguar fleet during Operation Desert Storm. The squadron were guests of 222 Tactical Fighter Brigade which flew ex-USAF F-4E Phantoms.

During the deployment approximately 90 sorties were flown over the two weeks and were mostly Combined Air Operations leading the Egyptian units. These operations were comprised of up to ten Jaguars, eight F-16s and four F-4Es ranged against a variety of targets including HMS Invincible which was operating in the region at that time. Other missions included air-to-air refuelling (AAR) with VC10 tankers. The Egyptian Air Force took advantage of the tanker to practice AAR with their Mirage 2000s as up to this time they had little or no experience in the 'hose to basket' technique.

February 1997 saw the Jaguars return to Gioia De Colle to resume the policing of the former Yugoslavia. Once

again, 41 Squadron led the Coltishall Wing in replacing the Harrier GR.7 force, a role reversal of July 1995. All three of Coltishall's squadrons then began their regular rotation to Italy.

The Jaguar has gone through many modification and development phases during its 25 years of service. These ranged from the early addition of in-flight refuelling probes, the modification of the nose to house the Laser Rangefinder & Marked Target Seeker (LRMTS), with its distinctive chisel window below the pitot probe, and the Radar Warning Receiver on the tail. 'Operation Granby' saw 31 Jaguar GR.1As modified for service in the Gulf.

The 'Granby' modifications were carried out in three phases, with the final phase being the provision of over-wing AIM-9L Sidewinder missiles. The three-phase programme was deemed to be temporary and in fact some aircraft were de-modified before operations in Italy and Turkey were introduced for the Jaguar, then, it became obvious that the de-modification of the programme should be halted and it should even be extended to even more of the fleet.

Next saw an urgent requirement for the Jaguar to be modified to undertake Laser Designation operations. Twelve aircraft, including two T.2s, were drawn from the fleet to be modified with various up-grades including a display screen in the cockpit capable of displaying Thermal Imaging and Laser Designation (TIALD) or moving map imagery. Both the Defence Experimental Research Agency (DERA) and the RAF undertook the modification programme with the first three modified at Boscombe Down and the remainder at St Athan. The designation of the modified GR.1s and T2s being GR.1B and T.2B respectively.

The upgraded 'Jaguar 96' ensured the types future well into the 21st Century.

More modifications to the venerable Jaguar saw an upgraded version, with new avionics and improved flight safety features designed to take the aircraft into the next century, take to the air for the first time at Coltishall in March 1997.

The first front-line pilot to fly 'Jaguar 96' was Flt Lt Jez Milne, a Qualified Weapons Instructor from 54(F) Squadron. After the one and half hour sortie he said that it took a matter of minutes to adjust to the new hands-on-throttle and stick facilities, particularly the twin radio and change-destination navigational features. This, coupled with the user-friendly heads-up display, fostered instant confidence in the navigation system and substantially reduced the cockpit workload in the single-seat, low-level environment.

The upgrade was designed, and trial installation completed, by DERA at Boscombe Down in 1996. After test flying, the aircraft was evaluated at the DERA facility for flight clearances. The modifications to the Jaguar were incorporated by the engineers of 3 Squadron at St Athan, where up to six aircraft were upgraded at any one time. Each aircraft took on average 55 days to complete by an eight-strong team.

Following on from this successful programme, the Royal Air Force of Oman officially announced on 7 July 1997 that it was to upgrade its own fleet of Jaguars to the latest RAF standard under an agreement with the UK MoD.

Following on from the highly successful Jaguar '96 modification programme it was the turn of GEC-Marconi and Honeywell Military Avionics to develop and provide the next modification to the Jaguars capabilities. The

Helmet Mounted Sighting System (HMSS) fitted to the aircraft made the jaguar one of the first fixed-wing aircraft to be operational with this system.

HMSS used the GEC-Marconi Alpha Sight and the Honeywell Advanced Metal Tolerant Tracking System mounted on the current in-service Mk.10B Flying Helmet. The managing director of GEC-Marconi's Mission Avionics Division, Mike Sweeny, said that the RAF would benefit from having the latest helmet sighting system technology for application on a wide range of fixed-wing aircraft. At the same time it also firmly established the GEC-Marconi and Honeywell team as a world leader in helmet-display technology.

The Jaguar Upgrade was subject to widespread media attention and was held up by Sir Robert Walmsley, Chief of Defence Procurement, as 'a shining example of Smart Procurement in action.' Even the mainstream 'Fleet Street' press had been almost embarrassingly effusive in its praise of the Jaguar Upgrade, producing the kind of positive coverage rare in defence-related news stories.

When asked why this was the case, Wg Cdr Peter Birch MBE, the project manager at Coltishall Commented: "In short, the Jaguar Upgrade has been on time, on budget and above specification. It certainly has become an RAF Success Story."

The last time that Coltishall witnessed any significant works disruption was in the early 1980s when the main runway was re-surfaced. With constant use ever since that time, 1997 was to see the same happen again, only on this occasion, the taxiways were to be included in the works programme.

On 25 July, the Jaguars left Coltishall and took up residence across the border at Honington in Suffolk. They were to remain there carrying out their daily duties as per normal until the November when they returned home.

A total of 5500 tonnes of concrete and asphalt were laid to provide the runway with a special skid-resistant surface. All the recovered concrete was re-cycled on the airfield thus reducing significantly the traffic in and around Coltishall and the local area. The wet concrete was laid using a computer controlled skipform power machine that was capable of laying 90 cubic metres per hour. During the runway-resurfacing programme itself, there were carefully planned windows in the work where certain Jaguars were rotated in and out of Coltishall for routine maintenance.

A postscript to the move away from Coltishall, and the subsequent return, became apparent when a local resident, who had moved into the area whilst the Jaguars

Jaguar GR.1A XZ382/AE the first of its type to end up in civilian hands. Seen here, still at Coltishall in October 1998.

were away, phoned up to ask what was happening. She was unaware that Coltishall was in fact an active operational base. Apparently the unsuspecting purchaser of the house assumed that Coltishall was in fact closed!

For the Jaguar pilots at Coltishall, time in the Flight Simulator was almost an everyday occurrence. However, for Flt Lt Mark Discombe of 54 (F) Squadron, being crowned the champion in the Breitling Fighter Challenge at the Royal International Air Tattoo (RIAT) at Fairford in 1997, proved to be a completely different simulator experience.

The Breitling Challenge was open to pilots from all Nations taking part in the RIAT that year. Of the many scenarios in the virtual simulation, dogfights were carried out using high-tech software, virtual reality goggles and joystick controls that simulated a single-seat fast jet aircraft. Mark claimed victory flying against an Italian pilot, winning two matches to one in a hard fought and fairly contested final.

The Power and the Glory certainly belonged to Cpl Matt Saunders of the Engine Bay at Coltishall during July 1997 as he claimed the world 100-kilo power lifting title. This title marked the end of a sensational summer for Matt who had continuously been smashing records as he returned to competitive lifting in magnificent style. The July RAF Championships yielded no less that eight new RAF records with Matt taking the 100-kilo and overall title. The Guinness Book of Records also has 15 stone Matt on their books courtesy of the nine-man team that smashed the 24-hour bench press record with his own contribution being a mind-boggling 11,000 50 kilo lifts. For the record, Matt Saunders' current bench press personal best is 190 kilos equivalent to lifting a 30 stone man to the elbow-lock position whilst lying with his back on a bench!

In late 1997, it was announced that Coltishall was to become the home of the entire fleet of Jaguar aircraft.

Following the recent upgrades to the aircraft, this decision was to make Coltishall one of the most important airbases in Great Britain, ensuring its future as a front-line base for at least another ten years. Coupled with this announcement, it was also declared that a further eight Jaguars from Lossiemouth in Scotland would be transferred within the next two years.

At a local press conference, the new Station Commander, Gp Capt Stephen Dalton stated that the technology now being incorporated in the Jaguar was quite outstanding and that the recent announcements would ensure the airfields future into the 21st Century.

During November 1997, the Officers' Mess at could rightfully claim to have the best Chef in the British Armed Services; Sgt Marc Cornell. His Commanding culinary skills beat the best Chefs from the Army, Navy and Air Force to earn him this prestigious title at a competition held aboard HMS Nelson in Portsmouth. Marc had just 60 minutes to cook the gourmet meal of Highland Salmon and Exotic Fruit Baba that won him the Supercook Competition. But for Marc, his own taste in food was far less extravagant his favourite meal was French Bread, butter and Marmite!

An article in the magazine Flight International in February 1998 once again brought into the spotlight the uncertainty of Coltishall's future. Speculations that seem to have dogged the base since the end of WWII. The article claimed that defence budget cuts would spell the end for Coltishall and the Jaguars. This statement was quickly dismissed by the MoD as 'Pure Speculation.' It was suggested in the article that the cuts would be brought forward to 2000 or 2001 for cost-cutting rather than defence reasons.

The first Jaguar aircraft to end up in private hands was sold at auction by Phillips in London for £12,000, a fraction of the £2 millions it cost originally. After flying over 1000 sorties out of Germany and Gibraltar, XZ382/AE was retired to become a Battle Damage Repair (BDR) airframe at Coltishall. Over the subsequent years, the airframe was peppered with holes to allow the engineers to perfect their BDR skills, a vital task that made this particular Jaguar look like a patchwork quilt and certainly less than airworthy. Aircraft collectors and enthusiasts from all over the world were out in force to snap up the first Jaguar to be disposed of in this way. But despite much local interest and efforts to keep the aircraft in Norfolk, it was an American collector that pushed the price up to £10,500 within minutes of the bidding starting. With the buyer's premium added to the final bid, £12,000 was the selling price.

Following some cosmetic surgery and a coat of paint prior to the aircraft being exported, it was found that due to problems with US Customs, specifically with the importation of a single-seat warplane, it would not find itself across the pond. Instead the owner made a deal with the British Aviation Heritage Collection at Bruntingthorpe in Leicestershire where the aircraft is now on display.

The end of a 47 year career with the RAF both as a Regular and as a Reserve Officer came for Sqn Ldr Jack Love in April 1998, just a month before his 65th birthday. Jack had been the public voice and face of Coltishall for over twelve years as the CRO.

Over the years he had dealt with literally thousands of enquiries about the Jaguar and the base from the public and press and during the Gulf crisis in 1991 he worked around the clock to handle calls from the world's media. Tributes to Jack's outstanding career were led by Wg Cdr Mike Kemley, OC Admin Wing at a farewell lunch in the Officers' Mess at Coltishall. He commented that Jack was a man with great passion for the RAF and Coltishall in particular.

The RAF's commitment over the former Yugoslavia was scaled down on 6 April 1998 when six Jaguars based at Gioia del Colle in Italy and their supporting Tristar tanker based at Ancona, also in Italy, redeployed back to the UK. The Jaguars had been tasked with flying patrols over Bosnia as part of Operation Deliberate Guard, the Stabilisation Force operating in the region.

The initial Jaguar deployment had been in 1993 when nine aircraft went to Gioia in the July tasked with providing air cover at the UNs request and to conduct air strikes against targets threatening the UN safe area.

The redeployment away from Italy was short-lived as on 12 June the Jaguars were ordered back to the Balkans as Serbia was given four days to stop 'ethnic cleansing' in Kosovo or face air strikes. This deployment took them back to their recently vacated base at Gioia del Colle where they were once again within striking distance of Kosovo.

About 150 personnel from 6 Squadron accompanied the Jaguars and Hercules spent the weekend of 13/14 June flying out personnel and vital equipment. No sooner had the Jaguars arrived than they were tasked to show force over nearby Macedonia and Albania in the company of F-16s from the USAF and F/A-18 Hornets of the Spanish Air Force.

The first tasking for the Jaguars over the target area was at 0950 hours when they took-off from Gioia for their 90-minute sortie. The air component was controlled by the 5th Tactical Air Forces Combined Air Operations Centre at Vincenza in Italy the same centre that supported the NATO Stabilisation Force missions over Bosnia.

Like other participants, the Jaguars were refuelled over the Adriatic. In this case by a Tristar of 216 Squadron flying out of its base at Ancona, before entering the Former Yugoslav Republic of Macedonia airspace. Most of the exercise was carried out at medium levels, up to within 15 miles of national boundaries, but the aircraft descended to over fly Albania's capital, Tarna at 2000 feet.

After the aircraft safely returned, Wg Cdr Mick Roache, OC 6 Squadron and Jaguar Detachment Commander, commented that this proved to be an ideal opportunity to show the Jaguar at its best. Able to deploy rapidly to the area, closely followed by the first sortie in theatre. From the receipt of notice to move, people worked continuously to generate seven aircraft in the appropriate fit and all the aircraft deployed in theatre within 36 hours of our first deployment meeting. As far as he was aware, this was the quickest time in which the Jaguar Force had ever deployed and was well within national and NATO criteria for such actions.

On a Balkan patrol.

XZ108 whilst serving with 2 Squadron in Germany.

The safety record of the Jaguar was once again being defended after a Coltishall based aircraft, XZ108/GL from 54(F) Squadron crashed into the sea 13 miles off Cromer whilst on a training mission with two other aircraft on 3 September 1998. The pilot, Flt Lt Whittaker of 41(F) Squadron, ejected and was rescued by a Sea King from Leconfield. He was taken to the Norfolk and Norwich Hospital for check-ups, but thankfully he was no worse for wear following his experience.

Up to this crash, four Jaguars had been lost in the past five years and as with all the other incidents a Board of inquiry was established to find out the cause of this particular accident. The aircraft was eventually recovered from 200 feet down on the seabed to allow the full investigation to begin.

Whilst involved in the salvage operations over the crash site a Royal Navy Sea King helicopter from RNAS Culdrose ditched into the seat at 1820 hours over the same spot as the Jaguar on the previous day. The four crewmen were picked up by a Wattisham based Sea King at about 1910 hours after spending about an hour in the water and were taken to the Norwich and Norfolk Hospital suffering from mild hypothermia and burns. Helicopters from Wattisham in Suffolk and Leconfield in Yorkshire were scrambled and the Cromer and Sheringham Lifeboats launched, but it was a commercial helicopter that was first to spot the crew, who were floating in individual life rafts beside the floating wreck of their helicopter.

That evening a Royal Naval Auxiliary Salvage Vessel went to the scene of the accident to recover the Sea King that was still afloat thanks to the floatation equipment that had been deployed at the time of the ditching.

'The memory of a baby twin boy who was the victim of cot death will always live on through a sponsored walk and cycle ride to raise cash for research.' These were the leading words of an article that recorded the efforts of a young mother and father from Coltishall who had lost a child so tragically.

SAC Simon Waters set off with many of his colleagues on a 100-mile challenge from Coltishall to Lowestoft in memory of his son Kieran who died on his christening day aged just nine weeks. Simon, who worked in the Communications Engineering Section, raised over £1000

XZ396 displaying the anniversary logo in October 1998.

The 25th Anniversary of the Jaguar was well-supported by aircraft from both home and abroad.

for cot death prevention and the Norfolk & Norwich Special Baby Care Unit in 1997. One year later in July 1998 he set out to do it all again for the Foundation of the Study of Infant Deaths and the Norfolk Autistic Society. Again his team broke the £1000 barrier with £300 being collected in a raffle alone. Simon and the team of eleven cycled from Coltishall to Lowestoft on a Friday and returned by foot via the Weavers Way over the weekend.

The Jaguar celebrated its 25th Anniversary in RAF service on 12 October 1998 and to mark the occasion the tail of XZ396 was specially painted with a logo designed by an engineer from 41(F) Squadron, Cpl 'Robbo' Robinson.

Prior to the actual anniversary date, a Families Day was organised for the 3 October with a flying display that culminated in a 16-ship diamond formation flypast of Jaguars and a roaring Hangar Party later that day.

The day before, a special event was organised to allow aircraft enthusiasts to view and photograph the aircraft, many of which were adorned with the markings of previous Jaguar squadrons. This event also attracted numerous international visitors, all with Jaguar links. These included a Dutch Air Force F-16 flown by an ex-Coltishall Jaguar pilot who was on exchange duties with the Dutch Air Force. An Italian AMX flown by another exchange pilot and aircraft familiar to Coltishall during the 1960s and 1970s; the Spitfire, Hurricane and Lancaster of the BBMF. The 'stars' of the show were undoubtedly a pair of Jaguar Es of the French Air Force who gave a breathtaking demonstration of close formation aerobatics.

A 16 year-old boy from Belarus fulfilled his dream on 10 November 1998 when he marshalled a Jaguar safely into its parking slot at Coltishall. Victor Bobr was invited to the base by Sqn Ldr Guy Stockill, who had met the teenager in Jersey where he has lived with his guardians since 1994. The youngster was just four years old when the Chernobyl disaster struck and the long-term low-level exposure to radiation had left Victor with a list of medical problems including stunted growth, brittle bones, impaired kidneys and Hepatitis C.

Victor made regular trips to Southampton Hospital for treatment to try and halt the effects of radiation poisoning. Guy Stockhill was impressed that Victor was not letting his illness hold him back. At the time Victor was an active member of the ATC in Jersey and as a lad could speak no English when he arrived four years ago. But with gritted determination he soon learnt the language and at the same time took great interest in everything RAF, impressing all who met him at Coltishall with his knowledge of everything aviation.

For the second year running a Chef from the Officers' Mess was named as the RAF's Chef of the Year. SAC Darran Benham was following in the footsteps of his Sergeant, Marc Cornell who was the Top Chef in 1997. Once again the task was to produce a meal for two in under an hour. His dishes of Lattice of Salmon and Turbot served on a bed of freshly made Pesto Pasta with char-grilled Mediterranean Vegetables and Brandy and Ginger sauce, followed by Hot Grand Marnier Crème Anglaisse and Crystallised Orange segments convinced the judge's taste buds that he was the best! This was the first major cookery award that Darren had won although he did finish third in a Junior Chef competition in 1997.

During war and peace their cheerful chats and homely fresh cook-ups were legendary at Coltishall. Bridget Smith and Ann Holland gave unstinting service to the base when they ran the busy social centre for serviceman's wives. Apart from its hub of the community role, the HIVE (Help Information Volunteer Exchange) also raised £10,000 over a ten-year period. These efforts brought recognition in November 1998 when Bridget was presented with a commendation from the C-in-C after nine years service to the HIVE and local Community and an AOC Commendation for Ann for her two and a half years service. Bridget had also received a commendation after the Gulf War when the HIVE operated as a mini operations centre when the families of Coltishall personnel who were serving in the region came in to find out what was happening.

19 January 1999 saw two Jaguars of 6 Squadron, flown by Flt Lts Mark Discombe and Jason Easthope, provide an escort for King Hussein of Jordan. The Jaguars shepherded the King who was flying his Gulfstream out of Heathrow Airport on his final journey home after nine months in America for cancer treatment. The squadron was chosen for this sad task because of its close ties with the Jordanian Royal Family having served in Jordan and the Middle East on peacekeeping duties from 1920-1956.

In 1950, King Hussein's father, King Abdullah, presented 6 Squadron with his Royal Standard at his palace in Amman in recognition of its peacekeeping role. This bond of friendship was strengthened in 1995 when King Hussein visited Coltishall to present a Flag of Friendship to the squadron.

Just short of a month after the King was escorted out of United Kingdom airspace, personnel of 6 Squadron

King Hussein salutes the 6 Squadron standard only a few weeks before his death.

King Hussein inspects 6 Squadron.

who were on detachment in the Middle East, learned with sadness of his death on 7 February 1999. At Coltishall his death was also greeted with sadness and with many fond memories. The Station Commander, Gp Cap Stephen Dalton, said that the sudden death of King Hussein had a significant impact on the Jaguar Force at Coltishall and most poignantly for the members of 6 Squadron. King Hussein managed a keen and personal interest in 6 Squadron and will be fondly remembered every time the Royal Standard is on parade with the squadron.

WO Bill Ogilvie, a revered figure, retired in March 1999 as the SWO after 37 years in the Service. Bill was in one of the first groups of RAF Regiment personnel to qualify as a parachutist in the RAF. Together with eleven other colleagues, the twelve became known as the 'Dirty Dozen' once they had completed their training in 1962. Eight of the original twelve were amongst seventy of Bill's service friends and their wives who spent a reunion weekend at Coltishall to be with Bill and his wife Jackie before they emigrated to Australia. Bill was 'seen-off' the Station in style. A trip in a Jaguar, flown by the Station Commander Gp Capt Stephen Dalton, included a pass over Catterick, the RAF Regiments Training Depot where Bill's career began in 1962.

Next saw the ceremonial drive around the Station

suitably dressed in his original parachutist smock and wearing a bowler hat adorned with corks. This event did not pass without incident. Firstly the Land Rover was ambushed by Coltishall's Regiment Flight and Bill was captured; then, before he could recover his breath he was met by a piper, Flt Sgt John Welton MBE and drummer WO Andy Kilner in full ceremonial dress and the rest of Coltishall's Warrant Officer Fraternity. The last duty he performed was an inspection of the Regiment Flight, which after his capture earlier in the afternoon could have been a time for revenge! But in true SWO's tradition, the only fall-out was in a few personnel requiring the attention of the Station Barber!

For Her Majesty the Queen's official birthday on 12 June 1999 a diamond formation of sixteen Jaguars were to fly up the Mall and then over the Buckingham Palace balcony at 1000 feet and exactly 1300 hours. Operational Commitments, including the Kosovo crisis, meant that the usual mixed formation of aircraft in the fly-past was reduced to the Jaguars from Coltishall to represent the 'front-line.'

The aircraft took-off from Coltishall and formed up over the sea and then headed back across Cromer, Coltishall, Norwich and Lowestoft before making their run in to the heart of London. However, after being airborne for 40 minutes, thunderstorms and lightning forced the formation leader, Gp Capt Dalton, to abandon the flypast. Despite the disappointment for all concerned, on the way back into Coltishall, the children and supporters of the nearby Worstead School were to get their own mini flypast by four Jaguars.

A Memorial Plaque to honour 'The Few' who flew from RAF Coltishall during World War 2 was presented to the Sergeants Mess in June 1999. The plaque was commissioned and donated by a Battle of Britain

41 Squadron keep close formation on a Polish Air Force Sukhoi Su-22 Fitter.

Historical Society member Mr Bill Bond, and was presented on behalf of the Society by another member, Sqn Ldr Joe Leigh. Bill, an Honorary Life Member of the Mess, instructed many of the Battle of Britain airmen whist stationed at Sealand with 5 FTS and Joe Leigh flew Spitfires during the Battle with 72 Squadron at Biggin Hill and occasionally from Coltishall as well. During the war Joe shot down seven enemy aircraft, was commissioned in 1941 and received the DFC in 1944. The plaque was accepted on behalf of the members of the Sergeants Mess by WO Andy Anderton, the Deputy Chairman of the Messing Committee and was witnessed by more than 60 SNCO's.

During an official Royal Visit to on 8 July 1999, HRH The Duke of Kent saw at first hand the Jaguar GR.3A. He was shown this latest variant of the Jaguar by Wg Cdr Pete Birch, the Jaguar Update Project Officer, who told the Duke it was like turning an old Ford Anglia into a new BMW 5 Series.

At the start of his visit the Duke was welcomed by the Station Commander, Gp Capt Dalton and the pupils and teachers from the Coltishall Airfield First School. All waving their Union Jacks with gusto. HRH also met wives and children of Station personnel. He was briefed on the role of the HIVE, including the recent addition of an Internet site that allowed the families to stay in touch with those on detachment around the world at a fraction of the cost of a normal telephone call.

Whilst visiting the Training and Development Section, the Duke was invited by the Station Commander to open the newly created History Room; a proud moment for the author of this book. The History Room had been created over the previous months having amassed a comprehensive record of the Station through models, photographs and memorabilia displayed in the main briefing room. HRH was also presented with a copy of the book 'RAF Coltishall Fighter Station'; a history of the base written and published by the author of this version just prior to the visit.

The day ended with an operational rapid re-arm and turnaround of a Jaguar in a simulated deployed location. This saw the demonstration of the Station Combined Incident Team, made up of volunteers from all trades and flights on the unit who are trained and held at a high state of readiness to deploy anywhere in the world to support the Jaguar Force.

The 1999 Lord Mayors procession of carnival floats bands and dancers through the streets of Norwich raised more than £8000 for the Macmillan Cancer Relief Nurse Appeal. Amongst the winning floats in the procession was Coltishall's entry, winning the best community arts, non-commercial award. Personnel from the AMF and other sections at Coltishall entered three models of aircraft and a Lightning cockpit to represent aircraft through the century. The models, a Sopwith Camel, Hawker Hurricane and Red Arrows Hawk were all hand-made by the team in their spare time. Dressed in clothing depicting aviators through the ages, they collected a handsome trophy and a cheque for £300 which they presented to their adopted charity, the Edinburgh Road School for Children with Learning Difficulties.

On 6 September 1999, Gp Capt Chris Harper took over command from Gp Capt Stephen Dalton. For the new 'boss' it was almost 20 years to the day that he first took off from the base as a junior pilot on his first operational tour with 41(F) Squadron in 1979. One of his first official duties was to hand over a cheque for £500 to the 'We Care' Appeal run by the EDP. The appeal chairperson, Mrs Paddy Seligman was delighted that Gp Capt Harper had marked the beginning of his time back at Coltishall with such a generous gesture.

Coltishall earned itself a place in the history books on 18 November 1998 when six Jaguars of 41(F) Squadron left Coltishall for a one hour and ten minute flight to Poland. The Jaguars took-off from the base at 0900 hours for a ten-day detachment. The first involving a British squadron since Poland joined NATO in March 1999. The aircraft took part in joint air exercises, Ulan Eagle 99, with Sukohi Su-22 Fitters of the Polish Air Forces 8th Fighter Bomber Regiment at Miroslaweic airbase and it was the first time the two Air Forces had carried out joint operations in support of a major exercise on the Polish/German border. 41 Squadron's boss, Wg Cdr Graham Wright, commented that from a NATO perspective it was an historic occasion for the squadron as it was the first time in its long and distinguished history that the squadron had flown in Poland.

Links between the Polish Air Force and Coltishall went back more than 50 years. After the Second World War, the base was wholly run as a Polish unit under the command of Gp Capt A K Gabszewic DSO DFC. Coltishall was then handed back to the RAF and 12 Gp Fighter Command in February 1946.

A former Spitfire pilot took a nostalgic step back in time on 11 November 1999 when he returned to Coltishall. Polish-born Konrad Stembowicz, who now lived in Horstead was invited to the base after a letter he had sent to the Evening News had been published. Konrad felt inspired to put pen to paper after reading an article about Jaguar pilots from Coltishall who were going to fly in Poland and said that everyone from 41 Squadron should expect a warm welcome from the Poles. He served with the Polish Air Force during WWII and once flew from Coltishall.

After accepting the offer of a visit, Konrad spent several hours touring the base and meeting service personnel. 'The day was fantastic, just smelling the aircraft made me think back to 1944. The visit was a great pleasure and an honour. Visiting Coltishall was just like going back in time. I felt quite at home.'

Following a study into the future basing requirements for the Eurofighter, it was announced by the Defence Minister Geoff Hoon on 13 December 1999 that Coltishall was not amongst those bases to have been selected for the new fighter. Coltishall had been widely tipped to receive the aircraft that was still under development to replace the Jaguar amongst others. If the move had come about it would have ensured the bases survival well into the 21st century. The news came as a shock to many associated with the base and with the wider community as a whole, especially those who worked at Coltishall or depended on the base for their livelihoods. Once again a niggling doubt as to the long-term future of the historic Battle of Britain base was at the forefront of everyone's minds.

The news prompted both the North Norfolk and Broadlands councils to act in a hope to safeguard hundreds of jobs in order to secure what was North Norfolk's largest employer. It was stated that the economic implications of closing the base were unimaginable, given it was worth about £17.5 millions to the local economy. Estimates suggested that about £10 million was being spent by the base employees and families in the local shops, with £6 million going to local contractors and £1.5 millions to civilian employees.

A Jaguar pilot and a Tornado navigator were the first aircrew to have reached 2000 flying hours, celebrated in the year 2000. Wg Cdr Bob Judson, the CO of 6 Squadron reached his milestone whilst flying a Jaguar from Coltishall on a local training sortie. Two days earlier Flt Lt Chris Stradling of 15(R) Squadron based at Lossiemouth in Scotland reached his 2000th hour of flying. During his 20 years of Service, Wg Cdr Judson had served on five Jaguar Squadrons as well as an exchange tour with the Luftwaffe flying F-4 Phantoms. He had also completed two operational detachments to Operation Warden and four to Operation Deny Flight.

Sqn Ldr Mark Discombe welcomes Lt Col Jacek Lazarczyk.

Trains and boats and planes ferried an Air Force scroll on a milestone journey around the country as the Royal Air Forces Association (RAFA) Millennium Link was being passed between RAFA branches during the summer months of 2000. The scroll had travelled by the horse-drawn Holt Flyer bus, by steam train on the North Norfolk Railway and by the Sheringham Lifeboat. Earlier in the region it moved by tank, motorcycle, police car, autogyro, traction engine, light aircraft and was even dropped by parachute from 3000 feet. In the following weeks it was flown in a Jaguar, by mail coach to RAF Neatishead, by paddle steamer to Potter Heigham and on to Yarmouth in the cockpit of a Lightning fighter before leaving the country. This parchment along with eight others from across the country was to end up in London in September to mark the RAFA's biggest annual fund-raising drive, the Battle of Britain Wings Appeal.

Coltishall was awarded the 'Millennium Award for MoD Energy Efficiency' from BG Energy Services, part of the BG Group plc, in June. The awards, judged by the Buildings Research Establishment, are designed to promote the efficient use of energy throughout the MoD and Coltishall was selected as a result of recent energy projects that were aimed at improving its utility management and minimising consumption. Over the past decade Coltishall had reduced its consumption by 20% and the achievement earned it the £3000 prize which was distributed to three charities; The East Angian Children's Hospice at Quidenham, The Nancy Oldfield Trust and the Station Charities Fund at Coltishall. In addition to the prize money, the Station Energy manager Marc Harris also received an engraved crystal bowl and a certificate to recognise his personal achievement in introducing many of the energy efficiency measures.

June 2000 witnessed 60th Anniversary of Coltishall. Throughout the June and July there were many events to celebrate the sixty glorious years, but the arrival of the Polish Air Force on the 28 June and the Families Day on 8 July were the highlights.

Two Polish Air Force Sukhoi Su-22 Fitters of 8 Fighter Bomber Regiment from Miroslaweic arrived at Coltishall having accepted an invitation from 41(F) Squadron to pay a visit after the very successful deployment of the Jaguars to Poland as part of Exercise Ulan Eagle 99. Coltishall was an appropriate venue for the Poles as it ensured that the visit would not only Commemorate the vital contribution that their forerunners made to the victory in the Battle of Britain, but also to recognise the fact that Coltishall was a Polish base from 1945 to 1946.

For many of Norfolk's Polish Community, the visit of their countrymen brought back many happy and sad memories. One of the wartime pilots to witness the arrival of the Sukhois was Tony Brent, a Pole who had joined his national air force after fleeing his troubled country at the beginning of WWII. He had many fond memories of post-war Coltishall when it was a Polish base and was deeply moved by the experience of welcoming his fellow countrymen to the United Kingdom.

Mr Brent, who retired to Taverham in 1991, enjoyed meeting with the present-day pilots during their week-long stay at Coltishall, as did the widows of two Polish airmen. Beryl Paleolog and Jean Grabowski fondly remember those days especially when they met their late husbands Vic and Fran at the Samson and Hercules Dance Hall in Norwich.

Tony Brent with fellow countryman, Major Bogus Zych.

As a child, Halinka Szymanska's fondest memory was when she sat on her father's lap in the cockpit of his Mustang III at Coltishall that he proudly named after her. Years later, Halinka rekindled the proud memories of her father on a visit to the base where both the RAF and Poles recreated that precious moment when she smiled for the camera whilst sitting in her father's aircraft.

In 1944 her father, Tadeuz Szymanski, was flying Mustangs with 316 (City of Warsaw) Squadron. The squadron and Tadeuz in particular were to gain notoriety in the way they dispatched the deadly V-1 Flying Bombs. On hearing the story, the Polish aircrew happily invited Halinka to sit in the cockpit of one of the Sukhois and for the photograph, the aircraft was named 'Halinka' in her honour, just like her father's Mustang half a century earlier.

The Families Day on 8 July was a time when the extended Coltishall family reacquainted themselves with the base and friends of old. Without doubt, the Polish contingent stole the show. They stood proudly in front of their aircraft talking to one and all and extending the kind of friendship that was the hallmark of their countrymen 60 years earlier.

Apart from the Polish, the event attracted aircraft from Germany, Italy, Belgium and Denmark as well as the RAF. The BBMF recalled the wartime exploits of Coltishall squadrons and its pilots such as Douglas Bader and Bob Stanford Tuck. The Flight, having been based at Coltishall from 1962 to 1976, had come 'home' to celebrate this special birthday.

Although the Families Day was closed to the public, nothing could stop enthusiasts from enjoying the event from outside the wire. Hundreds lined the roads around

A young Halinka Szymanska with her father, Tadeuz in the cockpit of his Mustang III in 1944.

the edge of the airfield and standing on the bonnets of their cars with cameras, binoculars and their eyes glued skywards.

For 1300 lucky enthusiasts, the Friday prior to the Families Day gave them the opportunity to witness and photograph the arrival of the visiting aircraft as well as the Coltishall based Jaguars. F-4 Phantoms from Germany, F-104 Starfighters and AMXs from Italy, an F-16 and Alpha Jet from Belgium and an F-16 from Denmark as well as Harriers, Tornadoes, Hawks and Tucanos from the RAF were on the menu. Each had paid for this unique opportunity and a total of in excess £13,000 was raised for Station Charities.

Veterans, villagers and personnel from Coltishall gathered at the hamlet of Meeting Hill to celebrate 60 years of friendship and to dedicate a memorial in the Baptist Chapel. The contingent from Coltishall paraded with the three resident Squadron Standards and were joined by representatives from the Royal British Legion, RAFA and a host of civil dignitaries, including Liz Cornwall, the Mayor of North Walsham and Roy Haynes, deputy leader of North Norfolk District Council.

During the service, the station Chaplain, Sqn Ldr Jonathan Beach, said that one reason why Coltishall was one of the most popular postings, and why many ex-RAF personnel retire to the area, was because of the warmth and friendship shown by the local communities. He accepted that the RAF were not the quietest of neighbours. The day of the silent jet had yet to come but he said, at least we can be honest about things that annoy us and remain friends nevertheless.

Sylvia Pearce, a Meeting Hill resident gave a moving account of her wartime memories in the area. As a seven-year-old she recalled how she waved at a pilot who had flown low above her and he waved back. Later she learned

Halinka recreates the moment in the cockpit of a Polish Air Force Su-22.

The Memorial Plaque at Meeting Hill.

The parade at Meeting Hill.

that it was a German pilot flying a Messerschmitt Bf109 and he had been shot down over the sea off Bacton. She also paid tribute to the crew of Venom NF.3 WX879 from 23 Squadron that went out of control over Meeting Hill on 2 January 1956. The aircraft had skimmed the roof of the chapel and of her neighbourhood home before crashing into a field. The crew, Flg Off I Jarvis and H Parsons died in the accident after trying to avoid crashing into the buildings.

Wg Cdr Jon Taylor, OC Ops Wing, unveiled a Memorial Plaque that was to be placed on a cairn that was being built behind the 18th-century chapel to celebrate the long friendship between the Meeting Hill residents and Coltishall. David Fox, the Baptist Minister, reminded the congregation that there were complaints about the noise made by the RAF jets. But he said, 'Praise God for that noise because it is the sound of freedom.'

A solitary Jaguar from 41 (F) Squadron assisted the Sussex Police in their search for the missing schoolgirl Sarah Payne. Photographs taken by the Jaguar on 15 July helped police officers starting the third week of the search for the eight-year old girl. The aircraft joined in the hunt on the Saturday in a rare move by the police asking for military assistance in the desperate search to find Sarah, who it was feared had been abducted.

The Jaguar scanned a 60-mile corridor between London and Worthing during seven low passes at between 1000 and 2000 feet taking dozens of pictures. Detectives hoped to piece together the images onto an up-to-date map so that no possible hideaway was left unchecked by the search teams. The techniques used on the search mission were the same as those used every day by the Jaguars policing Northern Iraq from their base at Incerlik in Turkey.

Photographic Analysts from 41 Squadron RIC made an initial assessment of the results before passing them to the Sussex Police. Chief Inspector Mike Alderson said that the RAF help enabled the police to plan searches based on the crystal clear photographs. Sadly, little Sarah Paynes body was found on 17 July 2000.

The 20 July saw the arrival of eight Jaguars from Lossiemouth belonging to 16(R) Squadron, the OCU for the Jaguar Force. Their arrival at Coltishall with the jets and around 100 personnel meant that the base was now the home to the RAF's entire front-line Jaguar fleet. On landing, the jets were welcomed by the Station Commander Gp Capt Chris Harper and a lone piper, Flt Sgt John Welton MBE who heralded this new episode in the history of Coltishall with a stirring rendition of 'The Green Hills of Tyrol.' The crews, under the command of Wg Cdr Andy Sudlow, were welcomed with a champagne reception where he Commented that Coltishall had always had a reputation as a friendly base and to some

Flt Sgt John Welton MBE heralds the arrival of 16(R) Squadron.

extent it was like coming home because most of the squadron had served at the base before.

The 8 September 2000 was to be an historic day for the Airfield School for it was on this day that the widow of the legendary fighter pilot Sir Douglas Bader officially re-named the school after her late husband.

Lady Joan Bader officiated at the newly-christened Sir Douglas Bader School in the shadow of the base where Sir Douglas served back in 1940. The historic name-change marked the move to primary school status for the former Coltishall Airfield First School with the increase of pupils from 78 to 150. She said that her late husband would have been very proud to have been able to open the school, and that she was equally proud to do so - on his behalf.

More than 100 pupils listened intently as Lady Joan joked about her late husband's famous tin legs. She said that considering the number of legs that had been dropped to him whilst he was being held POW by the Germans, she could have given every pupil one to keep as he must have been a centipede!

The new identity was suggested by one of the parents as the perfect 'figurehead' for the pupils. The Head teacher Diana Ellis noted that being the 60th Anniversary of Douglas Bader being at Coltishall and because he was a real good role model being disabled yet never letting anything hold him back, the suggestion was perfect. The day's celebrations continued into the evening with a Battle of Britain 60th Anniversary Pageant that was held in front of the hangars on the base.

Joining Lady Bader at the pageant were four Battle of Britain veterans, Wg Cdr Tom Neil, Sqn Ldr Andy Anderson, Sqn Ldr Joce Millard and Flt Lt Ron Smythe. They all witnessed a moving ceremony that consisted of music by the Band of the RAF College Cranwell and the City of Norwich Pipe Band, followed by a stunning drill display by the Queen's Colour Squadron and a series of fly-bys by a Spitfire from nearby Duxford. The finale saw all the participants joined by dancers from the newly named Douglas Bader School. After the pageant there was a sunset ceremony in front of the Officers' Mess that concluded with a Jaguar flypast before the distinguished guests were escorted into the mess for a formal dinner.

Despite the historical celebrations that unfolded during its 60th Anniversary, fears were once again being centred on the long-term future of the Jaguar and the historic base. Speculation was rife that the Jaguars were now favourites to be axed as part of the MoD drive to plug an alleged £1.5 billion shortfall. An MoD spokesperson was quick to emphasise that there were no plans to shut the base early and that the worries were fuelled by a leaked report looking at possible defence savings that included measures such as scrapping an entire aircraft type.

The Mid-Norfolk MP Keith Simpson urged ministers to 'come clean' over the document, as having been at the 60th Anniversary celebrations he knew that the base and its personnel were 'getting on with the job.' But he also recognised that the speculation, claims and counter claims were not helpful for those whose livelihoods depended on the long-term future of the base.

Flt Lt 'Torch' Clarke, a New Zealander on exchange with 6 Squadron was forced to eject from his Jaguar XZ111, which crashed at Shield Hill, Dumfries just before 1100 hours on 27 October following a multiple bird-strike. The bird-strike disabled both engines giving Flt Lt Clarke seconds to react. He valiantly tried to re-light the engines whilst pointing his aircraft away from populated areas but in the end had no option but to eject. His aircraft came down in a remote field occupied by cows, luckily none of which were killed or injured.

The pilot landed in a field close to the wreckage of his aircraft and was soon joined by a local farmer Mr John Kerr who had witnessed the accident. Mr Kerr stayed with Flt Lt Clarke until a Royal Navy Sea King from Prestwick arrived on the scene to take the pilot to hospital for check-up before being released from hospital to rejoin his squadron on 29 October.

It was announced in November 2000 that 29-year old Flt Lt James Heald was to receive the Queen's Commendation for Bravery in the Air for his act in recovering his Jaguar following a double engine failure whilst over hostile territory. Heald, of 41(F) Squadron suffered the engine failure during a busy ten minutes whilst on a routine sortie over Northern Iraq. He found himself dropping like a stone and just ten seconds from ejecting when an engine relit enabling him to recover to a friendly base.

The incident started shortly after a routine air-to-air refuelling link up. As he backed away from the tanker there were two big bangs and the number two engine immediately shut down. The failure was due to air disturbance caused by the refuelling probe and following the emergency shut-down drill, practiced on a regular basis in the flight simulator, he jettisoned his fuel tanks and then increased the other engine to full re-heat power.

After regaining height and speed Flt Lt Heald eased out of re-heat, this action caused the second engine to fail as he flew at around 2000 feet. Following all his drills he radioed that he was going to eject in 30 seconds, but at the same time keeping his finger on the re-light button; it eventually worked. The seriousness of the situation did not occur to the pilot at the time, as he was too busy in the cockpit. It was not until the next day safely back at Incerlik that it finally hit home. The prospect of parachuting down into Iraq was not one that pilots looked forward to.

In typical fashion, James Heald played down the bravery award by simply saying that 'it was what anyone else with a sense of self-survival would have done.'

Two RAF Regiment Instructors from Coltishall confirmed to their colleagues at the base what had been suspected for a very long time, they both enjoy the gas chamber! Cpls Geordie Rothwell and Rick Jollands spent 24 hours in the 'gas chamber' to raise money for charity. They both decided that after many happy months of placing station personnel through the chamber on their annual CCS course that they would show them how it was really done. Not just for a few short minutes, but for a whole day and what better benefactor for their self-induced pleasure than the RAF Regiments own 'Hope and Homes for Children' Charity.

Fully kitted-out and with a CS pellet being lit every four hours, the two raised more than £400 for the charity that helps to rebuild the lives of orphans of war or disaster by giving them a foundation for the future and a family for life. A fire bucket left outside the chamber collected more cash and with visits from other Regiment staff and a TV to keep them company, they survived the ordeal none the worse for their experience.

"Royal Air Force, Kungliga Brittiska flygvapnet, gastar F21 med sju spaningsplan av typ Jaguar. Besoket ar ett led I forberedleserna for Sveriges deltagande I FN: s fredsbevarande aktioner. Men vadret satte stopp for samovningar."

This was the headline of the Swedish newspaper welcoming members of 41(F) Squadron to the Swedish Air Force Base at Kallax near Lulea. The base, part of the most northern Swedish Air Force Wing, Norbotten, played host to the first bi-lateral operational training deployment to Sweden by an RAF Unit. Five Jaguars deployed to Kallax for Exercise LONE WOLF, named after F21 Viggen squadron who hosted the visit that involved around 100 members of 41 Squadron. Expecting to be met with temperatures well below freezing with a liberal sprinkling of snow, the RAF lads were disappointed to be in an all too familiar situation with rain and low cloud keeping the jets firmly on the ground for most of the week.

Despite the frustration, no opportunity was missed to exchange ideas and information with their Swedish hosts who had been tasked by their government with providing an air reconnaissance capability to international peace support operations from the beginning of the new millennium.

The Viggen squadrons included F21, equipped with the SH.37 reconnaissance variant of the double-delta fighter. The squadron was keen to benefit from the wide experience that 41 Squadron had gained in a decade of operational sorties over the Middle East and Balkans.

Conducted 'in the spirit of Partnership for Peace' the exercise certainly fostered a close working relationship between 41 Squadron and F21. It was hoped that the deployment would form the basis of a continuing relationship for the future.

The first RAF parade of its kind since 1949 was conducted at Coltishall on 10 May 2001 when airmen of 54(F) Squadron 'Trooped' their Squadron Standard at the Station's Annual Formal Inspection by AVM

41 Squadron in company with a pair of Swedish Air Force SH.37 Viggens.

Glen Torpy, the AOC 1 Gp. The parade of the Standard was carried out as part of the celebrations to mark 54 Squadron's 85th anniversary.

Following the historic parade Wg Cdr Edward Stringer paid tribute to the personnel of his squadron by saying that his staff had just come back from 100 days flying around Northern Iraq and only had a few days to practice for the parade. He went on to say that he wanted the Standard to be trooped because the squadron would not be anything without the young men and women who keep the aircraft going and fly them night and day. This was for them.

The Defence Secretary Geoff Hoon reassured families of Coltishall pilots under fire in Iraq that they would

Vicon Recce Pod under a Jaguar GR.3.

not be forgotten. His comments were made during an election campaign visit to Oulton Broad on 28 May 2001 where he went on to say that they were performing an extraordinarily important job there and have been doing so ever since the invasion of Kuwait and the Gulf War.

Families of personnel who were serving in the region at the time of Mr Hoons visit were becoming concerned at the increase in heavy anti-aircraft artillery and missile launches that the Jaguars were facing on a daily basis whilst patrolling the no-fly zone over Northern Iraq. Tensions were said to be high at this time over the region and in one recent attack a Jaguar pilot from

54(F) Squadron came close to being shot down over the Kurdish safe haven.

The capabilities of the Jaguar force flying missions over the Iraqi northern no-fly zone were significantly enhanced by the introduction of the GR.3A variant and the new Jaguar Reconnaissance Pod during the middle months of 2001. Flying out of Incerlik in Turkey, the Jaguar GR.3's on detachment there were gradually replaced by the GR.3A and with 41(F) Squadron completing the first sorties with the new combination of aircraft and recce pod, they were quick to praise the upgrades.

The Jaguar GR.3A is an upgraded version of the GR.3 fitted with a range of sophisticated avionics and unlike the GR.3, which flies with the older Vicon Reconnaissance Pod that uses 'wet-film', the GR.3A's pod uses an electro-optical system that records onto video tape.

Since the arrival of the GR.3A in theatre the system very quickly proved its worth in the operational environment and the detachment was able to complete the transition from wet-film to electro-optical operations within one week without a break in the operational tempo. The Detachment Commander, Wg Cdr Graham Wright commented that the smooth transition was only possible because of some excellent work by personnel at 1 Group, the Integrated Project Team at Coltishall and by those on the ground at Incerlik.

During July, a scheme that saw RAF Volunteers team-up

Handover of the first Jaguar GR.3.

with the ambulance service proved crucial in saving lives across Norfolk began. Personnel from Coltishall, together with their colleagues from Marham joined forces with the East Anglian Ambulance NHS Trust to be part of the nationwide First Response charity.

Trained volunteers, all unpaid and working from 1800 hrs to midnight, including weekends, respond to emergency situations in specially marked and equipped cars, cutting the response times considerably. The First Response teams were not designed to replace the regular ambulance services, as for every call the responders receive, a land ambulance would also be sent. But it was soon recognised that in some cases the RAF responders may be closer to the scene than the normal ambulance, often proving crucial for the patients.

Whilst on detachment at Eielson Air Force Base in Alaska on Exercise Cope Thunder, 54(F) Squadron lost one of its most enthusiastic and gifted young pilots in a tragic accident. 28 year-old Flt Lt Jason Hayes died during a routine training exercise over the vast wilderness of Alaska near the remote settlement of Eagle, close to the Canadian border on the morning of 26 July 2001.

Back home, it was difficult to describe the shock and sadness that people on the close-knit station felt and for the pilots, groundcrews and support personnel at Eielson this tragic and devastating event was greeted with silence and deep reflection.

Prior to every sortie, Jason Hayes made it his business to 'say hello' to the numerous support staff that were there to help run the detachment and to the groundcrews of his own squadron. The morning of 26 July was no different. A gentleman to the core, and always smiling, Jason greeted everyone with the same enthusiasm and utmost respect. The Jaguars on the mission that morning were on a simulated ground attack as part of the exercise when Jason's aircraft disappeared from the radar screens. With the other Jaguars landing back at Eielson and with no sign of the missing aircraft after 15 minutes the worst was feared.

SAR assets from both Eielson and Elmendorf Air Force Base near Anchorage were scrambled. They included helicopters, OA-10A Thunderbolts, F-16s, C-130s and a KC-135 Stratotanker followed the planned route of the Jaguars until they finally located the wreckage of the Jaguar at 1400 hours British Standard Time, six hours after the others had landed safely back at Eielson.

The funeral of Flt Lt Hayes was held on a bright sunny day at Norwich Cathedral. Dozens of his RAF colleagues, family and friends gathered to pay tribute with the

Coltishall First Responders.

perfectly observed silence being broken as four Jaguars flew over the cathedral spires in formation to honour their comrade. Once overhead the lead Jaguar pulled up and away to enact the 'missing man' formation that traditionally marks the passing of an airman.

41(F) Squadron celebrated its 85th Anniversary in September with pilots from each decade from the 1920s onwards, sharing experiences with squadron colleagues during a nostalgic weekend. On 1 September, they gathered for a Families Day at the base that included a flying display and ground demonstrations. From a display by a Spitfire recalling the part that 41 Squadron played in the Battle of Britain and WWII, to the Jaguars of today in a formation of their squadron emblem, the Cross of St Omer, the young and old reflected on 85 years of distinguished history.

Coltishall bade farewell to Gp Capt Chris Harper on 5 October 2001, and following his final Jaguar flight he handed over control of the base to Gp Capt Ricci Cobelli after two years in command. Leaving Coltishall on promotion to Air commodore, Chris Harper was posted to HQ Strike command with the responsibility of bringing on stream the Eurofighter. The aircraft that will eventually replace the Jaguar in front line service towards the end of the decade.

Gp Capt Cobelli was no stranger to the Jaguar as he flew the aircraft from Brüggen before moving on to the Tornado. His last posting before taking command of Coltishall was as the Personal Staff Officer to the Commander Air North at Ramstein AFB in Germany.

Olympic gold and silver medal cyclist Jason Queally was certainly not used to riding tandem on his state-of-the-art competition bicycle. But he had to take a back seat when he was flown in a Jaguar whilst on a visit to the base to talk to the RAF cycling team on 25 October.

His flight with Sqn Ldr Johnny Stringer included a series of dummy bombing runs over the Wash. On his return and beaming from ear to ear, Jason commented that he was nervous before the flight. Just like he is prior to any race, but once airborne he described the experience as fantastic, topping anything he had done in the past year and fulfilling a dream that he had ever since he was a boy.

Sqn Ldr Jez Milne of 54(F) Squadron, described the award of the DFC for bravery in the Operational Honours List on 30 October 2001 as being 'somewhere between acute embarrassment and dying of pride.' He was awarded the DFC for his professional leadership and bravery after facing a barrage of anti-aircraft fire whilst on a mission to patrol the no-fly zones over Northern Iraq. His citation also commended him for his courage and motivation of other crews through his actions.

Sqn Ldr Jez Milne DFC.

Sqn Ldr Milne was the Jaguar Detachment Commander with coalition forces at Incerlik Air Base in Northern Turkey in March 2001 when on one mission he faced particularly heavy fire. At the time, British and American aircraft involved in patrols and reconnaissance missions to protect the Kurds in the safe haven above the 36th parallel in Iraq, were being shot at on a daily basis. On a mission on the 20 March, his aircraft faced prolonged fire and came close to being shot down. He recalled that at one stage there was a call from another pilot for him to break right with Triple A, anti-aircraft artillery, right on his nose. The Triple A was four seconds ahead of his aircraft and there was no question that this was a close call.

For most people a flight in a Jaguar is probably an amazing experience, but for one VIP passenger the trip of a lifetime would be remembered for a long time. Sheila Kefford, the Sheriff of Norwich, had been invited to fly in a Jaguar T.2 of 41(F) Squadron as part of her civic duties. However, during mid-flight the aircraft developed a hydraulic problem and returned to base. On landing the brakes failed, the parachute was deployed and the aircraft came to a stop off the side of the runway.

After soothing her nerves with a cup of sweet tea, and declining the offer of a whiskey, Mrs Kefford recalled that the pilot, Wg Cdr Graham Wright, told her that they had to turn back just as they made it to the Humber Bridge some 20 minutes into the flight. Whilst she was nervous at seeing all the flashing lights in the cockpit, she remained calm as Wg Cdr Wright explained what was happening and kept reassuring her as they transited back to Coltishall. On passing the Norfolk coast she said that she had never been so pleased to see the Cromer Pier! Despite the experience she had nothing but praise for Wg Cdr Wright. 'He kept reassuring me I'd be all right. He was first rate.'

Exceptional airmanship and skill shown by Sqn Ldr Toby Craig, the Jaguar Standards and Evaluation pilot at Coltishall during an emergency on 2 April 2001 resulted in a Green Endorsement to his Flying Log Book. On the day in question Sqn Ldr Craig was tasked to fly as the wingman in a pairs formation on a weapons range sortie. His aircraft was configured with drop tanks, a Container Bomb Light Stores (CBLS) with two 14 kilogramme practice bombs and a second CBLS with four three kg practice bombs.

Very shortly after getting airborne whilst still within the airfield boundary, Sqn Ldr Craig saw, in his peripheral vision, an object pass down the left-hand side of his aircraft. Almost immediately there was a loud bang and he, aware that the aircraft had stopped accelerating and was now descending, selected full power on both engines. At this stage he contemplated ejecting but, assessing that there was only just sufficient time to clear his aircraft using the emergency jettison button, he raised the undercarriage in an attempt to climb away.

With the aircraft clear of external stores, he established a climb but, on checking his engine instruments, noted that the port engine RPM was decreasing and that the temperature was well above 1000 degrees. It subsequently transpired that the port engine had suffered catastrophic damage following the ingestion of at least one wood pigeon. He shut the engine down immediately, declared a MAYDAY and called for a visual inspection from the lead aircraft. With seemingly only minor damage to the airframe, Sqn Ldr Craig jettisoned fuel and, after a low speed handling check, landed safely from a textbook single engined approach.

His citation read: 'Sqn Ldr Craig demonstrated exceptional clarity of thought, airmanship and skill throughout the emergency. Faced with a catastrophic engine failure in arguably the most critical phase of flight, he understandably considered ejection and would have been fully justified in doing so; however, his rapid and accurate assessment of the situation allowed him to complete the appropriate drills expediously and, consequently, save a valuable aircraft. In recognition of his outstanding professionalism, and exceptional skill and judgement that he displayed during this emergency, Sqn Ldr Craig is awarded the Green Endorsement to his Flying Log Book.'

The Operational Honours List promulgated in early 2002 saw two Jaguar pilots Mentioned in Despatches for bravery whilst operating in the no-fly zone over Northern Iraq.

The former CO of Coltishall, Air Cdre Christopher Harper received his honour for bravery for his part in a reconnaissance mission during May 2001 when his aircraft came under attack from anti-aircraft artillery and surface-to-air missiles and a missile that exploded less than 500 metres behind his aircraft. Not phased by his experience, he returned the next day to gather more photographic data that resulted in an attack on an Iraqi missile system; this was destroyed as a result.

Also Mentioned in Despatches was Sqn Ldr Dave Foote of 41(F) Squadron. His award was in recognition of an act of bravery and providing a substantial contribution to Operation RESINATE (NORTH) in support of the overall Operation Northern Watch.

Sqn Ldr Foote led a significant number of sorties during April 2001 over the no-fly zones. He also played a key role in the changeover to the new reconnaissance equipment, volunteering to stay on with the operation longer than required to ensure the smooth transition from one system to the other. He was shot at by anti-aircraft artillery and surface-to-air missiles on ten out of twelve occasions and reflecting this his citation said that he was 'utterly unflappable and demonstrated a focus and total disregard for his own personal safety in the face of enemy fire.'

A team of young engineering students who had been working on a new way of testing a stabiliser system for RAF Jets were told their research would be used in trials by RAF engineers working on Jaguars.

The team from Paston College at North Walsham were taking part in a national engineering education scheme, The Best Programme, designed to encourage students to consider engineering as a career. Members, Howard Lomax, Tim Mindham, Elliott Bird and Ben Hicks, all 17 years old, worked with the engineers for six months where they was given the problem of testing a Jaguar plane stabilising system automatically, rather than the manual way used at the time. Their ideas led to the RAF evaluating and modifying their prototype system in the hope that further development may lead to the equipment being used in the future.

During the Annual Formal Inspection of Coltishall by the AOC 1 Gp, AVM Glenn Torpy, nineteen personnel, representing every rank on the station, received their Queen's Golden Jubilee Medal from the AOC at a parade to mark the occasion. Among the recipients was the SWO, WO 'Ginge' Roffey, who also held the Queen's Silver Jubilee Medal.

WO Roffey is one of the most decorated Warrant Officers in the RAF; he has been awarded the MBE and amongst his other medals he has been decorated for operational service with the RAF Regiment in Bosnia, Oman and Northern Ireland.

LONE CAT 02 was designed as another routine out-of-area exercise for 6 Squadron, aimed at enhancing the unit's flexibility to deploy and immediately commence operations in an unfamiliar region. For their hosts, the Bulgarian Air Force however, Lone Cat 02 was regarded as something of a challenge. The first time its fighter and strike pilots had taken part in an exercise involving such close co-operation with a NATO member air arm. Moreover, it was to be the first time that the Bulgarian pilots would have operated in conditions resembling a real-life operation with scenarios similar to those developed in and around Iraq by mid-2002.

The exercise was planned in late 2001 as the most important event in the British-Bulgarian military co-operation plan. Eight Jaguars, 14 pilots and over 100 technicians and support personnel deployed to the biggest of the Bulgarian Air Force bases at Graf Ignatievo, five miles north of Bulgaria's second largest city, Plovdiv.

Much of the equipment to support the Jaguars went overland on an eight-day drive across Europe and was all in place when the aircraft arrived on 19 August. The Jaguars flew missions each day with their Bulgarian hosts, dropping practice bombs on a nearby range and familiarising the Bulgarian pilots with NATO procedures and tactics.

16(R) Squadron display jet at play.

Bulgaria was one of a number of former Warsaw Pact countries who were actively seeking membership of an expanding NATO. The exercise, as designed, gave the Bulgarian pilots an insight as to how they would fly if they were to gain membership. Second Lt Lubomir Slaov, a Mig-21 Lancer pilot commented that all the training objectives had been met and the achievements were greater than the expectations.

The Freedom of the City of Norwich had been enjoyed by Coltishall for the past 35 years and to commemorate this honour the badge of Norwich was placed on the tail of the 16(R) Squadron display jet. The Lord Mayor of Norwich, Councillor Derek Wood, joined Gp Capt Ricci Cobelli and the Jaguar display pilot, Flt Lt Mike Hayes to unveil the new badge.

The Jaguar display aircraft had taken part in over 30 air shows up to this time in locations as far a field as Denmark, Malta and the Channel Islands. The symbolic gesture of adding the badge served to strengthen the bond between Norwich and Coltishall.

He was a brave fighter pilot who fought for the freedom of his native Poland as well as in the Battle of Britain. For five years WO Jan Rogowski's grave had been unmarked, but on Thursday 12 September 2002, scores of people including friends and dignitaries surrounded his grave at a touching service to unveil a headstone and pay tribute to a man who earned his country's equivalent of the VC.

Jan Rogowski had survived being shot down over Beckenham, been successful in shooting down enemy aircraft and as part of 306 (Polish) Squadron. Had flown in combat against the V-1 Doodlebugs over Kent. He had always appeared to shun any public recognition of his achievements and was said to be an intensely private man who lived in a flat in Queen's Street Ipswich above a bakery next door to the Falcon Pub. But despite his privacy, those who knew Jan said that he would have been extremely proud of his service. He died in 1997 at the age of 79.

Representatives of the Royal British Legion and Honington attended the service and as the Last Post was played a Jaguar from Coltishall, his old wartime station whilst with 306 Squadron, flew over Ipswich Lawns Cemetery in a mark of respect for a very, very honourable gentleman.

A routine and long-planned exercise with the Royal Jordanian Air Force in January 2003 fuelled speculation that the involvement of the Jaguars spelled something more sinister, especially as there had been a marked build-up of the British military presence in the region for possible operations against Saddam Hussein.

41 Squadron RIC, located immediately behind the squadron line.

Exercise DESERT THUNDERCAT saw crews from 6 Squadron taking part in simulated ground attack and troop support sorties with their Jordanian hosts. The detachment itself lasted for two weeks with the pilots and support personnel living in Spartan conditions in tents and it being winter, having to endure sub-zero temperatures at night. Desert conditions such as heat and dust put human and equipment endurance to the test, but in Jordan the crews had to adapt to bad winter weather as well.

Despite returning to Coltishall as planned following DESERT THUNDERCAT, the press speculation regarding the possible deployment of aircraft, personnel and equipment back to the Gulf region from the base heightened as the diplomatic arguments continued at the United Nations and elsewhere with regards to an invasion of Iraq. For Coltishall, the preparations for possible conflict were being planned just in case there was a requirement to reinforce the Jaguar detachment at Incerlik who were already involved in patrolling the no-fly zone over Northern Iraq.

As world diplomatic pressures increased over the possible conflict with Iraq, the Turkish Government introduced a ban on warplanes using their airspace in the fear that any conflict might spill over into the country across their border with Iraq.

Since October 1998 four Jaguars have been based at Incerlik enforcing the no-fly zone over Northern Iraq. But with the advent of the new war in Iraq and the Turkish enforcement of the flight ban over their own territory, the zones had now become obsolete and there was no longer an operational role for the aircraft in that region.

Following their return April 2003, the aircraft and pilots went onto immediate standby for possible involvement in the new conflict. As it was, 50 personnel from the base had already deployed to the Gulf region to carry out support duties such as catering, driving, supply and policing roles.

In 1947, Norfolk missed the chance to witness a piece of history that came in the form of an intricately-crafted lace tapestry commemorating the Battle of Britain. Back then the tapestry bypassed the county on a national tour even though Coltishall played a significant part in the battle. During the war Dobsons & Browne had devoted most of its output to the production of Mosquito and camouflage netting. As a means of retaining the skills and standards of their highly trained designers and draughting staff that were under-employed by the wartime production requirements, the firm took up the idea of making a large commemorative lace panel.

The design of the panel took two years and the drafting for the jacquards (pattern cards) another 15 months. The pattern required 40,000 cards, weighing a tonne altogether. Each panel took a week to produce and required 4,200 threads and the preparation of 975 bobbins for the loom. A total of 41,830 kilometres of fine Egyptian cotton went into making each panel which measured 15 feet x five feet when completed.

The panel depicts scenes of the bombing of London, and types of aircraft used in the battle, as well as badges of the Allied forces involved and the floral emblems of Great Britain and the Commonwealth. Also included are the names of the firm and the craftsmen from Dobsons & Browne who created the work. At the bottom of the scroll are Sir Winston Churchill's famous words: "Never was so much owed by so many to so few." A cottage and a castle are also depicted, to indicate that rich and poor suffered alike. The edging of the curtain is composed of ripening ears of corn representing the season during which the Battle of Britain took place. Interwoven with these are Tudor roses, thistles, shamrocks and oak leaves.

Thirty-eight panels were woven before the jacquards were destroyed. King George VI and Sir Winston Churchill were each presented with one and others were distributed to various RAF units and to Westminster Abbey, the City of Nottingham, City of London and personnel from Dobsons & Browne. As airmen from New Zealand, South Africa, Canada and Australia had been attached to various RAF squadrons, these countries also received a panel.

The Officers' Mess at Coltishall housed one of the panels that were made which had arrived at the station wrapped in a brown paper parcel in 1972. By 1973 the lace was mounted in a hardwood frame but had to be folded to fit as the height of the mess ceiling prevented it from being displayed in its full glory. It would not be until 1975 that the full lace could be seen. To ensure this could happen, a team led by WO Smith carefully removed the lace from its wooden frame and mounted it in a new metal-framed cabinet. To make room for the extra height, a corner of the foyer ceiling was removed and re-plastered around the new frame.

For Reg Sheppard from Horning, the lace was well known as he was in charge of a 20-month tour that allowed hundreds of thousands of people to view the stunning work after its official unveiling in London. Reg Commented that he thought Norfolk deserved to see it because everyone from the area knew someone in the war as a result of there being 36 aerodromes in the county.

Reg hatched a plan to show this lace to the people of Norfolk by re-locating it from the Officers' Mess to the Forum at Norwich during the Battle of Britain week in September. It was later realized it was going to be a problem getting the framed lace out of the mess as part of the ceiling had to be removed when it arrived at the base in the 1970's.

Not deterred, Reg managed to track down the actual lace he toured with to a woman living in Shropshire whose father had been presented with it after the display had ended. She agreed to bring the lace that had been stored in a bottom drawer for 40 years, to Norwich for the weeklong display in the Forum.

All seemed well until it came to funding the event, as £1500 was needed for insurance, transportation from Shropshire and hiring the Forum. Thankfully, with the support of various groups and the dogged determination and enthusiasm of Reg Shepperd, the lace that passed Norfolk by in 1947 was eventually on show for all to see in September 2003.

The Operational Honours List released in April 2003 saw the award of the DFC to Flt Lt James Heald of 41(F) Squadron for Operations over Iraq. His award stated that during Operation RESINATE (North) he was tasked to recce anti-aircraft batteries. His aircraft came under intensive fire and was surrounded by exploding FLAK which was only avoided by carrying out a series of high G-force turns, dives and climbs. Nevertheless the target was successfully photographed and he returned to allied controlled airspace to re-fuel air-to-air from a tanker aircraft. Taking on the required fuel load to return to Incerlik, Flt Lt Heald was in fact tasked once again to fly back into the danger zone to check another anti-aircraft battery instead of returning to base.

This was the second occasion that Flt Lt Heald had been recognised for operations over Iraq. He received the Queen's Commendation for Bravery in the Air three years previously. Both awards reflected the dangers faced by Coltishall's Jaguar pilots at that time.

May 2003 saw more than a dozen Jaguars grounded at Coltishall after a mid-air emergency, the aircraft had all received a recent engine upgrade or were about to be worked on. The pilot of the Jaguar GR.3A involved in the emergency was alerted to a problem with the engine by his cockpit warning system; the aircraft landed safely. The Adour Mk106 engine was relatively new and the incident was the first since its introduction to the Jaguar fleet. At the time the exact problem was not known and Rolls Royce, the manufacturers, carried out an investigation into the incident that resulted in further modifications being made to the engine.

During his Annual Formal Inspection of on 30

The RIC on det.

May 2003, the AOC 1 Gp, AVM Glenn Torpy assured personnel that the Jaguar, and with it, the base, had a bright future ahead of them. The annual inspection combined with celebrations to commemorate the 30th Anniversary of the Jaguar in RAF Service.

Fears over the Jaguar's future, and with it that of Coltishall had grown in recent years as the aircraft reached the end of its working life. These worries had been compounded after the Jaguar was not actively involved in the second Gulf War despite spending most of the last decade patrolling the skies over Northern Iraq. The decision not to deploy the Jaguar on this occasion was primarily due to the political sensitivities surrounding the continuing use of the base at Incerlik in Turkey rather than the ability of the Jaguar to carry out its task.

The AOC added at an address after the formal inspection that the Jaguar had a significant life ahead of it and that it was versatile, adaptable and still one of the most important and potent frontline aircraft.

3 July saw the final RIC at Coltishall pass into history after a long and distinguished past. 41 Squadron RIC was formed at Coningsby in 1973 to support Phantoms before a move to Coltishall to provide reconnaissance support for the newly formed 41 Squadron's Jaguars. Since then the centre had been involved worldwide, from the cold inside the Arctic Circle to the heat of the desert. Bahrain, Incerlik and Gioia del Colle were amongst operational deployments that the RIC had made in recent years.

The summer of 2000 witnessed the phasing out of wet-film on the Jaguars as the old BAE pod was withdrawn and replaced with the state-of-the-art Joint Reconnaissance

Pod (JRP) and associated computer-based Ground Imagery Exploitation System. Having brought the JRP into service, the centre returned to Incirlik with the medium level JRP replacing the Vinten Vicon GP1 wet-film pod that the Jaguars had been flying at the time. Earlier in 2000 the centre deployed to Kuwait having only 24 hours notice to move. This time to support the Harrier Force, operating with the JRP.

The handover of 41 Squadron RIC took place at Coltishall when Wg Cdr Mark Hopkins handed over control of the RIC to Gp Capt Graham Pearson of the Marham-based Tactical Imagery Intelligence Wing.

The City of Norwich witnessed an historic flypast over the city by sixteen Jaguars in a diamond formation on 19 September 2003 when the formation flew directly over Norwich Castle at 1500 feet at exactly 1715 hours.

Photo Interpreter at work.

The formation was part of the celebrations to mark the 30th anniversary of the Jaguar in RAF Service that culminated in a weekend where former flyers and groundcrews joined those charged with flying and maintaining the aircraft today.

This was a belated birthday party for the aircraft as the actual 30th anniversary happened back in July but celebrations had to be postponed due to the conflict in Iraq. The formation and celebrations also provided a poignant end to the Battle of Britain week, as Coltishall was the only surviving base from that vital conflict that had remained a fighter base throughout its entire history.

A change of command on 28 November saw Gp Capt Ricardo Cobelli hand over to an individual who had been well connected with the station and the Jaguar over many years, in fact for the majority of his RAF career. Gp Capt Graham Wright whose last tour at Coltishall saw him in command of 41(F) Squadron.

February 2004 saw the 90th Anniversary celebrations for 6 Squadron start off in style with a visit by His Majesty, King Abdullah II of Jordan. The visit was the first of many events organized for the Squadrons 90th birthday celebrations. The King was welcomed by a flypast of nine

Jaguars before attending a parade held in 6 Squadron's hangar. The parade itself was an all-6 Squadron affair, where both Her Majestys Squadron Standard and the Royal Jordanian Standard were proudly borne in front of the Royal guest.

Following the review of the parade by King Abdullah, Wg Cdr Mike Sears spoke of 6 Squadron's proud history and unique relationship with Jordan which started back in 1950 when King Abdullah I presented the Royal Jordanian Standard. After the parade, the Royal party and other dignitaries gathered in the Officers' Mess for luncheon where the King made a heart-warming speech praising 6 Squadron, and the RAF, for their contribution to world peace and Middle Eastern stability.

Prior to departing in his private jet, King Abdullah re-visited the squadron where he met Chief Technician Taff Collins, the Squadron Historian, who showed him an extensive and impressive collection of 6 Squadron memorabilia and historical information. The display boards alone reflected the proud history of the 'Flying Canopeners.' Following this, the entire squadron also had their photograph taken with the King and Prince Faisal in front of the specially marked 90th Anniversary Jaguar.

EM & EJ of 6 Squadron on the line with a pair of 41 Squadron machines.

Chapter 14

THE FINAL COUNTDOWN

The Defence White Paper of December 2003, *'Delivering Security in a Changing World'*, set out the MoD's analysis of the future security environment and how the UK's strategic interests should be prioritised in the light of this assessment. It was regarded as a baseline from which the decisions on the future size as and composition of the Armed Forces would be made.

In July 2004 an additional chapter to the White Paper entitled *'Future Capabilities'* was published. It set out in detail the intended changes to the structure and role of the Armed Forces and identified where specific cuts were to be made. It was this paper that confirmed what many had feared in the months leading up to the official announcement; the axe was to fall on Coltishall.

On Wednesday 21 July 2004, the Defence Secretary, Geoff Hoon, announced to the House of Commons that Coltishall was to close as part of large cuts in the Armed Forces. Apart from the closure of the station by the end of 2006 and the withdrawal of the Jaguar from front-line service at the end of 2007, the overall manpower requirement for the RAF was to be reduced to about 41,000 personnel by 2008.

Prior to the official announcement in the Houses of Parliament, the Station Commander, Gp Capt Graham Wright, told personnel about the impending announcement that morning. He said that a lot of pride and loyalty was at stake when this sort of announcement was made but it was inevitable that changes would have to be made as the Jaguar Force came to the end of its life. He went on to say that he had spoken to the Chief of Air Staff that morning and understood that the decisions that had been made were not done lightly. They were painful decisions at all levels within the RAF. He added that they now had to ensure that the Jaguar Force and Coltishall went out in a style appropriate to their respective histories.

Despite the announcement, life had to carry on with preparations for forthcoming exercises and deployments. One such exercise was held on 18/19 August - EXCALIBUR 2004, the United States Air Forces in Europe (USAFE) bombing competition being held at Lakenheath. All USAFE units and NATO forces within the USAFE area of responsibility were invited to compete. The RAF competitors were made up of four Tornadoes from 2(AC) Squadron from Marham and four Jaguar GR.3A's from the Coltishall Wing.

The competitors from Coltishall were Sqn Ldr 'D Reg' Bhasin, Flt Lts Paul Littlejohn and Derek Sington from 16(R) Squadron and Flt Lt Mark Flewin from 41(F) Squadron. Personnel from 16(R) and 41(F) squadrons prepared the aircraft and the competition entry was made under the Jaguar Force, a wing effort rather than any one squadron.

The competition was comprised of seven different attack profiles, two passes on each profile and a weapons release on each pass. New attack profiles had to be designed from first principles by the 16(R) Squadron Qualified Weapons Instructors. To fit in with the American rules, these attack profiles were flown as new range patterns on the day, so all of the pilots were well out of their comfort zones. The missions were flown from Coltishall and then video footage was sent to Lakenheath for analysis and scoring.

Come the competition, the Jaguars were unfortunately only able to complete three of the seven attack profiles due to bad weather. Despite this the Jaguars were placed third overall as a flight, beating all the F-15Es, Tornado GR.4s from 2(AC) Squadron, A-10s and half of the F-16 units taking part. Being the highest scoring RAF participants, the team proved that, despite the announcement of the end of the Jaguar in RAF Service, the jet/pilot combination was still able to excel.

The lead Jaguar pilot, Sqn Ldr 'D Reg' Bhasin, said: "We took effectively a brand new set of circumstances, developed a method of solving the problem using our QWI experience, and then went out and flew the best we could. Participating just felt like doing our job. The results prove that what we do is world class."

On an individual level, Sqn Ldr Bhasin's superb performance won him the 'Best Low Altitude High Drag' trophy. He said, "We weren't expected to do massively well." The fact that we won something, and came third overall, validates the training in the RAF and in particular the Jaguar Force.

The presentation of Sqn Ldr Bhasin's trophy was made by Gen Robert H Foglesong, Commander USAFE, on 19 August in the presence of AVM John Cliffe, the Chief of Staff Operations, HQ Strike command.

From 20 September to the 1 October 2004, 6 Squadron took part in Exercise LONE CHEETAH, the first chance the Jaguar Force had to fly with the Romanian Air Force. Flying from Constanta, about a three-hour drive from Bucharest on the coast of the Black Sea, the Jaguars flew

OPEVAL at St Mawgan.

daily missions with the unit's Mig-21 Lancers. The Lancer, a reworked version of the Mig-21 Fishbed, boasting new radar and upgraded avionics, proved to be a worthy platform.

Coltishall successfully led the RAF back into the NATO Operational Evaluation (OPEVAL) programme after a number of years absence in November 2004. The Station's preparation was intense with an immensely challenging training programme, which included Sector Level Training and Enhanced Sector Level Training exercises as well as 'Thursday Wars', and a MAXEVAL. The rigorous training programmed fully equipped, in all respects, Coltishall personnel for the main event.

Challenges were met with agile thinking and a lateral approach, such as the creation of the Deployed Operating Base Web-Site, otherwise known as 'DOB Web', to enhance command and control. For OPEVAL, a Force Element of ten Jaguars deployed to a simulated Deployed Operating Base at St Mawgan in Cornwall supported by 877 Strike command personnel of which 500 were from Coltishall. Against a demanding scenario, many 'excellent' grades were received in many key areas, in particular the command and control element. The OPEVAL Team considered the leadership to be 'strong and positive' providing 'proactive, focused and a mission orientated direction.'

Coltishall, supported by Strike command personnel, was the first force returning to the NATO evaluation process to pass first time in recent years. Moreover, the OPEVAL Team stated that all Unit personnel demonstrated 'exemplary capability to adopt a wartime posture' and 'showed the ability to accomplish its task to a level that is an example for deployable forces.'

It was a poignant day at Coltishall when, on Friday 11 March 2005, two of its squadrons said farewell after 170 years of combined service to the Crown. In a parade of 550 personnel, the largest to be held at a single station for many years, all four of Coltishall's squadrons together with

a flight of station personnel, paraded on a cold, blustery apron in front of the Chief of the Air Staff, ACM Sir Jock Stirrup, who reviewed the parade which was also attended by the AOC 1 Gp, AVM Chris Moran.

Battling against a cold stiff breeze the parade was led by the Station Commander, Gp Capt Graham Wright, a Jaguar pilot himself since 1985. In fact Gp Capt Wright had never done a flying tour at any other station other than Coltishall.

The spirits of those gone by, Douglas Bader, Bob Stanford-Tuck and Johnnie Johnson, could almost be felt as the parade formed up in front of the wartime 'C' type hangars that once saw Hurricanes, Spitfires, Venoms and Lightnings grace the concrete. But on the day it was 16(R) and 54 (F) Squadrons that all were here to see and say farewell to. In front of a stunning backdrop of 15 Jaguars the parade and ceremonial paid a fitting tribute to both squadrons whose history began back in the early days of World War One. The most poignant moment of the parade for those who braved the cold morning was when Wg Cdrs Guy Stockill and Neil Connell led 16 and 54 Squadrons respectively through the ranks of the three flights on parade in their support. For many, including the gathered media, a surreal silence fell and many tears were shed as they proudly 'trooped' their Standards.

Just before the two squadrons marched-off for the last time, Sir Jock Stirrup in his address said: "Today is not about looking back but looking forward, because the spirit of 16 and 54 Squadrons does not end, this spirit is part of the RAF's future." Gp Capt Wright reflecting on the day's events, commented that he wanted to ensure that the disbandment of the two squadrons was made in a style appropriate to their illustrious histories, the tradition of the Jaguar Force and Coltishall, "I think we did just that. The fact that Sir Jock attended added gravitas to the occasion."

For the members, ex-members, families and friends of both squadrons the celebrations continued over this very special weekend as the Families Day held on the Saturday was another chance for them to gather to mark the passing of their squadrons. A varied flying and static display, together with ground displays in the hangars, kept the visitors occupied throughout the day but perhaps most importantly the event was another opportunity to see 'old-pals' meeting for the first time in many a year and to chat about old times. Some looked back with pride and others with anger at the passing of their old squadrons. For one, his answer to a press question was short and to the point: "What do you think? They've taken away my squadron!"

Impressive disbandment parade at Coltishall in March 2005.

At the end of the Families Day, Gp Capt Wright took the salute at a sunset ceremony where a single Jaguar climbed into the threatening skies just as the RAF Ensign was lowered. This was followed by a moving fly-past of a single Spitfire from the BBMF flanked by a Jaguar from each of the disbanding squadrons. The day's celebrations came to a fitting end with an all-ranks hangar dance when once again families and friends were able to relax, enjoy each other's company and exchange yet more tales. For the two squadrons the final act was to lay-up their most treasured possession, the squadron Standards.

It was 54 Squadron which was the first to carry out this ceremony on Sunday 13 March at Norwich Cathedral, symbolizing the unit's long association with the County of Norfolk. Following a moving sermon by Coltishall's Padre, Flt Lt Stephen Lamond. The Squadron Standard bearer. Flg Off Reuben Cholmondley-Smith, with his escorts marched forward to the sanctuary of the cathedral to be received by the Dean, the Very Reverend Graham Smith, as the band of the RAF College Cranwell played the RAF March Past. There, the symbol of 54(F) Squadron was handed over for safe keeping.

For 16 Squadron, a similar event took place at the Cathedral of St. Omer in France on 20 March 2005. A fitting end to a squadron that was formed at St-Omer on 10 February 1915 under the command of Mjr F V Holt DSO.

Apart from the disbandment of 16(R) and 54(F) Squadrons being a very visible sign that Coltishall was

about to close, many individuals wrote to the station requesting permission to visit their old haunts before the final day. Hundreds of visitors were given the opportunity to pay their respects both with organised groups representing Veterans Organisations and as individual visitors. Brian Mawdesley was one of those individuals who visited in April 2005 and as a way of thanking the station he wrote the following. This reaction was typical of those who came back for the last time:

Ask any youngster today whether they know who Stanford Tuck, Sailor Malan or Douglas Bader was they

Flg Off Cholmondley-Smith laying up the 54 Squadron Standard at Norwich Cathedral.

will probably answer you with a blank stare. Perhaps Bader will ring a bell with those who have seen the film "Reach for the Sky" but for the most part they will have no idea that they may well owe their lives and freedom to these and others like them, and who can blame them!

Time waits for no man, unless you are just old enough to drag it back by the tail. Yesterday gets filed away in the dusty archives of history and rapidly becomes reference. Both time and change, however, combined recently for me to revisit a scene from the past.

My wife and I were invited to share a holiday cottage in Norfolk and Coltishall was not far away. "Coltishall!" "RAF Coltishall!" My mind was immediately turned upside down and memories, buried for over a half a century, tumbled out. A small boy on the back of his father's motorbike, passing through the entrance gates, privileged beyond comprehension to be an eye-witness to scenes of a great moment! The year - 1940. England fighting for her life against the overwhelming might of the Luftwaffe.

It is easy, in retrospect, to make comparisons with "The Spanish Armada", "Trafalgar" or "Waterloo", where the underdog triumphed against all odds, but there can surely be no greater example in our long history of warfare than "The Battle of Britain." The facts and figures may now speak for themselves and a reinforced from film archives, but the atmosphere cannot be recorded, and unless one was there, those extra, magic ingredients of the senses are missing. The difference is just as subtle as attending a live concert or hearing a recording. I was there, and proud and glad that those sights and sounds, smells and emotions of laughter, tears and fears are imprinted on my mind indelibly and will remain with me always. But I digress!

This was 2005 and arrangements have to be made in order to visit a modern airfield. It took a lot of phone calls to make an appointment.

I had very mixed feelings as we drove up to the guardroom; was this a waste of time? There could be surely little of interest for me after all these years, and I am not particularly keen on present day planes. I confess to feeling rather a "Dodo." We walked pass the guard, clutching his very real machinegun and were photographed. Having our passports scrutinised we were issued with a Station Pass and told to wait for our guide. In the interval we were nearly deafened by the roar of Jaguars taking off on training flights. It was strange to realise that they could be over our home in Wales in twenty minutes!

Our guide duly arrived. I was expecting a WAAF in familiar blue. Silly of me! She was a young, tall and beautiful girl in battle-dress, in charge of showing visitors round the station. She took us first to the Ops Room, after our passes had again been scrutinised; comforting to realise that security is uppermost on the agenda.

Here the various flights were recorded on a huge board at the front of the room, whilst a battery of computers ticked away under the watchful eyes of their minders. I found all this far removed from the time when I watched, with my father, from a gallery high above, as he had directed the pilots onto "Bandits" which were shown up on a huge map below where blue-bloused girls were busy with long handled pushers, adjusting markers of this or that squadron according to their positions.

It was not until we reached the Control Tower that I realised I was treading on hallowed ground, for it was pointed out to me that the concrete steps up which we were climbing were those that had led to the 1940 building. A continuation of these steps had been added when the new tower had been built. This was now entered. The glass sided room gave a panoramic view of the whole airfield. Grass runways had given place to concrete and we could look down on the jets as they scurried past to hurtle skywards. From this vantage point I could see the hangars, still the same, all but one which had been bombed in the war. More staff here, studying more computers, but no door out onto a balcony from which, so long ago, I had watched a Spitfire or a Hurricane returning to base, trailing the debris of a shattered wing like a broken bird, whilst the fire tenders were already racing to the scene of the inevitable crash.

But it was time to leave modern Coltishall where it's up to date technology and its thunder of jet engines. I was caught between two worlds. How could I have expected to walk back in time, to see faces long dead, gone, grave by grave, where I must surely follow! Grateful as I was to have this opportunity, I was disappointed. We had been shown every kindness by our hosts, guided around this historic aerodrome, which is soon to close forever. We had met some charming young people who had gone out of their way to make us welcome, and yet, with my mind alive with memories far beyond their comprehension; I felt a vast vacuum of years. And then! And then!

As we walked back towards the entrance, our guide took us to the museum. This had been compiled with devotion and detail by Mick Jennings who was about to retire. He had collated, in photographs and manuscripts, the history of Coltishall from its birth in 1939, as a proposed bomber station but eventually to be used for fighters.

In a vestibule, set out on a table, were arranged models of World War Two planes. Here I was in my element, for I found myself identifying each one with ease. The huge

Flying Fortress, twin-tailed Lightning, Wellington and Beaufighter, painted black as the night it had flown in to surprise and pluck its prey out of the skies.

If I was unprepared for this initial kindling of my emotions, then how much greater my feelings upon entering the museum itself? I would not say that I was greeted by that strange sense of damp and devotion found in old churches, yet here, in the warm, altar less display of memorabilia, I felt the same need for silence and respect which always surrounds the dead! Rather this was a Chapel of Rest.

As I began to recognise the faces before me the floodgates of memory was opened and I became truly lost in a time and dimension which excluded my companions. The vibrations of jets gave way to that unmistakeable, sweet purr of throttled-back engines as the ghosts of 242 Squadron came into land once more. There was Douglas Bader, whose hand I had shaken with pride.

Here a photo of Tedak! Tedak Koletski of 303 fame, with his crumpled cap proudly displaying the Polish Eagle. He, more than any other pilot, was my friend, for he loved children and wrote me many letters at school, usually teasing me about the many girlfriends he imagined I must have. I once had a book of this wonderful squadron, signed by all the pilots, but alas it was stolen.

Here, the story of a yellow-nosed Bf109 which had persistently streaked low across the village, blasting off its guns at anything that moved. This confirmed a story which my father used to tell in the Mess. He had been ambling over the village green one foggy morning on his way to the local pub. He had almost reached it when out of the gloom came a low flying German fighter. He hurled himself through the door and slid under the nearest table, mush to the astonishment of the landlord and several ancient locals. He swore he never entered an inn so quickly and never had a whisky and soda been so urgently required!

Here also I found a photo of the great, cumbersome looking Walrus sea-plane which had always stood by fro rescuing and pilots shot down in the sea. I had been promised a ride in this but the weather had turned foul and I never did get to fly.

Finally there was a page from the Operational Records Book for 1940 with my father's name, Pilot Officer Robert Mawdesley. What more could I have asked for this day?

It was with difficulty that I tore myself away and still dazed, like a medium coming out of a trance, returned to everyday life. I had wandered at will through echoing hangars, relived the frantic efforts of the mechanics striving to patch up damaged aircraft and to get them flying again, recalled the heady smell of aviation fuel, oil and dope. I had shaken the hands of those long gone and blessed them. It was time to go.

I turned as we reached the guardroom for the last look behind, with tears in my eyes, a Hurricane. High above the ground, poised upon its pinnacle in a steep banking turn, frozen for eternity.

In a carefully coordinated training exercise held on 28 April, the Station and members of the local Emergency Services discovered how they could work together in the event of a major incident.

Participants included large numbers from the Norfolk Constabulary, Norfolk Fire Service, the Norfolk NHS Ambulance Trust in addition to the County and District Emergency Planning Departments. The exercise also saw helicopter support from 22 Squadron based at Wattisham in Suffolk with a Sea King HAR.3, the Norfolk Air Ambulance and the Norfolk Police Air Support Unit, the latter hovering over the exercise crash site providing a TV downlink into the Crisis Management Centre.

The incident itself was based around a Jaguar T.4 that had suffered catastrophic results following a bird strike whilst landing at Coltishall. Following the successful ejection of the crew, flying wreckage from the disintegrating aircraft hit a bus carrying personnel and a tanker full of aviation fuel. With 22 exercise casualties involved in the incident the crash scene exercised every aspect of the scenario as well as giving the Emergency Services realistic training; one that would hopefully never happen for real.

With the draw down of the Jaguar Force and the closure of Coltishall there were many events held to remember those who had served at the unit since it was officially declared operational on 23 June 1940. One such ceremony took place on 20 May 2005 when Coltishall paid tribute to six members of 41(F) Squadron who were tragically killed as a result of a coach crash at Sasbachwalden in the Black Forest near Stuttgart in Germany on 21 May 1983.

The event on 23 June, the 22nd Anniversary of the accident, was to be the last opportunity for the squadron to parade with their Squadron Standard at the memorial cairn on the Station before the squadron disbanded. Families, friends, former and serving squadron members gathered around the cairn, backed by the six cherry trees planted in their memory shortly after the crash, to celebrate the lives of their colleagues. The sights and sounds of the Last Post played by Chief Technician Dave

Swann from Wyton and a lament on the pipes by Mr Geoff Taylor from Marham added to the poignancy as an impeccable flypast by four Jaguars flew a missing-man formation over the parade.

In his short sermon, Padre, Flt Lt, The Reverend, Steve Lamond paid tribute to those lost. He remembered them as "brothers in arms who lost their lives not in active service but in service to their country." Wg Cdr Dick MacCormac, OC 41(F) Squadron, who led the parade, commented, "With the closure of Coltishall and the disbandment of the squadron before next year's anniversary of the crash we thought it fitting to mark the occasion in a special way." The Squadron Warrant Officer, Pete Ingram, who organized the event, said that the families were hugely affected on this occasion and having visited the memorial on many occasions over the years he was determined to ensure that the cairn was moved to a suitable location after the Station had closed, thus enabling families and friends to continue paying their respects to those lost in the years to come.

6 Squadron were the hosts of the Polish Air Force on Exercise Lone Cat 05, 9-17 June 2005. 7 Eskadra Lotnictwa Taktycnego (7ELT) from Powidtz Air Base arrived on 9 June with four Sukhoi Su-22M-4 Fitters for the exercise under the command of Lt Col Jacek Lazarczyk, 7ELT's Squadron Commander.

Lone Cat 05 was a two-phased exercise with 6 Squadron

41 Squadron Jaguars flypast over the memorial cairn outside the Airmen's Mess.

making a reciprocal visit to Powditz for eight days from 19 July. Six Jaguars were deployed to Poland where they worked with the Su-22s as well as the Polish Air Force MiG-29 Fulcrum fleet in Close Air Support missions. During their time at Coltishall the Fitters flew a mixture of Simulated Attack Profile and Close Air Support missions, the latter mainly over the old USAF base at Sculthorpe near Fakenham. Composite Air Operation packages were flown all over the UK, the Lake District, Spadeadam Ranges, Devon and Cornwall with nearly all the profiles being at low-level, that for the exercise was set at 350 feet.

A social event held at 6 Squadron on 10 June saw the Station Commander, Gp Capt Graham Wright, OC 6 Squadron, Wg Cdr Willie Cruickshank and Lt Col Jacek Lazarczyk welcome Polishs guest from the local community, one of whom was Stephan Gabszewicz, son of the last Polish Station Commander at Coltishall, Gp Capt A K Gabszewicz DSO DFC.

To celebrate its long and distinguished association with the County of Norfolk, Coltishall was invited to provide the Guard of Honour at the closing ceremony of the 2005 Royal Norfolk Show. The guard, with their coveted Squadron Standards, consisted of personnel from 6 and 41(F) Squadrons under the watchful eye of the SWO Mike 'Ginge' O'Hara.

Gp Capt Graham Wright escorted the Bishop of Norwich, The Right Reverend Graham James, President of the Royal Norfolk Show, to the Dais where he took the salute from the Parade Commander, Sqn Ldr Kevin Marsh, a pilot from 6 Squadron. A formation of Jaguars from both 6 and 41(F) Squadrons performed a diamond nine fly past as the Parade Commander ordered the General Salute and at the end of the ceremony, five Jaguars in a vic-five flew overhead whereupon a single aircraft climbed away in a missing man formation to signify the end of the 2005 show and the forthcoming closure of Coltishall.

For Gp Capt Wright and the personnel under his command, being asked to take part in the 2005 Royal Norfolk Show was a great honour, in itself being a fitting tribute to the close relationship that the base had enjoyed with the people of the County of Norfolk.

The National Commemoration Week to mark the end of World War II culminated in a day of celebrations in London on 10 July 2005. The Reflections of WWII Commemorative Show was held on Horseguards Parade in front of Her Majesty the Queen and other members of the Royal Family in addition to hundreds of veterans invited to take part in the extravaganza.

The Polish Su-22s of 7 ELT returned to Coltishall in June 2005.

Celebrities from film and television entertained the audience in a show that took those present back in time. As the show progressed the focus moved from Celebration to Remembrance. Her Majesty gave an address to all the veterans on behalf of a grateful nation which was followed by a Two-Minute Silence in Remembrance of the fallen. The start signalled by the guns of HMS Belfast.

It was at the end of the two minutes that Jaguars played their part in the celebrations by flying a missing man formation of four aircraft over Horseguards Parade. The Station Commander, Gp Capt Graham Wright, led the formation that was comprised of Wg Cdrs Simon Blake, OC Ops Wing, Willie Cruickshank, OC 6 Squadron and Dick MacCormac, OC 41(F) Squadron.

Gp Capt Wright described the opportunity to take part in the Horseguards event as an honour and a privilege and that Coltishall's involvement was particularly relevant because of its role in the Battle of Britain and WWII.

Alice Baker celebrated her 107th birthday on 28 July 2005 and was the oldest surviving member of the Women's Auxiliary Air Force at that time having started her basic training at Blackpool in 1917. During her time in the RFC, Alice was a 'Doper', repairing fabric on aircraft such as the Avro 504, Sopwith Camel and RE8. After WWI, Alice and her husband worked until their retirement for various members of the Royal Household at the Sandringham Estate in Norfolk. Following the death of her husband she lived independently until she was 105 years old when she moved in to the All Hallows Hospital Home at Ditchingham near Beccles.

It was at the home that Coltishall's Royal Air Forces Association Liaison Officer, Sqn Ldr Andy Quick of 41(F) Squadron, presented Alice with a birthday card and specially made cake decorated with the WAAF Emblem. Kindly made by the catering Flight at Coltishall. Also present was Air Cadet Gaby Wells, the youngest member of the Norwich ATC. To cap her birthday celebrations off, an immaculate flypast of Jaguars from 41(F) Squadron flew over in her honour.

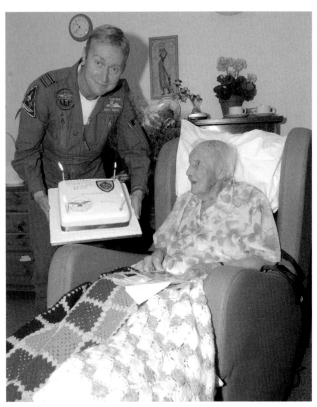

Sqn Ldr Andy Quick with Alice Baker on her 107th birthday.

Sadly, Alice passed away on 1 March 2006 and was laid to rest on Thursday 10 March at Hempnall, a village where Alice had spent so many happy years and played an active role in village life. As her family and members of the South Norfolk Community gathered at her graveside to pay their last respects, a flypast by two Jaguars of 41(F) Squadron was a fitting tribute for the last surviving woman to have served in the First World War.

On 28 and 29 July, Coltishall played host to a number of aircraft taking part in the annual seafront airshow at Lowestoft in Suffolk. Apart from Coltishall's own solo Jaguar Display flown by Flt Lt Derek Sington, the airshow had a large variety of displays in the programme ranging from the Utterly Butterly Wing walking Team with their Boeing Stearmans through to the ultra-modern Eurofighter Typhoon T.1.

Many of the fast-jet aircraft were flown from Coltishall including the Typhoon of 29 Squadron from Coningsby, Tornado F.3 of 56(R) Squadron from Leuchars, F-16 Fighting Falcon from the Royal Netherlands Air Force and the Red Arrows, being led for the 2005 season by an ex-Coltishall Jaguar pilot, Sqn Ldr Dicky Pastounas. Flt Lt Jim Turner, Red 5, was also back on familiar territory, having flown with 16(R) Squadron as the Jaguar Solo Display pilot in 2004.

Flt Lt Derek Sington, 41(F) Squadron display pilot.

The weather on the 28th disrupted the flying programme to an extent that the Red Arrows and Typhoon stayed firmly on the ground at Coltishall. However, the weather on the 29th proved the opposite with a full display being flown for the 100,000 spectators.

During August 2005, engineers, painters and finishers from Coltishall gave a much needed makeover to Norwich's SOS bus that provides a safe haven for young people on nights out in the city. The restoration team carried out the refurbishment of the bus in conjunction with their normal day-to-day duties over a period of weeks. The bendy-bus was introduced to the city in 2001 after the tragic river death of two young revellers and for its operations manager, PC Colin Lang, the transformation was more than he ever dreamed of. He said, "It's such an eye-catching design the young people will definitely not miss it."

Gp Capt Graham Wright, Coltishall's Station Commander said it was nice to be able to contribute to things like this, "we have a number of people who volunteer their time to do such projects and from their point of view it's good to see and looks fantastic. We have always had a good relationship with the local Community and to be able to assist in such a manner and for people to volunteer their time to do projects such as this is great." Following the formal handover by the Station Commander to PC Lang the bus was once again on duty in the City of Norwich providing a valuable service to the citizens and visitors to the City.

JT Kieron Taylor, an armourer with 41(F) Squadron was awarded the Queens Commendation for Bravery in the Operational Honours List released on 9 September 2005 for his bravery following a tragic accident in Iraq. On Monday 19 July 2004, whilst serving on Operation

TELIC, JT Taylor witnessed the crash of an RAF Puma helicopter on the dispersal at Basra Airport. Ignoring all the dangers to his personal safety, Taylor responded immediately by assisting in the rescue of the three crewmen on board the helicopter at the time. Sadly one of the crew died at the scene, but the other two, whilst seriously burned, were rescued from the wreckage and survived thanks to the courage of their rescuers.

26-year-old Kieron joined the RAF in November 1998 and served on 56(R) Squadron at Coningsby on the Tornado F.3 before being posted to 16(R) Squadron at Coltishall in May 2002. On 1 April 2005 following the disbandment of 16(R) Squadron, he joined 41(F) Squadron. In addition to his primary duties with the squadron Kieron was also a member of the Jaguar Solo Display Team and it was whilst he was with the team at Leuchars for the annual air show that he was told of this prestigious award.

For Coltishall, the 2005 Battle of Britain celebrations saw personnel from the Station take part in events to commemorate the 65th Anniversary of this epic battle as well as the 65th Anniversary of Coltishall itself as a front line Station; its last prior to closure in 2006.

On Thursday 8 September the last annual Battle of Britain Cocktail Reception was held at the Officers' Mess where Station officers were able to host members of the local Community, dignitaries and long-standing neighbours. The Station Commander, Gp Cap Wright, said: "As the last Battle of Britain Reception at Coltishall it has a special poignancy because it was a Battle of Britain base in the first place." In a special gesture, Gp Capt Wright was joined on the saluting dais by a Battle of Britain veteran; 84 year old Flt Lt Ron Smythe who, as

JT Kieron Taylor.

a 19 year old flew Hurricanes from bases around London during the battle and who now lives in Norwich.

Two parades were held in the City of Norwich on 12 September, with the opening ceremonies of Battle of Britain Week taking place at Norwich City Hall in front of an appreciative crowd. That evening, Coltishall once again provided a Guard of Honour and paraded the Standards of 6 and 41(F) Squadrons at a reception held at County Hall where, as with the morning parade, the Central Band of the RAF provided the music and a lone Spitfire from the Battle of Britain Memorial Flight flew over the parade in honour of all those who fought in the battle.

With aircraft from many RAF Squadrons as well as from our NATO allies arriving on Friday 16 September to display at the Families Day on the Saturday, 700 aircraft enthusiasts were invited to the Station to view and photograph the aircraft as they arrived. Despite the odd squally shower, the sun shone through allowing the enthusiasts unprecedented photographic opportunities.

The Families Day on 17 September provided Station personnel, their families and friends, as well as invited guests, with a display second-to-none. With a six-hour flying display, opened by Coltishall Jaguars and closed by a Hurricane, with a wide variety of historic and modern types in between, the gathered crowds were treated to a spectacular afternoon. For many, the Chinook display was the highlight, who could argue, it was breathtaking. It even impressed four year-old Dylan Edwards, a true aircraft enthusiast in the making, who excitedly observed, and told everyone that would listen, that "it's got two spinners!" Apart from the flying in glorious autumnal weather, there was a wide and interesting variety of ground displays and exhibits that entertained those present throughout the day. The RAF Regiment's face painting department proved to be very popular!

That evening, an equally popular Hangar Dance was held where once again Station personnel and their guests were able to soak up the atmosphere and enjoy the company. From music of Glenn Miller played by the Jonathan Wyatt Big Band to the energetic 'Booze Brothers' who took the spectrum of music up to the present day. All in keeping with the theme of the weekends celebrations.

Battle of Britain Sunday was to be another busy day for the Station and its personnel. From 0700-1300 hours over 300 vintage and classic motorcars passed through the gates on the annual Memorial Run organised by the Norfolk MG Owners Club. With vehicles ranging from a 1930's MG TF through to the modern MGF. As well as many other types and models, the rally then toured other RAF and USAAF bases and memorials throughout Norfolk to remember those that had fallen during WWII.

At Norwich Cathedral, personnel from Coltishall, RRH Neatishead and the Band of 231 (Norwich) Squadron ATC paraded in the Cathedral close before the Service of Thanksgiving. Following the service and at the conclusion of the parade a Spitfire from the BBMF from Coningsby flew over as the reviewing officer took the salute.

Another 'end of an era' milestone was reached on Monday 10 October 2005 when Flt Lt Matt D'Aubyn graduated from 41(F) Squadron Jaguar Training Flight, the last ever pilot to be trained to fly the Jaguar in the RAF. Matt D'Aubyn joined the RAF in October 2001 and, following his Initial Officer Training at the RAF College Cranwell, he was posted to 1 FTS at Linton-on-Ouse in the Vale of York during May 2002 to start his Basic Flying Training on the Tucano T.1.

After completing his training on the Tucano, Matt was posted to the NATO Flying Training Programme in Canada for his Advanced Flying Training where he flew the BAe Systems Hawk 115 from both the Canadian Forces Base at Moose Jaw and Cold Lake. Successfully

Flt Lt Matt D'Aubyn.

completing his Advanced Flying Training, he was then posted back to the UK and to Coltishall in April 2005 for conversion onto the Jaguar. After six months with 41(F) Squadron Jaguar Training Flight he successfully completed the course and was posted to 6 Squadron where he will remain on the Jaguar until the aircraft is finally retired from front line service.

Jaguar pilot training started in the RAF in May 1973. At that time pilots were taught to fly the Jaguar by 226 OCU at Lossiemouth in Scotland with 16(R) Squadron taking over the training role there in November 1991.

In July 2000, 16(R) Squadron re-located to Coltishall where they continued to train Jaguar pilots until March 2005 when the Squadron was disbanded. The training commitment for the Jaguar Force then became the responsibility of 41(F) Squadron. A role they retained until the end of October 2005.

For the Station Commander, Gp Capt Wright, who himself passed through Jaguar training with both 226 OCU and 16(R) Squadron no less than four times. His thoughts at this time were common to all Jaguar pilots past and present:

"The graduation of Matt D'Aubyn as the last Jaguar pilot to be trained on the aircraft, despite the fact that it had been planned for some time, forces home the realization that the end of an era has dawned on the Jaguar fraternity."

"Since my initial training on the Jaguar with 226 OCU at Lossiemouth in 1985, I have undertaken refresher courses as a Flight Commander, Squadron Commander and most recently as preparation to take command of Coltishall and this continued contact with the OCU is typical of all of us who have served on the Jaguar Force. Indeed it is sobering to think that every Jaguar pilot has passed through that unit in its various forms as 226 OCU, 16(R) Squadron and finally as the Jaguar Training Flight of 41(F) Squadron. The OCU therefore has a great history of its own and everybody involved in the Jaguar training process over the years should be immensely proud of their achievements."

"It is sad that this proud tradition is now at an end. Having successfully graduated from 41(F) Squadron Jaguar Training Flight and now beginning his operational flying career with 6 Squadron, Flt Lt D'Aubyn now has a place in history."

The last few months for Flight Lt D'Aubyn prior to his graduation were so busy that being the last Jaguar pilot to be trained in the RAF had not really crossed his mind. About a week after the event he commented:

"It has only been over the last few days that have made

Her Majesty The Queen at Coltishall in November 2005.

me realise the historic significance of being the last pilot to be trained on the aircraft. Whilst I knew that I was in fact the last pilot to convert to the Jaguar, my focus was totally towards graduating from the Jaguar Training Flight. It is only now that I realised that I am the last of over 800 pilots to be trained on the Jaguar; an honour indeed."

For the record, there were 1038 students who passed through the Jaguar training programme with the three squadrons, of which 841 were new pilots converting onto the aircraft for the first time. Prior to the first course at Lossiemouth in May 1973, a number of pilots were trained to fly the Jaguar by the manufacturer, BAC, from their factory airfield at Warton in Lancashire. They went on to become the core of Instructor Pilots with 226 OCU at Lossiemouth.

Her Majesty The Queen visited Coltishall on 17 November 2005 to mark the 65th Anniversary of the base and The Battle of Britain. Her Majesty was formally welcomed by Mr Jewson, Her Majesty's Lord Lt of Norfolk and the Station Commander, Gp Capt Graham Wright. A Guard of Honour made up of personnel from the Station and the Squadron Standards of 6 and 41(F) Squadrons under the command of Sqn Ldr Andy Quick, Executive Officer on 41(F) Squadron, music from the Band of the RAF Regiment and a flypast of nine Jaguar

aircraft from 6 and 41(F) Squadrons welcomed the Queen at the start of her visit.

Following the inspection of the Guard of Honour, Her Majesty took a short walkabout where she was greeted by enthusiastic flag-waving pupils from the Douglas Bader School and met personnel and families from the base.

The Queen's visit then continued with a series of displays in No 2 Hangar demonstrating the capabilities of the Jaguar Force that was based around a backdrop depicting various aspects of a Deployed Operating Base. Individual displays included Force Protection, Jaguar Munitions, Jaguar Network Enabled Capability and Imagery Exploitation.

After the Royal Luncheon in the Officers' Mess, Her Majesty continued with her visit to the Station gymnasium where she was presented to a cross-section of Station personnel who had achieved a high level of personal excellence whilst stationed at Coltishall. Catering, Sport, Charities and a Photographic display gave Her Majesty an insight into the many extra curricular activities that Coltishall personnel have been involved with over the years. Those presented included Sgt Matt Saunders, the world power-lifting champion and JT Matt Gildersleeve the World Martial Arts champion in the discipline Haidong Gumbo.

The penultimate part of the Queen's visit was to the Station History Room where she met children from the Douglas Bader School together with Coltishall veterans in an interactive display depicting aspects of the Station's illustrious history. Displays included 'Scramble', where ex-Polish Air Force pilot Tony Brent explained to the children what it was like to be on a flight line waiting for the call to go into action, rationing and the Home Front with Miss Joan Osborne-Walker, a sprightly 84 year-old who served as a stewardess in the Officers' Mess in WWII, as well as SAR, Current Operations and Coltishall's continued affiliation with Veterans Agencies. Another individual presented to Her Majesty in the History Room was JT Kieron Taylor who had recently been awarded the Queen's Commendation for Bravery in Iraq.

Just prior to Her Majesty leaving the Station on an aircraft from 32 (The Royal) Squadron she was presented with a bouquet by the Station Commander's daughter, nine-year old Emma Wright.

On 12 December 2005, the headlines in the local press saw another impact that the closure of Coltishall was to have on the local population. It had almost been expected and inevitable that with the loss of the base, the closure of the Douglas Bader School would follow, especially as by September 2006 the number of pupils was expected to drop from its current level of 114 to just nine.

Norfolk County Council reported that only seven people had responded to a recent public consultation on the proposal to close the school in August 2006. Of those, no one opposed the closure, just one asking for it to remain open until the December of that year. The report stated that retaining the school for nine pupils was neither good for the provision of good education, nor is it an effective use of resources. It was preferable to move the remaining pupils to another school to protect the quality of education for them.

The council report also addressed how to use the school site and buildings. As an interim measure it stated that it might be possible that another children's service or county council user could be found. Once the future of the Coltishall site and its housing had been determined by the MoD, the County Council could then decide on retaining the site for future use as a school, use it for other purposes or to sell it. Subsequently, it was announced in the local press in July 2006 that following the closure of the Douglas Bader School the facilities would become a Pupil Referral Unit for those with behavioural difficulties in the County of Norfolk. This facility opened in September 2006 and replaced those units at Aylsham, North Walsham, Bawdeswell and Dereham.

The memorial to the six airmen killed in the Sasbachwalden re-dedicated at the Scottow Military Cemetery.

With the closure of any station, certainly in Coltishall's case, there are many clubs, societies and groups that all have to be wound up or disbanded. For some, years of hard work and effort disappear overnight.

One such club was 'Theatre 101', a theatrical group whose company was made up of 40 civilians and servicemen. Their home since 1987 being the old Station Cinema, a building that traced its lineage back to the very beginning when the base was built where many famous, and not so famous, patrons watched films and newsreels on a daily basis.

Saturday 21 January 2006 saw the theatre 'sign-off' with their last pantomime, Goldilocks and the Three Bears. The director, Martin Truss said: "The RAF has a great history of putting on shows. It was very emotional, but the final show was great fun."

In the years that Theatre 101 has been entertaining its audiences it has won ten awards including a RAFTA (the RAF's equivalent of a BAFTA) and nurtured the talent of budding actors and playwrights. It was not just the players of today that were upset about the demise of the venue. There was said to be a phantom that also trod the boards and was very unhappy, having himself been part of the scenery since WWII.

Station parade on to mark the end of 66 years of flying operations from Coltishall.

A poignant service took place at Coltishall away from the pomp and parades of the Station's closing ceremonies on 23 March 2006 when a memorial cairn was rededicated at the nearby Scottow military cemetery by Coltishall's padre, Flt Lt Steve Lamond. The cairn, recently moved from outside the Airmen's Mess on the Station, commemorates six airmen from 41(F) Squadron who were killed in a coach crash in Germany in May 1983.

The cemetery contains the graves of many airmen from a number of nations who lost their lives in and around Coltishall during the Second World War and over the subsequent years. It is cared for by Scottow Parish Council whose clerk, Granville Yaxley, said their duty of care was an honour.

Speaking on behalf of the whole parish council Mr Yaxley said he wanted to thank the RAF for a long and valued relationship. He added: "It has been a privilege to have Coltishall as part of our community and they really have been just that. The bulk of the station lies within the parish of Scottow. Some of the old boys still call the base Scottow Aerodrome and one of our parish councillors is a co-opted governor from the Douglas Bader School on the camp and the residents of the married quarters appear on the electoral role. This is a sad day for us and we just want to express our gratitude for everything the RAF has done over the years for Scottow. We are going to miss them very much."

Following the re-dedication by Padre Lamond, Flt Sgt John Parkes laid a wreath on behalf of the Squadron, continuing the tradition of remembrance by 41(F) Squadron that has been an annual occasion ever since the original cairn was dedicated on the Station just after the tragic accident in 1983.

Squally showers and winds greeted the thousands of visitors and invited guests who gathered at Coltishall on 1 April 2006 to witness the end of flying operations from this famous Battle of Britain Station. However, as predicted by the Met Man, a window of dry sunny weather appeared over the parade ground in front of 6 Squadron's old wartime 'C' Type hangar just after 1100 hours when the first of three formal parades began.

6 Squadron, the only squadron in the RAF never to have been disbanded and reformed, were the first on parade to receive a new Standard from the Reviewing Officer on the day, Chief of the Air Staff, ACM Sir Jock Stirrup. On the second parade over 600 servicemen and women from Coltishall marched on under the command of the Deputy Station Commander, Gp Capt Simon Blake, to formally mark the end of 66 years of flying operations from the Norfolk base. Finally, the second of Coltishall's resident Jaguar squadrons, 41(F) paraded in front of their own hangar to hand over their Standard to the Fast Jet & Weapons Operational Evaluation Unit, which thus became 41(R) Squadron. At the General Salute, a trio of aircraft, Harrier GR.9, Tornado GR.4 and Tornado F.3 from the unit over flew the parade to mark the transition.

Sadly high winds caused the cancellation of the Spitfire and Hurricane flypast over the Coltishall parade, two types synonymous with Coltishall and the Battle of Britain, but a superbly executed 'Diamond Nine' formation of Jaguars launched from Coningsby flew over in salute as the main parade marched off. This formation also signified the end of a 32-year association between Coltishall and the Jaguar; truly the end of an era.

WO John Welton marshalls 'almost' the last Jaguar from Coltishall.

For many of the gathered media their reports told of immeasurable pride and emotions that had been forged at Coltishall across wars and during peacetime; history that will not end with the eventual closure of the Station.

The principle guest of honour, ACM Sir Jock Stirrup, said after reviewing the main parade in his address to those gathered: "It is always a very sad moment when you have to close and say farewell to a station, a much-loved station. And when it is the last Battle of Britain Fighter Station, then the moment is even more poignant. It has served in splendid fashion and with enormous success."

For Sir Jock, who served at Coltishall himself, his closing words encapsulated what the day meant to so many: "In a few months the gates will close and that will be sad. But the spirit of Coltishall will not close, that will be part of us forever."

Following the three parades, and after many ex-Coltishall veterans were able to reacquaint themselves with long lost friends, it was time for the last ceremony of the day, the departure of the last Jaguars. As the pilots walked to their aircraft they were greeted with spontaneous applause from the crowds, acutely aware that this was the last time Jaguars would leave Coltishall.

Prior to leading the formation away from Coltishall to their new home at Coningsby, the Station Commander, Air Cdre Graham Wright, described the station as being 'very special.' He also summed up the emotions of many when he said, "My life, for one, has been inextricably linked with this place, but today has been better than I could have expected. This was a ceremony Coltishall had hoped it would never have to host, though it has been bracing itself for many years as talk of closure had surrounded the station long before the then Defence Secretary, Geoff Hoon confirmed the fact in 2004."

As the Jaguars taxied out, it was Air Comm Wright's aircraft that was last to leave the aircraft dispersal. He was marshalled out for the last time by WO John Welton, who, as a Corporal back in 1974 was the first serviceman at Coltishall to 'see-in' the new SEPECAT Jaguar. However, as fate would have it, just like the thousands of people who did not want to leave that day, one of the Jaguars had to return with an electrical problem, thus signifying that it also did not want the inevitable to happen.

Ironically, it was Jaguar GR.3A XZ112, the mount of Gp Capt Simon Blake and the aircraft that carried the 65th Anniversary markings, that was the aircraft to re-take its place on the aircraft dispersal; back where it belonged. As there was still a Harrier GR.9 of 41(R) Squadron and two Typhoons of 29 Squadron left at Coltishall, it would have been totally inappropriate for one of these types to have eventually been the last types to use the Coltishall runway.

As the remaining aircraft took to the air the heavens opened, but for those in the crowd this made no difference as they wanted to see the final flypast lead by Air Cdre Wright. Following a box-four formation, a 'missing-man' formation was flown where, on queue, a single Jaguar climbed into the skies in salute of all who had served and lost their lives in the Service of their Country from Coltishall. A fitting tribute to a truly remarkable station.

On Sunday 2 April, Norwich Cathedral was the scene of the last ceremony to mark the end of flying operations from Coltishall and to give thanks for the 66 years that the Station and the County of Norfolk had been so closely linked. The service also witnessed the laying-up of 6 Squadron's old Squadron Standard that had been replaced in a ceremony the day before. Here it joined the Standard of 54(F) Squadron that was laid up at the Cathedral after the squadron was disbanded in March 2005, thus continuing the link between the Station, the Cathedral and the County of Norfolk.

It was not until 1625 hours on 3 April that the last remaining Jaguar XZ112/GW, eventually took off from Coltishall to join the others of 6 Squadron at Coningsby. Once again, WO John Welton marshalled the aircraft from its parking spot on the northern dispersal. The pilot for this flight, who now has his own place in Coltishall's long and distinguished history, was Flt Lt Jim Luke.

After take-off, Flt Lt Luke made a couple of spectacular low-level passes over the Station before finally pulling up into the clouds to end this chapter in RAF and Coltishall's history. For those servicemen, women and civilian employees who turned out to watch this historic event, this was to be an even more poignant event, as this was personal, for them and them alone. At 1640 hours, the Senior Air Traffic Controller, Sqn Ldr Ian McDowell said: "This is RAF Coltishall Tower. Coltishall Airfield is Now Closed."

The RAF have always had a close relationship with the Horning Sailing Club; an affiliation that has remained for well over 40 years. Indeed, the club has witnessed the gradual draw down of the RAF in Norfolk over many years as personnel from West Raynham, Swanton Morley, Marham, Coltishall and Neatishead have all been members of the RAF Norfolk Sailing Club based at Horning.

To commemorate this long-standing association with the RAF and Coltishall in particular, a 'perpetual trophy' was handed over to the Horning Sailing Club for presentation to the 'Most Improved Junior Sailor.' A fitting trophy as the Coltishall Sailing Club strongly believed that the younger members represent the future in sailing.

Wg Cdr Paul Robins presented the new trophy to the first recipient, Holly Evans, during an informal ceremony in the Station History Room on 18 April. Holly was one of the first sailors to have graduated from the Club following the establishment of the Royal Yachting Association Training Centre at Horning.

Air Cdre Graham Wright formally handed over command of Coltishall to Wg Cdr Paul Robins at a ceremony on 24 April 2006.

Wg Cdr Robins, the 39th Station Commander at Coltishall, presented the Air Commodore's pennant to Air Cdre Wright when it was lowered for the last time, marking the end of a remarkable association between the outgoing Station Commander and Coltishall.

Following the ceremony Air Cdre Wright congratulated Wg Cdr Robins on his appointment and commented: "Having led the detailed planning for the closure as the Draw Down Manager and subsequently as OC Admin Wing, Wg Cdr Robins was the ideal person to oversee the final closure and handover of the Station to Defence Estates." In reply, Wg Cdr Robins thanked the Air Commodore by saying: "It is an enormous privilege to assume command of such a famous Station and I shall make sure the legacy of RAF Coltishall remains positive long after we depart."

Judge John Deed, AKA the actor Martin Shaw, visited Coltishall on 23 May to film an introduction to a BBC Documentary on the history of the Station. Mr Shaw agreed to film the introduction and to narrate the documentary after being contacted by its producer Dick Meadows. Being a keen aviator himself, owning and flying his own Boeing Stearman from the WWII USAAF airfield at Old Buckenham. Martin was no stranger to Coltishall having flown in the back seat of a 6 Squadron Jaguar in 1996 flown by Sqn Ldr Willie Cruickshank and then over the subsequent years commentating on the flying display at a number of Families Days.

After filming his piece at the end of the runway Martin spent some time with the Station Commander, Wg Cdr Paul Robins, before being jealously escort/guarded

The last Jaguar to leave Coltishall; GR.3A XZ112 on the 3 April 2006.

throughout Station Headquarters by Veronica Claxton, the Station Commander's PA. His time at Coltishall culminated in a short visit to the Cockpit Collection where Martin was able to re-acquaint himself with a Jaguar T.2A as well as less familiar types such as the Lightning, Phantom and Buccaneer.

The documentary, aired on BBC East on 7 June, followed the history of the Station from its construction through to the disbandment parades on 1 April 2006. Dick Meadows and his team filmed 41(F) Squadron in their preparations prior to 1 April and interviewed a number of Coltishall veterans as well as preparations for the final parade. As with all such undertakings, trying to get a balanced view of 66 years of history in a 30-minute documentary was a nightmare; what do you leave out? Dick said: "I have enough footage to make an hour documentary, which Coltishall deserves. Unfortunately many aspects of the history and several of those who have been interviewed, all of equal importance, have been left out to enable me to edit within the allocated 30 minutes."

The 24 May 2006 saw a Fluffy Green Bunny make its way home to Coltishall where its master flew many of his missions during the Battle of Britain. The Bunny was the mascot of Sqn Ldr Douglas Bader who flew from the Station in early 1940 whilst in command of 242 (Canadian) Squadron. However, this lucky mascot never flew in one of his Hurricanes, but was the co-pilot in his MG sports car.

The re-union of the Bunny and Coltishall happened thanks to the Chairman of the Sheringham RAFA whose family befriended the flier when he was stationed at Cranwell in Lincolnshire. Derek Shrigley's wife Madge's father got to know Douglas Bader when he was dating the daughter of a local brewery boss. They struck up a friendship, and Douglas Bader gave his Bunny to the family as a token of his gratitude for their support and comradeship during the time he was at Cranwell.

Mr Shrigley said "It used to sit with other stuffed animals in my office for years, but before Madge died last year she asked me to ensure the rabbit went home ; which he has now done."

Accepting the Bunny, following an after-dinner talk to the Sheringham RAFA, the author of this book told the audience that Douglas Bader was interwoven with the Station's history. "We have a replica of Douglas Bader's Hurricane proudly on display at the Main Gate and in 2000, the 60th Anniversary of Coltishall, Lady Joan Bader re-named the Coltishall Airfield First School, The Douglas Bader School. Having this mascot is very

poignant, especially with the closure of the Station almost upon us." Its journey home that day to Coltishall was far less glamorous than its open-top trips in the MG; it was this time in an RAF Pool Car; a Ford Focus!

Friday 30 June 2006 saw another significant closure in the draw down of the Station. The SPAR Shop, previously the NAAFI Families Shop, finally cleared the shelves of stock and closed the doors for the last time on that day.

The shop manager Gordon Robertson said it was 'an emotional moment' as it brought to an end many years of service to the men, women and families who served at the base, not forgetting the many local civilians who used the convenience of the store from early morning to late at night. In fact on locking the doors it also bought to an end a 43-year career for Gordon, himself who started with the NAAFI in Germany before being posted to Coltishall in 1989.

Mr Robertson said that the shop was popular with the local community but as the population dropped with the move of 6 Squadron to Coningsby, the disbandment of 41(F) Squadron and the posting of many other individuals and families as a result of the drawdown, the store lost most of its custom and the closure of the shop was inevitable; sadly with a dozen redundancies amongst those employed in the store.

In its place, providing a valuable service to those left at Coltishall, the former Community Police Station on the Station was renamed the 'Cop Shop.' Stocked with essential supplies from soap and toothpaste to bread, in addition to providing hot food, the facility was manned by volunteers during the time it was in operation. Non-profit making, the Cop Shop donated all its profits to local charities. The Station Commander, Wg Cdr Paul Robins, formally opened the facility on 6 June 2006 where, following tradition, he served the first customer with an old NAAFI favourite, a cup of char and a wad.

Celebrations during the week of 17 July 2006 saw the closure of two educational establishments linked with both Coltishall and the remote Radar Head at Neatishead. Throughout the week, the Douglas Bader School celebrated their long association with both stations. These celebrations culminated in a visit on 20 July by the widow of one of Coltishall's most celebrated sons, Sir Douglas Bader.

Lady Bader was at the school with Coltishall's Station Commander, Wg Cdr Paul Robins, Norfolk County Council Chairman Mr Patrick Hacon, the council's Deputy Director of Children's Services Mr Fred Corbett and Mr Keith Delderfield from the Douglas Bader Foundation. In an afternoon of celebrations the distinguished guests heard the children sing, saw a School Council presentation and were given a guided tour by the pupils of an exhibition of photographs and memorabilia.

Prior to the start of the celebrations, and following her welcome address, the Headmistress, Mrs Lin Wakeford, was able to announce that the name of the flying legend would live on in Norfolk, even though the event was to mark the closure of the school named in his memory. Mrs Wakeford told the audience that Lady Bader, through the Douglas Bader Foundation, had given permission for the Pupil Referral Unit that is taking over the school site to continue using her late husband's name. She said that the exact name of this referral unit had still to be confirmed, but Lady Bader's permission for the name to be used would continue the strong links between Sir Douglas, Coltishall and the County of Norfolk.

The final and most poignant event for the pupils, staff and parents was on 21 July. At 1520 hours just as the pupils marched out of the school behind pipers and drummers from the City of Norwich Pipe Band led by WO John Welton MBE, two Jaguar aircraft of 6 Squadron from Coningsby flew over the school in their honour. Earlier that morning, Wg Cdr Robins carried out a presentation to commemorate the closure of the Flying Start Nursery at Horsham St Faith.

This facility, located within the RAF Married Quarter patch on Spencer Road close to the City of Norwich, had served RAF Families for many years and had witnessed thousands of children pass through the doors in their early formative years. The closure of the nursery also marked the retirement of the Nursery Manager, Mrs Peggy Gower, who had been in charge for over 21 years having taken up the post on her return from Germany when her husband was posted to Coltishall. In presenting Peggy with a framed print of a Jaguar and Hurricane, Wg Cdr Robins said that the print was a small token of appreciation from all those parents whose children had passed through her safe hands. Whilst it was a sad occasion, he said that Mrs Gower should be very proud of the valuable role that she had played in the development of the young children over the past 21 years.

At the same event, the Station Commander also made a presentation to Carrie Morrison, Coltishall's HIVE Information Officer, for her valuable work over the past year. Carrie took over the post at a time when many families were planning to leave Coltishall on the closure of the Station. Wg Cdr Robins paid tribute to her hard work, much of which she carried out in her own time, saying that the help she had provided to many of the families had ensured a smooth transition to their new homes throughout the country.

Stories of vast dump sites scattered around Coltishall had been doing the rounds for many a year. Numerous eyewitnesses remembered vehicles, aircraft parts and even Rolls Royce Merlin engines being buried after the war. In fact, as with virtually every RAF and USAAF base in the country, these stories were true. Much of the equipment declared war surplus was in fact paid for or supplied by the Americans as part of the Lend-Lease agreement. Following the Victory in Europe and the rapid reduction of the Armed Forces, so much equipment was declared surplus that disposal by burying became the norm.

At Coltishall, the Free Polish Air Force took over the station in 1945 and remained incumbent on the base for a couple of years following the cessation of hostilities. The majority of their equipment stemmed from the American Lend-Lease programme; Mustang fighters, Jeeps and Harley Davidson motorcycles being just the tip of the iceberg. Therefore, when the Polish Air Force left Coltishall in 1947 most of their equipment was destined for disposal. Much of which ended up in large pits around the perimeter of the station.

As part of the 60th Anniversary celebrations of the station in 2000, a small trench was dug close to the Firing Range and POL Section following reports of a dump being located in that area. Ex-RAF WO Fred Prebble, a keen aviation enthusiast who resided at North Walsham was invited to Coltishall to help pinpoint the location. He vividly remembered the dump being used in the late 1940s and with his guidance the trench did in fact indicate that domestic rubbish had been buried there with the recovery of bottles, clothing, cutlery, plates and cups; small aircraft parts also came to light in the dig.

It was not until the announcement that Coltishall would be closed that a renewed interest in these dump sites was shown. This time by a group of civilian enthusiasts led by Malcolm Weale of Geofizz and Dennis Morris, a local aircraft enthusiast from North Walsham. Dennis had for many years been a friend of Fred Prebble and following his passing in 2005, he decided to continue with the quest to find the dumps around Coltishall.

Following a couple of leads and an unsuccessful dig at another location, the team eventually ended up on land farmed by Mr Austin Grey in July 2006. The location, behind the bomb dump, was in fact an extension of the wartime runway where in the post war years a lone Mosquito was parked-up for ground instructional use. In 1952, when 23, 141 and 264 Squadrons exchanged their Mosquitoes for the Venom and Meteor night-fighters, this particular aircraft was set on fire and unceremoniously buried.

It was here that Malcolm and Dennis proved that such dumps existed. Not only did they find substantial remains of the Mosquito. The main spar, engine mountings, undercarriage legs and numerous engine parts. But also other artefacts that gave a further insight to life at those times. Rolls Royce Merlin engine stubs, crockery, glass bottles, footwear, documents, bundles of window (metal foil) and ground equipment. Of particular interest was an undamaged china plate made by A. J. Wilkinson Limited in 1952 and marked 'E II R.' This may have been one of the first plates issued to the RAF with the markings of Her Majesty Queen Elizabeth II who only became Queen in February of that year.

Mr Grey visited the site every day to see how the dig was progressing. He, as a young lad, remembered the work being carried out by teams of RAF personnel on the

Coltishall Flying Clubs Cessna C150 G-JAGS.

site and specifically recalls that at least two large crates were buried in the area. It had been said that complete Merlin engines in their crates were buried around the airfield. What he witnessed could well be the same.

The team planned to work other sites around Coltishall and as far away as Skeyton where it was said that a substantial amount of equipment from Coltishall was buried in an old sand pit. With other known dumps located within the perimeter fence of the station, the mini Time-Team of aviation archaeologists will have plenty to keep them busy for years to come.

In 1938 the Shaw family were forced to sell a quarter of their land for around 30 pence an acre when the site for the new airfield at Scottow was confirmed. 66-years later with the closure of Coltishall the family hoped to buy back at least some of the land that they lost all those years ago. However, the MoD confirmed on 1

August 2006 that this opportunity would not be offered, prompting Mr Shaw to declare that he may challenge the decision.

The sale of the land that had been compulsorily purchased in the past and then became surplus to requirements is subject to a complicated and historic set of conditions called the Crichel Down Rules. These rules require government departments and other statutory bodies to offer back the former landowners any land previously acquired by compulsory purchase. Such an offer being made at the current market value for the land concerned. These rules were created in response to the Crichel Down affair, a political scandal involving such land in Dorset during the 1950s.

The MoD pointed out that under Rule 10 of the document, that land does not have to be offered back to the original owner if it had been 'materially changed.' Whilst Mr Shaw did not dispute that this, may be the case with much of the land such as housing, hangars, runway and other buildings on the site, he did feel that a substantial part of the remaining estate appeared to be untouched and should be offered back. In addition to Mr Shaw, a number of former owners had been named by Defence Estates as being affected by the decision, but it was not clear at the time whether any of them had any intention of pursuing claims for buying back the land.

Friday 3 August 2006 saw the departure of the last aircraft belonging to the Coltishall Flying Club when Cessna C150 G-JAGS took off for North Denes in the hands of Coltishall's Senior Medical Officer, Sqn Ldr Gus Cabre. Light aircraft flying clubs based at RAF Stations had been promoting General Aviation for many years but their efforts had been largely uncoordinated. Thanks to the foresight and vision of the then Junior Medical Officer at RAF Coltishall, Flt Lt Gus Cabre, the creation of the RAF Flying Clubs Association helped to enhance the profile of flying clubs service-wide and greatly improve the accessibility of flying for Service personnel of all ranks and trades and affiliated civilians.

It was during Gus's arrival interview with the Station Commander in March 2001 that he was asked what kind of Secondary Duty he would like to do whilst at Coltishall. Gus replied; "The RAF Flying Club", to which Gp Capt Chris Harper pointed out that the RAF did not have an established flying club and therefore it was very difficult for him to carry out a Secondary Duty in something that did not exist. When Gus explained his interest in General Aviation and that he wished to form an established club for the RAF, Gp Capt Harper said "OK, I will be your chairman!"

On 1 April 2001 at MoD Main Building, London, the formation of the RAF Flying Clubs Association was agreed when representatives from all the RAF Flying Clubs met for the first time as a group.

It was during a Fly-In and Activities Day at the Halton Flying Club on 7 July 2001 that the Association was officially inaugurated by AVM Philip Sturley, the Assistant Chief of Staff and President of the Association. From that day to the present, Gus Cabre had carried out the role of Secretary for the very successful Association he helped to establish in 2001.

Coltishall has always had a long and friendly association with the local community and on 31 August and 1 September an event was held at the station to reinforce this connection; A Charity Track Day. The purpose of the track day was to show support for the local Community by raising funds for local Children's Charities whilst allowing a wide range of 'petrol heads and machinery' to circulate the airfield at high speed. The amount of preparation required to set up the track together with the level of demand from the public dictated that the event would run over two days.

In all a total of 170 vehicles ranging from a Peugeot 205 to a Ferrari 360 Maranello and a whole selection of exotic motorcycles took to the track over the two days and helped to raise £10,000 for the Quidenham Children's Hospice, The Nancy Oldfield Trust, Swanton Abbott Primary School and Playgroup.

During the first week of September, local villages and businesses were given the opportunity to have their say on the future of the Coltishall site. Over the previous months, officials had been drawing up a list of possible uses for the base to help prospective purchasers and developers prior to the 750-acre site going on the open market. They ranged from a science park and warehousing to a sports academy, private airfield or housing. Other potentially controversial suggestions in the list of possible uses included migrant worker accommodation and a prison, both of which were thought unlikely to come to fruition.

David Hayman, the Coltishall Task Force Co-ordinator said that it was a chance for the local councils and Commerce to look at the options in detail and to assess the benefits and problems associated with each of the proposals. He said that there had been interest shown in using the hangars for grain storage and factory production lines, as well as talk of relocating the printing facilities from the Jarrolds Printing works in Norwich. However, suggestions of a prison and rumours of a relocated Norwich Airport had been ruled out due to the constraints that included the remote site's poor communications links.

The council's strategic director Steve Blatch said they were not voicing any preferences, just providing an objective list of possibilities under current planning policies. He added that Defence Estates were obliged to take the most reasonable, but not necessarily the highest offer for the site. However that might not be in line with the interests of the local community which it was the council's role to protect.

Despite the best efforts of the Coltishall Task Force and its aims with regard to the future use of Coltishall, fears that Norfolk's interest may not be best served were being raised by the council. Locals were pressing for the site to be sold to an organisation whose plans were most likely to claw back the million's of pounds that was being lost to the County's economy by the withdrawal of the RAF.

At the meeting, Julian Newman, who headed the team in charge of selling Coltishall on behalf of the MoD said that it was his team's duty is to the wider taxpayer as it's the wider taxpayer who has supported Coltishall to date. He added however that they would carry out their own financial checks about the suitability and track record of any bidder and that it was his intention to stipulate that bidders must give their plans and aspirations for the site. The highest bidders would be asked to make presentations to the council in the area, and the councils would be asked for feedback once the bidders had been ranked.

Mr Newman's Comments were followed by strong concerns from cabinet members. Peter Moore said that they were concerned that bidders making a realistic assessment of the investment that will deliver the best outcome for the area may not be the highest offer. The best offer for the area may not be the best for Defence Estates. Graham Jones added that he feared Defence Estates were looking for the best value and to hell with everything else!

Others at the meeting were there to specifically find out when the ex-Married Quarters would be placed on the open market. Nearly 350 houses were being sold separately by Annington Homes once they had been vacated by their occupants and improvements had been made. The first release of homes being expected on the market by mid-2007.

Delegates and visitors were then told that the remainder of the site was due to be put on the market in October 2006 with the aim of a sale being completed by April 2007. As the formal closure of Coltishall drew even nearer, two major steps were being taken to ensure that the spirit of this Battle of Britain station lived on.

On Saturday 9 September, the RAF Air Defence Radar Museum at Neatishead opened a new section dedicated to Coltishall within the award winning attraction. The RAF Coltishall Memorial Room was devoted to the memory of the station by displaying a collection of artefacts, memorabilia and documents celebrating the station's existence and was opened to the public for the first time as part of the Countrywide Heritage Weekend celebrations.

Many of the items on display were transferred from the Station History Room at Coltishall, but in addition, other items which were previously unseen by the General Public. Silverware, trophies and certificates presented to the station over many years now take pride of place in two large display cabinets. Bader's Bunny, Douglas Bader's lucky mascot is also placed on display having found its way home 66-years after the Ace flew from Coltishall.

RAF Coltishall Memorial Room at Neatishead.

The work to transform the former guardroom at Neatishead into the Memorial Room was carried out by the author of this book, Chief Technician Kev Starling and WO John Welton MBE, an engineer who first worked on Lightnings at Coltishall in the early 1970s but latterly was responsible for the drawdown of the engineering aspects of the station prior to closure.

Having established and managed the History Room since 1995, it was a sad day for the author when he had to finally close and dismantle the displays after the last formal visit to the Coltishall History Room saw its 15,000th visitor. However, sadness was tempered with the opening of the Memorial Room. Doug Robb MBE, the Curator and General Manager of the RAF Radar Museum said that the addition of the RAF Coltishall Memorial Room would continue the link between the two stations that went back to WWII when the Ground Interception

Controllers from Neatishead would direct the Coltishall pilots on to enemy aircraft. Its establishment would also ensure that the name of Coltishall and its exploits over the past 66-years would be preserved for future generations.

For more than 30 years the Battle of Britain Lace had graced the entrance to the Officers' Mess at Coltishall, a poignant and lasting reminder to the young officers of today of the bravery of those who went before them, especially those who flew from the station during the Battle of Britain itself.

On Friday 15 September, Battle of Britain Day, the lace was formally handed over to the Dean at Norwich Cathedral. Wg Cdr Paul Robins who was in command of Coltishall at the time of the transfer together with Air Cdre Graham Wright who commanded the station from November 2003 until the cease of flying were both instrumental in ensuring that this national treasure was preserved and remained in the County of Norfolk.

It was considered that the Cathedral was an apt choice because of its close links with Coltishall and their joint relationship with the people of Norfolk. Soon after the announcement that the station was to close, many had been trying to find a way of recognising its close connection with the people of Norfolk, bearing in mind that Coltishall was a Battle of Britain Station. The lace represented what everyone considered to be the most appropriate and lasting legacy of this connection.

On accepting the lace, the Dean of Norwich, the Very Reverend Graham Smith, said that it was important that the lace remained in Norfolk. What he wanted to do was remind a future generation not just of what was achieved during those dark days in 1940. How, every day, men and women rise above themselves in acts of courage and comradeship to protect freedom. It shows what people are capable of, but it is not just a war memorial. It is a statement about what the people of Norfolk together with the RAF have achieved. There is a tremendous affection from the people of Norfolk for the Royal Air Force and the lace is a way of remembering that.

The move of the one and half tonne lace in its case proved to be an interesting logistical exercise. Not possible without the expert advice and direction of Mervyn Cousens, Service Delivery Manager of Babcock DynCorp, Coltishall's prime contractor. Merv, working with Flt Sgt Tony Singleton and a joint RAF/Babcock team, ensured that the removal from the Officers' Mess, transportation and re-erection at the Cathedral went without hitch.

That same evening another 'last' was marked at

Coltishall as personnel and invited dignitaries gathered for arguably the most memorable celebration of the Battle of Britain to be held at the station. In past years, guests were hosted at the Officers' Mess with the sunset ceremony taking place at the front of the mess. However, the parade on the 15 September 2006 used the Hurricane and the station flagpole as the backdrop and the Gymnasium, suitably bedecked with a montage of wartime photographs, host the reception. Whereas in the past the Station's Officers hosted honoured and distinguished guests, on this occasion it was all hands to the pumps where all ranks played their part in what was a very enjoyable but poignant occasion.

The evening ceremony featured a performance by the City of Norwich Pipe Band followed by a Sunset Parade with the Guard of Honour commanded by Flt Lt Sarah Wells parading in front of Station Headquarters. At the General Salute, and prior to the lowering of the RAF Ensign to a lament played on the pipes by WO John Welton MBE, a single Jaguar from Coningsby, flown by Sqn Ldr Ian 'Smithy' Smith, flew low overhead before rising sharply into the thin grey cloud in honour of those who made the ultimate sacrifice in that battle.

The Station Commander, Wg Cdr Paul Robins said: "It is always a poignant time when we reflect on the significant impact the 'Few' had on the outcome of the Second World War and subsequently the shaping of future generations. Perhaps, however, for us here the occasion is ever more moving as this will be the last time that the Battle of Britain will be formally commemorated at RAF Coltishall."

Over the weekend of 16/17 September, Terry Owen of the RAF Amateur Radio Society held an Amateur Radio Special Event Station in the Battle of Britain Hall to commemorate the closure of Coltishall which during their time on air had contacted 350 Stations over the two-day period. Those contacted included the IWM at Duxford and at Bletchley Park. Many memories from contacts were exchanged between the Stations, one, which was of particular interest being from a former baker who used to deliver bread to the NAAFI Shop in 1950. Hundreds of other contacts were made with former airmen, airwomen and civilians who had all been connected with, or had served at Coltishall over the previous 66-years.

The Radio Station closed down at 1750 hours GMT on Sunday 17 September with the following message:

"This is GBORAE (the call-sign of the Radio Special Event Station). This is Royal Air Force Coltishall in Norfolk closing down 1940-2006 with EGYC which is now going

'Silent Key.' This will be the final radio transmission from RAF Coltishall, God Bless Coltishall we will miss you - Out."

The wording 'Silent Key' denotes a morse key when used in the Radio World for an operator that has passed away.

As marketing packs were sent out to parties interested in the Coltishall site, North Norfolk MP Norman Lamb called for the land to remain in public rather than private hands. He called upon the East of England Development Agency (EEDA) to make the most of the opportunity provided by its sale. Mr Lamb wanted the body to buy the land and work with local authorities to dispose of it piecemeal while ensuring development was in the best interest of the public. He feared that if it were allowed to fall into a private developer's hands, its potential would not be maximised. He added that even if they did not want to purchase the site, EEDA should at least explore the opportunity, which up to that point they had failed to do.

Following a meeting of the Coltishall Task Force held at Norfolk County Council's Headquarters in Norwich a few days later, Norman Lamb reacted furiously to the behaviour of EEDA over the future use of the Coltishall site. He attacked the agency for the way it had failed to discuss properly its intentions over the site, instead presenting a number of decisions in recent months as pre-determined. He said that the cross-interest task force had been set up specifically as a forum for discussion of all issues to do with the base. However, Mr Lamb said that EEDA had repeatedly notified the task force of their decisions 'after the event', much to his frustration. He said "All EEDA seems to do is present us with a series of fait accompli instead of taking part in discussion. They have not engaged with the issue with a sufficient degree of commitment. It is not the right way to proceed. It makes me very angry; we seem to be treated as peripheral. I wonder whether attending these meetings is a complete waste of my time."

In reply, an EEDA spokesperson said that as a member of the task force EEDA is committed to finding the best solution for the future use of the Coltishall site. Any decision not to purchase the site does not demonstrate a lack of commitment to the Coltishall site and the local Communities. Indeed this now enables EEDA to work with the task force and other public sector parties to secure a more ambitious vision for the site. This would be the most effective way of ensuring real and long-lasting benefits are delivered for local people. We will support this work in every way we can.

V7467 being lowered back to earth by the ATRF.

The Hurricane prepares to leave for High Wycombe.

Another part of the Coltishall story closed on 17 September 2006 when the replica Hurricane that stood guard at the entrance to the Station was moved to pastures new. The aircraft, V7467/LE-D, was unveiled on 9 June 1989 by Lady Joan Bader and since that date has proudly remained in the markings of her late husbands aircraft that he flew from Coltishall with 242(Canadian) Squadron in 1940. However, with the closure of the station a new home had to be sought for this symbolic part of Coltishall's history.

A team from the Aircraft Transportation & Recovery Flight ARTF from St Athan under the leadership of Sgt Max Morrell were tasked with the move, and after an initial survey, they began the lift at 1000 hours that day. After lifting the aircraft from its mount, they lowered it onto trestles to remove the wings for transportation. This proved an interesting task in itself as after 27-years on display the wing bolts proved a little reluctant to move. However, this small problem was soon overcome and the task went ahead.

Whilst the team and Sqn Ldr Martin Exely, the Project Officer from High Wycombe, were satisfied with the recovery process, not everyone was pleased to see the aircraft go. Of the many that came to see the aircraft leave was 84-year old Don Juler who had travelled from his home at Lowestoft. In 1939 he had helped to build the new station and proudly said that he had seen the first Hurricanes and Spitfires arrive and witnessed the last Jaguar to leave. He said: "I felt that I had to come here today to see the Hurricane go, it was an essential part of Coltishall and now it's gone; it's a very sad day."

The spirit of Douglas Bader and Coltishall will now continue with the Hurricane at its new home where it will guard the entrance to the Combined Headquarters at High Wycombe.

Yet another chapter in the modern history of Coltishall came to an end on 30 September 2006 when the Coltishall First Response Team, call sign 661, fulfilled their last emergency shift. It was in July 2001 that the First Response Team was set up at Coltishall to provide emergency medical care in conjunction with the East Anglian Ambulance Trust (EAAT). The team then consisted of 20 volunteers, all RAF personnel who were trained by EAAT to provide Trauma Care, Advanced Life Support and high-speed emergency driving on blue lights and sirens.

Since its establishment, the First Response Team completed 1800 shifts and attended in excess of 4600 '999' calls throughout East Norfolk. These calls have ranged from simple falls, medical emergencies and sadly, the all too regular road traffic accidents.

Out of all the emergency responses over the past years, one in particular stands out. On this occasion, it was a call to a house fire in which reports stated that two occupants were still in the premises. Once on the scene, the Fire Service quickly evacuated the occupants; a fire crew treated one female at the scene. The other occupant was passed to the First Response Team; not a male or female person, but the occupant's pet cat that had sadly succumbed to the smoke and was assumed dead. However, with oxygen and lots of TLC from those at the scene, the lucky cat and her owner made full recoveries.

Towards the end and with the ever-increasing requirement for service personnel to deploy away from their stations, the Coltishall First Response Team had lost 75% of its establishment and only seven responders remained when they disbanded. Despite the extra burden placed on those seven individuals, their dedication and commitment continued and they remained an active part of the EAAT by managing to man and maintain their Rapid Response Vehicle for at least six priority shifts in a seven-day period.

Following their last emergency shift, some of the team were posted to Marham where they joined Marham's own First Response Team. For the remainder, postings throughout the UK meant an end to their valuable voluntary work in this field.

Coltishall ensured its spirit would remain long after its impending closure when the Station Commander handed over £20,000 to good causes on Thursday 12 October. This staggering amount of money was raised by a variety of activities and individual challenges throughout the previous year, including the popular track day, cycle rides and sponsored walks by staff and volunteers. The 10 good causes to receive donations were the East Anglia Air Ambulance, Quidenham Children's Hospice, Swanton Abbott School and Swanton Abbott playgroup, the Nancy Oldfield Trust, the Benjamin Foundation, Break, Buxton & Lamas Youth, the Royal Air Forces Association and the Royal Air Force Benevolent Fund.

Wg Cdr Paul Robins said that he was very proud to hand this money over to such worthwhile good causes, but he explained it was like a swansong as it was one of the last public events prior to the station closure in November. He said "I like to think that we have played a strong part in the Community during our time here and it will be with great sadness when we leave it behind."

Liz Holman from Break said that they were so grateful to Coltishall for the support that her own charity and many others have received over the years, and that Break were honoured to have been given the money today. She went on: "They've been an integral part of the Community for so many years and it will always be Coltishall, whatever is here next."

The £20,000 presented today represented the last to have been raised for charity by personnel from Coltishall. Over 40 years the station had generously given to good causes and an estimated £4.5 million had been raised over that period for local and national charities.

A lunchtime civic reception was held at Norwich City Hall on 13 October to mark the handing back of the station's Freedom of the City parchment. In his last official public engagement as the 39th Station Commander, Wg Cdr Paul Robins gave back the parchment awarded to Coltishall in 1967 giving the station the Freedom of Norwich. The event also gave the Lord Mayor of Norwich, Felicity Hartley, the chance to bid the station an official farewell on behalf of the people of Norwich. At the same time, the Lord Mayor ensured that the freedom certificate was not lost to the history of the city by placing it on display with others in the Mayoral Parlour at City Hall.

At the end of the reception, Wg Cdr Robins thanked the Lord Mayor and other city dignitaries for their kind gesture. He went on to say that Coltishall's history and the strong links with the city will always be something to be proud. Personnel from the station present at the reception were grateful for the opportunity to say a final farewell and to ensure that Coltishall's part in the history of the city was never forgotten. He said "It is a privilege, tainted with great sadness, for me to be able to return the Freedom before I hand over command of Coltishall this afternoon."

Back at Coltishall, Wg Cdr Robins handed over the Station Commander's pennant to the 40th and last man to hold the post, Sqn Ldr Jason Hughes. On assuming command, Sqn Ldr Hughes recounted that he had read about the station when he was a small child and that he found it humbling to be the last station Commander of such an enormously famous establishment. He went on to say that, his main aims were now to close Coltishall in a timely and efficient manner. But also to ensure that the dignity of the station was preserved during that process. Sqn Ldr Hughes took over command of approximately 160 serving personnel and civilian staff on that day.

The 9th of November witnessed a small but sombre ceremony at the end of the now-silent runway 22 as Coltishall honoured those who paid the ultimate sacrifice during World War Two. Normally, Coltishall would have been represented at more than 20 Remembrance parades throughout Norfolk, but with the rapid drawdown of the station and with only a small number of personnel remaining it was decided to honour those who lost their lives close to home at the Scottow Military Cemetery. The ceremony led by the Station Commander, Sqn Ldr Jason Hughes with a parade of eight personnel and with WO John Welton playing a lament on the pipes, demonstrated that, even with the station closing in a matter of days, personnel would never forget the sacrifices of those who went before them.

This cemetery is the last resting place for 43 World War Two airmen and more than a dozen others who have been laid to rest since, including Flt Lt Greg Noble who tragically lost his life only yards from his final resting place when his Jaguar aircraft crashed on take-off in 1995. Also buried in the well manicured grounds are

Poles, Czechs, Australians and New Zealanders. Next to them lie five Germans whose aircraft were shot down locally and who were never repatriated.

Over a period of weeks following the active marketing of the 750-acre site by the Defence Estates appointed agent, Drivers Jonas. A number of potential purchasers had visited Coltishall to view what was on offer. But all the hard work by the agents, Defence Estates and those left on the station was put into turmoil on 22 November following the headlines in the EDP that read "Shock over proposed use of former RAF base - IMMIGRATION 'JAIL' PLAN FOR NORFOLK!"

The news from an under pressure Home Office that the site could become a detention centre for illegal immigrants sent shock-waves around the local area. The eleventh hour approach made by the Home Office to potentially convert the station into such a facility, surprised officials and politicians alike who had been working together on the Coltishall Task Force to develop the station after its closure. One local MP said the news was 'a bolt from the blue' which would open a 'Pandora's Box' of concerns from the local Community. One local councillor said it would spark strong objections and that a 'monster' of an institution like the government taking over the site had 'reared its head.'

The Home Office intervention came after it had earlier ruled out any interest in the site, along with the MoD and other government departments. However, with the failure by the Home Office to secure the site of the former Connaught Barracks in Dover earlier in the month, their attention was suddenly drawn back towards Coltishall as a matter of urgency. This shock move threw the whole sale process into confusion. Raising concerns that the spectre of such a centre might blight not only the solemn closing ceremonies at the end of the month but also the possible use of any remaining parts of the station and the neighbouring former Families Married Quarters, which were being planned to be sold off as affordable housing.

Over the following days, senior Norfolk politicians and community leaders demanded answers to a raft of questions about the controversial plan to build the detention centre as grassroots anger began to mount in Communities around the station following the revelations about the site in the EDP on 22 November. MP Norman Lamb and MP Keith Simpson to help build a clearer picture of what economic, social arranged two key meetings and security impact the centre could have. However, in the midst of widespread local anger at the proposal, both MPs insisted that their efforts to establish the facts revealed a truly negative picture; they would back their constituents to the hilt in battling against the proposal.

Opponents of the proposed immigration centre were urged to speak out even if the controversial plan seemed inevitable. This rallying call was made at a public meeting in Coltishall village when residents voiced fears ranging from security to plummeting property prices. The meeting heard Mid Norfolk MP Keith Simpson say that he thought the Home Office was keen on the Norfolk site and, providing the figures stacked up, would be moving quickly to drive it ahead with a decision due in mid-December. Nevertheless, parish councillor Paul Thomas urged local people to follow the lead of Coltishall's Battle of Britain aircrews and fight on "even if defeat seems to be inevitable", adding they should write to the authorities with their concerns and keep up the pressure.

The community closest to Coltishall packed a local pub on 29 November to add its voice to the concerns that the station could become an immigration detention centre. About 100 people crowded into the Three Horse Shoes at Scottow to hear David Hayman, the official who co-ordinated the Coltishall Task Force, say that if the Home Office pressed ahead with the plans for the centre, the first 500 detainees could be arriving by next summer. Scottow parish council vice-chairman Trevor Bunting said that the village had "put up with a lot" from the airbase including aircraft noise, and was prepared to fight as it "looked forward to some peace and quiet" in its next use.

At another meeting, Buxton and Lamas parish council also condemned the Home Office for its "knee-jerk reaction" to immigration detention problems. They insisted that the best use for the former RAF base would be by companies and businesses generating long-term employment to help restore some of the £20 million a year lost to the local economy through the closure. "The detention centre may serve as a short-term answer to a current problem, but there is no guarantee that the proposed 500 jobs would remain after the minimum three to five years suggested as the life of the detention centre," said a statement from the council.

The final chapter in Coltishall's 66-year history came to an end on Thursday 30 November 2006 when the gates to this famous Battle of Britain Fighter Station were closed for the last time. Over 6000 members of the General Public witnessed the Closure Ceremony of Coltishall that began with a spectacular flypast by a solo Hurricane and a four-ship formation of Jaguars within

AVM Walker takes the salute on the 30 November 2006.

seconds of the Parade Commander ordering the General Salute to welcome the Reviewing Officer to the Saluting Dais.

The Reviewing Officer, AVM David Walker CBE AFC RAF, the AOC 1 Gp, in his address, paid tribute to the special relationship that Coltishall had enjoyed with its close neighbours and with the wider communities in the County of Norfolk. In recounting the history of the station and the unique place it had in the history of the RAF, AVM Walker said that the names of Douglas Bader, Bob Stanford Tuck, Johnnie Johnson and John 'Cats Eyes' Cunningham would remain part of its legacy forever. As would aircraft such as the Hurricane, Lightning and Jaguar. In recognising that the closure was a sad and difficult task, he praised those who were responsible for overseeing the operation that had been achieved ahead of schedule and £10 million below budget. His final comments however encapsulated the mood of all those gathered: "Rarely will a station be as much missed as Coltishall will be in the years ahead. We leave with a heavy heart and with great memories."

Following the address, the Parade Commander, Flt Lt John Podmore, who himself had spent around ten years of his 17-year RAF career at Coltishall during three postings, gave the orders for the final act in the ceremony; the lowering of the ensigns. Accompanied by a lament on the pipes played by WO John Welton MBE, the Station commanders pennant was lowered. The RAF Ensign was then solemnly drawn down for the last time to the haunting sound of the Last Post played by SAC Ruth Sydney, a trumpeter with the RAF College Band Cranwell.

Led by the City of Norwich Pipe Band and followed up by the Ensign Party and the Station Commander Jason Hughes, the parade marched off the station to the sound of 'Auld Lang Syne' accompanied by rapturous applause from the gathered crowd. As the parade reached the Main Gate, the four Jaguars of 6 Squadron led by Sqn Ldr Mark Discombe roared overhead in salute. A final farewell from a squadron and aircraft type that had called Coltishall home for 32 years. Coming to a halt just outside the Main Gate, the parade turned to face the Jaguar Gate Guard that just a day before was christened 'Spirit of Coltishall.' It was then that the SWO, WO Pat Chapman, locked the gates and passed the key to the Station Commander. In turn Sqn Ldr Hughes passed the key and RAF Coltishall to James Ryley of Defence Estates to mark the first stage of the handover of the site.

For many however, the solo display by the Hurricane at the end of the ceremony was the highlight of a very emotional and poignant day. Sqn Ldr Al Pinner MBE, the OC BBMF, flew the Hurricane XII from its home at Duxford with the Historic Aircraft Collection to lead the flypast before his solo display. After five minutes of breathtaking and evocative flying, he flew the Hurricane low over the locked gates and climbed into a barrel roll over the Station before returning to Duxford. This was the ultimate honour to all those who served at Coltishall over the past 66-years.

In summing up the days events, the Station Commander, the 40th and last of a long and distinguished line, said

The RAF Ensign is lowered for the final time.

The SWO, WO Pat Chapman locking the gates after the final parade.

Sqn Ldr Jason Hughes hands the station keys to James Ryley.

RAF Coltishall airfield and estate from Headquarters Strike command to Defence Estates. These formalities were based around the RAF Form 2, Royal Air Force Proceedings of a Board of Officer's, where members, under Sqn Ldr Hughes as President, formally signed the handover document that in effect transferred the site from RAF control to Defence Estates, who from that time would act as Head of Establishment until the final disposal of the site.

Thus with that act, the story of Royal Air Force Coltishall comes to an end. At the time of writing, no formal decision had been made on the future of the site, although the Home Office option seems to be at the fore; only time and the continuing history of the site itself will provide the answer.

that it had been a great privilege to have held that position. "But it is not about me or those on parade" he added. "It is us as the Royal Air Force celebrating the history of RAF Coltishall in the right way. I am just 37-years old and I am shutting the station that Douglas Bader flew from. It has been a very emotional and moving day for us all."

Following the parade a small reception was held for invited guests and VIPs. Amongst those present were the Lord Lt of Norfolk, Mr Richard Jewson TD, AVM John Howe CB CBE AFC RAF (Retd) who commanded 74 Squadron, the first squadron to accept the English Electric Lightning into service at Coltishall in 1960. Tony Brent, a Polish Air Force pilot who flew from Coltishall with 306 Squadron during WWII and Joan Osborne-Walker, who as a young 18 year-old served as a steward in the Officers' Mess from 1941-1943. At the end of the reception, guests witnessed a presentation where Sqn Ldr Hughes presented three civilian members of staff with their Imperial Service Medals. They were Carole Swan, Colin Pye and Sheila Govan who, between them, had clocked up 90 years in the civil service.

In a day of lasts, the final act took place at 1500 hours when the Station Commander handed over

THE END OF AN ERA!

Chapter 15

SATELLITE AIRFIELDS
MATLASKE

RAF Matlaske was prepared during the summer of 1940 as a dispersed satellite airfield for Coltishall. The site of the airfield was on a small estate close to the North Norfolk village of the same name, and located approximately six miles from the market towns of Aylsham, Holt and Sheringham.

It first came into use during October of that year, when the Spitfires of 72 Squadron deployed from Coltishall. Ground support for the dispersed squadrons came initially from Coltishall, with personnel and equipment making the daily journey. It was not until sufficient manpower and supplies had been well established that the airfield became an independent unit, although still under the overall control of the Coltishall Sector.

Being a grass airfield, without any concrete runways, taxiways or peri-tracks, numerous problems were encountered from the outset; especially after heavy or prolonged rainfall. Water settled on many areas of the airfield due to the poor drainage. 'Sommerfield Tracking' was laid over the grass runways in an attempt to eliminate the problems, however, this too proved to be ineffective. It soon became obvious that many improvements were required before successful operations could be mounted from the airfield and just a few days after their arrival 72 Squadron returned to Coltishall.

With no flying from the airfield, many of the vital improvements could be addressed. A narrow perimeter track was constructed around the field that connected new fighter pens and dispersals with the three grass runways.

The establishment and construction of this new airfield soon caught the attention of the Luftwaffe, and soon they

AFDU Airacobra I at Duxford in September 1941.

were to make their first visit, on 29 October 1940, when a force of five enemy aircraft, Dornier Do17s, bombed and strafed the airfield, thankfully causing few casualties and very little damage.

During November 1940, 222 Squadron began to use Matlaske on a daily basis, flying their Spitfire Is in from Coltishall each morning. They continued this daily ritual until taking up permanent residence on 6 June 1941, by which time they had re-equipped with the Spitfire IIa and IIb. The squadron carried out regular convoy patrols, escort duties and fighter sweeps over the Norfolk coast until 1 July 1941, when the squadron re-located to Manston in Kent.

Hurricane IIbs of 601 (County of London) Squadron, under command of Sqn Ldr Gracie, replaced the Spitfires and continued with the familiar sweeps and escorts. With the start of the bomber offensive against Germany, the majority of escort missions were generally in support of the bomber forces launched from East Anglian stations.

On 13 August 1941, Matlaske, and 601 Squadron in particular, were to witness the arrival of a new American-designed aircraft, the Bell P-39 Airacobra. Whilst still operating their Hurricanes, 601 Squadron had been chosen to test this new fighter for possible use by the RAF. As soon as sufficient P-39s became available to start testing, the squadron and their new aircraft moved to Duxford in August 1941.

The squadron was destined to be the only RAF unit to fly this mid-engined fighter. For the RAF, the aircraft was unusual in that it had a tricycle undercarriage instead of the familiar tail-wheel configuration. Despite early optimism, the aircraft failed to impress the RAF and following a series of accidents that were attributed to the design the P-39s were withdrawn in early 1942.

Spitfire II of 222 Squadron.

137 Squadron Whirlwinds at Matlaske.

Whirlwinds parked on a freshly laid perimeter track.

With the departure of 601 Squadron to Duxford with their mixture of Hurricanes and Airacobras, 19 Squadron arrived with the Spitfire II to continue with the fighter sweeps and bomber escort missions. However, their stay at Matlaske was to be short-lived, as by the end of December the squadron had re-equipped with the Spitfire LF.VB and moved to Coltishall's second satellite field, Ludham.

By then, Matlaske housed some of the most talked of, most curious and always fascinating aeroplanes; the twin-engined Westland Whirlwind I fighter. Only two squadrons in the RAF used the Whirlwind, 137 and 263 Squadrons. 137 Squadron moved into Matlaske from Coltishall on 1 December 1941, and commenced operations only a few hours after their arrival on that same day. The Whirlwinds' first operational sortie was to patrol the East Coast convoys, mainly off the Yarmouth area, and whilst they encountered several enemy aircraft on this mission, none were shot down or damaged.

The Whirlwinds shared Matlaske at this time with Lysanders, Walrus, Defiants and Anson's of 278 Squadron who moved in from Coltishall in October 1941. 278 Squadron was an ASR unit who formed at Coltishall as 5 ASR Flight, with two Supermarine Walrus and three Lysander IIIAs. The squadron, which at the time was the largest unit in the RAF, with detachments at many Coastal Command units throughout the UK, continued to use Matlaske as their HQ until they moved to Bradwell Bay in April 1944.

On 29 December 1941, two Spitfires of 485 Squadron, which had taken off from Matlaske at 1400 hours, saw a Junkers Ju88 at 2000 feet over a convoy. At 1415 hours, as the Spitfires went in for the attack they were 'bounced' by a pair of Messerschmitt Bf109s. Accurate fire from the Bf109s soon disabled the Rolls Royce Merlin engine of one of the Spitfires, its pilot having no alternative but

to take to the silk and parachute to safety over the sea. Luckily, a Rescue Launch soon picked him up. The other Spitfire headed back to Matlaske at full speed after expending all of its ammunition.

A fateful day always to be remembered in the annals of Matlaske history was 12 February 1942. Soon after noon, the pilots of 137 Squadron were brought to readiness and at 1310 hrs; four of the squadron's Whirlwinds were scrambled. Their task was to protect and patrol a group of British destroyers racing to intercept the German Battleships, Scharnhorst and Gneisenau, which were passing through the English Channel.

The weather at the time was very poor, but the Whirlwind pilots caught sight of the German convoy some 20 miles off the Belgian coast. As they dived to investigate, a flight of about 20 Messerschmitt Bf109s descended on the scene where a fierce dogfight ensued. Two Whirlwinds, P7093/SF-A flown by Flg Off Hughes, and P7107 with Flt Sgt Robertson at the controls were shot down as were two relieving aircraft, P7106 and P7050.

Flt Sgt Mercer in his Whirlwind P7055, succeeded in lining up one of the Bf109s in his gun sight, only to develop a stoppage in his cannons. Another of the German fighters tailed Mercer and raked his aircraft with dire consequences. For Mercer, together with two more Whirlwinds their fight had ended. The fourth aircraft in the flight, with Plt Off de Houx at the helm, fared no better. He had fired all of his ammunition without success.

A second detail left Matlaske at 1340hrs, but nothing more was heard of them. This left Plt Off Bryan and Sgt Ashton to keep watch over the British destroyers, for a further 30 minutes prior to returning to safety.

On 15 March, Whirlwinds of 137 Squadron were scrambled from Matlaske to assist a flight of Spitfires

Tending the vegetable patch at Matlaske.

Sgt Roberts RNZAF in his personal Whirlwind.

of 412 RCAF Squadron. The Canadians were attacking German E-Boats which had earlier, at 0430 hours, sunk the destroyer HMS Vortigern while escorting a convoy. As the Whirlwinds reached the scene, they found that British Motor Torpedo Boats were already attacked their German equivalent. However; the enemy was certainly not going to give up easily. Shortly after, a Junkers Ju88D, who had earlier witnessed the battle, reported back to its base in Holland with details of the convoy strength and the subsequent British response. That evening 28 Dornier Do217Es attempted, unsuccessfully, to destroy the convoy. The Whirlwinds were soon to find themselves engaged in the constant battle against the E-boats off the East Coast.

The first victory for the Whirlwinds came on 25 June 1942, when Plt Off McClure and WO Smith were on patrol east of Smiths Knoll. Both spotted a Junkers Ju88, and two bursts from McClure's cannons saw the unfortunate Ju88 crash into the sea.

Whilst much of Fighter Command was operating as part of the Dieppe raid in August, 137 Squadron went into action once again off the East Coast. Flg Off J M Bryan and Sgt Roberts were scrambled during the morning and some 50 miles off Happisburgh dived upon, and attacked a lone Dornier Do217. The crew of the Do217 had no choice but to bale out from their burning bomber.

Apart from the odd incident, such as the Ju88 and Do217, the role of the squadron had been mainly defensive. However, on 3 September the squadron was to take part in their first 'Rodeo.' Eleven Whirlwinds, together with 24 Spitfires of 411 and 485 Squadrons, mounted a feint on Lille. It was hoped that the enemy fighter defences would launch an attack against the incoming fighters. The Luftwaffe on this day did not rise to the bait and the raid failed to fulfil its aim.

Within days of this raid, on 24 August 1942, 137 Squadron and their unique aircraft left Matlaske for Snailwell in Cambridgeshire.

The early months of 1942 saw flights and sections of Coltishall's resident squadrons dispersing to Matlaske. Lysanders of 1489 Gunnery Flight, a target-towing unit, arrived in June 1942 to provide facilities for gunnery practice for the squadrons at Coltishall, Matlaske and Ludham.

From the 2 to 11 August the Typhoon IBs of 266 Squadron based at Duxford arrived on detachment. The squadron was moved to Matlaske as a forward operating base whilst attacking German shipping, which was particularly active in the North Sea at that time.

56 Squadron, another Typhoon-equipped unit, under command of Sqn Ldr 'Cocky' Dundas, moved in from Snailwell in August as a replacement for 137 Squadron. Sqn Ldr Dundas was destined to command the squadron at Matlaske for only a short time, as on the 10 November he was promoted to Wing Commander, and left to take over command of the Typhoon Wing. The squadron made history on 14 September 1942 when it shot down a Junkers Ju88, this being the first enemy aircraft destroyed by a Typhoon. The new squadron Commander, Sqn Ldr Johnston, did not arrive to take command until 23 November. However, in the meantime, 56 Squadron were far from idle.

On 17 November, for instance, three Typhoons flew 'Rhubarbs' to Flushing airfield, damaging two Messerschmitt Bf109s on the ground as well as a steam train and some huts. One of the Typhoons, flown by Flg Off Bob Duego, flew so low during the attack on a gun position that he hit one of the German gunners with his wing as the unfortunate individual jumped over the sandbag wall of a gunpit! This type of mission was

56 Squadron in late 1942.

now being flown daily against targets in Belgium and Holland.

On 12 May 1943, thirteen Focke Wulf Fw190s made a low-level attack on Lowestoft. In response, six Typhoons were scrambled from Matlaske to intercept the raiders. On this occasion the Typhoons were scrambled too late, however, one Fw190 was downed by anti-aircraft fire on the coast. Bombs from this raid fell on the town and harbour causing minor damage. A similar raid, carried out, again by Fw190s, saw a similar result with the Typhoons failing to intercept. However, on this occasion the damage to a Gas holder at Lowestoft caused extensive damage and claimed the lives of twenty three people with a further twenty nine seriously wounded.

The British reaction to these raids was swift. The next day, 13 May, additional Typhoons from 245 Squadron were rushed into Matlaske from Gravesend. In addition, 195 Squadron joined the reinforcements from their home base at Woodvale on Merseyside. This squadron flew from Ludham, the second satellite station under Coltishall's control.

Sector patrols and standbys were now the order of the day, but the Typhoons of 56 Squadron soon resumed their offensive operations flying 'Rhubarbs', 'Roadsteads' and concentrating on anti-shipping operations.

It was on one such mission, being mounted from Ludham, that 56 Squadron lost their CO, Sqn Ldr Johnston, whilst attacking targets over Holland on 13 January 1943. A second Typhoon, flown by Flg Off Rouse, was also lost on the same mission. This was the start of a bad day for the squadron as later they were to lose another of their pilots.

That evening four Fw190s attempted an attack on Great Yarmouth. Luckily, the Typhoons from Matlaske were already on station and went in for the attack. During the engagement, Flt Sgt Clucas flying one of the Typhoons was shot down into the sea. Despite atrocious weather conditions, a Walrus of 278 Squadron with a Spitfire escort was scrambled to rescue him. This rescue attempt proved to be costly in its own right, as, soon after take off, Plt Off Libby in his Spitfire crash-landed in a field after engine failure. The Walrus continued on its own, without fighter cover, but regretfully without success.

As part of a visit to the airfields within the Coltishall Sector, HM King George VI and Queen Elizabeth visited Matlaske on 28 January 1943. After being received in the Matlaske Officers' Mess at Itteringham Hall by the Camp commandant, Sqn Ldr C W Cudmore MC, DFC, the Royal Party visited 56 Squadron and 1489 Gunnery Flight; the latter who were equipped with Lysanders and Miles Masters.

Escorted by the Camp commandant and the respective

squadron commanders, Sqn Ldr T H V Pickering of 56 Squadron and Sqn Ldr H H A Ironside of 1489 Gunnery Flight, the Royal Party toured Matlaske for an hour before departing for Coltishall.

During the period March to April 1943, the 56th FG, USAAF, equipped with Republic P-47D Thunderbolts were at Matlaske before moving to Horsham St Faith

On 23 April 1943, another of the squadron pilots had a miraculous escape. Plt Off Cramer landed his Typhoon DN317, very heavily at Matlaske and his aircraft bounced and slow-rolled before crashing inverted. As his aircraft hit the ground, the wings sheared off and the fuselage, with the pilot still strapped inside, ended up 30 yards further on. Despite fire, exploding ammunition and the crumpled mess around him, Plt Off Cramer managed to struggle out with only slight damage to one of his knees.

Black and white stripes were soon applied to the wings of Matlaske Typhoons, not invasion stripes, but identification stripes as many Typhoons had been previously attacked by Spitfires, mistaken for Fw190s. To which they bore some resemblance, especially in the heat of battle. One of 56 Squadron pilots, Flg Off E Haabjoern, had in fact been shot down over the North Sea by a Spitfire and this incident caused the hasty introduction of the ID stripes.

The Typhoons of 56 Squadron remained at Matlaske until the 22 July 1943, when they re-located to Manston in Kent. July was to see the arrival of a further Spitfire Squadron, when 611 Squadron, flying the Mark IX variant, joined the resident squadrons for a two-week rest period. During their short stay, the squadron re-equipped with the low-level Spitfire before moving on to Ludham.

Matlaske was placed under Care and Maintenance on the 24 August 1943. All the fighter squadrons having flown south to be nearer the current scene of activity. Despite being non-operational, the airfield and the surrounding villages were attacked on 24 October. Maybe having been mistaken for Coltishall. An unusual load of nine 50kg mines and three SBC50 bombs fell around Matlaske and Toft's Monk from two highflying raiders, causing very little damage.

Some bombing training took place at Matlaske between March and April 1944. In addition, the 3rd Engineer Battalion of the USAAF practised here for their forthcoming duties in France. 1944 was a quiet year for the station but only until the autumn. Bomber command was now operating in daylight, and support was needed for the airborne landings in Holland. Tempest Vs of 150

Wing, comprising 3, 56 and 486 Squadrons, spent a few days at Matlaske before proceeding to Grimbergen.

Their place was soon taken by a Mustang Wing, comprised of 19, 65 and 122 Squadrons operating from Matlaske in the September and October of 1944. The three squadrons flew mainly long-range escort missions to RAF and USAAF bombers, with the occasional fighter sweep in between. The wing left for Andrewsfield in Essex on 14 October.

Matlaske was totally unsuitable for Mosquito operations, and thus the station was not in a position to mount night operations against the V-1 menace. However, by October 1944, V-2 rockets were falling in Norfolk and the only effective defence against this threat was to find and destroy their launching sites.

Since the sites were mobile, this would be a difficult task. Spitfires on armed reconnaissance missions had proved to be ideal for this mission and soon Matlaske was to become involved in operations against these Terror Weapons.

229, 453 RAAF and 602 Squadrons flew into Matlaske during the third week of October 1944 with their Spitfire IXs to carry out the armed reconnaissance raids. 229 Squadron, whilst carrying out the occasional armed recce raid, flew the majority of their missions in support of 100 Gp bomber aircraft over enemy territory. By 20 November, the squadron had in fact moved to a 100 Gp station, namely Swannington. Soon after arriving at Matlaske, 453 and 602 Squadrons changed their Spitfire IXs for the new Mk XVI version of the fighter which was powered by the American-built Packard Merlin engine.

Matlaske had always suffered with water drainage problems and when the field became water-logged for the umpteenth time, 453 and 602 Squadrons joined 226 Squadron in operating from the nearby Mosquito base at Swannington until the surface at Matlaske improved.

602 Squadron continued to operate in the armed reconnaissance role from Matlaske until 23 February 1945 when they moved to Ludham. It was 453 Squadron who proved to be the final occupants of Matlaske, in fact, they did not leave until April 1945.

By October 1945, the airfield was vacated, never to see flying again. Matlaske was to be one of the earliest airfields to be returned to farming after the Second World War. Today, sections of the perimeter track and the odd Pill Box remain as a reminder of the days when this forgotten airfield played such an important role as a satellite to Coltishall.

LUDHAM

Ludham, the second satellite airfield of Coltishall, came into use in the last quarter of 1941 as a forward operating base for fighter squadrons under the control of Coltishall. Its proximity to the coast made it an ideal base for maritime operations, escorting bombers raiding the Continent and for scrambles against raiders.

In mid November 1941, 152 Squadron were sending sections of Spitfire IIAs forward from Swanton Morley for convoy escorts and operations against the E-Boat threat. Then, on 1 December 1941, 19 Squadron moved in with their Spitfire LF.VBs carrying out shipping reconnaissance flights, 'Circuses', and sweeps under 12 Gp's control. The Squadron left Ludham on 4 April 1942.

610 (County of Chester) Squadron arrived from Hutton Cranswick with their Spitfire Vb and Vc in April 1942 to replace 19 Squadron. They continued with 'Circus' sorties and escorts to 2 Gp's light bombers on operations over Holland and Belgium.

The Squadron quickly drew their first blood at dawn on 27 April 1942, when a Junkers Ju88D, Wrk No 430215 coded F6+HL, was shot down over the sea off Great Yarmouth. This Ju88 was credited to both Plt Off Hokan, who was flying Spitfire Vb BL267/DW-H and Sgt S G Creagh in BL484/DW-K.

An unusual visitor dropped in to Ludham on 12 May. WO Matte, a Free Frenchman of 235 Squadron based at Hibaldstow, had been ordered to make a sector reconnaissance. Evidently, finding this task somewhat unexciting, he skimmed off to Holland where he shot up a gasometer at The Hague, setting it ablaze before turning his attention to a nearby barge during his private 'Rhubarb.' Landing at Ludham short of fuel he was suitably greeted by a less than enthusiastic representation from his Group Headquarters!

Convoy patrols represented a considerable proportion of the effort. There were a number of engagements such as the evening of 14 May when another two Spitfire Vbs, flown by Sqn Ldr G S K Haywood flying BL564/DW-E and Sgt F Mares in W3128/DW-B, found some Junkers Ju88s mine laying close to Convoy 'Smilax.' One of the intruders was intercepted and damaged. The next day, in cloud and rain, six of the squadron's pilots destroyed two Dornier Do217s of KG2, Wrk No 5378 coded U5+CL and Wrk No 5373 coded U5+BL. At the same time, a Whirlwind of 137 Squadron damaged a Ju88.

During the night attacks on Norwich, detachments from Ludham operated Fighter Night patrols, but without success. When not on patrol, 610 Squadron were operating over Europe flying 'Rhubarbs', sweeps and escorts. During the Dieppe raid, the squadron moved forward to West Malling, to take part in operations with 411 and 485 Squadrons, jointly commanded by Wg Cdr Jameson.

Three days later Sqn Ldr Haywood, again flying BL564 and Flt Sgt Mares, this time in BL267/DW-H, were patrolling off Yarmouth when they saw a Junkers Ju88 coming head on. Long bursts from both Spitfires hit the nose and tail of the Junkers before a third Spitfire from Coltishall, flown by Wg Cdr Hanks, joined in the fight. The Ju88 was last seen entering a mist bank with a silent rear gun and smoke belching from both engines. Another Ju88 was damaged off Lowestoft at dawn on 21 May. Plt Off P B Wright in Spitfire Vb, BL564/DW-E and Sgt J H Turner in BL262/DW-L, both from 610 Squadron, shared the claim.

The middle part of 1942 saw Ludham's squadrons continue with their patrols and escorts. On the night of 31 May, Spitfires of 610 Squadron left Ludham to give rear cover to the returning bombers after the 1000 bomber raid on Cologne. On 14 October, 167 Squadron arrived in their Spitfires and two Harrows after a long journey from Castletown near the North East tip of Scotland.

The squadron was destined to stay at Ludham for seven months. Its role, more offensive than defensive, reflected the current role of Fighter Command. Much of their work related to escorting the Venturas of 2 Gp, who continued making daily raids to the Continent. Escorting Coastal Command Beaufighters from the Langham Wing, giving rear cover to returning USAAF B-17s and B-24s. Also, shipping reconnaissance off Holland and escorting the Walruses of 278 Squadron on Search and Rescue missions.

'Rhubarbs' continued on a daily basis, and whilst on such a mission they lost Sqn Ldr Lane to a Focke Wulf Fw190 on 13 December 1942. Such sorties were becoming increasingly dangerous now that the Fw190 was in plentiful supply. In fact, the day after Lane was shot down, this type of mission was suspended whilst revised tactics were tested.

The 28 January 1943 saw the visit of the King and Queen to the Coltishall Sector airfields of Matlaske and Ludham. The suspense and drama that unfolded this day could not have been better scripted, in fact, it is doubted that Alfred Hitchcock could have plotted such a script!

Shortly after 1500 hours, HM King George VI and Queen Elizabeth were due to arrive at Ludham. As they

'Just a Sanappin' at Ludham.

set out on their journey through the Norfolk Broads on their way to the airfield, events unfolding across the North Sea were to coincide with their arrival. At about the same time, a Junkers Ju88 of KG6 took off from its base at Soesterberg in Holland, intent on attacking shipping off the East Anglian coast.

Just as their Majesties were due to arrive, Plt Off Tommy Cody and Sgt Nash flying a pair of Spitfire VBs, were scrambled from their dispersal at Ludham. Nine minutes later, the two pilots returned; Tommy Cody, celebrated with a 'victory roll' over the airfield before landing and reporting for his de-brief. He had claimed his first victim, the Ju88 from Soesterberg.

Their landing coincided with the arrival of the Royal Party who were met by the Camp commandant, Flt Lt N E Hext and OC 167 Squadron, Sqn Ldr D S Edwards. Cody was naturally elated with his victory, and the King made no attempt to conceal his delight on meeting the two pilots.

Activity for 167 Squadron reached a memorable peak in May 1943. Shortly before 1700 hours on 3 May, 167 Squadron took off to join 118 Squadron. The Coltishall Wing was airborne en-masse, under the command of Wg Cdr 'Cowboy' Blatchford. They met up with the Venturas of 487 Squadron from Methwold and set course for Holland. Soon after entering Dutch airspace over 20 enemy fighters swooped upon them from ahead, dived below the Spitfires and set upon the Venturas which were by now cut off from their fighter escort.

In vain, the Spitfires tried to shield the bombers but each Section was repeatedly 'jumped' by groups of the enemy fighters until eventually the whole fighter force mingled. The Spitfires were badly mauled and 167 Squadron claimed one solitary 'kill.'

That morning, a sudden sharp raid was made on Lowestoft by Focke Wulf Fw190 fighter-bombers, which raked the town and fled before the defenders could attack them. In fact, the Spitfire Vs were no match for this type of operation and were soon withdrawn.

195 Squadron was rushed in from Woodvale on Merseyside with Hawker Typhoon Is to fill the void. There were more such raids on the coast, but never was the warning early enough to give the Typhoons a chance to fight. Instead the Typhoons undertook convoy patrols and Beaufighter escorts before making way for the Spitfire VBs of 611 Squadron which arrived in July from Matlaske.

The fighters vacated Ludham on 4 August 1943. The base was then transferred to the Ministry of Works on 13 August. It was decided to hand the airfield over to the Americans, however, no flying units ever moved in.

Ludham lay virtually unused until August 1944, when the Royal Navy began to use the station, renaming it HMS Flycatcher. However, in the meantime, Ludham still played host to damaged aircraft returning from raids on the continent.

On 27 September 1943, a battle damaged B-17 Flying Fortress of the 96th BG based at Snetterton, crash landed after a raid on Emden. On 8 October a 100th BG B-17 from Thorpe Abbots, 'Just a Snappin', also crash-landed after a raid on Bremen.

Ludham village played host to an unwelcome visitor on 13 December when a P-38H-3 Lightning, 42-67053 'Vivacious Vera', crashed on the high street after a bomber escort mission on the North German port of Kiel. The aircraft belonged to the 55th FG at Wormingford and was being flown by Lt Hugh James Gouldock. Over the target area the aircraft suffered port engine failure as a result of FLAK or a mechanical malfunction. With over 400 miles between himself and Wormingford, Jim Gouldock had to call on all of his skill and training to get his aircraft back home.

As he approached the coast of England, he saw the welcome sight of an unknown airfield some ten miles away. However a dead transmitter precluded the pilot from talking to the control tower at Ludham. His wing-man, Lt Sorace, gained permission for his colleague to make a landing but he was unable to advise Jim Gouldock of the situation.

On a single engine, and with only one hydraulic pump to extend his undercarriage and flaps, things were looking desperate. However, 90 degrees to the runway at 1800 feet, his aircraft was flying well. With only one more turn, Gouldock banked his P-38 into the final approach only to have his one remaining Allison engine stop. So near, yet so far, the P-38 crashed in a cloud of dust and debris. The aircraft ploughed through trees and buildings, but miraculously Jim Gouldock was still alive, only to find himself trapped in his burning cockpit.

Were it not for the bravery and quick thinking of Ludham residents Russell Brooks, Cyril Thrower and airfield worker Robert Utting, Lt Hugh James Gouldock would have certainly perished in the wreckage.

HMS Flycatcher, as Ludham had been re-named, was the Headquarters of the Mobile Naval Air Base (MONAB) organisation. MONABs were mobile, self-contained units able to repair and prepare aircraft, engines and components as required by the fleet. The first five were formed at Ludham before embarking on ships for Australia.

MONAB No.1 was commissioned on 28 October 1944 and embarked for Australia on the "Empress of Scotland" on 20 November. MONAB No.2 formed on 11 November 1944, embarking for Australia later that month. No.3 was commissioned on 4 December 1944, embarking on SS "Windsor Castle" on the 20 December. MONAB No.4

The Spitfire XXI prototype.

commissioned on 1 January 1945, embarking on the "Dominion Monarch" fifteen days later. The final unit, No.5, was formed on 1 February 1945, embarking on the "Stirling Castle" later in that month, again for Australia. Transportable Aircraft Maintenance Yard (TAMY) No.1 was also formed at Ludham on 1 February 1945, joining MONAB No.5 on the "Stirling Castle" to Australia.

HMS Flycatcher moved to Middle Wallop on 16 February 1945 with the station reverting to RAF hands that same day. RAF fighters returned 22 February 1945 with the arrival of 603 (City of Edinburgh) Squadron, which had been re-numbered from 229 Squadron at Coltishall on 7 January 1945.

The squadron resumed its attacks on V-2 launching sites, undertook armed reconnaissance and escorted the Beaufighters of the Langham Strike Wing. These duties were continued from Ludham, which they shared with the Spitfire XVIs of 602 (City of Glasgow) Squadron, who had moved in from Matlaske on 23 February 1945.

603 Squadron suffered a string of accidents during March 1945 both self imposed and enemy action. On 9 March, on a mission over Holland, Spitfire XVI SM405, was hit by flak near Wassenaar. The pilot managed against all odds to recover his aircraft back to Ludham, however, such was the damage that it was struck-off charge as being beyond repair.

The next day, Spitfire XVI SM464 suffered a jammed undercarriage whilst attempting to land. After a couple of passes for Flying Control to assess the situation from the ground, the pilot made a wheels-up landing which resulted in the aircraft being written-off. A week later on 17 March, Spitfire XVI SM473, failed to return from a fighter sweep over the continent.

Unfortunately, worse was to come on 24 March when two Spitfires, SM396 and TB396 collided in mid-air whilst on a sortie from Ludham. The pilot of SM396 managed to land his aircraft on the foreshore two miles North East of Sea Palling whilst the other crashed two miles North West of the same village. Both aircraft were destroyed.

Early April 1945 saw the departure of both 602 and 603 Squadrons back to Coltishall and the subsequent arrival of a new version of the Spitfire, the Mk XXI. The first operational sortie with this new mark was launched from Ludham on 10 April 1945. This time, their task was to seek out the midget submarines that were being used for the first time against mainland England. The first two sorties on 26 April were flown by Spitfires LA252 and LA223. This was a particularly good sortie as they claimed a midget submarine destroyed.

The Spitfire XXIs flew their 152nd and last sortie from Ludham on 1 May 1945. Maintenance problems brought the two operational Mk XXI Squadrons together at Ludham on 14 May 1945 when 1 Squadron joined 603 Squadron. Both stayed until 14 July, after which Ludham lay quiet.

The base was handed back to 60 Gp for Care and Maintenance in September of that year. During the remaining months of 1945, Ludham gradually began to run down and since the late 1940s, much of the airfield returned to agricultural use.

In the 1950s, the feature film "Conflict of Wings" was made in the village of Ludham and the surrounding area of Broadland. The film starred John Gregson as a Vampire pilot whose squadron wanted to use the local nature reserve as a bombing range. Even with Ludham airfield close at hand, it was not used during the filming.

Today, the odd crop spraying aircraft flies from the last remaining strip of concrete that used to be one of the runways. In the mid-90s, the Control Tower was re-built as a museum, re-kindling the memories of Britain's most easterly airfield, but sadly has since closed with the building falling into disrepair.

RAF COLTISHALL COMMANDING OFFICERS

Wg Cdr W K Beisiegal	15 May 1940	-	9 Jan 1941
Gp Capt R B Lees	9 Jan 1941	-	11 Sep 1942
Gp Capt G D Harvey	11 Sep 1942	-	20 Apr 1943
Gp Capt A V Harvey	20 Apr 1943	-	10 Dec 1943
Gp Capt A H Donaldson	0 Dec 1943	-	25 May 1945
Gp Capt A H Dunn	25 May 1945	-	9 Aug 1945
Gp Capt T H Polski	9 Aug 1945	-	27 Feb 1946
Gp Capt A K Gabszewic	27 Feb 1946	-	13 Feb 1947
Wg Cdr R R Stanford-Tuck	13 Feb 1947	-	22 Jan 1948
Wg Cdr Spotswood	22 Jan 1948	-	6 Mar 1950
Wg Cdr E L Colbeck-Welch	6 Mar 1950	-	1 Feb 1951
Gp Capt A H Smythe	1 Feb 1951	-	8 May 1953
Gp Capt P P Hanks	8 May 1953	-	12 Dec 1955
Gp Capt J C Sisson	12 Dec 1955	-	25 Nov 1958
Wg Cdr W Laing	25 Nov 1958	-	1 Jun 1959
Gp Capt H Bird-Wilson	1 Jun 1959	-	15 Nov 1961
Gp Capt L H Malins	15 Nov 1961	-	1 Nov 1963
Gp Capt R L Topp	1 Dec 1963	-	3 Jun 1966
Gp Capt M E Hobson	4 Jun 1966	-	3 Jan 1969
Gp Capt W J Stacey	3 Jan 1969	-	20 Nov 1969
Gp Capt J T Jennings	20 Nov 1969	-	18 Nov 1971
Gp Capt J A Gilbert	18 Nov 1971	-	28 Dec 1973
Gp Capt L Swart	28 Dec 1973	-	6 Aug 1976
Gp Capt J H Honey	6 Aug 1976	-	6 Sep 1978
Gp Capt T H Stonor	6 Sep 1978	-	15 Oct 1980
Gp Capt T J Nash	15 Oct 1980	-	3 Dec 1982
Gp Capt G R Profit	3 Dec 1982	-	8 Feb 1985
Gp Capt M R French	8 Feb 1985	-	4 Jun 1987
Gp Capt F J Hoare	4 Jun 1987	-	2 Aug 1989
Gp Capt M J Abbott	3 Aug 1989	-	16 Aug 1991
Gp Capt J P Dacre	16 Aug 1991	-	5 Jul 1993
Gp Capt N C Rusling	5 Jul 1993	-	28 Jul 1995
Gp Capt T C Hewlett	28 Jul 1995	-	5 Sep 1997
Gp Capt S G G Dalton	5 Sep 1997	-	5 Sep 1999
Gp Capt C N Harper	6 Sep 1999	-	5 Oct 2001
Gp Capt R D Cobelli	6 Oct 2001	-	28 Nov 2003
Gp Capt G A Wright	28 Nov 2003	-	3 Dec 2005
Air Cdre G A Wright	3 Dec 2005	-	24 Apr 2006
Wg Cdr P D Robins	24 Apr 2006	-	13 Oct 2006
Sqn Ldr J Hughes	13 Oct 2006	-	30 Nov 2006

SQUADRONS BASED AT RAF COLTISHALL

Unit	Date In	Date Out	Code
66 Sqn	29-05-1940	03-09-1940	LZ
242 Sqn	20-06-1940	26-10-1940	LE
604 Sqn, 'B' Flt	07-1940	08-1941	NG
616 Sqn	03-09-1940	09-09-1940	YQ
74 Sqn	09-09-1940	15-10-1940	ZP
72 Sqn	13-10-1940	30-10-1940	RN
64 Sqn	15-10-1940	10-11-1940	SH
72 Sqn	02-11-1940	29-11-1940	RN
222 Sqn	12-11-1940	06-06-1941	ZD
242 Sqn	30-11-1940	16-12-1940	LE
257 Sqn	15-12-1940	7-11-1941	DT
93 Sqn Dets	12-1940	11-1941	HN
42 Sqn Dets	03-1941	06-1942	AW
151 Sqn Det	22-04-1941	03-05-1941	DZ
29 Sqn Dets	04-1941	05-1943	RO
225 Sqn Dets	04-1941	09-1941	YD
151 Sqn Det	21-05-1941	25-01-1942	DZ
5 ASR Flt	07-1941	01-10-1941	MY
133 'Eagle' Sqn	29-07-1941	15-08-1941	MD
12 Gp TT Flt	08-1941	08-12-1941	12
604 Sqn Det	08-1941	21-09-1941	NG
255 Sqn	20-09-1941	02-03-1942	YD
137 Sqn	18-11-1941	01-12-1941	SF
152 Sqn	17-12-1941	17-02-1942	UM
1489 TT Flt	08-12-1941	10-1942	
226 Sqn Dets	01-1942	08-1942	UO
154 Sqn	12-03-1942	05-04-1942	HT
154 Sqn Dets	04-1942	05-1942	HT
266 Sqn Dets	03-1942	08-1942	UO
278 Sqn	10-04-1942	21-04-1944	MY
610 Sqn	14-04-1942	14-10-1942	DW
68 Sqn	01-03-1942	05-02-1944	WM
56 Sqn	24-08-1942	22-07-1943	US
488 Sqn Dets	09-1942	03-1943	ME
167 Sqn	15-10-1942	13-05-1943	VL
346th FG Dets	11-1942	06-1943	
Mandrel Screen Unit	12-1942	07-1943	
118 Sqn	18-01-1943	15-08-1943	NK

288 Sqn Dets	01-1943	11-1944	RP
841 Sqn FAA (Det 3)	07-02-1943	23-06-1943	
409 Sqn Dets	02-1943	02-1944	KP
613 Sqn	03-05-1943	27-05-1943	SY
FIU	06-1943	03-1944	ZQ
288 Sqn	06-1943	07-1943	RP
611 Sqn	02-08-1943	29-04-1944	FY
195 Sqn	21-08-1943	23-09-1943	JE
64 Sqn	25-09-1943	24-01-1944	SH
234 Sqn	28-01-1944	18-03-1944	AZ
64 Sqn	03-02-1944	29-04-1944	SH
25 Sqn	05-02-1944	01-10-1944	ZK
316 (Polish) Sqn	29-04-1944	25-10-1944	SZ
307 (Polish) Sqn	01-05-1944	30-01-1945	EW
229 Sqn	01-07-1944	25-09-1944	9R
312 (Czech) Sqn	11-07-1944	27-08-1944	DU
NFDU	09-1944	05-1945	
80 Sqn	20-09-1944	29-09-1944	W2
274 Sqn	20-09-1944	29-09-1944	JJ
303 (Polish) Sqn	25-09-1944	09-08-1945	RF
453 Sqn	29-09-1944	06-04-1945	FU
602 Sqn	29-09-1944	18-10-1944	LO
125 Sqn	18-10-1944	24-04-1945	VA
26 Sqn	11-1944	04-1945	XC
315 (Polish) Sqn	24-10-1944	01-11-1944	PK
68 Sqn	27-10-1944	08-02-1945	WM
229 Sqn	02-12-1944	10-04-1945	9R
603 Sqn	10-01-1945	28-04-1945	XT
124 Sqn	10-02-1945	07-04-1945	ON
602 Sqn	19-02-1945	23-02-1945	LO
68 Sqn	27-02-1945	15-03-1945	WM
602 Sqn	05-04-1945	15-05-1945	LO
1 Sqn	08-04-1945	22-07-1945	JX
303 (Polish) Sqn	16-05-1945	19-08-1945	RF
316 (Polish) Sqn	16-05-1945	10-08-1945	SZ
307 Sqn	18-05-1945	24-08-1945	EW
315 (Polish) Sqn	08-08-1945	19-11-1945	PK
306 (Polish) Sqn	10-08-1945	08-10-1945	UZ
309 (Polish) Sqn	10-08-1945	08-10-1945	WC
309 (Polish) Sqn	16-11-1945	06-01-1947	WC
306 (Polish) Sqn	18-11-1945	06-01-1947	UZ
315 (Polish) Sqn	20-12-1945	14-01-1947	PK
141 Sqn	17-06-1946	21-11-1949	TW

318 Sqn	19-08-1946	12-12-1946	LW
23 Sqn	01-04-1947	19-11-1949	YP
264 Sqn	13-01-1948	19-11-1949	PS
109 Sqn	04-09-1948	29-09-1948	HS
23 Sqn	22-09-1950	15-02-1952	YP
141 Sqn	22-09-1950	12-10-1956	TW
264 Sqn	02-10-1950	24-08-1951	PS
809 Sqn FAA	31-08-1951	10-12-1951	
228 OCU Det	26-01-1952	04-07-1952	
23 Sqn	04-07-1952	12-10-1952	
85 Sqn	03-11-1952	11-12-1952	
275 Sqn Det	12-10-1956	23-11-1956	
23 Sqn	25-05-1957	07-09-1958	
141 Sqn	28-05-1957	31-01-1958	
41 Sqn	01-02-1958	03-07-1958	
23 Sqn	05-06-1959	31-03-1960	
74 Sqn	08-06-1959	31-03-1960	
AFDS	01-09-1959	04-04-1960	
23 Sqn	11-07-1960	09-03-1963	
74 Sqn	11-07-1960	02-03-1964	
AFDS	07-1960	10-1962	
228 Sqn Det	05-04-1963	29-08-1964	
HAF/BBMF	04-1962	01-03-1976	
226 OCU	13-04-1964	30-09-1974	
202 Sqn 'D'Flt	30-08-1964	02-04-1973	
65 Sqn	01-09-1970	03-07-1974	
849 Sqn FAA	27-09-1971	30-09-1971	
22 Sqn 'B' Flt	01-04-1973	05-1979	
54 Sqn	09-08-1974	13-03-2005	
6 Sqn	06-11-1974	01-04-2006	
202 Sqn 'C' Flt	05-1979	29-07-1982	
41 Sqn	01-04-1977	01-04-2006	
22 Sqn 'E' Flt	01-08-1983	02-09-1985	
202 Sqn 'C' Flt	02-09-1985	28-08-1988	
22 Sqn 'E' Flt	28-08-1988	18-09-1994	
39 (1 PRU) Sqn	07-1995	01-1996	
16 (R) Sqn	20-07-2000	13-03-2005	

III

AIRCRAFT USED BY SQUADRONS BASED AT RAF COLTISHALL

Unit	Aircraft Types
1 Sqn	Spitfire LF.IXb, F21
5 ASR Flt	Walrus I, II
	Lysander IIa
	Anson I
6 Sqn	Jaguar (All marks)
16 (R) Sqn	Jaguar GR.3, GR.3A, T.2A, T.4A
12 Gp TT Flt	Lysander I, II
22 Sqn	Beaufort I, II, Whirlwind HAR.2, HAR.10, Wessex HAR.2
23 Sqn	Mosquito NF.36, Vampire NF.10, Venom NF.2, NF.3, Javelin FAW.4, FAW.7, FAW.9R
25 Sqn	Mosquito VI, XVII, NF.XXX
29 Sqn	Beaufighter IF, VIF
39 Sqn	Canberra T.4, PR.7, PR.9
41 Sqn	Javelin FAW.4, Jaguar (All marks)
42 Sqn	Beaufort I, II
54 Sqn	Jaguar (All marks)
56 Sqn	Typhoon Ia, Ib
64 Sqn	Spitfire I, Vb, LFVc
66 Sqn	Spitfire I
68 Sqn	Beaufighter IF, VI, Mosquito XVII, XIX, XXX
72 Sqn	Spitfire I
74 Sqn	Spitfire IIa, Hunter F.6. Lightning F1/F3
80 Sqn	Tempest V
85 Sqn	Meteor NF.11
93 Sqn	Havoc I
118 Sqn	Spitfire Vb
124 Sqn	Spitfire XI
125 Sqn	Mosquito XIV, XXX
133 Sqn	Hurricane IIb
137 Sqn	Whirlwind I
141 Sqn	Mosquito NF.36, Meteor NF.11, Venom NF.3, Javelin FAW4
151 Sqn	Hurricane I, IIb, IIc, Defiant I
152 Sqn	Spitfire IIa
154 Sqn	Spitfire Va, Vb
167 Sqn	Spitfire Vb, Vc
195 Sqn	Typhoon Ib
202 Sqn	Whirlwind HAR.10, Sea King HAR.3
222 Sqn	Spitfire Ia, IIa, IIb
226 OCU	Lightning F.1,F.1A, F.3, T.4, T.5, T.55
234 Sqn	Spitfire Vb, Vc

228 OCU	Mosquito (various marks), Meteor (various marks)
228 Sqn	Whirlwind HAR.10
229 Sqn	Spitfire XI, XVI
242 Sqn	Hurricane I
255 Sqn	Beaufighter IIF
257 Sqn	Hurricane I, IIa, IIb, IIc
264 Sqn	Mosquito NF.36
266 Sqn	Typhoon Ia, Ib
274 Sqn	Tempest V
275 Sqn	Sycamore HR.13, HR.14
278 Sqn	Lysander IIa, Walrus I, II, Anson I
288 Sqn	Hurricane I, Defiant TT II/III, Spitfire V, IX, XVI
303 Sqn	Spitfire IX, Mustang IV
306 Sqn	Mustang III
307 Sqn	Mosquito XXX
309 Sqn	Mustang III, IV
312 Sqn	Spitfire XI
315 Sqn	Mustang III
316 Sqn	Mustang III
318 Sqn	Spitfire IX
409 Sqn	Beaufighter VI
453 Sqn	Spitfire IX
488 Sqn	Beaufighter II
602 Sqn	Spitfire IX, XVI
603 Sqn	Spitfire XVI
604 Sqn	Beaufighter I
610 Sqn	Spitfire Vb, Vc
611 Sqn	Spitfire IX
616 Sqn	Spitfire I
809 Sqn FAA	Sea Hornet F.20, NF.21
841 Sqn FAA	Albacore I, Swordfish I, II
849 Sqn FAA	Gannett AEW.3, COD.4, T.5
1489(TT) Flt	Lysander II, III, Henley III
346th FG	Spitfire Vb, P-39 Airacobra
AFDS	Javelin (various marks), Hunter (various marks), Lightning (various marks)
HAF/BBMF	Hurricane IIc, Spitfire IIa, Va, PR.XIX, Lancaster B.I
Mandrel Screen Unit	Defiant II
FIU	Mosquito (various marks)
NFDU	Mosquito (various marks), Firefly 1

IV

SQUADRONS BASED AT RAF MATLASKE

Unit	Date In	Date Out	Code
72 Sqn	30-10-1940	02-11-1940	SD/RN
222 Sqn	06-06-1941	01-07-1941	ZD
601 Sqn	02-07-1941	16-08-1941	UF
19 Sqn	16-08-1941	01-12-1941	OV
5 ASR Flt	01-10-1941	10-04-1942	MY
137 Sqn	09-11-1941	24-08-1942	SF
266 Sqn	01-08-1942	28-08-1942	ZH
56 Sqn	24-08-1942	22-07-1943	US
245 Sqn Det	19-03-1943	11-05-1943	MR
1489 TT Flt	13-04-1943	02-06-1943	
19 Sqn	04-06-1943	20-06-1943	QV
611 Sqn	01-07-1943	31-07-1943	FY
609 Sqn	22-07-1943	18-08-1943	PR
195 Sqn	31-07-1943	21-08-1943	JE
Care & Maintenance	24-08-1943	18-09-1944	
486 Sqn	19-09-1944	28-09-1944	SA
3 Sqn	21-09-1944	28-09-1944	JF
56 Sqn	23-09-1944	28-09-1944	US
19 Sqn	28-09-1944	14-10-1944	QV
122 Sqn	28-09-1944	14-10-1944	MT
65 Sqn	29-09-1944	14-10-1944	YT
453 Sqn	18-10-1944	06-04-1945	FU
602 Sqn	18-10-1944	20-11-1944	LO
229 Sqn	22-10-1944	20-11-1944	9R
451 Sqn	23-02-1945	06-04-1945	NI
658 Sqn	10-07-1945	02-10-1945	
659 Sqn	10-07-1945	02-10-1945	

V

AIRCRAFT USED BY SQUADRONS BASED AT RAF MATLASKE

Unit	Aircraft Types
3 Sqn	Tempest V
19 Sqn	Spitfire IIa, Vb, Vc, Mustang III, IV
56 Sqn	Typhoon Ia, Ib, Tempest V
65 Sqn	Mustang III
72 Sqn	Spitfire Ia, Ib
122 Sqn	Mustang III
137 Sqn	Whirlwind I
195 Sqn	Typhoon Ib

222 Sqn	Spitfire IIa, IIb
229 Sqn	Spitfire XI
245 Sqn	Typhoon Ib
451 Sqn	Spitfire XVI
453 Sqn	Spitfire IX, XVI
486 Sqn	Tempest V
601 Sqn	Hurricane IIb
602 Sqn	Spitfire XI, XVI
609 Sqn	Typhoon Ia, Ib
611 Sqn	Spitfire Vb, Vc, IX
658 Sqn	Auster IV, V
659 Sqn	Auster IV, V
5 ASR Flt	Walrus I, II, Lysander IIa, Anson I

VI

SQUADRONS BASED AT RAF LUDHAM

Unit	Date In	Date Out	Code
19 Sqn	01-12-1941	04-04-1942	QV
610 Sqn	04-04-1942	15-10-1942	DW
167 Sqn	14-10-1942	01-03-1943	VL
245 Sqn	03-1943	05-1943	MR
195 Sqn	13-05-1943	04-08-1943	JE
611 Sqn	31-07-1943	04-08-1943	FY
HMS Flycatcher	31-07-1943	16-02-1945	
602 Sqn	23-02-1945	05-04-1945	LO
603 Sqn	24-02-1945	05-04-1945	XT
91 Sqn	08-04-1945	11-07-1945	DL
1 Sqn	14-05-1945	23-07-1945	JX

VII

AIRCRAFT USED BY SQUADRONS BASED AT RAF LUDHAM

Unit	Aircraft Types
1 Sqn	Spitfire IXb, XXI
19 Sqn	Spitfire Vb, Vc
91 Sqn	Spitfire XXI
167 Sqn	Spitfire Vb, Vc
195 Sqn	Typhoon Ib
245 Sqn	Typhoon Ib
602 Sqn	Spitfire XVI
603 Sqn	Spitfire XVI
610 Sqn	Spitfire Vb, Vc
611 Sqn	Spitfire Vb, Vc, IX

RAF COLTISHALL HISTORY TIMELINE

Construction began at the Scottow Aerodrome site in **1939** as a bomber base for 2 Group Bomber Command. The airfield was officially re-named Coltishall shortly after construction started.

Before completion as a bomber station the site was handed to 12 Group Fighter Command and was declared operational by Wg Cdr W K Beisiegal on **23 June 1940**.

During **August 1941** 255 Squadron, the first permanently based night-fighter squadron, arrived at Coltishall to take up their nocturnal duties. Prior to their arrival, Defiant night fighters of 151 Squadron were flown in to Coltishall on a daily basis from Wittering.

During **October 1942**, the 346th FS of the USAAF formed at Coltishall with pilots from the recently disbanded RAF 'Eagle' Squadrons.

28 January 1943. His Majesty King George presents 5 (ASR) Flight with their new Squadron Badge ; 278 (ASR) Squadron. The only time in the Service's history that a RAF squadron has been presented with a new badge by a Reigning Monarch.

8 August 1945 saw Coltishall handed over to 133 Wing of the Free Polish Air Force. The only time that an operational airfield in the UK has been handed over in to a foreign country.

Coltishall was handed back to 12 Group RAF Fighter Command by the Polish Air Force in **February 1946**.

1935

1940

1945

1950

First recorded enemy aircraft shot down during the Battle of Britain fell to Sgt F N Robertson of 66 Squadron, Coltishall. He successfully intercepted and destroyed the Dornier Do17 at 0510 hours off Winterton on **10 July 1940**.

133 'Eagle' Squadron formed at Coltishall on **29 July 1941**. The last of three RAF Squadrons manned by American Volunteer pilots.

19 November 1941. Matlaske, to the south of Holt, opened as the first satellite airfield for Coltishall. The second satellite airfield for Coltishall; Ludham was opened in 1943. At the time, Ludham was the most easterly airfield in the UK and was situated close to the Norfolk Broads.

12 February 1942. Coltishall was a launch platform for attacks on the German Battleships during the 'Channel Dash'. Coastal Command Bristol Beauforts from Leuchars, Lossiemouth and St Eval operated from Coltishall during that time.

Throughout **1944**, 45 different squadrons of the Coltishall Wing were involved in anti-V-1 and V-2 missions over the Continent in addition to supporting Allied troops as they moved through Europe following the Normandy invasion.

20 March 1945. The last enemy aircraft to be shot down over the UK was a Junkers Ju88 shot down off Cromer by a Mosquito of 125 Squadron from Coltishall. Flt Lt Kennedy and Flg Off Morgan flew this particular aircraft.

Following the re-occupation by the RAF, Coltishall was to be a dedicated Night-Fighter unit within Fighter Command. Squadrons were initially equipped with the Mosquito NF.30 and NF.33 and then with the advent of the jet-age, the Venom and Meteor.

Coltishall was to become the first Wing in the RAF to accept the Gloster Javelin into service. 23 and 141 Squadrons converted to their new aircraft at Horsham St Faith whilst Coltishall was being upgraded to accept the new aircraft.

December 1959 saw the first pre-production Lightning delivered to the AFDU at Coltishall. By January 1960 the squadron had its full compliment of four Lightning's

In July 1963, 23 Squadron became the first squadron of any Air Force in the world to deploy overseas using air-to-air refuelling. Operation Dyke saw the Javelins deploy from Coltishall to Tengah in Singapore supported by Valiant tankers of 214 Squadron based at Marham.

1964 saw the departure of the Javelins of 23 Squadron and the Lightnings of 74 Squadron to Leuchars. 226 OCU from RAF Middleton St George replaced both squadrons at Coltishall.

1973 saw the arrival of the last remaining airworthy Avro Lancaster B.I from Waddington. That year also saw the Historic Aircraft Flight renamed The BBMF.

The Jaguar era began at Coltishall with the arrival of 54(F) Squadron in **mid-1974**. 6 Squadron followed later that year after conversion from the McDonnell Douglas Phantom.

1955

1960

1965

1970

Sqn Ldr John Howe became the first operational Lightning Squadron CO in the RAF when 74 (Tiger) Squadron converted to the aircraft at Coltishall in **June 1960**.

April 1963 saw the arrival of the RAF Historic Aircraft Flight with two Spitfires and a single Hurricane together with the Sycamore helicopters of 228 (SAR) Squadron from Horsham St Faith when that unit closed as an operational RAF Station.

During **1968**, four Lightning T.55s of the Royal Saudi Air Force joined the Lightning OCU.

226 OCU disbanded on **1973** when the training commitment for the Lightning moved toBinbrook. From 1964 to 1974, the OCU at Coltishall trained 810 new pilots to fly the Lightning.

The BBMF moved to RAF Coningsby in **1976**.

May 1979 saw the Westland Sea King HAR.3 replace the venerable Whirlwinds of 202 Squadron in the SAR role. The Whirlwind had been in residence since mid-1956.

41(F), the third and last operational UK Jaguar Squadron, arrived in **April 1977**.

In **1982**, 'C' Flt 202 Squadron deployed to the South Atlantic to provide SAR cover for the Falkland Islands following conflict with the Argentinean Forces. They were replaced by the Westland Wessex HAR.2 of 'E' Flight, 22 Squadron.

January 1982. Coltishall was identified as being a suitable site for the seventh base to house the Bloodhound anti-aircraft missile. Eventually West Raynham was chosen as a more suitable location.

1975

1980

1985

1990

Jaguars from Coltishall were used in anger for the first time during Operation GRANBY; the first Gulf War in **1990**.

Since the end of Operation GRANBY, the Jaguar Wing was involved in numerous operations that included the policing of Northern Iraq and support to the United Nations Stabilisation Force over the Balkans.

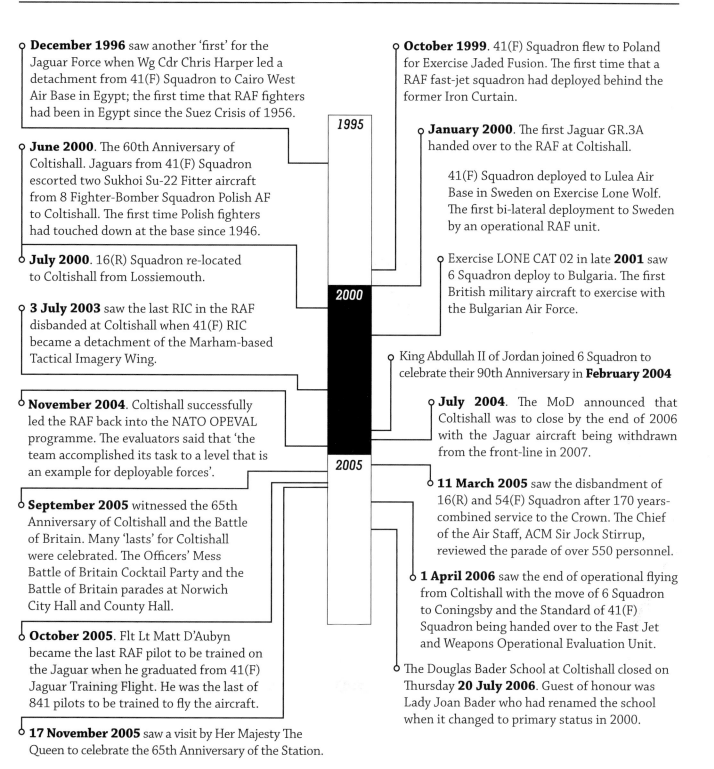

December 1996 saw another 'first' for the Jaguar Force when Wg Cdr Chris Harper led a detachment from 41(F) Squadron to Cairo West Air Base in Egypt; the first time that RAF fighters had been in Egypt since the Suez Crisis of 1956.

June 2000. The 60th Anniversary of Coltishall. Jaguars from 41(F) Squadron escorted two Sukhoi Su-22 Fitter aircraft from 8 Fighter-Bomber Squadron Polish AF to Coltishall. The first time Polish fighters had touched down at the base since 1946.

July 2000. 16(R) Squadron re-located to Coltishall from Lossiemouth.

3 July 2003 saw the last RIC in the RAF disbanded at Coltishall when 41(F) RIC became a detachment of the Marham-based Tactical Imagery Wing.

November 2004. Coltishall successfully led the RAF back into the NATO OPEVAL programme. The evaluators said that 'the team accomplished its task to a level that is an example for deployable forces'.

September 2005 witnessed the 65th Anniversary of Coltishall and the Battle of Britain. Many 'lasts' for Coltishall were celebrated. The Officers' Mess Battle of Britain Cocktail Party and the Battle of Britain parades at Norwich City Hall and County Hall.

October 2005. Flt Lt Matt D'Aubyn became the last RAF pilot to be trained on the Jaguar when he graduated from 41(F) Jaguar Training Flight. He was the last of 841 pilots to be trained to fly the aircraft.

17 November 2005 saw a visit by Her Majesty The Queen to celebrate the 65th Anniversary of the Station.

1995

2000

2005

October 1999. 41(F) Squadron flew to Poland for Exercise Jaded Fusion. The first time that a RAF fast-jet squadron had deployed behind the former Iron Curtain.

January 2000. The first Jaguar GR.3A handed over to the RAF at Coltishall.

41(F) Squadron deployed to Lulea Air Base in Sweden on Exercise Lone Wolf. The first bi-lateral deployment to Sweden by an operational RAF unit.

Exercise LONE CAT 02 in late **2001** saw 6 Squadron deploy to Bulgaria. The first British military aircraft to exercise with the Bulgarian Air Force.

King Abdullah II of Jordan joined 6 Squadron to celebrate their 90th Anniversary in **February 2004**

July 2004. The MoD announced that Coltishall was to close by the end of 2006 with the Jaguar aircraft being withdrawn from the front-line in 2007.

11 March 2005 saw the disbandment of 16(R) and 54(F) Squadron after 170 years-combined service to the Crown. The Chief of the Air Staff, ACM Sir Jock Stirrup, reviewed the parade of over 550 personnel.

1 April 2006 saw the end of operational flying from Coltishall with the move of 6 Squadron to Coningsby and the Standard of 41(F) Squadron being handed over to the Fast Jet and Weapons Operational Evaluation Unit.

The Douglas Bader School at Coltishall closed on Thursday **20 July 2006**. Guest of honour was Lady Joan Bader who had renamed the school when it changed to primary status in 2000.

On **30 November 2006** over 6000 members of the General Public witnessed the formal closure of Coltshall. The Reviewing Officer for the small, but poignant ceremony was the AOC 1 Group, AVM David Walker. Four Jaguars of 6 Squadron and a Hurricane from the Historic Aircraft Company, Duxford, carried out flypasts over the parade. The Hurricane, flown by Sqn Ldr Al Pinner, later flew a solo display as the keys to the Station were handed over by the Station Commander, Sqn Ldr Jason Hughes, to James Ryley of Defence Estates.This brought to an end a 66-year history of a Battle of Britain Station; the only Station in the RAF to have remained in the fighter role for its whole existence.

BIBLIOGRAPHY

Airfield Focus 22 – Coltishall	Stewart Scott	GMS Enterprises
Airfield Focus 36 – Ludham	Peter Foster	GMS Enterprises
Airfields of Norfolk	Merv Hambling	Norfolk Aviation Society
Air Raid against East Anglia	Michael J Bowyer	Patrick Stephens
Battle over Britain	Francis Mason	McWhirter Twins
Bomber Squadrons of the RAF	Philip Moyes	Macdonald & Janes
British Military Airfields	David Smith	Patrick Stephens
Coastal Command Squadrons	John Rawlings	Janes
Confound & Destroy	Martin Streetly	Macdonald & Janes
East Anglia at War 1939-45	Derek Johnson	Jarrold Publishing
English Electric Lightning	Martin Bowman	Crowood
Fighter Command Losses in WWII	Norman Franks	Midland Counties
Fighter Squadrons of the RAF	John Rawlings	Macdonald & Janes
Final Flights	Ian McLachlan	Patrick Stephens
Fly for your Life	Larry Forrester	Cerberus
Invaders over Britain	Simon Parry	Air Research Publications
Jaguar – Endangered Species	Peter Foster	Tempus
John 'Cats Eyes' Cunningham	John Golley	Airlife Classic
Lightnngs Live On	Hugh Trevor	Lightning Preservation Group
Military Airfields British Isles	Willis & Hollis	Enthusiast Publications
No 2 Group RAF	Michael J Bowyer	Faber
Norfolk Air Crashes 1939-45	Merv Hambling	Norfolk Aviation Society
Norfolk Air Crashes 1946-2000	Merv Hambling	Norfolk Aviation Society
Norfolk Airfields in WWII	Graham Smith	Countryside Books
Norfolk Military Airfields	Peter Walker	Privately Published
Norfolk Military Airfields	Merv Hambling	Norfolk Aviation Society
Pursuit through Darkened Skies	Michael Allen	Airlife Classic
RAF at War	Martin Bowman	Patrick Stephens
RAF Bomber Command Losses	W R Chorley	Midland Counties
RAF Squadrons	C G Jefford	Airlife
RAF Squadrons Battle of Britain	Anthony Robinson	Brockhampton Press
Reach for the Sky	Paul Brickhill	Companion Book Club 1955
Short History of RAF Ludham	Mervyn Hinton	Privately Published
Spitfire Command	Bobby Oxpring	Cerberus
Spitfire MkV in Action	Peter Caygill	Airlife
The Canadian Years	Hugh Halliday	Midland Counties
The men who flew the Mosquito	Martin Bowman	Patrick Stephens
The Mighty Eighth	Roger Freeman	Arms & Armour
The Source Book of the RAF	Ken Delve	Airlife
Thunder & Lightning	Charles Allen	HMSO
World Air Power Journal Vol 11	Jon Lake	Aerospace Publishing

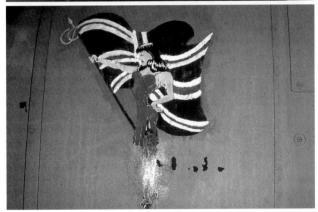

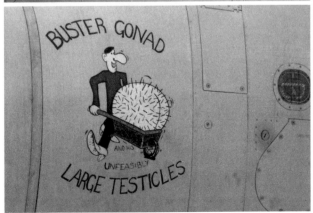

1st Lt	1st Lieutenant
2nd Lt	2nd Lieutenant
AA	Anti-Aircraft
AC	Aircraftsman
AC1	Aircraftsman First Class
AC2	Aircraftsman Second Class
ACM	Air Chief Marshal
AEF	Air Experience Flight
AFB	Air Force Base
AFC	Air Force Cross
AFDS	Air Fighting Development Squadron
AI	Airborne Interception
Air Cdre	Air Commodore
ALG	Advanced Landing Ground
AM	Air Marshal
AMF	Aircraft Maintenance Flight
AOC	Air Officer Commanding
APC	Armament Practice Camp
ARP	Air Raid Precautions
ARTF	Alkaline Removable Temporary Finish
ASR	Air Sea Rescue
ASV	Air Surface Vessel
ATAF	Allied Tactical Air Force
ATC	Air Training Corps
ATC	Air Traffic Control
ATRF	Aircraft Transportation & Recovery Flight
AVM	Air Vice Marshal
AWACS	Airborne Warning And Control System
AWOL	Absent Without Leave
BAC	British Aircraft Corporation
BBMF	Battle of Britain Memorial Flight
BDR	Battle Damage Repair
BEF	British Expeditionary Force
BEM	British Empire Medal
BG	Bomber Group
BS	Bomber Squadron
BSc	Bachelor of Science
CAACU	Civilian Anti-Aircraft Co-operation Unit
CAP	Combat Air Patrol
Capt	Captain
CB	Companion of the Order of the Bath
CBE	Commander of the Order of the British Empire
CCS	Common Core Skills
CFE	Central Fighter Establishment
CFI	Chief Flying Instructor
CFS	Central Flying School
C-in-C	Commander-in-Chief
CO	Commanding Officer
Cpl	Corporal
CRO	Community Relations Officer
CSBM	Confidence and Security Building Measure
CT	Chief Technician
DERA	Defence Experimental Research Agency
DF	Direction Finding
DFC	Distinguished Flying Cross
DFM	Distinguished Flying Medal
DSO	Distinguished Service Order
EAAT	East Anglian Ambulance Trust
ECM	Electronic Counter Measures
EDP	Eastern Daily Press
EEDA	East of England Development Agency
FAA	Fleet Air Arm
FCTU	Fighter Command Trials Unit
FG	Fighter Group
FIU	Fighter Interception Unit
Flg Off	Flying Officer
Flt	Flight
Flt Lt	Flight Lieutenant
Flt Sgt	Flight Sergeant
FS	Fighter Squadron
FTS	Flying Training School
Fw.	Feldwebel
GCA	Ground Controlled Approach
GCI	Ground Controlled Interception
GEC	General Electric Company
Gefr.	Gefreiter
Gen	General
GG	Ground Gunners
GI	Government Issue
GMT	Greenwich Meantime
Gp	Group
Gp Capt	Group Captain
HAF	Historic Aircraft Flight
HAS	Hardened Air Shelter
HCU	Heavy Conversion Unit
HE	High Explosive
HIVE	Help Information Volunteer Exchange
HM	His/Her Majesty
HMS	His/Her Majesties Ship
HMSS	Helmet Mounted

HRH	His/Her Royal Highness	RAFVR	Royal Air Force Volunteer Reserve
HQ	Head Quarters	RCAF	Royal Canadian Air Force
ILS	Instrument Landing System	RDF	Radar Direction Finder
ITW	Initial Training Wing	RFC	Royal Flying Corps
IWM	Imperial War Museum	RIAT	Royal International Air Tattoo
JRP	Joint Reconnaissance Pod	RIC	Reconnaissance Intelligence Centre
JT	Junior Technician	RNAS	Royal Naval Air Service
KBE	Knight of the Order of the British Empire	RNAS	Royal Navy Air Station
		RNLI	Royal
LAC	Leading Aircraftsman	RNZAF	Royal New Zealand Air Force
LACW	Leading Aircraftwoman	ROC	Royal Observer Corps
LOROP	Long-Range Oblique Photography	RRH	Remote Radar Head
LRMTS	Laser Rangefinder and Marked Target Seeker	RSM	Regimental Sergeant Major
		R/T	Radio/Transmitter
Lt	Lieutenant	SAC	Senior Aircraftsman
Lt.	Leutnant	SACEUR	Supreme Allied Commander Europe
Lt Col	Lieutenant Colonel	SEO	Senior Executive Officer
MALM	Master Air Load Master	Sgt	Sergeant
MBE	Member of the Order of the British Empire	SIO	Station Intelligence Officer
		SOE	Special Operations Executive
MC	Military Cross	SoTT	School of Technical Training
Mjr	Major	S/Lt	Sub Lieutenant
MO	Medical Officer	SNCO	Senior Non Commissioned Officer
MOD	Ministry of Defence	Sqn Ldr	Squadron Leader
MONAB	Mobile Naval Air Base	SSgt	Staff Sergeant
MoU	Memorandum of Understanding	Stabsfw	Stabsfeldwebel
MT	Motor Transport	SWO	Station Warrant Officer
MU	Maintenance Unit	TIALD	Thermal Imaging And Laser Designation
NAAFI	Navy Army Air Force Institue		
NATO	North Atlantic Treaty Organisation	TRE	Telecommunications Research Establishment
NCO	Non Commissioned Officer		
NFIU	Night Fighter Interception Unit	TRS	Tactical Reconnaissance Squadron
Obfw.	Oberfeldwebel	TRW	Tactical Reconnaissance Wing
Oblt.	Oberleutnant	TSgt	Technical Sergeant
OCU	Operational Conversion Unit	TTF	Target Towing Flight
Ogefr.	Obergefreiter	TTTE	Tri-National Tornado Training Establishment
ORB	Operational Records Book		
OTU	Operational Training Unit	TWCU	Tactical Weapons Conversion Unit
PAF	Polish Air Force	Uffz.	Unteroffizier
Plt Off	Pilot Officer	UN	United Nations
POL	Petrol Oil and Lubricants	USAF	United States Air Force
POW	Prisoner of War	USAAF	United States Army Air Force
PR	Photographic Reconnaissance	USN	United States Navy
QFI	Qualified Flying Instructor	VDU	Video Display Unit
QRA	Quick Reaction Alert	VHF	Very High Frequency
QWI	Qualified Weapons Instructor	WAAF	Womens Auxiliary Air Force
RAAF	Royal Australian Air Force	Wg Cdr	Wing Commander
RAE	Royal Aircraft Establishment	WO	Warrant Officer
RAF	Royal Air Force	WO2	Warrant Officer Class 2
RAFA	Royal Air Force Association		

Index

X, Y, Z